MW00947589

FEDERAL CIVIL PRETRIAL PRACTICE AND PROCEDURE
THIRD EDITION

Benjamin V. Madison III

Kindle Direct Publishing (KDP)

Copyright © 2019 Benjamin V. Madison III
All Rights Reserved

ISBN-13 978-1088577349

Printed by Kindle Direct Publishing, An Amazon.com Company
www.kdp.amazon.com

In memory of the Honorable Walter E. Hoffman,
someone who taught me the importance of procedure
and who loved the law more than anyone I've known

Acknowledgments

I thank my wife, Judy, and my children, Daniel, Andrew, Mary, Stephen, and Eliza. Any book project involves some time in which the author is either away from home or, if there, asking for silence in order to work on the book. I appreciate my family's support on this project.

I would also like to sincerely thank the following graduate assistants who have worked on parts of this book over the several years it took to complete it: Andrew Butler, Kourtney Coker, Michael Sevy, Krista Sheets, Ashley Simmons, Lauren Stroyeck, Melanie Sanders, and Konstantin Oschepkov. I particularly appreciate the help of Courtney Hitchcock, my current graduate assistant, for her close reading of this book, corrections, and suggested improvements of this edition.

Thanks too, to Julia Drake, for her illustration of the district court circuit map used throughout this text and the graphical design of this book's cover. Finally, I appreciate the help of the multitalented Lisa Marie Otto who helped to revise the cover and provided technical assistance whenever needed.

A Note on Citations

The reader needs to recognize that some citations in this Casebook are by the author and some are by the courts deciding one of the cases featured in this book. The reader can distinguish the author's cites from those of courts by their location. If the cites are outside the context of a case, they are the author's citation of authority. If they are in footnotes or otherwise within a case, however, these are the courts' citations of authorities for their opinions.

Often in casebooks, citations are either completely edited out or are left in the text. The author chose a compromise of putting citations in footnotes for a reason. The reader needs to see that courts decide opinions based on previous authority and that the norm is to cite such authority. However, the citation in text can make reading the case difficulty. Hence, my compromise: cite the authorities in the footnotes rather than the text of the featured case. Thus, when reading a featured case, most of the footnotes have been added by the author to move the authorities from the text of the case to the footnotes.

TABLE OF CONTENTS

Chapter 8: Understanding the Steps in a Lawsuit, the Role of the Rules of Civil Procedure, and When Particular Rules Apply

TABLE OF FEATURED AUTHORITIES

Cases

CHAPTER 1:
FOUNDATIONAL CONCEPTS

This book offers an introduction to the system of dispute resolution known as federal civil litigation. Before taking up the necessary doctrines, rules, and procedures that a litigator must know to handle federal civil cases, this chapter addresses certain concepts foundational to an understanding of the American system of federal civil justice. These are in Part One. The topics in Part One may seem broad and distant from the practicalities of litigation. However, the themes introduced here are important to a full understanding of how to handle a federal civil case. Part Two of this chapter explains the structure of this book. There, you will see that each chapter of the book relates to questions a litigator must resolve as the stages of a civil action proceeds. Here, you should understand that you will be called on to answer these questions at some point. Knowing the point in a case at which an issue arises is as important as mastering the analysis of that issue.

I. Foundational Concepts

This part of the chapter addresses, in order, the following core subjects:

- Subpart 1   Civil Procedure's Role in Law
- Subpart 2   The Structure of the Federal Court System
- Subpart 3   Federalism
- Subpart 4   The Adversary System
- Subpart 5   Further Inheritance from English Law
- Subpart 6   Other Sources of Law
- Subpart 7   The Higher Purpose of Civil Litigation

A. Civil Procedure's Role in Law

Civil procedure is about the rules and hurdles a party must navigate in a civil lawsuit. You will learn in other courses about substantive rights. For instance, the breach of a valid contract gives rise to a right on which the party who suffered loss from the breach can sue. Someone injured by another's negligence has the right to sue under tort law for compensation arising from her injuries. A federal statute that prohibits racial discrimination will, if violated, give rise to a claim under that statute. Each of these—contract, tort, and anti-discrimination statutes—are substantive rights. They arise either from the common law of the state (court-made law) in which the breach occurs (*e.g.*, contract, tort) or from a statute (*e.g.*, Title VII of the Civil Rights Act of 1964 which prohibits discrimination based on race, religion, sex). Civil procedure deals with the rules and requirements involved in such a suit for relief based on a violation of one or more of these substantive rights. Please keep in mind, as you study the following cases or fact patterns, that there are both substantive rights and procedural rules at issue. Because civil procedure focuses on the requirements for bringing or defending civil claims, there will be more emphasis on the procedural issues rather than the parties' substantive rights in these cases.

Criminal law is different from civil litigation. A civil case involves disputes between two private parties, the "plaintiff," who is the party seeking relief based on a right established by the Constitution, statutes, or common law, and the "defendant," who is the party against whom the suit is brought. Civil plaintiffs seek money damages to compensate the plaintiff. If money damages would not right the wrong, the plaintiff in a civil suit can seek equitable relief, such as an injunction ordering the defendant to stop doing something the defendant should not be doing or to do something the defendant ought to be doing. In criminal cases, the government stands in a position analogous to a plaintiff. The United States (in federal prosecutions) or a state (in state prosecutions) brings charges against an accused, also referred to as a "defendant." Instead of claims for relief, the government seeks convictions for those charged with violating statutes. Criminal procedure governs the way the government prose-cutes the defendant. The defendant can be fined, imprisoned, or even sentenced to death for "capital" crimes. You will study the substantive criminal law and criminal procedure involved in these cases in other courses.

The same events can give rise to both civil claims and criminal charges. An example can be found in something as routine as a car accident. Someone injured by the negligent operation of a car can sue the driver in a civil suit and seek damages. If the injured person dies because of the driver's negligence, her estate's representative can bring what is called a wrongful death action, which is also a civil action for damages. Additionally, the governmental jurisdiction in question can also bring charges against the driver. In the car accident example, a defendant who drove recklessly in violation of a state statute would be prosecuted in state court. The federal government prosecutes when a federal criminal statute was violated. In other cases, state and federal prosecutions can in fact overlap when both the state and federal government have statutes criminalizing the same conduct. Such a scenario is not unusual in drug cases. Then, there are federal criminal statutes that apply in prosecutions in federal court. An example would be intentional contamination of the environment in violation of federal statutes.

The standard of proof differs in criminal and civil cases. The government must prove the violation of a criminal statute "beyond a reasonable doubt." By contrast, a plaintiff in a civil case need only prove her claim by a "preponderance of the evidence." The preponderance standard is likened to a scale in which the plaintiff's proof tips the scale to one side, even if it is but fifty-one percent of a lean toward having proved the plaintiff's case. Beyond a reasonable doubt requires the fact-finder to be far more certain that the government has proved the elements of a crime. Thus, just because a civil suit results in a plaintiff's recovery, it does not automatically mean prosecution of the conduct will result in a criminal conviction. The judge and/or jury could conclude in the civil suit that it is more likely than not that the defendant's negligence caused the plaintiff's injuries. Conversely, the judge or jury in a criminal trial may not be satisfied that the government's evidence established beyond a reasonable doubt that the defendant committed the crime(s) alleged. The higher standard of proof in criminal cases can explain the seemingly inconsistent verdicts in some cases. For instance, say a defendant is accused of murder. The jury may find the defendant "not guilty." Many mistakenly believe such a verdict is a finding of innocence. It is not. The verdict means that the jury concluded that the government failed to prove violation of a statute beyond a reasonable doubt. The same defendant can then be sued by the family, referred to as the "survivors," of the victim who was the subject of the criminal trial, in a "wrongful death" suit. The burden, as suggested, does not require the plaintiffs to show beyond a reasonable doubt that the defendant killed the victim. All the plaintiffs must do is show by a preponderance of the evidence that it is more likely than not that the defendant killed the victim.

This book addresses solely civil litigation and procedure. The discussion of criminal law and procedure here should be taken only as a basis for distinguishing the two areas of law.

B. The Structure of the Federal Court System

The federal government has a system of courts derived from Article III, Section 2 of the United States Constitution. Three levels of courts comprise the federal system. These are the (1) United States district courts, (2) intermediate courts of appeals, and (3) the United States Supreme Court.

The United States district courts are the first level of courts in this system. These are called courts of "original jurisdiction," because they are the ones in which a case is first filed and in which the parties present evidence to the factfinder (the judge and/or jury) who reaches a decision. In other words, these are the trial courts of the federal system.

The intermediate courts of appeals are federal appellate courts that review decisions of the trial courts. Of the thirteen circuit courts of appeals, twelve are geographically assigned to hear appeals from decisions of the U.S. district courts within states or districts of a given region. For instance, the United States Court of Appeals for the Fourth Circuit hears appeals from district courts in Maryland, North Carolina, South Carolina, Virginia, and West Virginia. The following map illustrates the federal circuits, with designations of the circuit courts of appeals for each circuit's applicable region.[1]

Figure 1-1

Geographic Boundaries
of United States Courts of Appeals and United States District Courts

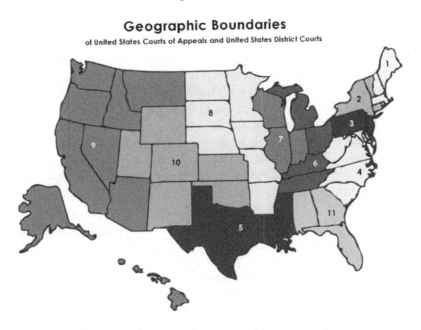

The remaining circuit court of appeals, the United States Court of Appeals for the Federal Circuit, hears appeals based on the type of case rather than the district court's geographic region. Regardless of where the case is decided, appeals in certain types of cases (including patents, international trade, government contracts, trademarks, and similar types of cases) go to the Court of Appeals for the Federal Circuit. Thus, regardless of whether such a case is decided in a geographic region that ordinarily would

---

[1] This map was illustrated by Julia Drake. There are two additional circuit courts of appeals not depicted, the District of Columbia Circuit and the Federal Circuit. Each of these circuits have specialized jurisdiction. The Federal Judiciary also offers a geographical map distinguishing individual districts within the federal circuits. *See* U.S. Federal Courts Circuit Map, Uscourts.Gov, http://www.uscourts.gov/sites/default/files/u.s._fed-eral_courts_circuit_map_1.pdf.

hear all other appeals from that district court, the appeal will go to the Court of Appeals for the Federal Circuit. In other words, a patent case decided in a district court in California will be appealed to the Federal Circuit in the same way a patent case decided in Virginia would do so. Therefore, some refer to the Federal Circuit's jurisdiction as nationwide in scope.

The United States Supreme Court hears appeals from the intermediate courts of appeals. The Court has original jurisdiction in a narrow class of cases, primarily disputes between states about land. The Court also has appellate jurisdiction, meaning it must accept the appeal, only in a rare type of case in which the intermediate appellate court has granted or failed to grant certain relief. The most common path of cases that are heard by the Court is by writ of certiorari. The Court would be overwhelmed if it reviewed every decision of every federal circuit court of appeals and every petition of a decision of the highest court of a state. The Court traditionally grants a small percentage of such writs and bases its decision on the novelty of a question of federal law raised, whether there is a split among the intermediate circuit courts of appeals on a point of federal law, or other compelling reasons to hear the case.

C. Federalism

We live in a country in which our conduct is regulated simultaneously by the federal government and by state and local governments. This is because the United States Constitution provides for a federal government of limited powers to pass laws, execute laws, and resolve disputes that fall within the federal prerogative. Such a system has many implications. For instance, conduct over which a party may wish to sue may give rise to a claim under federal law and under state law. Moreover, Article III, Section 2 of the Constitution sets forth nine types of cases that can be brought in federal courts. If a case falls within both the constitutional grant and the enabling statutes passed to effectuate the authority granted in the Constitution, then the case can be litigated in the federal system.[2] The phrase "enabling statute" simply means that the statute takes the potential jurisdiction created by constitutional grant and makes that jurisdiction available in a federal statute. The key is that the enabling statute often does not enact the entirety of a category of potential jurisdiction. Thus, the limits of the enabling statute—such as the general diversity of citizenship statute, 28 U.S.C. § 1332, and the general federal question statute, 28 U.S.C. § 1331, will be the focus of one's analysis as to whether, on a given set of facts, suit can be filed under the statute in federal court.

Cases that fall outside the federal grant of subject matter jurisdiction can always be brought in state court. As opposed to the limited jurisdiction of federal courts, state courts have what is called "general jurisdiction." They can hear virtually any kind of civil case. Indeed, most cases that can be filed in federal court may also be heard in state court—a concept known as "concurrent jurisdiction."[3]

Concurrent jurisdiction allows the plaintiff to have a choice of whether to file in federal court or state court. Why is it important to know that cases often may be brought in either federal or state court? Attorneys who litigate on a regular basis know that there are differences in trying a case in federal court

---

[2] Subject matter jurisdiction, addressed in Chapters 3 and 4, explains why one must not only satisfy the constitutional grant but also a federal enabling statute to invoke the jurisdiction of federal courts. The "enabling" statute takes the potential jurisdiction allowed by the constitutional grant and enacts a statute that allows the potential to become actual. Nevertheless, as we will see, these statutes are typically narrower in what they permit than the full potential of a category in the constitutional grant. Thus, the statutes will drive the analysis of whether the category of subject matter jurisdiction for a given statute are satisfied.

[3] The only exceptions to concurrent jurisdiction are the few areas in which federal court jurisdiction is exclusive, such as federal antitrust suits, copyright cases, and patent actions.

and a given state's court. Such differences may make it preferable to go to federal court. However, the attorney will not know whether there is even a choice unless she is able to confirm that a case is one that satisfies one of the limited bases for federal jurisdiction. If so, then there is a choice of forum in which to file and the attorney will need to advise her client of the pros and cons of filing in the federal system versus the state system.

What if a case involves a federal question and it is filed and tried in state court? Does that mean no federal court will ever pass on a ruling that affects the federal question in the case? No, but it will take some work to have the federal question heard. The only federal court that can, in these circumstances, review a decision on a federal question is the United States Supreme Court. If a state court is the trial court, then the appeal of a state trial court's decision—even one with a federal question involved—goes to the appellate courts of the state and ultimately to the state's highest court. The party who loses in the state system can petition the Supreme Court for a writ of certiorari. As noted above, the Supreme Court grants only a small percentage of such writs. However, this avenue ensures that the Supreme Court can still review a question of federal law ruled on in the state system if the Supreme Court believes the matter is sufficiently important to address. Note, however, that the Supreme Court can only rule on matters of federal law. The Supreme Court cannot rule on matters purely related to state law. Therefore, there must be some federal question involved for the Supreme Court to grant a writ of certiorari.

An example will make clearer how even the Supreme Court cannot decide state law but can decide questions of federal law raised in state proceedings. Say a utility company seeks a ruling in state court on whether a landowner owns the airspace 150 feet above her property. In other words, the utility company was using said airspace over the objection of the plaintiff landowner. The utility company brought suit in state court and asked the court to determine whether it needed to compensate the plaintiff if the airspace was within the plaintiff's right as the owner of the property, and, if so, what compensation the landowner should be paid for the use of that airspace. Under state law, the state court finds that 150 feet above one's property was beyond the amount of airspace that a landowner could reasonably use. Therefore, according to the state court's ruling, the landowner is not entitled to any compensation. The Supreme Court cannot review a decision as to state law. The determination of what constitutes property—e.g., how much airspace above one's land a landowner owns—is a matter of state law. By contrast, if the state court had ruled that the utility lines were within the landowner's property rights, and the landowner included in her state court case a claim that the lines were a "taking" of property in violation of the Fifth and Fourteenth Amendments to the U.S. Constitution, then a decision on whether the use of the lines was a "taking" and the appropriate remedy would be something the Supreme Court could review on a writ of certiorari.

Supreme Court decisions appear throughout this book. At times, cases will have arisen through the federal system—from district courts, to courts of appeals, and then to the Supreme Court. However, in other cases, particularly in the area of personal jurisdiction, much of the governing case law derives from cases on writ of certiorari from a state supreme court. Therefore, an understanding of how the Supreme Court renders decisions in both cases is important.

D. The Adversary System

Litigation in the United States is based on an adversarial system, which has its roots in English law. In this system, the plaintiff presents evidence of the violation of a right that justifies relief (e.g., money damages or an injunction). The defendant opposes the plaintiff and offers the defendant's own proof. Both the plaintiff and defendant cross-examine each other's witnesses and otherwise counter each other's case through a variety of means. The judge in an adversarial system is a neutral decision maker and does not decide claims that are not brought before the court. Because the adversarial system contemplates that the interests of each side will produce the matters necessary to be litigated, the parties shape the case. A plaintiff asserts claims, a defendant asserts defenses, and both plaintiff and defendant present these claims and defenses to a factfinder (judge or jury) who ultimately decides the results. The judge serves as the source of law affecting the path of a case, such as by ruling on motions dealing with the case (e.g., evidentiary objections) and, if the case involves a jury trial, by giving jury instructions on the law, ruling on matters such as the proof necessary to establish whatever claim(s) brought, the appropriate means of applying the facts the jury finds as proved, and the like.

The adversary system is distinctly an Anglo-American approach. It derives from the common law of England that American adopted.[4] Generally, European countries follow an alternative model in both criminal and civil cases in which the judge serves an inquisitorial role, actively participating in defining the issues to be resolved, investigating the facts of the case, and resolving the issues. This inquisitorial model derives from Roman law.[5]

The phrase "adversary system" suggests that the system is one in which the parties can wreak whatever havoc on each other that they can imagine. The approach of some lawyers seems to imply such an understanding of the system.[6] To make such an inference is a mistake—one that has many consequences. First, the lawyer who puts all considerations aside other than winning for the client is ignoring the Model Rules promulgated by the American Bar Association dictating the multiple interests lawyers should consider in advocating for their client. The Preamble to the Model Rules also makes clear that the Rules do not provide everything a lawyer needs to resolve ethical dilemmas. The lawyer must not only rely on "personal conscience" but also on "sensitive professional and moral judgment."[7] Indeed, the Preamble acknowledges that all difficult ethical decisions arise from a conflict between the lawyer's duties to the client, to the legal system, and to "the lawyer's own interest in remaining an ethical person."[8] Anyone who thinks that the Rules by themselves should serve as a lawyer's sole guidance for making ethical decisions is, therefore, mistaken. The Rules set a minimum threshold for conduct that will avoid discipline. For the many areas left to the lawyer's discretion, the Rules give little direction. For that reason, you will be asked throughout your time in law school to develop your internal sense of ethical values by which you want to abide. You will also be asked to reflect on the method in which you can work through the more difficult ethical questions that can arise. This book will present you with some opportunities to begin this process.

In one of the last sections of this chapter entitled "The Higher Purpose of Civil Litigation," the role of a lawyer who believes in a fair judicial system and fair treatment of everyone else in it—not just her client, but the opposing party, opposing counsel, the judge, witnesses, etc.—will be discussed.

E. Further Inheritance from English Law

The previous section discussed the adversary system that Americans inherited from the English.

---

[4] RUSSEL KIRK, THE ROOTS OF AMERICAN ORDER 186 (2003).

[5] *Id.*

[6] *See, e.g.*, Allen K. Harris, *The Professionalism Crisis: The "Z" Words and Other Rambo Tactics: The Conference of Chief Justices' solution*, 53 S.C.L. REV. 549, 569 (2002) ("The phrase 'zealous advocacy' is frequently invoked to defend a 'Rambo,' or 'win at all costs,' attitude.").

[7] MODEL RULES OF PROF'L CONDUCT, PREAMBLE ¶¶ 7, 9 (AM. BAR ASS'N 2016). The American Bar Association Model Rules are a model for state Rules of Professional Conduct. Some states adopt the Rules almost verbatim and others make changes in certain provisions.

[8] *Id.* at ¶ 9.

This section will discuss in broad terms the other aspects of English law adopted in America, requiring a brief review of English history.

English law developed what is called a common-law system. Common law is judge-made law deriving from the facts and ruling in a case. The judges were not making up law but rather, on a set of facts, the judge would apply whatever "precedent"—i.e., previous decisions on similar facts—to reach a decision that likely added to whatever body of law the case concerned. Thus, the law grew incrementally over time through such decision-making.

Royal courts such as the Court of Common Pleas and the Court of the Exchequer decided cases at common law during the Thirteenth and Fourteenth Centuries. These courts became known for the rigidity by which they ruled, especially in the form of remedy. Generally, these courts would provide money damages as the sole means of remedy. If the plaintiff could not be made whole by money damages, the plaintiff had nowhere to turn. The following excerpt from the famous English historian, William Maitland, describes this dilemma and how the Court of Chancery, which came to be a source of equitable relief, arose:

The Origin of Equity
F.W. Maitland

In Edward I's day, at the end of the thirteenth century, three great courts have come into existence, the King's Bench, the Common Bench or Court of Common Pleas and the Exchequer. Each of these has its own proper sphere, but as time goes on each of them attempts to extend its sphere and before the middle ages are over a plaintiff has often a choice between these three courts and each of them will deal with his case in the same way and by the same rules. The law which these courts administer is in part traditional law, in part statutory law. Already in Edward I's day the phrase 'common law' is current. It is a phrase that has been borrowed from the canonists – who used 'jus commune' to denote the general law of the Catholic Church; it describes that part of the law that is unenacted, non-statutory, that is common to the whole land and to all Englishmen. It is contrasted with statute, with local custom, with royal prerogative. It is not as yet contrasted with equity, for as yet there is no body of rules which bears this name.

. . .

[Describing the rise of the Court of Chancery, in which the judge was the Chancellor, Maitland explains how this court of equity developed as a means of providing justice when the courts of law left someone without a remedy at law.] But by another route the Chancellor is brought into still closer contact with the administration of justice. Though these great courts of law have been established [,] there is still a reserve of justice in the king. Those who [cannot] get relief elsewhere present their petitions to the king and his council praying for some remedy. Already by the end of the thirteenth century the number of such petitions presented in every year is very large, and the work of reading them is very laborious. In practice [,] a great share of this labour falls on the Chancellor. He is the king's prime minister, he is a member of the council, and the specially learned member of the council. It is dealing with these petitions that the Chancellor begins to develop his judicial powers.

. . .

In the course of the sixteenth century [,] we begin to learn a little about the rules that the Chancellors are administering in the field that is thus assigned to them. They are known as 'the rules of equity and good conscience [.'] As to what they have done in remoter times we have to draw inferences from vary sparse evidence. One thing seems pretty plain. They had not considered themselves strictly bound by precedent.

. . .

Injunctions

Let us see what an injunction is. It is an order made by the Court forbidding a person or class of persons from doing a certain act, or acts of a certain class, upon pain of going to prison for an indefinite time as contemners of the Court. This penalty will not be mentioned in the injunction, but if knowing of an injunction you break it, then the Court has a large discretionary power of sending you to prison and keeping you there.

. . .

In general, an injunction forbids a defendant to do certain acts, but sometimes it forbids him to permit the continuance of a wrongful state of things that already exists at the time when the injunction is issued. The Court does not merely say "'Do not build any wall to the injury of the plaintiff's right of light'; it can say 'Do not permit the continuance of any wall to the injury of the plaintiff's right to light.'"[9]

As Maitland's discussion suggests, separate courts existed for parties seeking legal relief in a common law court (e.g., money damages) and equitable relief in the Court of Chancery (e.g., an injunction). That system carried over to early American Jurisprudence. In federal courts prior to 1938, a party had to bring her action as either a law action or an equity action. It was not until the Federal Rules of Civil Procedure were adopted in 1938, that the federal system recognized a unified suit in which the plaintiff could seek both law and, in addition or alternatively, equitable damages.

In modern practice, a plaintiff can plead both legal and equitable claims and relief in the same suit. However, one must still assert in one's pleading a "lack of adequate remedy at law" to receive equitable relief. Thus, you would need to know this when you get to Chapter 8 on pleading claims. Moreover, when we address in Chapter 14 the test for whether a party can demand a jury, you will see that whether a party has a right to a jury trial on a claim requires a determination of whether the claim would have been solely in equity (where a judge, not a jury, would be the only fact finder and decision-maker) or at law (where a jury could be demanded by the party seeking relief and the jury would be the fact finder and decision-maker). Thus, although the merger of law and equity has now become standard practice, the vestiges of

---

[9] Excerpt from F. W. MAITLAND, EQUITY: A COURSE OF LECTURES, (A. H. Chaytor & W. J. Whittaker eds., Cambridge Univ. Press rev. ed. 1936) (reprt. 1969).

differences between law and equity still play a role in handling a federal lawsuit.

1. Other Sources of Law

Most of the first-year curriculum in law schools include courses on common law topics— contracts, property, torts, etc. That means the law you will be learning in most cases derives from decisions made over centuries. However, especially in federal civil procedure, you need to realize there are other sources of law. These include the United States Constitution, federal statutes, and federal rules. A bit about these three categories of sources should help.

a. United States Constitution

As previously discussed in Section IV on Federalism, the United States Constitution provides the entire basis for the limited federal government, including the limited jurisdiction of federal courts. The United States Constitution also provides the basis for several rights that we will address in civil procedure. For instance, the Due Process Clause of the Fourteenth Amendment is the basis for the requirement that nonresident defendants have sufficient contacts with the state in which suit is filed. Moreover, the Seventh Amendment provides the right to a jury trial—a quintessential part of the Anglo-American tradition.

i. Federal Statutes

Federal statutes play different roles in federal civil procedure. Some statutes are jurisdictional. For instance, the diversity statute—28 U.S.C. § 1332—provides that federal courts can hear cases between parties from different states if the amount in controversy exceeds $75,000 exclusive of interests and costs. In addition, the general federal question statute—28 U.S.C. § 1331—provides that federal courts have jurisdiction over suits arising under federal law, such as the Constitution, federal statutes, and federal regulations. For example, the Age Discrimination in Employment Act (ADEA),[10] is a type of federal statute that provides rights on which a person or entity can sue as well as remedies for violations. Under the ADEA, a plaintiff who was discharged from employment can prove an ADEA claim if she shows: (a) that her employer is within the group of employers covered by the ADEA, (b) that she is within the group of persons protected by the ADEA, (c) that she had performed and was performing her job satisfactorily; and (d) that she was discharged due to her age. If the plaintiff proves her ADEA claim, the statutory remedies available to her are broad: reinstatement, back pay, front pay (lost future earnings), compensatory damages, punitive damages, attorneys' fees, and prejudgment interest. Thus, a federal statute like the ADEA[11] is the corollary to common law rights under tort, contract, and property law. The difference is, of course, that those are developed in a case-by-case fashion over time, whereas statutes enacted by the legislature automatically provide the basis for claims and the remedies available.

ii. Federal Rules

Congress can pass statutes that enable the United States Supreme Court to adopt rules. The Supreme Court has adopted federal rules on a variety of matters. These include the Federal Rules of Civil Procedure, Federal Rules of Evidence (applicable in U.S. district courts when evidence is taken, usually at trial), Federal Rules of Appellate Procedure (for appeals to the intermediate courts of appeals), and Rules of

---

[10] 29 U.S.C. § 621 et seq. (2017)

[11] *Id.*

Practice before the United States Supreme Court, etc.

The Rules are first developed by an Advisory Committee appointed by the Supreme Court. The Advisory Committee publishes proposed Rules and seeks comment on them. The Advisory Committee then revises the Rules in response to comments. The Rules then go to the Supreme Court for review and, if the Supreme Court adopts them, they are sent to Congress. Congress has ample time to make changes to the Rules, but if they have not been changed by a specified date, they become effective as written. Because the Rules are adopted through Congress' authority and Congress has the ultimate decision on whether to adopt them, the Rules are law. Some find it odd to call such Rules "law" and believe they are little less weighty than statutes. However, if a Federal Rule and a state statute conflict on a matter of procedure in how a case is handled in the federal system, the Federal Rule will qualify as "law" that trumps the state law under the Constitution's Supremacy Clause. In Article VI, the Supremacy Clause provides that federal law shall be deemed supreme. Thus, when federal and state law conflict, federal law governs.

F. The Higher Purpose of Civil Litigation

The federal judicial system rests on deep, fundamental principles. Many never appreciate these principles. Often, law students and attorneys alike see the system as a random series of rules that somehow must be understood to avoid malpractice. However, if you see the broader purposes of the procedural system that serve the needs of society, you will be more likely to find purpose in your work.

What are these transcendent principles underlying the system? At its core, two principles underlie the system. First is the reality that human beings are flawed and will make errors. As the Framers of our Constitution knew, we need institutional protections to protect us from one another. James Madison's remarks regarding the need for governmental checks and balances in the following excerpt from The Federalist No. 51 easily applies to our nation's judicial system:

If men were angels, no government would be necessary. If angels were to govern men, neither external nor internal controls on government would be necessary. In framing a government which is to be administered by men over men, the great difficulty lies in this: You must first enable the government to control the governed; and in the next place, oblige it to control itself.[12]

Some of the "checks" in our procedural system are, indeed, constitutional checks. For instance, the jury is a check on judges, due process is a check on the governmental exercise of authority, and the right to appeal is a check on the trial court's power. Innumerable other instances exist in the judicial system in which parties can rely on procedural rules and doctrines to avoid unfair treatment. While these checks and balances may be less celebrated, they are still of great importance.

These procedural rules and doctrines help protect us from ourselves. As with constitutional checks and balances, the need for a set of procedural rules and doctrines that apply to each litigant rests on implicit foundations such as those which the Framers based the Constitution. Any system run by human beings will inevitably fall short of providing impartial justice. The procedural system recognizes that even the best human beings have biases, prejudices, and other character traits that can affect the impartial administration of justice. Although procedure cannot possibly offset the human factor in all its manifestations, it serves to ensure that most litigants get a fair opportunity to have their claims heard or their defenses presented.

---

[12] THE FEDERALIST NO. 51, at 262 (James Madison) (Buccaneer Books, 1992).

The second deeply rooted principle of the American judicial system is the flipside of the one previously discussed. If a lawyer is not aware of procedures that could offset bias and prejudice or are generally aware but lack the discipline to use these procedures, the client suffers. Provisions designed to offset bias and prejudice remain dormant. The client has less of a chance for impartial justice than if the lawyer knew how to use the system to protect her client. It is the notion that all persons are equal in dignity and deserve equal justice under the law. Intuitively, we know that justice hinges on our embracing such equality. Thus, we create a procedural system that in a variety of ways promotes the values of dispensing justice impartially. Parties have the opportunity, where applicable, to choose a jury by the same terms as the other side, allowing a jury of one's peers to decide the dispute versus a single judge. Indeed, the standard for summary judgment or judgment as a matter of law pays credence to this notion. A judge can only decide the case as a matter of law if she determines that fair-minded, reasonable jurors cannot disagree on the evidence. If the judge oversteps her bounds and substitutes her own judgment, the appellate process informs the trial judge of the error. Ultimately, the cases that deserve their day in court will get their day in court.

Problems arise when lawyers are not aware of the procedures that allow them to "check" the human factor in litigation. That should be motivation enough for a lawyer to learn procedure—and learn it well. As most experienced judges and lawyers know, a lawyer who knows the procedural system well is a formidable adversary. You need not wait until practice to develop the skills of such an adversary. If a new lawyer will integrate the decision-making process outlined in this book into his or her handling of every case, the odds are that the lawyer's client will not be the one disadvantaged by a procedural matter. To the contrary, the client will more likely end up in a position of strength by following the proper procedures. If the odds continue to play out according to form, your opponent will then end up at a disadvantage. At the very least, a lawyer who follows the steps outlined in this book should get cases with merit to a decision on the merits. She may not win every case on the merits; few lawyers do. However, she will have done her job to get the case to a decision, or if appropriate, to advise the client at an earlier stage to settle. The key here is that the lawyer will have intelligently handled the case. Over time, clients (and other lawyers) will realize that a lawyer who handles cases intelligently is a lawyer worth retaining.

II. Structure of this Book

Up to this point, this chapter has addressed the foundational principles necessary to understand the American civil justice system. This section will explain the organization of this book. Knowing the structure of this book will help you to learn the concepts discussed. Indeed, pedagogical research affirms that students learn best when they have a context in which to engage topics.[13] The principle underlying the remaining chapters is that civil lawsuits follow a predictable pattern. This book is, therefore, organized around the progress of a civil suit. Structuring the book in this way serves at least two goals. First, educational experts have shown repeatedly that those who learn information within a context tend to not only absorb that information more effectively, but that they also retain what they learn. Second, the process of going through the stages of a civil suit itself teaches you a valuable lesson. By following the progress of a case, you will know which issues may arise at the outset of a case, in the pretrial phase, and during or after trial. Those limited issues that can arise any time in the process are discussed at the end.

At the beginning of each chapter, you will see the following depiction of the stages of a civil action:

---

[13] *See* Benjamin V. Madison, III, *The Elephant in Law School Classrooms: Overuse of the Socratic Method as an Obstacle to Teaching Modern Law Students*, 85 U. DET. MERCY L. REV. 293, 320–23 (2008).

Figure 1-2

Cause of Action (events leading to suit)	Pre-Filing Tasks (items to begin representation, interviewing, and related matters)	Choice of Forum (subject matter jurisdiction, removal, personal jurisdiction, and venue)	Notice and Service of Process (completing the process of ensuring the forum court can enter a valid judgment)	Pleading the Case and Joinder of Claims and Parties (including supplemental jurisdiction)

Responding to Claims by Motion or by Answer	Discovery (developing proof to establish claims and learn your adversary's case)	Right to Jury (pretrial motions and practice)	Final Pretrial Conference (events within last month before trial)	Trial (procedures and motions during trial)	Verdict	Post-Trial Motions (motions for a new trial and/or judgment as a matter of law)	Appeal

This chapter provides an overview of the topics that are addressed in detail in the remainder of this book. Because the big picture will help you understand how a procedural doctrine or rule fits in the system, this chapter should help in several ways. First, it provides you with a context to begin studying the procedural topics that follow. Second, you can return to this section on the stages of a civil action regularly—indeed, every time you reach a new chapter—to ensure you appreciate where the topic you are studying fits within the broader scheme.

The following subsections summarize the stages of a civil action, and thus, the remaining chapters of this book.

Chapter 2: Cause of Action and Pre-filing Tasks

Chapter 2 explains how a case is born. Any lawsuit must begin with what lawyers and judges refer to as a "cause of action." The phrase is a bit enigmatic. However, the word "cause" gives a clue as to what it means. The cause of action comprises the events leading to a suit that are joined with a "right of action" (common law, statutory, etc.). This chapter recognizes that too many law students go through law school without being exposed to the array of issues and tasks that arise at the outset of a case. This chapter shows that there is plenty to do when the case is only a cause of action, and no suit has been filed. Thus, this chapter discusses the practical matters a lawyer must consider in taking on representation of a client. All law schools require Professional Responsibility. At some point, the tasks of ensuring that there are no conflicts of interest for the lawyer in representing a party, and some other specific issues, are covered. Many of the other topics addressed in Chapter 2, however, are not in required courses. A competent lawyer must know them to do her job. Anyone who reads Chapter 2 should have a sense of the matters that must be addressed before suit is ever filed.

Chapters 3, 4, 5, and 6:
Choice of Forum—Subject Matter Jurisdiction, Personal Jurisdiction, and Venue

Chapter 3 discusses how to determine whether limited federal subject matter jurisdiction exists. Only if it does will a client have a choice whether to file in federal court or state court. If the case is not the kind of case that can be heard in federal court, it must be filed in state court. As discussed in Subpart 3, "The Structure of the Federal System" and Subpart 4 "Federalism" above, the lawyer needs to determine quickly whether a case fits within the criteria of the limited jurisdiction of federal courts. If it does, then she almost always has a choice of filing in federal court or in state court. If the lawyer does not know how to determine whether federal jurisdiction exists, she cannot even get to the point of knowing there is a choice. Some less-than-diligent lawyers do not bother to analyze such matters because they file every case in state court because they prefer state court. Such lawyering is irresponsible. An effective lawyer files the case in the forum most advantageous to her client. The lawyer must be able and willing to handle a case in federal court or in state court—whichever best serves the interests of the client, not the lawyer.

Chapter 4 deals with "Removal Jurisdiction," a variation on subject matter jurisdiction. In Chapter 4, we will explore whether a defendant in a suit filed in state court can remove the case to a U.S. district court. As Chapter 4 will explain, the first step in that process will be to determine whether the federal court would have had subject matter jurisdiction, had the plaintiff filed suit in federal court instead of state court. If so, concluding the case could have been filed in federal court is only the beginning of removal analysis. For a plaintiff to satisfy diversity of citizenship jurisdiction or federal question jurisdiction, there are limited hurdles to clear. By contrast, a defendant seeking to remove a case from state court to federal court must not only show that the hurdles for subject matter jurisdiction are met, but also that many other hurdles permit the defendant to remove the case. Thus, the analysis of removal is far more detailed than the subject-matter-jurisdiction analysis addressed in Chapter 3, even though it is incorporated as the threshold part of the removal analysis.

Chapter 5 addresses the question of whether the court in which the plaintiff has sued has "personal jurisdiction," such that the court can adjudicate the rights and liabilities of a nonresident defendant. In terms of personal jurisdiction, federal and state courts within the same state are analyzed in the same way. If a federal court in a state can exercise personal jurisdiction, then a state court could as well, and vice versa.

Chapter 6 is related to personal jurisdiction. It deals with the important question of which venues (or areas) of the federal system or state can hear a case. The federal venue statutes and state venue statutes funnel a case to a location in which there is a logical connection, usually where it is most convenient for parties and witnesses. Chapters 3 through 6 thus deal with the question of choosing the forum—i.e., the court in which to file suit. That choice, obviously, is a crucial one.

Chapter 7: Notice and Service of Process

Chapter 7 explains the requirements for serving a party under the applicable service of process provisions of the Federal Rules of Civil Procedure, whether in federal or state court. Although pleading the complaint would logically come before the topic of notice and service, the connection between the necessity for notice to a defendant and the first chapters of the book—all of which discuss matters that must the accomplished for the court to be able to hear and resolve the dispute—support discussing notice here. If a defendant is not properly notified of a suit, the Due Process Clause will be violated to the same degree as if the court lacks personal jurisdiction. Thus, Chapter 7 asks you to recognize that we will turn immediately after this topic to pleading the plaintiff's case. However, the last piece of the puzzle is ensuring the court where the suit is filed can enter a valid judgment—something that requires us to explore the necessity for notice. As we will see, Rule 4's methods for service, if followed, will ensure proper notice. Notice that dips below the means provided by Rule 4 and which violates principles of due process can lead to a void, unenforceable judgment.

Chapters 8-18: Civil Litigation After Service of Process

Chapter 8 describes the process of a civil case after filing and service. It describes the stages of litigation that typically flow in sequence from that point. The chapter also emphasizes the Federal Rules of Civil Procedure applicable at each stage.

Chapters 8 through 18 describe the progress of a civil action after service of process. Typically, the topics in these chapters are reserved for the second semester of law school, or the latter half of a course if the school teaches Civil Procedure solely in one semester. Chapters 1 through 7 are best understood as addressing where to file a suit and how to provide notice through service of process. Chapter 8 through 18 are best understood as outlining the stages of the litigation process once the defendant or defendants have been served. The author believes it best for a student to have a separate introduction to the latter stage of the litigation process. Therefore, Chapter 8 will summarize the stages of litigation after service of process, beginning with Chapter 9 and ending with Chapter 18. These latter stages in the process of a civil case more heavily involve the Rules of Civil Procedure. Chapter 8 will explain the Federal Rules that apply at each stage so that the student can see how these rules form an integral part of the sequence of stages leading to trial.

CHAPTER 2: CAUSE OF ACTION AND PRE-FILING TASKS.

I. How the Topics in this Chapter Fit in the Overall Progress of a Civil Action

Below is a diagram of the stages of a civil action showing in bold where the topics addressed in this chapter fall in the progress of a civil case.

Figure 2-1

Cause of Action (events leading to suit)	Pre-Filing Tasks (items to begin representation, interviewing, and related matters)	Choice of Forum (subject matter jurisdiction, removal, personal jurisdiction, and venue)	Notice and Service of Process (completing the process of ensuring the forum court can enter a valid judgment)	Pleading the Case and Joinder of Claims and Parties (including supplemental jurisdiction)

Responding to Claims by Motion or by Answer	Discovery (developing proof to establish claims and learn your adversary's case)	Right to Jury (pretrial motions and practice)	Final Pretrial Conference (events within last month before trial)	Trial (procedures and motions during trial)	Verdict	Post-Trial Motions (motions for a new trial and/or judgment as a matter of law)	Appeal

Lawsuits do not appear out of thin air. Someone breaches a contract. Someone commits a tort. Perhaps a company violates a statute under which the plaintiff can sue. Events such as these—the events of everyday life—are the stuff of which lawsuits are made. The technical term for facts that give rise to a legal claim are the "cause of action." When these cause-of-action facts are combined with a legal basis for relief, whether it be a common-law right to recover for breach of contract, for injury due to tortious conduct, or violation of a statute, the plaintiff can have a lawyer file a lawsuit that sets forth in pleadings how the facts violate the law in question and give rise to claims for which the plaintiff seeks relief.

Before filing suit, however, several steps occur that are transparent to most. Unless you are a lawyer or someone who has had the opportunity to litigate, you are not be likely to even know about these steps. However, as you go through law school, you will have courses that equip you to take these steps. They are introduced here so that you realize that you will need to learn these steps to be a competent and professional lawyer. For instance, you will learn in your upper-level Professional Responsibility course, that a lawyer must perform a "conflicts check" before hearing a word from the prospective client—other than the identities of the parties who would be the potential client's adversaries. The Model Rules of Professional Responsibility preclude a lawyer from representing a party who is adverse to an existing client, or a previous client if the previous representation is sufficiently related such that the lawyer would have confidential information of the former client.[14]

Once you have confirmed that you can ethically represent the client, you can hear the client's story, decide whether the facts give rise to claims, and discuss with the client whether you are willing to undertake representation. In other words, you do not have to take every case. You discuss with the client whether you will agree to undertake representation, the terms of such representation, especially how you will be compensated (*e.g.*, whether it be on an hourly rate or a share of the recovery contingent on prevailing—called a "contingent fee" case). If you agree to representation, you prepare, and both the client and you sign a representation agreement setting forth these terms.

You will also take in your first year of law school a legal research and writing course. You may not at first realize all the reasons such a course is so crucial to your development. For the purpose of handling a civil suit, you need—at the point of undertaking representation—to be able to research all legal bases on which the facts you have been given can give rise to claims. Only in that way can you file a complaint that includes all the grounds for relief available, and there are in most cases at least two or more claims arising from the same set of facts. You will need to know how to draft a complaint that would be filed to start a lawsuit and be served on the defendant or defendants. As such, this civil procedure course will teach you how to draft a complaint, how to file it, and how to serve it properly. Thus, you see how different courses in law school combine to provide you with the proficiencies you will need to be successful in law practice.

Only lawyers and judges know that there are other issues that need to be researched as soon as one takes on a case. In addition to identifying the claims, you need to determine if there is anything you must do before filing suit as a prerequisite to suing. For instance, some claims require a party to send notice within a specified period to the prospective defendant of the events for which the plaintiff will sue. Certain statutes likewise require a party to go through seeking resolution of the dispute outside of litigation before filing suit. This type of requirement is called exhausting remedies. If you do not know about these prerequisites to advise your client to do them before filing suit, you can bet the defendant will challenge the suit for failing to observe the prerequisites.

Another critical area of research is the statutes of limitations—the time from the events giving rise to a claim and the date on which a complaint is filed—on each claim. Different claims will have different statutes of limitations. You will want to file the complaint before the earliest statute of limitations runs out. Of course, this assumes you will have satisfied any prerequisites your research shows as required to bring one or more of the claims.

As will be explained later in the course of our hypothetical lawsuit, you will make choices on how to serve the complaint on the defendant. Another pretrial consideration in preparing one's suit for trial is the idea of informal discovery and investigation.

These are a brief summary of the kinds of considerations a lawyer routinely does at the outset of a case. It's a juggling process that becomes routine. The point here is to alert you to these additional matters so that you do not believe you can simply file a complaint on anything at any time. But the main considerations of a plaintiff's lawyer bringing a claim, specifically one in the federal system, are reserved for the next four chapters. Chapters 3 and 4 address the question of whether the case is one that is within

---

[14] The Rules of Professional Responsibility prohibit a lawyer from representing someone against a party the lawyer is currently representing, even if it is on an unrelated matter. MODEL RULES OF PROF'L CONDUCT, R. 1.7 (AM. BAR ASS'N 2016). Moreover, lawyers have to do a check of all former clients because the Rules of Professional Conduct prohibit representing a former client in matters "substantially related" to a former case. *Id.* at r. 1.9.

the jurisdiction of federal courts. Because the Constitution limits the jurisdiction of federal courts to certain kinds of cases, the lawyer needs to know whether the case qualifies as one that can be brought in federal court. If not, the suit can be brought in state court. Here, we focus on the criteria for federal court cases. Chapter 5 focuses on whether the specific court in which the lawyer plans to file suit is one that has personal jurisdiction over the defendant or defendants named. A court cannot exercise power over nonresident defendants, even a federal court, unless the criteria exists for that court to exercise power over the defendant. Finally, in the choice-of-forum (i.e., where the suit is filed) analysis, the lawyer filing in the federal system needs to understand that there are 94 federal districts, that many states have more than one district, and that the suit must be filed in a district for which the federal venue statues provide a basis for venue. The choice-of-forum issues will take up most of the first semester of Civil Procedure. The process of pursuing a suit once filed, and of defending if you represent a defendant sued in federal court, comprise the second semester.

II. Initial Steps in Evaluating the Case

A. First Meeting with the Prospective Client

The single most important aspect of your first meeting with the prospective client, regardless of whether you agree to take the case, is that the client comes away from that meeting believing that you care. Being empathetic does not mean that the lawyer has no boundaries. In their excellent book, RELATIONSHIP CENTERED LAWYERING, Susan Brooks and Robert Madden describe this balance:

> Empathy is the capacity to feel with and think about the client. Empathic lawyers recognize the motives and feelings of clients by considering the situation from the perspective of their experiences. This allows clients to feel heard and respected and increases the opportunities for lawyers to address the most important client needs. However, lawyers must be clear about their boundaries in managing a lawyer-client relationship as there is a danger in extending oneself beyond what is appropriate. Being empathetic is different from being a therapist to a client. Being an advocate is different from creating dependency in clients. The scope of the lawyer's intervention should always be related to the legal issue for which the client is seeking services.[15]

Every person is different. Law students and lawyers will thus vary in the degree to which they possess the ability to be empathetic. Make no mistake: authenticity is essential. We are not talking about pretending to care about the client. Regardless of your views on the importance of empathy in a lawyer-client relationship, you are encouraged to talk to lawyers who have become pillars of the legal community. Ask them about the importance of listening to the client, looking at the world from the client's perspective, and how that develops trust. Better yet, find clients who have had lawyers they trust and clients who have not connected with their lawyers. Again, the single most important thing to convey to the client is that you care about the client and, within proper boundaries, would like to help.

How can empathy be developed in law students and young lawyers? The good news is that emotional intelligence, of which empathy is one aspect, can be gained with effort.[16] Those serious about

---

[15] RELATIONSHIP-CENTERED LAWYERING: SOCIAL SCIENCE THEORY FOR TRANSFORMING LEGAL PRACTICE 151 (Susan L. Brooks & Robert G. Madden eds., 2010).
[16] *See* DANIEL GOLEMAN, EMOTIONAL INTELLIGENCE 34 (1995).

their faith recognize that Daniel Goleman neither discovered "empathy" nor that it is a quality that can increase over one's life.[17] The development of virtue has long been part of the Christian tradition—and the typical pattern for such development is a process over time.[18]Nevertheless, Goleman and others have influenced the academic community to teach more than information. In this area, medical education may be ahead of many other graduate fields. For example, medical schools have students play the role of patient so that they can experience what it is like for patients to deal with doctors who often use terms the patient does not understand. Students thereby gain the patient's perspective.[19] Law schools can just as easily have law students play the role of the client. As mock clients, law students can see things from the client's perspective. Perhaps they may be subjected to questioning in which the "lawyer" seems not to be listening to the "client," or where the "lawyer" uses legal terms with which the "client" is not familiar, etc. Indeed, some schools are beginning to implement such creative approaches to cultivating interpersonal skills. Perhaps it is no coincidence that key studies within the last decade have identified these skills as being as important as analytical ability to effective lawyering.[20] Consistent with the caution from RELATIONSHIP-CENTERED LAWYERING, law schools believe that empathy has to be paired with cultivating the ability to detach while empathizing such that the lawyer can provide objective judgment.[21] If you have been successful in the first goal of meeting with the client, you have begun to build a relationship of trust.

The best approach in dealing with a prospective client is to learn as much as possible about the events that led the client to seek legal assistance. A helpful rule of thumb on questioning one's client is to find answers to the five W's: Who, What, When, Where, and Why. Who are all the persons and entities involved in the events over which the client has come to see you? (Note that, if any names or entities come up that were not previously mentioned, and they are potentially adverse, you as the attorney must suspend the interview until another conflicts check has been run.) What happened? When did the events occur? Where did they occur? Why has the client come to you? While the client cannot be expected to explain why these events give rise to a claim, you can determine what the client's goals are and what the client wants as the outcome of your representation.

Having the broad outline provided by the five W's with which to begin, counsel can flesh out more facts in follow-up conversations. Counsel will want to ask the client for all pertinent documents and get the client to sign a release to all medical providers so that she can gather medical records. In addition, the proactive lawyer will determine if there is any physical evidence and secure it; visit any accident scene; determine what changes, if any, have been made to the scene and identify persons who can testify to facts, such as the condition of the scene at the time of the accident. Many lawyers refer to such investigation as

---

[17] *Id.*

[18] *See* THOMAS KEATING, INVITATION TO LOVE: THE WAY OF CHRISTIAN CONTEMPLATION (20th ed. 2012) (describing growth in the Christian faith as a process of progressive dismantling human attachment to the world, to status, and to power and control—a process that the Holy Spirit accomplishes but in which the person can either refuse to participate or surrender to the process).

12 Available at http://www.law.berkeley.edu/files/LSACREPORTfinal-12.pdf (last visited June 24, 2016).

[19] *See* Neil Hamilton & Verna Monson, *Legal Education's Ethical Challenge: Empirical Research on How Most Effectively to Foster Each Student's Professional Formation (Professionalism)*, 9 U. ST. THOMAS L.J. 325, 358 (2011).

[20] Lawrence S. Krieger & Kenneth M. Sheldon, *What Makes Lawyers Happy?: A Data-Driven Prescription to Redefine Professional Success*, 83 GEO. WASH. L. REV. 554 (2015); MAJORITE M. SHULTZ & SHELDON ZEDECK, FINAL REPORT: IDENTIFICATION, DEVELOPMENT, AND VALIDATION OF PREDICTORS FOR SUCCESSFUL LAWYERING 55 (2008).

[21] Benjamin V. Madison, III, and L.O. Natt Gantt, *The Emperor Has No Clothes, But Does Anyone Really Care: How Law Schools Are Failing to Develop Students' Professional Identities and Practical Judgment*, 27 REGENT U.L. REV. 339, 390–406 (2015).

"informal discovery." The topic of informal discovery, and the other steps counsel would take in a thorough effort, are described briefly in this chapter,[22] and in much more detail later at the beginning of Chapter 13, the chapter devoted entirely to the discovery process in litigation. However, the discussion here is designed to allow you to understand that lawsuits do not just begin with a complaint containing claims. Many steps precede that.

Often, in an interview, the lawyer will prompt the client: "Please tell me more about (something the client mentioned)." It also helps in reinforcing your empathy to use a technique called reflective listening as you gather more information. For instance, say the prospective client talks for ten minutes or more detailing negotiations with the fictional Smith Corporation that led to a contract that someone breached. You can tell from the person's description that she's frustrated by the entire series of events. You can summarize: "As I understand it, on [fill in date] you began negotiations with Smith Corporation to [describe the service or goods to be provided]. You followed up with telephone calls on the following dates: [fill in dates]. As you got closer on the terms, the negotiations were put on paper. You recall several letters back and forth and then a signing a contract. Then, Smith Corporation failed to do what it promised. I can see how that understandably frustrates you." Here, you are not only interviewing, but also reinforcing your empathy. You also give the client the opportunity to clarify or add facts if you do not recite them accurately, even as you express your recognition of their frustration. As lawyers, we need to remember we are representing human beings with emotional reactions. If we treat prospective clients like computers that provide data and that is all we look for, we are ignoring the human element. The client needs to know we care, and the first meeting is a good time to convey this.

The practice of law will present you with real-life problems in people's lives. Over time, a lawyer can become impassive. Indeed, indifference is one psychological defense to facing the problems and distress that clients bring to the lawyer. An impassive lawyer will not project much of any response, much less empathy. The approach that will yield more of a connection to one's clients is to grow in empathy while maintaining professional boundaries. A lawyer can care about others without taking on the client's problems as her own. Prospective and actual clients alike will respond favorably to someone who cares. Even more importantly, you will know that you are treating others with respect by showing empathy. In maintaining such an approach to client relations, you will maintain self-respect and your own sense of humanity. You will avoid becoming impassive or, worse, cynical.

Your first-interview outline should also have reminders to have the client sign any forms necessary for you to gather documents. For instance, medical providers will not provide you with your client's medical documents without a consent form signed by the client. You can ask the client to sign these forms before or after the interview. The point is to have a plan and to follow the plan. By so doing, you will project that you are someone that knows what she is doing. If you are not ready to enter a formal representation, make it clear to the client that you are asking these questions and gathering the documentation so as to make a judgment, and that only upon signing a formal agreement will the attorney-client relationship arise.

At the conclusion of the initial meeting, reaffirm how pleased you are to have met the client and how you hope that your further investigation will lead you and your firm to the decision to represent her. Some clients may expect the lawyer to have legal answers on the spot at the first interview. It is a false assumption that lawyers carry around in their heads everything they need to know about the law. As much as the client may want to receive an immediate evaluation, you do not want to create any false impressions or expectations. You can, however, give the prospective client a date by which you will explain whether

---

[22] *Infra* Part II.3.

19

the client has a case, what claims can be brought, and the other details that would follow undertaking representation. Some inexperienced lawyers feel the need to please the client. Resist that urge. A professional makes sound judgments, and it is a rare case when one can decide whether to take a case and outline the claims in an initial meeting.

B. Following Up on Initial Meeting and Deciding Whether to Represent a Prospective Client

One other reason for deferring on whether to enter representation and providing advice is a fact that surprises some students and new lawyers. The reality is that clients do not always provide a clear picture of events. That does not mean the client is lying. People tend to perceive events and present them to someone they want to be their advocate, in a manner that is often slanted in a way that suggests the client has a better case than may be true. Others will not disclose everything because they are afraid the lawyer will not take their case. Here is where the boundaries and detachment come in. You have been empathetic. However, that does not mean you have to be gullible. One way to encourage prospective clients to provide all information is to confirm that you are in a lawyer-client relationship for at least the limited purpose of determining whether to pursue the case and that anything the client tells you about past events will be protected by privilege. That often leads to other facts being disclosed. Another way to encourage clients is to ask: "Please tell me about any facts that worry you. I need to know those, too." Regardless of what you hear, stay objective and remember that events may or may not turn out as the prospective client represents.

1. Initial Investigation

Thus, after meeting with the potential client, and setting a date by which you will get back to the client, you ought to do some initial investigation. Check out whether facts that the client related are accurate. You can go to the scene of an accident, for instance, and see whether the physical layout fits with the client's account. You can also get an accident report and perhaps interview the officer who responded. If there were emergency personnel who responded, you could interview them as well. Whatever it takes to help you gain enough confidence that a case is there—or not—will be worth the effort. What if you find out from the accident report and the policeman that beer cans were found inside your prospective client's car? If the officer determined your client was inebriated, you have just saved yourself a great deal of effort.

2. Factors that May Affect Whether to Take a Case

Some lawyers, especially inexperienced ones, are too inclined to believe that every client's case should be taken. However, to practice law effectively, you must develop sound judgment in determining the cases you undertake.

What are some other factors you should consider when deciding whether to represent a client? If the client's case seems to have merit, that will certainly factor into the equation. Aside from probability of success, what is the potential recovery? How much time and effort would it take to get the case through trial and, if necessary, an appeal? Will the client pay an hourly rate at your normal hourly billing rate? Is the client in favor of a contingent fee? Will the case require significant expert testimony (typically fronted as expenses by the plaintiff's firm)?

The lawyer should also be aware of certain predictable warning signs. Although such warning signs may not preclude representation, you should investigate further to ensure you do not regret committing to the case. If the prospective client spoke with other lawyers before you, you can legitimately ask whether these other lawyers turned down the case for a reason. Perhaps the case is without merit. Perhaps the client is extremely passionate, but the stakes are not that high. You'll know, then, that you have a case that could be a problem to handle. If you represent the client on an hourly basis, the client will end up realizing that she is paying you every time she calls or comes in. Even then, the client's expectations can be out of line. What if the client tells you, "I have no doubt we can win." Any trial lawyer who has worked for any length of time will tell you there is always doubt, even in the best cases. You'll want to ensure you tell clients with high expectations that the process of litigation is a long and arduous one, that the American rule[23] on attorney's fees means that the client will have to pay the fees and costs, and that the process can take significant time. Moreover, even if the client can win, the ability to collect on a judgment (if monetary damages are the goal) depends on the defendant's ability to pay. The process just described is what lawyers call "managing the client's expectations." The average person is not aware of the array of procedures involved in a suit, the uncertainties attendant to any litigation, and the length of time resolution can take, not to mention the cost. Unreasonable expectations by a client are not unusual. The client needs to be educated on all these points.

Other facts can signal potential troublesome cases. If the client comes to you well after the events in question occurred, you should immediately be concerned about the statute of limitations. Some lawyers will do a limited engagement solely to evaluate whether the statute of limitations has run before they take a case. If they conclude the limitations period has run, the lawyer could decline representation. Although statutes of limitation are an affirmative defense that must be raised by the opponent, rarely will a defendant not raise the defense when applicable.

What about the client's financial ability to pay? If the case is a potentially large recovery for personal injury, or if the case is under a statute in which attorney's fees are awarded (*e.g.*, federal discrimination cases, civil rights cases), then one may overlook the client's financial state because of the potential for a reward for the client and the attorney on prevailing. Such situations usually require a contingent fee agreement. In such cases, the client should be told that you would not be handling the litigation if it were not for the prospects of recovery and/or fee shifting under a statute. Again, that offsets any sense that the lawyer is capitalizing on the client's misfortune. The client should realize that you will put significant time in the case and take a major risk of not recovering and having that time go unpaid.

Everything you say to the client should be put in writing. If you decide not to represent the client, that should be confirmed in a letter. If you take the case on an hourly basis, that arrangement and all the other conditions of representation should be spelled out in a written, signed agreement. A monthly reflection of the time spent on matters related to the case should be sent to the client regardless of whether the client signs an hourly representation agreement. That will, in the hourly scenario, allow for regular payments. In other scenarios, the client will be apprised of the amount of work one is doing on a case. Laypeople often have little idea how much time and effort go into litigation. By documenting time and effort spent on a case, the client can more clearly appreciate your representation. They will see, for instance, when the opponent has developed an aggressive discovery approach to which you're having to respond in written responses and in-person depositions. The likelihood of an objection when you receive your share of a contingent fee is far less likely if you have adopted this transparent approach.

If you have decided to take on a case and have met with the client and performed an initial

---

[23] The approach to recovery of attorneys' fees in civil litigation typically compares the English Rule, in which the loser in a civil case pays the winner's legal fees and costs, versus the American Rule, in which the parties bear their own legal fees and costs regardless of the result.

investigation, you can send an initial plan of action letter. This is beneficial on many levels and is recommended by many practicing attorneys. The action letter will confirm everything you have told the client about the vagaries of the litigation process, particularly the time factor. Moreover, you can outline the claims that you plan to bring on the client's behalf. You can inform the client of the elements of those claims that will need to be proved. You can ask the client for documents and witnesses that will support each element. If experts are necessary, you can ask the client if anyone in their company or business would be a potential expert. You can tell the client that experts are generally expensive, but in certain cases essential (*e.g.*, product liability cases). If the client is not willing to hire experts in such a case, the client may not be successful, and should reconsider filing suit. You can note that, in addition to whatever evidence the client, friendly witnesses, client documents, and experts can provide, you will be performing "formal discovery" of the opponent. The client should be told that it is essential to perform discovery to find out what the opponent has in the way of documents and witnesses. Moreover, you can note that the process will not only protect you and the client from surprise, but usually turns up documents and witness testimony that you can use later in the case. All in all, taking the extra step to provide the client with an initial plan of action letter will lead to repeat business and word-of-mouth referrals.

After the plan of action letter, meet with the client and see what the client can do to provide what you have asked for. You will thus have formed a partnership in moving forward and likely reduced some costs. Then, as the litigation proceeds, send the client regular update letters. These can refer to the initial letter and explain how you have furthered the goals outlined in that letter. Moreover, you can bring to the client's attention any developments not foreseen at the outset.

C. Informal Discovery

Informal discovery is simply another way to refer to further investigation. If, upon preliminary investigation, you and your firm are ready to represent the client, advise the client and have her sign an appropriate agreement on the terms of representation. Such an agreement will vary depending on whether you will be charging an hourly rate, a flat fee, or handing the case on a contingent fee.

Informal discovery should be the place where every lawyer starts building her case and developing a case strategy. Informal discovery is more efficient and less costly than using the methods provided by the procedural rules. It allows the lawyer to begin locating all favorable and unfavorable information she can on the case. Then, the lawyer can target formal discovery to obtain the necessary evidence to support the strong points of her case while negating the weak points.

Conferring with the client has already started the informal discovery process. At the initial meeting, you probably requested documents and materials. If the client was injured, you will also want to get any medical records from health care providers who examined the client.[24] These documents will educate you about the issues at hand, the damages incurred, and possible future damages. A client's documents may also lead to third-party witnesses who can testify to important facts. For injured clients, the medical documents obtained will provide a record of health care professionals who examined or treated the client. These persons often serve as a cross between factual and expert witnesses because they provide factual background about treatment, but also may offer expert opinions.

---

[24] In order for you to obtain your client's medical records, which are protected under the Health Insurance Portability and Accountability Act of 1996 (HIPAA), your client will have to sign a release authorization form, known as a "HIPAA release." *See* 45 C.F.R. §§ 160, 164 (2017). This release should specify the extent of information sought and deadline in which the authorization expires. Be prepared, however. Depending on the facility, it can take a few days to several months to process a HIPAA release and receive the requested information.

Informal discovery need not stop with your own client. For example, in a personal injury case, an attorney should visit the scene of the accident as soon as possible. The attorney can make a record of the accident scene, gather facts, take photographs from different viewpoints, and measure pertinent distances, heights of objects, etc. Often the location of an accident undergoes physical changes by the time a case is tried. A proactive attorney will preserve evidence at the accident site as close to the time of the accident as possible. If a witness can testify that whatever photograph or diagram depicts the scene at the time of the events in question, you can get these into evidence. Having done so may prove to be invaluable when the case goes to trial and may prevent the attorney from having to rely on a witness's recollection of the condition of the scene.

Each time an attorney gathers information informally, she advances her client's case. Bit by bit, she learns more about the case. The difference between hearing a description of an accident scene and visiting the scene is comparable to the difference between listening to someone describe the taste of an apple and to experience the taste of an apple. At an accident scene, the lawyer can view it from every angle, measure relevant distances, and observe physical conditions that simply could not be appreciated without being on the scene. Indeed, the wise lawyer would visit the site at the same time of day as an accident happened, under similar weather conditions, and may in the process pick up valuable information such as traffic flow, witnesses who travel the route, etc. Throughout the remainder of the case, the lawyer who has visited the scene and gathered evidence will continue to benefit from that effort. When she drafts the written discovery requests, or questions witnesses under oath in the depositions, she will draft more intelligent document requests and ask better questions than an attorney who handles the case from her desk. Informal investigation may, and should, involve more than merely visiting an accident scene and recording facts from there alone. For example, if vehicles or other physical evidence have been towed away or placed in a location other than the accident site, the attorney should secure this evidence. Securing such evidence may require placing it in storage. Although doing so may come at an additional fee, it allows the attorney to preserve the evidence exactly as found. If the physical evidence is owned by others, the attorney can ask the nonparty for the evidence so that it can be preserved. However, if a nonparty or a party has physical evidence and will not agree to preserve it, the attorney may have to seek an immediate court order requiring such preservation on filing suit.

What if people live near the location where events giving rise to the suit occurred? The attorney or someone on her team should interview these persons. Did they see the events? Do they know anyone who did? How long has a physical condition, such as a hole in the ground or a sharp pipe sticking out of the ground, existed? Do they know of anyone who has been hurt there? After speaking with witnesses, the attorney or other agent often asks these people if they are willing to sign a statement reciting the facts related.

Finally, the attorney can investigate sources of information and documents that can supply additional background regarding the case. These can include national websites, such as the National Weather Service website,[25] which has a vehicle for determining past weather on a given day, or the National Transportation Safety Board,[26] which has accident data as well as other data that may be useful in examining whether a vehicle is safe. Other sources include state websites for the state involved, such as the Department

---

[25] *See Finding Past Weather…Fast*, NAT'L OCEANIC AND ATMOSPHERIC ADMIN., http://www.weather.-gov/help-past-weather (last visited May 28, 2017).
[26] *See* Accident Reports, NAT'L TRANSP. SAFETY BD., http://www.ntsb.gov/investigations/Acciden-tReports/Pages/AccidentReports.aspx (last visited May 28, 2017).

of Motor Vehicles,[27] which has crash information data and links to requesting police reports, among other useful information. One can determine information about a corporation by checking the State Corporation Commission website for that any state. In addition to national and state websites, one can find information on local government websites, at the offices of local agencies, at state and local libraries, as well as many other sources, depending on the information needed. Indeed, public databases available for investigation of facts are more accessible by the Internet now than ever before.[28]

Follow-Up Questions and Comments

1. You are working late and receive a call from someone. You confirm that you are a lawyer, and the person begins to tell you about an incident where he slipped and fell at a local grocery store. He starts going into details when you stop him. Why would you stop the person?

2. At a cocktail party, you meet a doctor who learns you are a lawyer. The doctor informs you that he has just given his two-week notice of resignation to the medical center he works for. The doctor asks you whether the medical center can enforce a covenant-not-to-compete in his employment contract that prohibits him from practicing within a 50-mile radius for one year after leaving the medical center. How would you respond? What, if any, implications would flow from providing the doctor your view and/or opinion have?

III. Checking Urgent Dates: Pre-Suit Notice of Claims, Calculating Deadlines, and Statutes of Limitations

You will learn that handling a lawsuit can be quite complicated. Preliminary legal research will always be appropriate. Researching the elements of all potential claims under the substantive law must be done on any potential case to (1) determine whether any pre-suit notice requirements apply to a particular claim, requiring notice to be given prior to a suit being filed; and (2) how to apply the applicable statute of limitations analysis to each claim.

A. Is there a Pre-Suit Notice or Exhaustion Requirement before Filing Suit?

During your meeting with the client, you explain that your first research priority will include determining the statutes of limitations for each viable claim and identifying claims which require provision of notice prior to filing suit. You realize that deadline calculations will be required for both and begin to wonder how one determines the start date for counting a specified period. How does one know the latest date on which a statute of limitations or notice deadline falls? Your questions raise the subject of how to calculate deadlines in court proceedings. Many refer to this as "judicial counting" to distinguish it from ordinary counting. It is wise to give judicial counting a separate label because it is decidedly different from ordinary counting. As your research reveals, calculating judicial deadlines requires one to ignore the date an event occurred (*e.g.*, an accident date, date of diagnosis, date of breach, etc.). "Day 1" of the applicable notice or limitations deadline applies on the day after the event. Failure to master these fundamental rules

---

[27] *See* Highway Safety, VA. DEPT. OF MOTOR VEHICLES, http://www.dmv.state.va.us/safety/ (last visited May 28, 2017).

[28] *See* Paul Meyers, Online Research Tools and Investigative Techniques, GLOBAL INVESTIGATIVE JOURNALISM NETWORK, http://gijn.org/2015/05/05/online-research-tools-and-investigation-techniques/ (May 5, 2015).

of counting can result in missing a deadline that might prejudice your client, or worse, lead to dismissal of the case.

1. Learning to Count the Judicial Way

a. Calculation of Deadlines Expressed in Days: Rule 6

Computation of days in federal court is governed by Federal Rules of Civil Procedure 6. In pertinent part, Rule 6 provides as follows:

> **(a) Computing Time.** The following rules apply in computing any time period specified in these rules, in any local rule or court order, or in any statute that does not specify a method of computing time.
>> **(1) Period Stated in Days or a Longer Unit.** When the period is stated in days or a longer unit of time:
>>> (A) exclude the day of the event that triggers the period;
>>> (B) count every day, including intermediate Saturdays, Sundays, and legal holidays; **and**
>>> (C) include the last day of the period, but if the last day is a Saturday, Sunday, or legal holiday, the period continues to run until the end of the next day that is not a Saturday, Sunday, or legal holiday.
>> **(2) Period Stated in Hours.** When the period is stated in hours:
>>> (A) begin counting immediately on the occurrence of the event that triggers the period;
>>> (B) count every hour, including hours during intermediate Saturdays, Sundays, and legal holidays; *and*
>>> (C) if the period would end on a Saturday, Sunday, or legal holiday, the period continues to run until the same time on the next day that is not a Saturday, Sunday, or legal holiday.[29]

Some federal statutes, for instance, require a plaintiff to give notice to other parties before filing suit. The Federal Water Pollution Control Act,[30] is one such example. The Act authorizes private citizens to bring claims for water pollution, but only after giving pre-suit notice to certain parties:

> No action may be commenced . . . prior to sixty days after the plaintiff has given notice of the alleged violation (i) to the Administrator [of the Environmental Protection Agency], (ii) to the State in which the alleged violation occurs, and (iii) to any alleged violator of the standard, limitation, or order[31]

Now, let's assume you are researching a claim under the Federal Water Pollution Control Act. You are aware that Rule 6 governs this deadline because the Act specifies an act must be done within a prescribed amount of time, specifically a suit cannot be commenced until sixty days after giving notice. But, what is Day 1 in the counting of 60 days? The day of the notice cannot be "Day 1" because that would directly contradict Rule 6's direction to "exclude the day or event that triggers the period." Thus, you would start

---

[29] FED. R. CIV. P. 6 (emphasis added).
[30] 33 U.S.C. § 1251, et seq.
[31] 33 U.S.C. § 1365(b) (1) (A) (2017).

counting "Day 1" on the day after the notice was given and proceed to count until Day 60. Then, you must check to see whether the last day is a Saturday, Sunday, or legal holiday. If so, the deadline will carry over to the next business day. A seasoned litigator handily analyzes each of these steps without really thinking about them as a step-by-step process because the analysis has become second nature. However, at one point she too was a novice and had to navigate each individual step. Once you have calculated the date beyond sixty days, you will then know when suit can be brought under the Act.

b. Calculation of Deadlines Expressed in Terms of "Years" or "Months" - Rule 6

Although Federal Rules of Civil Procedure 6 does not expressly address calculation of years or months, the same rule that applies to days also applies to all longer units. When counting months and years, the calendar year method governs.[32] Under this method, one goes from the date in one month (e.g., February 2) to the same date in the month that falls however many months after that which the deadline states (e.g., six months after February 2 is August 2), even though if one counted the days it would not equal six 30-day periods. Likewise, statutes of limitations follow the calendar year method such that, if a statute of limitations requires suit to be filed within two years, one would have to file on the same month and day as the events two years afterward.

Additionally, several federal statutes contain an exhaustion of remedies requirement. Consider the following language from the Federal Tort Claims Act, under which the government must waive immunity in certain tort actions:

An action shall not be instituted upon a claim against the United States for money damages for injury or loss of property or personal injury or death caused by the negligent or wrongful act or omission of any employee of the Government while acting within the scope of his office or employment, unless the claimant shall have first presented the claim to the appropriate Federal agency and his claim shall have been finally denied by the agency in writing and sent by certified or registered mail.[33]

Follow-Up Questions and Comments

1. What is the difference between a pre-suit notice and filing suit: in terms of (a) what the documents will look like; (2) how they will be sent; and (3) whether they will be filed? Research the law of the state where you intend to practice and determine how you can typically satisfy applicable pre-suit notice requirements.

2. In every case that lands on your desk, how can you remember to research whether the applicable law will require pre-suit notice as a prerequisite to filing a complaint? What is the risk for not recognizing such claims? Who will bear responsibility for dismissal of the suit if the time for notice ran out after counsel undertook representation and before filing suit?

---

[32] *See* 4B CHARLES ALAN WRIGHT & ARTHUR R. MILLER, FEDERAL PRACTICE AND PROCEDURE § 1162 (4th ed. 2018).
[33] 28 U.S.C. § 2675; *see also* 42 U.S.C. § 2000 e-5(f) (1) (2017) (restricting a party from bringing a claim for employment discrimination under Title VII of the Civil Rights Act of 1964 until obtaining a right to sue letter from the Equal Employment Opportunity Commission).

Practice Problems

Practice Problem 2-1

Megan Mailwoman is delivering mail in a neighborhood in Norfolk, Virginia on June 17, 2016. Due to lengthened workdays and increased demands on postal workers, Megan and many of her fellow postal workers are chronically fatigued. While driving to her next set of mailboxes, Megan runs through a stop sign and hits Pete Parker, severely injuring him. Because the accident occurred in the course of Megan's employment, Parker's case falls within the Federal Tort Claims Act, meaning the government waives its immunity up to a certain dollar amount for negligence cases. Parker comes to you and asks when he can file suit in federal court. How would you advise Parker to proceed if he wanted to file suit?

Practice Problem 2-2

Molly Manager works at Old Virginia, Inc., a company that specializes in providing products related to Virginia. Her supervisor has repeatedly, over the last year, put his arm around her while giving her instructions to pass on to her subordinates. His hand had recently started moving closer to her breast. Molly raises the issue with Human Resources, and within six months she is notified that she is being fired. She comes to you and asks whether she can bring a lawsuit in federal court for sexual discrimination and harassment under Title VII of the Civil Rights Act of 1964. You research whether there is anything you must do before filing the federal suit. How would you advise Molly?

B. What are the Applicable Statutes of Limitations?

The statute of limitations analysis requires a lawyer to determine the time period allocated by law for a kind of claim. Typically, this period varies in length depending on the type of claim. For state claims heard in federal court based on diversity jurisdiction, the state statute of limitations will govern, and the state sets its own statute of limitations period for types of claims (i.e., property, contract, tort, equitable). See 4 AM. JUR. Trials § 441 (2017). In many states, the statute of limitations for personal injury actions is two years, while the statute of limitations for property damage is five years.[34]

In many states, shorter limitation periods apply for intentional torts (*e.g.*, one year), as compared to negligence claims (*e.g.*, two to three years), contract claims (often four or five years), and property claims (*e.g.*, five or more years).[35]

Federal statutes, at times, contain their own specified statutes of limitations. For instance, the federal False Claims Act provides a six-year statute of limitations for claims under that Act.[36] Some federal

---

[34] *See, e.g.*, VA. CODE ANN. § 8.01-243 (A)-(B) (2016). For examples of other statutes of limitations, *compare* CAL. CIV. PROC. CODE §§ 335-335.1 (Deering 2017) (establishing a two-year statute of limitations period for actions other than the recovery of real property) *with* CAL. CIV. PROC. CODE § 315 (Deering 2017) (establishing a ten-year statute of limitations period for actions seeking recovery of real property); *see also* N.Y. C.P.L.R. §§ 212(a)(Consol. 2017) (establishing a ten-year statute of limitations period for actions seeking recovery of real property); *id.* § 214(a) (establishing a two-year-and-six-months statute of limitations period for actions seeking recovery for medical malpractice).

[35] *See e.g.*, 4 AM. JUR. TRIALS APP. § 441 (2017). States vary, however, in the length of time prescribed for a particular kind of action. Thus, an attorney must be careful to check her state's limitations period for each claim in a case.

[36] *See* 31 U.S.C. § 3731 (2017).

statutes, however, do not include a statute of limitations. In such instances, the applicable statute of limitations will be the limitations period in the forum state's law for a claim most analogous to the federal statutory claim.[37] For instance, when a plaintiff was sued under the Individuals with Disabilities Education Act,[38] the federal court had to resort to the most analogous state law of the forum (Montana) because the federal statute lacks a limitations period.[39] Similarly, in an action under Title IX of the Education Amendments Act of 1972,[40] by a high school student based on sexual abuse by a teacher in Georgia, the court applied the forum state's two-year personal injury statute of limitations.[41]

Practice Problems

Practice Problem 2-3

Well-Mart is a large retailer with stores in all 50 states. H2O Association, an advocate for clean water, learns that Well-Mart employees are routinely pouring pesticides down the sink at stores nationwide. H2O seeks to bring a citizens' suit against Well-Mart under the Clean Water Act. The Act requires that the plaintiffs provide 60 days' notice to the party who committed the violation.

The forum state has a statute of limitations of five years for damage to someone's property, including contamination of water (*e.g.* ponds) on their property. H2O gives notice to all required parties on Earth Day, April 22, 2016. What is the earliest date on which H2O can bring the citizens suit against Well-Mart? What is the latest date on which H20 can bring suit?

Practice Problem 2-4

Assume all the facts of Practice Problem 2-2 involving Molly Manager's employment discrimination claim apply. Assume further that the Equal Employment Opportunity Commission gives Molly Manager a "Notice of Right to Sue" letter on June 23, 2016. Title VII of the Civil Rights Act of 1964 allows a plaintiff to bring a claim within 90 days of the date of the letter. By what date must Molly Manager bring her Title VII claim against her employer?

---

[37] *See* 19 CHARLES ALAN WRIGHT & ARTHUR R. MILLER, FEDERAL PRACTICE AND PROCEDURE § 4519 (4th ed. 2018).
[38] 20 U.S.C. §§ 1400 et. seq. (2017).
[39] *See e.g.*, Livingston School District Numbers. 4 and 1 v. Keenan, 82 F.3d 912, 916 (9th Cir. 1996).
[40] *Id.* §§ 1681 et. seq.
[41] M.H.D. v. Westminster Schools, 172 F.3d 797 (11th Cir. 1999).

CHAPTER 3: CHOOSING THE FORUM: SUBJECT MATTER JURISDICTION

I. How the Topics in this Chapter Fit in the Overall Progress of a Civil Action

Below is a diagram showing the point when the issue of choosing a forum will arise in a civil case.

Figure 3-1

Cause of Action (events leading to suit)	Pre-Filing Tasks (items to begin representation, interviewing, and related matters)	**Choice of Forum (subject matter jurisdiction,** removal, personal jurisdiction, and venue)	Notice and Service of Process (completing the process of ensuring the forum court can enter a valid judgment)	Pleading the Case and Joinder of Claims and Parties (including supplemental jurisdiction)

Responding to Claims by Motion or by Answer	Discovery (developing proof to establish claims and learn your adversary's case)	Right to Jury (pretrial motions and practice)	Final Pretrial Conference (events within last month before trial)	Trial (procedures and motions during trial)	Verdict	Post-Trial Motions (motions for a new trial and/or judgment as a matter of law)	Appeal

The overall context you should keep in mind is that this book follows the stages of a civil suit in the federal system. As shown in Chapter 1, a diagram appears at the head of each chapter, with the stage of a civil action bolded to show at which point in the progression of a case the topic or topics arise.

The choice of a forum, one of the first stages, involves several major concepts. These include subject matter jurisdiction—the legal phrase used to answer the question of whether a case meets the criteria for a court's jurisdiction. Because this book addresses federal lawsuits, subject matter jurisdiction means whether the case is one federal courts are authorized to hear. Because federal courts have jurisdiction limited to the categories set forth in the Constitution, and further limited by the federal statutes that enable courts to hear the cases, this book helps you to determine the questions to ask to determine whether a case can be brought to federal court.

Even if a case is within federal subject matter jurisdiction, the court where the case is filed must have a basis for exercising its power over the defendant If the defendant is a nonresident of the state in which the suit is filed (in a federal court located in that state), the court can exercise personal jurisdiction over the defendant only if certain prerequisites are met. Thus, personal jurisdiction is also a matter addressed in the "choice of forum" stage of a case. The term "forum" simply means the court in which suit is brought.

Finally, choice of the forum also requires analysis of whether the case is filed in a district within the state consistent with federal venue statutes. The federal system is divided into 94 districts—with some states having four districts, others having three districts, others having two districts, and some with but one district for the entire state. The process of analyzing whether suit is filed in the correct forum may thus require you to confirm subject matter jurisdiction, personal jurisdiction, and venue. These concepts, though related in the broadest sense, have very different analyses. They also happen to be among the most involved analyses you will see in federal civil procedure. Hence, they each get their own chapter even though they are addressing the question of whether the court in question is in the proper location.

This chapter will address subject matter jurisdiction by exploring the applicable criteria involved in a plaintiff's decision to bring suit in either federal or state court. Chapter 4 will address how to analyze personal jurisdiction over defendants, whether it be in federal or state court. Then, Chapter 5 will address the question of which federal district within a state would be an appropriate venue, if a claim is filed in federal court.

Traditional teaching on subject matter jurisdiction tends to ignore the evaluation that goes into considering (a) all the potential courts in which a plaintiff can sue, and (b) the strategic evaluation of both the advantages and disadvantages of suing in federal versus state court. An experienced litigator has likely internalized the process of deciding on a forum such that she often may not even articulate each step. The problem for a student, or a junior lawyer, is that experienced lawyers are inconsistent in the degree to which they vocalize their thought processes. Because lawyers tend to be busy folks, too often senior lawyers do not take the time to articulate their reasoning so that the junior lawyer can learn without having to figure out, from observing how cases are handled, how the process of deciding on a forum works.[42]

So, what are the kinds of questions that a lawyer will consider in choosing whether to file suit in federal or state court? Unfortunately, for many lawyers the leading factor is their level of comfort with the system and its rules, including the degree to which courts in that system enforce the rules.[43] In other words, many lawyers prefer the state system over the federal, or vice versa, for reasons in tension with the best interests of the client. For instance, consider a lawyer who is more familiar with the state court system than the federal system and that the federal courts in her area dispose of cases quickly by strictly enforcing deadlines and compliance with discovery rules. If that lawyer chooses the state system because of her comfort in having more time to litigate the case, and to avoid being held accountable for complying with discovery in a timely and responsive manner, the choice serves the lawyer's interest and not the client's. Within reason, the faster a case is resolved the better it is for a client. The expression "justice delayed is justice denied" may not always hold true, but one thing is certain: the earlier a trial, the earlier a settlement is likely to occur—or, if not, then the earlier the client will receive a resolution through trial.

The client's interests, not the lawyer's comfort, ought to lead the lawyer to the preferred forum. The comparative speed of resolution in each system and the difference in cost to litigate in each system are significant factors. However, other factors also enter the decision. As we shall see in this chapter, if a case satisfies one of the limited criteria for filing suit in federal court, concurrent jurisdiction in federal or state

---

[42] Even if a law firm is on a billable hour arrangement, partners are less likely now than ever to take time discussing a case with an associate. Judge Patrick Schilz has keenly observed this phenomenon. If clients will not pay for senior and junior lawyers conferring about issues in a case, "every hour that a senior lawyer spends mentoring a junior lawyer costs the law firm whatever one or both of the attorneys would have billed had they not been talking with each other." Patrick J. Schiltz, *Legal Ethics in Decline: The Elite Law Firm, the Elite Law School, and the Moral Formation of the Novice Attorney*, 82 MINN. L. REV. 705, 743 (1998).

[43] *See infra* Professional Identity Question

court can exist. The beauty of concurrent jurisdiction is that the plaintiff can then choose to file suit in either federal or state court. For instance, in a suit where the plaintiff is suing in a state in which two of the defendants are citizens, but which the plaintiff is not, the plaintiff may be concerned she will experience bias favoring the in-state defendants. As such, the Framers of the Constitution included provisions that could influence the plaintiff to choose federal court, which is less likely to be partial and more likely to be neutral. One of the key provisions encouraging a neutral forum for non-residents in federal court are those that ensure federal judges' independence. Under Article III, Section 1, federal judges are appointed for life "during good behavior"[44] and are protected against having their salaries reduced.[45]Thus, a lawyer who is weighing the optimal system—not choosing based on the lawyer's own interests—will also consider whether her client, as a nonresident of the state where the accident occurred, would benefit from the constitutional protections afforded by federal courts. A system that promotes the independence of its judges could be important in a case in which the nonresident will likely litigate in the state where the accident occurred. Although not as influential to some lawyers, federal courts draw juries from a much larger geographic area than the region from which a state court would draw. Some state locales are known for larger verdicts and for being oriented more toward plaintiffs, while other state juries are more conservative and more oriented to defendants—or at least lawyers will tell you so. If one is in doubt, a jury drawn from a broad geographical area is less likely to have a bias and may be the safer choice.[46]

The plaintiff's decision of whether to file in federal or state court implicates many other factors. The list that follows includes several reasons that experienced litigators often give for preferring federal over state court. Some of these have been discussed above; others are new. In no order of significance, they include but are not limited to:

(1) Speed of resolution is often quicker in the federal system, e.g., typically there is less time between filing a claim and receiving a resolution, whether through trial or settlement;

(2) Federal courts allow for more judicial independence due to judges having lifetime appointments and protections against salary reduction under Article III, Section 1 of the U.S. Constitution;

(3) In some federal courts, verdicts are higher than in state courts in the same area;

(4) As federal practice is national, there is a certain level of uniformity to the rules in the federal system, e.g., the same jurisdictional statutes such as the Federal Rules of Civil Procedure, etc. apply in every federal court (note, however, that many federal courts also have Local Rules that one must also become familiar);

(5) Unlike state systems, every litigant in the federal system gets an appeal as a matter of right for every case;

(6) Federal judges have more familiarity with federal law, which could be beneficial if your case involves a federal claim;

(7) Traditionally, summary judgment motions are granted at a higher rate in federal court than in most state courts;

(8) Federal courts, as a rule, are known to hold parties to rules, deadlines, and particularly

---

[44] The level of misconduct that would violate the "good behavior" clause is essentially criminal conduct. *See, e.g.*, James E. Pfander, *Removing Federal Judges*, 74 U. CHI. L. REV. 1227, 1230–33 (2007).

[45] U.S. CONST. art. III, § 1.

[46] *See* Benjamin V. Madison, III, *Color-Blind: Procedure's Quiet but Crucial Role in Achieving Racial Justice*, 78 U.M.K.C. L. REV. 617, 617–19 (2010) (comparing the result in first Rodney King jury trial, in Simi Valley, CA, state court versus the results of the federal jury trial in which jurors were drawn from the seven regions comprising the U.S. District for the Central District of California).

discovery matters strictly, making it more feasible for a party facing significant discovery to accomplish such discovery more effectively and efficiently than in state courts;

(9) While not always true in state court, litigants in federal court receive written opinions as a matter of course; and

(10) Federal courts generally have more resources than state courts, *e.g.*, court reporters are provided in all federal cases, whereas counsel in state civil cases often must arrange court reporters themselves.

Conversely, considerations that may lead experienced litigators to prefer state court over federal court include:

(1) A case may not be ready to be put on a federal court's "fast track;"

(2) Because judges in the state system are either elected or appointed by the Governor with the consent of the state legislature, and do not serve unlimited terms, sometimes an appearance of impartiality can arise. However, filing in state court may still be justified if the lawyer believes the perceived lack of independence is more helpful than harmful to her client's case;

(3) There is greater flexibility in "targeting" a specific city/county in which to file suit in a state court. This is because a U.S. district court covers up to half a state in most cases, and, even though the court will have divisions, the jury composition will not come from one, but from many counties/cities. Additionally, in state practice, many states have certain venues that are known for returning extremely high verdicts;

(4) Some believe that summary judgment is more difficult to obtain, particularly in states where the highest court has expressed a preference for cases to go to trial rather than to be dismissed on a pretrial motion;

(5) If a case is primarily a state law case, state court judges typically will have more familiarity with the law;

(6) If a case is on the "cutting edge," seeking to make a claim where the law has not yet been extended, some believe state courts are more willing to adopt new causes of action than federal courts;

(7) While in the long run fees and costs may even out, federal court cases will bring relatively higher fees and costs in a shorter time period than in state court. This is a reality factor that the client and lawyer need to discuss. For instance, if the client needs to be able to pay over time, then state court may result in payments being spread over a longer time;

(8) Trial counsel are generally given more reign to conduct voir dire (questioning of jurors before selection) by state judges while federal judges are often perceived as less flexible. For instance, some federal judges will only allow counsel to submit questions that the judge will then ask the potential jurors; and

(9) Closing arguments are typically conducted before the jury is instructed in federal court while many state courts allow closing arguments after instructions, and many trial counsel prefer arguments after the jury has been instructed.

The above considerations may or may not be relevant in any matter. However, experienced litigators consider these kinds of factors routinely, even if the lawyer does not vocalize each step in her decisions. On the matter of preferences of judges, many litigators would rather not say anything, even to her client, out of the fear that such comments may somehow get back to a judge. Make no mistake, however, that the independence of judges and their tendencies play a role in a lawyer's decision.

As the above discussion demonstrates, the strategic question of deciding in which system to sue is rich with learning opportunities. One of the first lessons for the inexperienced lawyer is that not all "forum shopping" is illegitimate. In the first year of law school, students will undoubtedly hear the phrase "forum shopping" in discussions of the Erie doctrine—that malleable doctrine designed to maintain state rules of decision in diversity cases filed in federal court. However, based on the famous decision of *Erie Railroad Company v. Tompkins*,[47] and its progeny, the Court's opinions are not necessarily aligned against forum shopping per se. Instead, the Court seeks to avoid allowing parties to gain an unfair advantage by filing in federal court and to reserve the benefit of the impartial forum for parties who qualify for diversity jurisdiction.[48] In other words, the *Erie* doctrine avoids forum shopping that undermines principles of federalism, not all forum shopping.

Lawyers should explain to clients the advantages and disadvantages of filing suit in alternative courts. Lawyers are entitled to discuss the potential courts in which a suit may be filed and weigh the strategic options with one's client. In providing such advice, an attorney can face difficult questions—ones that test her professional identity. As such, lawyers should consider these questions before addressing the issues with her client. It is better for the lawyer to decide ahead of time what kind of professional identity she will have and how she will respond to an issue of forum selection, which can implicate her value system, than to allow a strong-willed client to pressure her into a decision inconsistent with her values. For example, how will you respond if your client asks you about the racial composition of juries in the alternative jurisdictions in which suit can be filed? In *Batson v. Kentucky*,[49] the Supreme Court held that litigants who exercise peremptory strikes based on the race of jury members violate the Constitution. Would you tell your client that you believe it is inappropriate to consider race as part of the forum selection process? Is there a context in which you feel it is appropriate to discuss racial composition of juries? If you resolve that under no circumstances do you believe it to be an appropriate subject to discuss, is there a way to express your opinion to your client without suggesting that your client is a racist for even asking the question? Or, do you believe your client should be confronted for asking a question along these lines? How can you confront someone about a delicate issue such as this, but do so in a civil manner?

Although perhaps less emotionally charged, discussions with a client about judges on various courts are also ones that implicate a lawyer's principles. Lawyers are obliged to not denigrate the judicial system. Will you criticize judges or offer specific personality characterizations of them to your client? If you do, will you consider how to describe the composition of a court, or judges, without denigrating that court, the judges, or the judicial system? Can you discuss the compositions of courts by prefacing your discussion with a well-thought-out description of the legal system as one that attempts to provide justice but which, as a result of human vulnerabilities, can never do so perfectly?

II. Subject Matter Jurisdiction of Federal Courts

Jurisdiction refers to the power of a court to resolve a case or controversy. To hear and decide a case, the court in which suit is filed must have both subject matter jurisdiction and personal jurisdiction. Subject matte jurisdiction, however, is different from personal jurisdiction, which will be covered in Chapter 4. Subject matter jurisdiction refers to the kind of case brought before the court. If the plaintiff files in a U.S. district court in Tennessee, but none of the categories of federal jurisdiction apply, then not only

---

[47] 304 U.S. 64 (1938).
[48] Hanna v. Plumer, 380 U.S. 460 (1965).
[49] 476 U.S. 79 (1986).

would the U.S. district court in Tennessee lack subject matter jurisdiction, but every federal court in the country would also lack subject matter jurisdiction over the case. Simply put, the case does not meet the criteria for one of the limited categories of jurisdiction that federal courts can hear. Because the case is not the kind of case over which federal courts are granted authority to decide, no federal court will have the power to decide the case. Conversely, personal jurisdiction deals with the power of the court but in a court-and-state-specific way. As we will see in the next chapter, a U.S. district court in Tennessee may have subject matter jurisdiction in a case but lack personal jurisdiction over the defendant. In these cases, the nonresident has insufficient contacts with the state in which suit is brought for a court in that state to exercise power over that defendant. At the same time, another federal court, in a different state in which the defendant has enough contacts, will have personal jurisdiction. The difference between subject matter jurisdiction and personal jurisdiction will become clearer as we progress.

A. The Source of Federal Courts' Subject Matter Jurisdiction

In Article III, Section 1, the Constitution provides that the "judicial power of the United States, shall be vested in one Supreme Court, and in such inferior courts as the Congress may from time to time ordain and establish." These so-called "inferior" courts are the thirteen federal courts of appeal and numerous district courts across the nation. Recall, district courts are the trial courts in which cases are heard and decided in the federal system and appellate courts review the decisions of lower courts. No federal court, however, can hear a case unless it is within the limited grant of jurisdiction in Article III, Section 2 of the Constitution.[50] That article sets forth the so-called nine heads, or fonts, of federal jurisdiction:

> The judicial Power shall extend to all Cases, in Law and Equity, [1][51] arising under this Constitution, the Laws of the United States, and Treaties made, or which shall be made, under their Authority; [2] to all Cases affecting Ambassadors, other public Ministers and Consuls; [3] to all Cases of admiralty and maritime Jurisdiction; [4] to Controversies to which the United States shall be a Party; [5] to Controversies between two or more States;[6] between a State and Citizens of another State; [7] between Citizens of different States; [8] between Citizens of the same State claiming Lands under Grants of different States, and [9] between a State, or the Citizens thereof, and foreign States, Citizens or Subjects.[52]

The challenges in subject matter jurisdiction arise in determining whether a case fits within the limited category of cases that qualify for federal jurisdiction. If a case qualifies for federal jurisdiction, the case may still be filed in either state court or federal court in most instances.[53] The great majority of cases that qualify for federal jurisdiction also qualify for state jurisdiction. Thus, courts say that there is "concurrent jurisdiction" over such matters. This observation applies not only to diversity of citizenship but also to federal question cases. Unless a case is in the relatively rare category of exclusively federal cases, then state courts can adjudicate federal questions in the same fashion as federal courts.

---

[50] U.S. CONST. art. III, § 2.

[51] The bracketed numbers in the above quote have been added for ease of reference. [1] is the constitutional basis for federal question jurisdiction. Most cases filed in federal court fall under this category. [7] refers to diversity of citizenship jurisdiction. The second most filings in federal court fall under this category.

[52] The bracketed numbers have been added to divide Article III, Section 2 into nine categories.

[53] A limited number of federal matters are considered exclusively federal and can be heard only in federal courts, such as disputes raising antitrust laws, bankruptcy protections, patents, and limited other categories.

The first question in analyzing any case filed in federal court, therefore, is this: Can the case qualify for one of the limited categories of federal jurisdiction? If so, the case is likely one that can be brought in both state and federal court and the plaintiff must choose where to file. If not, the case can only be filed in state court. So how does one answer whether a case fits the limited category of federal question jurisdiction? Although the seven other categories in Article III, Section 2 can supply federal jurisdiction, they are nowhere near as common as federal question jurisdiction and diversity of citizenship jurisdiction. Thus, our analysis will focus on these two categories.

Before we launch into an analysis of general federal question jurisdiction and diversity jurisdiction, it is worth noting that some of the other categories are ones that provide an easy basis for federal jurisdiction. The key is to know what factual scenarios trigger these. For instance, if the United States is a plaintiff, the case will be in federal court. If the United States is a defendant, the same is true. These provisions account for a fair number of the cases in federal courts. However, general federal question jurisdiction and diversity of citizenship jurisdiction account for more filings than any of the other categories. Far from simple, the analysis for determining whether a case fits within one of these categories requires a disciplined evaluation of many questions. Before we delve into that analysis, let us consider why it is important to know the jurisdiction of federal courts and to be willing to litigate in them if they are the best court in which to bring your client's case.

Professional Identity Question

Professional identity formation has become a focus in legal education after the publication of the Carnegie Institute's Educating Lawyers *and a companion study,* Best Practices in Legal Education. *Both reports concluded that law schools do not sufficiently challenge students to consider their values, whether those values are consistent with the legal profession's stated values, and to reflect on how they would (will) apply those values in practice, and thus to form a professional (ethical/moral) identity. The notion is novel in the sense that it recognizes the process is internal and not something someone can just be told: "Do this because it's the professional thing." Instead, it asks the person to consider why he or she may want to decide in ways consistent with his or her values. Too often lawyers fall into the trap of thinking that the Model Rules of Professional Conduct—basically minimum standards that, if a lawyer dips below them, he or she is disciplined—is the standard for ethical behavior. Even the drafters of those Model Rules say they never intended the Model Rules to be ethical norms and that the discretion accorded lawyers in so many areas requires lawyers to make "sensitive" questions of "personal conscience" and to reconcile "conflicting interests."[54]*

Plaintiff's counsel is a solo practitioner who has chosen personal injury law as her primary focus. She has been practicing for a little under five years. All the cases she has filed to date have been in state court. She has had good success there, either resolving cases favorably before trial or, in some instances, winning jury verdicts for her clients. She has also lost a couple of cases that were close ones. She likes the state system because it does not put great pressure on counsel. Cases go to trial at a deliberate pace. The federal court in her area is different. That court has a mandatory pretrial conference, sets cases for trial as soon as the court deems it feasible, and is known for imposing firm deadlines. Despite these differences, neither federal nor state juries in the area are sympathetic to plaintiffs or to defendants and the amount of

---

[54] MODEL RULES OF PROF'L CONDUCT, R. 1.7 (AM. BAR ASS'N 2016). For an advanced civil pretrial practice book that contains more than 55 professional identity questions, each placed at the point in the progress of a civil suit that ethical, moral, and professional identity challenges arise. *See* BENJAMIN V. MADISON, III, CIVIL PROCEDURE FOR ALL STATES: A CONTEXT AND PRACTICE CASEBOOK (Carolina Academic Press 2010).

jury awards are within the same range.

Plaintiff's counsel has found a mentor through the local bar association. The mentor is an established trial lawyer experienced in litigating in the federal system. A few months ago, this lawyer had offered to be co-counsel with plaintiff's counsel in her first federal court case when the opportunity arose. This lawyer has told plaintiff's counsel that, by working together, she could help the less experienced lawyer get over her apprehension of federal court. As the more seasoned lawyer noted, sometimes federal court is a better forum in which to sue because of the faster pace and no-nonsense approach to case management.

In the case at issue, the product that severely injured plaintiff was manufactured by a company incorporated and with its headquarters in the forum state. Away from home when injured, plaintiff lives in a neighboring state. Thus, plaintiff's counsel could sue in federal court in the forum based on diversity of citizenship. Plaintiff's counsel thinks at one point that this plaintiff really needs a recovery as soon as possible. Although insurance had paid for most of the medical treatment to date, the bills are mounting, and plaintiff had little income on which to live. Plaintiff's counsel considered talking to her mentor about whether this case is a good candidate for federal court. She then wondered if the other lawyer would want to split the contingent fee to which she had agreed with plaintiff. She concludes not to call her mentor. Plaintiff's counsel reasons that her experience on the other state court cases has prepared her for this case— the biggest she had handled so far in her career. She told herself she would team up with the other lawyer at the next opportunity, but that she was filing this case in state court and handling it herself.

What are the values in tension in this scenario? Did the less experienced lawyer show good judgment? If so, how? If not, why not? What can the lawyer do to ensure she is aware of her own motives and analyze whether they should be playing a role in decisions such as this? What steps could a lawyer in such a case take to better ensure she has considered all competing values, determined the effect of each potential decision, and exercise sound judgment to reach the optimal decision?

B. Federal Question Jurisdiction (also known as Federal "Arising Under" Jurisdiction)

The United States Constitution states that federal judicial power extends to cases that "arise under this Constitution, the laws of the United States, or Treaties made, or which shall be made, under their authority."[55] If a federal law is involved in a case, then it fits within federal jurisdiction, right? Not so fast. Here, we need to realize that the Constitution grants potential jurisdiction, but it takes Congress, through a jurisdictional statute, to implement actual jurisdiction. Often, Congress' jurisdictional statutes place more stringent requirements for getting into federal court than the categories of Article III, Section 2 that are the basis on which Congress creates the statute (i.e., "enabling" constitutional potential jurisdiction to be used).[56] "How dare you, Congress!" some might protest, "That's unconstitutional!" The opposite is true. The Constitution is designed to give Congress a reservoir of jurisdiction from which to draw. However, nothing in the Constitution says that Congress must draw every drop from the reservoir. By understanding that the Constitution represents the potential scope of jurisdiction from which Congress may enact jurisdictional statutes, the matter becomes clearer. Nothing prevents Congress from enabling, in the jurisdictional statutes taking potential jurisdiction and making it available, from choosing to not enact all the potentially available jurisdiction under a category. Congress can go to the limit of potential jurisdiction or, if it chooses, authorize cases in any of the nine categories but less than all the potential jurisdiction. This

---

[55] U.S. CONST., art. III, § 2.

[56] See supra note 10 and accompanying text for a discussion of the meaning of an enabling statute, and how it can enact less than the full potential jurisdiction authorized by the Constitution.

implicit power of Congress to limit the cases that come into lower federal courts derives from the constitutional text that grants to Congress the power to create lower federal courts. However, Article I, Section 8 lists among Congress' enumerated powers, "[t]o constitute tribunals inferior to the Supreme Court."[57] Because Congress has the power to create lower federal courts, Congress likewise has the power to prescribe the scope of such lower court's jurisdiction under each the categories in Article III, Section 2.

In the two main categories of jurisdiction we will study—general federal question jurisdiction and diversity of citizenship jurisdiction—we will start with a case that shows that the constitutional grant of jurisdiction is broader than the actual grant by Congress's jurisdictional statute. Thus, we will see that the federal question category of cases has a potentially broader scope than the one that litigators must meet in filing a federal question case. Likewise, we will see that the constitutional scope of diversity of citizenship jurisdiction is also broader than the actual statutory grant by Congress. Most cases that come into federal court are those filed under federal question jurisdiction: "arising under the Constitution, laws of the United States" category.[58]

As noted above, we ought to first recognize that the constitutional scope of the arising-under-federal-law category set forth in Article III, Section 2 is broader than the typical case brought under the general federal question statute, 28 U.S.C. § 1331. To see how broad the constitutional limits of "arising under" jurisdiction actually are, we are aided by the decision by Chief Justice John Marshall in *Osborn v. Bank of the United States*.[59] In *Osborn*, the question arose whether, if the federal question at issue was not part of the plaintiff's claim, but rather was raised by the defendant in opposing the case, such a question was within Article III, Section 2 arising-under-federal-law jurisdiction. The Court ruled that the "arising under" grant of Article III was satisfied—for Constitutional purposes—when either (a) the plaintiff's suit raised a federal question, or (b) the defendant raised a federal question in his or her defense. The Court stated that, so long as a federal question was an "ingredient" in the case, it arose under Article III.[60]

Practice Problem

Practice Problem 3-1

Eliza had a farm next to Harry's farm. Harry decided to stop farming and to allow a sewage disposal company to come on his property, dig craters, and dispose of waste. After a few years Eliza developed cancer. Her doctor determined it was from exposure to toxic waste. She brought suit against Harry for state common law nuisance, the elements of which are (a) defendant's use of her property, (b) in a way that substantially interferes, (c) with plaintiff's use of her property and/or causes injuries to plaintiff from defendant's use of property. Damages recoverable are property damages and/or, if the use causes personal injury, then personal injury damages. Eliza's counsel drafts a complaint alleging that Harry's use of the property for sewage disposal was a use that, through migration underground, substantially interfered with Eliza's use of her property, particularly the contamination of her private water supply. Assume for purposes of this Problem that there is a federal statute immunizing property owners who allow for their property to be used for sewage disposal due to a shortage of such sites. Eliza sues Harry based solely on state law

---

[57] U.S. CONST., art. III, § 8.

[58] *See, e.g.,* 13 RICHARD D. FREER & EDWARD H. COOPER, WRIGHT AND MILLER'S FEDERAL PRACTICE AND PROCEDURE § 3526 (3d ed. 2014) ("Certainly, there has never been a serious challenge to the basic idea that Congress has wide power to regulate the jurisdiction of the lower federal courts.").

[59] 22 U.S. (9 Wheat.) 738 (1824).

[60] *See Federal Judicial Caseload Statistics,* USCOURTS.GOV, at http://www.uscourts.gov/statistics-re-ports/analysis-reports/federal-judicial-caseload-statistics (last visited June 13, 2017).

nuisance. In defense, Harry raises the federal statute as a basis for immunizing him from liability. Under the *Osborn* test, would this case be within the "arising under" federal question jurisdiction in Article III?

C. General Federal Question Statute

Pretend for a second that Article III, Section 2—the reservoir of jurisdiction for cases "arising under" federal law—could justify jurisdiction in every case filed in federal court that either included federal law in the plaintiff's case or as part of the defendant's defense. That would allow more cases into the federal courts than would be true if something required that the federal question be part of the plaintiff's case. And there is reason, beyond docket control of filings, for the limitation in the federal question statute requiring that the federal question be a necessary part of the plaintiff's complaint—the well-pleaded complaint rule addressed later in this chapter.[61] With that rule, the trial court can determine at the time of the filing of the complaint whether there is jurisdiction. Conversely, if the court had to wait until the defendant filed her answer to see whether a federal question was an "ingredient" in the case, courts would have less of a bright-line time frame in which to determine whether federal jurisdiction exists. It may seem insignificant whether the court determines such a question on filing of the complaint, or in reviewing the defendant's response. However, you will find later that the defendant's ability to file motions can delay a court's seeing the defendant's response to the case on non-technical grounds for months. Hence, the important question of whether the federal court even has subject matter jurisdiction could be likewise delayed.

For the reasons suggested, Congress does not want the full reservoir of general federal question jurisdiction under Article III, Section 2 to be tapped. Thus, Congress enacted the general federal question statute, 28 U.S.C. § 1331, and has reenacted the statute after the *Mottley* decision below, the one in which the Supreme Court articulated the well-pleaded complaint rule. By reenacting the federal question statute after that decision, and by not explicitly allowing federal question jurisdiction to extend to federal issues raised by the defense, Congress has ratified the well-pleaded complaint rule.

1. Hurdle Number One: The Well-Pleaded Complaint Rule

So, what does the general federal question statute provide? Here it is (all of it):

The district courts shall have original jurisdiction of all civil actions arising under the Constitution, laws, or treaties of the United States.[62]

The Supreme Court has found two limitations on general federal question claims even though they are not apparent on the statute's text. One such limitation is the well-pleaded complaint rule. The other limitation is that, even if the well-pleaded complaint rule is satisfied, the federal component of the case must be sufficiently central to the federal system that it warrants federal jurisdiction.

We will call these the two hurdles to general federal question jurisdiction. We will turn first to Hurdle One.

The first of the limitations in 28 U.S.C. § 1331 is the so-called well-pleaded complaint rule. That

---

[61] *See infra*, for a complete discussion of the well-pleaded complaint doctrine and how the statute limits the cases that can be filed in federal court under the general federal question statute in a manner that is narrower than the constitutional grant of federal question jurisdiction

[62] 28 U.S.C. § 1331 (2017).

rule is itself poorly worded because the rule has nothing to do with how well the complaint is pleaded. Instead, the analysis has everything to do with what a hypothetical complaint would plead. A plaintiff can include language in her complaint alleging federal law as an issue in the case even if the plaintiff is not suing on federal law. If the court simply asked whether the complaint had language in it asserting an issue of federal law, many a plaintiff could bootstrap her way right into federal court. However, the Supreme Court has rejected such an approach. The test focuses on whether the plaintiff's claim(s), if pled properly, must (hypothetically, not as actually pled) include a federal question. Then—and here is where the hypothetical part comes in—the court asks: "Regardless of what is actually in the plaintiff's complaint, when we look at what claim(s) the plaintiff is asserting, would the plaintiff be required to prove federal law as part of the plaintiff's claim(s)?" Here, the court is asking, in light of the claim (let's say breach of contract), would the plaintiff be required to prove federal law to prove the elements of her breach of contract claim. If the answer is "yes," then the complaint will satisfy Hurdle One and meet the well-pleaded complaint rule, even if its grammar is terrible and its punctuation worse. However, if the answer is "no," then the case will not satisfy the requirements of the general federal question statute and be dismissed. Because breach of contract is a state law claim not involving any federal law, a claim for breach of contract will fail the well-pleaded complaint test. Plaintiff can always sue in state court if the plaintiff wants to continue. After all, state courts have jurisdiction to hear federal claims in most cases as already explained.

The leading Supreme Court case on the well-pleaded complaint rule, featured below, is *Mottley Louisville Railway*. The decision will make a bit more sense with some background. More than thirty years before the case bearing their name, Erasmus and Annie Mottley were in an accident on the Louisville & Nashville Railroad. In a settlement, they dropped their claims for personal injuries in return for lifetime passes to ride the Louisville & Nashville Railroad wherever they wanted, whenever they wanted. They did so for quite a while. Congress, however, passed a statute—referred to in the decision—prohibiting free passes on railroads or passengers riding for any compensation other than the tariff applied to all passengers.

A settlement agreement is a contract. Under state law, all that needed to be alleged to plead and prove breach of contract was (a) existence of the contract, and (b) breach of the contract. The Mottleys did plead that the Railroad breached the contract. However, breach of contract is a state law claim and they sued in federal court. Notice how the Mottleys' lawyer cleverly sought to invoke federal-question-statute-arising-under jurisdiction by anticipating the Railroad's defense (i.e., the Act of Congress made free passes void so the Act was unconstitutional). If we envision the hypothetical claim the Mottleys were required to plead to sue on breach of contract, the question becomes whether the Mottleys had to raise the federal statute at all in their complaint. If not, their doing so could not create federal jurisdiction simply because they chose to make allegations about how the Act the defense would rely on was unconstitutional. With that background, see how the Supreme Court resolved whether the Mottleys' complaint passed Hurdle One.

LOUISVILLE & NASHVILLE RAILROAD CO. v. MOTTLEY
Supreme Court of the United States, 1908
211 U.S. 149

APPEAL from the Circuit Court of the United States for the Western District of Kentucky.

The appellees (husband and wife), being residents and citizens of Kentucky, brought this suit in equity in the circuit court of the United States for the western district of Kentucky against the appellant, a railroad company and a citizen of the same state. The object of the suit was to compel the specific performance of the following contract:

. . .

The bill [another term for "complaint"] alleged that in September, 1871, plaintiffs, while passengers upon the defendant railroad, were injured by the defendant's negligence, and released their respective claims for damages in consideration of the agreement for transportation during their lives, expressed in the contract. It is alleged that the contract was performed by the defendant up to January 1, 1907, when the defendant declined to renew the passes. The bill then alleges that the refusal to comply with the contract was based solely upon that part of the act of Congress of June 29, 1906 . . . which forbids the giving of free passes or free transportation. The bill further alleges: First, that the act of Congress referred to does not prohibit the giving of passes under the circumstances of this case; and, second, that, if the law is to be construed as prohibiting such passes, it is in conflict with the 5th Amendment of the Constitution, because it deprives the plaintiffs of their property without due process of law. The defendant demurred [a demurrer is an old term for moving to dismiss] to the bill. The judge of the circuit court overruled the demurrer, entered a decree for the relief prayed for, and the defendant appealed directly to this court.

Mr. Justice MOODY, after making the foregoing statement, delivered the opinion of the court:

Two questions of law were raised by the demurrer to the bill, were brought here by appeal, and have been argued before us. They are, first, whether that part of the act of Congress of June 29, 1906 (34 Stat. at L. 584, chap. 3591, U. S. Comp. Stat. Supp. 1907, p. 892), which forbids the giving of free passes or the collection of any different compensation for transportation of passengers than that specified in the tariff filed, makes it unlawful to perform a contract for transportation of persons who, in good faith, before the passage of the act, had accepted such contract in satisfaction of a valid cause of action against the railroad; and, second, whether the statute, if it should be construed to render such a contract unlawful, is in violation of the 5th Amendment of the Constitution of the United States. We do not deem it necessary, however, to consider either of these questions, because, in our opinion, the court below was without jurisdiction of the cause. Neither party has questioned that jurisdiction, but it is the duty of this court to see to it that the jurisdiction of the circuit court, which is defined and limited by statute, is not exceeded.

There was no diversity of citizenship, and it is not and cannot be suggested that there was any ground of jurisdiction, except that the case was a "suit . . . arising under the Constitution or laws of the United States." It is the settled interpretation of these words, as used in this statute, conferring jurisdiction, that a suit arises under the Constitution and laws of the United States only when the plaintiff's statement of his own cause of action shows that it is based upon those laws or that Constitution. It is not enough that the plaintiff alleges some anticipated defense to his cause of action and asserts that the defense is invalidated by some provision of the Constitution of the United States. Although such allegations show that very likely, in the course of the litigation, a question under the Constitution would arise, they do not show that the suit, that is, the plaintiff's original cause of action, arises under the Constitution. In *Tennessee v. Union & Planters' Bank*,[63] the plaintiff, the state of Tennessee, sued in the circuit court of the United States to recover from the defendant certain taxes alleged to be due under the laws of the state. The plaintiff alleged that the defendant claimed an immunity from the taxation by virtue of its charter, and that therefore the tax was void, because in violation of the provision of the Constitution of the United States, which forbids any state from passing a law impairing the obligation of contracts. The cause was held to be beyond the jurisdiction of the circuit court, the court saying, by Mr. Justice Gray: 'A suggestion of one party, that the other will or may set up a claim under the Constitution or laws of the United States, does not make the suit one arising under that Constitution or those laws.' Again, in *Boston & M. Consol. Copper & S. Min. Co. v. Montana*

---

[63] 152 U. S. 454 (1894).

Ore Purchasing Co.,[64] the plaintiff sued in the circuit court of the United States for the conversion of copper ore and for an injunction against its continuance. The plaintiff then alleged, for the purpose of showing jurisdiction, in substance, that the defendant would set up in defense certain laws of the United States. The cause was held to be beyond the jurisdiction of the circuit court, the court saying, by Mr. Justice Peckham:

> It would be wholly unnecessary and improper, in order to prove complainant's cause of action, to go into any matters of defense which the defendants might possibly set up, and then attempt to reply to such defense, and thus, if possible, to show that a Federal question might or probably would arise in the course of the trial of the case. To allege such defense and then make an answer to it before the defendant has the opportunity to itself plead or prove its own defense is inconsistent with any known rule of pleading, so far as we are aware, and is improper. The rule is a reasonable and just one that the complainant in the first instance shall be confined to a statement of its cause of action, leaving to the defendant to set up in his answer what his defense is, and, if anything more than a denial of complainant's cause of action, imposing upon the defendant the burden of proving such defense.

> Conforming itself to that rule, the complainant would not, in the assertion or proof of its cause of action, bring up a single Federal question. The presentation of its cause of action would not show that it was one arising under the Constitution or laws of the United States.

The application of this rule to the case at bar is decisive against the jurisdiction of the circuit court.

It is ordered that the judgment be reversed[,] and the case remitted to the circuit court with instructions to dismiss the suit for want of jurisdiction.

Follow-Up Questions and Comments

1. Breach of contract (i.e., the Railroad's failure to continue abiding by the settlement agreement with the Mottleys) was the only claim on which the Mottleys could sue. The elements of breach of contract are (1) existence of a valid contract, and (2) breach of that contract. Considering this, what was essential to a complaint by the Mottleys?

2. Considering the claim that the Mottleys were suing on, what did they absolutely have to allege (and later, to prove) to state a claim against the defendant? Did they need to even mention in their complaint that the federal statute banning lifetime passes was a violation of their constitutional due process rights? Were those allegations superfluous to their complaint? Do you now see that your evaluation of whether Hurdle One is met needs to avoid reading what a complaint has alleged, and instead determining what the plaintiff's claim is and what was essential to plead to make that claim?

3. It is often said that in a well-pleaded complaint, the plaintiff cannot anticipate defenses and plead a federal question as an anticipated defense. The rule is better stated by asking: (a) what claim(s) the plaintiff has; (b) what are the elements (essential allegations) to support the plaintiff's claim(s);

---

[64] 188 U. S. 632 (1903).

and (c) whether federal law is included in the elements that must be alleged. If the answer is that federal law is not essential to pleading a claim, then the complaint cannot satisfy Hurdle One. If the answer is that the plaintiff is required to plead federal law to assert her claim, then the plaintiff will clear Hurdle One and move on to Hurdle Two.

4. Return to Practice Problem 3-1 regarding Eliza's nuisance claim against Harry. Even though a federal question is an ingredient in that case, does the federal question satisfy the well-pleaded complaint rule?

5. Declaratory judgment actions present special challenges for applying the well-pleaded complaint rule. In the federal system, the Federal Declaratory Judgment Act,[65] is the procedural mechanism that someone threatened with violation of a right by another could institute to bring suit and have the controversy resolved. Prior to declaratory judgment statutes, a person or entity threatened with a suit could not do anything until the party sued. That could be a concern, other than simply when someone wanted resolution, because businesses often must report threatened claims, even if they do not consider them as having merit.

6. Thus, a declaratory judgment action allows a person or entity that ordinarily would be a defendant to initiate suit against the one who asserts a violation of law. You can see how this will present problems for the well-pleaded complaint analysis. Whereas the analysis typically asks whether the plaintiff has stated on the face of her complaint a federal question that had be pled to assert the claim, the "plaintiff" in a declaratory judgment action would ordinarily be a defendant if the threatening party had gotten down to business and filed suit. No worries, we can say, however. We just remember in any declaratory judgment action not to focus on who the plaintiff or defendant happens to be. Instead ask who has the substantive right that, if proved, would result in recovery. The party threatening suit will be the one who has such a right, if there indeed is a basis for the claim. Thus, having found the party and claim on which to focus, you should simply ask the same well-pleaded complaint question as you ask in typical suits: if the party with the right to sue brought suit, would a federal question necessarily be included in the complaint. As with a traditional well-pleaded complaint analysis, the question is a hypothetical one that does not key in on the actual pleadings. The only difference here is that, instead of asking whether the plaintiff's complaint needed to include a federal question as part of the claim, we ask whether the defendant in the declaratory judgment suit—the one with the right—needs to plead a federal question to recover.

7. Some wonder why the fact that suit is being brought under a federal statute—the Declaratory Judgment Act—is not sufficient to create a federal question. The answer lies in the peculiar nature of the Declaratory Judgment Act. The act does not create any substantive right, but rather merely creates a remedy. Thus, the Supreme Court in *Skelly Oil Co. v. Phillips Petroleum Co.*,[66] held that a suit under the federal declaratory judgment act does not, simply by invoking the act, raise a federal question. Instead, as noted, the well-pleaded complaint analysis must be applied to the substantive right claimed to be violated and whether, if that had been brought by the party who is threatening, a federal question would have to be pled to bring the claim.

8. Congress could expand the general federal question statute to allow jurisdiction in federal court over cases in which the federal question is a defense in the case and not part of the required elements

---

[65] 28 U.S.C. §§ 2201, 2202.
[66] 339 U.S. 667 (1950).

of the case. Why might Congress have chosen not to allow jurisdiction to the full scope of the "arising under" federal law provision?

9. Was not the question of the constitutionality of the federal statute also an ingredient in the *Mottley* case? Why was that not enough for the Court to hold that a federal court could hear the case? For those concerned that a federal court would never have the opportunity to review the federal question raised by the defendant, have no fear. Hurdle One (or the well-pleaded complaint rule) will send many cases to state court, where the federal question will be resolved as a part of the defendant's case. If a party disagrees with the ruling on federal law, the party can appeal to the highest court of that state. Then, if the party is still not satisfied after the highest court rules on the federal question, the party can petition for certiorari to the United Sates Supreme Court.[67] The percentage of cases in which the Supreme Court grants certiorari is admittedly low. However, you will see in Chapter 4 addressing personal jurisdiction below (a concept that invokes a federal question defense, *i.e.*, whether a nonresident being subjected to jurisdiction in another state violates due process of law) that many of the cases took the route just described. In other words, as much personal jurisdiction jurisprudence derives from cases that went through the state system and then to the Supreme Court as those that originated in federal courts. The *Mottley* case ended up in the state system and was reviewed by the Supreme Court on certiorari. The Court held that the statute was not an unconstitutional taking. *Figure 3-2*, the following chart showing how a federal question can get to the Supreme Court—through the federal system or, as in *Mottley*, through the state system— follows in *Figure 3-2*.

---

[67] *See* 28 U.S.C. § 2101.

Figure 3-2

U.S. Supreme Court jurisdiction allows review of a Federal Question that is merely part of a case but must also be among the small percentage of cases for which the Supreme Court grants certiorari i.e., agrees to hear under 28 U.S.C. § 1257. If the case is decided by a federal district court, and then appealed to a federal circuit court of appeal, the losing party may petition for certiorari under 28 U.S.C. § 1254. Far more cases make it to the Supreme Court through the federal system—shown vertically on the left in the diagram below, than through the state system, shown on the right below. However, a federal question, even if decided by a state court and appealed to the highest court of that state, can always reach the United States Supreme Court.

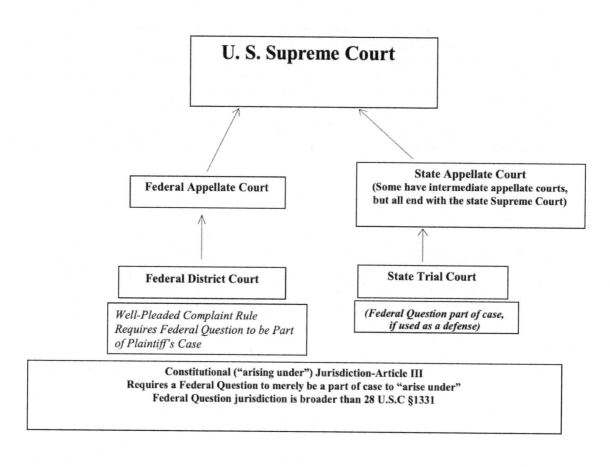

Practice Problems

Practice Problem 3-2

Carp Corporation sues Gar, a former employee, in tort for business libel. The elements of business libel are (a) a statement in written form, (b) that is false, (c) damaging to the business of the company or business that is the subject of the communication; and (d) is read or received by a third party. The suit is brought in federal court, and Carp alleges that Gar falsely reported to the Better Business Bureau (BBB) that Carp was using watered-down concrete on a construction project. Carp's complaint further alleges that Gar claims his report to the BBB was protected under the First Amendment to the United States Constitution, but as further alleged in Carp's complaint, Carp contends that libelous statements are outside First Amendment protection. Gar filed an answer, admitting that it had made a report to the BBB, but alleging in his affirmative defenses that its report was protected by the First Amendment to the United States Constitution, which guarantees the right of free speech. Assume that there is no jurisdiction based on diversity of citizenship and general federal question jurisdiction is the plaintiff's only hope for filing in federal court. Does Carp's complaint satisfy the well-pleaded complaint rule, a/k/a Hurdle One, in the general federal question analysis?

Practice Problem 3-3

You are hired by Bob (VA),[68] who was stopped by and, according to a video of the events, beaten to the ground by Hulk (VA), even though Bob did not put up any fight. Your suit is for excessive force in violation of the plaintiff's federal civil rights (guaranteed by the Federal Civil Rights Act) and is brought under the statute typically used for vindicating civil rights, 42 U.S.C. § 1983 (called a "Section 1983 claim"). According to the federal statute, the elements of a Section 1983 claim are: (1) that a right secured by the Constitution or laws of the United States was violated, and (2) that the alleged violation was committed by a person acting on behalf of the government (called a "state actor"). Why will such a case always satisfy the well-pleaded complaint rule if the plaintiff chooses to sue under the federal statute?

Practice Problem 3-4

Based on the same events as described in the immediately preceding Practice Problem (excessive beating, etc.), the plaintiff instead chooses to file solely a state-law battery claim but asks you to file it in federal court (even though he and the defendants are no of diverse citizenship). The elements of a battery claim are (1) acting with intent to cause harmful or offensive contact with another; and (2) actual harmful or offensive contact with the other, directly or indirectly. Does this battery claim satisfy the well-pleaded complaint rule? As the "master of his claim," the plaintiff can choose what claim or claims to plead in a complaint. The plaintiff still must plead all the elements of the claim that he or she chooses to pursue. Moreover, being the master of his claims does not entitle the plaintiff to be able to add language to his complaint to force the case into federal court by going beyond what the elements of the claim requires to be pled. For example: What if there was a federal statute that provided immunity to police in broad circumstances from suits against them under state law or federal law? Here, let's assume our plaintiff who tells you to file a battery claim in federal court alleges not only that the defendants acted intentionally to cause harmful or offensive contact to him and that harmful/offensive contact resulted from defendants' intentional acts, but also that the federal law granting immunity to police officers did not apply because the circumstances, according to plaintiff, were such an example of gross misconduct that it could not apply.

---

[68] Citizen of Virginia. From here on, citizenship may at times be denoted by a parenthetical with the abbreviation of state of citizenship.

Why would this complaint fail to satisfy the well-pleaded complaint rule?

2. Hurdle Number Two (if Applicable): Even if the Complaint Satisfies the Well-Pleaded Complaint Rule, Is the Federal Component Central Enough to the Federal System to Warrant Its Being Considered a Federal Question?

Courts have read a second limitation in the language of 28 U.S.C. § 1331—the so-called centrality of the federal component hurdle. Centrality is never a problem when the suit is brought under a federal statute giving the plaintiff the right to sue on the claim. Yet, some cases present state law claims that include federal law as a component of the claim. Technically, such cases would satisfy the well-pleaded complaint rule because federal law would be part of what is required to prove a claim. However, these state-law claims with a federal component typically will not satisfy the centrality requirement. The reason is that "centrality" here refers to the federal system, not simply to the case. Otherwise, a federal court would automatically have federal question jurisdiction over every state-law claim that incorporated federal law to satisfy an element of the state claim (e.g. federal statute or regulation used, as in many state-law negligence per se cases, to define the "duty." By limiting state-law claims to ones that are significant to interests of the federal system, Hurdle Number Two serves a valuable role. Courts applying the centrality hurdle ask whether the federal issue is important in the broad scheme of the federal system as set forth in the Constitution. The centrality requirement has also been called the requirement of a "substantial" federal question. The concept of centrality, however, perhaps better captures the essence of the courts' analysis of whether the federal issue relates to something central to the federal system. Often, state law claims with embedded federal law as an element fail at this stage of the analysis. They end up being litigated in state court rather than federal court.

Many apply the centrality hurdle to every federal question analysis. However, as noted above, the only time this second hurdle will come into play is when a state-law claim has a federal component—i.e., to satisfy the well-pleaded complaint test, the plaintiff does have to prove federal law in pursuing her state-law claim. The classic example is a state-law negligence per se claim. Negligence per se, under state law, requires proof of: (a) a duty defined by state or federal statute or regulation; breach of that duty; (c) which has proximately caused; (d) injury to the plaintiff. At times a federal statute or regulation will define a duty that allows the plaintiff to incorporate it into a state law negligence per se claim. Just because a state law tort claim incorporates federal law to define "duty" does not transform the state-law claim into a federal one. It's still a state law tort claim.

Perhaps the best example of such a case with a federal component that was not central to the federal system occurred in *Merrell Dow Pharmaceuticals, Incorporated v. Thompson*.[69] There, plaintiffs sued a drug manufacturer in state court alleging negligence per se. Negligence per se, as noted above, is simply a variation of a negligence claim in which the plaintiff attempts to establish duty and breach through a state or federal statute. If a defendant violates a state or federal statute placing a duty on the defendant, then the court will presume that there was a duty and a breach of the duty. Plaintiff will still have to show proximate cause and damages, but the case is more easily proved. In *Merrell Dow*, plaintiffs' negligence per se claim, was a state-law claim because it was a tort under Ohio law. Duty to avoid injury to others or their property was a state-law duty. Breach of that duty was also part of the state-law elements. However, plaintiff attempted to prove that breach by showing that a violation of the Federal Food, Drug, and Cosmetic Act (FDCA) represented the breach of duty that supported a negligence per se claim. The Court in *Merrell Dow* held, however, that state tort law could not transform a claim that was based on state tort law into a federal

---

[69] 478 U.S. 804 (1986).

claim. The federal issue in the case was not sufficiently central to allow the case to fall under the general federal question statute.

The Court held that the issue of federal law here was not central to the federal system. Similar cases incorporating federal law as part of state negligence per se claims have been viewed as efforts to take "garden variety" state-tort claims and make them into federal causes of action.[70] As suggested, if a federal issue is incorporated into what otherwise is a state-law claim, then the odds are that the federal issue will not be sufficiently central to pass the centrality test. But you should always check to be sure.

However, the Court has also held that some state-law claims incorporating a federal issue can satisfy the centrality requirement. To understand when that may be appropriate, we must review the Court's decision in *Grable & Sons Metal Products, Incorporated v. Darue Engineering & Manufacturing*.

GRABLE & SONS METAL PRODUCTS, INC v. DARUE ENGINEERING & MANUFACTURING
Supreme Court of the United States, 2005
545 U.S. 308

Justice SOUTER delivered the opinion of the Court.

The question is whether want of a federal cause of action to try claims of title to land obtained at a federal tax sale precludes removal to federal court of a state action with non-diverse parties raising a disputed issue of federal title law. We answer no, and hold that the national interest in providing a federal forum for federal tax litigation is sufficiently substantial to support the exercise of federal-question jurisdiction over the disputed issue on removal, which would not distort any division of labor between the state and federal courts, provided or assumed by Congress.

I

In 1994, the Internal Revenue Service seized Michigan real property belonging to petitioner Grable & Sons Metal Products, Inc., to satisfy Grable's federal tax delinquency. Title 26 U.S.C. § 6335 required the IRS to give notice of the seizure, and there is no dispute that Grable received actual notice by certified mail before the IRS sold the property to respondent Darue Engineering & Manufacturing. Although Grable also received notice of the sale itself, it did not exercise its statutory right to redeem the property within 180 days of the sale, § 6337(b) (1), and after that period had passed, the Government gave Darue a quitclaim deed, § 6339.

Five years later, Grable brought a state, quiet title action in state court, claiming that Darue's record title was invalid because the IRS had failed to notify Grable of its seizure of the property in the exact manner required by § 6335(a), which provides that written notice must be "given by the Secretary to the owner of the property [or] left at his usual place of abode or business." Grable said that the statute required personal service, not service by certified mail.

Darue removed the case to Federal District Court as presenting a federal question, because the claim of title depended on the interpretation of the notice statute in the federal tax law. The District Court declined to remand the case at Grable's behest after finding that the "claim does pose a 'significant question of federal law,'" . . . and ruling that Grable's lack of a federal right of action to enforce its claim against

---

[70] *See, e.g.*, Hampton Corman R.R. Switching Co., 683 F.3d 708, 712 (6th Cir. 2012).

Darue did not bar the exercise of federal jurisdiction.

The Court of Appeals for the Sixth Circuit affirmed. On the jurisdictional question, the panel thought it sufficed that the title claim raised an issue of federal law that had to be resolved, and implicated a substantial federal interest (in construing federal tax law). The court went on to affirm the District Court's judgment on the merits. We granted certiorari on the jurisdictional question alone . . . to resolve a split within the Courts of Appeals on whether *Merrell Dow Pharmaceuticals Inc. v. Thompson* . . . always requires a federal cause of action as a condition for exercising federal-question jurisdiction. We now affirm.

II

Darue was entitled to remove the quiet title action if Grable could have brought it in federal district court originally . . . as a civil action "arising under the Constitution, laws, or treaties of the United States," § 1331. This provision for federal-question jurisdiction is invoked by and large by plaintiffs pleading a cause of action created by federal law . . . . There is, however, another longstanding, if less frequently encountered, variety of federal "arising under" jurisdiction, this Court having recognized for nearly 100 years that in certain cases federal-question jurisdiction will lie over state-law claims that implicate significant federal issues. The doctrine captures the commonsense notion that a federal court ought to be able to hear claims recognized under state law that nonetheless turn on substantial questions of federal law, and thus justify resort to the experience, solicitude, and hope of uniformity that a federal forum offers on federal issues.

The classic example is *Smith v. Kansas City Title & Trust Co.*,[71] . . . a suit by a shareholder claiming that the defendant corporation could not lawfully buy certain bonds of the National Government because their issuance was unconstitutional. Although Missouri law provided the cause of action, the Court recognized federal-question jurisdiction because the principal issue in the case was the federal constitutionality of the bond issue. Smith thus held, in a somewhat generous statement of the scope of the doctrine, that a state-law claim could give rise to federal-question jurisdiction so long as it "appears from the [complaint] that the right to relief depends upon the construction or application of [federal law]."

The Smith statement has been subject to some trimming to fit earlier and later cases recognizing the vitality of the basic doctrine, but shying away from the expansive view that mere need to apply federal law in a state-law claim will suffice to open the "arising under" door. . . . It has in fact become a constant refrain in such cases that federal jurisdiction demands not only a contested federal issue, but a substantial one, indicating a serious federal interest in claiming the advantages thought to be inherent in a federal forum.[72]

But even when the state action discloses a contested and substantial federal question, the exercise of federal jurisdiction is subject to a possible veto. For the federal issue will ultimately qualify for a federal forum only if federal jurisdiction is consistent with congressional judgment about the sound division of labor between state and federal courts governing the application of § 1331. Thus, Franchise Tax Bd. explained that the appropriateness of a federal forum to hear an embedded issue could be evaluated only after considering the "welter of issues regarding the interrelation of federal and state authority and the proper management of the federal judicial system."[73]. Because arising-under jurisdiction to hear a state-law claim always raises the possibility of upsetting the state-federal line drawn (or at least assumed) by

_____

[71] 255 U.S. 180 (1921)

[72] *E.g., Daubert v. Merrell Dow Pharms., Inc.,* 509 U.S. 579, 594, n.12 (1993).

[73] *Id.*

Congress, the presence of a disputed federal issue and the ostensible importance of a federal forum are never necessarily dispositive; there must always be an assessment of any disruptive portent in exercising federal jurisdiction.

These considerations have kept us from stating a "single, precise, all-embracing" test for jurisdiction over federal issues embedded in state-law claims between non-diverse parties. We have not kept them out simply because they appeared in state raiment, as Justice Holmes would have done,[74] but neither have we treated "federal issue" as a password opening federal courts to any state action embracing a point of federal law. Instead, the question is, does a state-law claim necessarily raise a stated federal issue, actually disputed and substantial, which a federal forum may entertain without disturbing any congressionally approved balance of federal and state judicial responsibilities.

III

This case warrants federal jurisdiction. Grable's state complaint must specify "the facts establishing the superiority of [its] claim," . . . and Grable has premised its superior title claim on a failure by the IRS to give it adequate notice, as defined by federal law. Whether Grable was given notice within the meaning of the federal statute is thus an essential element of its quiet title claim, and the meaning of the federal statute is actually in dispute; it appears to be the only legal or factual issue contested in the case. . . . The Government has a strong interest in the "prompt and certain collection of delinquent taxes," . . . and the ability of the IRS to satisfy its claims from the property of delinquents requires clear terms of notice to allow buyers like Darue to satisfy themselves that the Service has touched the bases necessary for good title. The Government thus has a direct interest in the availability of a federal forum to vindicate its own administrative action, and buyers (as well as tax delinquents) may find it valuable to come before judges used to federal tax matters. Finally, because it will be the rare state title case that raises a contested matter of federal law, federal jurisdiction to resolve genuine disagreement over federal tax title provisions will portend only a microscopic effect on the federal-state division of labor.

. . .

Merrell Dow . . . is not to the contrary. *Merrell Dow* considered a state tort claim resting in part on the allegation that the defendant drug company had violated a federal misbranding prohibition, and was thus presumptively negligent under Ohio law. The Court assumed that federal law would have to be applied to resolve the claim, but after closely examining the strength of the federal interest at stake and the implications of opening the federal forum, held federal jurisdiction unavailable. Congress had not provided a private federal cause of action for violation of the federal branding requirement, and the Court found "it would . . . flout, or at least undermine, congressional intent to conclude that federal courts might nevertheless exercise federal-question jurisdiction and provide remedies for violations of that federal statute solely because the violation . . . is said to be a . . . 'proximate cause' under state law."

Because federal law provides for no quiet title action that could be brought against Darue, Grable argues that there can be no federal jurisdiction here, stressing some broad language in *Merrell Dow* (including the passage just quoted) that on its face supports Grable's position. But . . . *Merrell Dow* cannot be read whole as overturning decades of precedent, as it would have done by . . . converting a federal cause of action from a sufficient condition for federal-question jurisdiction into a necessary one.

. . .

---

[74] *See Smith v. Kansas Cty. Title and Trust Co.*, 255 U.S. 180, 214 (Holmes, J., dissenting).

Accordingly, *Merrell Dow* should be read in its entirety as treating the absence of a federal private right of action as evidence relevant to, but not dispositive of, the "sensitive judgments about congressional intent" that § 1331 requires. The absence of any federal cause of action affected *Merrell Dow*'s result two ways. The Court saw the fact as worth some consideration in the assessment of substantiality. But its primary importance emerged when the Court treated the combination of no federal cause of action and no preemption of state remedies for misbranding as an important clue to Congress's conception of the scope of jurisdiction to be exercised under § 1331. The Court saw the missing cause of action not as a missing federal door key, always required, but as a missing welcome mat, required in the circumstances, when exercising federal jurisdiction over a state misbranding action would have attracted a horde of original filings and removal cases raising other state claims with embedded federal issues. For if the federal labeling standard without a federal cause of action could get a state claim into federal court, so could any other federal standard without a federal cause of action. And that would have meant a tremendous number of cases.

One only needed to consider the treatment of federal violations generally in garden variety state tort law. "The violation of federal statutes and regulations is commonly given negligence per se effect in state tort proceedings."[75] . . . A general rule of exercising federal jurisdiction over state claims resting on federal mislabeling and other statutory violations would thus have heralded a potentially enormous shift of traditionally state cases into federal courts. Expressing concern over the "increased volume of federal litigation," and noting the importance of adhering to "legislative intent," *Merrell Dow* thought it improbable that the Congress, having made no provision for a federal cause of action, would have meant to welcome any state-law tort case implicating federal law "solely because the violation of the federal statute is said to [create] a rebuttable presumption [of negligence] . . .under state law." . . . In this situation, no welcome mat meant keep out. *Merrell Dow*'s analysis thus fits within the framework of examining the importance of having a federal forum for the issue, and the consistency of such a forum with Congress's intended division of labor between state and federal courts.

As already indicated, however, a comparable analysis yields a different jurisdictional conclusion in this case. Although Congress also indicated ambivalence in this case by providing no private right of action to Grable, it is the rare state quiet title action that involves contested issues of federal law. Consequently, jurisdiction over actions like Grable's would not materially affect, or threaten to affect, the normal currents of litigation. Given the absence of threatening structural consequences and the clear interest the Government, its buyers, and its delinquents have in the availability of a federal forum, there is no good reason to shirk from federal jurisdiction over the dispositive and contested federal issue at the heart of the state-law title claim.

IV

The judgment of the Court of Appeals, upholding federal jurisdiction over Grable's quiet title action, is affirmed.

It is so ordered.

---

[75] RESTATEMENT (THIRD) OF TORTS § 14, Reporters' Note, Comt. a, 195 (Tent. Draft No. 1, Mar. 28, 2001)

Practice Problems

The following Practice Problems demonstrate, first, how the centrality question will not even arise if the claim is under a federal law. Other Practice Problems will demonstrate how, if the claim is under state law, and satisfies the well-pleaded complaint rule, a/k/a Hurdle One, you determine whether the case also satisfies the centrality hurdles to qualify for federal question jurisdiction. If the case with a state law claim satisfies the well-pleaded complaint rule, but does not satisfy the centrality test, a/k/a Hurdle Two, it will not be considered a federal question. In other words, the case would have to be brought in state court.

Practice Problem 3-5

The elements to bring a suit under the Federal Age Discrimination in Employment Act,[76] are: (1) the plaintiff must be a member of a protected class, usually persons over the age of 40 in these types of cases; (2) the plaintiff suffered some form of adverse employment action, usually demotion or discharge; (3) at the time of this adverse action, the employee was performing his or her job at a level which met the employer's legitimate expectations; and (4) following the adverse employment action, the employee was replaced by someone of comparable qualifications outside of the protected class (i.e., someone at or under the age of 40). Because this suit is under a federal statute enacted by Congress and each element is defined by federal law in order to allow for a federal claim and remedies deemed important within the federal system, is there any question that such a case not only satisfies the well-pleaded complaint rule, but also the centrality requirement? Why is this Problem not an example of a state-law claim with an embedded federal issue?

Practice Problem 3-6

The State of Texafornia had a Consumer Protection statute that made it actionable if a defendant failed to adhere to federal or state laws and regulations in manufacturing a product. Carrie Consumer sues Toys-for-U for allegedly manufacturing toys that were able to break easily into parts small enough to swallow. Carrie sued in federal court, arguing that the federal toy manufacturing regulations were not only required to show negligence (thus satisfying the well-pleaded complaint rule) but also were central to the federal system. Assume diversity of citizenship jurisdiction does not exist and the case must rest, if at all, on federal question jurisdiction. Defendant moves to dismiss the case for lack of federal jurisdiction. How should the court rule?

Practice Problem 3-7

Air Measurement Technologies, Inc. (AMT) sought the legal advice of Big Law Firm (BLF) on certain safety devices developed by AMT to allow oxygen to be carried in small containers and used in emergencies. When a competitor came out with a similar product, AMT sued for patent infringement. In the patent infringement case, the court ruled that AMT's patent was invalid because the patent claims (what a patent applicant must provide in seeking a patent) were inadequate. The alleged inadequacy hinged on an aspect of the patent statute that described what the patent applicant must include in a patent application. After losing on its patent infringement claims, AMT sued BLF for malpractice, arguing that it had opined to AMT that the patent claim BLF submitted would satisfy the new statute. AMT filed the malpractice suit in U.S. district court arguing that would be required to prove federal law as part of its case in showing BLF's malpractice (thus satisfying the well-pleaded complaint rule) and that the patent law was central to the federal system. Big Law Firm moved to dismiss for lack of jurisdiction. Assume there is no basis for

---

[76] 29 U.S.C. § 623 et seq.

diversity of citizenship jurisdiction. How should the Court rule?

Practice Problem 3-8

Al Accountant (NY) invests in Big Corporation (incorporated and with its principal place of business in NY) and receives dividends on shares he bought. Surprised at how low the dividends are, Al investigates Big Corporation's tax returns. Al finds that Big Corporation did not deduct certain business expenses that he believes, under the applicable Federal Internal Revenue Code provision, should have been deducted. Big Corporation interpreted the recently added Internal Revenue Code provision as not allowing the deduction. As of the time of these events, the IRS had offered no guidance on how to apply the deduction. Al sues Big Corporation in the United States District Court for the Southern District of New York, asserting that Big Corporation breached its contract with him under New York common law of contracts by failing to deduct the business expenses, misstating its income, and as a result paying a lower dividend to Al. Suits by shareholders against corporations alleging breach of contract represent at least 20% of the case load of New York state courts. Does Al's suit against Big Corporation satisfy the general federal question statute?[77] If so, why? If not, why not?

Follow-Up Questions and Comments:

1. The Supreme Court in *Grable* summed up the litmus for the category of cases involving state law claims with federal components that would be sufficiently central by asking: "[D]oes a state-law claim necessarily raise a stated federal issue, actually disputed and substantial, which a federal forum may entertain without disturbing any congressionally approved balance of federal and state judicial responsibilities [?]" Notice that the court uses the term "substantial" for the concept of "central" to the federal system. As noted before, if we asked whether the issue was "substantial" to a case in which the federal law was a required part of the case, it would always be substantial. Instead, we must consider whether the federal issue that is a component of the state claim is central—or substantial in the sense of considering the federal system as a whole—to the federal system.

2. Please review Article I, Section 8 of the United States Constitution. Do you see the general subject at issue in Grable in a clause? Does a provision of Article I, Section 8 must be implicated to satisfy the Grable test? Alternatively, if a provision in Article I, Section 8 is implicated in a case in which a state law claim incorporates a federal component, does that increase the likelihood that the case will satisfy the *Grable* test?

3. Regulatory laws such as those in Problem 3-6 (toy manufacturing) are enacted under Congress' power to regulate interstate commerce and the last clause of Article I, Section 8, the catchall clause, that allows Congress to enact laws "necessary and proper" to carry out its legislation. In *Grable*, however, the federal component of the state law related to interpretation of the tax laws—something specifically identified in Article I, Section 8. Problem 3-7 deals with patent laws, another area specifically mentioned in Article I, Section 8. Should courts consider legislation in areas specifically identified (*e.g.*, taxes, patents) as being central to the federal system, while laws under the general interstate commerce and necessary and proper clause as being less likely to be central for purposes of this jurisdictional analysis?

---

[77] 28 U.S.C. § 1331

4. *Grable* also mentions, in the key question identified in Follow-Up Question 1 above, that the analysis should ask whether finding that a federal component to a state claim would disturb the distribution of power to the federal system and to the state system.

5. If federal courts were to begin hearing traditionally state-law tort claims, simply because they incorporated federal law as a standard for whether a duty had been breached, would that not take away from the state system something that has been traditionally considered the state's domain? Conversely, when state law includes a component of federal law that is specifically identified in Article I, Section 8 as a matter for the federal system, would that make the case for centrality stronger?

D. Diversity of Citizenship Jurisdiction

Diversity of citizenship jurisdiction derives from Article I, Section 3 as the basis in the Constitution for the potential jurisdiction. Congress has enacted the general diversity statute,[78] to allow parties to sue in federal court. As with federal question jurisdiction, the statute does not go to the limits of the potential jurisdiction allowed by the Constitution. As we saw with federal question cases, one hurdle—the well-pleaded complaint rule—applies in every case in which someone seeks to establish federal subject matter jurisdiction based on federal question, also known as federal "arising under," jurisdiction. The second hurdle in federal question cases only comes into play if the claim is a state law claim that incorporates a federal component. By contrast, with the diversity of citizenship statute, there are two hurdles that apply in every case, and without which a party cannot satisfy diversity of citizenship jurisdiction. These are (a) complete diversity of citizenship (Hurdle One), and (b) exceeding the amount in controversy requirement set forth in the statute (Hurdle Two). If someone shows complete diversity but does not satisfy the amount in controversy requirement, diversity jurisdiction will fail. Likewise, if one shows a sufficient amount in controversy, but does not satisfy the complete diversity requirement, diversity jurisdiction will not exist.

1. Complete Diversity

The next most frequent basis for federal court subject matter jurisdiction is diversity of citizenship jurisdiction. Recall that in the Constitutional grant of Article III, Section 2, one of the nine fonts of federal jurisdiction is "suits . . . between citizens of different states." That represents the constitutional reservoir from which Congress can enact jurisdictional statutes. It has enacted a jurisdictional statute that, like the general federal question statute, includes hurdles a plaintiff must clear that are not in the constitutional provision. The diversity statute[79] states:

§1332. Diversity of Citizenship; Amount in Controversy; Costs.

(a) The district courts shall have original jurisdiction of all civil actions where the matter in controversy exceeds the sum or value of $75,000, exclusive of interest and costs, and is between

(1) Citizens of different States;

---

[78] 28 U.S.C. § 1332
[79] *Id.*

53

(2) Citizens of a State and citizens or subjects of a foreign state, except that the district courts shall not have original jurisdiction under this subsection of an action between citizens of a State and citizens or subjects of a foreign state who are lawfully admitted for permanent residence in the United States and are domiciled in the same State;

(3) Citizens of different States and in which citizens or subjects of a foreign state are additional parties; and

(4) A foreign state, defined in section 1603(a) of this title, as plaintiff and citizens of a State or of different States.

. . .

(c) For the purposes of this section . . . of this title—

(1) A corporation shall be deemed to be a citizen of every State and foreign state by which it has been incorporated and of the State or foreign state where it has its principal place of business, except that in any direct action against the insurer of a policy or contract of liability insurance, whether incorporated or unincorporated, to which action the insured is not joined as a party-defendant, such insurer shall be deemed a citizen of—

(A) Every State and foreign state of which the insured is a citizen;

(B) Every State and foreign state by which the insurer has been incorporated;

. . . .

The requirement of complete diversity of citizenship is not immediately apparent on reading the diversity statute. The requirement derives from Chief Justice John Marshall's interpretation of the original diversity statute discussed below. Because Congress has passed later versions of the statute that accepted without objection Justice Marshall's interpretation that requires complete diversity, that interpretation—if it ever was debatable—is no longer in question.

So, what does "complete diversity" of citizenship mean? We can start by considering a broader kind of diversity of citizenship, the "minimal" diversity that Article III, Section 2 of the Constitution requires. In minimal diversity, so long as the case has one citizen of a state different from one defendant, minimal diversity exists. The following, in other words, would satisfy minimal diversity:

Plaintiffs	**v.**	**Defendants**
P1 (State A)		**D1 (State B)**
P2 (State B)		**D2 (State A)**
P3 (State B)		**D3 (State A)**

Because in the above diagram at least one plaintiff (P1) is from a state different from at least one defendant (D1), minimal diversity exists. If the Constitution allows minimal diversity, then how can the diversity statute require more than minimal diversity? The same way that the general federal question statute draws from the constitutional reservoir but places the well-pleaded complaint as an additional barrier under the enabling statute, 28 U.S.C. § 1331. Congress need not grant jurisdiction to the full extent authorized by Article III, Section 2 of the Constitution.

Having seen minimal diversity, let's now review *Strawbridge v. Curtiss* the famous case in which Chief Justice Marshall found minimal diversity insufficient and complete diversity required.

In *Strawbridge*, the Court considered whether federal jurisdiction existed through diversity of citizenship when the plaintiff, a citizen of Massachusetts, brought action against defendant, a citizen of Vermont, and other defendants, who were residents of Massachusetts. The version of the general diversity statute referenced in this case, the Judiciary Act of 1789, is the predecessor to the modern statute, 28 U.S.C. §1332. However, the *Strawbridge v. Curtiss* holding applies to the modern statute as well. Chief Justice Marshall stated in his opinion:

The court has considered this case and is of opinion that the jurisdiction cannot be supported. The words of the act of congress are, "where an alien is a party; or the suit is between a citizen of a state where the suit is brought, and a citizen of another state." The court understands these expressions to mean that each distinct interest should be represented by persons, all of whom are entitled to sue, or may be sued, in the federal courts. That is, that where the interest is joint, each of the persons concerned in that interest must be competent to sue, or liable to be sued, in those courts. But the court does not mean to give an opinion in the case where several parties represent several distinct interests, and some of those parties are, and others are not, competent to sue, or liable to be sued, in the courts of the United States.[80]

A diagram of the parties in *Strawbridge* ought to help show how the Court required complete diversity rather than minimal diversity—the implication of its ruling that with minimal diversity "jurisdiction cannot be supported" and that complete diversity was essential.

Plaintiffs	**v.**	**Defendants**
P1 (Massachusetts)		**D1 (Vermont)**
		D2 (Massachusetts)
		D3 (Massachusetts)

Because the plaintiff was a citizen of Massachusetts and Curtis, one of the defendants, was a citizen of Vermont, there was minimal diversity. However, complete diversity means that every party on the plaintiff's side of the "v" must have a state citizenship different from every defendant on the defendant's side of the "v." Here, D2 and D3 are, like, P1, from Massachusetts. Thus, complete diversity was lacking.

---

[80] *Strawbridge v. Curtiss*, 7 U.S. 267 (1806).

Follow-Up Questions and Comments

1. Having seen this simple case, and understanding the difference now between minimal diversity and complete diversity, what does that tell you will be necessary in any situation in which you are called on to determine whether jurisdiction exists under the diversity of citizenship statute?

2. Could Congress change the diversity of citizenship statute to spell out that minimal diversity, rather than complete diversity, suffices? Why do you think Congress has not opened the door to all diversity cases that could be filed under the constitutional reservoir in Article III, Section 2?

3. If the citizenship of each party on each side of the case is crucial to determining whether complete diversity exists, how does one determine the citizenship of an individual, of a corporation, or of other entities? Different tests may apply depending on the type of person or entity is involved. Therefore, knowing what test to apply to determine citizenship is as important as knowing the complete diversity rule. Armed with knowledge of the rule, and with the criteria for each test applicable to each type of party, you will be able to figure out in any scenario whether complete diversity of citizenship exists.

4. Having emphasized the necessity of complete diversity under the general diversity statute, it is worth noting that there are specific federal statutes other than the general diversity statute that permit minimal diversity. The federal interpleader statute does not require complete diversity, but rather only minimal diversity. Instead of requiring that none of the plaintiffs in a suit be from the same state as any of the defendants, minimal diversity requires only that any one plaintiff in a suit reside in a different state from any one defendant in that suit. Thus, in a multi-party suit, the interpleader statute allows a plaintiff to bring suit against a defendant in federal court, even though both parties reside in the same state, as long as there is at least one plaintiff that resides in a different state from at least one defendant in the suit. In *State Farm Fire & Casualty Company v. Tashire*,[81] the Supreme Court explained:

> The interpleader statute, 28 U.S.C. § 1335, applies where there are 'Two or more adverse claimants, of diverse citizenship . . . .' This provision has been uniformly construed to require only "minimal diversity," that is, diversity of citizenship between two or more claimants, without regard to the circumstances that other rival claimants may be co-citizens. The language of the statute, the legislative purpose broadly to remedy the problems posed by multiple claimants to a single fund, and the consistent judicial interpretation tacitly accepted by Congress, persuade us that the statute requires no more. There remains, however, the question whether such a statutory construction is consistent with Article III of our Constitution, which extends the federal judicial power to 'Controversies . . . between citizens of different States . . . and between a State, or the Citizens thereof, and foreign States, Citizens or Subjects.' In *Strawbridge v. Curtiss*, this Court held that the diversity of citizenship statute required 'complete diversity': where co-citizens appeared on both sides of a dispute, jurisdiction was lost. But Chief Justice Marshall there

---

[81] State Farm Fire & Cas. Co. v. Tashire, 386 U.S. 523, 530–31 (1967).

purposes to construe only "The words of the act of congress," not the Constitution itself. And in a variety of contexts this Court and the lower courts have concluded that Article III poses no obstacle to the legislative extension of federal jurisdiction, founded on diversity, so long as any two adverse parties are not co-citizens. Accordingly, we conclude that the present case is properly in the federal courts.[82]

---

2. Tests for Determining Citizenship

As noted above, you need to be equipped with the tests that apply to determining citizenship of each party in a case. After you have used the applicable test to determine the citizenship of every party on the plaintiff's side and on the defendant's side, you can then look to see whether any plaintiff is a citizen of the same state as any defendant. If any are, then complete diversity will not exist and jurisdiction under the general diversity statute is thwarted. If each plaintiff is a citizen of a state different from every defendant, then you can confidently conclude that complete diversity of citizenship exists.

a. Citizenship of Individuals

As shown above, 28 U.S.C. § 1332(a) (2) uses the term "domiciled" in determining whether the federal courts have diversity jurisdiction over a party. The way to determine the state in which an individual is a citizen for diversity purposes is to determine that individual's domicile. In *Mas v. Perry*, the United States Court of Appeals for the Fifth Circuit explained that a person's domicile is "his true, fixed, and permanent home and principal establishment . . . to which he has the intention of returning whenever he is absent therefrom."[83] At the time this case was before the Fifth Circuit, a woman would customarily take the domicile of her husband (current citizenship rules no longer have a wife's citizenship be determined by her husband). In Mrs. Mas's case, however, her marriage to a citizen of France would, by the "old approach," have removed her United States citizenship. The Court held that a United States citizen does not lose her state domicile by marrying an alien. Each spouse is a citizen in the state in which his or her true, fixed, and permanent home exists, and where the spouse intends to be a citizen even when away from the state (i.e., has the intention to return).

MAS v. PERRY
United States Court of Appeals for the Fifth Circuit, 1974
489 F.2d 1396

AINSWORTH, Circuit Judge:

This case presents questions pertaining to federal diversity jurisdiction under 28 U.S.C. § 1332, which, pursuant to article III, section II of the Constitution, provides for original jurisdiction in federal district courts of all civil actions that are between, inter alia, citizens of different States or citizens of a State and citizens of foreign states and in which the amount in controversy is more than $10,000. [The amount in controversy requirement, which Congress first established by the Judiciary Act of 1789, was raised to $50,000 in 1988 and increased to its current amount of $75,000 in 1996.]

Appellees Jean Paul Mas, a citizen of France, and Judy Mas were married at her home in Jackson,

---

[82] *Id.*
[83] 489 F.2d 1396 (5th Cir. 1974).

Mississippi. Prior to their marriage, Mr. and Mrs. Mas were graduate assistants, pursuing coursework as well as performing teaching duties, for approximately nine months and one year, respectively, at Louisiana State University in Baton Rouge, Louisiana. Shortly after their marriage, they returned to Baton Rouge to resume their duties as graduate assistants at LSU. They remained in Baton Rouge for approximately two more years, after which they moved to Park Ridge, Illinois. At the time of the trial in this case, it was their intention to return to Baton Rouge. While Mr. Mas finished his studies for the degree of Doctor of Philosophy. Mr. and Mrs. Mas were undecided as to where they would reside after that.

Upon their return to Baton Rouge after their marriage, appellees rented an apartment from appellant Oliver H. Perry, a citizen of Louisiana. This appeal arises from a final judgment entered on a jury verdict awarding $5,000 to Mr. Mas and $15,000 to Mrs. Mas for damages incurred by them as a result of the discovery that their bedroom and bathroom contained "two-way" mirrors and that they had been watched through them by the appellant during three of the first four months of their marriage.

At the close of the appellees' case at trial, appellant made an oral motion to dismiss for lack of jurisdiction. The motion was denied by the district court. Before this Court, appellant challenges the final judgment below solely on jurisdictional grounds, contending that appellees failed to prove diversity of citizenship among the parties and that the requisite jurisdictional amount is lacking with respect to Mr. Mas. Finding no merit to these contentions, we affirm. Under section 1332(a)(2), the federal judicial power extends to the claim of Mr. Mas, a citizen of France, against the appellant, a citizen of Louisiana. Since we conclude that Mrs. Mas is a citizen of Mississippi for diversity purposes, the district court also properly had jurisdiction under section 1332(a)(1) of her claim.

It has long been the general rule that complete diversity of parties is required in order that diversity jurisdiction obtain; that is, no party on one side may be a citizen of the same State as any party on the other side.[84] This determination of one's State Citizenship for diversity purposes is controlled by federal law, not by the law of any State. As is the case in other areas of federal jurisdiction, the diverse citizenship among adverse parties must be present at the time the complaint is filed. Jurisdiction is unaffected by subsequent changes in the citizenship of the parties. The burden of pleading the diverse citizenship is upon the party invoking federal jurisdiction; and if the diversity jurisdiction is properly challenged, that party also bears the burden of proof.

To be a citizen of a State within the meaning of section 1332, a natural person must be both a citizen of the United States, and a domiciliary of that State. For diversity purposes, citizenship means domicile; mere residence in the State is not sufficient. A person's domicile is the place of "his true, fixed, and permanent home and principal establishment, and to which he has the intention of returning whenever he is absent therefrom" A change of domicile may be affected only by a combination of two elements: (a) taking up residence in a different domicile with (b) the intention to remain there.

It is clear that at the time of her marriage, Mrs. Mas was a domiciliary of the State of Mississippi. While it is generally the case that the domicile of the wife—and, consequently, her State citizenship for purposes of diversity jurisdiction—is deemed to be that of her husband, we find no precedent for extending this concept to the situation here, in which the husband is a citizen of a foreign state but resides in the United States. Indeed, such a fiction would work absurd results on the facts before us. If Mr. Mas were considered a domiciliary of France—as he would be since he had lived in Louisiana as a student-teaching assistant prior to filing this suit—then Mrs. Mas would also be deemed a domiciliary, and thus, fictionally at least, a

---

[84] Strawbridge v. Curtiss, 7 U.S. (3 Cranch) 267 (1806).

citizen of France. She would not be a citizen of any State and could not sue in a federal court on that basis; nor could she invoke the alienage jurisdiction to bring her claim in federal court, since she is not an alien. On the other hand, if Mrs. Mas's domicile were Louisiana, she would become a Louisiana citizen for diversity purposes and could not bring suit with her husband against appellant, also a Louisiana citizen, on the basis of diversity jurisdiction. These are curious results under a rule arising from the theoretical identity of person and interest of the married couple. [As noted, the wife's taking domicile of the husband is antiquated law.]

An American woman is not deemed to have lost her United States citizenship solely by reason of her marriage to an alien. Similarly, we conclude that for diversity purposes a woman does not have her domicile or State Citizenship changed solely by reason of her marriage to an alien.

Mrs. Mas's Mississippi domicile was disturbed neither by her year in Louisiana prior to her marriage nor as a result of the time she and her husband spent at LSU after their marriage, since for both periods she was a graduate assistant at LSU. Though she testified that after her marriage she had no intention of returning to her parents' home in Mississippi, Mrs. Mas did not effect a change of domicile since she and Mr. Mas were in Louisiana only as students and lacked the requisite intention to remain there. Until she acquires a new domicile, she remains a domiciliary, and thus a citizen, of Mississippi.

Appellant also contends that Mr. Mas's claim should have been dismissed for failure to establish the requisite jurisdictional amount for diversity cases of more than $10,000 [at the time the diversity of citizenship required only that the amount in controversy exceed $10,000; that amount has changed over time]. In their complaint Mr. and Mrs. Mas alleged that they had each been damaged in the amount of $100,000. As we have noted, Mr. Mas ultimately recovered $5,000.

It is well settled that the amount in controversy is determined by the amount claimed by the plaintiff in good faith. Federal jurisdiction is not lost because a judgment of less than the jurisdictional amount is awarded. That Mr. Mas recovered only $5,000 is, therefore, not compelling. As the Supreme Court stated in *St. Paul Mercury Indemnity Company v. Red Cab Company*.[85]:

The sum claimed by the plaintiff controls if the claim is apparently made in good faith. It must appear to a legal certainty that the claim is really for less than the jurisdictional amount to justify dismissal. The inability of the plaintiff to recover an amount adequate to give the court jurisdiction does not show his bad faith or oust the jurisdiction.

Having heard the evidence presented at the trial, the district court concluded that the appellees properly met the requirements of section 1332 with respect to jurisdictional amount. Upon examination of the record in this case, we are also satisfied that the requisite amount was in controversy.

Thus[,] the power of the federal district court to entertain the claims of appellees in this case stands on two separate legs of diversity jurisdiction: a claim by an alien against a State citizen; and an action between citizens of different States. We also note, however, the propriety of having the federal district court entertain a spouse's action against a defendant, where the district court already has jurisdiction over a claim, arising from the same transaction, by the other spouse against the same defendant. In the case before us, such a result is particularly desirable. The claims of Mr. and Mrs. Mas arise from the same operative facts, and there was almost complete interdependence between their claims with respect to the proof required and

---

[85] 303 U.S. 283, 288–90.

the issues raised at trial. Thus, since the district court had jurisdiction of Mr. Mas's action, sound judicial administration militates strongly in favor of federal jurisdiction of Mrs. Mas's claim.

Affirmed.

Follow-Up Questions and Comments

1. Note how the Court pinpoints a moment in time to determine the parties' citizenship? What is that point in time? Why do you think courts determining whether there is diversity need a bright-line rule concerning when to determine whether complete diversity of citizenship exists? After filing suit against Perry, Mrs. Mas and her husband moved to Illinois where they apparently intended to settle. Considering the rule stated in the case about time of filing and the comments in this Note, would the result of the courts' determination of diversity be different if Mr. and Mrs. Mas bought and moved into a home in Louisiana before suing Mr. Perry?

2. Note the evidence that courts consider in applying the domicile rule. Such evidence includes whether the individual pays taxes, votes, owns property, or has stated to someone else his intention to live in that state; all these factors may inform the court of a person's domicile. However, these facts alone are not determinative; the facts must always be applied to the domicile test. In stating the domicile test, students often go beyond the accurate statement of the test and include in their statement the evidence that can show domicile. The accurate approach is to state the domicile rule as it is stated in *Mas v. Perry*, and then apply the particular facts (evidence) to that test to reach a conclusion.

3. What if a party relocates to a state different from the party she is suing solely to establish citizenship diverse from her adversary so that she can qualify for diversity jurisdiction? The collusive joinder statute, 28 U.S.C. § 1359, provides that "[a] district court shall not have jurisdiction of a civil action in which any party, by assignment or otherwise, has been improperly or collusively joined to invoke the jurisdiction of such court." However, the Supreme Court has held that this statute is not violated if a party, before filing, changes her domicile solely for purposes of creating diversity jurisdiction.[86] The Court seems to be saying that, if someone is willing to go to the trouble of establishing a new residence in another state, then they will be able to obtain diversity of citizenship.

4. The collusive joinder statute is, however, violated if a party assigns a claim without sufficient consideration to another party diverse from the adversary. For instance, assume P1 has a debt claim against D, but both parties are domiciled in the same state. If P1 assigned the claim to P2, a party domiciled in a state different from P1 and D's state of domicile, the ability of P2 (the assignee of the claim) to sue in diversity would depend on the terms of the assignment. If P1 received fair value and would not have a stake in the outcome of P2's suit, the assignment would be valid and P2 could sue based on diversity. If instead, P2 was merely a conduit for P1's claim and P2 received merely a fraction of any recovery (*e.g.*, five percent), the arrangement would violate the collusive joinder statute.

Practice Problem

---

[86] Morris v. Gilmer, 129 U.S. 315 (1889).

The following Practice Problem will allow you to apply the above test on domicile of an individual to a fact pattern to ensure you understand the nuances of the principles set forth in *Mas v. Perry*.

Practice Problem 3-9

Marge had grown up and worked in North Carolina since she went into the airline business and had risen to manager level. An opportunity opened in her company, Southeast Airlines, for a regional manager position based in the Baton Rouge, Louisiana offices of the company. Marge applied for and was selected to be the regional manager. She had inherited her family home in North Carolina and did not want to sell it. Nevertheless, she knew she would need to relocate to Baton Rouge. She entered an annual lease for a condominium unit near her offices. She said that she wanted to do that for a while and look around for a home to buy. She obtained a Louisiana driver's license. She was pleased as could be for the first two weeks in Baton Rouge. One morning, however, she wandered into the garden area outside her condo with a cup of coffee. There, as she walked on a path, she couldn't believe what she saw—an alligator less than ten feet from the path. She screamed, turned, and ran to the condo manager's office. Mr. Perry, the condo manager, was in when Marge ran inside. She said: "Call the police! There's an alligator on the loose." Mr. Perry just laughed and said, "Ma'am if we called the police every time we saw an alligator, they wouldn't have time to catch any of the law-breakers. Alligators are all over Louisiana. You'll have to just keep an eye out for them." Disgusted, Marge went to her condo and called in sick to work because she was so upset. She decided that she could not live in Louisiana with its alligators. She told Mr. Perry that she was moving back to North Carolina. He told her she could do as she pleased but she was obligated to pay the full annual amount for the condo. Marge told him she would do no such thing and was packing up to leave next week, once she transferred back to her old job in North Carolina. Mr. Perry called his lawyer and asked him to serve Marge with a lawsuit before she left. The lawyer analyzed the situation and wonders whether Marge established citizenship in Louisiana, or whether she had never lost her North Carolina citizenship, in which case he could sue her in federal court because there would then be complete diversity of citizenship and the amount at issue was sufficient. What are the arguments that Marge never changed her citizenship from North Carolina? What are the arguments that she established domicile and thus citizenship in Louisiana? Which arguments, in your judgment, are superior and why?

---

b. Citizenship of Corporations

The diversity statute provides that the citizenship of corporations will be dual, thus including both the state of incorporation and the state of the corporation's principal place of business.[87] The state of incorporation does not require a test. However, courts struggled with tests to determine a corporation's principal place of business. Fortunately, the Supreme Court in *The Hertz Corporation v. Friend* provided a clear test to determine a corporation's principal place of business.

---

[87] *See* 28 U.S.C. § 1332(c) (1) (2017).

61

THE HERTZ CORP. v. FRIEND
Supreme Court of the United States, 2010
559 U.S. 77

Justice BREYER delivered the opinion of the Court.

The federal diversity jurisdiction statute provides that "a corporation shall be deemed to be a citizen of any State by which it has been incorporated and of the State where it has its principal place of business." 28 U.S.C. § 1332(c) (1). We seek here to resolve different interpretations that the Circuits have given this phrase. In doing so, we place primary weight upon the need for judicial administration of a jurisdictional statute to remain as simple as possible. And we conclude that the phrase "principal place of business" refers to the place where the corporation's high-level officers direct, control, and coordinate the corporation's activities. Lower federal courts have often metaphorically called that place the corporation's "nerve center." We believe that the "nerve center" will typically be found at a corporation's headquarters.

I

In September 2007, respondents Melinda Friend and John Nhieu, two California citizens, sued petitioner, the Hertz Corporation, in a California state court. They sought damages for what they claimed were violations of California's wage and hour laws. And they requested relief on behalf of a potential class composed of California citizens who had allegedly suffered similar harms.

Hertz filed a notice seeking removal to a federal court.[88] Hertz claimed that the plaintiffs and the defendant were citizens of different States.[89] Hence, the federal court possessed diversity-of-citizenship jurisdiction. Friend and Nhieu, however, claimed that the Hertz Corporation was a California citizen, like themselves, and that, hence, diversity jurisdiction was lacking.

To support its position, Hertz submitted a declaration by an employee relations manager that sought to show that Hertz's "principal place of business" was in New Jersey, not in California. The declaration stated, among other things, that Hertz operated facilities in 44 States; and that California—which had about 12% of the Nation's population—accounted for 273 of Hertz's 1,606 car rental locations; about 2,300 of its 11,230 full-time employees; about $811 million of its $4.371 billion in annual revenue; and about 3.8 million of its approximately 21 million annual transactions, i.e., rentals. The declaration also stated that the "leadership of Hertz and its domestic subsidiaries" is located at Hertz's "corporate headquarters" in Park Ridge, New Jersey; that its "core executive and administrative functions . . . are carried out" there and "to a lesser extent" in Oklahoma City, Oklahoma; and that its "major administrative operations . . .are found" at those two locations.

The District Court of the Northern District of California accepted Hertz's statement of the facts as undisputed. But it concluded that, given those facts, Hertz was a citizen of California. In reaching this conclusion, the court applied Ninth Circuit precedent, which instructs courts to identify a corporation's "principal place of business" by first determining the amount of a corporation's business activity State by State. If the amount of activity is "significantly larger" or "substantially predominates" in one State, then that State is the corporation's "principal place of business." If there is no such State, then the "principal place of business" is the corporation's "'nerve center,'" i.e., the place where "'the majority of its executive

---

[88] 28 U.S.C. §§ 1332(d) (2), 1441(a).
[89] §§ 1332(a) (1), (c) (1).

and administrative functions are performed.'"

Applying this test, the District Court found that the "plurality of each of the relevant business activities" was in California, and that "the differential between the amount of those activities" in California and the amount in "the next closest state" was "significant." Hence, Hertz's "principal place of business" was California, and diversity jurisdiction was thus lacking. The District Court consequently remanded the case to the state courts.

Hertz appealed the District Court's remand order. The Ninth Circuit affirmed in a brief memorandum opinion. Hertz filed a petition for certiorari. And, in light of differences among the Circuits in the application of the test for corporate citizenship, we granted the writ.

. . .

III

We begin our "principal place of business" discussion with a brief review of relevant history. The Constitution provides that the "judicial Power shall extend" to "Controversies . . .between Citizens of different States."[90] This language, however, does not automatically confer diversity jurisdiction upon the federal courts. Rather, it authorizes Congress to do so and, in doing so, to determine the scope of the federal courts' jurisdiction within constitutional limits.

Congress first authorized federal courts to exercise diversity jurisdiction in 1789 when, in the First Judiciary Act, Congress granted federal courts authority to hear suits "between a citizen of the State where the suit is brought, and a citizen of another State. The statute said nothing about corporations. In 1809, Chief Justice Marshall, writing for a unanimous Court, described a corporation as an "invisible, intangible, and artificial being" which was "certainly not a citizen." *Bank of United States v. Deveaux*.[91] But the Court held that a corporation could invoke the federal courts' diversity jurisdiction based on a pleading that the corporation's shareholders were all citizens of a different State from the defendants, as "the term citizen ought to be understood as it is used in the constitution, and as it is used in other laws. That is, to describe the real persons who come into court, in this case, under their corporate name."

In *Louisville, C. & C.R. Co. v. Letson*,[92] the Court modified this initial approach. It held that a corporation was to be deemed an artificial person of the State by which it had been created, and its citizenship for jurisdictional purposes determined accordingly. Ten years later, the Court in *Marshall v. Baltimore & Ohio R. Co.*,[93] held that the reason a corporation was a citizen of its State of incorporation was that, for the limited purpose of determining corporate citizenship, courts could conclusively (and artificially) presume that a corporation's shareholders were citizens of the State of incorporation. And it reaffirmed *Letson*. Whatever the rationale, the practical upshot was that, for diversity purposes, the federal courts considered a corporation to be a citizen of the State of its incorporation.

In 1928, this Court made clear that the "state of incorporation" rule was virtually absolute. It held that a corporation closely identified with State A could proceed in a federal court located in that State as long as the corporation had filed its incorporation papers in State B, perhaps a State where the corporation

---

[90] U.S. CONT. art. III, § 2.
[91] 5 Cranch 61 (1809).
[92] 43 U.S. 497 (1844).
[93] 461 F. Supp. 362 (1978).

did no business at all.[94] Subsequently, many in Congress and those who testified before it pointed out that this interpretation was at odds with diversity jurisdiction's basic rationale, namely, opening the federal courts' doors to those who might otherwise suffer from local prejudice against out-of-state parties. Through its choice of the State of incorporation, a corporation could manipulate federal court jurisdiction, for example, opening the federal courts' doors in a State where it conducted nearly all its business by filing incorporation papers elsewhere. ("Since the Supreme Court has decided that a corporation is a citizen . . . it has become a common practice for corporations to be incorporated in one State while they do business in another. And there is no doubt but that it often occurs simply for the purpose of being able to have the advantage of choosing between two tribunals in case of litigation"). Although various legislative proposals to curtail the corporate use of diversity jurisdiction were made, none of these proposals were enacted into law.

At the same time[,] as federal dockets increased in size, many judges began to believe those dockets contained too many diversity cases. A committee of the Judicial Conference of the United States studied the matter. And on March 12, 1951, that committee, the Committee on Jurisdiction and Venue, issued a report.

Among its observations, the committee found a general need "to prevent frauds and abuses" with respect to jurisdiction. The committee recommended against eliminating diversity cases altogether. Instead it recommended, along with other proposals, a statutory amendment that would make a corporation a citizen both of the State of its incorporation and any State from which it received more than half of its gross income. (requiring corporation to show that "less than fifty per cent of its gross income was derived from business transacted within the state where the Federal court is held"). If, for example, a citizen of California sued (under state law in state court) a corporation that received half or more of its gross income from California, that corporation would not be able to remove the case to federal court, even if Delaware was its State of incorporation.

During the spring and summer of 1951[,] committee members circulated their report and attended circuit conferences at which federal judges discussed the report's recommendations. Reflecting those criticisms, the committee filed a new report in September, in which it revised its corporate citizenship recommendation. It now proposed that "a corporation shall be deemed a citizen of the state of its original creation . . . [and] shall also be deemed a citizen of a state where it has its principal place of business.'" The committee wrote that this new language would provide a "simpler and more practical formula" than the "gross income" test.[95] It added that the language "ha[d] a precedent in the jurisdictional provisions of the Bankruptcy Act."

In mid 1957, the committee presented its reports to the House of Representatives Committee on the Judiciary. Judge Albert Maris, representing Judge John Parker (who had chaired the Judicial Conference Committee), discussed various proposals that the Judicial Conference had made to restrict the scope of diversity jurisdiction. In respect to the "principal place of business" proposal, he said that the relevant language "ha[d] been defined in the Bankruptcy Act." He added:

All of those problems have arisen in bankruptcy cases, and as I recall the cases—and I wouldn't want to be bound by this statement because I haven't them before me—I think the courts have generally

---

[94] *See Black and White Taxicab & Transfer Co. v. Brown* and *Yellow Taxicab & Transfer Co.* (refusing to question corporation's reincorporation motives and finding diversity jurisdiction).
[95] Sept. Committee Rept. 2.

taken the view that where a corporation's interests are rather widespread, the principal place of business is an actual rather than a theoretical or legal one. It is the actual place where its business operations are coordinated, directed, and carried out, which would ordinarily be the place where its officers carry on its day-to-day business, where its accounts are kept, where its payments are made, and not necessarily a State in which it may have a plant, if it is a big corporation, or something of that sort. But that has been pretty well worked out in the bankruptcy cases, and that law would all be available, you see, to be applied here without having to go over it again from the beginning.

The House Committee reprinted the Judicial Conference Committee Reports along with other reports and relevant testimony and circulated it to the general public "for the purpose of inviting further suggestions and comments." Subsequently, in 1958, Congress both codified the courts' traditional place of incorporation test and also enacted into law a slightly modified version of the Conference Committee's proposed "principal place of business" language. A corporation was to "be deemed a citizen of any State by which it has been incorporated and of the State where it has its principal place of business."

IV

The phrase "principal place of business" has proved more difficult to apply than its originators likely expected. Decisions under the Bankruptcy Act did not provide the firm guidance for which Judge Maris had hoped because courts interpreting bankruptcy law did not agree about how to determine a corporation's "principal place of business."

After Congress' amendment, courts were similarly uncertain as to where to look to determine a corporation's "principal place of business" for diversity purposes. If a corporation's headquarters and executive offices were in the same State in which it did most of its business, the test seemed straightforward. The "principal place of business" was located in that State.

But suppose those corporate headquarters, including executive offices, are in one State, while the corporation's plants or other centers of business activity are located in other States? In 1959, a distinguished federal district judge, Edward Weinfeld, relied on the Second Circuit's interpretation of the Bankruptcy Act to answer this question in part:

> Where a corporation is engaged in far-flung and varied activities which are carried on in different states, its principal place of business is the nerve center from which it radiates out to its constituent parts and from which its officers direct, control and coordinate all activities without regard to locale, in the furtherance of the corporate objective. The test applied by our Court of Appeals, is that place where the corporation has an "office from which its business was directed and controlled"— the place where "all of its business was under the supreme direction and control of its officers.

Numerous Circuits have since followed this rule, applying the "nerve center" test for corporations with "far-flung" business activities.

Scot's analysis, however, did not go far enough. For it did not answer what courts should do when the operations of the corporation are not "far-flung" but rather limited to only a few States. When faced with this question, various courts have focused more heavily on where a corporation's actual business activities are located.

Perhaps because corporations come in many different forms, involve many different kinds of business activities, and locate offices and plants for different reasons in different ways in different regions, a general "business activities" approach has proved unusually difficult to apply. Courts must decide which factors are more important than others: for example, plant location, sales or servicing centers; transactions, payrolls, or revenue generation.

The number of factors grew as courts explicitly combined aspects of the "nerve center" and "business activity" tests to look to a corporation's "total activities," sometimes to try to determine what treatises have described as the corporation's "center of gravity." A major treatise confirms this growing complexity, listing Circuit by Circuit, cases that highlight different factors or emphasize similar factors differently, and reporting that the "federal courts of appeals have employed various tests"—tests which "tend to overlap" and which are sometimes described in "language" that "is imprecise." Not surprisingly, different circuits (and sometimes different courts within a single circuit) have applied these highly general multifactor tests in different ways . . . (noting that the First Circuit "has never explained a basis for choosing between 'the center of corporate activity' test and the 'locus of operations' test"; the Second Circuit uses a "two-part test" similar to that of the Fifth, Ninth, and Eleventh Circuits involving an initial determination as to whether "a corporation's activities are centralized or decentralized" followed by an application of either the "place of operations" or "nerve center" test; the Third Circuit applies the "center of corporate activities" test searching for the "headquarters of a corporation's day-to-day activity"; the Fourth Circuit has "endorsed neither [the 'nerve center' or 'place of operations'] test to the exclusion of the other"; the Tenth Circuit directs consideration of the "total activity of the company considered as a whole").[96]

This complexity may reflect an unmediated judicial effort to apply the statutory phrase "principal place of business" in light of the general purpose of diversity jurisdiction, i.e., an effort to find the State where a corporation is least likely to suffer out-of-state prejudice when it is sued in a local court. But, if so, that task seems doomed to failure. After all, the relevant purposive concern—prejudice against an out-of-state party—will often depend upon factors that courts cannot easily measure, for example, a corporation's image, its history, and its advertising, while the factors that courts can more easily measure, for example, its office or plant location, its sales, its employment, or the nature of the goods or services it supplies, will sometimes bear no more than a distant relation to the likelihood of prejudice. At the same time, this approach is at war with administrative simplicity. And it has failed to achieve a nationally uniform interpretation of federal law, an unfortunate consequence in a federal legal system.

V

A

In an effort to find a single, more uniform interpretation of the statutory phrase, we have reviewed the Courts of Appeals' divergent and increasingly complex interpretations. Having done so, we now return to, and expand, Judge Weinfeld's approach, as applied in the Seventh Circuit. We conclude that "principal place of business" is best read as referring to the place where a corporation's officers direct, control, and coordinate the corporation's activities. It is the place that Courts of Appeals have called the corporation's "nerve center." And in practice it should normally be the place where the corporation maintains its headquarters—provided that the headquarters is the actual center of direction, control, and coordination, i.e., the "nerve center," and not simply an office where the corporation holds its board meetings (for example, attended by directors and officers who have traveled there for the occasion).

---

[96] *See also* 13F CHARLES ALAN WRIGHT & ARTHUR R. MILLER, FEDERAL PRACTICE AND PROCEDURE § 3625 (describing, in 73 pages, the "nerve center," "corporate activities," and "total activity" tests as part of an effort to locate the corporation's "center of gravity," while specifying different ways in which different circuits apply these or other factors).

Three sets of considerations, taken together, convince us that this approach, while imperfect, is superior to other possibilities. First, the statute's language supports the approach. The statute's text deems a corporation a citizen of the "State where it has its principal place of business."[97] The word "place" is in the singular, not the plural. The word "principal" requires us to pick out the "main, prominent" or "leading" place. . . . And the fact that the word "place" follows the words "State where" means that the "place" is a place within a State. It is not the State itself.

A corporation's "nerve center," usually its main headquarters, is a single place. The public often (though not always) considers it the corporation's main place of business. And it is a place within a State. By contrast, the application of a more general business activities test has led some courts, as in the present case, to look, not at a particular place within a State, but incorrectly at the State itself, measuring the total amount of business activities that the corporation conducts there and determining whether they are "significantly larger" than in the next-ranking State.

This approach invites greater litigation and can lead to strange results, as the Ninth Circuit has since recognized. Namely, if a "corporation may be deemed a citizen of California on th[e] basis" of "activities [that] roughly reflect California's larger population . . . nearly every national retailer—no matter how far flung its operations—will be deemed a citizen of California for diversity purposes." But why award or decline diversity jurisdiction on the basis of a State's population, whether measured directly, indirectly (say proportionately), or with modifications?

Second, administrative simplicity is a major virtue in a jurisdictional statute. Complex jurisdictional tests complicate a case, eating up time and money as the parties litigate, not the merits of their claims, but which court is the right court to decide those claims. Complex tests produce appeals and reversals, encourage gamesmanship, and, again, diminish the likelihood that results and settlements will reflect a claim's legal and factual merits. Judicial resources too are at stake. Courts have an independent obligation to determine whether subject-matter jurisdiction exists, even when no party challenges it. So courts benefit from straightforward rules under which they can readily assure themselves of their power to hear a case.

Simple jurisdictional rules also promote greater predictability. Predictability is valuable to corporations making business and investment decisions. Predictability also benefits plaintiffs deciding whether to file suit in a state or federal court

A "nerve center" approach, which ordinarily equates that "center" with a corporation's headquarters, is simple to apply comparatively speaking. The metaphor of a corporate "brain," while not precise, suggests a single location. By contrast, a corporation's general business activities more often lack a single principal place where they take place. That is to say, the corporation may have several plants, many sales locations, and employees located in many different places. If so, it will not be as easy to determine which of these different business locales is the "principal" or most important "place."

Third, the statute's legislative history, for those who accept it, offers a simplicity-related interpretive benchmark. The Judicial Conference provided an initial version of its proposal that suggested a numerical test. A corporation would be deemed a citizen of the State that accounted for more than half of its gross income. The Conference changed its mind in light of criticism that such a test would prove too complex and impractical to apply. That history suggests that the words "principal place of business" should

---

[97] 28 U.S.C. § 1332(c) (1).

be interpreted to be no more complex than the initial "half of gross income" test. A "nerve center" test offers such a possibility. A general business activities test does not.

B

We recognize that there may be no perfect test that satisfies all administrative and purposive criteria. We recognize as well that, under the "nerve center" test we adopt today, there will be hard cases. For example, in this era of telecommuting, some corporations may divide their command and coordinating functions among officers who work at several different locations, perhaps communicating over the Internet. That said, our test nonetheless points courts in a single direction, towards the center of overall direction, control, and coordination. Courts do not have to try to weigh corporate functions, assets, or revenues different in kind, one from the other. Our approach provides a sensible test that is relatively easier to apply, not a test that will, in all instances, automatically generate a result.

We also recognize that the use of a "nerve center" test may in some cases produce results that seem to cut against the basic rationale for 28 U.S.C. § 1332. For example, if the bulk of a company's business activities visible to the public take place in New Jersey, while its top officers direct those activities just across the river in New York, the "principal place of business" is New York. One could argue that members of the public in New Jersey would be less likely to be prejudiced against the corporation than persons in New York—yet the corporation will still be entitled to remove a New Jersey state case to federal court. And note too that the same corporation would be unable to remove a New York state case to federal court, despite the New York public's presumed prejudice against the corporation.

We understand that such seeming anomalies will arise. However, in view of the necessity of having a clearer rule, we must accept them. Accepting occasionally counterintuitive results is the price the legal system must pay to avoid overly complex jurisdictional administration while producing the benefits that accompany a more uniform legal system.

The burden of persuasion for establishing diversity jurisdiction, of course, remains on the party asserting it. When challenged on allegations of jurisdictional facts, the parties must support their allegations by competent proof. And when faced with such a challenge, we reject suggestions such as, for example, the one made by petitioner that the mere filing of a form like the Securities and Exchange Commission's Form 10–K listing a corporation's "principal executive offices" would, without more, be sufficient proof to establish a corporation's "nerve center. Such possibilities would readily permit jurisdictional manipulation, thereby subverting a major reason for the insertion of the "principal place of business" language in the diversity statute. Indeed, if the record reveals attempts at manipulation—for example, that the alleged "nerve center" is nothing more than a mail drop box, a bare office with a computer, or the location of an annual executive retreat—the courts should instead take as the "nerve center" the place of actual direction, control, and coordination, in the absence of such manipulation.

VI

Petitioner's unchallenged declaration suggests that Hertz's center of direction, control, and coordination, its "nerve center," and its corporate headquarters are one and the same, and they are located in New Jersey, not in California. Because respondents should have a fair opportunity to litigate their case in light of our holding, however, we vacate the Ninth Circuit's judgment and remand the case for further proceedings consistent with this opinion.

It is so ordered.

Practice Problem

The following Practice Problem allows you to apply the test for a corporation's principal place of business to a factual scenario different from that in *Hertz*.

Practice Problem 3-10

Saddles, Inc. is a leader in making and selling saddles for horse-riding. Saddles was incorporated in Delaware. Saddles' manufacturing facility is in Dallas, Texas. The offices of Saddles' officers, accountants, lawyers, and other employees is close to the manufacturing facility in Dallas. On a monthly basis, the officers meet at a ranch that Saddles owns in Arizona. There, they make all major decisions about the company, including its business plans, decisions to continue or discontinue saddle styles, areas in which they would continue or discontinue selling, and other major decisions. Twice a year, the directors of Saddles join the officers at the ranch and, together, the directors hear presentations from the officers on the status of the company and vote on questions concerning the long-term direction in which the company would head. Saddles' practice is to prepare minutes of the monthly meetings of the officers, and of the biannual board of directors' meeting, and to transmit these from the ranch to all managers in the company in various locations. The managers are expected to implement the officers and directors' decisions. Under the Hertz test, where is Saddles' principal place of business?

c. Citizenship of Unincorporated Entities

Unlike for corporations, the means of determining the citizenship of unincorporated entities is not set forth in the diversity statute. Thus, courts have developed guidance to allow litigants to determine such entities' citizenship.

d. The Test for Partnerships and Traditional Unincorporated Entities

Carden v. Arkoma Associates is the leading case for determining the citizenship for diversity purposes of partnerships and, by extension, other unincorporated entities. The test for Partnerships and Traditional Unincorporated Entities is derived from this case.

CARDEN v. ARKOMA ASSOCIATES
Supreme Court of the United States, 1990
494 U.S. 185

Justice SCALIA delivered the opinion of the Court.

The question presented in this case is whether, in a suit brought by a limited partnership, the citizenship of the limited partners must be taken into account to determine diversity of citizenship among the parties.

. . .

II

Article III of the Constitution provides, in pertinent part, that "[t]he judicial Power shall extend to . . . Controversies . . . between Citizens of different States." Congress first authorized the federal courts to exercise diversity jurisdiction in the Judiciary Act of 1789. In its current form, the diversity statute provides that "[t]he district courts shall have original jurisdiction of all civil actions where the matter in controversy exceeds . . . $50,000 . . . and is between . . . citizens of different States."[98] Since its enactment, we have interpreted the diversity statute to require "complete diversity" of citizenship. The District Court erred in finding complete diversity in this case unless (1) a limited partnership may be considered in its own right a "citizen" of the State that created it, or (2) a federal court must look to the citizenship of only its general, but not its limited, partners to determine whether there is complete diversity of citizenship. We consider these questions in turn.

A

We have often had to consider the status of artificial entities created by state law insofar as that bears upon the existence of federal diversity jurisdiction. The precise question posed under the terms of the diversity statute is whether such an entity may be considered a "citizen" of the State under whose laws it was created. A corporation is the paradigmatic artificial "person," and the Court has considered its proper characterization under the diversity statute on more than one occasion—not always reaching the same conclusion. Initially, we held that a corporation "is certainly not a citizen," so that to determine the existence of diversity jurisdiction the Court must "look to the character of the individuals who compose [it]."[99] We overruled *Deveaux* 35 years later in *Louisville, C. & C.R. Co. v. Letson*,[100] which held that a corporation is "capable of being treated as a citizen of [the State which created it], as much as a natural person." Ten years later, we reaffirmed the result of *Letson*, though on the somewhat different theory that "those who use the corporate name, and exercise the faculties conferred by it," should be presumed conclusively to be citizens of the corporation's State of incorporation.

While the rule regarding the treatment of corporations as "citizens" has become firmly established, we have (with an exception to be discussed presently) just as firmly resisted extending that treatment to other entities. For example, in *Chapman v. Barney*,[101] a case involving an unincorporated "joint stock company," we raised the question of jurisdiction on our own motion, and found it to be lacking:

"On looking into the record, we find no satisfactory showing as to the citizenship of the plaintiff. The allegation of the amended petition is, that the United States Express Company is a joint stock company organized under a law of the State of New York, and is a citizen of that State. But the express company cannot be a citizen of New York, within the meaning of the statutes regulating jurisdiction, unless it be a corporation. The allegation that the company was organized under the laws of New York is not an allegation that it is a corporation. In fact, the allegation is, that the company is not a corporation, but a joint stock company—that is, a mere partnership."[102]

Similarly, in *Great Southern Fire Proof Hotel Co. v. Jones*,[103] we held that a "limited partnership association"—although possessing "some of the characteristics of a corporation" and deemed a "citizen"

---

[98] 28 U.S.C.A. § 1332(a).

[99] Bank of United States v. Deveaux, 5 Cranch 61, 86 (1809).

[100] 2 How. 497, 558 (1844).

[101] 129 U.S. 677 (1889).

[102] *Id.* at 682.

[103] 177 U.S. 449 (1900).

by the law creating it—may not be deemed a "citizen" under the jurisdictional rule established for corporations. "That rule must not be extended." As recently as 1965, our unanimous opinion in *Steelworkers v. R.H. Bouligny, Inc.*,[104] reiterated that "the doctrinal wall of *Chapman v. Barney*," would not be breached.

The one exception to the admirable consistency of our jurisprudence on this matter is *Puerto Rico v. Russell & Co.*,[105] which held that the entity known as a sociedad en comandita, created under the civil law of Puerto Rico, could be treated as a citizen of Puerto Rico for purposes of determining federal-court jurisdiction. The sociedad's juridical personality, we said, "is so complete in contemplation of the law of Puerto Rico that we see no adequate reason for holding that the Sociedad has a different status for purposes of federal jurisdiction than a corporation organized under that law." Arkoma fairly argues that this language, and the outcome of the case, "reflec[t] the Supreme Court's willingness to look beyond the incorporated/unincorporated dichotomy and to study the internal organization, state law requirements, management structure, and capacity or lack thereof to act and/or sue, to determine diversity of citizenship." The problem with this argument lies not in its logic, but in the fact that the approach it espouses was proposed and specifically rejected in *Bouligny*. There, in reaffirming "the doctrinal wall of *Chapman v. Barney*," we explained Russell as a case resolving the distinctive problem "of fitting an exotic creation of the civil law . . .into a federal scheme which knew it not." There could be no doubt, after *Bouligny*, that at least common-law entities (and likely all entities beyond the Puerto Rican sociedad en comandita) would be treated for purposes of the diversity statute pursuant to what Russell called "[t]he tradition of the common law," which is "to treat as legal persons only incorporated groups and to assimilate all others to partnerships."

. . .

B

As an alternative ground for finding complete diversity, Arkoma asserts that the Fifth Circuit correctly determined its citizenship solely by reference to the citizenship of its general partners, without regard to the citizenship of its limited partners. Only the general partners, it points out, "manage the assets, control the litigation, and bear the risk of liability for the limited partnership's debts," and, more broadly, "have exclusive and complete management and control of the operations of the partnership." This approach of looking to the citizenship of only some of the members of the artificial entity finds even less support in our precedent than looking to the State of organization (for which one could at least point to Russell). We have never held that an artificial entity, suing or being sued in its own name, can invoke the diversity jurisdiction of the federal courts based on the citizenship of some but not all of its members. No doubt some members of the joint stock company in Chapman, the labor union in *Bouligny*, and the limited partnership association in Great Southern exercised greater control over their respective entities than other members. But such considerations have played no part in our decisions.

. . .

In sum, we reject the contention that to determine, for diversity purposes, the citizenship of an artificial entity, the court may consult the citizenship of less than all of the entity's members. We adhere to our oft-repeated rule that diversity jurisdiction in a suit by or against the entity depends on the citizenship

---

[104] 382 U.S. 145 (1965).
[105] 288 U.S. 476 (1933).

of "all the members,"[106] "the several persons composing such association," [107] "each of its members"[108]

C

The resolutions we have reached above can validly be characterized as technical, precedent-bound, and unresponsive to policy considerations raised by the changing realities of business organization. But, as must be evident from our earlier discussion that has been the character of our jurisprudence in this field after *Letson*. Arkoma is undoubtedly correct that limited partnerships are functionally similar to "other types of organizations that have access to federal courts," and is perhaps correct that "[c]onsiderations of basic fairness and substance over form require that limited partnerships receive similar treatment." Similar arguments were made in *Bouligny*. The District Court there had upheld removal because it could divine " 'no common sense reason for treating an unincorporated national labor union differently from a corporation,'"[109] and we recognized that that contention had "considerable merit,"[110] We concluded, however, that "[w]hether unincorporated labor unions ought to be assimilated to the status of corporations for diversity purposes . . . properly a matter for legislative consideration which cannot adequately or appropriately be dealt with by this Court". In other words, having entered the field of diversity policy with regard to artificial entities once (and forcefully) in *Letson*, we have left further adjustments to be made by Congress.

Congress has not been idle. In 1958[,] it revised the rule established in *Letson*, providing that a corporation shall be deemed a citizen not only of its State of incorporation but also "of the State where it has its principal place of business."[111] No provision was made for the treatment of artificial entities other than corporations, although the existence of many new, post-*Letson* forms of commercial enterprises, including at least the sort of joint stock company at issue in Chapman, the sort of limited partnership association at issue in Great Southern, and the sort of Massachusetts business trust at issue in Navarro, must have been obvious.

Thus, the course we take today does not so much disregard the policy of accommodating our diversity jurisdiction to the changing realities of commercial organization, as it honors the more important policy of leaving that to the people's elected representatives. Such accommodation is not only performed more legitimately by Congress than by courts, but it is performed more intelligently by legislation than by interpretation of the statutory word "citizen." The 50 States have created, and will continue to create, a wide assortment of artificial entities possessing different powers and characteristics and composed of various classes of members with varying degrees of interest and control. Which of them is entitled to be considered a "citizen" for diversity purposes, and which of their members' citizenship is to be consulted, are questions more readily resolved by legislative prescription than by legal reasoning, and questions whose complexity is particularly unwelcome at the threshold stage of determining whether a court has jurisdiction. We have long since decided that, having established special treatment for corporations, we will leave the rest to Congress; we adhere to that decision.

III

The judgment of the Court of Appeals is reversed, and the case is remanded for further proceedings consistent with this opinion.

---

[106] *Chapman*, 129 U.S. at 682.
[107] *Great Southern*, 177 U.S. at 456.
[108] *Bouligny*, 382 U.S. at 146.
[109] 382 U.S. at 146.
[110] *Id.* at 150.
[111] 28 U.S.C.A. § 1332(c).

It is so ordered.

Practice Problem

Practice Problem 3-11

Turing, Wizniak & Associates is a partnership that developed a variety of user-friendly computer related items. Turing and Wozniak are general partners in the partnership. The other partners are fifty limited partners that backed their venture. The business's official address, registered with the State Corporation Commission of California, is in Cupertino, California, and that is where the headquarters and principal decisions of the partnership are made. Turing lives in San Jose, California, and Wizniak lives in Palo Alto, California. The limited partners live in several states, including California, Washington, New Mexico, Nevada. Plaintiff is a citizen of Nevada and wants to sue the partnership. Is there complete diversity of citizenship? Why or why not?

---

e. The Test for Limited Liability Corporations

With the advent of limited liability corporations in many states, some wondered whether these entities would be treated like corporations or like non-corporate entities for diversity purposes. Following is a leading case that answered the question.

BELLEVILLE CATERING CO. v. CHAMPAIGN MARKET PLACE, L.L.C.
United States Court of Appeals for the Seventh Circuit, 2003
350 F.3d 691

EASTERBROOK, Circuit Judge.

Once again litigants' insouciance toward the requirements of federal jurisdiction has caused a waste of time and money.

Invoking the diversity jurisdiction,[112] the complaint alleged that the corporate plaintiff is incorporated in Missouri and has its principal place of business there, and that the five individual plaintiffs (guarantors of the corporate plaintiff's obligations) are citizens of Missouri. It also alleged that the defendant is a "Delaware Limited Liability Company, with its principle [sic] place of business in the State of Illinois." Defendant agreed with these allegations and filed a counterclaim. The parties agreed that a magistrate judge could preside in lieu of a district judge,[113] and the magistrate judge accepted these jurisdictional allegations at face value. A jury trial was held, ending in a verdict of $220,000 in defendant's favor on the counterclaim. Plaintiffs appealed; the jurisdictional statement of their appellate brief tracks the allegations of the complaint. Defendant's brief asserts that plaintiffs' jurisdictional summary is "complete and correct."

It is, however, transparently incomplete and incorrect. Counsel and the magistrate judge assumed that a limited liability company is treated like a corporation and thus is a citizen of its state of organization and its principal place of business. That is not right. Unincorporated enterprises are analogized to

---

[112] *See* 28 U.S.C. § 1332,

[113] *See* 28 U.S.C § 636(c).

partnerships, which take the citizenship of every general and limited partner.[114] In common with other courts of appeals, we have held that limited liability companies are citizens of every state of which any member is a citizen.[115] So who are Champaign Market Place LLC's members, and of what states are they citizens? Our effort to explore jurisdiction before oral argument led to an unexpected discovery: Belleville Catering, the corporate plaintiff, appeared to be incorporated in Illinois rather than Missouri!

At oral argument we directed the parties to file supplemental memoranda addressing jurisdictional details. Plaintiffs' response concedes that Belleville Catering is (and always has been) incorporated in Illinois. Counsel tells us that, because the lease between Belleville Catering and Champaign Market Place refers to Belleville Catering as "a Missouri corporation," he assumed that it must be one. That confesses a violation of Fed. R. Civ. P. 11. People do not draft leases with the requirements of § 1332 in mind—perhaps the lease meant only that Belleville Catering did business in Missouri—and counsel must secure jurisdictional details from original sources before making formal allegations. That would have been easy to do; the client's files doubtless contain the certificate of incorporation. Or counsel could have done what the court did: use the Internet. Both Illinois and Missouri make databases of incorporations readily available. Counsel for the defendant should have done the same, instead of agreeing with the complaint's unfounded allegation.

Both sides also must share the blame for assuming that a limited liability company is treated like a corporation. In the memorandum filed after oral argument, counsel for Champaign Market Place relate that several of its members are citizens of Illinois. Citizens of Illinois thus are on both sides of the suit, which therefore cannot proceed under § 1332. Moreover, for all we can tell, other members are citizens of Missouri. Champaign Market Place says that one of its members is another limited liability company that "is asserting confidentiality for the members of the L.L.C." It is not possible to litigate under the diversity jurisdiction with details kept confidential from the judiciary. So federal jurisdiction has not been established. The complaint should not have been filed in federal court (for Belleville Catering had to know its own state of incorporation), the answer should have pointed out a problem (for Champaign Market Place's lawyers had to ascertain the legal status of limited liability companies), and the magistrate judge should have checked all of this independently (for inquiring whether the court has jurisdiction is a federal judge's first duty in every case).

Failure to perform these tasks has the potential, realized here, to waste time (including that of the put upon jurors) and run up legal fees. Usually parties accept the inevitable and proceed to state court once the problem becomes apparent. Perhaps the most extraordinary aspect of this proceeding, however, is the following passage in defendant's post-argument memorandum:

Defendant–Appellee, Champaign Market Place L.L.C., prays that this Court in the exercise of its Appellate jurisdiction decide the case on the merits and affirm the judgment entered on the jury's verdict. Surely in the past this Court has decided a case on the merits where an examination of the issue would have shown a lack of subject matter jurisdiction in the District Court. It would be unfortunate in the extreme for Champaign Market Place L.L.C. to lose a judgment where Belleville Catering Company, Inc. misrepresented (albeit unintentionally) its State of incorporation in its Complaint. . . .[T]here was no reason for Champaign Market Place L.L.C. to question diversity of citizenship, since it is not, and never has been, a citizen of Missouri.

---

[114] *See* Carden Arkoma Associates, 494 U.S. 185 (1990).
[115] *See* Cosgrove v. Bartolotta, 150 F.3d 729 (7th Cir.1998).

74

This passage—and there is more in the same vein—leaves us agog. Just where do appellate courts acquire authority to decide on the merits a case over which there is no federal jurisdiction? The proposition that the Seventh Circuit has done so in the past—a proposition unsupported by any citation—accuses the court of dereliction combined with usurpation. "A court lacks discretion to consider the merits of a case over which it is without jurisdiction."[116] And while counsel feel free to accuse the judges of ultra vires conduct, and to invite some more of it, they exculpate themselves. Lawyers for defendants, as well as plaintiffs, must investigate rather than assume jurisdiction; to do this, they first must learn the legal rules that determine whose citizenship matters (as defendant's lawyers failed to do). And no entity that claims confidentiality for its members' identities and citizenships is well situated to assert that it could believe, in good faith, that complete diversity has been established.

One more subject before we conclude. The costs of a doomed foray into federal court should fall on the lawyers who failed to do their homework, not on the hapless clients. Although we lack jurisdiction to resolve the merits, we have ample authority to govern the practice of counsel in the litigation. The best way for counsel to make the litigants whole is to perform, without additional fees, any further services that are necessary to bring this suit to a conclusion in state court, or via settlement. That way the clients will pay just once for the litigation. This is intended not as a sanction, but simply to ensure that clients need not pay for lawyers' time that has been wasted for reasons beyond the clients' control. The judgment of the district court is vacated, and the proceeding is remanded with instructions to dismiss the complaint for want of subject-matter jurisdiction.

Practice Problem

Practice Problem 3-12

Birds Not Squirrels, LLC developed the first birdfeeder that foiled squirrels' efforts to get seeds. The LLC was formed in Minnesota. Minnesota law required that the formation papers be filed with the State Corporation Commission and that the principal office address be listed with the filing. Woody, Finch, and Jay were the members of the LLC. Woody lived in Minnesota, but Finch and Jay lived in North Dakota. A supplier of the wood used in the birdfeeders, Wood4You, Inc. was incorporated and had its principal place of business in North Dakota. The Supplier claims that Birds Not Squirrels failed to pay a $100,000 shipment unjustifiably. (Birds Not Squirrels claims the wood was defective, i.e., rotting when delivered.) If Wood4You sued Birds Not Squirrels in U.S. District Court in North Dakota, would there be complete diversity of citizenship?

---

f. Citizenship of Unions

The citizenship of unions illustrates the challenge of achieving diversity of citizenship when the organization has many members in many states and the citizenship of each member—not the headquarters of the organization—will count as the states in which the organization is a member.

---

[116] Firestone Tire & Rubber Co. v. Risjord, 449 U.S. 368, 379 (1981).

UNITED STEELWORKERS OF AMERICA, AFL-CIO v. BOULIGNY, INC.
Supreme Court of the United States, 1965
382 U.S. 145

Mr. Justice Fortas delivered the opinion of the Court.

Respondent, a North Carolina corporation, brought this action in a North Carolina state court. It sought $200,000 in damages for defamation alleged to have occurred during the course of the United Steelworkers' campaign to unionize respondent's employees. The Steelworkers, an unincorporated labor union whose principal place of business purportedly is Pennsylvania, removed the case to a Federal District Court. The union asserted not only federal-question jurisdiction, but that for purposes of the diversity jurisdiction it was a citizen of Pennsylvania, although some of its members were North Carolinians.

The corporation sought to have the case remanded to the state courts, contending that its complaint raised no federal questions and relying upon the generally prevailing principle that an unincorporated association's citizenship is that of each of its members. But the District Court retained jurisdiction. The District Judge noted 'a trend to treat unincorporated associations in the same manner as corporations and to treat them as citizens of the state wherein the principal office is located.' Divining 'no common-sense reason for treating an unincorporated national labor union differently from a corporation,' he declined to follow what he styled 'the poorer reasoned but more firmly established rule' of *Chapman v. Barney*.[117]

On interlocutory appeal the Court of Appeals for the Fourth Circuit reversed and directed that the case be remanded to the state courts. Certiorari was granted, so that we might decide whether an unincorporated labor union is to be treated as a citizen for purposes of federal diversity jurisdiction, without regard to the citizenship of its members. Because we believe this properly a matter for legislative consideration which cannot adequately or appropriately be dealt with by this Court, we affirm the decision of the Court of Appeals.

Article III, [Section] 2, of the Constitution provides: 'The judicial Power shall extend . . . to Controversies . . . between Citizens of different States. . . .'

Congress lost no time in implementing the grant. In 1789[,] it provided for federal jurisdiction in suits 'between a citizen of the State where the suit is brought, and a citizen of another State.' There shortly arose the question as to whether a corporation—a creature of state law—is to be deemed a 'citizen' for purposes of the statute. This Court, through Chief Justice Marshall, initially responded in the negative, holding that a corporation was not a 'citizen' and that it might sue and be sued under the diversity statute only if none of its shareholders was a co-citizen of any opposing party.[118] In 1844 the Court reversed itself and ruled that a corporation was to be treated as a citizen of the State which created it.[119] Ten years later, the Court reached the same result by a different approach. In a compromise destined to endure for over a century, the Court indulged in the fiction that, although a corporation was not itself a citizen for diversity purposes, its shareholders would conclusively be presumed citizens of the incorporating State.[120]

Congress re-entered the lists in 1875, significantly expanding diversity jurisdiction by deleting the requirement imposed in 1789 that one of the parties must be a citizen of the forum State. The resulting

---

[117] 129 U.S. 677 (1889).
[118] Bank of United States v. Deveaux, 5 Cranch 61 (1809).
[119] Louisville, C. & C.R. Co. v. Letson, 2 How. 497 (1844).
[120] Marshall v. Baltimore & O.R. Co., 16 How. 314 (1853).

increase in the quantity of diversity litigation, however, cooled enthusiasts of the jurisdiction, and in 1887 and 1888 Congress enacted sharp curbs. It quadrupled the jurisdictional amount, confined the right of removal to nonresident defendants, reinstituted protections against jurisdiction by collusive assignment, and narrowed venue.

It was in this climate that the Court in 1889 decided *Chapman v. Barney*, supra [sic]. On its own motion the Court observed that plaintiff was a joint stock company and not a corporation or natural person. It held that although plaintiff was endowed by New York with capacity to sue, it could not be considered a 'citizen' for diversity purposes.

In recent years, courts and commentators have reflected dissatisfaction with the rule *of Chapman v. Barney*. The distinction between the 'personality' and 'citizenship' of corporations and that of labor unions and other unincorporated associations, it is increasingly argued, has become artificial and unreal. The mere fact that a corporation is endowed with a birth certificate is, they say, of no consequence. In truth and in fact, they point out, many voluntary associations and labor unions are indistinguishable from corporations in terms of the reality of function and structure, and to say that the latter are juridical persons and 'citizens' and the former are not is to base a distinction upon an inadequate and irrelevant difference. They assert, with considerable merit, that it is not good judicial administration, nor is it fair, to remit a labor union or other unincorporated association to vagaries of jurisdiction determined by the citizenship of its members and to disregard the fact that unions and associations may exist and have an identity and a local habitation of their own. The force of these arguments in relation to the diversity jurisdiction is particularized by petitioner's showing in this case. Petitioner argues that one of the purposes underlying the jurisdiction—protection of the nonresident litigant from local prejudice—is especially applicable to the modern labor union. According to the argument, when the nonresident defendant is a major union, local juries may be tempted to favor local interests at its expense. Juries may also be influenced by the fear that unionization would adversely affect the economy of the community and its customs and practices in the field of race relations. In support of these contentions, petitioner has exhibited material showing that during organizational campaigns like that involved in this case, localities have been saturated with propaganda concerning such economic and racial fears. Extending diversity jurisdiction to unions, says petitioner, would make available the advantages of federal procedure, Article III judges less exposed to local pressures than their state court counterparts, juries selected from wider geographical areas, review in appellate courts reflecting a multistate perspective, and more effective review by this Court.

We are of the view that these arguments, however appealing, are addressed to an inappropriate forum, and that pleas for extension of the diversity jurisdiction to hitherto uncovered broad categories of litigants ought to be made to the Congress and not to the courts.

. . .

If we were to accept petitioner's urgent invitation to amend diversity jurisdiction so as to accommodate its case, we would be faced with difficulties which we could not adequately resolve. Even if the record here were adequate, we might well hesitate to assume that petitioner's situation is sufficiently representative or typical to form the predicate of a general principle. We should, for example, be obliged to fashion a test for ascertaining of which State the labor union is a citizen. Extending the jurisdiction to corporations raised no such problem, for the State of incorporation was a natural candidate, its arguable irrelevance in terms of the policies underlying the jurisdiction being outweighed by its certainty of application. But even that easy and apparent solution did not dispose of the problem; in 1958 Congress thought it necessary to enact legislation providing that corporations are citizens both of the State of incorporation and of the State in which their principal place of business is located. Further, in contemplating a rule which would accommodate petitioner's claim, we are acutely aware of the complications arising from the circumstance that petitioner, like other labor unions, has local as well as national organizations and that these, perhaps, should be reckoned with in connection with 'citizenship' and its jurisdictional incidents.

Whether unincorporated labor unions ought to be assimilated to the status of corporations for diversity purposes, how such citizenship is to be determined, and what if any related rules ought to apply, are decisions which we believe suited to the legislative and not the judicial branch, regardless of our views as to the intrinsic merits of petitioner's argument—merits stoutly attested by widespread support for the recognition of labor unions as juridical personalities.

We affirm the decision below.

g. Citizenship of Any Type of Unincorporated Entity

The following case illustrates well the theme of the cases on unincorporated entities. If an entity is not a corporation, the test to determine its citizenship will almost surely be to identify the citizenship of each of the entity's members. Following is a good example of that approach.

POLYCHRON v. AIRGO, INC.
United States Court of Appeals for the Seventh Circuit, 1993
985 F.2d 563 (Unpublished Disposition)

Before EASTERBOOK and KANNE, Circuit Judges, and PELL, Jr., Senior Circuit Judge.

ORDER

In this diversity of citizenship case, Penelope Polychron appeals from a partial summary judgment entered in favor of Leslie Erb and Airgo, Inc. ("Airgo").

I

After her son died in a skydiving accident, Polychron sued five defendants on his behalf in federal district court. Because Polychron's claims were grounded in Illinois negligence law, she pleaded diversity of citizenship as the basis for federal subject matter jurisdiction. 28 U.S.C. § 1332.

In support of her diversity allegations, Polychron claimed that the decedent, who attended school in Missouri, maintained a domicile in Pennsylvania. She further alleged that defendant Dave Verner was a domiciliary of Illinois and that defendant Airgo was "a foreign corporation licensed to and doing business in the State of Illinois." She labeled defendant Washington University a not-for-profit corporation registered in Missouri, and Washington University Student Union ("the Union") "an organization which is financially supported by Washington University and/or encouraged and fostered by the University." She never discussed the citizenship of defendant Erb.

Instead of challenging the district court's jurisdiction, Erb and Airgo moved for summary judgment. The court granted partial summary judgment in favor of the two defendants, noting that "[t]here being no just reason for delay, the Clerk is directed to enter judgment in favor of the [two defendants]." . . . the parties immediately appealed the summary judgment.

At oral argument, this court informed the parties that we could not determine whether the district court possessed diversity jurisdiction or whether it had complied with Rule 54(b). In an order of October 5, 1992, we asked the parties to brief these jurisdictional issues by October 19, 1992. On October 19, the appellee's responded to our request with a jurisdictional memorandum and a motion "to file amendments to the answers by interlineation." In the motion and memorandum, appellee Leslie Erb admitted that he was a citizen of Illinois, and Appellee Airgo, Inc. admitted that it was a Delaware corporation with its principal place of business in Illinois. The appellees never addressed the citizenship of the other defendants to this suit. On October 26, 1992, the appellant filed a jurisdictional memorandum, which discussed one of the other defendants. It alleged that Washington University Student Union was an unincorporated association. The memorandum also claimed that the decedent maintained a domicile in Pennsylvania immediately before his death, but it never discussed defendants Erb, Verner, or AirThis appeal raises two crucial jurisdictional issues: the finality of the judgment and the diversity of the parties. We must consider such jurisdictional issues on our own initiative, despite the parties' failure to address jurisdiction in their briefs.

B. Diversity Jurisdiction

Absent proof of diversity jurisdiction, this court lacks subject matter jurisdiction over this negligence suit. Diversity jurisdiction exists only when the parties are completely diverse-no plaintiff and no defendant may be citizens of the same state.[121] The existence of complete diversity is determined at the time that the complaint is filed.

. . .

[N]either party has established the citizenship of all the defendants named in the complaint. The most problematic of these defendants is the Washington University Student Union. The Union is, as the plaintiff points out, an unincorporated association "comprised of each student at Washington University that pays fees." As an unincorporated association, the Union possesses the citizenship of each of these members. Thus, if any of the Union's members maintains a domicile in Pennsylvania, this common citizenship will preclude diversity jurisdiction. This is true even though the Union is not a party to this appeal. Because diversity is determined at the time the complaint is filed, a plaintiff cannot create appellate jurisdiction by filing an appeal against only the diverse parties.

. . .

The order we issued required the parties to address the citizenship of all parties. This under the circum-stances could only have referred to all the parties in the suit which was filed, whether some of them were before this court of appeals or not. Nevertheless, the appellees elected to limit their discussion to defendants Erb and Airgo as if "complete diversity" meant diversity between the parties to the claims that are the subject of the Rule 54 appeal. The October 5 order also called for the parties to address specifically:

a. Of what state are defendants Erb and Verner citizens?

b. What kind of organization is the Washington University Student Union? If it is not a corporation, what is the citizenship of each of its members or partners?

No one addressed the citizenship of Verner but the plaintiff-appellant in a belated response did address the citizenship of the Washington University Student Union as follows:

---

[121] Carden v. Arkoma Assoc., 494 U.S. 185, 187 (1990).

Washington University Student Union, hereinafter referred to as "Union" is clearly an unincorporated association. It is comprised of each student at Washington University that pays student fees. To establish jurisdiction pursuant to 28 U.S.C. 1332, it is necessary to consider the citizenship of each member and to specifically allege each member's diversity relative to the Plaintiff.[122]. In Loss above, this Court reasoned that because the local could sue in its own name only the citizenship of the local members was considered, not the membership of each member of the National. Here, however, application of those same legal principals [sic] would require diversity as to each member of the "Union" at the time these pleadings were filed. Under applicable State law, the "Union" has several thousand members. Obviously, Plaintiff would never be able to establish the Decedent's diversity as to each member.

In a conclusion to this response, the plaintiff-appellant agreed that this court did not have subject matter jurisdiction under Section 1332. In light of the diversity problem presented by the Union and its membership of several thousand students, this concession by the plaintiff-appellant is understandable. According to the current World Almanac, Washington University has an enrollment of more than 9500 students. We know at least one member of the Union came from Pennsylvania. With an enrollment of this size in a nationally known university, it would be surprising if there were no other members of the Union who maintained a domicile in Pennsylvania. It was the plaintiff who made the Union a party. No amendments to the complaint concerning the Student Union have been submitted.

[W]e accordingly vacate the judgment and the case is REMANDED with instructions to dismiss for lack of subject matter jurisdiction.

Practice Problem

Practice Problem 3-13

Bo is a member of the Truck Drivers' Union, Local 228. Bo was dissatisfied with the union's representation of him in grievances against a trucking company for which he worked, and which relied on the union truck drivers. Bo believed that the trucking company was intentionally scheduling him and other drivers such that they could not get eight hours sleep a night and, to fulfill a haul, would have to go without sleep or rely on stimulants to stay awake. (Bo had recently left a treatment center for addiction to Adderall, something he had used to meet the truck company's demands). Bo sued Truck Drivers Union, Local 228 for more than $80,000 comprising lost wage and his emotional pain and suffering caused by the failure of the Union to represent him. He watched the proceedings and felt that the Union, who was supposed to advocate for him but who refused to refer his grievance to arbitration under the collective bargaining agreement or to take any action on his behalf. Accept for purposes of this question that a claim of breach of fair representation exists against the Union if what Bo claimed was true and that his damages were capable of being recovered if he proved the breach. Bo is a citizen of Texas. The Union's main office is in Baton Rouge, Louisiana. The Union has members in states throughout the southeastern United States and, indeed, in many other areas of the country. If Bo wants to sue the Union in U.S. district court and asks you if he can sue based on diversity of citizenship, what would your answer be? Can Bo get into federal court, however, under another type of jurisdiction?

---

[122] Loss v. Blankenship, 673 F.2d 942 (7th Cir. 1982).

3. Amount in Controversy

The second hurdle under the general diversity statute is the amount in controversy requirement. The current version of the statute[123] requires that the amount in controversy exceed $75,000 exclusive of interests and costs. The question we now explore is how a court, reviewing a complaint, decides whether that threshold has been met. The decision in the following case helps to illustrate how such a determination is much easier than one might expect.

a. General Rule: The Legal Certainty Test

Refer back to *Mas v. Perry*[124] in which the Fifth Circuit, in deciding that Mrs. Mas was of diverse citizenship, also cited the Supreme Court's decision in *St. Paul Mercury Indemnity Company v. Red Cab Company*,[125] the leading case on how to determine whether a party has satisfied the amount in controversy threshold. Notice that, in *Mas*, even though the plaintiff was asserting emotional harm only, the Fifth Circuit held that she met the test. That ruling is far more typical than ones in which a court finds that a plaintiff cannot satisfy the amount in controversy requirement. Following, however, is a case in which the court applying the same standard ruled that the amount in controversy requirement was not met.

COULTER v. PAUL LAURENCE DUNBAR COMMUNITY CENTER
United States Court of Appeals for the Third Circuit, 2017
685 Fed. Appx. 161

PER CURIAM

Jean Coulter appeals from the order of the District Court dismissing her amended complaint.

I.

Coulter alleges that she loaned $50,000 to the now-defunct Paul Laurence Dunbar Community Center ("Dunbar") in 2013. She later filed this suit against Dunbar, several of its former officers or employees, and numerous other individuals. Coulter invoked the District Court's diversity jurisdiction, and she asserted three kinds of claims. First, she asserted a claim for breach of contract seeking repayment of the loan and interest. Second, she asserted a claim for "gross mismanagement"/negligence based on alleged mismanagement of Dunbar. Finally, she asserted a claim for fraud and civil conspiracy based on representations allegedly made to her both before and after the loan. Coulter also requested punitive damages, and she demanded $250,000.

Defendants moved under Fed. R. Civ. P. 12(b)(6) for dismissal of all of Coulter's claims except her claim for breach of contract against Dunbar.

---

[123] Congress has set the amount in controversy under 28 U.S.C. § 1332, in the past at an amount exceeding $3,000, at an amount exceeding $10,000, and at an amount exceeding $50,000.
[124] 489 F.2d 1396 (5th Cir. 1974).
[125] 303 U.S. 283 (1938).

The District Court granted defendants' motion and dismissed all of the claims [except her claim for breach of contract against Dunbar]. The District Court then concluded that Coulter's remaining claim for breach of the $50,000 contract did not satisfy the $75,000 amount in controversy requirement for diversity jurisdiction.[126] Thus, the District Court dismissed her complaint for lack of jurisdiction.

Coulter challenges the District Court's dismissal of her amended complaint [on the ground that she failed to satisfy the amount in controversy requirement]. We vacate [that ruling] and remand for further proceedings.

A. The Order of Dismissal

Our review of the order of dismissal turns on the issue of jurisdiction, which we have an independent obligation to consider. It appears that the only potential basis for jurisdiction in the District Court was diversity jurisdiction, which requires both diversity of the parties and an amount in controversy of over $75,000. See 28 U.S.C. § 1332(a).

The District Court dismissed Coulter's claim for breach of contract against Dunbar for lack of such jurisdiction. In doing so, the District Court did not address diversity of the parties, though it appears that they are diverse. Instead, the District Court concluded that Coulter failed to satisfy the amount in controversy requirement because (1) the court dismissed all of her other claims under Rule 12(b)(6), and (2) her breach of contract claim sought less than $75,000.

That approach was erroneous. The amount in controversy for diversity purposes is determined as of the filing of the complaint. Thus, the District Court either had or did not have diversity jurisdiction at that time. If the District Court did not have jurisdiction, then it lacked jurisdiction to dismiss claims on the merits under Rule 12(b)(6). If the District Court had jurisdiction, by contrast, then its subsequent dismissal of some claims did not divest it of jurisdiction over Coulter's remaining claim. "When diversity exists at the time the case is filed, it is not affected by the dismissal of one of the claims even though the amount recoverable on the remaining claim is less than the required [$75,000]."[127]

Thus, we will vacate the District Court's dismissals under both Rule 12(b)(6) and for lack of jurisdiction and will remand for the District Court to consider in the first instance whether Coulter's claims satisfied the amount in controversy requirement as of the filing of her complaint.

We note that the Rule 12(b)(6) standard plays no role in that inquiry. In determining the amount in controversy, "the sum claimed by the plaintiff controls" unless it "appear[s] to a legal certainty" that the plaintiff cannot recover that amount. That inquiry is not governed by the Rule 12(b)(6) standard. As we have explained:

> [T]he question whether a plaintiff's claims pass the "legal certainty" standard is a threshold matter that should involve the court in only minimal scrutiny of the plaintiff's claims. The court should not consider in its jurisdictional inquiry the legal sufficiency of those claims or whether the legal theory advanced by the plaintiff is probably unsound; rather, a court can dismiss the case only if there is a legal certainty that the plaintiff cannot recover [the jurisdictional amount]

---

[126] *See* 28 U.S.C. § 1332(a).
[127] Lindsey v. M.A. Zeccola & Sons, Inc., 26 F.3d 1236, 1244 n.10 (3d Cir. 1994).

Thus, "the 'threshold to withstand a motion to dismiss [based on lack of subject matter jurisdiction and, in particular, whether the legal certainty test is met to satisfy the amount in controversy requirement, is far less demanding than the District Court's ruling suggests. On a motion to dismiss for lack of subject matter jurisdiction, a plaintiff] fails to invoke the District Court's jurisdiction only if it is "wholly insubstantial and frivolous."

In this case, Coulter demanded $250,000 in damages. Coulter based that demand on all of her claims and on her request for punitive damages, and it satisfies the amount in controversy requirement on its face. Thus, the District Court has and should exercise diversity jurisdiction if it is legally possible that any of her claims could yield the jurisdictional amount.

We further note that at least one of Coulter's claims appears to qualify. Coulter's amended complaint can be read to assert a claim that Dunbar fraudulently induced her to enter into the loan agreement. As the District Court noted, a claim for fraud under Pennsylvania law requires, inter alia, a fraudulent misrepresentation on which the plaintiff relied. The District Court concluded under Rule 12(b)(6) that Coulter failed to state a claim for fraudulent inducement because all of the misrepresentations she alleged occurred after she already had made the loan.

That is not the case. Coulter alleged in her amended complaint that, before she agreed to the loan, she had discussions with defendant Catherine Donnelly, Dunbar's former Executive Director, regarding why Dunbar needed the money and how Dunbar would use it. She further alleged that Donnelly's representations in that regard were false, and she later referred to "deceptions related to the source of [Dunbar's] supposed cash flow problems (at the time of the initial discussions about the loan) [.]"

Indeed, even the Dunbar defendants recognized in their motion to dismiss that "it appears that the plaintiff claims that she was misled into making the loan[.]" . . . They argued that this claim was deficient because Coulter did not allege any specific misrepresentation, but mere legal insufficiency does not constitute legal impossibility . . . and the failure to adequately plead a claim is the kind of defect that can be cured by amendment even under Rule 12(b)(6).

That point aside, we see nothing suggesting that Coulter's claim for fraudulent inducement is legally certain to fail. We also see nothing suggesting that Coulter is legally certain to recover less than the jurisdictional amount given the apparent availability of punitive damages on this claim, which must be considered in determining the amount in controversy.

For these reasons, we . . . vacate the District Court's dismissal of her complaint and will remand for further proceedings.

Follow-Up Questions and Comments

1. The court in *Coulter v. Dunbar* refers to motions under Rule 12(b)(1) seeking dismissal for lack of subject matter jurisdiction and under Rule 12(b)(6) seeking dismissal for failure to state a claim in the complaint. Chapter 11 explores in detail the motions a defendant can raise to a plaintiff's complaint. You need not know that detail to understand the court's basis for rejecting the district court's approach to evaluating whether the amount in controversy requirement had been met.

Coulter addresses the flaw in the district court's approach to determining whether the amount in controversy requirement is met. What is that flaw? In evaluating fact patterns, how will you avoid this flaw in evaluating whether the amount in controversy requirement is met?

2. Consider the typical personal injury case. A plaintiff will incur costs—i.e. damages—beyond the date of filing. Medical bills will likely have accrued. Moreover, the plaintiff can claim damages for pain and suffering, lost wages, and have other kinds of monetary damages—items of damage that would continue to mount. Why, in most personal injury cases, will the evolving nature of damages mean that the court—applying the approach of Coulter—rarely will be able to decide to a legal certainty that the plaintiff has failed to satisfy the amount in controversy requirement?

3. The Supreme Court has never answered the question whether punitive damages should be included in the amount in controversy. Circuit courts of appeal are split on the issue. If you are litigating in a circuit, therefore, you would want to research that circuit's approach to the question.

Practice Problems

The following Practice Problems are typical scenarios. After applying the legal certainty test to these Problems, you should be able to apply the amount in controversy requirement and reach a conclusion without difficulty.

Practice Problem 3-14

Plaintiff Tom, saw a tool advertised on television as the "SuperSaw" that could cut through any material. He ordered the tool because the ad said it was available at the price advertised "for a limited time only." When using the SuperSaw to cut through some rock foundation that Tom was going to reinforce, the saw blade broke, flew off, and impaled his arm. He was in the hospital for a week after surgery to remove the saw blade. He has permanent nerve damage and will never have full use of his arm again. The pain comes and goes, something the doctor says could happen for years until the nerves heal. SuperSaw is incorporated and has its principal place of business in Iowa, and Tom's domicile is Missouri. He sues SuperSaw, Inc. on a product liability claim in a U.S. district court in Missouri. The court cannot tell from the pleadings the exact amount of damages Tom will recover if he prevails. His complaint simply says that the damages will exceed $75,000 exclusive of interest and costs. If you were the judge, how would you analyze whether the amount in controversy requirement of the general diversity statute had been met?

Practice Problem 3-15

Explaining to the tattoo artist that she wants to let everyone know her patriotism, Polly asks for a tattoo of the American flag on her forehead. She falls asleep when Tats, Inc.'s tattoo artist is working on her. When she wakes, she sees that instead of a cross, the tattoo is a Nazi swastika. Polly is livid. The tattoo artist, when asked what happened, just said, "Dude, I guess I got confused." She sues Tats, Inc. on a theory of negligence and claims that she has suffered and will suffer emotional distress because of the blunder. Tats, Inc. is incorporated in Florida with its principal place of business in Jacksonville, Florida. Polly is from southern Georgia, where she has lived all her life. She sues in a U.S. district court in Georgia and asserts that the amount in controversy exceeds $75,000 exclusive of interest and costs. Under applicable law, a plaintiff can recover damages for emotional distress if the defendant's negligence is outrageous. Whether negligence is outrageous generally is a factual issue determined by the jury. Tats, Inc. moves to dismiss on the ground that the amount in controversy requirement of the general diversity statute has not been met. Should the motion be granted? Why or why not?

Practice Problem 3-16

Pauline took a flight on Southeast Airlines to New York. She got into an argument with the flight attendant after complaining about another passenger who kept falling asleep, snoring, and drooling when his head fell forward. Pauline asked the flight attendant to please do something. The flight attendant told her to "Quit being 'Miss Priss.' The guy probably is just tired from working, something you no doubt have never experienced!" Pauline is a citizen of Virginia, and Southeast Airlines is incorporated in Tennessee with its principal place of business in Nashville, Tennessee. Pauline sues in a U.S. district court in Virginia, alleges the above facts, and claims that she suffered emotional distress from the rude comment and that the amount in controversy exceeds $75,000 exclusive of interest and costs. Defendant Southeast Airlines moves to dismiss claiming that under no set of circumstances could the court award $75,000 based on these facts. Do you agree?

---

b. Aggregation of Amounts in Different Claims to Satisfy the Amount in Controversy Requirement

Later, we will discuss the ability of a plaintiff to join claims against a defendant. For now, the only thing you need to know is that the ability of a single plaintiff to join claims against a defendant is broad. For purposes of the amount in controversy requirement, a single plaintiff can join a claim that is under the required amount (say, a $50,000 contract claim) with an unrelated claim (say, a $30,000 property damage claim), to reach a total over the required threshold. In reviewing such a case, if the parties are of diverse citizenship, the court would have to conclude there is diversity jurisdiction because it could not say to a legal certainly the amount the plaintiff will recover is less than $75,000 exclusive of interest and costs.

Aggregation of damages, however, is more difficult when two plaintiffs are seeking to combine the damages to each of them to exceed the amount in controversy, or when a single plaintiff is trying to join damages from a claim against one defendant with damages from a claim against another defendant. The general rule is that aggregation will not be permitted in either of the above scenarios. Two plaintiffs cannot join their damages against a defendant to reach a total over $75,000 exclusive of interest and costs. Moreover, a single plaintiff cannot join damages against one defendant with damages against a second defendant to total more than $75,000 exclusive of interest and costs.

An exception exists, however, to the no-aggregation-with-multiple-parties rule. Traditionally, if two plaintiffs have joint claims against a single defendant—such as two promises on the same promissory note—they have been allowed to join those joint claims to exceed the amount in controversy.[128] Likewise, if a single plaintiff is suing two defendants who are joint tortfeasors that caused a single, undivided injury to the plaintiff, the plaintiff can rely on the total amount for which she is seeking from both joint tortfeasors.[129] These exceptions, especially the joint tortfeasor exception, arise frequently. Absent such situations, the only allowance of claims being joined by more than one party to satisfy the amount in controversy is in class actions.[130] In short, whereas the allowance of joinder by one plaintiff against one defendant is broad, the ability to join claims either by two plaintiffs or by one plaintiff against multiple defendants has proved to be difficult unless an exception applied.

---

[128] MILLER, FEDERAL PRACTICE AND PROCEDURE § 3704 (4th ed. 2018)

[129] *See id.*

[130] *See id.* § 3705.

Practice Problems

Practice Problem 3-17

Alan had entered into a contract with Bob in which Bob would take care of Alan's home while Alan was in Europe for a year. The contract allowed Bob to stay in the home free if he maintained it properly. When Alan returned from Europe, he found the house trashed. There were stains on his wood floors. Windows had been broken and replaced with new panes, obviously done by an amateur because the putty was so thick it was caked on the windowpanes. Several doors were broken, the sewage system was blocked, and the house was filthy. It took Alan $50,000 to fix all the problems. In addition, Bob had told several of their mutual friends that Alan was a thief and he saw evidence while living in the home that Alan had stolen from others (Alan is a financial advisor) in financial arrangements. This was untrue. Alan adds a claim for slander and alleges the damages are at least $100,000. Alan and Bob are citizens of different states. Alan sues in federal court and alleges that the amount in controversy exceeds $75,000 exclusive of interest and costs. Has the amount in controversy requirement been met here?

Practice Problem 3-18

Take the facts of Practice Problem 3-17 (above), except that the defamatory statements about Alan being a thief, and that the speaker had seen evidence of that, were spoken by Carl, a mutual friend of both Alan and Bob. There is no evidence that Bob said anything on the subject for which Carl defamed Alan or that Bob repeated anything he heard. Again, assume all parties are of diverse citizenship. Alan seeks to sue Bob and Carl in the same suit and to aggregate his claim against Bob and his separate claim against Carl. Will the amount in controversy requirement be met?

Practice Problem 3-19

Professor Smith and Professor Regali, both of whom are too frugal to pay for reserved parking spaces, find themselves at times roaming the university parking lots for a space. One day they are both "trolling" for a space and end up equally distant from an open space. They do not notice Professor Beckman, who is driving carefully, and who pulls into a parking space just as Smith and Regali's cars collide behind Professor Beckman's car. The force of Professor Smith and Regali's cars ramming together causes them, joined together, to smash into the rear of Professor Beckman's vehicle, causing Professor Beckman whiplash injuries. The injuries to Professor Beckman amount to $100,000. Knowing joint tortfeasor liability, and because he also knew Professor Smith and Regali had recently lived in North Carolina and commuted to Virginia (where Professor Beckman lived) to teach, he sued both Smith and Regali in U.S. district court. Is the amount in controversy requirement satisfied here?

Follow-Up Questions and Comments

1. In *Diefenthal v. Civil Aeronautics Bd.*,[131] the Court of Appeals for the Fifth Circuit dealt with a claim for $50,000 in damages at the time when the amount in controversy threshold was $10,000. The allegations were not that the plaintiffs had been physically injured. Their only allegation of harm was "brusque" treatment by a flight attendant that caused $50,000 worth of humiliation.[132] In that scenario, the court was willing to hold that to a legal certainty, the amount in controversy had not been met.

---

[131] 681 F.2d 1039 (5th Cir. 1982).
[132] *Id.* at 1052.

2. Another scenario in which the court can find to a legal certainty that the amount in controversy cannot be met is when the contract at issue has liquidated damages—*i.e.*, a max recovery of, say, $50,000 specified in the contract for a breach. In liquidated damages cases, the recovery can be for less or more than $75,000 exclusive of interest and costs, but when it is less, the court can say to a legal certainty that the amount in controversy requirement cannot be met. Most cases, however, involve what is called unliquidated damages, meaning that the amount to be recovered is not set, and will depend on the proof and verdict.

---

c. Determining Amount in Controversy
When Solely Equitable Relief (Money Amount Unstated)

In some cases, the plaintiff seeks solely equitable relief. For instance, a plaintiff could seek the court issue an injunction, which requires the defendant to act, such as to cease taking an action (e.g., foreclosing). The Supreme Court has not rule definitively on the approach that courts should take in this situation.[133] Circuits have taken the approach of assessing how much it would cost for the plaintiff to obtaining the equitable relief; other circuits determine how much it would cost the defendant to comply with the equitable relief; and many circuits say if either of these tests show that the amount is plausibly more than $75,000 exclusive of interests and costs, then the amount in controversy requirement is met.[134]

III. Necessity of Pleading in One's Complaint the Basis for Subject Matter Jurisdiction

Because federal courts are courts of limited jurisdiction, they will not assume that they have jurisdiction unless the complaint filed in a civil action sets forth in detail the basis for subject matter jurisdiction. Thus, most practitioners include a heading "Subject Matter Jurisdiction" at the beginning of their complaint. Moreover, they do not simply state "This court has subject matter jurisdiction based on diversity of citizenship jurisdiction under 28 U.S.C. § 1332." Such a conclusory allegation will get a case dismissed, albeit usually with leave to amend to state the basis for jurisdiction properly.

The proper way to allege a basis for subject matter jurisdiction is, in the paragraphs beginning a complaint, to state—if the basis is diversity—the citizenship of all parties so that the court can see that there is complete diversity of citizenship. Official Form 7 to the Federal Rules of Civil Procedure shows how to plead jurisdiction. If the basis is federal question jurisdiction, one identifies not only 28 U.S.C. § 1331 but also the federal law on which the claim in the case is based. Again, failure to be detailed can result in an unnecessary dismissal.

Lest you believe the requirement to be perfunctory, consider *Randazzo v. Eagle-Picher Industries, Inc.*,[135] plaintiff's counsel stated, instead of identifying the principal place of business of a party that its "registered office . . . situate[d] at 123 S. Broad Street, Philadelphia, Pennsylvania."[136] The district court dismissed the action because reference to a "registered office" is not a phrase recognized in the diversity statute. The court explained in the dismissal that allowed leave to amend, that the plaintiff needed to state the principal place of business of the corporation. Yet the plaintiff refiled the suit with the same reference

---

[133] See C. WRIGHT & A. MILLER, 14A WRIGHT & MILLER'S FEDERAL PRACTICE & PROCEDURE § 3703 (4th ed. 2019).
[134] *Id.*
[135] 117 F.R.D. 557 (E.D. Pa. 1987).
[136] *Id.* at 558.

to "registered office." Considering that refiling "disrespectful," the district court dismissed the action with prejudice.[137] The court explained that, because federal courts are courts of limited jurisdiction, the traditional rule has been that there is a presumption against subject matter jurisdiction unless the plaintiff alleges with sufficient clarity in the complaint a basis on which the court can conclude that federal subject matter jurisdiction exists.[138] As the court noted: "In the context of our federal system, to consider a case not properly within the jurisdiction of the Federal courts is not 'simply wrong but indeed an unconstitutional invasion of the powers reserved to the states.'"[139]

IV. Exceptions to Diversity of Citizenship Jurisdiction

Federal courts will refuse to exercise diversity of citizenship, even if complete diversity exists and the amount in controversy is satisfied, in certain narrow categories of cases. The most well-known are domestic relations and probate cases. Yet, the exceptions must be clearly confined to domestic relations or probate of a will. Recent cases have refused to apply the exception because, although cases could be characterized as domestic relations or probate cases, the claims involved claims that exceeded the typical domestic relations or probate case.

In *Ankenbrandt v. Richards*,[140] the mother of two children sued her husband and his partner for sexual abuse of the children. The Court found such claims to be beyond the limited traditional domestic relations cases.[141] Although the Court acknowledged the basis for refusing to hear cases traditionally within an area so closely governed by states, it stated a rule that made clear the domestic relations exception to diversity jurisdiction may not have been as broad as many thought: "[T]he domestic relations exception encompasses only cases involving the issuance of a divorce,[142] alimony, or child custody decree."[143]

Likewise, a recent case clarified that the probate exception should not be read too broadly. In *Marshall v. Marshall*,[144] a widow brought claims against the stepson of her husband for tortious interference with expectancy of gift or inheritance. In ruling that the probate exception did not apply, the ruling of the Court in Marshall was careful to limit the scope of the probate exception to diversity jurisdiction: "[T]he probate exception reserves to state probate courts the probate or annulment of a will and the administration of a decedent's estate; it also precludes federal courts from endeavoring to dispose of property that is in the custody of a state probate court. But it does not bar federal courts from adjudicating matters outside those confines and otherwise within federal jurisdiction."[145]

Practice Problem

Practice Problem 3-20
Plaintiff was married in Mexico but had separated from her husband and moved to New Mexico. There she met a wealthy Texan who convinced her to get a divorce in Mexico and to marry him. Later,

---

[137] *Id.* at 557–58.

[138] *Id.* at 558.

[139] *Id.* at 559 (quoting 13 RICHARD D. FREER & EDWARD H. COOPER, WRIGHT AND MILLER'S FEDERAL PRACTICE AND PROCEDURE § 3522 (1983)).

[140] 504 U.S. 689 (1992).

[141] *Id.* at 704–05 (1992).

[142] *Id.*

[143] *Id.* at 704.

[144] 547 U.S. 293 (2006).

[145] *Id.* at 311–12.

Plaintiff sued the Texan, who never followed through on his promise to marry her. She claimed fraud in inducing her to get the Mexican divorce and in moving to Texas, induced by the Texan's statement that he would marry her and provide "everything she asked for." Plaintiff then moved back to New Mexico. She sued the Texan in U.S. district court on the fraud claims, seeking $200,000. Does the federal court have jurisdiction?

CHAPTER 4: REMOVAL

I. How the Topics in this Chapter Fit in the Overall Progress of a Civil Action

Below is a diagram of the stages of a civil action showing in bold where the topics in this chapter fall in the progress of a case:

Figure 4-1

Cause of Action (events leading to suit)	Pre-Filing Tasks (items to begin representation, interviewing, and related matters)	**Choice of Forum** (subject matter jurisdiction, **removal**, personal jurisdiction, and venue)	Notice and Service of Process (completing the process of ensuring the forum court can enter a valid judgment)	Pleading the Case and Joinder of Claims and Parties (including supplemental jurisdiction)

Responding to Claims by Motion or by Answer	Discovery (developing proof to establish claims and learn your adversary's case)	Right to Jury (pretrial motions and practice)	Final Pretrial Conference (events within last month before trial)	Trial (procedures and motions during trial)	Verdict	Post-Trial Motions (motions for a new trial and/or judgment as a matter of law)	Appeal

Notice that the above diagram is the same as at the beginning of Chapter 3. In addressing removal, we are still in the same stage of a case as those cases initiated in federal court by a plaintiff. Removal jurisdiction is simply a subset of subject matter jurisdiction that allows a defendant to transfer a case filed in state court to federal court if federal subject matter jurisdiction exists. What, you may ask, is a case doing in state court if it qualifies for federal subject matter jurisdiction? Some are surprised by the answer to that question, but it is a fact: most cases that qualify for federal jurisdiction can be filed, if the plaintiff so chooses, in state court due to state and federal courts having concurrent jurisdiction over such cases. This is particularly true with diversity of citizenship jurisdiction. However, exceptions exist for federal question claims, even though most of these claims can be brought in state court just as easily as in federal court. These exceptions arise when federal statutes specify a claim that can be heard exclusively in federal court, such as cases involving patent actions, antitrust suits, etc.

Because the first question in a removal analysis is whether the case satisfies federal subject matter jurisdiction (usually the general federal question statute or the general diversity statute), removal builds on the concepts of subject matter jurisdiction we have already addressed. The analysis asks the question of subject matter jurisdiction at the outset because there is no point in analyzing the other requirements of removal if the case is not within the subject matter jurisdiction of federal courts. For instance, if the case falls within diversity of citizenship jurisdiction, then there is subject matter jurisdiction. As we will see, however, a defendant removing a case—even if subject matter jurisdiction exists—face many more hurdles to achieving removal to federal court than a plaintiff initiating suit in federal court. Some wonder why the statutes make it so challenging to remove a case and allow for remand for a slight misstep. The only answer seems to be that Congress view removal as a privilege, not a right, and if someone wants to remove a case she had better dot her I's and cross her T's.

Removing a case not only requires the defendant to ensure that both the subject matter jurisdiction analysis supports federal subject matter jurisdiction, but also that the removal statutes' requirements are met. These statutes are technical. If they permit removal and the defendant is careful to ensure all requirements are satisfied, then she can achieve removal. Removal is not something a U.S. district court has to "grant" or approve. The defendant just follows the steps laid out in removing a case. However, the defendant who misses something in the required steps will likely face a motion to remand the case to state court by the plaintiff. If the defendant has not shown in her removal papers that all requirements are satisfied, the federal court will remand for even minor failures to follow each requirement. Perhaps the best way to view removal is by remembering that it is a privilege accorded defendants if all requirements are met, but it is not an absolute right to have a case removed, even if the plaintiff could originally have filed in federal court. This principle should be kept in mind as you proceed through this chapter to better appreciate the nature of removal and the risk of remand.

II. The Law of Removal

A. Constitutional Basis for Removal and the Removal Statutes

The jurisdictional basis for a defendant's removal of a case from state court to federal court is the same basis on which plaintiffs can file in federal court—Article III, Section 2 and 28 U.S.C. § 1331 (for federal question cases) or 28 U.S.C. § 1332 (for diversity of citizenship cases). However, the jurisdictional enabling statutes that a defendant must satisfy to remove a case are very different. In other words, removal is not a separate jurisdictional basis for bringing a case in federal court. It is purely statutory and represents an effort to allow a defendant the opportunity to transfer a case from state court to federal court if the defendant satisfies all the statutory requirements. And the statutory requirements far exceed those of a plaintiff seeking to file in federal court based on the general federal question statute or the general diversity statute.

Only a defendant may invoke removal. If the defendant does so and shows that all the grounds for removal are met, the case is transferred from the state court in which it was filed to a federal court within the federal district in which the state court is located. At the point of removal, the state court loses jurisdiction and the federal court gains jurisdiction. However, a case may end up being remanded if (a) the federal court determines that it lacks subject matter jurisdiction or (b) the defendant has not satisfied all the statutory requirements for removal. In making this determination, the court must decide whether the removed case satisfies the requirements of the removal statutes: 28 U.S.C. §§ 1441, 1446, and 1447. Please read these statutes now. We will be studying the requirements of the removal statutes throughout this chapter.

28 U.S.C. § 1441(a) presents the first hurdle for removing a case to federal court. That provision states:

> Except as otherwise expressly provided by Act of Congress, any civil action
> brought in a State court of which the district courts of the United States have

original jurisdiction, may be removed by the defendant or the defendants, to the district court of the United States for the district and division embracing the place where such action is pending.

Thus, the initial removal analysis piggy-backs on the subject matter jurisdiction analysis. For example, a defendant seeking to remove must show in her notice of removal either that the parties are completely diverse and the amount in controversy is met, or that the case satisfies the general federal question statute by meeting the well-pleaded complaint rule. If the case does not satisfy subject matter jurisdiction, the case will be remanded.

Notice the other requirement in 28 U.S.C. § 1441(a). The provision states that a case that qualifies can be removed to the United States district court for the district "embracing the place where such action is pending." This second requirement is applicable to all cases that are removed. Thus, when you are asked to join the requirements of § 1441 and § 1446 later in this chapter, you should remember to include this requirement in the list.

B. The In-State Removal Bar

One of the most important hurdles to removal applies to cases in which subject matter exists based solely on general diversity of citizenship. Known as the in-state removal bar, 28 U.S.C. § 1441(b) (2) provides:

> A civil action otherwise removable solely on the basis of the jurisdiction under section 1332(a) of this title may not be removed if any of the parties in interest properly joined and served as defendants is a citizen of the State in which such action is brought.

If the sole basis for subject matter jurisdiction is diversity of citizenship, a defendant cannot remove a case to federal court if any defendant in the case is a citizen of the state in which suit was brought. We will now read *Brooks v. District of Columbia*, in which a personal injury action was brought against District of Columbia police officers as agents of the District of Columbia. The defendant police officers attempted to remove the case to federal court by asserting that complete diversity existed as the police officers were citizens of the District of Columbia, the plaintiff was a citizen of Virginia, and the amount in controversy requirement was met.[146] However, the court explained that 28 U.S.C. § 1441(b) (2) bars removal of cases when a defendant in the case is a citizen of the state where the case was brought.

---

[146] Plaintiff alleged damages in excess of $50,000, which was sufficient for the amount in controversy requirement at the time. The amount in controversy requirement under the general diversity of citizenship statute has changed over time. It has gone from $500 in 1789, to $2,000 in 1887, to $3,000 in 1911, to $10,000 in 1958, $50,000 in 1989 and, finally, to the current amount of $75,000 in 1986. 14A CHARLES ALAN WRIGHT & ARTHUR R. MILLER, FEDERAL PRACTICE AND PROCEDURE§ 3701 (4th ed. 2017).

BROOKS v. DISTRICT OF COLUMBIA
United States District Court for the District of Columbia, 1993
819 F. Supp. 67

CHARLES R. RICHEY, District Judge.

The above-captioned case is an action recently removed from the Superior Court of the District of Columbia pursuant to 28 U.S.C. § 1441. Upon review of the notice of removal, the Court finds that the removal is improper and remands the case to the Superior Court pursuant to 28 U.S.C. § 1447(c).

This case was originally filed in the Superior Court of the District of Columbia on December 21, 1992. The Plaintiff sued the Defendants for injuries sustained when the Plaintiff was allegedly shot as a bystander in an exchange of gunfire between D.C. police officers and third parties. The Plaintiff sought $1,000,000 in damages. On March 26, 1993, the District of Columbia filed a Notice of Removal in the case, claiming a right to remove pursuant to 28 U.S.C. § 1441. The District alleged that the Plaintiff was a citizen of Virginia, the three Defendants were all citizens of the District of Columbia, and the amount in controversy exceeded $50,000, thus satisfying the requirements for diversity jurisdiction.

The District of Columbia failed, however, to examine the words of the applicable removal statute. § 1441 provides:

Any civil action of which the district courts have original jurisdiction founded on a claim or right arising under the Constitution, treaties or laws of the United States shall be removable without regard to the citizenship or residence of the parties. Any other such action shall be removable only if none of the parties in interest properly joined and served as defendants is a citizen of the State in which such action is brought.

The first sentence of § 1441(b) refers to "federal question" jurisdiction pursuant to 28 U.S.C. § 1331. The second sentence refers to federal jurisdiction based on the diversity of the parties, as in this case. Thus, a case may be removed to federal court on the basis of diversity of the parties only if the Defendants are not citizens of the forum state.[147] "Even where an action could have been originally brought in federal court, the defendant may not remove the state action to federal court if the defendant is a citizen of the state in which the action was filed." In other words, a Defendant may not remove a case to federal court on the basis of diversity when the suit was filed in the Defendant's home state.

In this case, the two individual Defendants are, by their own admission, citizens of the District of Columbia. Consequently, by the terms of § 1441, the case is not one subject to removal and should be remanded pursuant to 28 U.S.C. § 1447(c).

Accordingly, it is, by this Court, this 15th day of April, 1993, ORDERED that the above-captioned case shall be, and hereby is, REMANDED to the Superior Court of the District of Columbia; and it is FURTHER ORDERED that the above-captioned case shall be, and hereby is, DISMISSED from the dockets of this Court.

---

[147] *Martin v. Snyder*, 148 U.S. 663 (1893).

Follow-Up Questions and Comments

1. The in-state removal bar may seem counter-intuitive. For example, although an initial subject matter jurisdiction analysis might reveal parties that are completely diverse with a sufficient amount in controversy in a case filed in state court which would ordinarily allow a defendant to remove the case to federal court, the in-state removal bar could preclude removal if the defendant is a citizen of the state in which the suit was originally brought, despite the existence of subject matter jurisdiction. For example, X (a citizen of North Carolina) sues Y (a citizen of Virginia) and Z (a citizen of West Virginia) in a Virginia federal court. Presuming the amount in controversy is met, the case would satisfy diversity of citizenship and would be allowed to remain in federal court. Yet, if the North Carolina plaintiff files the same case in a Virginia state court, the case cannot be removed to federal court and must stay in state court. The statute—28U.S.C. § 1441(b) (2)—precludes the defendant from taking the case to federal court.

2. One of the principles that supports the above result is that the plaintiff is the master of his or her lawsuit. Plaintiffs in the American civil justice system have traditionally been granted the latitude to assert claims as the plaintiff sees fit, even if that means leaving out a claim or a defendant. Likewise, the in-state removal bar supports allowing the plaintiff to choose to litigate in state court if the plaintiff has a legitimate claim against a citizen of the state in which suit is filed. That defendant may not have resources to ensure payment of a judgment, and hence the plaintiff often sues another defendant that does. Yet if there is a claim against at least one of the defendants in the state court action and that defendant is a resident of the forum state, § 1441(b) (2) will preclude removal. Of course, the defendant can always try to remove the case, but a motion to remand will ensure the case is sent back.

3. One might ask, "Does not the in-state removal bar undercut the policy behind diversity jurisdiction?" The result of the in-state removal rule is that parties from different states will end up having to try their case in state court, not in federal court with its added protections to ensure impartiality. If a case involves a nonresident plaintiff and a defendant who is a resident of the forum, we can easily see how barring removal would be consistent with diversity's purposes. In this scenario, the defendant is a citizen of the forum and ought not to suffer prejudice in her own state. Where the policy implications become more problematic is when a nonresident sues more than one defendant—with one of the defendants being aa citizen of the forum state and one or more other defendants not being citizens of the forum state. The nonresidents stuck in state court could claim unfairness. Here, the system essentially admits it cannot provide perfect justice. Instead, it presumes that, by having at least one defendant as a citizen of the forum state, potential prejudice to the nonresident defendants will be offset.

4. Now, put on your strategic plaintiff's lawyer hat. If, as plaintiff's counsel, you can find a defendant against which the plaintiff has a legitimate claim (e.g., a supervisor) who is a citizen of the state in which suit is filed, would you sue that supervisor, even though your plaintiff's primary target is the "deep pocket," nonresident corporation for which the supervisor works? You see the strategy, right—add an "in-state" defendant, even though that defendant is not the primary target, to ensure

the case is not removable? Do you consider that approach improper? We will discuss the potential for fraudulent joinder, also called improper joinder, of an in-state defendant. Nevertheless, you should realize that the strategy of adding a citizen of the state, even if that party is not a deep pocket, is legitimate so long as a viable claim exists against that defendant. Indeed, this practice is one by which intelligent plaintiffs' lawyers ensure that a case the plaintiff wants in state court will stay there.

5. If the plaintiff sues a party diverse from the plaintiff and adds a non-diverse party against whom the plaintiff fails to state a claim in her complaint for a viable cause of action, the in-state removable bar will not prevent removal. Courts reject such a ruse by various terms, including fraudulent joinder or improper joinder.[148] Because the defendant need not show that such joinder was motivated by an intent to deceive (which the phrase "fraudulent joinder" suggests), the phrase "improper joinder" is probably a better one to describe this scenario.

Practice Problems

The following Practice Problems should help you to apply the removal principles discussed up to this point.

Practice Problem 4-1
Police officer Wyatt Earp (AZ) sued Johnny Ringo (MO) and Curly Bill Brocius (IN) in state court in Missouri. Earp had spoken in favor of gun control and urged greater restrictions on weapons. Ringo and Brocius, who strongly opposed Earp's position on gun control, jumped him and beat him so badly that he required ongoing medical treatment and likely would have permanent injuries. Earp's suit was under federal statute 42 U.S.C. § 1983, which allows a person to sue for violation of civil rights including injuries received as a result of exercising one's constitutional right to free speech under the First Amendment. Earp sought $50,000 in damages. Can Earp's case be removed to federal court? Why or why not?

Practice Problem 4-2
Bob Smith (NC) went to Bosch Gardens for a day of fun. He rode the roller coasters, visited Dat Feasthaus where he chowed down on the great German food and watched polka dancing, and then went back out for more rides. He was on the swings that whirl one around such that one rises higher and higher. Unfortunately, his seat broke at the apex of the swinging and he fell to the concrete, breaking a leg. Upon investigation, his attorney found that the supervisor in charge of the ride had not inspected the swings that day as he was required to do. Under applicable law, the employer (or principal) is liable for the negligence of its employee (agent). Bosch Gardens is incorporated in Delaware and has its principal place of business at its headquarters in Miami, Florida. The supervisor, Dan Jones, is a citizen of Virginia. Bob sues Bosch Gardens and Dan Jones in a Virginia Circuit Court. Can the case be removed? Why or why not?

Practice Problem 4-3
Plaintiff (VA) bought an excavator at a dealership in North Carolina. Plaintiff is injured in an accident in which the excavator's arm holding the bucket breaks in half and falls on him. Plaintiff sues in state court both the manufacturer, incorporated and with its principal place of business in Illinois. There is a Virginia dealership that sells the same kind of excavator as Plaintiff bought, but this dealership was not

---

[148] 13F CHARLES ALAN WRIGHT & ARTHUR R. MILLER, FEDERAL PRACTICE AND PROCEDURE (3d ed. 2016).

involved in the purchase of the excavator in question. Plaintiff has a claim against the North Carolina dealer under the Uniform Commercial Code for breach of the implied warranty of merchantability (when a good is not fit for the purposes for which it is intended, an implied warranty exists in any sale between a merchant and a buyer). Plaintiff also has a product liability claim against the manufacturer. Plaintiff sues, in Virginia state court, both the excavator manufacturer, the North Carolina dealership, and the Virginia dealership. Could the Illinois manufacturer remove this case to federal court and have the Virginia dealer dismissed?

C. The Other Removal Prerequisites

Please read 28 U.S.C. §§ 1441 and 1446 and identify how many requirements a lawyer removing a case based on diversity of citizenship must satisfy, what he or she must file and where the filing will be, by what deadlines, and what must be provided to counsel for other parties in the case. Then read the same statutes and answer the same questions based on the assumption that a federal question is the basis for removal. The number of requirements for removal based on diversity of citizenship is different from the requirements for removal of a case based on federal question jurisdiction. You should interpret "requirements" as criteria you must check off your list. In other words, just because you can meet the requirement, do not fail in an analysis (or in real life, in your notice of removal) to explain that you have met the requirement and how you have done so.

The following are requirements of 28 U.S.C. §§ 1441 and 1446. See whether you can find where in the statutes these requirements exist. As we will see, lawyers know to dot their "i's" and cross their "t's" in removal because missing even one requirement—no matter how seemingly insignificant, leaves the case vulnerable to a plaintiff moving to remand to state court.

- **Location of Federal Court to Which Removed.** While the requirement that the case be one within the subject matter jurisdiction of federal courts has been discussed above, 28 U.S.C. § 1441(a) includes a second requirement. It provides that the case be removed to the federal district court for the district "embracing the place where such action is pending."

- **Filing.** "Filing" is a term of art in the Federal Rules. Mailing a pleading or paper to opposing counsel would not constitute filing. To be filed, the Clerk of the Court in which the paper is being filed must receive it. The Clerk will then stamp the date on which it is received and put it in a file to which a Civil Action Number will be assigned.

- **Removing to the U.S. District Court Covering the State Court from which the Suit is Being Removed.** The removing defendant cannot remove the state court suit to any court. Rather, 28 U.S.C. § 1441(a), requires removal to the U.S. district court "for the district and division in which such [state court] civil action is pending."

- **Notice of Removal.** The defendant must file a notice of removal with the U.S. district court. This notice is really a pleading. It will have the caption of the case and include numbered paragraphs in which the defendant cites the removal statutes under which she is removing. The grounds for jurisdiction should be included in the notice of removal. Moreover, each of these steps outlined in the removal statutes should be addressed in a paragraph to show the federal court you have done everything you are required to do to remove the case.

- *Signature.* The notice of removal must be signed. As we will see later, Federal Rule of Civil Procedure 11 provides that the signature of the lawyer signing the pleading constitutes certain certifications. You may ask, "Who would file a pleading without signing it?" Ask anyone who works in a Clerk's office and he will doubtless tell you about many pleadings and letters sent to the court that are not signed. On receiving such an unsigned pleading, the Clerk typically calls the lawyer and asks them to sign the necessary documents, but if the signing occurs after the time deadline below, that itself could be a basis for remand.

- *Statement of the Grounds for Jurisdiction.* The notice of removal, like a complaint, should state in enough detail that the court can, looking at the statement, know that the case satisfied federal subject matter jurisdiction. Thus, the notice should not simply provide that the U.S. district court has diversity jurisdiction but includes details of the citizenship of each party (including the state of incorporation and principal place of business of any corporate party) so that the court can determine for itself from what is stated that the court has subject matter jurisdiction. The requirement here parallels the requirements placed on plaintiffs alleging a complaint in federal court. Because federal courts are courts of limited jurisdiction, they will presume that they lack jurisdiction unless the complaint—or in the case of a removal, the notice of removal—include sufficient and appropriate details that the court can determine from what is pled that subject matter jurisdiction exists.

- *Attachment of all Process, Orders, and Pleadings in the State File.* The lawyer must obtain "all process, orders, pleadings" from the state court's file and copying everything in it. Process typically relates to service of process—the "summons" that is served with a complaint (which together constitutes "process" to be "served," along with the process servers "return" filled by the server indicating how and when each defendant was served, etc. Orders would be orders of the state court on any number of matters, such as the process by which the case will proceed. Pleadings would be the complaint and any other pleadings filed, etc. The safest course is to include everything in the state court's file and to attach those papers as an exhibit to the notice of removal.

- *Filed within 30 Days after the Defendant Was Served with Process in State Proceedings.* This requirement is the timing deadline for removal. When a nonresident defendant first contacts you and you are considering removal, you must determine promptly when service was made. It could be close to the 30-day deadline and you do not want to miss the opportunity to remove a case because you, the lawyer, did not act quickly enough. However, note the ability of a later-served defendant, in a multi-defendant case, to meet the 30-day deadline and thus "save" a previously served defendant who missed the deadline. While this is not something a lawyer should count on, it may be helpful in some cases.

- *All Defendants Consent to Removal.* The requirement of unanimity among defendants in removing a case is one that can prove a problem when a defendant would prefer to stay in state court. Sometimes the defendant's counsel leading the effort to remove must lobby other counsel. In any event, the first defendant to remove needs to include a statement in the notice of removal affirming that all defendants consent to removal. Then, other defendants should promptly file a "Consent to and Joinder in Removal," incorporating by reference everything in the lead defendant's notice of removal, affirming the codefendant's consent to removal, and including counsel for the codefendant's signature on the consent and joinder pleading. Some courts will not accept a mere representation of one defense counsel that another defendant (or her counsel) consents.

97

- *Notice to Adverse Parties.* When the defendant removes the case to federal court, she should put in her certificate of service of the notice of removal that it is being delivered (or mailed) to plaintiff's counsel (including the name of plaintiff's counsel, the address to which delivery or mailing will occur, by what means it will occur, and the date of such delivery/mailing. The cover letter to the Court should carbon copy all counsel for opposing parties or, if a defendant does not yet have counsel, to the defendant at the address on the state court complaint. Everything that the removing defendant files with the federal court or the state court should be copied in full to all counsel for all parties (or for unrepresented parties, to that party).

- *Notice to the State Court.* 28 U.S.C. § 1446 also requires that the removing party file with the state court a notice of removal. Typically, this is not the same as a copy of the notice filed with the federal court even though it is included in the package to the state court. Rather, this notice should include the caption of the case and provide that "Pursuant to 28 U.S.C. § 1446, counsel for [defendant, removing party] hereby provides notice that this action has been removed to the United States District Court for the District of. Thus, jurisdiction in such action has transferred to the U.S. district court." Some state courts (or clerks) do not understand that, when an action is removed, it automatically transfers jurisdiction from the state court system to the federal system. That is, however, exactly what happens. Even if the removed case has a defect in the removal, jurisdiction does not return to the state court unless and until the federal court remands the case.

Again, do not fool yourself into thinking that a federal court will overlook even a minor lapse in the above requirements. The following case is but one example of the degree of punctilious care one must show to ensure a case is removed.

MURPHY v. NEWELL OPERATING CO.
United States District Court for the District of Massachusetts, 2003
245 F. Supp. 2d 316

SWARTWOOD, United States Magistrate Judge.

. . .

This is a products liability case which was originally commenced in the Massachusetts Superior Court and later removed to this Court by a Third–Party Defendant pursuant to 28 U.S.C. §§ 1332, 1441 on the grounds that there is complete diversity of citizenship among all the parties and the amount in controversy exceeds Seventy–Five Thousand Dollars ($75,000).

Facts
1. On February 16, 1999, Plaintiff filed this products liability case against Newell Operating Company ("Defendant") in the Massachusetts Superior Court.
2. On or about August 21, 2001, Defendant filed a Third–Party Complaint against Crisa Industrial, LLC ("Crisa") and Vitrocrisa S.A.D.E.C.V. ("Vitrocrisa").
3. Crisa was served, through its registered agent, with a copy of the Third–Party Complaint on September 24, 2001. Crisa then filed a motion to dismiss which was denied by the Superior Court on March 27, 2002. On or about April 5, 2002, Crisa filed its answer to Defendant's Third–Party Complaint.

4. On March 18, 2002, Defendant's Third–Party Complaint was served upon Vitrocrisa.
5. On or about April 8, 2002, Vitrocrisa filed its answer to Defendant's Third–Party Complaint.
6. On April 9, 2002, Vitrocrisa filed its Removal Petition.
7. On May 7, 2002, Crisa filed its Assent to Removal.
8. There is diversity of citizenship for all parties and the amount in controversy is alleged to exceed Seventy–Five Thousand Dollars ($75,000).

Discussion

The federal removal statute, 28 U.S.C. § 1446(a) and (b), provides that in order to remove a state court action to federal court, a defendant shall file in the federal district court a notice of removal within thirty days after receipt by the removing defendant of the initial pleading or service of process. The removal statute is strictly construed. In cases involving multiple defendants, all defendants who have been served must join or assent in the removal petition [The notice of removal is sometimes referred to as a petition for removal]. This "rule of unanimity" requires that all defendants file their notice of removal or consent to removal within thirty days of being served. "Failure to do so constitutes a 'defect in the removal procedure' and is grounds for remand."

Defendant argues, in its motion to remand, that since Crisa did not file a notice of removal within 30 days of its having been served with process, Vitrocrisa was thereafter barred from removing this case. Alternatively, Defendant argues that even if this Court finds that Crisa's initial failure to file a timely notice of removal did not preclude Vitrocrisa from later seeking to remove this case, Crisa's failure to file its consent to Vitrocrisa's Removal Petition within thirty days of service of process on Vitrocrisa invalidates the removal and requires that this case be remanded to state court. Crisa argues in opposition that, since its counsel changed during the course of the litigation, any failure to timely seek or consent to the removal was an oversight of predecessor counsel which has been cured by it Assent to Removal filed on May 7, 2002.

The threshold issue raised in this motion is whether Vitrocrisa, a subsequently served third-party defendant, is foreclosed from removing this case because Crisa, served much earlier in the proceeding, did not itself file a timely notice of removal. The First Circuit Court of Appeals has not addressed this issue.

Under the circumstances of this case, it is not necessary for me to address whether Crisa's failure to timely seek removal bars Vitrocrisa from doing so, Crisa's failure to file its assent to removal within thirty days of Vitrocrisa's having been served renders such assent ineffective. Since Crisa did not timely consent to removal, the rule of unanimity has been violated and Vitrocrisa's Removal Petition is invalid. Accordingly, Defendant's Motion to Remand the case to the Massachusetts Superior Court is allowed.

Conclusion

Newell Operating Company's Motion to Remand is allowed and the clerk shall remand the case to Massachusetts Superior Court.

Follow-Up Questions and Comments:

1. It used to be that if the first-served defendant did not remove the case within 30 days of being served, any other defendants could not remove. That was true even if the other defendants had been served later and were within the 30-day removal period. Why was such a result unfair? How did 28 U.S.C. § 1446(b) (2) (B) change the result in such cases?

2. Nevertheless, even if a defendant is served later and removes the case within 30 days, each defendant must consent to the removal—regardless of whether it is a defendant who missed the 30-day deadline but was saved by another defendant's meeting the deadline. The safest course by which to consent is for each defendant to file a pleading entitled a "Consent to and Joinder in Removal," confirming the co-defendant's consent to removal. The removing defendant's notice of removal must state that all defendants consent to removal. However, such a statement without the follow-up of a pleading from each defendant confirming each defendant's consent, gives rise to grounds for a motion to remand. Is that the reason the court in *Murphy v. Newell Operating Company* remanded? Would it make any difference to the result if Crisa had talked to Vitrocrisa's counsel and told Vitrocrisa's counsel that Crisa consented, but Vitrocrisa forgot to mention that in the notice of removal and Crisa did not file a joinder in the removal indicating its consent? What if Crisa indicated consent to Vitrocrisa's counsel but did not file anything indicating the consent? What if Vitrocrisa's notice indicated Crisa had consented and Crisa's counsel filed a Consent to and Joinder in Removal?

3. In *Creekmore v. Food Lion, Inc.*,[149] a defendant was filing a notice of removal and received permission to sign on behalf of another defendant on the removal papers. However, the court held that each defendant had to file its own notice of removal. Even with permission from another party, counsel for a separate defendant could not achieve consent by signing "on behalf of" the other defendant. *But see Harper v. Auto Alliance Int'l. Inc.*,[150] The safest course is for each codefendant to file an independent consent and joinder in removal, signed by each codefendant's counsel.

4. What if one defendant in a multi-defendant case does not want to remove? Does that defendant have an absolute veto over removal?[151]

Practice Problems

The following Practice Problems include a defective notice of removal. Go through the steps for analyzing of whether removal is proper. Start with 28 U.S.C. § 1441 and ask (a) whether a basis in federal subject matter jurisdiction exists, and (b) whether any defendant is a citizen of the state in which suit is brought, such that the in-state removal bar will preclude a diversity case from being removed. Then, list the removal requirements to see which are satisfied and where the deficiency lies.

Practice Problem 4-4

Plaintiff, a Maine citizen, filed suit against a Minnesota citizen in Maine state court on a breach of contract claim seeking $100,000. (Maine has only one district court, the U.S. District Court for the District of Maine.) Within 30 days of being served, defendant filed a signed notice of removal with the United States District Court for the District of Maine. As is typical in state court complaints, there was no recitation of the citizenship of the parties.

After the caption, the notice stated the following:

---

[149] 797 F. Supp. 505 (E.D. Va. 1992).

[150] 392 F.3d 195, 201–02 (2004) (recognizing that Rule 11 did not require a defendant to submit a pleading, written motion, or other paper directly expressing concurrence with removal or prohibit counsel for other defendants from making such representations on a defendant's behalf).

[151] 28 U.S.C. § 1446(b) (2).

1. Plaintiff filed suit in state court.
2. This action is within the subject matter jurisdiction of the U.S. District Court under 28 U.S.C. § 1332.
3. Defendant is the only defendant and thus need not get consent of another.
4. This removal notice is timely.
5. Notice has been given to the state court and to all adverse parties.
6. All process, orders, and pleadings filed in the state court are hereby attached.

WHEREFORE, Defendant hereby removes the case to the U.S. District Court for the District and Division in which the state court is located.

Assuming Defendant's counsel signed the above notice, is it sufficient to effect removal or is the case vulnerable to a motion to remand? If it is vulnerable, how so? In this evaluation, recall what a plaintiff must include in a complaint filed in federal court.

Practice Problem 4-5

What if Plaintiff forgets to sign the notice of removal? To attach all process, orders, and pleadings filed in the state court by the time of removal? To give notice to the State Court and all adverse parties at the time of removal? Are the removal provisions really that picky that such failures could lead to remand?

D. Removal Based on Events After Initial Filing

Many cases are not able to be removed at the outset but become removable later due to developments in the case. Please read 28 U.S.C. §§ 1446(b) (3) and 1446(c). The following are the primary scenarios that, though not removable at the outset, allow for removal later based on the provisions you just read.

1. Plaintiff Amends Complaint to Add a Federal Question

A typical scenario after suit has been pending in state court that could trigger a defendant's right to remove the case is when a plaintiff amends her complaint to add, for the first time, a claim based on federal question jurisdiction. This form of removal is based on 28 U.S.C. § 1446(b) (3), which provides:

Except as provided in subsection (c), if the case stated by the initial pleading is not removable, a notice of removal may be filed within 30 days after receipt by the defendant, through service or otherwise, of a copy of an amended pleading, motion, order or other paper from which it may first be ascertained that the case is one which is or has become removable.

In *King v. Cardinal Health, Incorporated*,[152] the plaintiff filed an amended complaint that included a claim under the Family and Medical Leave Act (FMLA). Because the defendant filed a notice of removal within 30 days of the filing of the amended complaint, the notice was timely even though the plaintiff had alluded to the FMLA during earlier proceedings:

The presence or absence of federal question jurisdiction is governed by the well-pleaded complaint

---

[152] King v. Cardinal Health, 411, Inc., No. 5:10CV112, 2011 U.S. Dist. LEXIS 1469, *8-10 (N.D. W. Va. Jan. 2011)

rule, which provides that a federal question must be presented on the face of the plaintiff's properly pleaded complaint. Only those cases "in which a well-pleaded complaint establishes either that federal law creates the cause of action or that the plaintiff's right to relief necessarily depends upon resolution of a substantial question of federal law" are subject to removal. This Court finds that the plain language on the face of the plaintiff's amended complaint presents a federal question: whether the termination of the plaintiff's employment violated the FMLA. The plaintiff's allegation that Cardinal Health violated her rights under the FMLA, a federal law, is pled unambiguously. Accordingly, this Court has federal question subject matter jurisdiction over the plaintiff's action.

This Court further finds that the defendants timely filed the notice of removal. Because there is no mention of the FMLA or any federal law in the original complaint, the defendants could not determine the existence of a federal question until the filing of the plaintiff's amended complaint. Although the plaintiff referenced the FMLA in her response to the defendants' motion to dismiss, this response did not adequately set forth a FMLA claim such that the defendants should have been aware that a federal question may be implicated and a basis for removal existed. Rather, the plaintiff's response to the motion to dismiss cites the FMLA as a source of West Virginia public policy, not as a separate claim. This Court need look no further than the plaintiff's amended complaint in determining whether the lawsuit raises issues of federal law capable of creating federal question jurisdiction. Thus, because notice of removal was filed within thirty days of the amended complaint, this Court finds that removal is timely.[153]

Note that courts do not consider whether the amendment to add a federal question occurred more than one year after commencement of the action. The one-year rule applies only to cases based on diversity of citizenship. Thus, one need not worry about arguing bad faith failure to allege the federal claim earlier. If the federal claim is added, and the defendant removes within 30 days of service of the amended complaint and satisfies all the steps required in a removal, the removal will be permitted.

Note that the court applies a well-pleaded complaint analysis to determine whether the amended complaint adds a federal claim. If the amended complaint mentioned federal law, but federal law was not essential to plead any claim, the amended complaint would not be one on which removal could be based.

Practice Problem

The following Practice Problem tests your ability to apply the injection-of-a-federal-claim provision to a removal scenario:

Practice Problem 4-6

Assume that a plaintiff alleges a battery claim against a police officer who subdued him with a chokehold even though the plaintiff was far smaller than the officer and made no attempt to evade arrest. Battery is a state law claim and plaintiff filed in state court. During the trial, the plaintiff moves to amend to state a violation of his civil rights due to excessive force, under 42 U.S.C. § 1983, a federal statute. The court grants the plaintiff's motion and an amended complaint with the new claim is filed. Just before jury arguments, the defendant files a notice of removal and follows all the steps required for removal. Is this an instance in which the defendant can remove a case that was not originally removable? What happens to the

---

[153] *Id.*

2. Plaintiff Initially Joins a Non-Diverse Defendant but Dismisses Him More Than One Year After the Commencement of the Action.

Until recently, a plaintiff could include in a diversity case an in-state defendant in a case and prevent removal until one year from commencement of the case, at which point plaintiff often dropped the in-state defendant. The remaining defendant was stuck in state court because the one-year period for removal had run. However, 28 U.S.C. § 1446(c)(1) was amended to state:

A case may not be removed under subsection (b)(3) on the basis of juris-diction conferred by section 1332 more than 1 year after commencement of the action, unless the district court finds that the plaintiff has acted in bad faith in order to prevent a defendant from removing the action.

Following is a case interpreting the new "bad faith" provision:

AGUAYO v. AMCO INSURANCE CO.
United States District Court for the District of New Mexico, 2014
59 F. Supp. 3d 1225

JAMES O. BROWNING, District Judge.

The primary issue is whether the Court should grant the Motion and remand this case to state court, because it was pending there for "more than 1 year" at the time of removal; or deny the Motion and keep the case on the ground that the Plaintiffs "acted in bad faith in order to prevent [Defendant AMCO Insurance Company] from removing the action." The Court interprets the bad-faith exception—which is only two years old and which no court has yet comprehensively construed—to require an inquiry into whether the plaintiff kept a removal-spoiling party in the case only for the purpose of preventing removal. The Court construes this inquiry to entail a two-step standard. First, the Court assesses whether the plaintiff actively litigated its case against the removal spoiler in state court. A finding that the plaintiff did not actively litigate against the removal spoiler constitutes bad faith, and the Court will retain jurisdiction over the case. If, on the other hand, the Court finds that the plaintiff actively litigated against the removal spoiler, that finding creates a rebuttable presumption that the plaintiff acted in good faith. Second, the defendant may rebut the good-faith presumption, with evidence already in the defendant's possession, that the plaintiff kept the removal spoiler in the case to defeat removal; the defendant will not, however, receive discovery or an evidentiary hearing in federal court to obtain such evidence. The Court adopts an expansive view of active litigation: the plaintiff need not expect to recover damages from the removal-spoiling defendant; if the plaintiff keeps the removal spoiler joined to obtain discovery from him or her, to force a settlement, to pressure the removal spoiler to testify on the plaintiff's behalf against other defendants, or to obtain a judgment against the removal spoiler that the plaintiff knows the removal spoiler cannot pay, the Court will consider the plaintiff to have actively litigated against the removal spoiler, and unless the removing defendant can adduce other evidence of bad faith, such as communications from the plaintiff directly attesting to bad faith, the Court will presume good faith and remand the case. In this case, the Plaintiffs actively litigated both against Defendant Michael Trujillo, whom the Plaintiffs twice deposed, and against Defendants Trace Spoonhoward, the New Mexico State Police ("NMSP"), and the State of New Mexico (collectively, "the State Defendants"), with whom the Plaintiffs settled, thus entitling them to a rebuttable presumption of good faith. AMCO Insurance has introduced no direct or convincing circumstantial

103

evidence of bad faith and has therefore failed to rebut the presumption. The Court, accordingly, grants the Motion and remands the case to state court.

Factual Background

This case arises out of the July, 2010, murder of a young man, Christopher Aguayo, by another young man, Michael Trujillo, using a gun belonging to Trujillo's surrogate father, Spoonhoward, an officer with the NMSP. All events occurred in Santa Fe, New Mexico . . . and all persons involved are New Mexico citizens with the exception of AMCO Insurance, which is a foreign corporation.

Trujillo lived with his mother and Spoonhoward, who was not Trujillo's biological father, but to whom Trujillo would commonly refer as his "dad." Trujillo had disciplinary problems: in 2006, he was caught taking a pellet gun from his home to his school; in 2007, he was involved in a fight with another student at his high school; in 2009, his mother had reported him missing, and, when police found him, they reported that he was "belligerent, verbally abusive and that he referred to an officer as a pig." Trujillo's mother acknowledges that she had "extreme difficulties with her son" and worried that he might be in a gang. It is unclear what role Spoonhoward played in Trujillo's life over the years, but Spoonhoward was aware of Trujillo's disciplinary issues and of his possible gang affiliation.

The NMSP had issued Spoonhoward a .357 Smith & Wesson pistol. Pursuant to New Mexico Department of Public Safety ("NMDPS") policy, Spoonhoward was required to safely secure the firearm at all times, whether he was on-or off-duty. The policy provides:

When not secured on the officer's person or other department approved locking storage device or locked truck of an issued service vehicle, officers are to ensure that their service weapon is secured and/or stored in a safe manner; and the service weapon shall be secured so as to be inaccessible to children or unauthorized personnel at all times.

Trujillo was able to get his hands on this pistol, and, on July 8, 2010, he had his girlfriend arrange a meeting at the Santa Fe Place Mall between him and C. Aguayo. Trujillo was angry at C. Aguayo about cellular telephone communications that C. Aguayo had engaged in with Trujillo's girlfriend, and, when C. Aguayo arrived at the mall, Trujillo drove up to him, got out of the car, and shot him four or five times with the pistol. C. Aguayo collapsed to the ground, and Trujillo walked up to within three feet of him and emptied the rest of the gun's magazine into C. Aguayo. Trujillo and his girlfriend fled the scene, but Trujillo was picked up by police less than an hour after the shooting. Immediately upon apprehension, Trujillo told police that he "ha[d] to tell you guys I got the gun from my dad[;] he's a state cop."

Aguayo was bleeding, and slipping in and out of consciousness, when officers arrived at the scene. He was in great pain and at one point asked officers to shoot him to end his suffering. Officers rushed him to the hospital, but, shortly after his arrival, he succumbed to his injuries and died.

At the time C. Aguayo was murdered, the Aguayo family had an AMCO Insurance policy that provided them with uninsured motorist benefits. Because Trujillo used a vehicle in his commission of the crime, the Aguayo family submitted an insurance claim for the full amount of the policy limit. AMCO Insurance denied the claim without interviewing any witnesses or speaking with the Aguayo family.

Procedural Background

104

This case involves the Plaintiffs' Motion to remand the case to state court after AMCO Insurance removed it to federal court, arguing that, because the case was pending in state court "more than 1 year," AMCO Insurance's removal was improper. AMCO Insurance, for its part, contends that removal was justified under the recently passed bad-faith exception to the one-year limitation, which requires that the Plaintiffs' actions in state court were "in bad faith in order to prevent a defendant from removing the action." 28 U.S.C. § 1446(c) (1). As such, the relevant background to the resolution of this Motion are the parties' procedural actions while litigating this case in state court. The parties vary widely in the motives they ascribe to their own and each other's actions; the objective facts of how the litigation unfolded, however, are not in dispute.

[Plaintiffs, all citizens of New Mexico, sued in New Mexico state court both Trujillo and AMCO, alleging obviously wrongful death as to Trujillo and, as to AMCO, bad faith denial of insurance claims and violations of the insurance code. Because Trujillo was also a citizen of New Mexico, AMCO could not remove the case event though it is an Iowa citizen.]

. . .

AMCO Insurance argues that the "amendment effective January 6, 2012, now recognizes the right of a defendant to remove an action kept out of federal court for more than one year by bad-faith conduct of plaintiffs," and that "[t]he comments to the amendment indicate that it is intended to apply in circumstances such as those at bar."

. . .

The "Bad Faith" Exception to the One–Year Removal Bar for Diversity Cases.
Since 1988, 28 U.S.C. § 1446 has provided that no case that has been pending more than one year in state court can be removed on the basis of diversity jurisdiction. On January 6, 2012, Congress put into effect the Federal Courts Jurisdiction and Venue Clarification Act of 2011, Pub. L. No. 112–63, 125 Stat. 760, 762 ("JVCA"), which, among other changes, added a bad-faith exception to the one-year limitation. As a result, the current subsection (c) is almost entirely new; it reads as follows, with the sole sentence of the statute that pre-exists the JVCA underlined:

Requirements; removal based on diversity of citizenship:

A case may not be removed under subsection (b) (3) on the basis of jurisdiction conferred more than 1 year after commencement of the action, unless the district court finds that the plaintiff has acted in bad faith in order to prevent a defendant from removing the action.

. . .

For the reasons explained in the Analysis, the Court construes the bad-faith exception as a two-step standard. First, the Court inquires whether the plaintiff actively litigated against the removal spoiler in state court: asserting valid claims, taking discovery, negotiating settlement, seeking default judgments if the defendant does not answer the complaint, et cetera. Failure to actively litigate against the removal spoiler will be deemed bad faith; actively litigating against the removal spoiler, however, will create a rebuttable presumption of good faith. Second, the defendant may attempt to rebut this presumption with evidence already in the defendant's possession that establishes that, despite the plaintiff's active litigation against the removal spoiler, the plaintiff would not have named the removal spoiler or would have dropped the spoiler before the one-year mark but for the plaintiff's desire to keep the case in state court. The defendant may introduce direct evidence of the plaintiff's bad faith at this stage—*e.g.*, electronic mail transmissions in which the plaintiff states that he or she is only keeping the removal spoiler joined to defeat removal—but will not receive discovery or an evidentiary hearing in federal court to obtain such evidence.

Analysis

The Plaintiffs did not act in bad faith by keeping the removal-spoiling defendants, Trujillo and the State Defendants, joined past the one-year mark, because the Plaintiffs actively litigated against them, and AMCO Insurance has produced no direct evidence to rebut the presumption of good faith that this active litigation creates. The Court interprets the bad-faith exception to apply to plaintiffs who keep a removal-spoiling party in the case past the one-year mark for the purpose of defeating removal, i.e., it applies when the removal spoiler would not have been in the case at the one-year mark but for the plaintiffs' deliberate forum manipulation. To create a workable gauge for this inquiry—one that honors the bad-faith exception's statutory content and respects Congress' desire for additional removals, while protecting plaintiffs from unwelcome intrusions into their work-product and private litigation strategy—the Court construes the bad-faith exception to entail a two-step standard. First, the Court looks to whether the plaintiff actively litigated against the removal-spoiling defendant in state court: asserting valid claims, taking discovery, negotiating settlement, seeking default judgments if the defendant does not answer the complaint, et cetera. If the plaintiff did not actively litigate against the removal spoiler, then bad faith is established; if the plaintiff actively litigated against the removal spoiler, then good faith is rebuttably presumed. In the standard's second step, the defendant may attempt to rebut the good-faith presumption with direct evidence of the plaintiff's subjective bad faith. Although the Court will allow subjective evidence at the second step, the Court will only permit defendants to use the evidence they already have on hand and will not permit discovery or provide an evidentiary hearing on the bad-faith issue.

[Here, the court expressed its concern with finding "bad faith" unless it had a solid basis for doing so. As it related, the court was concerned that it would be] easy . . . for defendants to concoct a colorable bad-faith argument, remove the case to federal court, and then lose the remand battle without having costs assessed against them—a result that the Court fears many defendants will prefer over staying quietly in state court. The Court is thus concerned that the bad-faith exception is a recipe for many more improper removals. These removals, while doomed for remand, will produce significant judicial inefficiency and needless friction between federal and state courts. Ultimately, however, § 1446(c) (1)'s text demands a standard, and not a rule, and the Court must be faithful to the statutory text above all else. Similarly, current Supreme Court precedent forecloses the other method of which the Court could conceive to curb wasteful improper removals—presumptively imposing costs against defendants under
§ 1447(c) on all removals that result in remand.

I. The Court Construes the Bad–Faith Exception as a Two–Step Standard.

The Court fashions its two-step standard by first interpreting the statute's content and then forming a workable test to effectuate that content. Section 1446's historical development and present-day text elucidate the exception's content. The bad-faith exception does not codify fraudulent joinder doctrine or expand it to reach new claims; it has little to do with fraudulent joinder, and the plaintiff's assertion of legally or factually unsound claims does not trigger the exception. Rather, the bad-faith exception prohibits plaintiffs from asserting good claims in bad faith: it permits removal whenever a plaintiff keeps a removal-spoiling party in the case past the one-year mark, and the removal-spoiling party is one whom the plaintiff would not have kept in the case but for the plaintiff's desire to defeat removal.

This subjective inquiry into the plaintiff's intent is a difficult test for courts to apply and runs the risk of putting the plaintiffs' attorneys on the stand and asking them about their litigation strategy. Furthermore, this subjective inquiry—if it focused only on what is in the plaintiff's counsel's mind—could result in the Court almost never sustaining removal, because the plaintiff can virtually always articulate some basis other than forum manipulation for keeping the removal spoiler in the case; because there is no marginal expense to the plaintiff associated with naming or keeping an additional defendant in a case, the plaintiff could then argue that the non-forum manipulation reason that he or she articulated, however weak, outweighs the nonexistent costs of joining or keeping the removal-spoiling defendant. To craft a workable standard, the Court will not focus on whether the plaintiff was motivated by a desire to stay out of federal court but will instead approach the issue by looking primarily at objective criteria, evaluating whether the plaintiff in fact pursued a non-forum-manipulation reason for joining and keeping the removal-spoiling defendant, i.e., whether the plaintiff actively litigated against the removal spoiler.

The Court will define "actively litigate" broadly. The core incentive that the judicial system provides for plaintiffs to assert claims against defendants is money damages—plaintiffs name defendants with the goal of obtaining a judgment against them and, ultimately, of collecting on that judgment. Recovery is not the only permissible end for which a plaintiff can name a defendant, however, and plaintiffs often name defendants from whom they have no hope of recovering damages. Provided that the plaintiff has colorable claims against the defendant—and fraudulent joinder doctrine, not the bad-faith exception, permits removal when the plaintiff lacks a colorable claim—any of the following are permissible purposes for naming and keeping a defendant in a case: (i) recovering damages from the defendant pursuant to a judgment; (ii) obtaining a judgment against the defendant, even if the plaintiff knows the defendant will be unable to satisfy the judgment; (iii) obtaining a settlement from the defendant, even if the plaintiff has already decided that it would not under any circumstances be economical to take the defendant to trial; (iv) leveraging the claims against the defendant to encourage the defendant to testify on the plaintiff's behalf against other defendants; or (v) obtaining discovery from the defendant by virtue of the increased scope of discovery available against parties relative to nonparties. If the plaintiff shows that he or she pursued any of these ends, then the Court will presume that the plaintiff acted in good faith. At that point, the defendant may attempt to rebut the good-faith presumption with evidence of the plaintiff's subjective bad faith, but the defendant may only use evidence already in his or her possession and will not receive additional discovery or an evidentiary hearing to develop the bad-faith argument.

. . .

The Standard's First Step Is That Active Litigation Creates a Rebuttable Presumption of Good Faith.

The Court cannot usually discern the plaintiff's subjective intent, and the economic balancing test described immediately above, which would otherwise seem sensible, will almost invariably justify the plaintiff's actions. The Court will thus, instead, focus its inquiry on whether the plaintiff actively litigated against the removal spoiler in state court. The Court notes, at the outset, that this active litigation inquiry is a proxy for the statutory inquiry; it relies on circumstantial evidence of intent and is thus under-inclusive and, at least theoretically, over-inclusive. It is underinclusive because a plaintiff can actively litigate against a removal spoiler even though the plaintiff is only keeping the spoiler in the case for the forum manipulation purposes. While this course of action may have been irrational before the JVCA, the bad-faith exception incentivizes its own satisfaction, and plaintiffs will be able to defeat removal under the exception by jumping through the hoops of actively litigating in state court. The active-litigation standard is over-inclusive, because a plaintiff could keep a defendant in a case without litigating against him or her, but nonetheless desire the defendant's presence in the case for reasons other than forum manipulation. For example, if the case is slow-moving, the plaintiff may have been putting off taking discovery from the removal spoiler until after the one-year mark, and then received an acceptable settlement offer from the spoiler before any discovery was taken; given that discovery is not costless, naming and retaining a defendant is, in this scenario, perfectly plausible. That there are diverse parties, i.e., not removal spoilers, out there who have been joined to cases for over a year without being actively litigated against is a testament to the standard's over-inclusivity.

Still, the active-litigation proxy is not an unreasonable one, and it can be proven by factual evidence that the parties already have on hand when they enter federal court: the discovery taken against different parties, the hours spent negotiating settlements, and any motion practice in which the parties engaged in state court. As the Court has already stated, it takes a wide-open view of what constitutes active litigation; any one form of active litigation satisfies the standard's first step. Most often, the relevant factor will be whether the plaintiff took discovery from the defendant, although the plaintiff can satisfy the standard even if he or she did not take discovery if he or she engaged in any other form of active litigation, such as seeking a default judgment against a removal-spoiling defendant who does not respond to the complaint within the required timeframe or settling the case for more than nominal damages with a removal spoiler from whom the defendant has not yet taken discovery.

The Court will set forth a few firm principles for when a plaintiff's litigation efforts qualify him or her for the rebuttable presumption of good faith. Any non-token amount of discovery or other active litigation against a removal spoiler entitles the plaintiff to the presumption. In assessing whether a quantum of litigation is token, the Court will consider the amount of litigation commenced against the spoiler in light of: (i) the amount of time the spoiler spent joined to the case—the Court will expect less discovery taken from a spoiler joined for six months than from one joined for a year; and (ii) the size and money value of the case—the Court expects that discovery and motion practice bear some proportionality to the case's worth. The Court recognizes some danger in consideration (i); the Court does not want to incentivize plaintiffs to name and drop multiple removal spoilers over the course of the first year in state court, but, rather, thinks it preferable for at least one single removal spoiler to be present in the case throughout the first year—that way, if the plaintiff's claims against the spoiler are frivolous, the defendant has ample time to develop a fraudulent joinder argument without the plaintiff playing a shell game of rotating different removal spoilers through the case at different times. The Court will, thus, demand a separate showing of active litigation against every removal spoiler who is, at any time before the one-year mark, the only removal spoiler in the case.

2. In the Second Step, the Court Will Consider Evidence Offered to Rebut the Good–Faith Presumption Created in the First Step.

If the plaintiff can establish that he or she actively litigated against the removal spoiler, the plaintiff is entitled to a rebuttable presumption of good faith. The defendant may attempt to rebut this presumption with direct evidence of bad faith but is limited to the evidence that he or she has on hand: the defendant may not take discovery in federal court or call witnesses at a hearing to develop this rebuttal; the defendant may, however, produce affidavits. The Court gives five justifications for this evidentiary limitation. First and foremost, the Court does not want to open the plaintiff up to intrusions into its attorneys' strategy, their opinions about what avenues of discovery are likely to be fruitful, and their impressions regarding likely recovery from various defendants—otherwise known as attorney work-product. It would be unfair to disclose this proprietary information to the defendants, and, even if the bad-faith exception contemplated in camera review, the Court is resistant to demanding this information from an attorney who might subsequently have to prosecute his or her case in front of the Court. The Court generally avoids putting attorneys on the stand or otherwise in positions where they are obligated to waive privileges to bring out favorable evidence, which might occur if an attorney had good-faith reasons for joining a removal-spoiling party. Even indirect evidence of good faith comes perilously close to prying into the plaintiff's work-product and attorney-client relationship. For example, if the Plaintiffs in this case dismissed Trujillo because he offered to testify against AMCO Insurance, revealing that information at the motion-to-remand stage might undermine the Plaintiffs' plan to conceal Trujillo's cooperation until a later date. Courts assiduously avoid making this kind of inquiry, and if Congress had intended to open up plaintiffs' attorneys to mind-probing depositions on their strategies and overrule the common-law work-product doctrine, then it likely would have said so in clearer terms.

Second, and perhaps most obviously, the Court does not want to expend any more judicial or litigation resources on these issues than necessary. Direct evidence of subjective intent, *e.g.*, an electronic mail transmission from the plaintiff to the defendant saying "[removal spoiler] is only in the case because he keeps it non-diverse," will not exist in most cases, and the Court has no desire to set up a costly and time-consuming discovery period or evidentiary hearing when it will turn out fruitless in most cases. Third, and relatedly, even if some plaintiffs' attorneys were to honestly admit to bad-faith intentions on the stand, the Court dislikes the strong disincentives this creates regarding candor to the tribunal, particularly if this candor persists throughout a lengthy examination on the attorney's case strategy. Fourth, the statute requires that the defendant have evidence of bad faith to remove the case in the first place and not just to keep the case in federal court once it is removed. Congress could have placed the bad-faith exception in § 1447, the remand statute, but, instead, it put the exception in the removal statute. The result is normatively desirable, as well as textually sound: defendants cannot use removal under the bad-faith exception as a fishing expedition for evidence of the very basis of the removal. Fifth, the evidentiary limitation in step two effectuates something of a trade-off for the active-litigation standard of step one. As already discussed, the active-litigation standard is over-inclusive, and it results in more removals than a standard that requires direct evidence of subjective intent, which plaintiffs could usually satisfy by simply keeping quiet about their bad faith, or an economic balancing test, which plaintiffs could satisfy by pointing to any positive-value, non-forum-manipulation benefit to naming the removal spoiler. Prohibiting discovery is a fair counterbalance to the active-litigation standard for the Court to protect the plaintiff's sensitive strategic opinions, impressions, and litigation goals, from unwelcome, adversarial, nonreciprocal prying.

The substantive operation of the second step will vary depending on the quantity and quality of the defendant's evidence, but the Court will make a few points on the front end. First, the Court will draw all reasonable inferences in the plaintiff's favor. There is a general presumption against removal,[154] and a policy justification for keeping the bad-faith exception narrow . . . and, if the standard's first step is to mean anything, there is a need for the good-faith presumption to have bite. Second, the Court is more concerned with the quality of evidence than the quantity. The Court wants a smoking gun or close to it. The suspicious timing of a dismissal, a drop in a settlement offer to the removal spoiler after the one-year mark, or an ambiguous comment about how the plaintiff plans to drop the removal spoiler before trial, will not suffice. If a defendant wants the removal to stick, then he or she should be able to show either: (i) that the plaintiff did not litigate at all or engaged in a mere scintilla of litigation against the removal spoiler; or (ii) that the defendant has strong, unambiguous evidence of the plaintiff's subjective intent, for which the plain-tiff cannot offer any plausible alternative explanation.

---

[154] *See, e.g.*, Laughlin v. Kmart Corp., 50 F.3d 871, 873 (10th Cir. 1995).

. . .

[Based on the test it developed, the court held that it could not find that the bad faith exception to removing a diversity case after one year applied here.] IT IS ORDERED that the Plaintiffs 'Motion to Remand . . . is granted.

Practice Problem

Practice Problem 4-7

Assume all the facts in Practice Problem 4-2. Further assume the plaintiff, Bob Smith, after serving the supervisor, Dan Jones, litigated only with Bosch Gardens and did not serve another discovery document, make any requests, or depose the supervisor. More than one year after commencing the suit in state court, Bob Smith dismissed the supervisor from the suit. Defendant Bosch Gardens then removes the case, following all the requirements of 28 U.S.C. §§ 1441 and 1446 and alleges that the one year from commencement of the action rule did not apply because the joinder of the supervisor was in bad faith. If the court followed *Aguayo*, how would it rule?

---

3. Plaintiff in "bad faith" fails to disclose the amount in controversy within one year of commencement of action.

The previous section showed one type of bad faith that would allow a defendant to remove a diversity action more than one year after commencement. Another exception, also deemed "bad faith," will apply if the "district court finds that the plaintiff deliberately failed to disclose the actual amount in controversy to prevent removal . . . ."[155] The "deliberately fail to disclose" amount in controversy exception likely will have less impact than deliberately naming a defendant so as to spoil diversity. The reason is that the amount in controversy should, even if not stated in the original complaint, become clear at some point in discovery, likely before the one-year deadline on removing diversity suits.[156] Even if the case is not removable on filing because of the inability from the complaint to determine the amount in controversy, receipt of discovery materials that show the amount is likely greater than $75,000 exclusive of interests and costs triggers a 30-day deadline from the receipt of such "other paper from which it may first be ascertained that the case is one which is or has become removable."[157]

4. Plaintiff Voluntarily Dismisses Non-Diverse Defendant within One Year after the Commencement of the Action

A case can become removable when a non-diverse defendant is dismissed within one year of the commencement of the action. The question is whether the dismissal was voluntary or involuntary. Consider the following analysis from *Allen v. Independent Concrete Pipe Company*:

---

[155] 28 U.S.C. § 1446 (C)(2(B).
[156] C. WRIGHT & A. MILLER, 14AA FEDERAL PRACTICE & PROCEDURE § 3702.1 (4th ed. 2019).
[157] 28 U.S.C. §1446(b)(3).

110

ALLEN v. INDEPENDENT CONCRETE PIPE CO.
United States District Court for the Northern District of Ohio, March 9, 2004 No. 3:04CV7053, 2004 U.S. Dist. LEXIS 3580

OPINION BY: James G. Carr, United States District Judge.

. . .

Removal was premised on the understanding of a diverse defendant that the only non-diverse party had "apparently" been dismissed as a result of a settlement between the plaintiff and the non-diverse defendant.

Plaintiff does not contest the representation that the non-diverse party has been dismissed, nor does plaintiff contend that removal was not thereafter timely. Thus, the only issue is whether this case, having been non-removable (due to the presence of a non-diverse defendant) at its filing in state court became removable after the plaintiff dismissed the non-diverse defendant.

The answer depends on whether dismissal of the non-diverse party was voluntary or involuntary (i.e., on plaintiff's motion or on motion of the non-diverse party).[158] The reason for the distinction between voluntary and involuntary dismissal was set forth in *Wiacek v. Equitable Life Assurance Society. of U.S.*:[159]

This voluntary/involuntary distinction is grounded in the observation that when a non-diverse party is eliminated from an action pursuant to court order (i.e., involuntarily), the order of dismissal may be the subject of appeal; consequently, although diversity may temporarily exist between the parties, federal jurisdiction might ultimately be destroyed if the state appellate court reverses the order of dismissal. In contrast, a voluntary dismissal demonstrates a plaintiff's permanent intention not to pursue the case against the non-diverse defendant. As a result, unlike an involuntary dismissal, a voluntary dismissal does not present a threat to continued diversity, and courts will generally permit removal.

Dismissal following settlement is clearly voluntary, rather than involuntary. Thus, removal is appropriate, and the motion to remand must be denied.

It is, therefore, ORDERED THAT plaintiff's motion for remand be, and the same hereby is denied.

Practice Problems

Practice Problem 4-8

Pat James (WV) attended Big Time Amusement Park, Inc. in Fairfax, Virginia. Big Time Amusement is incorporated in Delaware and its principle place of business is in Florida. This park was one of its many holdings. Pat slipped on the steps climbing to a ride because someone had spilled a slippery substance on the steps. Other patrons said the slippery substance had been on the steps for at least a half hour and one said she even told a Big Time representative about it. Pat broke his leg and a disc in his back.

---

[158] *See* American Car & Foundry v. Kettelhake, 236 U.S. 311 (1915) (holding that cases with non-diverse and diverse parties become removable only if the plaintiff voluntarily dismisses the non-diverse parties).
[159] 795 F. Supp. 223, 225 (E.D. Mich. 1992).

He sued, in a Virginia state court, both Big Time Amusement Park, Inc. and Sam Supervisor (VA) who was responsible for the ride in question. Is the case removable at this point? If its removability depends on something, what? Assume the case is removed and that Pat reaches a settlement with Sam, after which Sam is dismissed from the case voluntarily. Can Big Time Amusement, Inc. remove the case then? If so, what steps must Big Time Amusement, Inc. take to remove? When does the deadline for removal after Sam's dismissal begin?

5. State Court Dismisses Non-Diverse Defendant Within One Year of the Commencement of the Action

This scenario is unlike the voluntary dismissal of a non-diverse defendant by the plaintiff. Here, the state court dismisses the non-diverse defendant. In such situations, the case is not removable regardless of the timing of the dismissal. The reason has to do with the potential for a reversal of the state trial court's dismissal. If that were to occur and the defendant could remove the case to the federal system, the result would be a mess: the state appellate court would reverse and remand, thus holding that the diversity destroying defendant should have remained in the state court litigation but the case would have been taken to the federal system. To prevent such a result, the system prevents removal based on a state trial court's dismissal of a defendant.[160]

Practice Problems

The following Practice Problem further illustrates the difference in a defendant's ability to remove following an involuntary dismissal by a court versus a voluntary dismissal by the plaintiff.

Practice Problem 4-9

Paul Jones (VA) went to Water World in Virginia for a day of fun. However, while sliding on the largest of the slides, the slide broke at a turn when Paul slid into it at a high rate of speed. Paul is 6'5" and 300 pounds, but the slides are supposed to handle persons of all sizes. When the slide broke, Paul fell 30 feet to the ground and suffered a concussion, sprained neck, and broke both arms. Water World, Inc. is incorporated in Delaware and has its principal place of business in St. Louis, Missouri. Sam Smith, who had lived in Williamsburg, Virginia, in the same home his entire life, was the supervisor in charge of safety on the slide in question. Paul sued Water World and Sam in Virginia state court and claimed $500,000 in damages. Paul had good faith claims against both defendants and pursued discovery against both. Sam filed a motion to dismiss on the grounds that there is no evidence he failed in any duty owed to Paul. The court granted Sam's motion and dismissed him as a defendant less than a year after commencement of the action in state court. Water World immediately proceeded to remove the case to the U.S. district court covering the area of the state court in question—following all the steps set forth for removal—and Paul then timely moved to remand to state court. Should the case be remanded? Why or why not?

---

[160] See, *e.g.*, R. FREER, INTRODUCTION TO FEDERAL PROCEDURE § 4.8, at 221 (2006).

6. Defendant Shows That Amount in Controversy Alleged by Plaintiff Is
Inaccurate, Thus Exceeding the Amount in Controversy Threshold,
With No Question About Diverse Parties.

If a plaintiff files in state court against a defendant who is of diverse citizenship but alleges damages that are less than the amount in controversy threshold, the defendant can still remove a case in most circuits if the defendant can show, by a preponderance of the evidence, that the amount in controversy exceeds the threshold requirement of $75,000 exclusive of interest and costs.[161]

Courts recognize that requiring the defendant to prove that the amount in controversy exceeds the threshold is a greater burden than the plaintiff bears in satisfying the St. Paul Mercury test.[162] Courts reconcile the inconsistency on the basis that the plaintiff typically is permitted reign, within limits, to be the master of her claim and choose the forum.[163] These "limits" obviously are that, if complete diversity exists and the court is satisfied that there is more than $75,000 exclusive of interest and costs at issue, the plaintiff cannot preclude a defendant's removal.

The following Practice Problem addresses removal in a situation in which the parties are diverse and the plaintiff claims less than the required amount in controversy, but the defendant challenges the amount at issue in support of removal.

Practice Problem 4-10

Phil Plaintiff (North Dakota citizen) sues Dexter Defendant (South Dakota citizen) in North Dakota state court and alleges $74,000 in damages. Dexter's timely notice of removal attaches, along with the usual requirements of process, orders, and pleadings, medical records showing that Phil sustained serious injuries in the accident over which he is suing, that he has incurred substantial medical expenses, and that he will continue to incur such expenses that they will exceed $75,000 exclusive of interest and costs. In support of his statement that the amount in controversy exceeds $75,000 exclusive of interest and costs, Dexter attaches an affidavit of persons who attended to Phil who verify the severity of his injuries. Defendant also attaches an affidavit of a physician that opines injuries such as the Phil's require ongoing treatment and often result in expenses exceeding far more than $100,000. Assume you are the judge and Dexter has satisfied every other requirement for removal. How would you rule on the question of whether, at the time of removal, the amount in controversy has been shown by a preponderance of the evidence (or more likely than not) to be more than $75,000?

---

[161] *See* 14C CHARLES ALAN WRIGHT & ARTHUR R. MILLER, FEDERAL PRACTICE AND PROCEDURE § 3725.1 (4th ed. 2018); *see also* Barker v. Dollar General, 778 F. Supp. 2d 1267 (M.D. Ala. 2011) (granting motion to remand, reasoning that when a plaintiff specifies an amount of damages in her complaint, a removing defendant must prove to a legal certainty that plaintiff's claim exceeds the jurisdictional amount requirement, but here the retailer failed to prove to a legal certainty that customer's damages, arising from injuries sustained when bottles of detergent fell from store shelf and hit her on the head, necessarily exceeded $75,000, since plaintiff's denial of request for admission that damages did not exceed $75,000 does not prove to a legal certainty that damages do exceed that sum, and medical bills that she produced indicated damages of only $4,118).

[162] 14C CHARLES ALAN WRIGHT & ARTHUR R. MILLER, FEDERAL PRACTICE AND PROCEDURE § 3725.1 (4th ed. 2018);

[163] *See id.*

113

*7. Removal Is More than One Year After Commencement of the Action,
and District Court Finds that the Plaintiff Deliberately Failed to Disclose
the Actual Amount in Controversy.*

A variation on the defendant's showing that the actual amount in controversy exceeds $75,000 exclusive of interest and costs is set forth in 28 U.S.C. § 1446(c) (2) (B). That provision states:

> If the notice of removal is filed more than 1 year after commencement of the action and the district court finds that the plaintiff deliberately failed to disclose the actual amount in controversy to prevent removal, that finding shall be deemed bad faith.

Thus, if the plaintiff's complaint in state court seeks less than the amount in controversy, but later in discovery or through other means (*e.g.*, a settlement demand letter from plaintiff's counsel) defendant learns that the amount in controversy exceeds $75,000 exclusive of interest and costs, then the defendant has thirty days from receipt of the discovery response (or settlement demand) to remove the case based on this version of the "bad faith" exception.[164] However, if the information supplied after the complaint merely confirms what the defendant reasonably should have ascertained from the complaint, the exception will not apply.[165]

Practice Problem

Practice Problem 4-11
On January 10, 2017, Pierre Plaintiff (South Carolina citizen), a forklift operator whose foot was caught under the forklift filed suit in South Carolina state court. He sued Lifts, Inc., a company incorporated in New Jersey with its principal place of business in Newark, New Jersey, for $74,500 After a long lapse discovery began. In discovery Lifts receives on May 1, 2018, for the first-time discovery responses from the plaintiff showing that several toes and part of Pierre's foot were cut off and that the cost of anticipated surgery, rehabilitation, and future treatment would likely exceed $500,000. Can Lift remove the case? Why or why not?

E. Move and Countermove: How the Plaintiff Can Move to Remand Back to State Court

As noted throughout this chapter, removal has many requirements that the defendant must satisfy or risk having the case remanded. The motion to remand can be based on an apparently minor defect, but if something is required by the removal statutes that is not satisfied, remand is possible. The characterization as "possible" is important because the plaintiff must, for all but limited

Grounds move for the remand within 30 days of receiving the notice of removal. Otherwise, the plaintiff will have been deemed to have waived the defect and the case will stay in federal court. Thus, not

---

[164] *See* 14A CHARLES ALAN WRIGHT & ARTHUR R. MILLER, FEDERAL PRACTICE AND PROCEDURE § 3725.1 (4th ed. 2018).
[165] *See id.*

only defendants but also plaintiffs must be well-versed in the requirements of removing a case. Only in this way can the plaintiff determine whether something has not been done that should have been and bring a timely motion to remand.

1. Determining the Defect at Issue

The deadline for a motion for remand will depend on whether the defect is a failure to follow the requirements of the removal statutes—a basis "other than subject matter jurisdiction." If the district court lacks subject matter jurisdiction, the motion to remand can be made at any time. What language in 28 U.S.C. § 1447 supports these statements?

In *Zerafa v. Montefiore Hospital Housing Company, Incorporated*, [166] the court held that the plaintiff waived a defect in removal by failing to timely make a motion to remand the case. Ironically, the basis of the plaintiff's motion was that removal was not timely:

The action against Louisville commenced on February 27, 2004. The one-year time period for removal of the case to federal court began to run on that date. The petition to remove was not filed until March 9, 2005, past the one-year removal deadline. After the case was removed plaintiff had 30 days to remand the case. Plaintiff sought remand on May 4, 2005, after the 30-day time limit had expired. This delay constitutes a waiver of the defect in removal procedure.

Practice Problems

Practice Problem 4-12
Review again Practice Problem 4-4 and Practice Problem 4-5. If the plaintiff files a motion to remand in federal court within 30 days of the notice of removal, pointing out the defects in the defendant's removal, how should the court rule? If, on the other hand, plaintiff files her motion to remand, pointing out the same defects in removal, 31 days after the notice of removal, how should the court rule? Is the difference in the outcomes of these scenarios fair?

Practice Problem 4-13
The Daily Times, Inc. printed a story referring to Hal Heckler, who is a local political activist, as a drug addict. Hal is a citizen of the same state in which the Daily Times is incorporated and has its principal place of business. When Hal's employer reads in the paper that Hal is a drug addict, Hal is fired from his job. Hal in fact is not a drug addict and sues the Daily Times for libel. The Daily Times has no basis for its claims of drug addiction other than the observations of a reporter that Hal seems to act like a drug addict when he's at political events. Libel requires a defamatory statement to be printed, communicated to others, and have the communication injure the subject of the defamation. The Daily Times, Inc. removes the case within 30 days of being served, asserting in its notice of removal that the case raises serious First Amendment questions that the federal court must resolve. Hal moves to remand 40 days after the notice of removal on the grounds that the U.S. district court lacks subject matter jurisdiction.

---

[166] 403 F. Supp. 2d 320 (S.D.N.Y. 2005).

CHAPTER 5: CHOOSING THE FORUM: PERSONAL JURISDICTION

I. How the Topics in this Chapter Fit in the Overall Progress of a Civil Action

Below is a diagram of the stages of a civil action showing in bold where the topic in this chapter falls in the progress of a case:

Figure 5-1

Cause of Action (events leading to suit)	Pre-Filing Tasks (items to begin representation, interviewing, and related matters)	**Choice of Forum** (subject matter jurisdiction, removal, **personal jurisdiction,** and venue)	Notice and Service of Process (completing the process of ensuring the forum court can enter a valid judgment)	Pleading the Case and Joinder of Claims and Parties (including supplemental jurisdiction)

Responding to Claims by Motion or by Answer	Discovery (developing proof to establish claims and learn your adversary's case)	Right to Jury (pretrial motions and practice)	Final Pretrial Conference (events within last month before trial)	Trial (procedures and motions during trial)	Verdict	Post-Trial Motions (motions for a new trial and/or judgment as a matter of law)	Appeal

You have determined whether the case in question fits within the limited categories of types of cases that can be brought in federal court. Questions about the kind of case a court can hear deal with subject matter jurisdiction—i.e., whether it is the type of subject matter the court is authorized to hear. Aside from lacking subject matter jurisdiction, a court's ability to enter judgment against parties also depends on whether that court has personal jurisdiction over the defendant. The question of *personal jurisdiction* is more specific to the state in which suit is brought—and to the court in that state—in which the suit was brought and to the nonresident defendant has been sued. The court in which suit is brought is known as the "forum" court. We focus here on the court and the defendant's contacts with the state in which the court is located. If there are enough contacts, the defendant can be subjected to the court's power without violating the Constitution's Due Process Clause. However, if there are no contacts or attenuated contacts, the court will not have the power to hear a case, even if subject matter jurisdiction exists, due to the nonresident defendant's lack of connections to the state. Of course, the defendant could be sued in some other state. However, that begs the question with which we will be presented repeatedly in this chapter: Can the defendant be subjected to personal jurisdiction consistent with due process principles in the forum the plaintiff has chosen?

II. The Law of Personal Jurisdiction

When a plaintiff submits a dispute to a court, she is asking the government to help resolve her dispute. Courts are part of the government and thus have limits on their power. A court's seeking to exercise power over a nonresident defendant often triggers challenge to the court's ability to exercise personal jurisdiction. The question is substantial. A court's judgment will be void if the court lacks personal jurisdiction that comports with due process. And, even then, the analysis is complicated by the requirement that, before satisfying the due process requirements, the plaintiff needs to show that the state's long arm statute—a statute enabling courts in the state (state or federal) to exercise jurisdiction over nonresidents—has been satisfied. Whether a court can exercise power over the nonresident under the state's long arm statute, and independently under a ground that satisfies principles of due process, represent threshold questions that must be answered. Any defense counsel should, if there is doubt of satisfaction of the statute or due process, challenge court's ability to proceed.

The analysis, as suggested, will follow a pattern. First, does a state long-arm statute authorize the exercise of personal jurisdiction over the suit? If the answer to this question is "no," the analysis must stop there. A court cannot exercise personal jurisdiction if the state statute authorizing jurisdiction over nonresidents itself has not been satisfied. If the answer is "yes," that the state statute authorizing jurisdiction over nonresidents has been satisfied, the inquiry continues. The forum court's exercise of jurisdiction over nonresidents must be consistent with the Due Process Clause of the Constitution. In other words, the requirements for establishing personal jurisdiction over a nonresident are conjunctive. The plaintiff must show that both (1) the forum state's long-arm statute authorizes jurisdiction and (2) the exercise of personal jurisdiction is consistent with the Due Process Clause.

The following sections will first address state long-arm statutes and then proceed with the due process analysis. Unless both requirements are met, personal jurisdiction will not exist. Traditionally, lawyers and judges analyze the long-arm requirement first because if it does not support jurisdiction, there is no need to analyze due process.

A. Statutory (Long-Arm) Analysis

As explained at the outset, analyses of personal jurisdiction should begin with the simple question of whether the statute of the state in which the suit is brought authorizes the exercise of jurisdiction over a nonresident. Long-arm statutes fall into three categories. The first type of long arm statutes, the traditional "to-the-limits-of-due-process statute," authorizes state courts to exercise jurisdiction to the full extent permitted by the Due Process Clause.[167] The second type of long-arm statute is a variation of the "to-the-limits-of-due-process statutes." This type of statute includes two parts. First, it enumerates various categories of conduct that will subject the nonresident to personal jurisdiction. Second, it then adds a catch-all provision that permits exercise of personal jurisdiction for any other conduct that would reach to the limits of the Due Process Clause. Effectively, these statutes operate in the same fashion as the first category because they allow any conduct, even if not enumerated, to satisfy the long-arm statute so long as it satisfies the Due Process Clause. The third category of statutes are true "enumerated long-arm statutes." These statutes permit state courts to exercise jurisdiction over a nonresident if certain criteria enumerated in the

---

[167] *See, e.g.*, CAL. CIV. PRO. CODE § 410.10 (West 2018) ("A court of this state may exercise jurisdiction on any basis not inconsistent with the Constitution of this state or of the United States.").

117

statute are met. They do not, however, have the catch-all "to-the-limits-of-due-process" provision that statutes in the second category contain. Common provisions in enumerated long-arm statutes include conducting business in the forum state, committing a tortious injury in the forum, owning property in the forum, and other similar contacts with the forum.[168]

Exercise to Synthesize the Topics in this Chapter

What is the first part of the personal jurisdiction analytical framework? How would you express this issue if you use a flow chart? How would you do so if you state this issue in outline fashion?

B. Constitutional (Due Process) Analysis

Even if the plaintiff satisfies a state's long-arm statute, she also must satisfy the United States Constitution. The reason is simple: even if a long-arm statute authorizes the exercise of personal jurisdiction, such exercise may infringe upon due process principles. Therefore, you must also ask whether the exercise of jurisdiction over a nonresident of a state comports with the Due Process Clause of the Constitution.

C. Threshold Questions

Most due process analyses require you to engage in the minimum contacts test of *International Shoe Co. v. Washington*,[169] and its progeny, which will be addressed in detail later in this chapter. However, before performing the minimum contacts analysis, certain threshold inquiries should be addressed. The constitutional analysis based on International Shoe requires an analysis of both the defendant's connections with a state and whether the suit arises from those connections. If one of the discrete grounds addressed in these threshold questions support personal jurisdiction, a more in-depth analysis is not necessary. These grounds, which tend to be historically based or confined in scope, can quickly solve the issue of personal jurisdiction if they apply. Therefore, the astute lawyer will ask a few simple questions before launching into a more elaborate analysis. If analyzing these threshold questions becomes a habit, the lawyer may find that personal jurisdiction exists on the simpler basis that these doctrines recognize. However, if the lawyer does not make it a habit to check these points first, they can be overlooked, resulting in much time, work, and money being lost in the process.

1. Consent to Jurisdiction

An important threshold question is whether the defendant has consented to jurisdiction. A defendant may consent to jurisdiction either expressly or impliedly.

2. Express (Contractual) Consent

A defendant expressly consents to a forum's exercise of personal jurisdiction when it enters into a contract in which the defendant consents to litigation in the forum through a "forum selection" clause. For

---

[168] *See* 4 CHARLES ALAN WRIGHT & ARTHUR R. MILLER, FEDERAL PRACTICE AND PROCEDURE § 1068 (4th ed. 2018).
[169] 326 U.S. 310 (1945).

example, in *Carnival Cruise Lines, Inc. v. Shute*,[170] the plaintiff, Mrs. Shute, was injured while a passenger traveling aboard a Carnival Cruise ship and sued the cruise line for negligence of the cruise line and its employees. The tickets issued to the Shutes by Carnival Cruise Lines, Inc., contained a forum selection clause that required any action against the cruise line to take place in Florida.[171] The clause specifically stated:

Terms and Conditions of Passage Contract Ticket

. . .

(a) The acceptance of this ticket by the person or persons named hereon as passengers shall be deemed to be an acceptance and agreement by each of them of all of the terms and conditions of this Passage Contract Ticket.

. . .

8. It is agreed by and between the passenger and the Carrier that all disputes and matters whatsoever arising under, in connection with or incident to this Contract shall be litigated, if at all, in and before a Court located in the State of Florida, U. S. A., to the exclusion of the Courts of any other state or country."[172]

The Supreme Court upheld the arbitration clause, finding that the Shutes had expressly consented to the clause when they purchased the tickets.[173] In determining whether the forum selection clause comported with basic principles of fundamental fairness, the Court noted:

In this case, there is no indication that petitioner set Florida as the forum in which disputes were to be resolved as a means of discouraging cruise passengers from pursuing legitimate claims. Any suggestion of such a bad-faith motive is belied by two facts: Petitioner has its principal place of business in Florida, and many of its cruises depart from and return to Florida ports. Similarly, there is no evidence that petitioner obtained respondents' accession to the forum clause by fraud or overreaching. Finally, respondents have conceded that they were given notice of the forum provision and, therefore, presumably retained the option of rejecting the contract with impunity.[174]

The *Carnival Cruise Lines* case illustrates express consent through a contractual provision. One must be careful to distinguish a choice-of-forum clause and a choice-of-law clause in a contract. The *Carnival Cruise Lines* case involved a choice-of-forum clause—i.e., a provision in which the parties agreed that any disputes that arose from the contract would be resolved in a specific state (Florida, in that contract). Often confused with choice-of-forum clauses are choice-of-law clauses. Following is an example of a choice-of-law clause:

---

[170] 499 U.S. 585 (1991).
[171] *Id.* at 587–88.
[172] Carnival Cruise Lines, Inc. v. Shute, 499 U.S. 585, 587–88 (1991).
[173] *Id.* at 593.
[174] *Id.* at 595.

The parties hereby agree that, in any case filed to resolve a dispute under this contract, the law of the State of Florida shall be applied by the court.

If the contract in Carnival Cruise Lines had only a choice-of-law clause, not a choice-of-forum clause, and the plaintiff sued the Cruise Line in, say California (where she boarded the ship), the question of whether the suit could be heard in California would be an open one in which the trial court would consider the defendant's contacts with the state. If the court decided it had personal jurisdiction over Carnival Cruise Lines, the choice of law clause would dictate only that the law of Florida would govern the claims in the case, even though the case was being litigated in California. In other words, a choice-of-law clause does not commit the parties to litigating a case in a forum in the same way that a choice of forum clause does.

3. Consent by Appointment of a Registered Agent?

It is doubtful that a corporation can consent to jurisdiction in a forum by appointing a registered agent for purposes of accepting service of process. The United States Court of Appeals for the Eighth Circuit held in *Knowlton v. Allied Van Lines, Inc.*,[175] that appointment of a registered agent for receipt of service constituted consent to personal jurisdiction. Most circuits that have addressed the issue, however, have held that appointing a registered agent in the forum does not provide a basis for personal jurisdiction.[176] Now twenty-five years old, the Eighth Circuit's decision in *Knowlton* has not been followed and has been the subject of frequent criticism. Most cases rejecting a finding of consent by a corporation's appointment of a registered agent typically observe at least two things. First, these decisions note that when a state requires a corporation to appoint a registered agent to do business there, it undercuts the idea of true consent. Second, the decisions resist the notion that a corporation could consent to any kind of case in a state before the claim arises. They observe that it is dubious to subject a corporation to personal jurisdiction in a state based on forced appointment of a registered agent, particularly when a minimum contacts analysis often would result in the conclusion that the corporation lacked sufficient minimum contacts with the state to make it foreseeable it could be sued over the claim at issue.[177] Thus, the better view is that appointment of a registered agent in a state does not establish consent.

4. Implied Consent by Actively Litigating.

Implied consent can arise when the defendant actively engages in litigation in the forum, despite raising personal jurisdiction as a defense.

CONTINENTAL BANK, N.A. v. MEYER
United States Court of Appeals for the Seventh Circuit, 1993
10 F.3d 1293

FAIRCHILD, Senior Circuit Judge:

In 1984, Continental Bank lent funds to Andrew C. Meyer, Jr., Donald M. Lubin and Philip J.

---

[175] 900 F.2d 1196 (8th Cir. 1990).

[176] *See, e.g.*, Siemer v. Learjet Acquisition Corp., 966 F.2d 179 (5th Cir. 1992); Ratliff v. Cooper Labs, Inc., 444 F.2d 745, 748 (4th Cir. 1971) ("[T]he application to do business and the appointment of an agent for service to fulfill a state law requirement is of no special weight . . . ."); Seymour v. Parke, Davis & Co., 423 F.2d 584 (1st Cir. 1970).

[177] *See, e.g.*, Tonya J. Monestier, *Registration Statutes, General Jurisdiction, and the Fallacy of Consent*, 36 CARDOZO L. REV. 1343 (April 2015).

Crowe, Jr. to invest in a horse-breeding limited partnership. In 1980, the bank sued each of these individuals to recover on the unpaid renewal notes. In July 1989, the actions were consolidated and the bank filed an amended consolidated complaint against all defendants. The defendants filed an answer including several affirmative defenses. The district court struck all the defenses but gave leave to amend the defense based on fraud. The defendants amended that defense and added another ("aiding a fraud") and a two-count counterclaim. The court dismissed the counterclaim and struck the affirmative defenses. The bank moved for summary judgment, and the defendants responded solely by challenging personal jurisdiction. The court found the defendants' active participation in the litigation for two-and-a-half years constituted a waiver of the personal jurisdiction defense and granted summary judgment.

. . .

On appeal, we address whether the district court properly struck the defendants most recent affirmative defenses and dismissed the counterclaims. We draw on defendants' pleading for the facts.

The three defendants were partners in a law firm in Massachusetts. They invested in and became limited partners in Sunrise Farm Breeding Partnership No. 3, operating in Illinois. The general partners were Charles Schmidt and Edward Zurek. The bank had financed two similar partnerships, Sunrise No. 1 and No. 2. Lubin and Meyer had invested in No. 2. The purpose of the partnership was "to breed world class and champion thoroughbred stallions to proven stakes broodmares with internationally recognized pedigrees so as to breed world class thoroughbred yearlings which would be sold at a profit."

Defendants' pleading is not very specific as to what happened. We gather that each defendant borrowed $200,000 from the bank and invested that amount. The breeding program is said to have "failed." It seems reasonable to assume that defendants claim they received no profits and their interests became valueless because in their counterclaim they seek to recover the part of the loans they had repaid, and their affirmative defenses sought to prevent the bank recovering the unpaid balances. Their allegations of information the bank failed to reveal suggests a claim that the failure was caused by Schmidt's selling to the partnership stallion breeding seasons which he owned for excessive fees and without arm's length negotiation. Other allegations suggest that the mares were not of good quality or value.

The claim of fraud includes alleged oral representations by a bank officer and failure to inform defendants of other facts, including untruths in a Private Placement Memorandum prepared by the General Partners, and approved by the bank officer and attorney. The representations were made before the defendants borrowed the money or the partnership began to operate.

. . .

The district court concluded that the defendants had failed to allege that the bank made any false statements of fact, as required for fraud under Illinois law. Instead, the court determined that the bank's representations were only opinions. The district court further decided that the defendants had not pled scienter with the required specificity. The district court also found that the defendants had failed adequately to plead loss causation. For these reasons, the court struck the defendants' fraud defense and dismissed the fraud count of the counterclaim.

In the second affirmative defense and second count of the counterclaim, defendants alleged that the bank assisted Schmidt and Zurek in their scheme to defraud defendants and other limited partners. The bank's motive allegedly was to help Schmidt and Zurek repay their own debts to the bank. They alleged

121

that Zurek orally made misrepresentations to defendants concerning the structuring of the partnership and the quality of the horses and made representations in the Private Placement Memorandum somewhat similar to the representations already referred to. The bank people allegedly knew of the representations and omissions, and knew they were false or had been made with reckless disregard of their truth. It was alleged that the bank assisted Schmidt and Zurek in perpetrating the fraud by "endorsing" Sunrise No. 3, confirming that Zurek's statements were correct, and failing to give information omitted by Schmidt and Zurek.

The district court struck the second affirmative defense and dismissed the second count of the counter-claim. The district judge's first reason was that they were not timely filed, noting defendants' admission that the "aiding a fraud" theory is "simply a new legal theory which arises out of the same facts of which Plaintiff [sic] has always been aware." She also concluded that defendants did not sufficiently allege that the bank benefitted from the fraud.

The bank then moved for summary judgment, and the defendants raised only their claim of lack of personal jurisdiction. This defense had been pled in the defendants' answer but had not been raised since that time. The court found that the defendants had waived the personal jurisdiction defense by extensively participating in litigation of the merits for two-and-a-half years before affirmatively pressing the challenge to personal jurisdiction.

. . .

The defendants contend that the district court erred in finding that they had waived their objection to personal jurisdiction. The district court held that although the defendants pled lack of jurisdiction in their answer, they had waived the defense by extensive participation in the merits of the lawsuit without raising the defense affirmatively.

Federal Rule of Civil Procedure 12(h) (1) provides that "[a] defense of lack of jurisdiction over the person . . . is waived . . . if it is neither made by motion under this rule nor included in a responsive pleading or an amendment thereof permitted by Rule 15(a) to be made as a matter of course." The defendants did raise the defense in their answer, and therefore the waiver provided for by Rule 12(h) did not occur. However, the privileged defenses referred to in Rule 12(h) (1) "may be waived by 'formal submission in a cause, or by submission through conduct.'" Indeed, "[a] party need not actually file an answer or motion before waiver is found."

Here, the defendants fully participated in litigation of the merits for over two-and-a-half years without actively contesting personal jurisdiction. They participated in lengthy discovery, filed various motions and opposed a number of motions filed by the bank. While the defendants literally complied with Rule 12(h), "they did not comply with the spirit of the rule, which is 'to expedite and simplify proceedings in the Federal Courts.'" The district court could properly conclude that the defendants' delay in urging this threshold issue manifests an intent to submit to the court's jurisdiction.

. . .

Accordingly, we AFFIRM.

5. Implied Consent: Failing to Raise Personal Jurisdiction Defense

At times, a defendant may simply fail to raise personal jurisdiction as a timely defense. For a complete discussion of the variety of ways in which a party can waive personal jurisdiction as a defense, see the discussion of waiver of personal jurisdiction under Federal Rule of Civil Procedure 11 below (pp. 324-34).

Exercises to Synthesize the Topics in This Chapter

You have now worked through the initial questions in a due process analysis. Why does it make sense to ask the above questions early in the analysis?

Is the due process analysis parallel to the long-arm analysis? In other words, if you had to satisfy both the state long-arm statute and the due process analysis, how would you show that in a flow chart or outline form?

D. Point of Divergence: Section of Due Process Analysis that Varies Depending on Whether the Defendant Is an Individual or a Corporation

To have reached this stage of the personal jurisdiction analysis, a litigator must have concluded that the long-arm statute is satisfied and that the defendant has not expressly or impliedly consented to jurisdiction. At this stage of the analysis, the type of defendant—whether, on one hand, an individual or, on the other, a corporation—influences the questions one asks. In other words, some of the "easy" ways to establish personal jurisdiction over an individual do not apply to a corporation. By contrast, the easiest way to gain personal jurisdiction over a corporation does not apply to individuals. Thus, the questions below are focused specifically on, first, individual defendants and, then, on corporations.

1. Personal Jurisdiction over an Individual Defendant

Assume the plaintiff's claim does not arise from an individual's jurisdictional connections to a state. The plaintiff is seeking to sue an individual defendant in the forum anyway. The plaintiff has two options. First, the plaintiff can seek to have the forum state's court invoke personal jurisdiction based on the individual's domicile status in a forum. Second, the plaintiff can rely on "transient jurisdiction," the term for obtaining service of the individual while within the territorial boundaries of the forum while the action is pending. It bears repeating that, if the plaintiff can establish personal jurisdiction over an individual based on either of these concepts, she has achieved the litigation equivalent of a lottery jackpot. The claim could have arisen a thousand miles away and have nothing to do with the forum. But if the plaintiff shows the defendant individual is domiciled in the state where suit is filed, or if the plaintiff serves the defendant individual within the boundaries of the state, the court will automatically have personal jurisdiction over the defendant.

a. Individual's Domicile in the Forum

An individual has long been subject to personal jurisdiction in courts of the state in which she is domiciled. A plaintiff may sue an individual defendant in the state in which she is domiciled for events that occurred outside the state.[178] The rationale here seems to be two-fold. First, if one is domiciled in a state,

---

[178] *See, e.g.*, Milliken v. Meyer, 311 U.S. 457 (1940).

she must have a reasonably strong connection to that state. Second, this jurisdictional basis assures a plaintiff that she can—if in no other state in the Union—sue an individual in at least one state.

Practice Problem

The following Practice Problem illustrates how an individual's domicile ensures that a plaintiff will be able to sue an individual in at least one state in which the plaintiff can be assured of getting personal jurisdiction, regardless of where the accident occurred.

Practice Problem 5-1

Wally Wildcatter had a home in Texas where he had been born and lived with his wife, Wanda Wildcatter. Wally and Wanda decided to drive to North Dakota and dig for oil wells on properties of landowners that would let them. On the way, Wally and Wanda had a car accident with Garth Broke in Oklahoma. Wanda and Wally spent the next couple of years in North Dakota searching for oil wells, staying in extended stay motels, sleeping at campgrounds, etc. They still maintained their home in Texas and intended to return there. Garth sued them in a U.S. district court in Texas, within the applicable statute of limitations. Would the court have personal jurisdiction over Wally and Wanda?

---

b. Service on an Individual Within State
Boundaries of the Forum (Transient Jurisdiction)

Although the question was not definitively answered when it came before the Supreme Court in *Burnham v. Superior Court*,[179] at least four justices concluded that "transient jurisdiction" may be established over an individual defendant when she is served within a state's territorial boundaries while the action is pending. According to Justice Scalia's opinion in Burnham, the length of time the defendant is within the forum's boundaries is irrelevant, as is the "reason" the defendant is within the forum's boundaries. The Court held that service on an individual within a state's boundaries has always passed constitutional muster.[180] Thus, by definition, Justice Scalia and the three justices who joined him concluded that "[t]he short of the matter is that jurisdiction based on physical presence alone constitutes due process because it is one of the continuing traditions of our legal system that define the due process standard of 'traditional notions of fair play and substantial justice.'"[181] However, Justice Scalia was careful to distinguish service on an individual defendant and service on a corporate officer within a state's boundaries, and refused to consider it as having the same effect as in-state service on an individual.[182]

2. Personal Jurisdiction over Corporation via General Jurisdiction

The doctrine of general jurisdiction is a means by which a plaintiff can obtain personal jurisdiction in a forum over a corporation if the forum state is the corporation's "home" state. If the plaintiff can establish general jurisdiction, she can sue the plaintiff in that forum regardless of whether the claim on which she is suing the corporation arose in that state. Indeed, the claim does not have to arise from any connection to the state of the forum court. The notion here is that, if general jurisdiction over the corporation

---

[179] 405 U.S. 604 (1990).
[180] *Id.* at 610–20.
[181] *Id.* at 619.
[182] *Id.* at 610, n.1.

in a state exists, the corporation can be sued for any claim, regardless of where it arose. Thus, it has the same effect as a plaintiff suing an individual in the state of the individual's domicile or if the individual is served in the forum. However, the analysis for general jurisdiction is different. An individual's "domicile" is analogous to a state in which a corporation is subject to general jurisdiction. The key, of course, is what criteria will determine whether a corporation is considered subject to general jurisdiction in a forum.

The genesis of general jurisdiction is *Perkins v. Benguet Consol. Mining Company*.[183] In Perkins, a company in the Philippines relocated to Ohio during World War II. The company's president, general manager, and primary shareholder opened a bank account and set up an office in Ohio. The Supreme Court upheld general jurisdiction over the company in Ohio for a claim arising from events in the Philippines.[184] The key to the Court's decision was that the company's principal place of business was in Ohio.[185]

Most observers assumed that, considering *Perkins*, a plaintiff could obtain general jurisdiction over a corporation not only in the state of its principal place of business, but also in its state of incorporation. For many years, lawyers and jurists believed general jurisdiction over a corporation could also exist if the corporation had extensive and substantial business operations and contacts in a state, even if that state was not its principal place of business or state of incorporation. The Supreme Court's most recent opinion on the subject suggests that, except in exceptional circumstances, general jurisdiction will apply solely to states in which the defendant corporation is "at home"—either incorporated in the state or with its principal place of business there. If the forum is not in a state in which the defendant corporation is "at home," the Court suggests that general jurisdiction will not apply—and that the more elaborate analysis of International Shoe will govern whether the corporation is subject to personal jurisdiction in the forum.

Following is one of the Supreme Court's most recent decisions on general jurisdiction over a corporate defendant:

BNSF RAILWAY CO. v. TYRRELL
Supreme Court of the United States, 2017
137 S. Ct. 810

JUSTICE GINSBURG delivered the opinion of the Court.

The two cases we decide today arise under the Federal Employers' Liability Act (FELA),[186] which makes railroads liable in money damages to their employees for on-the-job injuries. Both suits were pursued in Montana state courts although the injured workers did not reside in Montana, nor were they injured there. The defendant railroad, BNSF Railway Company (BNSF), although "doing business" in Montana when the litigation commenced, was not incorporated in Montana, nor did it maintain its principal place of business in that State.

. . .

I

In March 2011, respondent Robert Nelson, a North Dakota resident, brought a FELA suit against BNSF in a Montana state court to recover damages for knee injuries Nelson allegedly sustained while

---

[183] 342 U.S. 437 (1952).
[184] *Id.* at 438.
[185] *Id.* at 446–47.
[186] 35 Stat. 65, as amended, 45 U. S. C. §51 et seq.

working for BNSF as a fuel-truck driver. In May 2014, respondent Kelli Tyrrell, appointed in South Dakota as the administrator of her husband Brent Tyrrell's estate, similarly sued BNSF under FELA in a Montana state court. Brent Tyrrell, his widow alleged, had developed a fatal kidney cancer from his exposure to carcinogenic chemicals while working for BNSF. Neither plaintiff alleged injuries arising from or related to work performed in Montana; indeed, neither Nelson nor Brent Tyrrell appears ever to have worked for BNSF in Montana.

BNSF is incorporated in Delaware and has its principal place of business in Texas. It operates railroad lines in 28 States. BNSF has 2,061 miles of railroad track in Montana (about 6% of its total track mileage of 32,500), employs some 2,100 workers there (less than 5% of its total work force of 43,000), generates less than 10% of its total revenue in the State, and maintains only one of its 24 automotive facilities in Montana (4%). Contending that it is not "at home" in Montana, as required for the exercise of general personal jurisdiction under *Daimler AG v. Bauman*,[187] BNSF moved to dismiss both suits for lack of personal jurisdiction. [The Montana Supreme Court held that there was personal jurisdiction in Montana.]

. . .

III

We therefore inquire whether the Montana courts' exercise of personal jurisdiction . . . comports with the Due Process Clause of the Fourteenth Amendment. In International Shoe, this Court explained that a state court may exercise personal jurisdiction over an out-of-state defendant who has "certain minimum contacts with [the State] such that the maintenance of the suit does not offend 'traditional notions of fair play and substantial justice.'" Elaborating on this guide, we have distinguished between specific or case-linked jurisdiction and general or all-purpose jurisdiction.[188]

. . .

Because neither Nelson nor Tyrrell alleges any injury from work in or related to Montana, only the propriety of general jurisdiction is at issue here.

Goodyear and Daimler clarified that "[a] court may assert general jurisdiction over foreign (sister-state or foreign-country) corporations to hear any and all claims against them when their affiliations with the State are so 'continuous and systematic' as to render them essentially at home in the forum State."[189] The "paradigm" forums in which a corporate defendant is "at home," we explained, are the corporation's place of incorporation and its principal place of business. The exercise of general jurisdiction is not limited to these forums; in an "exceptional case," a corporate defendant's operations in another forum "may be so substantial and of such a nature as to render the corporation at home in that State."[190]

. . .

BNSF, we repeat, is not incorporated in Montana and does not maintain its principal place of

---

[187] 571 U.S. 117 (2014).

[188] *See, e.g., Daimler*, 571 U.S. at 119. Goodyear Dunlop Tires Operations, S.A. v. Brown, 564 U. S. 915, 919 (2011).

[189] *Daimler*, 571 U.S. at 127 (quoting *Goodyear*, 564 U.S. at 919).

[190] *Daimler*, 571 U.S. at 139, n.19. We suggested that *Perkins v. Benguet Consolidated Mining Company*, 342 U. S. 437 (1952), exemplified such a case. *Daimler*, 571 U. S., at n.19 (slip op., at 20, n.19).

business there. Nor is BNSF so heavily engaged in activity in Montana "as to render [it] essentially at home" in that State. As earlier noted, BNSF has over 2,000 miles of railroad track and more than 2,000 employees in Montana. But, as we observed in Daimler, "the general jurisdiction inquiry does not focus solely on the magnitude of the defendant's in-state contacts." Rather, the inquiry "calls for an appraisal of a corporation's activities in their entirety"; "[a] corporation that operates in many places can scarcely be deemed at home in all of them." In short, the business BNSF does in Montana is sufficient to subject the railroad to specific personal jurisdiction in that State on claims related to the business it does in Montana. But instate business, we clarified in Daimler and Goodyear, does not suffice to permit the assertion of general jurisdiction over claims like Nelson's and Tyrrell's that are unrelated to any activity occurring in Montana.

. . .

For the reasons stated, the judgment of the Montana Supreme Court is reversed, and the cases are remanded

It is so ordered.

Follow-Up Questions and Comments

1. Most observers would agree that courts have always been reluctant to exercise general jurisdiction beyond clear bases such as a corporation's principal place of business and state of incorporation. A leading commentator observes that the "reluctance to exercise general jurisdiction over nonresident corporations has only increased in the wake of the Supreme Court's *Goodyear*[191] and *Daimler*[192] decisions."[193] Decided in the 2017 term, the Court's decision in *BNSF* appears to continue that trend.

2. We addressed above whether service on a registered agent operates as consent by the corporation who appointed the agent as a condition of doing business in the forum. The conclusion was that, though some authority supports otherwise, finding consent on this basis is difficult. Other courts have approached service on a registered agent as a question of whether the defendant is subject to general jurisdiction by having an agent appointed in the forum for receiving lawsuits. Courts disagree over whether service on an agent can establish general jurisdiction.[194] If such a registered agent is not in the state in which the corporation is incorporated or has its principal place of business, Daimler raises serious questions about whether general jurisdiction could be found based on appointment of a registered agent in a state.

3. Prior to *Daimler*, courts have held corporations subject to general jurisdiction in states other than their principal place of business and state of incorporation based on business and operations that likely could not be sustained now.[195] Generally, courts have been unwilling to allow the Internet

---

[191] *Goodyear Dunlop Tires Operations, S.A. v. Brown*, 564 U.S. 915 (2011).

[192] *Daimler AG v. Bauman*, 571 U.S. 117 (2014).

[193] RICHARD C. CASAD & WILLIAM M. RICHMAN, MOORE'S FEDERAL PRACTICE AND PROCEDURE § 108.41, at 10 (2018).

[194] *See id.* at 11–12.

[195] See *id.* at 10–11, n.1 (collecting and summarizing cases that found general jurisdiction over corporations in situations showing "lesser involvement" with states than Goodyear and Daimler suggest is necessary).

to create a basis for general jurisdiction.[196]

Practice Problems

The following Practice Problems should help determine when general jurisdiction over a corporate defendant is likely to apply and when it is not likely to apply.

Practice Problem 5-2

Jeri Signfuld, who lived in New Jersey, bought lunch at the Soup Kitchen Inc.'s New Jersey restaurant, the second in a budding chain of restaurants incorporated in and with its principal place of business in New York. Signfuld, who is severely allergic to shellfish, developed a severe allergic reaction from which he took several weeks to recover after he ate one spoonful of the crab bisque rather than the turkey chili he ordered. Signfuld sued Soup Kitchen, Inc. in a U.S. district court in New York. Does the court have general jurisdiction over Soup Kitchen, Inc.?

Practice Problem 5-3

Mordor, Inc. is incorporated in Delaware with its principal place of business in Las Vegas, Nevada. Having mastered the process of converting molten lava into transferable energy, the company supplies energy throughout the United States. It has factories (approximately two acres in size, but on twenty-acre sites with fences keeping unauthorized persons out) in each state, including New Mexico. These factories are designed to house the lava and transfer its heat into energy by which electricity is transferred to businesses and homes. Mordor also has salespersons who visit businesses to promote the use of its power supply over other alternatives. Bill Boggins has an accident with Sam Saron, one of Mordor's salespersons, in Ohio. Having been on vacation at the time from his home in Arizona, Bill decided to sue Mordor for his serious injuries in a U.S. District Court in Nevada. Does the court have general jurisdiction over Mordor, Inc.? Under recent Supreme Court precedent, if Bill instead sued Mordor in New Mexico over the accident in Ohio, would he be able to establish general jurisdiction?

Practice Problem 5-4

GrassEatnGoats, Inc. ("GEG"), incorporated two years ago in Georgia, with its principal place of business in Macon, Georgia, is a company that rents goats to those who wish to have their grass or pastures "cut" naturally. Part of the year GEG goes to states adjoining Georgia and rents the goats to small farms for two-month intervals. The goats had been at a farm rented in Alabama for a few months, where the goats were routinely out "mowing" yards and fields. Their time in Alabama over, they were heading to Tennessee when the trailer carrying them was involved in an accident just over the border in Tennessee with Bob Boxer. Bob, who lived in Alabama, sues GEG for the negligent operation of the truck and trailer by its employee resulting in injuries to him in federal court in Alabama. Does the court have general jurisdiction over GEG?

---

[196] *See, e.g.*, Tamburo v. Dworkin, 601 F.3d 693, 701 (7th Cir. 2010) ("Nor is the maintenance of a public Internet website sufficient, without more, to establish general jurisdiction."); Bird v. Parsons, 289 F.3d 865, 874 (6th Cir. 2002) (holding that defendants' operation of a website with nationwide access did not confer general jurisdiction); Revell v. Lidov, 317 F.3d 467, 471 (5th Cir. 2002) ("Though the maintenance of a website is, in a sense, a continuous presence everywhere in the world, the cited contacts . . . are not in any way 'substantial.'"); GTE New Media Servs. v. BellSouth Corp., 199 F.3d 1343, 1349 (D.C. Cir. 2000) ("[P]ersonal jurisdiction surely cannot be based solely on the ability of District residents to access the defendants' websites.").

Determine and be ready to explain ways to include the questions just addressed in your analytical framework—whether it be in the form of an outline with questions or a flow chart. How will your framework show the questions asked for an individual defendant (related to domicile) versus the questions you will ask if the defendant is a corporation and whether criteria exists to support general jurisdiction over the corporate defendant?

Why, if you were a plaintiff suing an individual, would it make litigation easier to show the defendant is domiciled in the forum? Why, if you were suing a corporation, would it make litigation easier if you can establish general jurisdiction exists over the corporation in the forum?

E. Specific Jurisdiction: The "Minimum Contacts" Analysis

If, as the litigator, you have reached this point in the personal jurisdiction analysis, you had better roll up your sleeves. You will have determined that the state long-arm statute of the forum court has been met. You will also have concluded that the less demanding means of establishing personal jurisdiction are fruitless. Thus, you must delve into an area in which your analysis tends to hinge on malleable concepts that require close evaluation of the specific facts and the law. In other words, this part of the analysis is an opportunity for advocacy that separates excellent litigators from mediocre ones. The more effectively you tie together facts showing that the claim arises from jurisdictional contacts, the more likely you are to convince the court to exercise personal jurisdiction. Conversely, if the defense lawyer demonstrates that the jurisdictional contacts are only marginally related to the claim, the court may well refuse to exercise jurisdiction. The good news for you, as the plaintiff's lawyer, is that the Supreme Court has been far more willing to sustain personal jurisdiction as constitutional when the defendant has contacts with a state and the claim in question arises from them. In other words, whereas general jurisdiction has become increasingly hard, specific jurisdiction— the subject of this chapter—is attainable in many cases.

The hallmark of the minimum contacts analysis is that the claim must always arise from the defendant's jurisdictional contacts.[197] When performing a minimum contacts analysis—another way of referring to a specific jurisdiction analysis—the plaintiff must demonstrate the existence of personal jurisdiction under the holding of *International Shoe v. Washington*,[198] and its progeny. As we will see in these cases, to establish personal jurisdiction over the defendant, the claim(s) in the suit must arise from the defendant's contacts with the forum. If you have reached this point in the minimum contacts analysis, the approach now becomes the same for individuals and for corporations. Regardless of the form the defendant takes, that defendant must have sufficient minimum contacts with the forum out of which the claim in the case arises for specific jurisdiction to exist.

In *Kulko v. California Superior Court*,[199] for instance, the Supreme Court applied the same minimum contacts tests that it had applied to corporations. In *Kulko*, a New York couple divorced in New York. The ex-husband kept custody of their two children and remained in New York, while the wife moved to California. Later, the ex-husband bought a one-way ticket for one child to fly and move in with his ex-wife in California, while she bought a ticket for the other child. The ex-wife then sued her ex-husband in

---

[197] *See* 4 CHARLES ALAN WRIGHT & ARTHUR R. MILLER, FEDERAL PRACTICE AND PROCEDURE § 1067.1 (2018).
[198] 326 U.S. 310 (1945).
[199] 436 U.S. 84 (1978).

California. Applying the same minimum contacts analysis that the Court had been applying in other circumstances, including those involving corporate defendants, the Court held that the exercise of personal jurisdiction by California would violate due process.

1. International Shoe's *Minimum Contacts Analysis*

Prior to *International Shoe*'s introduction of the minimum contacts test, courts viewed personal jurisdiction as a territorial concept. If a defendant was served within the forum, then personal jurisdiction existed; if the defendant was outside the forum, it did not. For example, the Supreme Court in *Pennoyer v. Neff*,[200] resolved a famous dispute between a property owner who was not present in the forum state when an action arose against him, although he owed property in the forum. In *Pennoyer*, there were two suits. In the first suit, Mitchell (a lawyer) sued Neff for legal service and recovered in a default judgment. Mitchell then, under Oregon law, attached the real property of Neff in Oregon and had it sold at a sheriff's sale. Mitchell bought the property for fair market value and then deeded it to *Pennoyer*. The Supreme Court vindicated Neff's ownership because he was not present in Oregon when the original proceedings occurred, holding that those proceedings were unconstitutional. As the Court stated: "The authority of every tribunal is necessarily restricted by the territorial limits of the State in which it is established. Any attempt to exercise authority beyond those limits would be deemed in every other forum . . . an illegitimate assumption of power and be resisted as mere abuse."[201] Because of the failure to observe the territorial limits of Oregon, the Court voided the judgment for Mitchell and the deed to Pennoyer. The property was thus returned to Neff.

In the years after that eighteenth-century decision, interstate travel in the United States grew considerably. The nineteenth century saw considerable advances in transportation among states.[202] In addition, while previously corporations had primarily operated within a state, with some exceptions, the twentieth century saw an expansion of corporations with presence in many states.[203] With these developments, not to mention the growing number of cars traveling between states, and the resulting greater interaction between residents of states in general, the concept of territorial jurisdiction became outmoded. Territorial jurisdiction, most clearly identified with Pennoyer, focused solely on whether a defendant was within the territorial boundaries of the state in which suit was brought. It did not account for a defendant's having been in the state prior to the suit and having acted in ways that led to the suit. Nor did territorial jurisdiction recognize that, as time passed, the notion that a defendant had to be physically present to have contacts with the forum state made less and less sense.

Hess v. Pawloski,[204] is a decision showing the Supreme Court's bending of the concept of territorial jurisdiction to recognize the changing realities within the country. In *Hess v. Pawlowsk*, a citizen of Pennsylvania, had driven on Massachusetts highways when he had an accident with Hess, a citizen of Massachusetts. Massachusetts had enacted a statute (now common among states) that appointed the Commissioner of the Division of Motor Vehicles an agent for anyone who drives on the highways of

---

[200] 95 U.S. 714 (1878).

[201] *Id.* at 720.

[202] *See* American Antiquarian Society, Historical Background on Traveling in the Early 19th Century, TEACHINGUSHISTORY.GOV, http://www.teachushistory.org/detocqueville-visit-united-states/articles/historical-background-trav-eling-early-19th-century (last visited June 14, 2017).

[203] *See* ANUP SHAH, *THE RISE OF CORPORATIONS*, GLOBAL ISSUES: SOCIAL, POLITICAL, ECONOMIC, AND ENVIRONMENTAL ISSUES THAT AFFECT US ALL, http://www.globalissues.org/article/234/the-rise-of-corporations (last visited June 14, 2017).

[204] 274 U.S. 352 (1927).

130

Massachusetts. The "appointment" was of course a legal fiction because Pawlowski did not actively appoint the Commissioner. It happened by operation of law. Under the *Pennoyer* test, Hess would not have been able to sue Pawlowski in Massachusetts because it was not within its territorial limits. Hess, however, represented a step away from strict territorial jurisdiction by upholding personal jurisdiction over Pawlowski under the statute by which he was virtually represented by the Commissioner. After *Hess*, the Supreme Court faced the question of whether a corporation that had been doing business in a state over a matter sued on in that state could be subject to personal jurisdiction despite (a) the lack of territorial jurisdiction, and (b) the lack of any implied consent statute. The Court broke from the strict thinking of these approaches to recognize that defendants could effectively be present in a state through their activities there. The test the Court developed—the "minimum contacts" test—remains the one used to this day to determine whether a defendant can, consistent with due process, be subjected to jurisdiction in a state due to the defendant's contacts with that state.

2. The Breakthrough: "Minimum Contacts"
as a Means of Determining a Defendant's Connection to a Forum

INTERNATIONAL SHOE CO. v. STATE OF WASHINGTON
Supreme Court of the United States, 1945
326 U.S. 310

CHIEF JUSTICE STONE delivered the opinion of the Court.

The questions for decision are (1) whether, within the limitations of the due process clause of the Fourteenth Amendment, appellant, a Delaware corporation, has by its activities in the State of Washington rendered itself amenable to proceedings in the courts of that state to recover unpaid contributions to the state unemployment compensation fund exacted by state statutes, and (2) whether the state can exact those contributions consistently with the due process clause of the Fourteenth Amendment.

The statutes in question set up a comprehensive scheme of unemployment compensation, the costs of which are defrayed by contributions required to be made by employers to a state unemployment compensation fund. The contributions are a specified percentage of the wages payable annually by each employer for his employees' services in the state. The assessment and collection of the contributions and the fund are administered by appellees.

In this case notice of assessment for the years in question was personally served upon a sales solicitor employed by appellant in the State of Washington, and a copy of the notice was mailed by registered mail to appellant at its address in St. Louis, Missouri. Appellant appeared specially before the office of unemployment and moved to set aside the order and notice of assessment on the ground that the service upon appellant's salesman was not proper service upon appellant; that appellant was not a corporation of the State of Washington and was not doing business within the state; that it had no agent within the state upon whom service could be made; and that appellant is not an employer and does not furnish employment within the meaning of the statute.

. . .

The facts as found by the appeal tribunal and accepted by the state Superior Court and Supreme Court, are not in dispute. Appellant is a Delaware corporation, having its principal place of business in St. Louis, Missouri, and is engaged in the manufacture and sale of shoes and other footwear. It maintains places of business in several states, other than Washington, at which its manufacturing is carried on and from which its merchandise is distributed interstate through several sales units or branches located outside the State of Washington.

Appellant has no office in Washington and makes no contracts either for sale or purchase of merchandise there. It maintains no stock of merchandise in that state and makes there no deliveries of goods in intrastate commerce. During the years from 1937 to 1940, now in question, appellant employed eleven to thirteen salesmen under direct supervision and control of sales managers located in St. Louis. These salesmen resided in Washington; their principal activities were confined to that state; and they were compensated by commissions based upon the amount of their sales. The commissions for each year totaled more than $31,000. Appellant supplies its salesmen with a line of samples, each consisting of one shoe of a pair, which they display to prospective purchasers. On occasion they rent permanent sample rooms, for exhibiting samples, in business buildings, or rent rooms in hotels or business buildings temporarily for that purpose. The cost of such rentals is reimbursed by appellant.

The authority of the salesmen is limited to exhibiting their samples and soliciting orders from prospective buyers, at prices and on terms fixed by appellant. The salesmen transmit the orders to appellant's office in St. Louis for acceptance or rejection, and when accepted the merchandise for filling the orders is shipped f.o.b. from points outside Washington to the purchasers within the state. All the merchandise shipped into Washington is invoiced at the place of shipment from which collections are made. No salesman has authority to enter into contracts or to make collections.

The Supreme Court of Washington was of opinion that the regular and systematic solicitation of orders in the state by appellant's salesmen, resulting in a continuous flow of appellant's product into the state, was sufficient to constitute doing business in the state so as to make appellant amenable to suit in its courts. But it was also of opinion that there were sufficient additional activities shown to bring the case within the rule frequently stated, that solicitation within a state by the agents of a foreign corporation plus some additional activities there are sufficient to render the corporation amenable to suit brought in the courts of the state to enforce an obligation arising out of its activities there. The court found such additional activities in the salesmen's display of samples sometimes in permanent display rooms, and the salesmen's residence within the state, continued over a period of years, all resulting in a substantial volume of merchandise regularly shipped by appellant to purchasers within the state. The court also held that the statute as applied did not invade the constitutional power of Congress to regulate interstate commerce and did not impose a prohibited burden on such commerce.

. . .

Appellant also insists that its activities within the state were not sufficient to manifest its "presence" there and that in its absence the state courts were without jurisdiction, that consequently it was a denial of due process for the state to subject appellant to suit. It refers to those cases in which it was said that the mere solicitation of orders for the purchase of goods within a state, to be accepted without the state and filled by shipment of the purchased goods interstate, does not render the corporation seller amenable to suit within the state. And appellant further argues that since it was not present within the state, it is a denial of due process to subject it to taxation or other money exaction. It thus denies the power of the state to lay the tax or to subject appellant to a suit for its collection.

Historically the jurisdiction of courts to render judgment in personam is grounded on their de facto power over the defendant's person. Hence his presence within the territorial jurisdiction of a court was

132

prerequisite to its rendition of a judgment personally binding him. But now that the capias ad respondendum has given way to personal service of summons or other form of notice, due process requires only that in order to subject a defendant to a judgment in personam, if he be not present within the territory of the forum, he have certain minimum contacts with it such that the maintenance of the suit does not offend "traditional notions of fair play and substantial justice."

Since the corporate personality is a fiction, although a fiction intended to be acted upon as though it were a fact, it is clear that unlike an individual its "presence" without, as well as within, the state of its origin can be manifested only by activities carried on in its behalf by those who are authorized to act for it. To say that the corporation is so far "present" there as to satisfy due process requirements, for purposes of taxation or the maintenance of suits against it in the courts of the state, is to beg the question to be decided. For the terms "present" or "presence" are used merely to symbolize those activities of the corporation's agent within the state which courts will deem to be sufficient to satisfy the demands of due process. Those demands may be met by such contacts of the corporation with the state of the forum as make it reasonable, in the context of our federal system of government, to require the corporation to defend the particular suit which is brought there. An "estimate of the inconveniences" which would result to the corporation from a trial away from its "home" or principal place of business is relevant in this connection.

"Presence" in the state in this sense has never been doubted when the activities of the corporation there have not only been continuous and systematic, but also give rise to the liabilities sued on, even though no consent to be sued or authorization to an agent to accept service of process has been given. Conversely it has been generally recognized that the casual presence of the corporate agent or even his conduct of single or isolated items of activities in a state in the corporation's behalf are not enough to subject it to suit on causes of action unconnected with the activities there. To require the corporation in such circumstances to defend the suit away from its home or other jurisdiction where it carries on more substantial activities has been thought to lay too great and unreasonable a burden on the corporation to comport with due process.

While it has been held, in cases on which appellant relies, that continuous activity of some sorts within a state is not enough to support the demand that the corporation be amenable to suits unrelated to that activity, there have been instances in which the continuous corporate operations within a state were thought so substantial and of such a nature as to justify suit against it on causes of action arising from dealings entirely distinct from those activities.

Finally, although the commission of some single or occasional acts of the corporate agent in a state sufficient to impose an obligation or liability on the corporation has not been thought to confer upon the state authority to enforce it, other such acts, because of their nature and quality and the circumstances of their commission, may be deemed sufficient to render the corporation liable to suit. True, some of the decisions holding the corporation amenable to suit have been supported by resort to the legal fiction that it has given its consent to service and suit, consent being implied from its presence in the state through the acts of its authorized agents. But more realistically it may be said that those authorized acts were of such a nature as to justify the fiction.

It is evident that the criteria by which we mark the boundary line between those activities which justify the subjection of a corporation to suit, and those which do not, cannot be simply mechanical or quantitative. The test is not merely, as has sometimes been suggested, whether the activity, which the corporation has seen fit to procure through its agents in another state, is a little more or a little less. Whether due process is satisfied must depend rather upon the quality and nature of the activity in relation to the fair and orderly administration of the laws which it was the purpose of the due process clause to insure. That clause does not contemplate that a state may make binding a judgment in personam against an individual or corporate defendant with which the state has no contacts, ties, or relations.

But to the extent that a corporation exercises the privilege of conducting activities within a state, it enjoys the benefits and protection of the laws of that state. The exercise of that privilege may give rise to obligations, and, so far as those obligations arise out of or are connected with the activities within the state, a procedure which requires the corporation to respond to a suit brought to enforce them can, in most instances, hardly be said to be undue.

Applying these standards, the activities carried on in behalf of appellant in the State of Washington were neither irregular nor casual. They were systematic and continuous throughout the years in question. They resulted in a large volume of interstate business, in the course of which appellant received the benefits and protection of the laws of the state, including the right to resort to the courts for the enforcement of its rights. The obligation which is here sued upon arose out of those very activities. It is evident that these operations establish sufficient contacts or ties with the state of the forum to make it reasonable and just, according to our traditional conception of fair play and substantial justice, to permit the state to enforce the obligations which appellant has incurred there. Hence, we cannot say that the maintenance of the present suit in the State of Washington involves an unreasonable or undue procedure.

We are likewise unable to conclude that the service of the process within the state upon an agent whose activities establish appellant's "presence" there was not sufficient notice of the suit, or that the suit was so unrelated to those activities as to make the agent an inappropriate vehicle for communicating the notice. It is enough that appellant has established such contacts with the state that the particular form of substituted service adopted there gives reasonable assurance that the notice will be actual.

. . .

Appellant having rendered itself amenable to suit upon obligations arising out of the activities of its salesmen in Washington, the state may maintain the present suit in personam to collect the tax laid upon the exercise of the privilege of employing appellant's salesmen within the state. For Washington has made one of those activities, which taken together establish appellant's "presence" there for purposes of suit, the taxable event by which the state brings appellant within the reach of its taxing power. The state thus has constitutional power to lay the tax and to subject appellant to a suit to recover it. The activities which establish its "presence" subject it alike to taxation by the state and to suit to recover the tax.

Affirmed.

3. International Shoe: *A Specific Jurisdiction Case*

It is imperative that you to understand the difference between a general jurisdiction case and a specific jurisdiction case. International Shoe is a prototypical specific jurisdiction case. Although it refers to other types of jurisdiction in dicta, including general jurisdiction, you should not be confused. The case is all about specific jurisdiction.

The hallmarks of specific jurisdiction are (1) the claim or claims in the case (2) arise from the conduct or contacts alleged as the basis for personal jurisdiction, then the case is a specific jurisdiction case. Here, International Shoe operated in the State of Washington where it had agents sell shoes, but never paid unemployment compensation such that, if any of these employees became unemployed and sought unemployment relief from the State, part of the funds received by the employees would have been supplied by International Shoe. The State of Washington did not think that International Shoe's failure to pay was fair. Nor did it want to go to Missouri, the state in which International Shoe's principal place of business was located. Thus, the State of Washington was the plaintiff in this civil suit to force International Shoe to pay unemployment compensation to the State. That was the claim. The basis for personal jurisdiction was the activity of the agents who sold shoes for International Shoe in Washington—the same agents who posed a risk of unemployment. Thus, the claim in the case arose from the conduct of the nonresident in having agents in Washington making money but failing to contribute to the State's unemployment compensation fund if any of these agents become unemployed. The nexus between the claim and the ground for jurisdiction was sufficiently close that the Court could apply the minimum contacts analysis.

The Supreme Court would not have applied the minimum contacts analysis if International Shoe, Inc. had not been selling shoes in the State of Washington. If International Shoe was selling shoes in, say, only its state of incorporation (Missouri), the State of Washington would have had to look to general jurisdiction to establish personal jurisdiction on a basis unrelated to the claim sued on. The teaching point here is that the minimum contacts analysis will always apply to specific jurisdiction cases. General jurisdiction assumes that there is no claim arising from a defendant's contacts. If no nexus exists between the claim or claims in the case and the jurisdictional contacts alleged to support personal jurisdiction, the plaintiff will rarely be able to establish jurisdiction. It would have to look to one of the "easy" grounds for establishing personal jurisdiction discussed above (*e.g.*, consent, general jurisdiction over the corporation), and such grounds typically do not exist (though one looks to be sure).

Practice Problem

The following Practice Problem varies the facts of *International Shoe*. The question is whether the variation makes a difference in the specific jurisdiction analysis.

Practice Problem 5-5

International Boot, Inc. is incorporated in Missouri and has its principal place of business in St. Louis, Missouri. International Boot developed the world's greatest rubber boots. Because the State of Washington experiences inclement weather much of the year, the State decided to buy rubber boots for the employees that had to go out around the State. The State's procurement agent called International Boot about supplying these boots to the State. International Boot said it was happy to do so, but its policy was that on contracts for major amounts of goods, it required all negotiations to occur at its headquarters, to have the buyer sign documentation at the Missouri factory and that all would agree that International Boot would not be held to assume that the shoes were being used in any particular jurisdiction. International Boot had the State of Washington sign a document acknowledging that, while International Boot might assume otherwise that the State of Washington was using its boots in Washington, the State understood that International Boot insisted on all negotiations occurring in Missouri and to an understanding that, regardless of where the boots were shipped, the buyer acknowledged that possession of the boots would be deemed transferred at the Missouri shipping location and that the party to whom the boots were being shipped had control thereafter and could redirect the boots to any other location.

When the boots were ready, they were shipped as agreed. The State of Washington employees began to use them. A good number of the boots began to develop cracks after a month of use. The State sued International Boot in Washington. Why is this not a specific jurisdiction case? Why will general jurisdiction not help the State of Washington? Where will the State need to sue if it wants to recover? How does this fact pattern compare with the facts of International Shoe? Do you now see why, in the actual case, the Plaintiff State of Washington could rely on specific jurisdiction to obtain jurisdiction over International Shoe in the State of Washington? What was different about the facts of the original case of International Shoe and the facts of this Practice Problem?

International Shoe introduced the minimum contacts test. Of all the cases that followed that seminal case, the Court's decision in *World-Wide Volkswagen v. Woodson* does more to flesh out the meaning, scope, and purpose underlying the minimum contacts case than any other case.

WORLD-WIDE VOLKSWAGEN v. WOODSON
Supreme Court of the United States, 1980
444 U.S. 286

MR. JUSTICE WHITE delivered the opinion of the Court.

The issue before us is whether, consistently with the Due Process Clause of the Fourteenth Amendment, an Oklahoma court may exercise in personam jurisdiction over a nonresident automobile retailer and its wholesale distributor in a products-liability action, when the defendants' only connection with Oklahoma is the fact that an automobile sold in New York to New York residents became involved in an accident in Oklahoma.

I

Respondents Harry and Kay Robinson purchased a new Audi automobile from petitioner Seaway Volkswagen, Inc. (Seaway), in Massena, N. Y., in 1976. The following year the Robinson family, who resided in New York, left that State for a new home in Arizona. As they passed through the State of Oklahoma, another car struck their Audi in the rear, causing a fire which severely burned Kay Robinson and her two children. The Robinsons subsequently brought a products-liability action in the District Court for Creek County, Okla., claiming that their injuries resulted from defective design and placement of the Audi's gas tank and fuel system. They joined as defendants the automobile's manufacturer, Audi NSU Auto Union Aktiengesellschaft (Audi); its importer, Volkswagen of America, Inc. (Volkswagen); its regional distributor, petitioner World-Wide Volkswagen Corp. (World-Wide); and its retail dealer, petitioner Seaway. Seaway and World-Wide entered special appearances, claiming that Oklahoma's exercise of jurisdiction over them would offend the limitations on the State's jurisdiction imposed by the Due Process Clause of the Fourteenth Amendment.

The facts presented to the District Court showed that World-Wide is incorporated and has its business office in New York. It distributes vehicles, parts, and accessories, under contract with Volkswagen, to retail dealers in New York, New Jersey, and Connecticut. Seaway, one of these retail dealers, is incorporated and has its place of business in New York. Insofar as the record reveals, Seaway and World-Wide are fully independent corporations whose relations with each other and with Volkswagen and Audi are contractual only. Respondents adduced no evidence that either World-Wide or Seaway does any business in Oklahoma, ships or sells any products to or in that State, has an agent to receive process there, or purchases advertisements in any media calculated to reach Oklahoma. In fact, as respondents' counsel conceded at oral argument, there was no showing that any automobile sold by World-Wide or Seaway has ever entered Oklahoma with the single exception of the vehicle involved in the present case.

Despite the apparent paucity of contacts between petitioners and Oklahoma, the District Court rejected their constitutional claim and reaffirmed that ruling in denying petitioners' motion for reconsideration. Petitioners then sought a writ of prohibition in the Supreme Court of Oklahoma to restrain the District Judge, respondent Charles S. Woodson, from exercising in personam jurisdiction over them. They renewed their contention that, because they had no "minimal contacts" with the State of Oklahoma, the actions of the District Judge were in violation of their rights under the Due Process Clause.

The Supreme Court of Oklahoma denied the writ, holding that personal jurisdiction over petitioners was authorized by Oklahoma's "long-arm" statute. Although the court noted that the proper approach was to test jurisdiction against both statutory and constitutional standards, its analysis did not distinguish these questions, probably because § 1701.03 (a) (4) has been interpreted as conferring jurisdiction to the limits permitted by the United States Constitution. The court's rationale was contained in the following paragraph:

> In the case before us, the product being sold and distributed by the petitioners is by its very design and purpose so mobile that petitioners can foresee its possible use in Oklahoma. This is especially true of the distributor, who has the exclusive right to distribute such automobile in New York, New Jersey and Connecticut. The evidence presented below demonstrated that goods sold and distributed by the petitioners were used in the State of Oklahoma, and under the facts we believe it reasonable to infer, given the retail value of the automobile, that the petitioners derive substantial income from automobiles which from time to time are used in the State of Oklahoma. This being the case, we hold that under the facts presented, the trial court was justified in concluding that the petitioners derive substantial revenue from goods used or consumed in this State.

We granted certiorari to consider an important constitutional question with respect to state-court jurisdiction and to resolve a conflict between the Supreme Court of Oklahoma and the highest courts of at least four other States. We reverse.

II

The Due Process Clause of the Fourteenth Amendment limits the power of a state court to render a valid personal judgment against a nonresident defendant. A judgment rendered in violation of due process is void in the rendering State and is not entitled to full faith and credit elsewhere. Due process requires that the defendant be given adequate notice of the suit and be subject to the personal jurisdiction of the court. In the present case, it is not contended that notice was inadequate; the only question is whether these particular petitioners were subject to the jurisdiction of the Oklahoma courts.

As has long been settled, and as we reaffirm today, a state court may exercise personal jurisdiction over a nonresident defendant only so long as there exist "minimum contacts" between the defendant and the forum State. The concept of minimum contacts, in turn, can be seen to perform two related, but distinguishable, functions. It protects the defendant against the burdens of litigating in a distant or inconvenient forum. And it acts to ensure that the States, through their courts, do not reach out beyond the limits imposed on them by their status as coequal sovereigns in a federal system.

The protection against inconvenient litigation is typically described in terms of "reasonableness" or "fairness." We have said that the defendant's contacts with the forum State must be such that maintenance

137

of the suit "does not offend 'traditional notions of fair play and substantial justice.'"[205]

The relationship between the defendant and the forum must be such that it is "reasonable . . . to require the corporation to defend the particular suit which is brought there." Implicit in this emphasis on reasonableness is the understanding that the burden on the defendant, while always a primary concern, will in an appropriate case be considered in light of other relevant factors, including the forum State's interest in adjudicating the dispute; the plaintiff's interest in obtaining convenient and effective relief, at least when that interest is not adequately protected by the plaintiff's power to choose the forum; the interstate judicial system's interest in obtaining the most efficient resolution of controversies; and the shared interest of the several States in furthering fundamental substantive social policies.

The limits imposed on state jurisdiction by the Due Process Clause, in its role as a guarantor against inconvenient litigation, have been substantially relaxed over the years. As we noted in *McGee v. International Life Insurance Company*, this trend is largely attributable to a fundamental transformation in the American economy:

> Today many commercial transactions touch two or more States and may involve parties separated by the full continent. With this increasing nationalization of commerce has come a great increase in the amount of business conducted by mail across state lines. At the same time modern transportation and communication have made it much less burdensome for a party sued to defend himself in a State where he engages in economic activity.

The historical developments noted in *McGee*, of course, have only accelerated in the generation since that case was decided.

Nevertheless, we have never accepted the proposition that state lines are irrelevant for jurisdictional purposes, nor could we, and remain faithful to the principles of interstate federalism embodied in the Constitution. The economic interdependence of the States was foreseen and desired by the Framers. In the Commerce Clause, they provided that the Nation was to be a common market, a "free trade unit" in which the States are debarred from acting as separable economic entities. But the Framers also intended that the States retain many essential attributes of sovereignty, including, in particular, the sovereign power to try causes in their courts. The sovereignty of each State, in turn, implied a limitation on the sovereignty of all of its sister States--a limitation express or implicit in both the original scheme of the Constitution and the Fourteenth Amendment.

Hence, even while abandoning the shibboleth that "[the] authority of every tribunal is necessarily restricted by the territorial limits of the State in which it is established,"[206] we emphasized that the reasonableness of asserting jurisdiction over the defendant must be assessed "in the context of our federal system of government,"[207] and stressed that the Due Process Clause ensures not only fairness, but also the "orderly administration of the laws." As we noted in *Hanson v. Denckla*:

> As technological progress has increased the flow of commerce between the States, the need for jurisdiction over nonresidents has undergone a similar increase. At the

---

[205] International Shoe Co. v. Washington, 326 U.S. 310, 320 (1945) (quoting Milliken v. Meyer, 311 U.S. 457, 463 (1940)).
[206] Pennoyer v. Neff, 95 U.S. 714 (1877).
[207] International Shoe Co. v. Washington, 326 U.S. 310 (1945).

same time, progress in communications and transportation has made the defense of a suit in a foreign tribunal less burdensome. In response to these changes, the requirements for personal jurisdiction over nonresidents have evolved from the rigid rule of *Pennoyer v. Neff* to the flexible standard of International Shoe. But it is a mistake to assume that this trend heralds the eventual demise of all restrictions on the personal jurisdiction of state courts. Those restrictions are more than a guarantee of immunity from inconvenient or distant litigation. They are a consequence of territorial limitations on the power of the respective States.

Thus, the Due Process Clause "does not contemplate that a state may make binding a judgment in personam against an individual or corporate defendant with which the state has no contacts, ties, or relations." International Shoe. Even if the defendant would suffer minimal or no inconvenience from being forced to litigate before the tribunals of another State; even if the forum State has a strong interest in applying its law to the controversy; even if the forum State is the most convenient location for litigation, the Due Process Clause, acting as an instrument of interstate federalism, may sometimes act to divest the State of its power to render a valid judgment.

III

Applying these principles to the case at hand, we find in the record before us a total absence of those affiliating circumstances that are a necessary predicate to any exercise of state-court jurisdiction. Petitioners carry on no activity whatsoever in Oklahoma. They close no sales and perform no services there. They avail themselves of none of the privileges and benefits of Oklahoma law. They solicit no business there either through salespersons or through advertising reasonably calculated to reach the State. Nor does the record show that they regularly sell cars at wholesale or retail to Oklahoma customers or residents or that they indirectly, through others, serve or seek to serve the Oklahoma market. In short, respondents seek to base jurisdiction on one, isolated occurrence and whatever inferences can be drawn therefrom: the fortuitous circumstance that a single Audi automobile, sold in New York to New York residents, happened to suffer an accident while passing through Oklahoma.

It is argued, however, that because an automobile is mobile by its very design and purpose it was "foreseeable" that the Robinsons' Audi would cause injury in Oklahoma. Yet "foreseeability" alone has never been a sufficient benchmark for personal jurisdiction under the Due Process Clause. In *Hanson v. Denckla*, it was no doubt foreseeable that the settlor of a Delaware trust would subsequently move to Florida and seek to exercise a power of appointment there; yet we held that Florida courts could not constitutionally exercise jurisdiction over a Delaware trustee that had no other contacts with the forum State. In *Kulko v. California Superior Court*,[208] it was surely "foreseeable" that a divorced wife would move to California from New York, the domicile of the marriage, and that a minor daughter would live with the mother. Yet we held that California could not exercise jurisdiction in a child-support action over the former husband who had remained in New York.

If foreseeability were the criterion, a local California tire retailer could be forced to defend in Pennsylvania when a blowout occurs there; a Wisconsin seller of a defective automobile jack could be haled before a distant court for damage caused in New Jersey; or a Florida soft-drink concessionaire could be summoned to Alaska to account for injuries happening there. Every seller of chattels would in effect appoint the chattel his agent for service of process. His amenability to suit would travel with the chattel.

---

[208] 436 U.S. 84 (1978).

. . .

    This is not to say, of course, that foreseeability is wholly irrelevant. But the foreseeability that is critical to due process analysis is not the mere likelihood that a product will find its way into the forum State.

    Rather, it is that the defendant's conduct and connection with the forum State are such that he should reasonably anticipate being haled into court there. The Due Process Clause, by ensuring the "orderly administration of the laws," International Shoe, gives a degree of predictability to the legal system that allows potential defendants to structure their primary conduct with some minimum assurance as to where that conduct will and will not render them liable to suit.

    When a corporation "purposefully avails itself of the privilege of conducting activities within the forum State," it has clear notice that it is subject to suit there and can act to alleviate the risk of burdensome litigation by procuring insurance, passing the expected costs on to customers, or, if the risks are too great, severing its connection with the State. Hence if the sale of a product of a manufacturer or distributor such as Audi or Volkswagen is not simply an isolated occurrence, but arises from the efforts of the manufacturer or distributor to serve, directly or indirectly, the market for its product in other States, it is not unreasonable to subject it to suit in one of those States if its allegedly defective merchandise has there been the source of injury to its owner or to others. The forum State does not exceed its powers under the Due Process Clause if it asserts personal jurisdiction over a corporation that delivers its products into the stream of commerce with the expectation that they will be purchased by consumers in the forum State.

    But there is no such or similar basis for Oklahoma jurisdiction over World-Wide or Seaway in this case. Seaway's sales are made in Massena, N. Y. World-Wide's market, although substantially larger, is limited to dealers in New York, New Jersey, and Connecticut. There is no evidence of record that any automobiles distributed by World-Wide are sold to retail customers outside this tristate area. It is foreseeable that the purchasers of automobiles sold by World-Wide and Seaway may take them to Oklahoma. But the mere "unilateral activity of those who claim some relationship with a nonresident defendant cannot satisfy the requirement of contact with the forum State."

    In a variant on the previous argument, it is contended that jurisdiction can be supported by the fact that petitioners earn substantial revenue from goods used in Oklahoma. The Oklahoma Supreme Court so found, drawing the inference that because one automobile sold by petitioners had been used in Oklahoma, others might have been used there also. While this inference seems less than compelling on the facts of the instant case, we need not question the court's factual findings in order to reject its reasoning.

    This argument seems to make the point that the purchase of automobiles in New York, from which the petitioners earn substantial revenue, would not occur but for the fact that the automobiles are capable of use in distant States like Oklahoma. Respondents observe that the very purpose of an automobile is to travel, and that travel of automobiles sold by petitioners is facilitated by an extensive chain of Volkswagen service centers throughout the country, including some in Oklahoma. However, financial benefits accruing to the defendant from a collateral relation to the forum State will not support jurisdiction if they do not stem from a constitutionally cognizable contact with that State. In our view, whatever marginal revenues petitioners may receive by virtue of the fact that their products are capable of use in Oklahoma is far too attenuated a contact to justify that State's exercise of in personam jurisdiction over them.

    Because we find that petitioners have no "contacts, ties, or relations" with the State of Oklahoma,

140

International Shoe, the judgment of the Supreme Court of Oklahoma is

Reversed.

Follow-Up Questions and Comments

1. Some wonder why *World-Wide Volkswagen* is treated as a specific jurisdiction case. If the court is applying the "minimum contacts" teste, you know the Court considers the case to be a specific jurisdiction analysis. By analyzing minimum contacts, the Court is evaluating the defendant's "contacts" (purposeful acts affecting the State, taking advantage of the benefits of the State's commerce, laws, etc.) and whether the claim in the case arises from those contacts. The answer as to *World-Wide Volkswagen* has to do with the nature of product liability litigation. The claim in the case was that the car was defectively manufactured. Sellers of the car can be liable, at least under implied warranties of merchantability, for selling a defective product. Here, the car made its way from the northeast to Oklahoma. And it was the car that was involved in the accident. The jurisdictional contact was the presence of the car in Oklahoma. The claims in the case related to the car that had been sold by the defendants in the case, the regional dealer (World-Wide Volkswagen) and the dealer (Seaway, Inc.). The manufacturer, Volkswagen, did not contest jurisdiction in Oklahoma. Thus, any time a manufacturer (or dealer) sells a product, even if it is bought in a state other than where the manufacturer (or dealer) is based, the plaintiff will deal with a specific jurisdiction analysis seeking to determine that the manufacturer's or dealer's contacts with the forum in which the manufacturer (or dealer) are sued.

2. *World-Wide Volkswagen* helps to illustrate that, just because a defendant may have to go through a specific jurisdiction analysis, if that defendant's contacts with the forum state are solely that the defect manifested itself in that forum state—with no other contacts that would put the defendant on notice that it could be sued there—specific jurisdiction under the minimum contacts test will not support personal jurisdiction.

3. One of the key passages in *World-Wide Volkswagen* provides very practical guidance to determine whether a defendant can, based on its conduct prior to the time suit is filed, be said to have purposefully availed itself of the benefits of another state—i.e., be on notice that it could be sued there:

   > When a corporation 'purposefully avails itself of the privilege of conducting activities within the forum State,' it has clear notice that it is subject to suit there and can act to alleviate the risk of burdensome litigation by procuring insurance, passing the expected costs on to customers, or, if the risks are too great, severing its connection with the State.[209]

4. What does the Court mean by referring to procuring insurance? Does that mean that a plaintiff can only establish specific jurisdiction over a nonresident if it has purchased insurance? Or does it mean that the plaintiff can establish jurisdiction over a nonresident defendant if a company or individual, considering its conduct prior to suit, could reasonably have given the defendant a reason to buy insurance to allow for litigation in the forum? Could World-Wide Volkswagen, with its tri-state

---

[209] World-Wide Volkswagen Corp. v. Woodson, 44 U.S. 286, 297 (1980).

region in the Northeast, have reasonably expected to purchase insurance to protect against suit in Oklahoma? If the facts were different—and *World-Wide Volkswagen* distributed cars to dealers throughout the eastern United States up to every state on the border of the Mississippi River, could the defendant in those circumstances have reasonably anticipated suit in Oklahoma and purchased insurance protecting it against costs of such litigation?

Exercise to Synthesize the Topics in this Chapter

Develop an analytical framework that includes the initial questions by which the forum court can have personal jurisdictions—what has been referred to as the "easy" grounds for establishing jurisdiction. Then, assume that none of those grounds exist, and include the steps in the analysis—whether it be in the form of a flow chart or outline, one would need to analyze to conclude whether specific jurisdiction exists. As you consider the next series of cases, consider whether your analytical framework should have subsections devoted to different kinds of fact patterns—called "analogous contexts" below.

---

4. Fleshing Out Specific Jurisdiction in Various Factual Contexts

The key to a specific jurisdiction analysis is, first, to identify the claims(s) on which the plaintiff is suing and, then, to determine whether the claim(s) arise from the defendant's jurisdictional contacts. Does the claim (whether it be tort, contract, etc.) arise from the defendant's conduct—the defendant's jurisdictional activity—in the state? If so, then you have a shot at specific jurisdiction. If not, then the only place a plaintiff can sue would be to go to the individual defendant's domicile or to a corporation's principal place of business or state or incorporation.

The following discussion will refer to "analogous contexts," as a means of applying the specific jurisdiction analysis in a factual scenario. However, the phrase is not something derived from language in cases. Instead, the "analogous contexts" approach is an analytical tool to help you recognize that, in some factual contexts, the Court has suggested certain questions and factors will help to answer the more general questions of *International Shoe* and *World-Wide Volkswagen*. However, please do not use the analogous contexts as a reason to skip a statement of the overarching principles of *International Shoe* and *World-Wide Volkswagen*. These overarching principles of the minimum contacts analysis, and the policies underlying those principles, are fully included in the *International Shoe* and *World-Wide Volkswagen* cases.

The progeny of those two seminal cases may be viewed as branches of the same tree. However, the Court in each of these later cases is applying the principles outlined in *International Shoe* and *World-Wide Volkswagen* in different scenarios that typically lead to questions applicable to a specific factual setting. Thus, for purposes of organization, they are treated as contexts that are analogous to International Shoe and *World-Wide Volkswagen*. This book uses the phrase "analogous contexts" to mean that the Supreme Court applied the principles of International Shoe to specific types of facts patterns that allow for analogous reasoning. In other words, every one of these other cases is simply an elaboration of *International Shoe* and *World-Wide Volkswagen*. If you are preparing a memorandum to a colleague, or writing a brief, you would not refer to "analogous contexts" as if the reader would understand what they are, unless you explained what you meant by the phrase "analogous context." If you wanted to use the phrase, you would need to explain what you mean by the term. Again, it is a tool that can be useful in organizing the cases and seeing how the analysis, in a factual context, will focus on specific facts and questions that derive from the main cases, but are geared to the factual context.

For instance, we will see that in the contract context, the Supreme Court asks where the negotiations occurred and for how long, the length of the time the parties anticipated dealing with one an-other, whether the contracts specified a state's law as governing its interpretation, and how the parties in general carried out their dealings, etc. If you analyze a contract case involving the question of whether the defendant is subject to the jurisdiction of another state's court, you will see that these questions flow naturally from the principle that a party has to have meaningfully foreseen that the party could be brought into court in the state as in International Shoe. You will also see that questions such as "whether the nonresident dealt with the plaintiff by negotiating in the forum state" is a more specific way—in the context of a contractual dispute—of asking whether the defendant "structured his primary conduct" in a way that should have alerted him he could be sued in the forum as in *World-Wide Volkswagen*.

In short, these cases provide a frame of reference for you to compare the facts of your case to the application of the minimum contacts analysis in leading decisions. For each factual scenario in these decisions, you should know the specific criteria involved, such as the four factors discussed below in the "Contract Context." In addition, each analogous context illustrates the way the policies underlying the minimum contacts analysis play out situations. Although they should not be an artificial restriction on the application of the minimum contacts test, the analogous contexts should provide a framework for analyzing whether minimum contacts exist.

Finally, one should beware of tunnel vision. At times more than one factual context overlaps with another. If you have a case (or a law school essay) in which this occurs, just remember to first rely on the general principles *of International Shoe* and *World-Wide Volkswagen*. Then, apply the more specific questions from each of the decisions applying the minimum contacts analysis to specific factual situations. At times, each specific analysis will suggest the same result—either the existence of sufficient minimum contacts to exercise personal jurisdiction, or a lack thereof. In other cases, the analyses from different factual scenarios may not agree. The challenge then, is to consider the general principles and which of the contexts is most consistent with the overarching principles of International Shoe. If you approach the problem in this way and seek to find the best analysis and answer by consulting the underlying policies and concerns of personal jurisdiction, your answer should be an effective one.

With these caveats, viewing the cases following *International Shoe* and *World-Wide Volkswagen* as elaborations on these seminal cases in specific factual contexts will help you in your analysis. As you will see, the Court does emphasize, depending on the type of case, certain factors that ought to serve as a guide in reviewing cases that contain a factual scenario analogous to that of the case. The "contexts" below are not in any order of relative importance.

a. The Contract Context

In many instances, a plaintiff is suing a nonresident for breach of contract and seeking to resolve the dispute on the plaintiff's home turf. Whether a plaintiff will be able to do that depends, in general, on the test set forth in *International Shoe* and elaborated on in *World-Wide Volkswagen*. The following represents the Supreme Court's leading case on how to apply this test.

Keeping in mind the context of this test—the parties negotiated a contract followed by a suit for breach—see whether you can find the four factors outlined by the Court. While these factors are easy to overlook in the text of the opinion, they are factors you should memorize. One must be able to recall and apply these four factors whenever faced with a case (or law school essay) involving personal jurisdiction arising from a contract dispute. As the following case shows, none of these factors are dispositive but they can lead to the best answer.

Burger King Corp. v. Rudzewicz
Supreme Court of the United States, 1985
471 U.S. 462

JUSTICE BRENNAN delivered the opinion of the Court.

The State of Florida's long-arm statute extends jurisdiction to "[any] person, whether or not a citizen or resident of this state," who, inter alia, "[breaches] a contract in this state by failing to perform acts required by the contract to be performed in this state," so long as the cause of action arises from the alleged contractual breach. The United States District Court for the Southern District of Florida, sitting in diversity, relied on this provision in exercising personal jurisdiction over a Michigan resident who allegedly had breached a franchise agreement with a Florida corporation by failing to make required payments in Florida. The question presented is whether this exercise of long-arm jurisdiction offended "traditional [conceptions] of fair play and substantial justice" embodied in the Due Process Clause of the Fourteenth Amendment.[210]

. . .

Burger King Corporation is a Florida corporation whose principal offices are in Miami. It is one of the world's largest restaurant organizations, with over 3,000 outlets in the 50 States, the Commonwealth of Puerto Rico, and 8 foreign nations. Burger King conducts approximately 80% of its business through a franchise operation that the company styles the "Burger King System" a comprehensive restaurant format and operating system for the sale of uniform and quality food products." Burger King licenses its franchisees to use its trademarks and service marks for a period of 20 years and leases standardized restaurant facilities to them for the same term. In addition, franchisees acquire a variety of proprietary information concerning the "standards, specifications, procedures and methods for operating a Burger King Restaurant." They also receive market research and advertising assistance; ongoing training in restaurant management; and accounting, cost-control, and inventory-control guidance. By permitting franchisees to tap into Burger King's established national reputation and to benefit from proven procedures for dispensing standardized fare, this system enables them to go into the restaurant business with significantly lowered barriers to entry.

In exchange for these benefits, franchisees pay Burger King an initial $40,000 franchise fee and commit themselves to payment of monthly royalties, advertising and sales promotion fees, and rent computed in part from monthly gross sales. Franchisees also agree to submit to the national organization's exacting regulation of virtually every conceivable aspect of their operations. Burger King imposes these standards and undertakes its rigid regulation out of conviction that "[uniformity] of service, appearance, and quality of product is essential to the preservation of the Burger King image and the benefits accruing therefrom to both Franchisee and Franchisor."

Burger King oversees its franchise system through a two-tiered administrative structure. The governing contracts provide that the franchise relationship is established in Miami and governed by Florida

---

[210] International Shoe Co. v. Washington, 326 U.S. 310, 320 (1945).

law, and call for payment of all required fees and forwarding of all relevant notices to the Miami headquarters. The Miami headquarters sets policy and works directly with its franchisees in attempting to resolve major problems. Day-to-day monitoring of franchisees, however, is conducted through a network of 10 district offices which in turn report to the Miami headquarters.

The instant litigation grows out of Burger King's termination of one of its franchisees and is aptly described by the franchisee as "a divorce proceeding among commercial partners." The appellee John Rudzewicz, a Michigan citizen and resident, is the senior partner in a Detroit accounting firm. In 1978, he was approached by Brian MacShara, the son of a business acquaintance, who suggested that they jointly apply to Burger King for a franchise in the Detroit area. MacShara proposed to serve as the manager of the restaurant if Rudzewicz would put up the investment capital; in exchange, the two would evenly share the profits. Believing that MacShara's idea offered attractive investment and tax-deferral opportunities, Rudzewicz agreed to the venture.

Rudzewicz and MacShara jointly applied for a franchise to Burger King's Birmingham, Michigan, district office in the autumn of 1978. Their application was forwarded to Burger King's Miami headquarters, which entered into a preliminary agreement with them in February 1979. During the ensuing four months it was agreed that Rudzewicz and MacShara would assume operation of an existing facility in Drayton Plains, Michigan. MacShara attended the prescribed management courses in Miami during this period, and the franchisees purchased $165,000 worth of restaurant equipment from Burger King's Davmor Industries division in Miami. Even before the final agreements were signed, however, the parties began to disagree over site-development fees, building design, computation of monthly rent, and whether the franchisees would be able to assign their liabilities to a corporation they had formed. During these disputes Rudzewicz and MacShara negotiated both with the Birmingham district office and with the Miami headquarters. With some misgivings, Rudzewicz and MacShara finally obtained limited concessions from the Miami headquarters, signed the final agreements, and commenced operations in June 1979. By signing the final agreements, Rudzewicz obligated himself personally to payments exceeding $1 million over the 20-year franchise relationship.

The Drayton Plains facility apparently enjoyed steady business during the summer of 1979, but patronage declined after a recession began later that year. Rudzewicz and MacShara soon fell far behind in their monthly payments to Miami. Headquarters sent notices of default, and an extended period of negotiations began among the franchisees, the Birmingham district office, and the Miami headquarters. After several Burger King officials in Miami had engaged in prolonged but ultimately unsuccessful negotiations with the franchisees by mail and by telephone, headquarters terminated the franchise and ordered Rudzewicz and MacShara to vacate the premises. They refused and continued to occupy and operate the facility as a Burger King restaurant.

B

Burger King commenced the instant action in the United States District Court for the Southern District of Florida in May 1981, invoking that court's diversity jurisdiction pursuant to 28 U. S. C. § 1332 (a) and its original jurisdiction over federal trademark disputes pursuant to § 1338(a). Burger King alleged that Rudzewicz and MacShara had breached their franchise obligations "within [the jurisdiction of] this district court" by failing to make the required payments "at plaintiff's place of business in Miami, Dade County, Florida," and also charged that they were tortiously infringing its trademarks and service marks through their continued, unauthorized operation as a Burger King restaurant. Burger King sought damages, injunctive relief, and costs and attorney's fees. Rudzewicz and MacShara entered special appearances and argued, inter alia, that because they were Michigan residents and because Burger King's claim did not

145

"arise" within the Southern District of Florida, the District Court lacked personal jurisdiction over them. The District Court denied their motions after a hearing, holding that, pursuant to Florida's long-arm statute, "a non-resident Burger King franchisee is subject to the personal jurisdiction of this Court in actions arising out of its franchise agreements." Rudzewicz and MacShara then filed an answer and a counterclaim seeking damages for alleged violations by Burger King of Michigan's Franchise Investment Law.

After a 3-day bench trial, the court again concluded that it had "jurisdiction over the subject matter and the parties to this cause." Finding that Rudzewicz and MacShara had breached their franchise agreements with Burger King and had infringed Burger King's trademarks and service marks, the court entered judgment against them, jointly and severally, for $228,875 in contract damages. The court also ordered them "to immediately close Burger King Restaurant Number 775 from continued operation or to immediately give the keys and possession of said restaurant to Burger King Corporation," found that they had failed to prove any of the required elements of their counterclaim and awarded costs and attorney's fees to Burger King.

Rudzewicz appealed to the Court of Appeals for the Eleventh Circuit. A divided panel of that Circuit reversed the judgment, concluding that the District Court could not properly exercise personal jurisdiction over Rudzewicz pursuant to FLA. STAT. § 48.193(1) (g) because "the circumstances of the Drayton Plains franchise and the negotiations which led to it left Rudzewicz bereft of reasonable notice and financially unprepared for the prospect of franchise litigation in Florida." Accordingly, the panel majority concluded that "[jurisdiction] under these circumstances would offend the fundamental fairness which is the touchstone of due process."

. . .

The Due Process Clause protects an individual's liberty interest in not being subject to the binding judgments of a forum with which he has established no meaningful "contacts, ties, or relations." International Shoe. By requiring that individuals have "fair warning that a particular activity may subject [them] to the jurisdiction of a foreign sovereign,"[211] the Due Process Clause "gives a degree of predictability to the legal system that allows potential defendants to structure their primary conduct with some minimum assurance as to where that conduct will and will not render them liable to suit,"[212]

Where a forum seeks to assert specific jurisdiction over an out-of-state defendant who has not consented to suit there, this "fair warning" requirement is satisfied if the defendant has "purposefully directed" his activities at residents of the forum, *Keeton v. Hustler Magazine, Inc.*,[213] and the litigation results from alleged injuries that "arise out of or relate to" those activities, *Helicopteros Nacionales de Colombia, S.A. v. Hall*,[214] Thus "[the] forum State does not exceed its powers under the Due Process Clause if it asserts personal jurisdiction over a corporation that delivers its products into the stream of commerce with the expectation that they will be purchased by consumers in the forum State" and those products subsequently injure forum consumers.[215] Similarly, a publisher who distributes magazines in a distant State may fairly be held accountable in that forum for damages resulting there from an allegedly defamatory story. And with respect to interstate contractual obligations, we have emphasized that parties who "reach out beyond one state and create continuing relationships and obligations with citizens of another state" are

---

[211] Shaffer v. Heitner, 433 U.S. 186, 218 (1977) (Stevens, J., concurring).

[212] World-Wide Volkswagen v. Woodson, 444 U.S. 286, 297 (1980).

[213] 465 U.S. 770, 774 (1984).

[214] 466 U.S. 408, 414 (1984).

[215] *World-Wide Volkswagen*, 444 U.S. at 297–98.

subject to regulation and sanctions in the other State for the consequences of their activities.

We have noted several reasons why a forum legitimately may exercise personal jurisdiction over a nonresident who "purposefully directs" his activities toward forum residents. A State generally has a "manifest interest" in providing its residents with a convenient forum for redressing injuries inflicted by out-of-state actors. Moreover, where individuals "purposefully derive benefit" from their interstate activities, it may well be unfair to allow them to escape having to account in other States for consequences that arise proximately from such activities; the Due Process Clause may not readily be wielded as a territorial shield to avoid interstate obligations that have been voluntarily assumed. And because "modern transportation and communications have made it much less burdensome for a party sued to defend himself in a State where he engages in economic activity," it usually will not be unfair to subject him to the burdens of litigating in another forum for disputes relating to such activity.[216]

. . .

Notwithstanding these considerations, the constitutional touchstone remains whether the defendant purposefully established "minimum contacts" in the forum State.[217] Although it has been argued that foreseeability of causing injury in another State should be sufficient to establish such contacts there when policy considerations so require, the Court has consistently held that this kind of foreseeability is not a "sufficient benchmark" for exercising personal jurisdiction.[218] Instead, "the foreseeability that is critical to due process analysis . . . is that the defendant's conduct and connection with the forum State are such that he should reasonably anticipate being haled into court there." In defining when it is that a potential defendant should "reasonably anticipate" out-of-state litigation, the Court frequently has drawn from the reasoning of *Hanson v. Denckla*:[219]

> "The unilateral activity of those who claim some relationship with a nonresident defendant cannot satisfy the requirement of contact with the forum State. The application of that rule will vary with the quality and nature of the defendant's activity, but it is essential in each case that there be some act by which the defendant purposefully avails itself of the privilege of conducting activities within the forum State, thus invoking the benefits and protections of its laws."

This "purposeful availment" requirement ensures that a defendant will not be haled into a jurisdiction solely as a result of "random," "fortuitous," or "attenuated" contacts, or of the "unilateral activity of another party or a third person." Jurisdiction is proper, however, where the contacts proximately result from actions by the defendant himself that create a "substantial connection" with the forum State. Thus where the defendant "deliberately" has engaged in significant activities within a State, or has created "continuing obligations" between himself and residents of the forum, he manifestly has availed himself of the privilege of conducting business there, and because his activities are shielded by "the benefits and protections" of the forum's laws it is presumptively not unreasonable to require him to submit to the burdens of litigation in that forum as well.

Jurisdiction in these circumstances may not be avoided merely because the defendant did not physically enter the forum State. Although territorial presence frequently will enhance a potential

---

[216] McGee v. International Life Insurance Co., 355 U.S. 220, 223 (1957).
[217] *International Shoe Co. v. Washington*, 326 U.S. at 316.
[218] *World-Wide Volkswagen*, 444 U.S. at 295.
[219] 357 U.S. 235, 253 (1958).

defendant's affiliation with a State and reinforce the reasonable foreseeability of suit there, it is an inescapable fact of modern commercial life that a substantial amount of business is transacted solely by mail and wire communications across state lines, thus obviating the need for physical presence within a State in which business is conducted. So long as a commercial actor's efforts are "purposefully directed" toward residents of another State, we have consistently rejected the notion that an absence of physical contacts can defeat personal jurisdiction there.

. . .

Applying these principles to the case at hand, we believe there is substantial record evidence supporting the District Court's conclusion that the assertion of personal jurisdiction over Rudzewicz in Florida for the alleged breach of his franchise agreement did not offend due process. At the outset, we note a continued division among lower courts respecting whether and to what extent a contract can constitute a "contact" for purposes of due process analysis. If the question is whether an individual's contract with an out-of-state party alone can automatically establish sufficient minimum contacts in the other party's home forum, we believe the answer clearly is that it cannot. The Court long ago rejected the notion that personal jurisdiction might turn on "mechanical" tests, or on "conceptualistic . . . theories of the place of contracting or of performance." Instead, we have emphasized the need for a "highly realistic" approach that recognizes that a "contract" is "ordinarily but an intermediate step serving to tie up prior business negotiations with future consequences which themselves are the real object of the business transaction." It is these factors— [(1) prior negotiations and (2) contemplated future consequences, along with (3) the terms of the contract and (4) the parties' actual course of dealing]—that must be evaluated in determining whether the defendant purposefully established minimum contacts within the forum.

In this case, no physical ties to Florida can be attributed to Rudzewicz other than MacShara's brief training course in Miami. Rudzewicz did not maintain offices in Florida and, for all that appears from the record, has never even visited there. Yet this franchise dispute grew directly out of "a contract which had a substantial connection with that State." Eschewing the option of operating an independent local enterprise, Rudzewicz deliberately "[reached] out beyond" Michigan and negotiated with a Florida corporation for the purchase of a long-term franchise and the manifold benefits that would derive from affiliation with a nationwide organization. Upon approval, he entered into a carefully structured 20-year relationship that envisioned continuing and wide-reaching contacts with Burger King in Florida. In light of Rudzewicz' voluntary acceptance of the long-term and exacting regulation of his business from Burger King's Miami headquarters, the "quality and nature" of his relationship to the company in Florida can in no sense be viewed as "random," "fortuitous," or "attenuated." Rudzewicz's refusal to make the contractually required payments in Miami, and his continued use of Burger King's trademarks and confidential business information after his termination, caused foreseeable injuries to the corporation in Florida. For these reasons it was, at the very least, presumptively reasonable for Rudzewicz to be called to account there for such injuries.

The Court of Appeals concluded, however, that in light of the supervision emanating from Burger King's district office in Birmingham, Rudzewicz reasonably believed that "the Michigan office was for all intents and purposes the embodiment of Burger King" and that he therefore had no "reason to anticipate a Burger King suit outside of Michigan." This reasoning overlooks substantial record evidence indicating that Rudzewicz most certainly knew that he was affiliating himself with an enterprise based primarily in Florida. The contract documents themselves emphasize that Burger King's operations are conducted and supervised from the Miami headquarters, that all relevant notices and payments must be sent there, and that the agreements were made in and enforced from Miami. Moreover, the parties' actual course of dealing repeatedly confirmed that decision making authority was vested in the Miami headquarters and that the district office served largely as an intermediate link between the headquarters and the franchisees. When problems arose over building design, site-development fees, rent computation, and the defaulted payments, Rudzewicz and MacShara learned that the Michigan office was powerless to resolve their disputes and could only channel their communications to Miami. Throughout these disputes, the Miami headquarters and the Michigan franchisees carried on a continuous course of direct communications by mail and by telephone, and it was the Miami headquarters that made the key negotiating decisions out of which the instant litigation arose.

Moreover, we believe the Court of Appeals gave insufficient weight to provisions in the various franchise documents providing that all disputes would be governed by Florida law. The franchise agreement, for example, stated:

> This Agreement shall become valid when executed and accepted by BKC at Miami, Florida; it shall be deemed made and entered into in the State of Florida and shall be governed and construed under and in accordance with the laws of the State of Florida. The choice of law designation [[A choice of law provision differs significantly from a forum selection provision, such as the one in Carnival Cruise Lines, supra.]] does not require that all suits concerning this Agreement be filed in Florida.

The Court of Appeals reasoned that choice-of-law provisions are irrelevant to the question of personal jurisdiction, relying on *Hanson v. Denckla* for the proposition that "the center of gravity for choice-of-law purposes does not necessarily confer the sovereign prerogative to assert jurisdiction." This reasoning misperceives the import of the quoted proposition. The Court in *Hanson* and subsequent cases has emphasized that choice-of-law analysis—which focuses on all elements of a transaction, and not simply on the defendant's conduct—is distinct from minimum-contacts jurisdictional analysis—which focuses at the threshold solely on the defendant's purposeful connection to the forum. Nothing in our cases, however, suggests that a choice-of-law provision should be ignored in considering whether a defendant has "purposefully invoked the benefits and protections of a State's laws" for jurisdictional purposes. Although such a provision standing alone would be insufficient to confer jurisdiction, we believe that, when combined with the 20-year interdependent relationship Rudzewicz established with Burger King's Miami headquarters, it reinforced his deliberate affiliation with the forum State and the reasonable foreseeability of possible litigation there. As Judge Johnson argued in his dissent below, Rudzewicz "purposefully availed himself of the benefits and protections of Florida's laws" by entering into contracts expressly providing that those laws would govern franchise disputes.

. . .

The Court of Appeals also concluded, however, that the parties' dealings involved "a characteristic disparity of bargaining power" and "elements of surprise," and that Rudzewicz "lacked fair notice" of the potential for litigation in Florida because the contractual provisions suggesting to the contrary were merely "boilerplate declarations in a lengthy printed contract." . . . To the contrary, Rudzewicz was represented by counsel throughout these complex transactions and, as Judge Johnson observed in dissent below, was himself an experienced accountant "who for five months conducted negotiations with Burger King over the terms of the franchise and lease agreements, and who obligated himself personally to contracts requiring overtime payments that exceeded $1 million." Rudzewicz was able to secure a modest reduction in rent and other concessions from Miami headquarters; moreover, to the extent that Burger King's terms were inflexible, Rudzewicz presumably decided that the advantages of affiliating with a national organization provided sufficient commercial benefits to offset the detriments.

. . .

Notwithstanding these considerations, the Court of Appeals apparently believed that it was necessary to reject jurisdiction in this case as a prophylactic measure, reasoning that an affirmance of the District Court's judgment would result in the exercise of jurisdiction over "out-of-state consumers to collect payments due on modest personal purchases" and would "sow the seeds of default judgments against franchisees owing smaller debts."

For the reasons set forth above, however, these dangers are not present in the instant case. Because Rudzewicz established a substantial and continuing relationship with Burger King's Miami headquarters, received fair notice from the contract documents and the course of dealing that he might be subject to suit in Florida, and has failed to demonstrate how jurisdiction in that forum would otherwise be fundamentally unfair, we conclude that the District Court's exercise of jurisdiction pursuant to FLA. STAT. § 48.193(1) (g) did not offend due process. The judgment of the Court of Appeals is accordingly reversed, and the case is remanded for further proceedings consistent with this opinion.

It is so ordered.

Practice Problems

The following Practice Problems serve to help solidify your understanding of the specific jurisdiction minimum contacts analysis as applied to contracts.

Practice Problem 5-6

Aldo lived and worked as an engineer in North Carolina before deciding to attend Harvard Business School. While in a product development course there, he developed a plan to introduce a new product. Unfortunately, he became ill and went to his parents' home in Norfolk, Virginia to recover. As he recovered, Aldo kept busy by working to make his product (an escape ladder named "X-IT ladder") a commercial reality. Using all his savings, Aldo developed the X-IT ladder and displayed it at the national fire safety trade show. The X-IT ladder was such a hit at the trade show that Aldo soon heard from Safety Products, Inc. ("SPI"). SPI is incorporated in Texas and has corporate headquarters in Dallas, Texas.

Aldo met several times with SPI to negotiate an agreement. All these meetings occurred at the home of Aldo's parents in Norfolk, Virginia. The negotiations explored both SPI's purchase of Aldo's X-IT ladder rights, and the prospect of Aldo serving as a consultant to SPI on future design matters. Between meetings, Aldo made several calls to representatives of SPI at its headquarters to clarify the parameters of an agreement. The parties ended up agreeing in principle to an arrangement by which (1) SPI would pay Aldo $300,000 up front in return for the right to make, market, and sell the X-IT ladder for five years; (2) in addition, SPI would pay an annual consulting fee of $100,000 to Aldo; and (3) Aldo's failure to provide consulting services would constitute a breach of contract and render him liable to SPI for $150,000.

SPI and Aldo signed the contract at a final meeting in Virginia. SPI then began making, marketing, and selling the X-IT ladder. It initially became a success, but SPI needed consulting help from Aldo so that SPI could adjust the product when competitors started to develop similar versions of the ladder. However, SPI could not get any response from Aldo despite its requests for consulting assistance. SPI ultimately sent Aldo a letter advising him that SPI considered him in breach of the contract. SPI filed suit against Aldo in state court in Texas. The suit claimed that Aldo breached the contract with SPI by failing to provide consulting services as required by the contract. The suit demanded $150,000 from Aldo. Aldo filed a motion challenging personal jurisdiction. Should the motion be granted? Fully explain your answer.

Practice Problem 5-7

Tom Edson lives in New Jersey. After entering a purchase contract without negotiating it, Edson buys a $500 stereo system from a California manufacturer. Edson had seen the stereo system advertised in one of the "SkyMall" catalogs that airplanes make available to passengers. He called the 800-number listed and asked about the stereo. The company sent him a contract that provided "California law shall apply to any disputes arising from this contract." Edson signed the contract, and the manufacturer shipped the stereo equipment with an invoice for payment. The equipment did not work to Edson's satisfaction (the volume would randomly change when playing), so he sent the equipment back and refused to pay. The company sued him in California state court and argued that the court there had personal jurisdiction over Edson. Is this accurate in light of the governing law?

---

b. The Stream-of-Commerce Context

So-called "stream-of-commerce" cases present a more complicated situation. These cases involve a product originating with a manufacturer and moving—in the most basic context—through commerce via some form of middle-man (usually a wholesale distributor) to a retailer and ultimately to the consumer. The more complicated variety of stream-of-commerce cases occurs when a component part manufacturer supplies the part to a finished product manufacturer who incorporates the component into the finished product, and after traveling through more and more distributors, a consumer buys the product. In either form of these stream-of-commerce scenarios, the consumer typically is injured and brings a products liability suit against a manufacturer in the consumer's home state.

The following two opinions demonstrate plurality opinions of the United States Supreme Court. A plurality opinion is one in which the most justices join when no opinion is joined by a majority. Thus, with a full complement of nine justices, a majority would be an opinion in which five justices join while a plurality typically is one in which four justices join. If there are, as at times happens, two opinions with four justices joining each, the justice who agrees with the result of one of the pluralities will determine the holding of the Court. Plurality opinions do not carry the same precedential weight as a majority opinion. However, it is a mistake to believe that a Supreme Court plurality lacks precedential effect:

The Supreme Court itself . . . has provided guidance on how to interpret only one type of plurality decision, that in which the opinions offered in support of the result appear to be of varying scope or breadth. In such a situation, the Supreme Court has indicated that the opinion concurring in the judgment on the "narrowest grounds" represents the highest common denominator of majority agreement, and thus should be regarded as authoritative for future cases.[220]

---

[220] Linda Novak, *The Precedential Value of Supreme Court Plurality Opinions*, 80 COLUM. L. REV. 756, 760-61 (1980) (footnotes omitted).

ASAHI METAL INDUSTRY CO. v. SUPERIOR COURT OF CALIFORNIA
Supreme Court of the United States, 1987
480 U.S. 102

JUSTICE O'CONNOR announced the judgment of the Court and delivered the unanimous opinion of the Court with respect to Part I, the opinion of the Court with respect to Part II-B, in which THE CHIEF JUSTICE, JUSTICE BRENNAN, JUSTICE WHITE, JUSTICE MARSHALL, JUSTICE BLACKMUN, JUSTICE POWELL, and JUSTICE STEVENS join, and an opinion with respect to Parts II-A and III, in which THE CHIEF JUSTICE, JUSTICE POWELL, and JUSTICE SCALIA join.

This case presents the question whether the mere awareness on the part of a foreign defendant that the components it manufactured, sold, and delivered outside the United States would reach the forum State in the stream of commerce constitutes "minimum contacts" between the defendant and the forum State such that the exercise of jurisdiction "does not offend 'traditional notions of fair play and substantial justice.'"

I

On September 23, 1978, on Interstate Highway 80 in Solano County, California, Gary Zurcher lost control of his Honda motorcycle and collided with a tractor. Zurcher was severely injured, and his passenger and wife, Ruth Ann Moreno, was killed. In September 1979, Zurcher filed a product liability action in the Superior Court of the State of California in and for the County of Solano. Zurcher alleged that the 1978 accident was caused by a sudden loss of air and an explosion in the rear tire of the motorcycle, and alleged that the motorcycle tire, tube, and sealant were defective. Zurcher's complaint named, inter alia, Cheng Shin Rubber Industrial Co., Ltd. (Cheng Shin), the Taiwanese manufacturer of the tube. Cheng Shin in turn filed a cross-complaint seeking indemnification from its codefendants and from petitioner, Asahi Metal Industry Co., Ltd. (Asahi), the manufacturer of the tube's valve assembly. Zurcher's claims against Cheng Shin and the other defendants were eventually settled and dismissed, leaving only Cheng Shin's indemnity action against Asahi.

California's long-arm statute authorizes the exercise of jurisdiction "on any basis not inconsistent with the Constitution of this state or of the United States." Asahi moved to quash Cheng Shin's service of summons, arguing the State could not exert jurisdiction over it consistent with the Due Process Clause of the Fourteenth Amendment.

In relation to the motion, the following information was submitted by Asahi and Cheng Shin. Asahi is a Japanese corporation. It manufactures tire valve assemblies in Japan and sells the assemblies to Cheng Shin, and to several other tire manufacturers, for use as components in finished tire tubes. Asahi's sales to Cheng Shin took place in Taiwan. The shipments from Asahi to Cheng Shin were sent from Japan to Taiwan. Cheng Shin bought and incorporated into its tire tubes 150,000 Asahi valve assemblies in 1978; 500,000 in 1979; 500,000 in 1980; 100,000 in 1981; and 100,000 in 1982. Sales to Cheng Shin accounted for 1.24 percent of Asahi's income in 1981 and 0.44 percent in 1982. Cheng Shin alleged that approximately 20 percent of its sales in the United States are in California. Cheng Shin purchases valve assemblies from other suppliers as well and sells finished tubes throughout the world.

In 1983, an attorney for Cheng Shin conducted an informal examination of the valve stems of the tire tubes sold in one cycle store in Solano County. The attorney declared that of the approximately 115 tire tubes in the store, 97 were purportedly manufactured in Japan or Taiwan, and of those 97, 21 valve stems were marked with the circled letter "A", apparently Asahi's trademark. Of the 21 Asahi valve stems, 12 were incorporated into Cheng Shin tire tubes. The store contained 41 other Cheng Shin tubes that

152

incorporated the valve assemblies of other manufacturers. An affidavit of a manager of Cheng Shin whose duties included the purchasing of component parts stated: "'In discussions with Asahi regarding the purchase of valve stem assemblies the fact that my Company sells tubes throughout the world and specifically the United States has been discussed. I am informed and believe that Asahi was fully aware that valve stem assemblies sold to my Company and to others would end up throughout the United States and in California.'" An affidavit of the president of Asahi, on the other hand, declared that Asahi "'has never contemplated that its limited sales of tire valves to Cheng Shin in Taiwan would subject it to lawsuits in California.'" The record does not include any contract between Cheng Shin and Asahi. Primarily based on the above information, the Superior Court denied the motion to quash summons, stating: "Asahi obviously does business on an international scale. It is not unreasonable that they defend claims of defect in their product on an international scale."

The Court of Appeal of the State of California issued a peremptory writ of mandate commanding the Superior Court to quash service of summons. The court concluded that "it would be unreasonable to require Asahi to respond in California solely on the basis of ultimately realized foreseeability that the product into which its component was embodied would be sold all over the world including California."

The Supreme Court of the State of California reversed and discharged the writ issued by the Court of Appeal. The court observed: "Asahi has no offices, property or agents in California. It solicits no business in California and has made no direct sales [in California]." Moreover, "Asahi did not design or control the system of distribution that carried its valve assemblies into California." Nevertheless, the court found the exercise of jurisdiction over Asahi to be consistent with the Due Process Clause. It concluded that Asahi knew that some of the valve assemblies sold to Cheng Shin would be incorporated into tire tubes sold in California, and that Asahi benefited indirectly from the sale in California of products incorporating its components. The court considered Asahi's intentional act of placing its components into the stream of commerce--that is, by delivering the components to Cheng Shin in Taiwan--coupled with Asahi's awareness that some of the components would eventually find their way into California, sufficient to form the basis for state court jurisdiction under the Due Process Clause. We granted certiorari, and now reverse.

II A

The Due Process Clause of the Fourteenth Amendment limits the power of a state court to exert personal jurisdiction over a nonresident defendant. "[T]he constitutional touchstone" of the determination whether an exercise of personal jurisdiction comports with due process "remains whether the defendant purposefully established 'minimum contacts' in the forum state."[221] Most recently we have reaffirmed the oft-quoted reasoning of *Hanson v. Denckla*,[222] that minimum contacts must have a basis in "some act by which the defendant purposefully avails itself of the privilege of conducting activities within the forum State, thus invoking the benefits and protections of its laws.[223] "Jurisdiction is proper . . . where the contacts proximately result from actions by the defendant himself that create a 'substantial connection with the forum State.'"

. . .

The reasoning of the Supreme Court of California in the present case illustrates the former interpretation of World-Wide Volkswagen. The Supreme Court of California held that, because the stream

---

[221] Burger King Corp. v. Rudzewicz, 471 U.S. 462, 474 (1985).
[222] 357 U.S. 235, 253 (1958).
[223] *Burger King*, 471 U.S., at 475.

of commerce eventually brought some valves Asahi sold Cheng Shin into California, Asahi's awareness that its valves would be sold in California was sufficient to permit California to exercise jurisdiction over Asahi consistent with the requirements of the Due Process Clause. The Supreme Court of California's position was consistent with those courts that have held that mere foreseeability or awareness was a constitutionally sufficient basis for personal jurisdiction if the defendant's product made its way into the forum State while still in the stream of commerce.

Other courts, however, have understood the Due Process Clause to require something more than that the defendant was aware of its product's entry into the forum State through the stream of commerce in order for the State to exert jurisdiction over the defendant. In the present case, for example, the State Court of Appeal did not read the Due Process Clause, as interpreted by *World-Wide Volkswagen*, to allow "mere foreseeability that the product will enter the forum state [to] be enough by itself to establish jurisdiction over the distributor and retailer." In *Humble v. Toyota Motor Co.*,[224] an injured car passenger brought suit against Arakawa Auto Body Company, a Japanese corporation that manufactured car seats for Toyota. Arakawa did no business in the United States; it had no office, affiliate, subsidiary, or agent in the United States; it manufactured its component parts outside the United States and delivered them to Toyota Motor Company in Japan. The Court of Appeals, adopting the reasoning of the District Court in that case, noted that although it "does not doubt that Arakawa could have foreseen that its product would find its way into the United States," it would be "manifestly unjust" to require Arakawa to defend itself in the United States.

We now find this latter position to be consonant with the requirements of due process. The "substantial connection," between the defendant and the forum State necessary for a finding of minimum contacts must come about by an action of the defendant purposefully directed toward the forum State. The placement of a product into the stream of commerce, without more, is not an act of the defendant purposefully directed toward the forum State. Additional conduct of the defendant may indicate an intent or purpose to serve the market in the forum State, for example, designing the product for the market in the forum State, advertising in the forum State, establishing channels for providing regular advice to customers in the forum State, or marketing the product through a distributor who has agreed to serve as the sales agent in the forum State. But a defendant's awareness that the stream of commerce may or will sweep the product into the forum State does not convert the mere act of placing the product into the stream into an act purposefully directed toward the forum State.

Assuming, arguendo, that respondents have established Asahi's awareness that some of the valves sold to Cheng Shin would be incorporated into tire tubes sold in California, respondents have not demonstrated any action by Asahi to purposefully avail itself of the California market. Asahi does not do business in California. It has no office, agents, employees, or property in California. It does not advertise or otherwise solicit business in California. It did not create, control, or employ the distribution system that brought its valves to California. There is no evidence that Asahi designed its product in anticipation of sales in California. On the basis of these facts, the exertion of personal jurisdiction over Asahi by the Superior Court of California exceeds the limits of due process.

B

The strictures of the Due Process Clause forbid a state court from exercising personal jurisdiction over Asahi under circumstances that would offend "'traditional notions of fair play and substantial justice.'"

We have previously explained that the determination of the reasonableness of the exercise of

---

[224] 727 F.2d 709 (CA. 1984).

jurisdiction in each case will depend on an evaluation of several factors. A court must consider the burden on the defendant, the interests of the forum State, and the plaintiff's interest in obtaining relief. It must also weigh in its determination "the interstate judicial system's interest in obtaining the most efficient resolution of controversies; and the shared interest of the several States in furthering fundamental substantive social policies."[225]

A consideration of these factors in the present case clearly reveals the unreasonableness of the assertion of jurisdiction over Asahi, even apart from the question of the placement of goods in the stream of commerce.

Certainly, the burden on the defendant in this case is severe. Asahi has been commanded by the Supreme Court of California not only to traverse the distance between Asahi's headquarters in Japan and the Superior Court of California in and for the County of Solano, but also to submit its dispute with Cheng Shin to a foreign nation's judicial system. The unique burdens placed upon one who must defend oneself in a foreign legal system should have significant weight in assessing the reasonableness of stretching the long arm of personal jurisdiction over national borders.

When minimum contacts have been established, often the interests of the plaintiff and the forum in the exercise of jurisdiction will justify even the serious burdens placed on the alien defendant. In the present case, however, the interests of the plaintiff and the forum in California's assertion of jurisdiction over Asahi are slight. All that remains is a claim for indemnification asserted by Cheng Shin, a Tawainese corporation, against Asahi. The transaction on which the indemnification claim is based took place in Taiwan; Asahi's components were shipped from Japan to Taiwan. Cheng Shin has not demonstrated that it is more convenient for it to litigate its indemnification claim against Asahi in California rather than in Taiwan or Japan.

Because the plaintiff is not a California resident, California's legitimate interests in the dispute have considerably diminished. The Supreme Court of California argued that the State had an interest in "protecting its consumers by ensuring that foreign manufacturers comply with the state's safety standards." The State Supreme Court's definition of California's interest, however, was overly broad. The dispute between Cheng Shin and Asahi is primarily about indemnification rather than safety standards. Moreover, it is not at all clear at this point that California law should govern the question whether a Japanese corporation should indemnify a Taiwanese corporation on the basis of a sale made in Taiwan and a shipment of goods from Japan to Taiwan. The possibility of being haled into a California court as a result of an accident involving Asahi's components undoubtedly creates an additional deterrent to the manufacture of unsafe components; however, similar pressures will be placed on Asahi by the purchasers of its components as long as those who use Asahi components in their final products, and sell those products in California, are subject to the application of California tort law.

. . .

Considering the international context, the heavy burden on the alien defendant, and the slight interests of the plaintiff and the forum State, the exercise of personal jurisdiction by a California court over Asahi in this instance would be unreasonable and unfair.

---

[225] *World-Wide Volkswagen*, 444 U.S. at 292.

III

Because the facts of this case do not establish minimum contacts such that the exercise of personal jurisdiction is consistent with fair play and substantial justice, the judgment of the Supreme Court of California is reversed, and the case is remanded for further proceedings not inconsistent with this opinion.

It is so ordered.

Follow-Up Questions and Comments

1. In a more recent decision, J. *McIntyre Machinery, Ltd., v. Nicastro*,[226] the Supreme Court reaffirmed the reasoning in Asahi. In Nicastro, a New Jersey citizen injured his hand while using a metal-shearing machine manufactured by J. McIntyre Machinery, Ltd. ("McIntyre"), an English company. The plaintiff sued in New Jersey state court and relied on a stream of commerce theory to support jurisdiction. The evidence showed that a United States distributor agreed to sell McIntyre's equipment in the U.S.; that McIntyre attended trade shows in the U.S., though not in New Jersey, and that no more than four McIntyre machines (including the one on which plaintiff was injured) ended up in New Jersey. On these facts, the New Jersey Supreme Court held that personal jurisdiction existed under a stream of commerce theory. In yet another plurality decision, Justice Kennedy cited *Asahi* and observed that to satisfy due process a manufacturer would have to have more than merely putting its product into commerce.[227] The key question was whether the defendant's conduct was "directed at" the state in question.[228] Thus, the reasoning of Nicastro reaffirms the approach of the O'Connor plurality in *Asahi*.

Practice Problem

The following Practice Problem will help you evaluate the minimum contacts analysis in a stream-of-commerce setting.

Practice Problem 5-8

Ruby Red Slippers, Inc. ("RRS") is a company incorporated and based in Texafornia. It makes ruby red slippers that have become immensely popular with young women. Indeed, the Wall Street Gazette ran an article recently about how the ruby red slippers have been such a remarkable product because of their "crossover" appeal to girls ranging in ages from toddlers to teenagers. The product had become so popular that it was difficult to go out in public without seeing some young woman wearing sparkling ruby red slippers.

While RRS has done business in virtually every state, states on the eastern seaboard have been responsible for more sales than any other region. RRS has non-permanent kiosk stations set up in every mall in and around the state in which you plan to practice. RRS hires employees who dress up as a princess who wears the ruby red slippers, as guards for the princess, and even as a witch who entreats the princess to eat a special apple. Miranda attends high school in the state in which you plan to practice. She buys RRS's slippers at a mall kiosk. Unfortunately, the first time that she wore the slippers the heel unexpectedly

---

[226] 564 U.S. 873 (2011).
[227] *Id.* at 881–82.
[228] *Id.* at 884.

fell off the shoe. As a result, Miranda fell, hit her head, and went into a coma. Miranda's Uncle Prospero practices law in Virginia. Uncle Prospero consulted with an expert on shoes, known by plaintiffs' lawyers as Caliban the Cobbler, who confirmed that the shoes were defectively manufactured. The expert advised that the shoe design was such that the heel would easily come off if someone wearing them stepped on uneven surfaces, something that all shoe manufacturers must anticipate.

Miranda was still in a coma at the time Uncle Prospero filed suit against RRS in federal court in Virginia. RRS timely filed a motion to dismiss for lack of personal jurisdiction. You are the law clerk for the Judge. She asks you to write a memorandum objectively analyzing the issues raised by RRS's motion and her options in ruling. What would you advise the Judge?

c. Torts Contexts (Other Than Stream of Commerce)

Tort claims other than those arising from stream of commerce are often the basis of suits in which personal jurisdiction is challenged. In some of these cases, the analysis is relatively easy. For instance, if a person commits a negligent act (*e.g.*, causes a car accident) in a state, she ought to expect to be answerable in that state for her negligence. Likewise, someone who commits fraud, an assault or battery, or other tortious conduct within a state can hardly claim to lack notice. The more challenging cases are those like defamation cases, where the events are triggered out of the forum but have an impact within the forum.

For example, in *Calder v. Jones*,[229] the Supreme Court found sufficient minimum contacts to support personal jurisdiction over a Florida-based nationally distributed magazine and its staff. The magazine, The National Enquirer, published an article impugning a plaintiff's reputation as an entertainer. It used sources in California and California was the focal point of the article and the state where the magazine had its largest circulation. Hence, the Court found, the brunt of the article's effects would be expected—and were felt—in California. Because the magazine's efforts were calculated to cause injury to the plaintiff in California, the magazine and its responsible personnel could reasonably anticipate being haled into court there.[230]

The following case is an influential one that, as you will see, relies on *Calder v. Jones* and interprets it to require both effect on the defendant in the forum and knowledge of defendant's presence there to establish personal jurisdiction. You should realize, however, that unlike the series of Supreme Court case opinions in this chapter, the United States Court of Appeals for the Fifth Circuit does not bind courts in other circuits.

---

[229] 465 U.S. 783, 791 (1984).
[230] *Id.* at 788–91.

REVELL v. LIDOV
United States Court of Appeals for the Fifth Circuit, 2002
317 F.3d 467

HIGGINBOTHAM, Circuit Judge:

Oliver "Buck" Revell sued Hart G.W. Lidov and Columbia University for defamation arising out of Lidov's authorship of an article that he posted on an internet bulletin board hosted by Columbia. The district court dismissed Revell's claims for lack of personal jurisdiction over both Lidov and Columbia. We affirm.

I

Hart G.W. Lidov, an Assistant Professor of Pathology and Neurology at the Harvard Medical School and Children's Hospital, wrote a lengthy article on the subject of the terrorist bombing of Pan Am Flight 103, which exploded over Lockerbie, Scotland in 1988. The article alleges that a broad politically motivated conspiracy among senior members of the Reagan Administration lay behind their willful failure to stop the bombing despite clear advance warnings. Further, Lidov charged that the government proceeded to cover up its receipt of advance warning and repeatedly misled the public about the facts. Specifically, the article singles out Oliver "Buck" Revell, then Associate Deputy Director of the FBI, for severe criticism, accusing him of complicity in the conspiracy and cover-up. The article further charges that Revell, knowing about the imminent terrorist attack, made certain his son, previously booked on Pan Am 103, took a different flight. At the time he wrote the article, Lidov had never been to Texas, except possibly to change planes, or conducted business there, and was apparently unaware that Revell then resided in Texas.

Lidov has also never been a student or faculty member of Columbia University, but he posted his article on a website maintained by its School of Journalism. In a bulletin board section of the website, users could post their own works and read the works of others. As a result, the article could be viewed by members of the public over the internet.

Revell, a resident of Texas, sued the Board of Trustees of Columbia University, whose principal offices are in New York City, and Lidov, who is a Massachusetts resident, in the Northern District of Texas.

Revell claimed damage to his professional reputation in Texas and emotional distress arising out of the alleged defamation of the defendants and sought several million dollars in damages. Both defendants moved to dismiss for lack of personal jurisdiction under Federal Rule of Civil Procedure 12 (b)(2). The district court granted the defendants' motions, and Revell now appeals.

. . .

Answering the question of personal jurisdiction in this case brings these settled and familiar formulations to a new mode of communication across state lines. Revell first urges that the district court may assert general jurisdiction over Columbia because its website provides internet users the opportunity to subscribe to the Columbia Journalism Review, purchase advertising on the website or in the journal, and submit electronic applications for admission.

This circuit has drawn upon the approach of *Zippo Manufacturing Co. v. Zippo Dot Com, Inc.*,[231] in determining whether the operation of an internet site can support the minimum contacts necessary for

---

[231] 952 F. Supp. 1119 (1997).

the exercise of personal jurisdiction. *Zippo* used a "sliding scale" to measure an internet site's connections to a forum state. A "passive" website, one that merely allows the owner to post information on the internet, is at one end of the scale. It will not be sufficient to establish personal jurisdiction. At the other end are sites whose owners engage in repeated online contacts with forum residents over the internet, and in these cases personal jurisdiction may be proper. In between are those sites with some interactive elements, through which a site allows for bilateral information exchange with its visitors. Here, we find more familiar terrain, requiring that we examine the extent of the interactivity and nature of the forum contacts.

While we deployed this sliding scale in *Mink v. AAAA Development LLC*,[232] it is not well adapted to the general jurisdiction inquiry, because even repeated contacts with forum residents by a foreign defendant may not constitute the requisite substantial, continuous and systematic contacts required for a finding of general jurisdiction--in other words, while it may be doing business with Texas, it is not doing business in Texas.

Irrespective of the sliding scale, the question of general jurisdiction is not difficult here. Though the maintenance of a website is, in a sense, a continuous

. . .

Turning to the issue of specific jurisdiction, the question is whether Revell has made out his prima facie case with respect to the defendants' contacts with Texas. *Zippo*'s scale does more work with specific jurisdiction—the context in which it was originally conceived.

Revell urges that, given the uniqueness of defamation claims and their inherent ability to inflict injury in far-flung jurisdictions, we should abandon the imagery of *Zippo*. It is a bold but ultimately unpersuasive argument. Defamation has its unique features but shares relevant characteristics with various business torts. Nor is the *Zippo* scale, as has been suggested, in tension with the "effects" test of *Calder v. Jones* for intentional torts, which we address in Part II. D.

For specific jurisdiction we look only to the contact out of which the cause of action arises—in this case the maintenance of the internet bulletin board. Since this defamation action does not arise out of the solicitation of subscriptions or applications by Columbia, those portions of the website need not be considered.

The district court concluded that the bulletin board was "Zippo-passive" and therefore could not create specific jurisdiction. The defendants insist that Columbia's bulletin board is indistinguishable from the website in *Mink*. In that case, we found the website would not support a finding of minimum contacts because it only solicited customers, provided a toll-free number to call, and an e-mail address. It did not allow visitors to place orders online. But in this case, any user of the internet can post material to the bulletin board. This means that individuals send information to be posted and receive information that others have posted. In *Mink* and *Zippo*, a visitor was limited to expressing an interest in a commercial product. Here the visitor may participate in an open forum hosted by the website. Columbia's bulletin board is thus interactive, and we must evaluate the extent of this interactivity as well as Revell's arguments with respect to *Calder*.

. . .

---

[232] 190 F.3d 333 (5th Cir. 1999).

Revell urges that, measured by the "effects" test of *Calder*, he has presented his prima facie case for the defendants' minimum contacts with Texas. At the outset we emphasize that the "effects" test is but one facet of the ordinary minimum contacts analysis, to be considered as part of the full range of the defendant's contacts with the forum.

We find several distinctions between this case and *Calder*—insurmountable hurdles to the exercise of personal jurisdiction by Texas courts. First, the article written by Lidov about Revell contains no reference to Texas, nor does it refer to the Texas activities of Revell, and it was not directed at Texas readers as distinguished from readers in other states. Texas was not the focal point of the article or the harm suffered, unlike *Calder*, in which the article contained descriptions of the California activities of the plaintiff, drew upon California sources, and found its largest audience in California. This conclusion fits well with our decisions in other intentional tort cases where the plaintiff relied upon Calder. In those cases, we stated that the plaintiff's residence in the forum, and suffering of harm there, will not alone support jurisdiction under Calder. We also find instructive the defamation decisions of the Sixth, Third, and Fourth Circuits in *Reynolds v. International Amateur Athletic Federation*, *Remick v. Manfredy*, and *Young v. New Haven Advocate*, respectively.[233]

In *Reynolds*[,] a London-based association published a press release regarding the plaintiff's disqualification from international track competition for two years following his failure of a drug test. The plaintiff, an Ohio resident, claimed that the alleged defamation had cost him endorsement contracts in Ohio and cited *Calder* in support of his argument that personal jurisdiction over the defendant in Ohio was proper. The court found *Calder* inapposite because, inter alia, the allegedly defamatory press release dealt with the plaintiff's activities in Monaco, not Ohio; the source of the report was a urine sample taken in Monaco and analyzed in Paris; and the "focal point" of the release was not Ohio. We agree with the Reynolds court that the sources relied upon and activities described in an allegedly defamatory publication should in some way connect with the forum if Calder is to be invoked. Lidov's article, insofar as it relates to Revell, deals exclusively with his actions as Associate Deputy Director of the FBI--just as the offending press release in Reynolds dealt only with a failed drug test in Monaco. It signifies that there is no reference to Texas in the article or any reliance on Texas sources. These facts weigh heavily against finding the requisite minimum contacts in this case.

In *Remick*[,] the plaintiff, a Pennsylvania lawyer, sued several individuals for defamation arising out of two letters sent to the plaintiff in Pennsylvania containing oblique charges of incompetence and accusations that the plaintiff was engaged in extortion of the defendants. The letters concerned the termination of the plaintiff's representation of one of the defendants, a professional boxer. One of the two letters was read by individuals other than the plaintiff when it was faxed to the plaintiff's Philadelphia office. The court held, however, that since there was nothing in the letter to indicate that it was targeted at Pennsylvania residents other than the plaintiff, personal jurisdiction could not be obtained under *Calder*. Furthermore, the court noted that allegations that the charges in the letter had been distributed throughout the "boxing community" were insufficient, because there was no assertion that Pennsylvania had a "unique relationship with the boxing industry, as distinguished from the relationship in Calder be-tween California and the motion picture industry, with which the *Calder* plaintiff was associated."

Similarly, in *Young v. New Haven Advocate*,[234] two newspapers in Connecticut posted on the

---

[233] *See Revell*, 373 F.3d at 473–76 (discussing the Third, Fourth, and Sixth Circuit decisions).
[234] *Young*, 315 F.3d at 256.

internet articles about the housing of Connecticut prisoners in Virginia that allegedly defamed a Virginia prison warden. The Fourth Circuit held that Virginia could not exercise personal jurisdiction over the Connecticut defendants because "they did not manifest an intent to aim their websites or the posted articles at a Virginia audience." Following its decision in *ALS Scan, Inc. v. Digital Service Consultants*, it reasoned that "application of *Calder* in the Internet context requires proof that the out-of-state defendant's Internet activity is expressly directed at or directed to the forum state." It observed that more than simply making the news article accessible to Virginians by defendants' posting of the article on their internet sites was needed for assertion of jurisdiction: "The newspapers must, through the Internet postings, manifest an intent to target and focus on Virginia readers."

As with *Remick* and *Young*, the post to the bulletin board here was presumably directed at the entire world, or perhaps just concerned U.S. citizens. But certainly, it was not directed specifically at Texas, which has no especial relationship to the Pan Am 103 incident. Furthermore, here there is nothing to compare to the targeting of California readers represented by approximately 600,000 copies of the Enquirer the *Calder* defendants knew would be distributed in California, the Enquirer's largest market.

. . .

As these cases aptly demonstrate, one cannot purposefully avail oneself of "some forum someplace." Rather, as the Supreme Court has stated, due process requires that "the defendant's conduct and connection with the forum State are such that he should reasonably anticipate being haled into court there." Lidov's affidavit, uncontroverted by the record, states that he did not even know that Revell was a resident of Texas when he posted his article. Knowledge of the particular forum in which a potential plaintiff will bear the brunt of the harm forms an essential part of the Calder test. The defendant must be chargeable with knowledge of the forum at which his conduct is directed in order to reasonably anticipate being haled into court in that forum, as Calder itself and numerous cases from other circuits applying Calder confirm. Demanding knowledge of a particular forum to which conduct is directed, in defamation cases, is not altogether distinct from the requirement that the forum be the focal point of the tortious activity because satisfaction of the latter will oft times provide sufficient evidence of the former. Lidov must have known that the harm of the article would hit home wherever Revell resided. But that is the case with virtually any defamation. A more direct aim is required than we have here. In short, this was not about Texas. If the article had a geographic focus it was Washington, D.C.

. . .

In sum, Revell has failed to make out a prima facie case of personal jurisdiction over either defendant. General jurisdiction cannot be obtained over Columbia. Considering both the "effects" test of *Calder* and the low-level of interactivity of the internet bulletin board, we find the contacts with Texas insufficient to establish the jurisdiction of its courts, and hence the federal district court in Texas, over Columbia and Lidov. We AFFIRM the dismissal for lack of personal jurisdiction as to both defendants.

Affirmed.

Follow-Up Questions and Comments

1. Defamation cases have presented a challenge in the area of personal jurisdiction. Do you see a limiting principle developed in Revell and the circuit court opinions it analyzes that help to place

some limits on the jurisdictions in which a defendant can be sued for defamation? Are these limits consistent with *Calder*?

2. Battery and defamation are both torts. A person who comes into a state and punches another, even if the defendant has no other connections and is there for less than a half hour, will always be subject to personal jurisdiction in the state in which he commits battery. A person who defames another by, for instance, posting a defamatory comment on social media also commits a tort. Many social media applications are accessible in every U.S. state and indeed outside the U.S. Should that mean that the defendant is subject to personal jurisdiction in every U.S. state for the defamation? If not, what are the states in which the defendant should be subject to personal jurisdiction (be sure to analyze beyond transient jurisdiction and the individual's domicile)?

---

d. The Property Ownership Context

Shaffer v. Heitner,[235] is the leading case on property ownership as a basis for specific jurisdiction. This case illustrates a shareholder derivative action, a specialized kind of lawsuit ordinarily covered in upper-level courses. For present purposes, note that a shareholder derivative suit allows a shareholder to sue a third-party in the corporation's name—often company officers whom the shareholder believes to have breached a fiduciary duty to the company. In these cases, the shareholders need not wait for the company to sue. That is what happened here.

In *Shaffer*, the "property" on which the plaintiff sought to establish personal jurisdiction were shares of stock in the Greyhound Corporation representing ownership interest in the corporation. The reality, however, is that these shares were not in the forum. Instead, the plaintiff, as you will see, relied on a Delaware statute that deemed shares in any Delaware corporation "located" in Delaware. Even though the property ownership in this case was attenuated, the Court used this as an opportunity to discuss how claims in a case must arise from the ownership of the property that is the subject of the dispute for purposes of specific jurisdiction.

SHAFFER v. HEITNER
Supreme Court of the United States, 1977
433 U.S. 186

JUSTICE MARSHALL delivered the opinion of the Court.

The controversy in this case concerns the constitutionality of a Delaware statute that allows a court of that State to take jurisdiction of a lawsuit by sequestering any property of the defendant that happens to be located in Delaware. Appellants contend that the sequestration statute as applied in this case violates the Due Process Clause of the Fourteenth Amendment both because it permits the state courts to exercise jurisdiction despite the absence of sufficient contacts among the defendants, the litigation, and the State of Delaware and because it authorizes the deprivation of defendants' property without providing adequate procedural safeguards. We find it necessary to consider only the first of these contentions.

I

---

[235] 433 U.S. 186 (1977).

Appellee Heitner, a nonresident of Delaware, is the owner of one share of stock in the Greyhound Corp., a business incorporated under the laws of Delaware with its principal place of business in Phoenix, Ariz. On May 22, 1974, he filed a shareholder's derivative suit in the Court of Chancery for New Castle County, Del., in which he named as defendants Greyhound, its wholly owned subsidiary Greyhound Lines, Inc., and 28 present or former officers or directors of one or both of the corporations. In essence, Heitner alleged that the individual defendants had violated their duties to Greyhound by causing it and its subsidiary to engage in actions that resulted in the corporations being held liable for substantial damages in a private antitrust suit and a large fine in a criminal contempt action. The activities which led to these penalties took place in Oregon.

Simultaneously with his complaint, Heitner filed a motion for an order of sequestration of the Delaware property of the individual defendants pursuant to DEL. CODE ANN., Tit. 10, § 366 (1975). This motion was accompanied by a supporting affidavit of counsel which stated that the individual defendants were nonresidents of Delaware. The affidavit identified the property to be sequestered as:

> common stock, 3% Second Cumulative Preferred Stock and stock unit credits of the Defendant Greyhound Corporation, a Delaware corporation, as well as all options and all warrants to purchase said stock issued to said individual Defendants and all contractual [sic] obligations, all rights, debts or credits due or accrued to or for the benefit of any of the said Defendants under any type of written agreement, contract or other legal instrument of any kind whatever between any of the individual Defendants and said corporation.

The requested sequestration order was signed the day the motion was filed. Pursuant to that order, the sequestrator "seized" approximately 82,000 shares of Greyhound common stock belonging to 19 of the defendants, and options belonging to another 2 defendants. These seizures were accomplished by placing "stop transfer" orders or their equivalents on the books of the Greyhound Corp. So far as the record shows, none of the certificates representing the seized property was physically present in Delaware. The stock was considered to be in Delaware, and so subject to seizure, by virtue of DEL. CODE ANN., Tit. 8, § 169 (1975), which makes Delaware the situs of ownership of all stock in Delaware corporations.

All 28 defendants were notified of the initiation of the suit by certified mail directed to their last known addresses and by publication in a New Castle County newspaper. The 21 defendants whose property was seized (hereafter referred to as appellants) responded by entering a special appearance for the purpose of moving to quash service of process and to vacate the sequestration order. They contended that the ex parte sequestration procedure did not accord them due process of law and that the property seized was not capable of attachment in Delaware. In addition, appellants asserted that under the rule of *International Shoe Co. v. Washington*,[236] they did not have sufficient contacts with Delaware to sustain the jurisdiction of that State's courts.

The Court of Chancery rejected these arguments in a letter opinion which emphasized the purpose of the Delaware sequestration procedure:

> The primary purpose of 'sequestration' as authorized by 10 Del. C. § 366 is not to secure possession of property pending a trial between resident debtors and creditors on the issue of who has the right to retain it. On the contrary, as here

---

[236] 326 U.S. 310 (1945).

employed, 'sequestration' is a process used to compel the personal appearance of a nonresident defendant to answer and defend a suit brought against him in a court of equity. It is accomplished by the appointment of a sequestrator by this Court to seize and hold property of the nonresident located in this State subject to further Court order. If the defendant enters a general appearance, the sequestered property is routinely released, unless the plaintiff makes special application to continue its seizure, in which event the plaintiff has the burden of proof and persuasion.

This limitation on the purpose and length of time for which sequestered property is held, the court concluded, rendered inapplicable the due process requirements enunciated in *Sniadach v. Family Finance Corp.; Fuentes v. Shevin* and *Mitchell v. W. T. Grant Co.*[237] The court also found no state-law or federal constitutional barrier to the sequestrator's reliance on DEL. CODE ANN., Tit. 8, § 169 (1975). Finally, the court held that the statutory Delaware situs of the stock provided a sufficient basis for the exercise of quasi in rem jurisdiction by a Delaware court.

On appeal, the Delaware Supreme Court affirmed the judgment of the Court of Chancery.

II

The Delaware courts rejected appellants' jurisdictional challenge by noting that this suit was brought as a quasi in rem proceeding. Since quasi in rem jurisdiction is traditionally based on attachment or seizure of property present in the jurisdiction, not on contacts between the defendant and the State, the courts considered appellants' claimed lack of contacts with Delaware to be unimportant. This categorical analysis assumes the continued soundness of the conceptual structure founded on the century-old case of *Pennoyer v. Neff.*[238]

. . .

Although this Court has not addressed this argument directly, we have held that property cannot be subjected to a court's judgment unless reasonable and appropriate efforts have been made to give the property owners actual notice of the action. This conclusion recognizes, contrary to Pennoyer, that an adverse judgment in rem directly affects the property owner by divesting him of his rights in the property before the court. Moreover, in Mullane we held that Fourteenth Amendment rights cannot depend on the classification of an action as in rem or in personam, since that is "a classification for which the standards are so elusive and confused generally and which, being primarily for state courts to define, may and do vary from state to state."

It is clear, therefore, that the law of state-court jurisdiction no longer stands securely on the foundation established in Pennoyer. We think that the time is ripe to consider whether the standard of fairness and substantial justice set forth in International Shoe should be held to govern actions in rem as well as in personam.

. . .

The primary rationale for treating the presence of property as a sufficient basis for jurisdiction to adjudicate claims over which the State would not have jurisdiction if International Shoe applied is that a

---

[237] 395 U.S. 337 (1969); 407 U.S. 67 (1972); 416 U.S. 600 (1974).
[238] 95 U.S. 714 (1878).

164

wrongdoer "should not be able to avoid payment of his obligations by the expedient of removing his assets to a place where he is not subject to an in personam suit."[239] This justification, however, does not explain why jurisdiction should be recognized without regard to whether the property is present in the State because of an effort to avoid the owner's obligations. Nor does it support jurisdiction to adjudicate the underlying claim. At most, it suggests that a State in which property is located should have jurisdiction to attach that property, by use of proper procedures, as security for a judgment being sought in a forum where the litigation can be maintained consistently with International Shoe. Moreover, we know of nothing to justify the assumption that a debtor can avoid paying his obligations by removing his property to a State in which his creditor cannot obtain personal jurisdiction over him. The Full Faith and Credit Clause, after all, makes the valid in personam judgment of one State enforceable in all other States.

It might also be suggested that allowing in rem jurisdiction avoids the uncertainty inherent in the International Shoe standard and assures a plaintiff of a forum. We believe, however, that the fairness standard of International Shoe can be easily applied in the vast majority of cases. Moreover, when the existence of jurisdiction in a particular forum under International Shoe is unclear, the cost of simplifying the litigation by avoiding the jurisdictional question may be the sacrifice of "fair play and substantial justice." That cost is too high.

We are left, then, to consider the significance of the long history of jurisdiction based solely on the presence of property in a State. Although the theory that territorial power is both essential to and sufficient for jurisdiction has been undermined, we have never held that the presence of property in a State does not automatically confer jurisdiction over the owner's interest in that property. This history must be considered as supporting the proposition that jurisdiction based solely on the presence of property satisfies the demands of due process, but it is not decisive. "[T]raditional notions of fair play and substantial justice" can be as readily offended by the perpetuation of ancient forms that are no longer justified as by the adoption of new procedures that are inconsistent with the basic values of our constitutional heritage. The fiction that an assertion of jurisdiction over property is anything but an assertion of jurisdiction over the owner of the property supports an ancient form without substantial modern justification. Its continued acceptance would serve only to allow state-court jurisdiction that is fundamentally unfair to the defendant.

We therefore conclude that all assertions of state-court jurisdiction must be evaluated according to the standards set forth in International Shoe and its progeny.

IV

The Delaware courts based their assertion of jurisdiction in this case solely on the statutory presence of appellants' property in Delaware. Yet that property is not the subject matter of this litigation, nor is the underlying cause of action related to the property. Appellants' holdings in Greyhound do not, therefore, provide contacts with Delaware sufficient to support the jurisdiction of that State's courts over appellants. If it exists, that jurisdiction must have some other foundation.

Appellee Heitner did not allege and does not now claim that appellants have ever set foot in Delaware. Nor does he identify any act related to his cause of action as having taken place in Delaware. Nevertheless, he contends that appellants' positions as directors and officers of a corporation chartered in Delaware provide sufficient "contacts, ties, or relations" with that State to give its courts jurisdiction over appellants in this stockholder's derivative action. This argument is based primarily on what Heitner asserts to be the strong interest of Delaware in supervising the management of a Delaware corporation. That interest

---

[239] RESTATEMENT § 66, cmt. a.

is said to derive from the role of Delaware law in establishing the corporation and defining the obligations owed to it by its officers and directors. In order to protect this interest, appellee concludes, Delaware's courts must have jurisdiction over corporate fiduciaries such as appellants.

This argument is undercut by the failure of the Delaware Legislature to assert the state interest appellee finds so compelling. Delaware law bases jurisdiction, not on appellants' status as corporate fiduciaries, but rather on the presence of their property in the State. Although the sequestration procedure used here may be most frequently used in derivative suits against officers and directors, the authorizing statute evinces no specific concern with such actions. Sequestration can be used in any suit against a nonresident and reaches corporate fiduciaries only if they happen to own interests in a Delaware corporation, or other property in the State. But as Heitner's failure to secure jurisdiction over seven of the defendants named in his complaint demonstrates, there is no necessary relationship between holding a position as a corporate fiduciary and owning stock or other interests in the corporation. If Delaware perceived its interest in securing jurisdiction over corporate fiduciaries to be as great as Heitner suggests, we would expect it to have enacted a statute more clearly designed to protect that interest.

. . .

Appellee suggests that by accepting positions as officers or directors of a Delaware corporation, appellants performed the acts required by *Hanson v. Denckla*. He notes that Delaware law provides substantial benefits to corporate officers and directors, and that these benefits were at least in part the incentive for appellants to assume their positions. It is, he says, "only fair and just" to require appellants, in return for these benefits, to respond in the State of Delaware when they are accused of misusing their power.

But like Heitner's first argument, this line of reasoning establishes only that it is appropriate for Delaware law to govern the obligations of appellants to Greyhound and its stockholders. It does not demonstrate that appellants have "purposefully avail[ed themselves] of the privilege of conducting activities within the forum State" in a way that would justify bringing them before a Delaware tribunal. Appellants have simply had nothing to do with the State of Delaware. Moreover, appellants had no reason to expect to be haled before a Delaware court. Delaware, unlike some States, has not enacted a statute that treats acceptance of a directorship as consent to jurisdiction in the State. And "[i]t strains reason… to suggest that anyone buying securities in a corporation formed in Delaware 'impliedly consents' to subject himself to Delaware's… jurisdiction on any cause of action." Appellants, who were not required to acquire interests in Greyhound in order to hold their positions, did not by acquiring those interests surrender their right to be brought to judgment only in States with which they had had "minimum contacts."

The Due Process Clause "does not contemplate that a state may make binding a judgment . . . against an individual or corporate defendant with which the state has no contacts, ties, or relations." [240]

Delaware's assertion of jurisdiction over appellants in this case is inconsistent with that constitutional limitation on state power. The judgment of the Delaware Supreme Court must, therefore, be reversed.

It is so ordered.

---

[240] *International Shoe*, 326 U.S. at 319.

Practice Problems

Practice Problem 5-9
Carl lives in California but owns a home in Delaware, where he used to live but moved. He still owes a mortgage on that home to Mad Mortgage, Inc. He defaults on the mortgage and, according to the loan agreement, Mad Mortgage, Inc. sues under foreclosure law to sell the property to satisfy Carl's debt. Would a court in Delaware have personal jurisdiction over Carl in such a suit?

Practice Problem 5-10
General Zaroff lives in Texas most of the year. However, he owns real estate in a relatively unpopulated part of Delaware. He has on the property obstacle courses. In one part he even has a sunken pit with foliage right up to the edge so that, if someone did not know that it is there, she could fall in. Rainsford is an adventurer and ends up on Zaroff's property. He falls in the pit and breaks his leg badly and, as a result, sues Zaroff for maintaining a hazardous condition on his property, which under Delaware premises liability law could support liability. Would a court in Delaware have personal jurisdiction over this suit?

---

e. The Internet Factor (Typically Not a "Context" Unto Itself)

The Internet has added a new twist to personal jurisdiction analyses. *Zippo Manufacturing Company v. Zippo Dot Com, Incorporated*[241] is one of the first and most influential decisions dealing with the effect of Internet sites on personal jurisdiction. In *Zippo*, the court introduced a "sliding scale" approach in which the degree of an Internet site's interactivity represents the key factor in determining jurisdiction. Following is oft-quoted language describing this sliding scale:

At one end of the spectrum are situations where a defendant clearly does business over the Internet. If the defendant enters into contracts with residents of a foreign jurisdiction that involve the knowing and repeated transmission of computer files over the Internet, personal jurisdiction is proper. At the opposite end are situations where a defendant has simply posted information on an Internet Web site which is accessible to users in foreign jurisdictions. A passive web site that does little more than make information available to those who are interested in it is not grounds for the exercise of personal jurisdiction. The middle ground is occupied by interactive Web sites where a user can exchange information with the host computer. In these cases, the exercise of jurisdiction is determined by the level of activity and commercial nature of the exchange of information that occurs.[242]

Later cases have shown that in virtually every case the Internet component will supplement another factual context (with its own governing precedent for applying the minimum contacts test). For instance, *Revell v. Lidov*[243] addressed the ability of a plaintiff to establish personal jurisdiction in the plaintiff's home state of Texas over both an individual who lived in Massachusetts and an incorporated university located in New York. The individual posted allegedly defamatory comments about the plaintiff on a bulletin board hosted on a server maintained by a university incorporated under New York law. The district court rejected personal jurisdiction in part because it deemed the Internet bulletin board in question to be "Zippo-passive." The United States Court of Appeals for the Fifth Circuit disagreed and held that the Internet bulletin board

---

[241] 952 F. Supp. 1119 (W.D. Pa. 1997).
[242] *Id.*
[243] 317 F.3d 467 (5th Cir. 2002).

was "interactive" because "any user of the Internet [could] . . . send information to be posted, and receive information that others may have posted. . . [and] participate in an open forum."[244] Accordingly, based on the internet analysis alone, the Fifth Circuit theoretically could have upheld personal jurisdiction, but in Revell it did not. Therefore, we see that the Internet context may help courts bolster their conclusion that personal jurisdiction exists in cases where another factual context applies. However, for the reasons explored below, when the other factual context does not support personal jurisdiction, the Internet context usually will not overcome the lack of jurisdiction based on other grounds. Following is an example of how courts currently approach the existence of an Internet web site in a case.

MILLENNIUM ENTERPRISES, INC. v. MILLENNIUM MUSIC
United States District Court for the District of Oregon, 1999
33 F. Supp. 2d 907

AIKEN, Judge:

Plaintiff, Music Millennium, is a business incorporated in Oregon with its principal place of business located in Portland, Oregon. Plaintiff opened its first retail outlet under the name "Music Millennium" in 1969. Plaintiff now operates two retail music stores in Portland and also sells products through mail and telephone orders and its Internet Web site.

Defendant Millennium Music, Inc., is a South Carolina corporation and general partner of defendant Millennium Music, L.P., a South Carolina limited partnership. Defendants operate retail music stores in South Carolina under the name "Millennium Music." Defendants sell products through their retail outlets and their Internet Web site, although the vast majority of sales occur at their retail stores. From March 1998 through September 1998, defendants sold fifteen compact discs to nine separate customers in six states and one foreign country. The sales totaled approximately $225. During the same period, defendants' retail sales were $2,180,000. Defendants also offer franchising circulars through the Inter-net and have two franchised stores in North Carolina.

Defendants have purchased a small amount of compact discs from Allegro Corporation ("Allegro"), a distributor located in Portland, Oregon. Defendants' purchases from Allegro in 1994-1997 totaled approximately one-half of one percent of defendants' inventory purchases for those years.

On or about July 7, 1998, plaintiff received a credit document from Allegro. The credit was mailed to plaintiff in error; the document apparently was intended for defendants.

On August 21, 1998, an Oregon resident, Linda Lufkin, purchased a compact disc from defendants through their Web site. During oral argument on defendants' motion to dismiss, the court learned from defendants that an attorney at the law firm for which Ms. Lufkin works requested that she purchase a compact disc from defendant. Apparently, the attorney is an acquaintance of plaintiff's counsel. Plaintiff did not dispute these facts. Defendants have sold no other merchandise to any Oregon resident.

Plaintiffs filed suit on August 28, 1998. According to plaintiff's complaint, defendants' use of the name "Millennium Music" in connection with the sale of goods in interstate commerce violates plaintiff's

---

[244] *Id.* at 472.

state and common law trademark rights. Plaintiff further alleges that consumers familiar with plaintiff will likely be confused as to the source or origin of defendants' goods, thereby causing plaintiff harm.

. . .

[Plaintiff contends that the Court has specific jurisdictions over Defendant on the following grounds: Defendant sold one compact disc to Linda Lufkin, an Oregon resident; (2) Defendant purchased discs from an Oregon supplier; and (3) Defendant's infringing conduct targeted Oregon under the effects test. The Court, however, rejects Plaintiff's arguments.]

Plaintiff's remaining ground asserted in support of specific jurisdiction is defendants' Internet Web site through which persons can purchase compact discs, request franchising information and join a discount club. According to plaintiff, the fact that defendants maintain an interactive, rather than passive, Web site is a sufficient contact with this forum to establish personal jurisdiction. In other words, plaintiff argues that purposeful availment is satisfied by an Internet Web site which allows for the exchange of information between the Web user and the Web site, regardless of whether an actual exchange of information occurred with residents of this forum.

The facts of this case coupled with plaintiff's argument raise questions that have yet to be answered in this Circuit. Because the answers to these questions will have far-reaching implications for those who utilize the Internet for commercial purposes, the court takes a comprehensive look at the current state of the law with respect to personal jurisdiction and Internet contacts.

. . .

One of the first cases to address the question of personal jurisdiction and the Internet was Inset Systems, Inc. v. Instruction Set, Inc..[245] In that case, the plaintiff alleged trademark infringement as a result of the defendant's alleged use of plaintiff's trademark as its Internet domain address. The defendant did not have employees or offices or conduct business regularly within the forum state. Rather, the plaintiff claimed that the defendant's Internet Web site, which contained advertising and a toll-free telephone number, constituted sufficient minimum contacts for purposes of federal due process.

In discussing the defendant's Web site, the court remarked:

> In the present case, [defendant] has directed its advertising activities via the Internet and its toll-free number toward not only the state of Connecticut, but to all states. The Internet as well as toll-free numbers are designed to communicate with people and their business in every state. Advertisements on the Internet can reach as many as 10,000 Internet users within Connecticut. Further, once posted on the Internet, unlike radio and television advertising, the advertisement is available continuously to any Internet user.

Although these findings tend to show that the defendant did not target its Web site at the forum state in any particular manner, the court concluded that, through its Web site, defendant had "purposefully availed itself of the privilege of doing business within Connecticut."

---

[245] 937 F. Supp. 161 (D. Conn. 1996).

From this rather inauspicious beginning, the trend has shifted away from finding jurisdiction based solely on the existence of Web site advertising. Instead, "something more" is required to show that the defendant purposefully directed its activities at the forum. After Inset, two district courts endeavored to set standards the majority of courts now have adopted.

In *Bensusan Restaurant Corp. v. King*,[246] the operator of a New York jazz club, Bensusan, brought suit against the owner of a small Missouri jazz establishment, King, claiming that King infringed on Bensusan's right to the trademark "The Blue Note." Bensusan alleged that jurisdiction over King was properly asserted in New York, because King maintained a Web site that was accessible to New York residents. The court disagreed: "The mere fact that a person can gain information on the allegedly infringing product is not the equivalent of a person advertising, promoting, selling or otherwise making an effort to target its product in New York."

The court further found that assertion of jurisdiction over King would violate the Due Process Clause, reasoning that King had not purposefully availed himself of the benefits of New York when he "simply created a Web site and permitted anyone who could find it to access it." "Creating a site, like placing a product into the stream of commerce, may be felt nationwide — or even worldwide — but without more, it is not an act purposefully directed toward the forum state." Finally, the court found Bensusan's argument "that King should have foreseen that users could access the site in New York and be confused as to the relationship of the two Blue Note clubs" did not satisfy the requirements of due process.

In *Zippo Manufacturing Co. v. Zippo Dot Com, Inc.*,[247] ("Zippo"), the plaintiff alleged trademark dilution and infringement based on the defendant's Web site domain names. In determining whether jurisdiction was proper, the court applied a "sliding scale" under which "the likelihood that personal jurisdiction can be constitutionally exercised is directly proportionate to the nature and quality of commercial activity that an entity conducts over the Internet."

. . .

Most courts follow the reasoning set forth in Bensusan and Zippo and decline to assert jurisdiction based solely on Web site advertising.

Those courts which have asserted jurisdiction in cases involving passive Web sites did so because the defendant had additional contacts with the forum which related to the plaintiff's claim.[248]

Likewise, courts generally have exercised jurisdiction in cases at the other end of the scale, where the defendant "conducted business" over the Internet by engaging in repeated or ongoing business transactions with forum residents or by entering into a contract with the plaintiff through the Internet.[249]

Further, courts have found purposeful availment when the claim involves an intentional tort

---

[246] 937 F. Supp. 295 (S.D.N.Y. 1996).

[247] 952 F. Supp. 1119, 1123 (W.D. Penn. 1997)

[248] *See* Gary Scott International, Inc. v. Baroudi, 981 F. Supp. 714 (D. Mass. 1997) (jurisdiction based on sales of infringing products to Massachusetts retailer in addition to Web site advertising); Heroes, Inc. v. Heroes Foundation, 958 F. Supp. 1, 3-5 (D.D.C. 1996) (jurisdiction based on Web site and advertisement in local newspaper soliciting donations).

[249] *See* Thompson v. Handa-Lopez, Inc., 998 F. Supp. 738 (W.D. Tex. 1998) (defendant operated casino-type arcade game through its Web site and entered into contract with plaintiff to play the game).

allegedly committed over the Internet, such that the defendant intentionally directed its tortious activities at the forum state. These cases are based on the "effects test" articulated in *Calder v. Jones*,[250] where the Supreme Court found personal jurisdiction properly asserted over a defendant whose libelous actions were directed at the plaintiff resident of the forum state.

Courts have reached differing conclusions with respect to those cases falling into the middle "interactive" category identified in Zippo. As declared by one commentator, the "current hodgepodge of case law is inconsistent, irrational, and irreconcilable." In these cases, some courts find that an interactive Web site alone is sufficient to establish minimum contacts. Others find minimum contacts through additional non-Internet activity in the forum, regardless of whether the activity is related to the underlying claim. Finally, some courts require additional conduct in the forum that is related to the plaintiff's cause of action.

. . .

The court first determines where defendants' Web site corresponds on the sliding scale of interactivity. Through defendants' Web site, Web users may purchase compact discs, join a discount club and request franchising information.

Arguably, the capability of selling compact discs through the Web site could constitute "doing business" over the Internet and confer personal jurisdiction almost as a matter of course. However, the court finds such designation intended for those businesses which conduct a significant portion of their business through ongoing Internet relationships; for example, by entering "into contracts with residents of a foreign jurisdiction that involve the knowing and repeated transmission of computer files over the Internet."

. . .

On its face, the site would appear to suffice for personal jurisdiction under the middle category in Zippo; the level of potential interactivity, while not necessarily high, is not insubstantial. Further, the potential exchange of information can be commercial in nature. However, the court finds that the middle interactive category of Internet contacts as described in Zippo needs further refinement to include the fundamental requirement of personal jurisdiction: "deliberate action" within the forum state in the form of transactions between the defendant and residents of the forum or conduct of the defendant purposefully directed at residents of the forum state. This, in the court's view, is the "something more" that the Ninth Circuit intended in *Cybersell* and *Panavision*.

Although *Cybersell* involved an "essentially" passive home page, the court's reasoning easily applies in this case. In declining to assert jurisdiction, the court noted:

Cybersell FL did nothing to encourage people in Arizona to access its site, and there is no evidence that any part of its business (let alone a continuous part of its business) was sought or achieved in Arizona. . .. It entered into no contracts in Arizona, made no sales in Arizona, received no telephone calls from Arizona, earned no income from Arizona, and sent no messages over the Internet to Arizona.[251] Although the court noted the lack of commercial activity associated with the defendant's web site, the court concluded: "In short, Cybersell FL has done no act and has consummated no transaction, nor has it

---

[250] 465 U.S. 783, 788–90 (1984).
[251] *Cybersell*, 130 F.3d at 419.

171

performed any act by which it purposefully availed itself of the privilege of conducting activities in Arizona, thereby invoking the benefits and protections of Arizona law." In other words, "simply registering someone else's trademark as a domain name and posting a web site on the Internet is not sufficient to subject a party domiciled in one state to jurisdiction in another."

Here, defendants have "consummated no transaction" and have made no "deliberate and repeated" contacts with Oregon through their Web site. Defendants maintain a Web site which allows users to purchase products, thus rendering it foreseeable that residents of Oregon, or any other state or country for that matter, could purchase a product from defendants. However, it is well-established that foreseeability alone cannot serve as the constitutional benchmark for personal jurisdiction. "The foreseeability that is critical to due process analysis is not the mere likelihood that a product will find its way into the forum state. Rather, it is that the defendant's conduct and connection with the forum state are such that he should reasonably anticipate being haled into court there."[252]

. . .

A review of defendants' Web site furthers the conclusion that defendants did not intentionally or purposefully target its activities at Oregon. The site proclaims: "Come Visit Us!" and provides a map of the location of defendants' stores. The maps are local in nature, providing little more than a showing of the cross-streets surrounding the stores. Nothing published on the Web site suggests that defendants intended to target Oregon residents, some 3,000 miles away, any more than they intended to target residents of other states. Rather, from defendants' invitation to visit their retail outlets, one could reasonably infer that defendants intended to target residents in their area. In sum, the court finds that this, too, is a case where "something more" is required.

. . .

For all of these reasons, this court will not abandon the basic principle that defendants must have taken some action to direct their activities in the forum so as to "purposely avail" themselves of the privilege of doing business within Oregon. The timeless and fundamental bedrock of personal jurisdiction assures us all that a defendant will not be "haled" into a court of a foreign jurisdiction based on nothing more than the foreseeability or potentiality of commercial activity with the forum state. Until transactions with Oregon residents are consummated through defendants' Web site, defendants cannot reasonably anticipate that they will be brought before this court, simply because they advertise their products through a global medium which provides the capability of engaging in commercial transactions. It is therefore "presumptively . . . unreasonable to require [them] to submit to the burdens of litigations" in this forum.

. . .

Plaintiff fails to show the defendants have sufficient minimum contacts with this forum to allow the exercise of personal jurisdiction in accordance with federal due process. Therefore, defendant's Motion to Dismiss is GRANTED and all pending motions are DENIED as moot. Plaintiff's Complaint is HEREBY DISMISSED.

---

[252] *World-Wide Volkswagen*, 444 U.S. at 297.

Practice Problem

Practice Problem 5-11

Stephen Sotello (NY) sued AbelWare, Ltd., a company incorporated and with its principal place of business in New Mexico. Sotello had purchased software on AbelWare's website. Although Sotello was not aware, some of the software was bundled with spyware and other software of which Sotello was told nothing about. Moreover, this spyware transmitted to AbelWare information about Sotello's Internet use and, even worse, damaged his computers by clogging it and making it run more slowly, among other things. Purchasing the software required Sotello to visit AbelWare's website and contact their sales representative to let them know which of the multiple variations of software packages he wanted. The software would then be downloaded through the Internet.

Sotello wanted AbelWare's software on his twenty computers that he maintained at training site that taught young children and teenagers how to use them and eventually how to program. The sales representative said AbelWare was just what Sotello needed. The representative obtained personal information on Sotello, including his New York City address where he was located. Upon receiving credit card payment, the AbelWare representative transmitted the software through the Internet site.

Sotello downloaded the software from the Internet site using the code provided to him by the AbelWare representative, unaware that he was also downloading spyware and other dangerous programs that could harm his computer system.

When Sotello hires a computer whiz, Alex Turing, to fix his computers, Turing soon told Sotello he might as well throw the computers out. Known as a computer genius, even Turing could not undo the deviously intricate AbelWare software. Sotello's computers were all ruined, resulting in damages of over $150,000. Sotello sued AbelWare, Ltd. in the United States District Court for the Southern District of New York. AbelWare brought a motion to dismiss for lack of personal jurisdiction because its location was in New Mexico. How should the Court rule?

f. Combination of Contexts in Same Fact Pattern

Many cases and essays will not present scenarios with a neat, single context to analyze. In real life, fact patterns often include two or more of the contexts outlined above. Therefore, your evaluation should analyze the question of whether there is personal jurisdiction with the *International Shoe/World-Wide Volkswagen* framework in mind, as well as the factors applied in specific contexts. One approach may point against personal jurisdiction and another may point toward personal jurisdiction. In such situations, you would do well to go back to the underlying teaching of International Shoe and ask the questions that *World-Wide Volkswagen* has taught us to ask.

Practice Problem

The following Practice Problem presents a personal jurisdiction scenario involving different "contexts" to help you practice analyzing a more sophisticated personal jurisdiction analysis. This Problem gives you the opportunity to demonstrate your command of the law of personal jurisdiction by dealing with a complicated fact pattern in the form of an essay answer.

Practice Problem 5-12

Tina owned "Tina's Trout Ponds, Inc." (TTP), which was incorporated in and had its principal place of business in Ohio. TTP had 10 pay-trout ponds. Tina decided to get a supply of rods, reels, and fishing lures for customers to rent. Tina found "BROOK BROWN's FISHING SUPPLIES" Internet Website (Website). The Website was on a computer server at a company in the U.S. district for the Northern District of West Virginia (WV). The site's home page had a link by which one could electronically send a message. If someone clicked on this link and typed a message, the message would be routed electronically through the computer server to the computer at Brook's office attached to her home. Brook's home was in the U.S. district for the Southern District of West Virginia. When Brook responded to a Website message, it likewise was routed through the computer server and then to the original message sender's computer, wherever that computer happened to be. The Website had the features of a typical "shopping" site (*e.g.*, a shopping cart, order information, secured payment and shipping options, etc.). Upon placement of an order, the Website would not only automatically send an order confirmation to the computer of the ordering party, but also route the order electronically to Brook's home office. Upon receiving an order, Brook filled the order and shipped it according to the customer's preference. Brook was incorporated as "Brook Brown's Fishing Supplies, Inc." in West Virginia, where it also had its principal place of business.

Tina clicked on the link to contact Brook and expressed interest in buying rods, reels, and lures. In a series of ten communications back and forth via the Website over the next couple of months, the question whether Tina would order from Brook turned on Brook's willingness to develop new lures for fishing in the spring and summer. (Brook's stock had only lures used in the fall and spring. Both ladies knew that trout throughout the U.S. liked certain lures in the spring and summer different from the fall and winter.) Ultimately, Brook sent a message via the Website telling Tina that she would develop new lures if Tina was willing to sign a written agreement under which Tina would agree to order, for at least five years, (1) 300 fishing rods and reels a year, at $100 per rod and reel (for a total of $30,000 in rod and reel purchases a year), and (2) 500 fishing lures a year at $5 per lure (for a total of $2,500 in lure purchases a year). After discussing the proposed contract with a lawyer, Tina sent a message via the Website back to Brook agreeing to the above terms but insisting that the agreement specify that OH law govern the agreement. Tina sent or received five of the ten communications described above on her laptop while in the U.S. District for the Northern District of West Virginia. The other five communications were sent by or received by Tina on her laptop while in the U.S. District for the Southern District of Ohio.

Brook mailed the agreement incorporating the above terms to Tina's home in the U.S. District for the Southern District of Ohio. Tina signed on behalf of the corporation, as did Brook when Tina returned it. Tina placed her first order of 300 fishing rods and reels, and 250 fall and winter lures. When the spring and summer lures were ready, Tina ordered 250 of those. For two more years Tina ordered, as agreed, 300 rods and reels and 500 fishing lures. Tina made these orders on her laptop from her home, upon which Brook filled and shipped them. Essentially, all rod and lures at Tina's ten ponds were, at that point, supplied by Brook. Unfortunately, rods began to break often during ordinary use. Rods broke at each pond and in large numbers. In the process, customers were injured and told Tina they would never fish there again.

Tina knew that the average life of fishing poles was at least 15 years. Tina called Brook and told her what was happening. Brook responded that Tina she was letting amateurs misuse the rods and that it was all Tina's problem. Moreover, Brook reminded Tina of her agreement to continue ordering rods and lures, and that she had "better begin to give lessons to her customers on how to fish carefully." Recognizing that Brook was unyielding, but afraid to continue using the rods due to risk of injury and losing more customers, Tina immediately ordered replacement poles from another company. TTP filed suit in the U.S.

174

District Court for the Southern District of Ohio. The suit named Brook's corporation as the sole defendant and claimed breach of contract. The suit requested damages of $100,000 based on having to replace rods that should have lasted much longer, lost business, etc. A process server personally served the defendant by serving Brook, in West Virginia, with the lawsuit.

Ohio's long arm statute provides that a nonresident is subject to jurisdiction in any court within the boundaries of the state if, among other things, the nonresident enters into a contract with an Ohio citizen or business entity. If the defendant challenges personal jurisdiction in the suit described above, how should the Court rule? Fully explain your answer.

F. The Last Step of the Due Process Analysis: Reasonableness

Regardless of whether you find purposeful minimum contacts, you still have to ask one more question before your due process analysis is complete: Would the exercise of personal jurisdiction in the forum be unreasonable even if the contacts between the defendant and the forum satisfy the International Shoe test and the defendant could have foreseen being sued there? In Asahi, the Court disagreed over whether there were purposeful minimum contacts. A majority of the Court held, however, that requiring the Japanese defendant to litigate in the United States would be unreasonable in light of due process.[253] And the Court make clear that true unreasonableness would violate due process regardless of whether the Japanese defendant had sufficient minimum contacts. The Court reiterated the following five factors listed in *World-Wide Volkswagen* for courts to consider in determining this reasonableness of the exercise of jurisdiction:

A court must consider [1] the burden on the defendant, [2] the interests of the forum state . . . [3] the plaintiff's interest in obtaining relief . . . [4] "the interstate judicial system's interest in obtaining the most efficient resolution of controversies; and [5] the shared interest of the several States in furthering fundamentally substantive social policies."[254]

In *Burger King*,[255] the Court applied these same factors and held it reasonable to exercise personal jurisdiction despite the burden on a Michigan individual forced to litigate in Miami. Conversely, the burden on a Japanese defendant was extreme.[256] As the Court observed, "The unique burdens placed upon one who must defend oneself in a foreign legal system should have significant weight in assessing the reasonableness of stretching the long arm of personal jurisdiction over national borders."[257] Moreover, the Court observed that the Japanese defendant had been brought in as a third-party defendant to the claim of the original defendant, a Taiwanese company that manufactured tire assemblies, so that the interests of the State of California in providing a forum were minimal.[258] Although less significant, the remaining three factors also counseled against the reasonableness of exercising personal jurisdiction.

---

[253] Asahi Metal Indus. Co. v. Superior Court of California, 480 U.S. 102, 113–14 (1987).
[254] *Id.* at 113 (quoting World-Wide Volkswagen, 444 U.S. 286, 292 (1980) (brackets added); *see also* Burger King Corp. v. Rudzewicz, 471 U.S. 462, 476–77 (1985) (recognizing the same five factors).
[255] *Burger King Corp.*, 471 U.S. at 476–77.
[256] *Asahi*, 480 U.S. at 114.
[257] *Id.*
[258] *Id.* at 113–14.

CHAPTER 6: CHOOSING THE FORUM: VENUE

I. How the Topics in this Chapter Fit in the Overall Progress of a Civil Action

Below is a diagram of the stages of a civil action showing in bold where the topic discussed in this chapter fall in the progress of a case.

Figure 6-1

Cause of Action (events leading to suit)	Pre-Filing Tasks (items to begin representation, interviewing, and related matters)	**Choice of Forum** (subject matter jurisdiction, removal, personal jurisdiction, and **venue**)	Notice and Service of Process (completing the process of ensuring the forum court can enter a valid judgment)	Pleading the Case and Joinder of Claims and Parties (including supplemental jurisdiction)

Responding to Claims by Motion or by Answer	Discovery (developing proof to establish claims and learn your adversary's case)	Right to Jury (pretrial motions and practice)	Final Pretrial Conference (events within last month before trial)	Trial (procedures and motions during trial)	Verdict	Post-Trial Motions (motions for a new trial and/or judgment as a matter of law)	Appeal

Choosing a proper venue in which to sue can easily be overlooked after analyzing the seemingly more challenging subjects of confirming subject matter jurisdiction and personal jurisdiction. However, the experienced litigator knows better than to neglect the significance of venue. True, the court a plaintiff chooses cannot enter an enforceable judgment unless it has both subject matter jurisdiction and personal jurisdiction. The catch is that, unlike subject matter jurisdiction, a court can have the power to exercise personal jurisdiction based on a party's waiver of its right to object. Thus, the judgment is enforceable because there is subject matter jurisdiction (which is not waivable) and because there is personal jurisdiction either by existence of one of the grounds outlined in Chapter 5 or by waiver of one's right to object.

Proper venue, too, is the right of parties. The right derives from statutory authority rather than the Constitution. However, if one challenges improper venue, her challenge is as valid as an objection to personal jurisdiction. Nevertheless, the ability to waive the right to challenge venue can be waived just as the right to personal jurisdiction can be waived.[259]

---

[259] As explained in the Chapter 5, a defendant who expressly or impliedly consents to a court's handling of a case by, for instance, failing to raise an objection in a timely fashion, can waive their objection to personal jurisdiction.

Yet, the experienced litigator will evaluate venue as thoroughly as she does subject matter jurisdiction and personal jurisdiction. Venue is about picking the specific court in a part of the state that has personal jurisdiction. It focuses not simply on a defendant's connections to the entire state. It focuses on the subdivisions within the state that are appropriate under the venue statute. The map shown in *Figure 6-2* indicates the circuits associated with states.[260]Additionally, each state can be divided into more than one district. For example, California, Texas, and New York have four districts; Oklahoma, Alabama, and Georgia have three districts; Washington, Missouri, and Virginia have two districts; and Maine, New Hampshire, and South Carolina each have one district for their entire state. Therefore, venue is about the proper *district* in which a suit can be brought. The policy behind venue is to funnel cases to districts in which the suit has the most connection and, thus, is likely to be most convenient to parties, witnesses, etc.

Figure 6-2 [261]

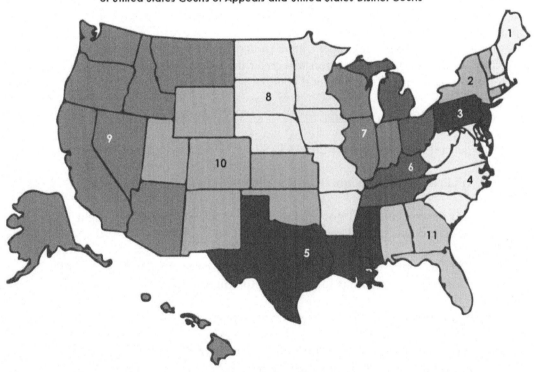

Geographic Boundaries
of United States Courts of Appeals and United States District Courts

Most defendants do not waive venue, and good lawyers do not count on their opponents' mistakes. Instead, an effective plaintiff's lawyer will consider all potential venues that are proper and evaluate the

---

[260] The Federal Judiciary also offers a geographical map distinguishing individual districts within the federal circuits. To see the states that are divided into two, three, and four districts, please see U.S. Federal Courts Circuit Map, USCOURTS.GOV, http://www.uscourts.gov/sites/default/files/u.s._federal_courts_circuit_map_1.pdf.

[261] The above map, moreover, does not depict the two other federal courts of appeal with specialized jurisdiction— the United States Court of Appeals for the District of Columbia Circuit and the Court of Appeals for the Federal Circuit.

one in which her client's case would have the best chance of succeeding. An experienced defense lawyer also recognizes the importance of venue as well. Venue is rarely a defense that will result in dismissal.[262]More often, the experienced defense counsel objects to the venue a plaintiff has chosen and moves to transfer to another venue. Whether the defendant can show that the transfer is warranted due to substantial inconvenience to the parties or to witnesses will determine whether the case is transferred. The motive of the defense counsel in seeking transfer usually is not based solely for the convenience to parties and witnesses. In moving to transfer venue, counsel has decided that the venue where the case would be transferred is more favorable to the defendant. Thus, the jockeying for venue in which parties seek to have the case tried is part of the strategy experienced trial lawyers consider even before suit is filed (if plaintiff's counsel) or immediately upon service on a defendant (if defense counsel). As the matter is so central to practice, you should learn well the requirements of a proper venue and how to seek transfer of venue.

II. The Law of Venue

The overall purpose of venue provisions is to direct a case to a location where it is most convenient for the parties and the witnesses. This discussion of applicable law will discuss federal venue concepts and how to interpret the general venue statute to determine a proper venue, as defined there. Because federal venue statutes permit transfer from one proper venue to another that satisfies the statute (and in which personal jurisdiction would exist), the discussion will cover the federal transfer of venue statutes first and conclude with forum non conveniens in the federal context.

A. "Proper" Venues According to the General Venue Statute

The general federal venue statute, 28 U.S.C. § 1391, provides as follows:

(a) **Applicability of Section.** Except as otherwise provided by law—

> (1) this section shall govern the venue of all civil actions brought in district courts of the United States; and

> (2) the proper venue for a civil action shall be determined without regard to whether the action is local or transitory in nature.

(b) **Venue in General.** —A civil action may be brought in—

> (1) a judicial district in which any defendant resides, if all defendants are residents of the State in which the district is located;

> (2) a judicial district in which a substantial part of the events or omissions giving rise to the claim occurred, or a substantial part of property that is the subject of the action is situated; or

> (3) if there is no district in which an action may otherwise be brought as provided in this section, any judicial district in which any defendant

---

[262] Dismissal of a case based on venue typically occurs only if a federal lawsuit has no connection to the United States. The concept of forum non conveniens requires dismissal when no connection exists to the state at all and every good defense lawyer will raise that defense if available. Forum non conveniens will be discussed later in this chapter.

is subject to the court's personal jurisdiction with respect to such action.

(c) Residency. For all venue purposes-

> **(1)** a natural person, including an alien lawfully admitted for permanent residence in the United States, shall be deemed to reside in the judicial district in which that person is domiciled;

> **(2)** an entity with the capacity to sue and be sued in its common name under applicable law, whether or not incorporated, shall be deemed to reside, if a defendant, in any judicial district in which such defendant is subject to the court's personal jurisdiction with respect to the civil action in question and, if a plaintiff, only in the judicial district in which it maintains its principal place of business; and

> **(3)** a defendant not resident in the United States may be sued in any judicial district, and the joinder of such a defendant shall be disregarded in determining where the action may be brought with respect to other defendants.

(d) Residency of corporations in States with multiple districts.--For purposes of venue under this chapter, in a State which has more than one judicial district and in which a defendant that is a corporation is subject to personal jurisdiction at the time an action is commenced, such corporation shall be deemed to reside in any district in that State within which its contacts would be sufficient to subject it to personal jurisdiction if that district were a separate State, and, if there is no such district, the corporation shall be deemed to reside in the district within which it has the most significant contacts.[263]

B. First Venue Option: District in Which Defendant Resides

The first basis for venue is to determine where the defendant(s) reside. The heading notes that this is a "potential" basis for venue. If the case has one defendant, then the provision will be a definite option. However, if there are two or more defendants and any one of them does not reside in the same state as every other defendant, then the residence option cannot apply. When § 1391(b) (1) states that venue is proper in "a judicial district in which a defendant resides, if all defendants are residents of the State in which the district is located." The "if" in this sentence is the key. When there are two or more defendants and one is a resident of another state, then the condition for subsection (b) (1) is impossible to meet and will not apply.

To determine whether § 1391(b) is applicable, you must apply the proper test to determine a defendant's residence. Courts choose the domicile of the defendant if the defendant is an individual. The term "residence" is thus defined in subsection (c) of the venue statute.[264] On the other hand, if the defendant is an entity such as a corporation, the court determines where the entity could be subjected to personal

---

[263] 28 U.S.C. § 1391(a)-(d) (2017).
[264] *See* 28 U.S.C. § 1391(c) (1)

179

jurisdiction in a district. In other words, you must apply the personal jurisdiction analysis set forth in Chapter 5 to a district, as if it were a state, to determine the residence of a corporation.[265] If the connections of the defendant would be sufficient to subject it to personal jurisdiction in the district if it were a state, then the defendant entity "resides" in that district.[266] Sometimes, however, the defendant's contacts in a state are so spread out that there is no contact in an individual district that would support personal jurisdiction. In such cases, the statute provides that the defendant corporation will reside in the district in which it has the "most significant contacts."[267]

Practice Problems

The following Practice Problems are designed to allow you to work through the residence provision—§ 1391(b) (1)—of the venue statute.

Practice Problem 6-1

Ashe, who lives in the Western District of North Carolina, sues Washington, who lives in the Eastern District of Virginia and has his surveying offices there, for negligence in a survey Washington performed. Under the terms of their contract, Washington agreed to survey and accurately identify the amount of land extending from the home Ashe owned in Asheville, North Carolina. Ashe relied on Washington's survey in building an addition on the home. The City of Asheville later determined the addition exceeded the boundaries of Ashe's property and forced him to tear it down. Under 28 U.S.C. § 1391(b) (1), is venue proper in the Eastern District of North Carolina? In the Eastern District of Virginia?

Practice Problem 6-2

Franklin, who lives in the Eastern District of Pennsylvania, sues Madison, who lives in the Eastern District of Virginia, and Jefferson, who lives in the Western District of Virginia, for allegedly infringing Franklin's copyrighted works in Madison and Jefferson's respective memoirs. Under 28 § 1391(b) (1), is venue proper in the Eastern District of Virginia? In the Western District of Virginia?

Practice Problem 6-3

Jackson, who lives in the Middle District of Tennessee, sued Dickinson, who lived in the District of Maryland, and The Nashville Times, Inc., a newspaper with its principal place of business in the Middle District of Tennessee and whose circulation is limited to the Middle District of Tennessee. The suit claimed that Dickinson and The Nashville Times defamed Jackson and should be held liable for damages for such defamation, lest Jackson should have to resort to repairing his honor by dueling. Under 28 U.S.C. § 1391(b) (1), is venue proper in the District of Maryland? In the Middle District of Tennessee? In any district under § 1391(b) (1)?

Practice Problem 6-4

Jefferson's Macaroni and Cheese, Inc. had become a profitable business. The headquarters and business operations of the company, and thus its principal place of business, were all located in the Western District of Virginia. The company had advertising on signs mostly in the Western District of Virginia. A few signs advertising the product, however, were in the Eastern District of Virginia. Ninety five percent of the purchases and business derived from the Western District of Virginia and five percent from the Eastern

---

[265] *See id.* § 1391(c) (2).
[266] *See id.* § 1391(d).
[267] *See id.*

District of Virginia.

Van Buren, from New York, was sure that northerners would fall in love with the delightful combination of macaroni and cheese produced by the machine Jefferson invented to create the macaroni and to mix just the right amount of cheese. Van Buren negotiated with Jefferson while passing through the Western District of Virginia to buy the rights to use Jefferson's invention to open macaroni and cheese restaurants in New York. The two reduced their agreement to a written contract and both signed it before Van Buren left. When Van Buren sent the agreed purchase amount, Jefferson sent it back and said he had changed his mind. However, Van Buren had already bought buildings in which to make the macaroni and cheese and began to outfit restaurants. Under 28 U.S.C. § 1391(b) (1), would Van Buren be able to sue in either the Eastern District of Virginia or the Western District of Virginia? If only in one district and not both, which district does § 1391(d) suggest would be the appropriate venue? Are the times in which § 1391(d) is likely to be at issue a relatively small percentage? What are the most likely scenarios in which § 1391(d) is likely to be at issue?

Practice Problem 6-5

Mary Washington, a citizen of Virginia, is on vacation touring the southern and coastal United States during the times described below. Gators Galore, Inc., is a company started by John Adams, who had, after keeping a pet alligator at the White House during his term as President, decided they were such interesting creatures that more people should see them. Gators Galore, Inc. raises alligators and takes them for annual monthly displays in the following federal districts: the Southern, Middle, and Northern Districts of Georgia; the Eastern District of Tennessee; the District of South Carolina; the Eastern District of Virginia; the Eastern District of North Carolina; and the District of Louisiana. Gators Galore, Inc., is incorporated in the District of Delaware and its corporate headquarters are in the Middle District of Georgia. These headquarters are where Gators Galore, Inc. houses its gators between tours; employs specialized trainers between tours; and has other employees, including handlers to get the gators from the trailers to the display cases at the sites where the tour stops. Calhoun is one of the Gators Galore, Inc. employees who takes the gators on tour. He lives in the Northern District of Georgia and only temporarily goes to headquarters when the tour season starts. He then serves as a handler on the road at various spots along the tour.

Mary's suit is for a gator bite injury she suffered when Calhoun negligently allowed a gator to escape at a carriage stop in the Eastern District of North Carolina as the company was traveling on its annual tour. Mary was hospitalized for a month, has had to undergo treatment to regain her health, and still suffers pain and emotional distress related to the gator bite.

Under the residency prong of the statute—§ 1391(b) (1) as defined in § 1391(c)-(d), what federal districts could be used as proper venues if Mary sued both Gators Galore, Inc. and Calhoun? Must you employ a personal jurisdiction analysis in this prong? If so, how is the scope of the geographic area you are considering different from a traditional personal jurisdiction analysis?

C. Most Common Venue Option: Where Acts/Omissions Occurred

The general venue statute, in subsection (b) also offers, as an alternative basis for proper venue(s), the option of suing where the events that gave rise to claims in the case occurred. Please read the following pertinent language:

<u>D. Venue in General</u>

A civil action may be brought in a judicial district in which a substantial part of the events or omissions giving rise to the claim occurred, or a substantial part of property that is the subject of the action is situated. As we have seen, the residency prong of the statute will not always allow for a proper venue. For instance, if all defendants are not residents of the state of the district court where the suit is filed, § 1391(b) (1) cannot apply by its own terms. However, the provision in § 1391(b) (2) is applicable in every case because some act or omission will have to have occurred for a claim to arise. However, it is possible that neither § 1391(a) nor § 1391(b) apply because the cause of action arose outside of the United States. In that rare case, one would fall back on § 1391(c). Thus, trial lawyers often consider § 1391(b) (2) first and then see whether the residency provision offers another alternative. That they do so underscores another important point—that the choice of a proper venue is not hierarchical, requiring one to go to § 1391(b) (1) first and then to § 1391(b) (2) only if necessary. Instead, you can go straight to § 1391(b) (2) to identify proper venues. However, as students analyzing cases (or fact patterns for exams) for the first time, pay attention to the question you are asked. If you are asked to identify all potential venues, you should analyze whether any districts are available under § 1391(b) (2) and, after determining that, turn to § 1391(b) (1) to identify the potential venues pursuant to that provision.

The following case illustrates well how an act or omission giving rise to a claim will assure a proper basis for venue.

EMPLOYERS MUTUAL CASUALTY CO. v. BARTILE ROOFS, INC.
United States Court of Appeals for the Tenth Circuit, 2010
618 F.3d 1153

OPINION BY: Holmes, Circuit Judge

. . .

Background

EMC is an insurance company organized under the laws of Iowa and has its principal place of business in Des Moines, Iowa. Bartile is organized under the laws of Utah and has its principal place of business in Centerville, Utah. Between 2001 and 2003, EMC issued three commercial general liability ("CGL") insurance policies to Bartile, providing coverage in the aggregate from November 1, 2001, to November 1, 2004. Although Bartile renewed the CGL policy each year, the policies provided liability insurance via a standard coverage form and contained the same language in all relevant terms, conditions, and definitions. These CGL policies were negotiated in Utah, underwritten in Colorado, and executed in Utah.

In mid–2001, FS Jackson Hole Development Company, LLC (the "Owner"), hired Jacobsen Construction Company ("Jacobsen") to construct the Four Seasons Resort Jackson Hole in Teton Village, Wyoming. As the general contractor, Jacobsen subcontracted the roofing work for this luxury hotel to Bartile. Bartile began work on the construction project in November 2002 and substantially completed its activities in February 2004. Bartile finished all of its work on the hotel in October 2005.

On March 11, 2004, Jacobsen filed a civil action against the Owner in California state court. The Owner countered with a cross-complaint against Jacobsen, alleging various defects in the construction. On

October 4, 2004, Jacobsen filed a cross-complaint against Bartile and other subcontractors. The project architect also filed a cross-complaint against Bartile on April 27, 2006, which was amended on July 24, 2007, alleging essentially the same claims as Jacobsen.

On November 22, 2004, Bartile requested defense and indemnification [Author's Note: indemnification is a legal concept by which one party, either by explicit agreement or indemnification imposed by law, such as where a principal is held liable for the act of an agent, is made to reimburse or make whole someone who suffers a loss; in litigation, a claim for indemnification can be filed before the results of the litigation in anticipation of a loss that, if it results the demanding party seeks to "pass off" the loss to the indemnifying party] against these claims, pursuant to the relevant CGL policies. On October 25, 2005, EMC agreed to provide a defense. However, EMC reserved its right to investigate the claims further and "to deny coverage for part or all of the claimed damage." On August 17, 2007, EMC issued a second letter to Bartile in which it announced that the claims "[we]re not covered by [the] policy." Although EMC stated that it would "continue to defend Bartile in this litigation," EMC reserved the right "to enforce any rights it may have to recoup defense costs from Bartile should it be determined that EMC had no duty to defend Bartile in this litigation."

On August 20, 2007, EMC filed a declaratory judgment action in the U.S. District Court for the District of Wyoming. EMC argued that it was not obligated to defend or indemnify Bartile for the claims and damages asserted in the underlying state-court action. EMC also sought to recoup the costs it had incurred in defending Bartile against those claims. On December 21, 2007, EMC moved for summary judgment. On the same day, Bartile moved to dismiss the federal claims for lack of personal jurisdiction and improper venue and, in the alternative, asked the district court to transfer the action to the U.S. District Court for the District of Utah.

On March 4, 2008, the district court denied the motion to dismiss and the motion to transfer venue. On August 6, 2008, the district court granted the motion for summary judgment in part and denied it in part. Although the district court held that the underlying state-court action did not trigger EMC's duty to defend Bartile, it denied EMC's request for recoupment of the defense costs.

Bartile now appeals the district court's orders denying its motion to dismiss and motion to transfer venue. Bartile also challenges the district court's grant of partial summary judgment in favor of EMC. EMC cross-appeals the order denying its motion for summary judgment on the recoupment of defense costs.

. . .

Improper Venue

We review de novo the district court's decision not to dismiss an action for improper venue. The district court held that "[v]enue is proper in Wyoming," pursuant to § 1391([b]) (2), because "[t]he events giving rise to this litigation all concern [Bartile's] actions in [Wyoming]." For the following reasons, we agree.

In a diversity action, venue lies in a judicial district where any defendant resides . . . (2) a judicial district in which a substantial part of the events or omissions giving rise to the claim occurred . . . or (3) a judicial district in which any defendant is subject to personal jurisdiction at the time the action is commenced, if there is no district in which the action may otherwise be brought.

The only possible ground for venue at issue here is under §1391 ([b]) (2). Under that provision, venue is not limited to the district with the most substantial events or omissions. Section 1391([b]) (2) instead "contemplates that venue can be appropriate in more than one district . . .[and] permits venue in multiple judicial districts as long as a substantial part of the underlying events took place in those districts."

We conduct a two-part analysis when reviewing challenges to venue under § 1391([b]) (2). First, we examine the nature of the plaintiff's claims and the acts or omissions underlying those claims. In this action, EMC requested a declaratory judgment that the CGL policies imposed no duty to defend or indemnify Bartile against claims pending in California state court. This declaratory judgment action arose from a series of acts and omissions that occurred in Utah, Colorado, and Wyoming. For example, the record suggests that the CGL policies were negotiated in Utah, underwritten in Colorado, and executed in Utah. Bartile performed allegedly negligent roofing work on the luxury hotel in Wyoming. Bartile also filed a claim through a Utah-based insurance broker to demand that EMC defend it from the state-court action and indemnify it from any adverse judgments. Although EMC sent a letter from Colorado announcing that the CGL policies did not cover the alleged damages, it agreed to provide a defense subject to a reservation of its right to recoup its defense costs.

Second, we determine whether substantial "events material to those claims occurred" in the forum district. The substantiality requirement is satisfied upon a showing of "acts and omissions that have a close nexus" to the alleged claims.

In this action, the substantial events include Bartile's allegedly negligent work on the luxury hotel. Courts have held that the alleged damages or loss under an insurance policy may constitute a substantial event for purposes of the venue analysis. Although Bartile contends that the location of the allegedly negligent work is irrelevant to the interpretation of the CGL policies, this work is still part of the "entire sequence of events underlying the claim" because it forms the basis of Bartile's request for a defense and indemnification, Thus, venue is proper under 28 U.S.C. § 1391([b]) (2).

. . .

Conclusion

For the foregoing reasons, we AFFIRM the district court's orders denying the motions to dismiss, denying the motion to transfer . . . and denying summary judgment to EMC on the recoupment-of-costs issue.

Follow-Up Questions and Comments

1. 28 U.S.C. § 1391(b) (2), and the *Bartile Roofs* case help to illustrate why someone performing venue analysis needs to remember that the question of where "a substantial part of the events giving rise to the claim" occurred is a distinct analysis. When analyzing whether a defendant is subject to specific personal jurisdiction from claims filed in a state, the court will not aggregate events that occur in different states, even states adjacent to the forum. Under § 1391(b) (2), however, the statutory language authorizes the court to consider venues in which "a substantial part of the events or omissions giving rise to the claim occurred." Thus, the court could determine—in a venue analysis—that districts in different states are proper under this standard.

2. *Bates v. C & S Adjusters, Inc.*,[268] provides another example of § 1392(b) (2) applying to more than one state. There, a collection agency sent a letter demanding payment of a debt to an address in the Western District of Pennsylvania for Bates, the debtor. However, unbeknownst to the collection agency, Bates had moved to the Eastern District of New York. The postal service forwarded the letter to Bates' new address. He received it and sued in the Eastern District of New York under the Fair Debt Collection Practices Act.[269] The defendant forgot to challenge personal jurisdiction in New York, but oddly enough did file a timely motion challenging venue. Relying on the version of § 1391(b) (2) then in effect, the court held that a substantial part of the events giving rise to the claim occurred both in the Western District of Pennsylvania and the Eastern District of New York (by receipt of the collection letter). The Court specifically noted the difference between personal jurisdiction, in which it would have been pertinent that the collection agency did not intend the letter to go to New York, and venue, where the court merely looks at the events giving rise to the claim to determine districts that are proper venues.

3. In *Bates*, the defendant raised the issue that the collection letter had been mailed by the defendant in Pennsylvania to another Pennsylvania address and, thus, the defendant could not have been intending conduct in New York, where the letter was forwarded. As the court in *Bates* concluded, "The statutory standard for venue focuses not on whether a defendant has made a deliberate contact—a factor relevant in the analysis of personal jurisdiction—but on the location where events occurred."[270]

Practice Problem

Following is a Practice Problem designed to test application of § 1391(b) (2).

Practice Problem 6-6

Schrank developed the plan to assassinate Theodore Roosevelt. Following Roosevelt's campaign speaking trail preceding the presidential election, Schrank bought the 38-caliber revolver that he ultimately used to shoot Roosevelt in the Eastern District of New York, telling the gun seller that he planned to use the gun for that purpose. Then, in Chicago, located in Northern District of Illinois, Schrank bought bullets for the gun, telling the ammunition supplier that he planned to use the ammunition to shoot Roosevelt. While Roosevelt rose to give a speech in Milwaukee, located in the Eastern District of Wisconsin, Schrank shot Roosevelt in the chest. Fortunately, Roosevelt had put his 100-page speech inside his coat pocket where the bullet entered. Although the bullet penetrated the papers and lodged in Roosevelt's ribs, he was not mortally wounded. Indeed, after admitting he had been shot, Roosevelt stated that it would take more than one bullet to "stop the Bull Moose" and continued his 90-minute speech before going to the hospital. Schrank was captured in Milwaukee and admitted to shooting Roosevelt. Assume that all jurisdictions impose a civil penalty by statute on gun sellers and on ammunition suppliers when a buyer states he plans to use the gun or ammunition to shoot another person without provocation. In a suit by Roosevelt against Schrank for assault, what venues would be proper under 28 U.S.C. § 1391 (b)(2)?

---

[268] 980 F.2d 865 (2d Cir. 1992).
[269] 15 U.S.C. § 1692.
[270] 980 F.2d at 868.

1. The Last (Little-Used) Option: The "Fall-Back" Provision

The final option under the general venue statute, often referred to as the "fallback" provision, is as follows: [I]f there is no district in which an action may otherwise be brought as provided in this section, any judicial district in which any defendant is subject to the court's personal jurisdiction with respect to such action.[271]

Notice the conditional language at the beginning of this option: "if there is no district in which an action may otherwise be brought." In other words, the fallback provision can apply only if neither the residency provisions of § 1391(b)(1) nor the acts-or-omission provisions of § 1391(b)(2) apply. We have seen that the residency provisions might not apply if the plaintiff has sued multiple defendants who do not all reside in the same state. However, there should always be a district within the United States where an act or omission giving rise to the claim occurred. The scenario in which the fallback provision may apply, however, would be when the residency provisions do not apply and the acts or omissions giving rise to the claim occurred outside the United States. The scenarios in which the fallback provision dictates venue are rare.

Practice Problem

The following Practice Problem illustrates a scenario in which § 1391(b) (3) could apply. Note how narrow the circumstances are.

Practice Problem 6-7

When Lafayette claimed that he was more responsible for the Americans defeating the British than Washington, Franklin overheard the boast and punched Lafayette in the teeth. Even though Franklin lived in Europe, and no longer had a domicile in the U.S., Lafayette thought it was appropriate to seek justice through the American civil system by suing Franklin in the U.S. District for the District of Columbia based on alienage jurisdiction, in which an alien can sue an American in federal court just as citizens of different states can do under the diversity of citizenship provision. In this case, would venue be proper under 28 U.S.C. § 1391(b) (3)? Why or why not?

E. Transfer of Venue

Two statutes govern transfer of venue in the federal system.[272] The first statute, 28 U.S.C. § 1404(a), deals with transfer of a case from a district that is a proper venue to another district. The second statute, 28 U.S.C. § 1406(a), addresses transfer from a court in a district that is an improper venue to another district which is proper. The difference between these two statutes is apparent on reading them:

§ 1404. Change of Venue.

For the convenience of parties and witnesses, in the interest of justice, a district court may transfer any civil action to any other district or division where it might have been brought

---

[271] 28 U.S.C. § 1391(b) (3) (2017).

[272] "Transfer" refers to a case in the federal system being transferred from one federal district court to another federal district court. Do not confuse the concept with "removal," in which a case is taken from a state court and transferred to a U.S. federal district court.

or to any district or division to which all parties have consented.[273]

§ 1406. Cure or Waiver of Defects.

The district court of a district in which a case is filed a case laying venue in the wrong division or district shall dismiss, or if it be in the interest of justice, transfer such case to any district or division in which it could have been brought.[274]

The party objecting to venue needs to have done so at the outset. Thus, a party should not simply file a motion to transfer venue. Such a motion is not one recognized as a proper response, at least on its own, under Federal Rule of Civil Procedure 12. Instead, the defendant should file a motion to dismiss under Rule 12(b) (3) for improper venue or, alternatively, to transfer venue. The motion should specify which statute—§ 1404 or § 1406—supports the motion to transfer venue. If the court in which the case was filed is within a district that qualifies as a proper venue, then the motion to transfer will be under § 1404(a). If it is not within a district that qualifies as a proper one under § 1391, the general venue statute, then the motion to transfer will be under § 1406(a).

1. Supreme Court Decisions on the Transfer of Venue Statutes

Several Supreme Court decisions have answered questions about motions to transfer venue. The rulings in these cases generally apply to both § 1404 and § 1406. Our discussion will first address these decisions. Then, we will address the differences between the criteria courts consider when determining whether to transfer under § 1404 and the factors considered § 1406.

The first case of note deals with the effect of a so-called forum selection clause. In a contract with a forum-selection clause, the parties enter an agreement that dictates the forum in which the parties must sue if they litigate. One might think that a forum-selection clause is absolutely binding, and the only location can be the forum in the contract. However, the Court in *Stewart Organization, Inc. v. Ricoh*,[275] held that the forum-selection clause would be a factor that the district court should consider in deciding whether to transfer a case. However, the Court held that the district court, in considering the factors traditionally weighed in deciding whether to transfer a case from one district to another should consider the parties expression of the choice of a forum as one among the other factors and not treat the choice-of-forum clause as dispositive.

Another case, *Goldwar, Inc. v. Heiman*,[276] addresses the important question of whether, if a case is originally filed in a court that lacks personal jurisdiction, the court can enter an order transferring the case. In *Goldwar*, the Court faced this issue when the plaintiff had filed in an improper venue that also lacked personal jurisdiction. Hence, the motion to transfer in *Goldwar* was under § 1406. The Court held that, despite the lack of personal jurisdiction, the transferor court (venue parlance for the court of first filing addressing a motion to transfer) could rule on the motion to transfer.[277] Most federal circuit courts of appeal have held that the same should apply to § 1404 motions to transfer—*i.e.*, that the district court, even if it lacks personal jurisdiction, can rule on a motion to transfer under § 1404, just as it could do under § 1406.[278]

---

[273] 28 U.S.C. § 1404(a) (2017).

[274] *Id.* § 1406(a).

[275] 487 U.S. 22 (1988).

[276] 369 U.S. 463 (1962),

[277] *See id.* at 466.

[278] Compare Sidari v. Caesar's Pocono Resorts, 29 Fed. Appx. 845, 847 (3d Cir. 2002) (adopting the position of the

The Supreme Court dealt with the opposite scenario in *Hoffman v. Blaski*.[279] There, the case had been filed in a proper venue, but the motion sought transfer to a court that lacked both personal jurisdiction and venue over the defendant. The Court observed that § 1404's language provides for transfer to a district in which the suit "might have been brought." That language, the Court ruled, required that the court to which a case is transferred ("the transferee court") must have personal jurisdiction over the defendant and must be a proper venue.[280] Because § 1406 contains language stating that transfer may be to a court in which the action "might have been brought," i.e., the identical language as in § 1404, the *Hoffman* ruling applies to § 1406 transfers. In other words, regardless of whether the case is filed in a court with proper venue, a motion to transfer must designate a transferee court in which the case could have been filed originally, i.e., one that has both personal jurisdiction over the defendant and in which venue is proper.[281]

The Supreme Court has also ensured that a party has no incentive to seek more favorable law through venue transfer under 28 U.S.C § 1404. In *Van Dusen v. Barrack*,[282] the Court addressed whether the choice-of-law rules of the state of the transferor court or the transferee court would apply if a case is transferred. Choice-of-law rules, also referred to as "conflicts of law," are the rules by which a court decides which state's law applies to a case. Choice-of-law rules apply in any case, not just venue transfer cases. For instance, if suit is filed in a federal or state court in Virginia, the court will apply Virginia choice-of-law rules to decide whose state's law applies to the claims. Because Virginia follows the traditional choice-of-law approach for a tort (*lex locus delicti*), the forum court would look to the state in which the tort occurred and apply that state's law.[283] So, an action filed in Connecticut state court could end up applying the law of Virginia if that is where the tort occurred.[284] Landers was overruled when Connecticut started following the Conflict of Laws' Restatement's approach to determining choice of law, rather than the first RESTATEMENT, which is still followed in some states. Most states follow a more sophisticated analysis that analyzes a variety of factors outlined in the Restatement (Second) Conflict of Laws.[285]

With this synopsis of choice-of-law principles, one should be able to see how the doctrine can be used in venue transfer cases to avoid parties' seeking transfer to obtain more favorable law. The court in *Van Dusen* recognized that risk. The Court's ruling precludes a party from achieving more favorable law in the transferee court by holding that the transferee court must apply the same choice-of-law rules as would

---

majority of circuits by finding venue transfer possible under § 1404(a), even in the absence of personal jurisdiction) with Pittock v. Otis Elevator Co., 8 F.3d 325, 329 (6th Cir. 1993) (adopting minority position by recognizing, "a transfer under [§] 1404(a) may not be granted when the district court does not have personal jurisdiction over the defendants.").

[279] 363 U.S. 335 (1960).

[280] *Id.* at 343–44.

[281] One exception applies under the Federal Courts Jurisdiction and Venue Clarification Act of 2011 (supra note 10) which permits transfer "to any district or division to which all parties have consented." Under this portion of the statute, a case can be transferred, even to a district or division that would not have had proper venue or personal jurisdiction at the time the suit was filed. This exception is intended to further the interest of justice by allowing, for example, the enforcement of forum selection clauses between parties; however, it does not supplant a court's ability to allow transfers under a 1406 motion. Note, the parties must still first satisfy the requirements of § 1404(a) before a court will consider allowing transfer to a court to which the parties have consented.

[282] 376 U.S. 612 (1964).

[283] Richards v. United States, 369 U.S. 1, 11 (1962).

[284] Landers v. Landers, 216 A.2d 183 (Conn. 1966), overruled in part by O'Connor v. O'Connor, 519 A.2d 13 (Conn. 1986), and Reichhold Chems., Inc. v. Hartford Accident and Indem. Co., 703 A.2d 1132 (Conn. 1997).

[285] RESTATEMENT (SECOND) OF CONFLICT OF LAWS § 145 (1971). *E.g.*, *Schwartz v. Schwartz*, 447 P.2d 254 (Ariz. 1968).

the transferor court. Hence, the law applied in the case should end up being the same after a case is transferred. The benefit of transfer, therefore, would be limited to the purposes for which venue transfers exist, *e.g.*, convenience of parties and witnesses.

In summary, the Supreme Court's guidance has established: (1) that a forum-selection clause will be considered but not determinative of a transfer; (2) that the court in which an action is filed need not have personal jurisdiction over the defendant to grant a motion to transfer the case to another district; (3) that the district to which a case is transferred must have both personal jurisdiction over the defendant and be a proper venue, however; and, finally, (4) that the result of a transfer will not affect the law applied because the choice-of-law rules of the state in which the case originated will apply even if the case is transferred. These are useful guidelines for understanding many of the principles governing venue transfer. However, the most basic point in transfer of venue—what criteria the court should rely on to grant or deny a motion to transfer—will be explained in the next section.

2. Difference in Criteria for § 1404 and § 1406 Transfers

Under 28 U.S.C. § 1404, the movant has the burden of showing the appropriateness of a transfer.[286] The criteria a court will apply in ruling on a motion to transfer will depend on whether the motion is under § 1404 or under § 1406. If the case was filed in a proper venue, and the motion is under § 1404, the plaintiff's choice of forum is accorded deference.[287]

Under § 1406 [,] the court does not defer to the plaintiff's choice of forum.[288] The plaintiff's choice can be overcome if "the convenience of the parties and witnesses" and "the interests of justice" support a transfer. After all, these are the criteria identified in the venue statues as the basis on which a transfer decision should rest. Courts have taken the language of the statute and applied a variety of means to determine whether the criteria for transfer have been met. Following is a representative case from the Fourth Circuit.

CERTUSVIEW TECHNOLOGIES, LLC v. S & N LOCATING SERVICES, LLC
United States District Court for the Eastern District of Virginia, 2013
No. 2:13CV346, 2013 U.S. Dist. LEXIS 175339

DAVIS, United States District Judge.

This matter is before the Court on a motion to transfer venue filed by defendants S & N Locating Services, LLC, and S & N Communications, Inc. (collectively "Defendants" or "S & N"). Defendants' motion seeks transfer of this patent infringement action to Defendants' home forum of the Middle District of North Carolina. Plaintiff Certusview Technologies, LLC, ("Plaintiff" or "Certusview") opposes such transfer. For the reasons set forth below, the Court DENIES Defendants' motion to transfer venue.

Factual and Procedural Background
Plaintiff filed its complaint in the United States District Court for the Eastern District of Virginia on May 29, 2013. After the Court granted Defendants' unopposed motion to extend the time to file pleadings or a motion in response to the Complaint, Defendants filed the instant motion to transfer venue.

---

[286] Werner Mach. Co. v. National Coops., Inc., 289 F. Supp. 962 (E.D. Wis. 1968).
[287] Sutherland v. Cybergenics Corp., 907 F. Supp. 1218 (N.D. Ill. 1995).
[288] Rojas v. Trans States Airlines, Inc., 204 F.R.D. 265, 269 (D.N.J. 2001).

The parties again filed a motion requesting additional time, and this Court extended the briefing schedule on the instant motion. Nearly a month after this matter was fully briefed, Plaintiff filed a motion for leave to file a surreply.

. . .

Standard for Discretionary Transfer of Venue

Title 28 of the United States Code, Section 1404, establishes that, "[f]or the convenience of parties and witnesses, in the interest of justice, a district court may transfer any civil action to any other district or division where it might have been brought or to any district or division to which all parties have consented." 28 U.S.C. § 1404(a). Such statute "is intended to place discretion in the district court to adjudicate motions for transfer of venue according to an 'individualized, case-by-case consideration

To determine whether a transfer of venue to another district is appropriate under § 1404(a), "a district court must make two inquiries: (1) whether the claims might have been brought in the transferee forum, and (2) whether the interest of justice and convenience of the parties and witnesses justify transfer to that forum." In conducting the second inquiry, the Court considers several factors to determine whether to transfer venue, including: "'(1) ease of access to sources of proof; (2) the convenience of the parties and witnesses; (3) the cost of obtaining the attendance of witnesses; (4) the availability of compulsory process; (5) the interest in having local controversies decided at home; (6) in diversity cases, the court's familiarity with the applicable law; and (7) the interest of justice.'" The principal factors to consider, however, are: (1) Plaintiff's choice of forum; (2) witness convenience and access to sources of proof; party convenience; and (4) the interest of justice. Ultimately, the burden of proof is on the movant to show "that transfer does more than merely 'shift the inconvenience to the other party.'"

Discussion

Venue in Transferee Forum

"As an initial matter, the court must determine whether the proposed transferee court is one in which the action originally may have been brought." If the claims could have been brought in the transferee court initially, the subsequent decision to transfer venue is within the discretion of the court.

Under 28 U.S.C. § 1400(b), venue in patent infringement lawsuits is proper in any "district where the defendant resides, or where the defendant has committed acts of infringement and has a regular and established place of business."[289] A corporate defendant resides in any district in which it is subject to personal jurisdiction.[290]

In the instant matter, it is undisputed that Plaintiff's patent infringement action could have initially been filed in the Middle District of North Carolina as Defendants are residents of such district and their corporate headquarters are located therein. Accordingly, the Court finds that venue would have been proper in the proposed transferee court.

Section 1404(a) Convenience and Justice Factors

Although there are various ways to formulate the relevant considerations for determining whether a discretionary transfer is appropriate, the primary considerations are: (1) Plaintiff's choice of forum; witness convenience and access to sources of proof; (3) party convenience; and (4) the interest of justice.

---

[289] 28 U.S.C. § 1400(b).
[290] 28 U.S.C. § 1391(c).

Plaintiff's Initial Choice of Venue

"Generally, the first factor—a plaintiff's choice of venue—is given substantial weight as '[i]t is well settled that a court should rarely disturb a plaintiff's choice of forum unless the balance of hardships clearly favor transfer.'" However, the "weight given to plaintiff's choice of venue varies with the significance of the contacts between the venue chosen by plaintiff and the underlying cause of action." Furthermore, a plaintiff's selection of a foreign forum is typically given less weight than a plaintiff's selection of its home forum. This is so because "it is often more difficult for the plaintiff to show why such a forum is more convenient for the plaintiff."

Here, it is undisputed that Plaintiff's "home forum" is in Florida, not the Eastern District of Virginia. Accordingly, to determine whether substantial weight should be given to Plaintiff's chosen forum, this

Court's inquiry focuses on the degree of connection between Plaintiff's cause of action and the Eastern District of Virginia.

The parties present vastly divergent pictures of the connection between the instant dispute and the Eastern District of Virginia. Plaintiff contends that Defendants are engaged in large-scale infringement of Plaintiff's various patents almost exclusively in the Commonwealth of Virginia. Plaintiff seeks to justify its allegation by explaining that the disputed technology involves electronic mapping of underground utilities and that the Commonwealth of Virginia, through several of its largest utility companies, is at the forefront of adopting electronic mapping methods. In contrast, Plaintiff asserts that it is unaware of any utility companies in North Carolina that are utilizing such electronic mapping services.

In response, Defendants note that Plaintiff's alleged unawareness of sales by Defendants of their products or services in North Carolina is "irrelevant" and indicate that they perform electronic mapping services in several states, including Virginia, North Carolina, Maryland, and Ohio. Although Defendants are correct that the facts-not Plaintiff's knowledge or lack thereof-should drive the inquiry, curiously, Defendants offer no sales data or other information to refute Plaintiff's suggestion that the vast majority of all (purported) infringement is occurring in Virginia. Defendants' efforts to refute Plaintiff's claim that the instant suit bears substantial ties to Virginia falls flat because: 1) prior to discovery, Defendants are the sole possessors of any such evidence; 2) Defendants have submitted no such data or evidence; and 3) Defendants bear the burden of proving that venue should be transferred.

The Court further notes that Defendants seek to demonstrate the lack of a connection to Virginia by citing case law indicating that "[f]ederal courts are not solicitous of plaintiffs claiming substantial weight for their forum choice where the connection with the forum is limited to sales activity without more." However, the instant facts, as presented to this Court by Plaintiff, involve infringement that is occurring almost exclusively in Virginia. At least based on the information before the Court at this time, this is not a case where an infringing physical device is designed and manufactured in one state and the connection to the state in which suit is filed is merely claimed retail sales. Rather, it appears that Plaintiff's primary allegation of infringement is that Defendants are currently, on a daily basis, infringing Plaintiff's patent in Virginia by using Plaintiff's patented method of creating electronic maps of utility lines in Virginia, and that such electronic maps are specific to land surveyed in Virginia. It is also notable that Defendants have more than ten offices in Virginia which, according to Defendants, support both the accused purportedly infringing activities, as well as unrelated clearly non-infringing construction activities.

191

Although Defendants' filings suggest that the claimed infringement stems from Defendants' "product," the "SN LocSys System," which was designed and created in North Carolina, Defendants fail to articulate the type of product (i.e., software or hardware) and fail to effectively refute Plaintiff's assertion that the focus of the instant suit is on "method" claims being infringed in Virginia, rather than an infringing apparatus being designed and manufactured in one state and merely being sold in another. For example, in *Beam Laser Systems, Incorporated. v. Cox Communications, Incorporated*,[291] another Judge of this Court rejected the defendants' attempts to demonstrate a lack of significant ties to the Eastern District of Virginia. The Court began by noting that "[u]nder patent law, 'whoever without authority makes, uses, offers to sell, or sells any patented invention, within the United States . . . during the term of the patent therefor, infringes the patent.'"[292] Although in some cases, the "hub of activity" where an infringing product is designed and manufactured will have the strongest ties to the cause of action, such is true when the "patent infringement action alleg[es] violation of the 'makes' prong of the statute."[293] In contrast, the "center of the accused activity" in Beam Laser Systems was the Eastern District of Virginia, where the plaintiffs had asserted large-scale use of the purportedly "infringing . . . system."[294]

Considering the above, as in Beam Laser Systems, the Court finds that Plaintiff has advanced "significant ties" to the Eastern District of Virginia such that Plaintiff's choice of forum should be given substantial weight. Although various factors lead to such conclusion, most notable is the fact that the alleged infringement involves the use of a method (and/or apparatus) within the Eastern District of Virginia in order to map underground utility lines located within Virginia. Furthermore, Defendants fail to present any sales data or other evidence to refute Plaintiff's assertion that Virginia is at the forefront of adopting the disputed technology and is the primary locus of the use of the patented method to electronically map underground utilities. Accordingly, the Court finds that Plaintiff has demonstrated sufficient ties to this district to afford "substantial weight" to its selection of forum for litigating the instant lawsuit.

Parties/Witness Convenience and Access

The Court next performs a combined analysis of considering the convenience to the parties and witnesses in litigating in the instant venue rather than the proposed transferee venue. Assessment of this factor requires the court to consider, among other things, the "ease of access to sources of proof, the costs of obtaining witnesses, and the availability of compulsory process."

A party asserting witness inconvenience "has the burden to proffer, by affidavit or otherwise, sufficient details respecting the witnesses and their potential testimony to enable the court to assess the materiality of evidence and the degree of inconvenience." Additionally, "the convenience of non-party witnesses should be afforded greater weight [than the convenience of party witnesses] in deciding a motion to transfer." As the moving party, Defendants must demonstrate that the Eastern District of Virginia is "an inconvenient forum in which to litigate, not simply that the [Middle District of North Carolina] would be more convenient."

Here, Defendants motion and memoranda at best demonstrate why the Middle District of North Carolina would be more convenient for its witnesses and provide for easier access to Defendants' corporate files. Defendants do not, however, demonstrate why this Court, which is only 235 miles from the Middle District of North Carolina, Greensboro Division, is an "inconvenient forum." Notably, Defendants do not proffer, by affidavit or other evidence, sufficient details regarding the potential testimony of its proposed

---

[291] 117 F. Supp. 2d 515, 518–19 (E.D. Va. 2000).
[292] *Id.* at 518 (quoting 35 U.S.C. § 271(a)).
[293] *Id.* at 518–19.
[294] *Id.* at 519.

witnesses such that the Court can assess the materiality of such testimony and/or the extent of the inconvenience. Rather, Defendants focus primarily on the number of miles that need to be driven by Defendants' potential witnesses, as well as the assumed expense of meals and lodging. Furthermore, not only do Defendants fail to identify a single witness who is located more than 250 miles from this courthouse, but four of the eleven S & N witnesses identified by Defendants are actually closer to this courthouse than to the courthouse in Greensboro, North Carolina. As to the seven potential witnesses who are far closer to Greensboro, Defendants broadly assert that those individuals have "relevant knowledge . . . regarding the development, maintenance, advertising, and/or sales" of the accused technology. As the parties asserting inconvenience, Defendants' broad statements fall far short of the requirement that they "proffer by affidavit or otherwise, sufficient details respecting the witnesses and their potential testimony" to permit the Court to assess whether such testimony is "central to a claim," as well as whether it is "merely cumulative" to testimony offered by other witnesses.

Although Defendants have identified one third-party witness located 90 miles from the Greensboro courthouse and 240 miles from this Court, Defendants have not included an affidavit from that witness suggesting that traveling to Norfolk would be "inconvenient." Defendants vaguely identify additional third-party witnesses who live in Roanoke, Virginia (which is actually closer to Greensboro, North Carolina than to Norfolk, Virginia); however, Defendants' own facts suggest that one or more of those witnesses live more than 100 miles from Greensboro and would thus be outside the subpoena power of the Greensboro Court, but would still be within the subpoena power of this Court. Finally, Defendants do not persuasively demonstrate that air travel from Florida to Greensboro, North Carolina, as compared to air travel from Florida to Norfolk, Virginia, is any different in length of travel, price, or inconvenience.

Regarding "access to sources of proof," Defendants also assert that "S & N related documents" are housed in North Carolina and would need to be transported to Virginia. However, Defendants fail to identify such documents with any degree of particularity, fail to quantify the scope of the relevant documents, and fail to indicate whether the documents are paper or electronic. Furthermore, Defendants fail to provide any evidence rebutting Plaintiff's assertion that the bulk of the alleged infringement is occurring in Virginia, or that Defendants have more than ten offices in Virginia.

Considering the above information, the Court finds that the instant prong, at best, slightly favors transfer to the Middle District of North Carolina. That said, the limited information provided by Defendants does little to distinguish the facts of this case from almost any other lawsuit because transferring a case to a defendant's home forum is almost always more convenient for that defendant's witnesses.

Interest of Justice

"The interest of justice category is 'designedly broad,'" and "is intended to encompass all those factors bearing on transfer that are unrelated to convenience of witnesses and parties." To place a more practical framework on such a designedly broad test, district courts generally consider the following eight factors: (1) the pendency of a related action, (2) the court's familiarity with the applicable law, docket conditions, (4) access to premises that might have to be viewed, (5) the possibility of an unfair trial, (6) the ability to join other parties, (7) the possibility of harassment, and (8) the interest of having local controversies decided at home. Ultimately, the interest-of-justice factor "encompasses public interest factors aimed at 'systemic integrity and fairness,' with the most prominent considerations being "judicial economy and the avoidance of inconsistent judgments."

Here, Defendants focus solely on factor eight (local controversies decided at home), asserting that the other factors are "not at issue" in this case. The central dispute is which state has a "local" interest in the matter. Defendants assert that North Carolina has a "local" interest in this matter solely because Defendants are headquartered there and because the allegedly infringing technology was researched, designed, and developed there. Plaintiff offers an effective counterargument, however, asserting that, regardless of Defendants' physical location, Defendants are engaging in large-scale infringement in Virginia as they utilize patented technology on a daily basis to create electronic maps of underground utilities located in Virginia for large utility companies in Virginia. In other words, although Defendants may be headquartered in North Carolina, their alleged infringement is occurring in Virginia.

Defendants attempt to counter Plaintiff's point by vaguely asserting that they perform services in other states as well, including North Carolina, but Defendants fail to quantify in any way their activities in other states. It appears to this Court that the state with the most direct interest in the instant action is the state where its utility companies rely daily on the services of an alleged infringer rather than the state where such infringer has its home office. Accordingly, the interest-of-justice factor slightly favors Plaintiff.

In sum, Defendants have failed to demonstrate that transfer to the Middle District of North Carolina is warranted, based on the relevant factors present in this case. As detailed above, a transfer to the Middle District of North Carolina would simply shift the inconvenience from Defendants to Plaintiff, and Defendants have failed to demonstrate that "the interest of justice and convenience of the parties and witnesses justify transfer to" the Middle District of North Carolina. Accordingly, Defendants' motion to transfer venue is DENIED.

By contrast, a case such as the following considers some of the same factors as in a § 1404 analysis, as well as other factors.

DEE-K ENTERPRISES v. HEVEAFIL SDN. BHD.
United States District Court for the Eastern District of Virginia, 1997
985 F. Supp. 640

ELLIS, III, District Court Judge.

In this international antitrust action, plaintiffs allege a conspiracy between and among various foreign manufacturers of extruded rubber thread and their distributors to fix prices of the thread in the United States.

. . .

The matter now before the Court is a motion by several defendants to dismiss for improper venue pursuant to Rule 12 (b) (3), Fed. R. Civ. P. The facts pertinent to this motion may be succinctly stated. The named defendants fall into two groups: (i) Malaysian, Indonesian, and Thai manufacturers of extruded rubber thread, and (ii) the American distributors of the thread. None of these defendants is located in the Eastern District of Virginia. Moreover, no defendant transacts business in this District; defendant Consortium International Corp. ("Consortium") has supplied thread to plaintiff Dee-K Enterprises, Inc. ("Dee-K") in Virginia, but all of those transactions took place in the Western District of Virginia. Thus, certain defendants contend that venue is improper in this District. Several defendants also moved to dismiss this action for lack of personal jurisdiction and for failure to state a claim; these motions were denied by the earlier Memorandum Opinion. Left undecided by that Memorandum Opinion, however, was defendants' motion to dismiss for improper venue. Accordingly, by Order dated October 23, 1997, plaintiffs were directed to file a memorandum concerning the propriety of venue in the Eastern District of Virginia. Plaintiffs have filed such a memorandum, and defendants have filed their responses. Thus, the matter is now ripe for disposition.

. . .

[The court considered whether the venue objection had been waived (Dee-K had waived the objection, Consortium had not) and then if venue was proper in the Eastern District of Virginia.]

The inescapable conclusion is that venue does not properly lie in the Eastern District of Virginia.

. . .

When venue is improperly laid, the district court "shall dismiss, or if it be in the interest of justice, transfer [the] case to any district or division in which it could have been brought."[295] At the outset, it is worth noting that dismissal would be a proper remedy in this matter. When a plaintiff's attorney reasonably should have foreseen that the forum in which he filed an action was improper, dismissal is warranted. Lawyers, especially skilled attorneys such as plaintiffs' counsel, are expected to comply with the relatively straightforward jurisdictional and filing requirements set out in the Federal Rules of Civil Procedure. Here there was no plausible basis for believing venue was proper in this District. Although some of the alleged conspiratorial activity occurred in Floyd, Virginia, a cursory review of the configuration of the federal judicial districts would have revealed that city to be located in the Western District, not the Eastern District, of Virginia. Indeed, the only reasons one might discern for filing here are the celerity with which complex actions are disposed of in this District, and the proximity of the Alexandria courthouse to plaintiffs' counsel's offices in Washington, D.C. First, counsel's residence weighs little, if at all, in the venue inquiry. Second, while the potential for a prompt trial is not to be disregarded entirely in the interest-of-justice calculus, it certainly does not overcome the absence of proper venue.

Notwithstanding the conclusion that dismissal would be proper, a transfer is more appropriate in the circumstances. This is so given the substantial proceedings that have already occurred in this case, including, for example, initial discovery, entry of protective orders, briefing and resolution of Rule 12(b)(6) motions, and the filing of answers, counterclaims, and cross claims; and also given the accepted principle that every litigant is entitled to its day in court. Consortium suggests that, in the absence of dismissal, the case be transferred to the Western District of Virginia. The Malaysian defendants, by contrast, ask that if the action is not dismissed, it be transferred to the Western District of North Carolina. Thus, it is necessary to evaluate and balance the contacts each of those fora has with this matter.

Dee-K and other potential class members are located in the Western District of Virginia. Furthermore, Dee-K has filed a bankruptcy action in that District. Other facts, however, tip the scales decisively in favor of transfer to the Western District of North Carolina. First, plaintiff Asheboro Elastics Corp. and other potential class members are located in that District. Second, of the five U.S. defendants, three are located, or have their records, in or near Charlotte, which is in the Western District of North Carolina. Third, according to the Malaysian defendants' affidavits, more witnesses, and especially non-party witnesses, are located in the Western District of North Carolina than in any other District. Finally, a federal grand jury has been convened in Charlotte to investigate defendants' alleged conspiratorial conduct. Accordingly, the Western District of North Carolina is the appropriate transferee forum.

. . .

---

[295] 28 U.S.C. § 1406 (a).

For the reasons stated above, venue in this District is improper. In lieu of dismissal pursuant to Rule 12(b)(3), Fed. R. Civ. P., this action will be transferred to the Western District of North Carolina, pursuant to 28 U.S.C. § 1406(a).

An appropriate Order will issue.

Follow-Up Questions and Comments

1. Did you notice the reference in *Dee-K* to "potential class members"? That means the case is one in which the plaintiffs were seeking to proceed under Federal Rule of Civil Procedure 23 as a class action.[296] The suit cannot proceed as such until the court "certifies" that the requirements of Rule 23 have been met. A first-year course in federal pretrial practice and procedure generally does not delve too deeply into class actions under Rule 23. However, you should make it a point to know enough about class actions to realize when a client may present a scenario that could give rise to one. The class action is a powerful means of relief for numerous parties whose claims may, taken individually, seem insignificant, but together are formidable.

2. If an advanced procedure course in your school does not address this topic, you can explore the topic on your own. An essential resource on class actions is William Rubenstein, Alba Conte, and Herbert Newberg's *Newberg on Class Actions* (5th Ed. 2019). *Dee-K Enterprises* was a class action. Thus, named members representative of the class as a whole, presenting common questions of law and fact, were pursuing the claim. If you just skim Rule 23, you see that the process of handling a class action is sophisticated. When presented with a potential class action for the first time, you would be wise to associate with counsel who have handled class actions before. Having said that, you should not shy away simply because class actions are sophisticated. Lawyers typically will associate with less experienced lawyers. In class actions, the fees awarded to the lawyers provide more than enough compensation to go around. Class actions are discussed more fully in Chapter 11.

Practice Problems

Practice Problem 6-8

Lincoln represented the Illinois Central Railroad, Inc. in a suit against Mclean County, Illinois seeking to prevent the County from selling the Railroad's property. McLean County, and the property at issue, are in the Central District of Illinois. The Railroad is incorporated in Delaware and has its principal place of business in Carbondale, located in the Southern District of Illinois. Suit was filed in the United States District Court for the Southern District of Illinois. Is venue proper? If McLean County moves to transfer venue, what venue transfer statute should apply to the decision on whether to transfer? How should the court rule and why?

---

[296] Fed. R. Civ. P. 23.

Practice Problem 6-9

Roosevelt lives in the Southern District of New York. Taft lives in the Southern District of Ohio. Harding lives in the Northern District of Ohio. Roosevelt had planned to build a high-rise tower in the Western District of Ohio. Roosevelt sues Taft and Harding for breach of contract in failing to follow through on the multi-million-dollar financing needed for construction of the high rise. The negotiations for the financing took place in the Eastern District of Pennsylvania. Roosevelt's complaint alleges that Taft and Harding breached their contract with him because, after providing the first installment of the financing, and after Roosevelt had those under his supervision dig and construct the foundation of the high rise, Taft and Harding refused to provide further payments that Roosevelt needed to complete construction. Recognizing that this case qualifies as one to be filed in federal court under diversity of citizenship, answer the following questions:

Under § 1391, what federal districts qualify as proper venues for this suit?

If Roosevelt files suit in the United States District Court for the Middle District of Pennsylvania, and Taft and Harding timely object to venue there, what statute would govern whether the case is transferred to another federal district? What factors would determine whether the case could be transferred?

If Roosevelt files suit in the United States District Court for the Eastern District of Pennsylvania, and Taft and Harding timely object to venue there, what statute would govern transfer? What factors would determine whether transfer was granted?

Practice Problem 6-10

After he had been diagnosed with lung cancer, Grant sued S.F. Hess & Co. on the ground that the company not only knew of the addictive qualities of cigars and their tendency to cause cancer but that the company consciously withheld its knowledge of this information and failed to warn consumers such as Grant adequately. Grant had a home in Pennsylvania, but spent more time at a residence in Washington, D.C. than in Pennsylvania. S.F. Hess & Co. is incorporated in New York and has its principal place of business in Rochester, located in the Western District of New York. Grant sued in his home state, in the Southern District of Ohio. On S.F. Hess & Co.'s objection to venue and motion to transfer, the case was transferred to the U.S. District Court for the Western District of New York. What state's substantive law on tort liability and whether a duty to warn had been breached would apply in these circumstances?

F. Forum Non Conveniens

The phrase "forum non conveniens" is Latin for "the forum is not convenient." Here, however, the inconvenience is different from that considered in transferring cases under 28 U.S.C. § 1404 or § 1406. Although both § 1404 and § 1406 contemplate dismissal or transfer of a case, courts have interpreted the statutes such that dismissal is disfavored and transfer is the preferred means of dealing with a dispute about the appropriate venue within the districts in the United States. Conversely, if a court finds that the doctrine of forum non conveniens applies, that will rest on the conclusion that there is no federal district within the United States that is a convenient forum. Hence, dismissal of the case is the only option. The plaintiff can sue in a foreign tribunal.

In *Piper Aircraft Co. v. Reyno,*[297] the Supreme Court addressed forum non conveniens. This case is still the controlling precedent in the federal system on the applicability of forum non conveniens and the appropriateness of dismissal.

PIPER AIRCRAFT CO. v. REYNO
Supreme Court of the United States, 1981
454 U.S. 235

JUSTICE MARSHALL delivered the opinion of the Court.

These cases arise out of an air crash that took place in Scotland. Respondent, acting as representative of the estates of several Scottish citizens killed in the accident, brought wrongful-death actions against petitioners that were ultimately transferred to the United States District Court for the Middle District of Pennsylvania. Petitioners moved to dismiss on the ground of forum non conveniens. After noting that an alternative forum existed in Scotland, the District Court granted their motions. The United States Court of Appeals for the Third Circuit reversed. The Court of Appeals based its decision, at least in part, on the ground that dismissal is automatically barred where the law of the alternative forum is less favorable to the plaintiff than the law of the forum chosen by the plaintiff. Because we conclude that the possibility of an unfavorable change in law should not, by itself, bar dismissal, and because we conclude that the District Court did not otherwise abuse its discretion, we reverse.

I

In July 1976, a small commercial aircraft crashed in the Scottish Highlands during the course of a charter flight from Blackpool to Perth. The pilot and five passengers were killed instantly. The decedents were all Scottish subjects and residents, as are their heirs and next of kin. There were no eyewitnesses to the accident. At the time of the crash the plane was subject to Scottish air traffic control.

The aircraft, a twin-engine Piper Aztec, was manufactured in Pennsylvania by petitioner Piper Aircraft Co. (Piper). The propellers were manufactured in Ohio by petitioner Hartzell Propeller, Inc. (Hartzell). At the time of the crash the aircraft was registered in Great Britain and was owned and maintained by Air Navigation and Trading Co., Ltd. (Air Navigation). It was operated by McDonald Aviation, Ltd. (McDonald), a Scottish air taxi service. Both Air Navigation and McDonald were organized in the United Kingdom. The wreckage of the plane is now in a hangar in Farnsborough, England.

The British Department of Trade investigated the accident shortly after it occurred. A preliminary re-port found that the plane crashed after developing a spin and suggested that mechanical failure in the plane or the propeller was responsible. At Hartzell's request, this report was reviewed by a three-member Review Board, which held a 9-day adversary hearing attended by all interested parties. The Review Board found no evidence of defective equipment and indicated that pilot error may have contributed to the accident. The pilot, who had obtained his commercial pilot's license only three months earlier, was flying over high ground at an altitude considerably lower than the minimum height required by his company's operations manual.

In July 1977, a California probate court appointed respondent Gaynell Reyno administratrix of the estates of the five passengers. Reyno is not related to and does not know any of the decedents or their survivors; she was a legal secretary to the attorney who filed this lawsuit. Several days after her

---

[297] 454 U.S. 235 (1981).

appointment, Reyno commenced separate wrongful-death actions against Piper and Hartzell in the Superior Court of California, claiming negligence and strict liability. Air Navigation, McDonald, and the estate of the pilot are not parties to this litigation. The survivors of the five passengers whose estates are represented by Reyno filed a separate action in the United Kingdom against Air Navigation, McDonald, and the pilot's estate. Reyno candidly admits that the action against Piper and Hartzell was filed in the United States because its laws regarding liability, capacity to sue, and damages are more favorable to her position than are those of Scotland. Scottish law does not recognize strict liability in tort. Moreover, it permits wrongful-death actions only when brought by a decedent's relatives. The relatives may sue only for "loss of support and society."

On petitioners' motion, the suit was removed to the United States District Court for the Central District of California. Piper then moved for transfer to the United States District Court for the Middle District of Pennsylvania, pursuant to 28 U.S.C. § 1404(a). Hartzell moved to dismiss for lack of personal jurisdiction, or in the alternative, to transfer. In December 1977, the District Court quashed service on Hartzell and transferred the case to the Middle District of Pennsylvania. Respondent then properly served process on Hartzell.

B

In May 1978, after the suit had been transferred, both Hartzell and Piper moved to dismiss the action on the ground of forum non conveniens. The District Court granted these motions in October 1979. It relied on the balancing test set forth by this Court in *Gulf Oil Corporation v. Gilbert*,[298] and its companion case, *Koster v. Lumbermens Mut. Cas. Co.*[299] In those decisions, the Court stated that a plaintiff's choice of forum should rarely be disturbed. However, when an alternative forum has jurisdiction to hear the case, and when trial in the chosen forum would "establish . . . oppressiveness and vexation to a defendant . . . out of all proportion to plaintiff's convenience," or when the "chosen forum [is] inappropriate because of considerations affecting the court's own administrative and legal problems," the court may, in the exercise of its sound discretion, dismiss the case. To guide trial court discretion, the Court provided a list of "private interest factors" affecting the convenience of the litigants, and a list of "public interest factors" affecting the convenience of the forum.

After describing our decisions in *Gilbert* and *Koster*, the District Court analyzed the facts of these cases. It began by observing that an alternative forum existed in Scotland; Piper and Hartzell had agreed to submit to the jurisdiction of the Scottish courts and to waive any statute of limitations defense that might be available. It then stated that plaintiff's choice of forum was entitled to little weight. The court recognized that a plaintiff's choice ordinarily deserves substantial deference. It noted, however, that Reyno "is a representative of foreign citizens and residents seeking a forum in the United States because of the more liberal rules concerning products liability law," and that "the courts have been less solicitous when the plaintiff is not an American citizen or resident, and particularly when the foreign citizens seek to benefit from the more liberal tort rules provided for the protection of citizens and residents of the United States."

The District Court next examined several factors relating to the private interests of the litigants and determined that these factors strongly pointed towards Scotland as the appropriate forum. Although evidence concerning the design, manufacture, and testing of the plane and propeller is located in the United States, the connections with Scotland are otherwise "overwhelming." The real parties in interest are citizens of Scotland, as were all the decedents. Witnesses who could testify regarding the maintenance of the

---

[298] 330 U.S. 501 (1947).
[299] 330 U.S. 518 (1947).

aircraft, the training of the pilot, and the investigation of the accident--all essential to the defense--are in Great Britain. Moreover, all witnesses to damages are located in Scotland. Trial would be aided by familiarity with Scottish topography, and by easy access to the wreckage.

The District Court reasoned that because crucial witnesses and evidence were beyond the reach of compulsory process, and because the defendants would not be able to implead potential Scottish third-party defendants, it would be "unfair to make Piper and Hartzell proceed to trial in this forum." The survivors had brought separate actions in Scotland against the pilot, McDonald, and Air Navigation. "[It] would be fairer to all parties and less costly if the entire case was presented to one jury with available testimony from all relevant witnesses." Although the court recognized that if trial were held in the United States, Piper and Hartzell could file indemnity or contribution actions against the Scottish defendants, it believed that there was a significant risk of inconsistent verdicts.

The District Court concluded that the relevant public interests also pointed strongly towards dismissal. The court determined that Pennsylvania law would apply to Piper and Scottish law to Hartzell if the case were tried in the Middle District of Pennsylvania. As a result, "trial in this forum would be hopelessly complex and confusing for a jury." In addition, the court noted that it was unfamiliar with Scottish law and thus would have to rely upon experts from that country. The court also found that the trial would be enormously costly and time-consuming; that it would be unfair to burden citizens with jury duty when the Middle District of Pennsylvania has little connection with the controversy; and that Scotland has a substantial interest in the outcome of the litigation.

In opposing the motions to dismiss, respondent contended that dismissal would be unfair because Scottish law was less favorable. The District Court explicitly rejected this claim. It reasoned that the possibility that dismissal might lead to an unfavorable change in the law did not deserve significant weight; any deficiency in the foreign law was a "matter to be dealt with in the foreign forum."

C

On appeal, the United States Court of Appeals for the Third Circuit reversed and remanded for trial. The decision to reverse appears to be based on two alternative grounds. First, the Court held that the District Court abused its discretion in conducting the Gilbert analysis. Second, the Court held that dismissal is never appropriate where the law of the alternative forum is less favorable to the plaintiff.

The Court of Appeals began its review of the District Court's Gilbert analysis by noting that the plaintiff's choice of forum deserved substantial weight, even though the real parties in interest are nonresidents. It then rejected the District Court's balancing of the private interests. It found that Piper and Hartzell had failed adequately to support their claim that key witnesses would be unavailable if trial were held in the United States: they had never specified the witnesses they would call and the testimony these witnesses would provide. The Court of Appeals gave little weight to the fact that Piper and Hartzell would not be able to implead potential Scottish third-party defendants, reasoning that this difficulty would be "burdensome" but not "unfair," Finally, the court stated that resolution of the suit would not be significantly aided by familiarity with Scottish topography, or by viewing the wreckage.

The Court of Appeals also rejected the District Court's analysis of the public interest factors. It found that the District Court gave undue emphasis to the application of Scottish law: "'the mere fact that the court is called upon to determine and apply foreign law does not present a legal problem of the sort which would justify the dismissal of a case otherwise properly before the court.'" In any event, it believed that Scottish law need not be applied. After conducting its own choice-of-law analysis, the Court of Appeals

200

determined that American law would govern the actions against both Piper and Hartzell. The same choice-of-law analysis apparently led it to conclude that Pennsylvania and Ohio, rather than Scotland, are the jurisdictions with the greatest policy interests in the dispute, and that all other public interest factors favored trial in the United States.

In any event, it appears that the Court of Appeals would have reversed even if the District Court had properly balanced the public and private interests. The court stated:

"[It] is apparent that the dismissal would work a change in the applicable law so that the plaintiff's strict liability claim would be eliminated from the case. But . . . a dismissal for forum non conveniens, like a statutory transfer, 'should not, despite its convenience, result in a change in the applicable law.' Only when American law is not applicable, or when the foreign jurisdiction would, as a matter of its own choice of law, give the plaintiff the benefit of the claim to which she is entitled here, would dismissal be justified."

In other words, the court decided that dismissal is automatically barred if it would lead to a change in the applicable law unfavorable to the plaintiff.

We granted certiorari in these cases to consider the questions they raise concerning the proper application of the doctrine of forum non conveniens.

II

The Court of Appeals erred in holding that plaintiffs may defeat a motion to dismiss on the ground of forum non conveniens merely by showing that the substantive law that would be applied in the alternative forum is less favorable to the plaintiffs than that of the present forum. The possibility of a change in substantive law should ordinarily not be given conclusive or even substantial weight in the forum non conveniens inquiry.

> We expressly rejected the position adopted by the Court of Appeals in our decision in *Canada Malting Co. v. Paterson Steamships, Ltd.*.[300] That case arose out of a collision between two vessels in American waters. The Canadian owners of cargo lost in the accident sued the Canadian owners of one of the vessels in Federal District Court. The cargo owners chose an American court in large part because the relevant American liability rules were more favorable than the Canadian rules. The District Court dismissed on grounds of forum non conveniens. The plaintiffs argued that dismissal was inappropriate because Canadian laws were less favorable to them. This Court nonetheless affirmed:

"We have no occasion to enquire by what law the rights of the parties are governed, as we are of the opinion that, under any view of that question, it lay within the discretion of the District Court to decline to assume jurisdiction over the controversy. '[The] court will not take cognizance of the case if justice would be as well done by remitting the parties to their home forum.'"

The Court further stated that "[there] was no basis for the contention that the District Court abused its discretion."

It is true that *Canada Malting* was decided before *Gilbert*, and that the doctrine of forum non

---

[300] 285 U.S. 413 (1932).

conveniens was not fully crystallized until our decision in that case. However, *Gilbert* in no way affects the validity of *Canada Malting*. Indeed, by holding that the central focus of the forum non conveniens inquiry is convenience, *Gilbert* implicitly recognized that dismissal may not be barred solely because of the possibility of an unfavorable change in law. Under *Gilbert*, dismissal will ordinarily be appropriate where trial in the plaintiff's chosen forum imposes a heavy burden on the defendant or the court, and where the plaintiff is unable to offer any specific reasons of convenience supporting his choice. If substantial weight were given to the possibility of an unfavorable change in law, however, dismissal might be barred even where trial in the chosen forum was plainly inconvenient.

The Court of Appeals' decision is inconsistent with this Court's earlier forum non conveniens decisions in another respect. Those decisions have repeatedly emphasized the need to retain flexibility. In Gilbert, the Court refused to identify specific circumstances "which will justify or require either grant or denial of remedy." Similarly, in *Koster*, the Court rejected the contention that where a trial would involve inquiry into the internal affairs of a foreign corporation, dismissal was always appropriate. "That is one, but only one, factor which may show convenience." And in *Williams v. Green Bay & Western Railroad. Company*,[301] we stated that we would not lay down a rigid rule to govern discretion, and that "[each] case turns on its facts." If central emphasis were placed on any one factor, the forum non conveniens doctrine would lose much of the very flexibility that makes it so valuable.

In fact, if conclusive or substantial weight were given to the possibility of a change in law, the forum non conveniens doctrine would become virtually useless. Jurisdiction and venue requirements are often easily satisfied. As a result, many plaintiffs are able to choose from among several forums. Ordinarily, these plaintiffs will select that forum whose choice-of-law rules are most advantageous. Thus, if the possibility of an unfavorable change in substantive law is given substantial weight in the forum non conveniens inquiry, dismissal would rarely be proper.

Except for the court below, every Federal Court of Appeals that has considered this question after Gilbert has held that dismissal on grounds of forum non conveniens may be granted even though the law applicable in the alternative forum is less favorable to the plaintiff's chance of recovery.

The Court of Appeals' approach is not only inconsistent with the purpose of the forum non conveniens doctrine, but also poses substantial practical problems. If the possibility of a change in law were given substantial weight, deciding motions to dismiss on the ground of forum non conveniens would become quite difficult. Choice-of-law analysis would become extremely important, and the courts would frequently be required to interpret the law of foreign jurisdictions. First, the trial court would have to determine what law would apply if the case were tried in the chosen forum, and what law would apply if the case were tried in the alternative forum. It would then have to compare the rights, remedies, and procedures available under the law that would be applied in each forum. Dismissal would be appropriate only if the court concluded that the law applied by the alternative forum is as favorable to the plaintiff as that of the chosen forum. The doctrine of forum non conveniens, however, is designed in part to help courts avoid conducting complex exercises in comparative law. As we stated in Gilbert, the public interest factors point towards dismissal where the court would be required to "untangle problems in conflict of laws, and in law foreign to itself."

Upholding the decision of the Court of Appeals would result in other practical problems. At least where the foreign plaintiff named an American manufacturer as defendant, a court could not dismiss the

---

[301] 326 U.S. 549, 557 (1946).

case on grounds of forum non conveniens where dismissal might lead to an unfavorable change in law. The American courts, which are already extremely attractive to foreign plaintiffs, would become even more attractive. The flow of litigation into the United States would increase and further congest already crowded courts.

The Court of Appeals based its decision, at least in part, on an analogy between dismissals on grounds of forum non conveniens and transfers between federal courts pursuant to § 1404(a). In *Van Dusen v. Barrack*,[302] this Court ruled that a § 1404(a) transfer should not result in a change in the applicable law. Relying on dictum in an earlier Third Circuit opinion interpreting *Van Dusen*, the court below held that that principle is also applicable to a dismissal on forum non conveniens grounds.[303] However, § 1404(a) transfers are different than dismissals on the ground of forum non conveniens.

Congress enacted § 1404(a) to permit change of venue between federal courts. Although the statute was drafted in accordance with the doctrine of forum non conveniens,[304] it was intended to be a revision rather than a codification of the common law. District courts were given more discretion to transfer under § 1404(a) than they had to dismiss on grounds of forum non conveniens.

The reasoning employed in *Van Dusen v. Barrack* is simply inapplicable to dismissals on grounds of forum non conveniens. That case did not discuss the common-law doctrine. Rather, it focused on "the construction and application" of § 1404(a). Emphasizing the remedial purpose of the statute, *Barrack* concluded that Congress could not have intended a transfer to be accompanied by a change in law. The statute was designed as a "federal housekeeping measure," allowing easy change of venue within a unified federal system. The Court feared that if a change in venue were accompanied by a change in law, forum-shopping parties would take unfair advantage of the relaxed standards for transfer. The rule was necessary to ensure the just and efficient operation of the statute.

We do not hold that the possibility of an unfavorable change in law should never be a relevant consideration in a forum non conveniens inquiry. Of course, if the remedy provided by the alternative forum is so clearly inadequate or unsatisfactory that it is no remedy at all, the unfavorable change in law may be given substantial weight; the district court may conclude that dismissal would not be in the interests of justice. In these cases, however, the remedies that would be provided by the Scottish courts do not fall within this category. Although the relatives of the decedents may not be able to rely on a strict liability theory, and although their potential damages award may be smaller, there is no danger that they will be deprived of any remedy or treated unfairly.

III

The Court of Appeals also erred in rejecting the District Court's Gilbert analysis. The Court of Appeals stated that more weight should have been given to the plaintiff's choice of forum, and criticized the District Court's analysis of the private and public interests. However, the District Court's decision regarding the deference due plaintiff's choice of forum was appropriate. Furthermore, we do not believe that the District Court abused its discretion in weighing the private and public interests.

A

The District Court acknowledged that there is ordinarily a strong presumption in favor of the

---

[302] 376 U.S. 612 (1964).
[303] 630 F.2d, at 164, n.51.
[304] *See* Revisor's Note, H. R. Rep. No. 308, 80th Cong., 1st Sess., A132 (1947); H. R. Rep. No. 2646, 79th Cong., 2d Sess., A127 (1946).

plaintiff's choice of forum, which may be overcome only when the private and public interest factors clearly point towards trial in the alternative forum. It held, however, that the presumption applies with less force when the plaintiff or real parties in interest are foreign.

The District Court's distinction between resident or citizen plaintiffs and foreign plaintiffs is fully justified. In *Koster*, the Court indicated that a plaintiff's choice of forum is entitled to greater deference when the plaintiff has chosen the home forum. When the home forum has been chosen, it is reasonable to assume that this choice is convenient. When the plaintiff is foreign, however, this assumption is much less reasonable. Because the central purpose of any forum non conveniens inquiry is to ensure that the trial is convenient, a foreign plaintiff's choice deserves less deference.

B

The forum non conveniens determination is committed to the sound discretion of the trial court. It may be reversed only when there has been a clear abuse of discretion; where the court has considered all relevant public and private interest factors, and where its balancing of these factors is reasonable, its decision deserves substantial deference. Here, the Court of Appeals expressly acknowledged that the standard of review was one of abuse of discretion. In examining the District Court's analysis of the public and private interests, however, the Court of Appeals seems to have lost sight of this rule, and substituted its own judgment for that of the District Court.

(1)

In analyzing the private interest factors, the District Court stated that the connections with Scotland are "overwhelming." This characterization may be somewhat exaggerated. Particularly with respect to the question of relative ease of access to sources of proof, the private interests point in both directions. As respondent emphasizes, records concerning the design, manufacture, and testing of the propeller and plane are located in the United States. She would have greater access to sources of proof relevant to her strict liability and negligence theories if trial were held here. However, the District Court did not act unreasonably in concluding that fewer evidentiary problems would be posed if the trial were held in Scotland. A large proportion of the relevant evidence is located in Great Britain.

The Court of Appeals found that the problems of proof could not be given any weight because Piper and Hartzell failed to describe with specificity the evidence they would not be able to obtain if trial were held in the United States. It suggested that defendants seeking forum non conveniens dismissal must submit affidavits identifying the witnesses they would call and the testimony these witnesses would provide if the trial were held in the alternative forum. Such detail is not necessary. Piper and Hartzell have moved for dismissal precisely because many crucial witnesses are located beyond the reach of compulsory process, and thus are difficult to identify or interview. Requiring extensive investigation would defeat the purpose of their motion. Of course, defendants must provide enough information to enable the District Court to balance the parties' interests. Our examination of the record convinces us that sufficient information was provided here. Both Piper and Hartzell submitted affidavits describing the evidentiary problems they would face if the trial were held in the United States.

The District Court correctly concluded that the problems posed by the inability to implead potential third-party defendants clearly supported holding the trial in Scotland. Joinder of the pilot's estate, Air Navigation, and McDonald is crucial to the presentation of petitioners' defense. If Piper and Hartzell can show that the accident was caused not by a design defect, but rather by the negligence of the pilot, the plane's owners, or the charter company, they will be relieved of all liability. It is true, of course, that if Hartzell and Piper were found liable after a trial in the United States, they could institute an action for indemnity or contribution against these parties in Scotland. It would be far more convenient, however, to resolve all claims in one trial. The Court of Appeals rejected this argument. Forcing petitioners to rely on actions for indemnity or contributions would be "burdensome" but not "unfair." Finding that trial in the plaintiff's chosen forum would be burdensome, however, is sufficient to support dismissal on grounds of forum non conveniens.

(2)

The District Court's review of the factors relating to the public interest was also reasonable. On the basis of its choice-of-law analysis, it concluded that if the case were tried in the Middle District of Pennsylvania, Pennsylvania law would apply to Piper and Scottish law to Hartzell. It stated that a trial involving two sets of laws would be confusing to the jury. It also noted its own lack of familiarity with Scottish law. Consideration of these problems was clearly appropriate under Gilbert; in that case we explicitly held that the need to apply foreign law pointed towards dismissal. The Court of Appeals found that the District Court's choice-of-law analysis was incorrect, and that American law would apply to both Hartzell and Piper. Thus, lack of familiarity with foreign law would not be a problem. Even if the Court of Appeals' conclusion is correct, however, all other public interest factors favored trial in Scotland.

Scotland has a very strong interest in this litigation. The accident occurred in its airspace. All of the decedents were Scottish. Apart from Piper and Hartzell, all potential plaintiffs and defendants are either Scottish or English. As we stated in Gilbert, there is "a local interest in having localized controversies decided at home." Respondent argues that American citizens have an interest in ensuring that American manufacturers are deterred from producing defective products, and that additional deterrence might be obtained if Piper and Hartzell were tried in the United States, where they could be sued on the basis of both negligence and strict liability. However, the incremental deterrence that would be gained if this trial were held in an American court is likely to be insignificant. The American interest in this accident is simply not sufficient to justify the enormous commitment of judicial time and resources that would inevitably be required if the case were to be tried here.

IV

The Court of Appeals erred in holding that the possibility of an unfavorable change in law bars dismissal on the ground of forum non conveniens. It also erred in rejecting the District Court's *Gilbert* analysis. The District Court properly decided that the presumption in favor of the respondent's forum choice applied with less than maximum force because the real parties in interest are foreign. It did not act unreasonably in deciding that the private interests pointed towards trial in Scotland. Nor did it act unreasonably in deciding that the public interests favored trial in Scot-land. Thus, the judgment of the Court of Appeals is *Reversed*.

Practice Problem

Practice Problem 6-11

Pierce, who lived in Haiti, and was notorious for his inability to control horses, visited Argentina. There, he led a horse tour of over 50 persons with an Argentinian guide whom he ignored most of the tour. At one point, Pierce ran over several Argentinians with his horse. They were badly injured. While on an indefinite stay in New Hampshire with his sister, Pierce was sued by the Argentinians in the U.S. District Court for the District of New Hampshire. Pierce moved to dismiss based on forum non conveniens.

205

(a)   In light of the principles set forth in the *Piper* case, how should the court rule?

(b)   Can the district court place any conditions on its dismissal? What conditions did the defendants in Piper agree to? Why does dismissal subject to such conditions serve justice?

___

CHAPTER 7: NOTICE AND SERVICE OF PROCESS

I. How the Topics in this Chapter Fit in the Overall Progress of a Civil Action

Below is a diagram of the stages of a civil action showing in bold where the topics in this chapter fall in the progress of a case.

Figure 7-1

Cause of Action (events leading to suit)	Pre-Filing Tasks (items to begin representation, interviewing, and related matters)	Choice of Forum (subject matter jurisdiction, removal, personal jurisdiction, and venue)	**Notice and Service of Process (completing the process of ensuring the forum court can enter a valid judgment)**	Pleading the Case and Joinder of Claims and Parties (including supplemental jurisdiction)

Responding to Claims by Motion or by Answer	Discovery (developing proof to establish claims and learn your adversary's case)	Right to Jury (pretrial motions and practice)	Final Pretrial Conference (events within last month before trial)	Trial (procedures and motions during trial)	Verdict	Post-Trial Motions (motions for a new trial and/or judgment as a matter of law)	Appeal

Service of process is the last step in equipping the court in which you have filed with the power to resolve the dispute and enter a binding order. Technically, the topic of pleading the complaint should precede service because the complaint must be drafted before it is combined with a summons. The combination of a summons filled out by the clerk, with the complaint signed by counsel, creates what we call "process." Thus, the reference to "service of process" means service of the filled-out summons from the court clerk, attached to the front of the complaint signed by counsel.

However, in this chapter we deal with service of process first because its concepts are tied to the principles that we explored in the first half of this book requiring a case to be in a court that has the power to exercise jurisdiction over the parties and enter an order that binds them—i.e., a court with both subject matter jurisdiction and personal jurisdiction. Service of process is like subject matter jurisdiction and personal jurisdiction because it, too, is a necessary threshold for the court to enter a valid judgment.

There are constitutional requirements of notice under the Due Process Clause, as well. However, the constitutional underpinnings of notice are often overlooked because the service of process requirements under Federal Rule of Civil Procedure 4, which also incorporates by reference state service laws, typically demand more exacting standards than the due process standard.[305] The Due Process Clause requires only that the notice given to a defendant be reasonably calculated to bring home notice of the action to the defendant. Whereas, the service of process rule places stricter requirements than the Due Process Clause's general criteria. In other words, if you follow the rule on service of process, you will almost always satisfy due process.

As explained below, service of process is an integral step in gaining relief for your client. If a plaintiff does not make efforts reasonably calculated to provide notice to the defendant, any judgment in the suit lacks validity. The defendant in such circumstances will have a due process defense based on insufficient notice. Some say that without proper service of process the court does not really have jurisdiction, even if subject matter jurisdiction and personal jurisdiction exist, until the defendant is provided sufficient notice such that the court's power over the defendant becomes a reality. Little reason exists, however, for a plaintiff to fail to achieve the kind of notice that will pass constitutional muster. Laziness is probably the most common reason for ineffective notice. Rule 4—the service of process rule— offers many options for properly serving a defendant. Determining service requirements generally requires the plaintiff's lawyer to know two things: (1) whether the defendant is a resident of the state in which suit is filed, and (2) what type of defendant is being served, *e.g.*, an individual, municipality, corporation, etc. Although filing a complaint and serving process are not the most challenging decisions in a case, they are essential to obtaining a valid judgment.

A. Service of Process—Rule 4 and More

1. Basic Background for Understanding Service Concepts

To analyze service of process, you should first define what "process" means. Process must include both a summons and a complaint. For each defendant being served, a plaintiff will need a summons, a formal document completed and signed by the court's clerk, attached to a complaint. *See Figure 7-2* for the summons available at http://www.uscourts.gov/forms/notice-lawsuit-summons-subpoena/summons-civil-action. If a plaintiff serves only a complaint on a defendant, that accomplishes nothing. If a plaintiff serves a summons, signed by the Court Clerk, attached to a complaint, then service of process will have been achieved. As explained more fully below, there are many options in which a plaintiff can serve process. Yet, service by an accepted option is essential to obtaining jurisdiction over a defendant.

---

[305] *See* FED. R. CIV. P. 4.

Figure 7-2 Sample Summons

UNITED STATES DISTRICT COURT

for the

_____District of_____

	)	
	)	
_____	)	
Plaintiff(s)	)	
v.	)	**Civil Action No.** _____

_____

Defendant(s)

SUMMONS IN A CIVIL ACTION

To: (Defendant's name and address)

A lawsuit has been filed against you.

Within 21 days after service of this summons on you (not counting the day you received it)—or 60 days if you are the United States or a United States agency, or an officer or employee of the United States described in Fed. R. Civ. P. 12 (a) (2) or (3) — you must serve on the plaintiff an answer to the attached complaint or a motion under Rule 12 of the Federal Rules of Civil Procedure. The answer or motion must be served on the plaintiff or plaintiff's attorney, whose name and address are:

_____

_____

If you fail to respond, judgment by default will be entered against you for the relief demanded in the complaint. You also must file your answer or motion with the court.

CLERK OF COURT

Date: _____

_____

Signature of Clerk or Deputy Clerk

2. The Purpose of Service

Service of process rules derived from American common law "to protect state sovereignty and to assure that the defendant had actual notice of the lawsuit."[306] The modern approach to service of process tends to be less strict than in the past: "[T]he trend is away from an overly strict approach, with courts now tending to ignore service irregularities where there was actual notice of suitable tenor and content or where the manner of transmitting and form of notice substantially complied with the prescribed procedure."[307]

Nevertheless, the relaxation in manner of service does not mean that you can neglect making sure a defendant receives actual notice of a suit. In *Mullane v. Central Hanover Bank & Trust Co.*,[308] the United States Supreme Court underscored a party's constitutional right, under the Fourteenth Amendment's Due Process Clause, to have notice reasonably calculated to reach the party. Mullane involved a common trust fund formed under New York law. The New York statute allowed pooling of funds that were otherwise insufficient for instances in which there were numerous beneficiaries but the amount of holdings for each was minimal. Thus, the statute allowed the beneficiaries in Mullane to afford a trustee. Central Hanover Bank served as the trustee of the common trust in question. The bank, as trustee, sought a hearing to present an accounting that, once approved by the court, would cut off the trustee's liability to beneficiaries. Using the methods outlined in the New York statute, the trustee notified beneficiaries of the hearing by the only means required—by advertisement published in a newspaper for four weeks before the hearing.

A beneficiary challenged the constitutionality of the notice by publication. The Court held unconstitutional such notice to those beneficiaries whose addresses the trustee knew.[309] By contrast, the Court held constitutional notice by publication to those beneficiaries who could not be identified or whose addresses were unknown.[310] In so ruling, the Court issued certain guidelines for constitutional notice:

> An elementary and fundamental precept of due process in any proceeding which is to be accorded finality is notice reasonably calculated, under all the circumstances, to apprise interested parties of the pendency of the action and afford them an opportunity to present their objections. The means employed must be such as one desirous of actually informing the absentee might reasonably adopt to accomplish it. The reasonableness and hence the constitutional validity of any chosen method may be defended on the ground that it is in itself reasonably certain to inform those affected . . . or, where conditions do not reasonably permit such notice, that the form chosen is not substantially less likely to bring home notice than other of the feasible and customary substitutes.[311]

The Court specifically approved notice by first class mail as a "feasible and customary" substitute to formal service in notifying those beneficiaries for whom the bank had addresses.[312]

---

[306] James Weinstein, *The Federal Common Law Origins of Judicial Jurisdiction: Implications for Modern Doctrine*, 90 VA. L. REV. 169, 173, 195 (2004).

[307] GEOFFREY C. HAZARD, JR., ET AL., PLEADING AND PROCEDURE: STATE AND FEDERAL CASES AND MATERIALS, 326, 654 (8th ed. 1999).

[308] 339 U.S. 306 (1950)

[309] *Id.* at 314.

[310] *Id.* at 317–20.

[311] Mullane v. Central Hanover Bank & Trust Co., 339 U.S. 306, 315 (1950).

[312] *Id.* at 318.

Even though Mullane sets the constitutional minimum for notice, federal and state judicial systems are free to adopt rules or statutes that impose greater requirements on plaintiffs. As we shall see, Federal Rule of Civil Procedure 4 does impose more demanding requirements, except to the extent where it defers to state law on service. Nevertheless, most state service requirements, like Rule 4, require more stringent requirements than Mullane. Thus, a plaintiff who complies with the more stringent requirements will exceed the minimum due process requirements of Mullane and adequately provide notice to the defendant.

Follow-Up Questions and Comments

1. Do you know the addresses of the defendants to be named in the suit? If so, Mullane will allow you to send notice of the suit to them by first class mail. Does Rule 4, if you are litigating in federal court, typically require more than service by first class mail, thus requiring you to go beyond the due process minimum?

2. In what scenarios would service by publication in a newspaper satisfy Mullane's constitutional test?

B. Effective Service Needed to Enter Valid Judgment on a Defendant

MISERANDINO v. RESORT PROPERTIES, INC.
Court of Appeals of Maryland, 1997
691 A.2d 208

JOHN F. MCAULIFFE, Judge, Specially Assigned.

This case involves a constitutional attack by judgment debtors against a judgment entered against them by a state trial court in Virginia. The collateral attack on the judgment was made in the Circuit Court for Carroll County, Maryland, where the judgment creditor sought to enforce the judgment. The defendants challenge the basis for the exercise of long-arm personal jurisdiction by the Virginia court, as well as the constitutional sufficiency of the Virginia statutory scheme for the giving of notice to nonresidents proceeded against under that Commonwealth's long-arm jurisdiction statute.

I. Facts

Pursuant to the Uniform Enforcement of Foreign Judgments Act, Sections 11-801 to 807 of the Courts and Judicial Proceedings Article, Md. code . . . Resort Properties, Inc. (Resort), filed a judgment against Gerard and Karen Miserandino, (defendants) in the Circuit Court for Carroll County on June 3, 1993. The notice of filing of judgment, mailed by a court clerk to the defendants, simply informed them that a judgment of $4,211.82 against them had been filed by Resort. Thereafter, the defendants filed a motion to strike the entry of the foreign judgment. From their inspection of the court's file, the defendants knew that the judgment was obtained in Warren County, Virginia and that Resort was the assignee of North Fork Shenandoah Vacations, Inc.

In the motion, the defendants alleged by affidavit made on personal knowledge that they were not served with process, had no notice, and did not appear in the Virginia action. They alleged further, that:

211

Defendants were not subject to the jurisdiction of said Virginia Court in said action, nor was either of them. . . . Said foreign judgment is invalid, null, void and of no effect since said Virginia Court lacked in personam jurisdiction over defendants, or either of them, in the action in which that judgment was entered.

Specifically, the motion alleged that neither of the defendants resides in Virginia, neither is domiciled in Virginia, neither is employed in Virginia, and neither carries on any regular business, occupation, vocation in Virginia, or maintains a principal place of business in Virginia.

. . .

[The Maryland Court of Appeals rejected defendants first ground for challenging the judgment—that the defendants lacked sufficient minimum contacts with Maryland to satisfy the due process clause. The court held that the defendants had waived this argument. The court then went on to analyze the key issue here, i.e., whether the manner of service fell below the requirements of due process so as to void the judgment on that ground.]

II. Adequacy of Notice

The more difficult question with respect to the acquisition of personal jurisdiction by the Virginia court involves the constitutional adequacy of the means employed to give notice to the defendants. The procedure followed by the plaintiff was in accordance with the Virginia statute prescribing the method of service of process upon a nonresident individual in a case involving long-arm jurisdiction, but that will not be sufficient to confer jurisdiction unless the method authorized by the statute comports with the requirements of federal due process. Thus, we are required to address a question not yet resolved by the United States Supreme Court, and only rarely considered by other federal and state courts: whether initial and original service of process by first-class mail is constitutionally sufficient to confer in personam jurisdiction over a nonresident individual in a long-arm jurisdiction case.

The Due Process Clause of the 14th Amendment "at a minimum . . .require [s] that deprivation of life, liberty or property by adjudication be preceded by notice and opportunity for hearing appropriate to the nature of the case."[313] The importance of giving adequate notice cannot be overstated.

. . .

No particular procedure is required in all cases. "On the contrary, due process is flexible and calls only for such procedural protections as the particular situation demands. Procedures adequate under one set of facts may not be sufficient in a different situation."[314]

To determine whether notice in a particular case is constitutionally sufficient, the court "must balance the interests of the state or the giver of notice against the individual interest sought to be protected by the fourteenth amendment." At a minimum, the notice must be "reasonably calculated, under all the circumstances, to apprise interested parties of the pendency of the action and afford them an opportunity to present their objections."[315]

---

[313] Mullane v. Central Hanover Bank & Tr. Co., 339 U.S. 306, 313 (1950).

[314] Department of Transportation v. Armacost, 299 Md. 392, 416 (1984).

[315] *Mullane*, 339 U.S. at 314.

. . .

Section 8.01–329 of the Code of Virginia . . . provides an alternative method of service of process on a nonresident subject to long-arm jurisdiction by service "on the Secretary of the Commonwealth of Virginia . . . who, for this purpose, shall be deemed to be the statutory agent of such person." That section of the code further provides that service on the Secretary shall be sufficient upon the person to be served, provided that notice of such service, a copy of the process or notice, and a copy of the affidavit are forthwith mailed, by the Secretary to the person or persons to be served at the last known post-office address of such person, and a certificate of compliance herewith by the Secretary or someone designated by him for that purpose and having knowledge of such compliance, shall be forthwith filed with the papers in the action.

. . .

That the notice was sent, however, does not answer the question of whether the means employed for transmittal of the notice was constitutionally sufficient. Service on a state official or agency does not obviate the necessity for constitutionally sufficient notice to the defendant.

Personal delivery of process to a defendant, followed by the filing of written proof of that service, is a time-honored method of acquiring personal jurisdiction. This method of service, properly executed, provides a high degree of probability that the defendant received the required notice. An alternative method of "personal delivery" is to have an employee of the United States Postal Service deliver the process to the defendant. This method, service by mail, is often quicker and less expensive than service by a sheriff or private process server but may present a problem with respect to proof of service.

Postal regulations providing an optional service of restricted delivery of registered or certified mail do, however, offer a solution to the problem of proof of service. For an additional fee, a person mailing a letter may direct that the letter be handled as registered or certified mail, that the letter may be delivered only to the addressee or his duly authorized representative, and that the person accomplishing delivery return a receipt to the sender bearing the signature of the person receiving the letter and showing the date and address of delivery. When process is mailed in this fashion a return that includes a postal receipt bearing the signature of the defendant or his authorized agent and a copy of the process that was mailed is filed, and the court can proceed with a high level of confidence that the requisite notice has been given.

. . .

Courts in jurisdictions permitting personal service by registered or certified mail have generally held that a defendant cannot defeat service by an affirmative refusal to accept the letter, but that an "unclaimed" letter will not suffice to confer personal jurisdiction.

. . .

This history of recent amendments to Fed. R. Civ. P. 4 suggests the existence of an abiding congressional concern about the effectiveness about certain types of mail delivery as a primary means of service to acquire personal jurisdiction. Certainly, there has been no suggestion that the use of first-class mail alone to accomplish such service would be looked upon with favor.

. . .

213

[T]he concept of due process is not static—the process that is due may change according to the circumstances. Necessity may, therefore, be a valid factor in the due process equation in the balancing of the interest of the state against the interest of the individual. Historically, courts have permitted the employment of potentially less effective methods of service where more effective methods have been attempted and have failed, or are otherwise impractical. Notification of lien holders in tax sale proceedings by mail instead of individual personal service may be adequate because of the state's interest in facilitating tax sales, the presumption of reasonable interest in tax sale proceedings by the lien holders, and the difficulty and expenses of personal service, but notice by publication may not be sufficient when the identities of creditors are reasonably ascertainable.[316] Reasonable risks that the method of notice employed will not reach each individual affected may be tolerated when the action is against a class of persons and notice is reasonably certain to reach most of those interested in objecting.[317]

Turning to the case before us, we consider whether there are any special or unique circumstances that would justify relaxation of the ordinary and available methods of service that offer a considerably higher degree of probability of actual notice. In other words, given the availability of personal service by officials or private process servers, or service by restricted delivery mail, what state interest is present in this case that would justify resort to the significantly less certain procedure of first-class mail? We find but one circumstance that may distinguish this case from any other in personam action: the fact that the defendants are nonresidents of the Commonwealth of Virginia.

The Supreme Court has recognized that some distinctions may be drawn between the methods employed to serve residents and some to serve nonresidents.

> Personal service has not in all circumstances been regarded as indispensable to the process due to residents, and it has more often been held unnecessary as to nonresidents. We disturb none of the established rules on these subjects.

. . .

The heart of the question is whether the means adopted by the Virginia legislature to notify nonresident defendants of an in personam action against them amounted to "a reliable means of acquainting interested parties of the fact that their rights are before the courts" and "means . . .such as one desirous of actually informing the absentee might reasonably adopt to accomplish it,"[318] when "the reasonableness of the notice provided . . .[is] tested with reference provided to the 'feasible and customary' alternatives and supplements to the form of notice chosen."[319] We hold that the means selected by the Virginia legislature to accomplish notice of service of original process in this case does not measure up to this test, and are constitutionally inadequate to afford the due process required by the United States Constitution. The method chosen to acquire personal jurisdiction over nonresident individuals—notice by first-class mail— "is not reasonably calculated to reach those who could easily be informed by other means at hand."[320]

Accordingly, although the judgment may remain valid where entered until there is a contrary ruling by a court of competent jurisdiction, we decline to grant full faith and credit to the judgment because of our finding that the Virginia trial court did not acquire personal jurisdiction over these defendants because of

---

[316] Mennonite Bd. of Missions v. Adams, 462 U.S. 791 (1983).

[317] *Mullane*, 339 U.S. at 306.

[318] *Mullane*, 339 U.S. at 315

[319] *Greene v. Lindsey*, 456 U.S. 444, 454 (1982).

[320] *Mullane*, 339 U.S. at 319.

214

the constitutional inadequacy of notice.

Judgment of the court of special appeals *reversed*.

Follow-Up Questions and Comments

1. Following the above decision, the Virginia General Assembly modified Virginia's service statutes to require the Secretary of the Commonwealth to effect service on nonresidents by certified mail.[321]

2. The Supreme Court denied certiorari in *Resort Properties, Inc. v. Miserandino*.[322] Because the Court upheld first class mail in Mullane, there are some cases in which service by first class has been held to satisfy due process. Nonetheless, the careful practitioner will err on the side of serving by certified mail or another means that will avoid the question of whether service satisfies constitutional requirements. If a plaintiff wants to have an enforceable judgment, the plaintiff must satisfy due process not only in establishing sufficient minimum contacts, but also in serving process in a manner that is constitutionally sufficient.

3. Notwithstanding due process concerns, courts have been willing to recognize valid service through means that technology has made possible only recently.[323]

4. Note that many states have so-called "cure" statutes. These statutes provide that, if a defendant actually receives service of process in time to respond to the complaint, defects in the manner of service will be overlooked.[324] Many of the decisions regarding service by modern technology probably rest to some extent on the notion that the defendant actually received process through an active account and argued that such receipt was improper.

II. Commencing a Civil Action

The importance of knowing when a lawsuit is "commenced" such that it tolls (i.e., stops) the statute of limitations cannot be underestimated. Many assume that commencement equates to the date of the case's filing. Although that is true as a rule, it is dangerous to make this presumption because in some state-law claims the statute of limitations is not tolled until both suit is filed and the defendant is served.[325] As suggested, the more typical approach is for a suit to commence—and the statute of limitations to be tolled—

---

[321] *See* VA. CODE ANN. § 329 (2016).

[322] 118 S. Ct. 376 (1997).

[323] *See, e.g.*, Rio Props. v. Rio Int'l Interlink, 284 F.3d 1007, 1017 (9th Cir. 2002) (upholding service on foreign company by e-mail); *Popular Enters., LLC v. Webcom Media Group, Inc.*, 225 F.R.D. 560, 563 (E.D. Tenn. 2004) (upholding service by e-mail on foreign individual under FRCP 4(f) (3)). *Compare* Fortunato v. Chase Bank USA, *N.A.*, No. 11 Civ. 6608, 2012 U.S. Dist. LEXIS 80594, at *6–7 (S.D.N.Y. June 7, 2012) (rejecting argument that service by Facebook is reasonably calculated to provide actual notice) *with* Alyssa L. Eisenberg, *Keep Your Facebook Friends Close and Your Process Server Closer: Service of Process in Cases Involving Domestic Defendants*, 51 SAN DIEGO L. REV. 779 (2014) (citing cases in which the court upheld service of process by Facebook).

[324] *See, e.g.*, VA. CODE ANN. § 8.01-288.

[325] GEOFFREY C. HAZARD, JR., ET AL., PLEADING AND PROCEDURE: STATE AND FEDERAL CASES AND MATERIALS, 322 (8th ed. 1999).

when the suit is filed, even if the plaintiff does not complete service of process for some time.[326] An extreme example is California, in which filing the action tolls the statute of limitations, provided service is accomplished within three years."[327] Conversely, in other states, "a suit is commenced and the statute of limitations is tolled only when service of process is accomplished."[328] Be sure to know the position of your jurisdiction. If you are in a minority state where the statute of limitations continues running after filing the complaint until service is accomplished, your client's case may end up being time-barred if you delay service.

You will want to speed up the service of process (i.e., the summons and complaint) if you are practicing in such a jurisdiction.

Follow-Up Questions and Comments

1. Will you, as the lawyer, be able to fill out the entirety of the summons? What do you have to provide the Clerk of Court with? What must the clerk do before you serve the summons and complaint?

2. Does your state consider an action to be commenced upon filing of the complaint, regardless of when it is served, or require both filing and service of the summons and complaint for the action to be deemed commenced and the statute of limitations period to be tolled? In some states, service will operate as commencing an action for purposes of the statute of limitations for certain types of claims but not all claims. If yours is such a state, what are the claims that require service of the summons and complaint to toll the statute of limitations?

III. Service of Process Requirements

The requirements for service of process typically depend on the type of defendant. The requirements vary for serving individuals, business entities, or governmental entities. The following section first discusses service on individuals and then service on entities.

A. Service of Process on Individuals

In serving individuals, the approach of Federal Rule of Civil Procedure 4 is followed by most states. Please read Rule 4 now. Note the organization of the Rule. It includes general information applicable to service in a variety of situations at the beginning. Then it has separate subsections for service on types of defendants. We will focus on the options for serving (1) under Rule 4(e) an individual in the United States, and (2) the options for serving a corporation, partnership, or association under Rule 4(h). We also will address waiver of service under Rule 4(c). Nevertheless, you should be aware of the other provisions in Rule 4 if you end up having to serve a party that does not fit the typical categories we will cover.

As you read Rule 4(e) and Rule 4(h), notice the variety of ways permitted to serve an individual defendant or a corporation, partnership, or entity. Rule 4(e) and Rule 4(h) have several options separated

---

[326] *See id.*
[327] *Id.*
[328] *Id.*

by the disjunctive "or." Thus, the Rule is not hierarchical—it does not require that the plaintiff try the first option and then, only if unsuccessful, proceed to the next. As to serving an individual, Rule 4 describes the first three options in its own terms: (1) personally delivering a copy of the summons and complaint to "an individual other than a minor or incompetent person," leaving copies of process "at the individual's dwelling house or usual place of abode with some person of suitable age and discretion then residing therein" (typically called "substituted service"), or (3) delivering a copy of process "to an agent authorized by appointment or by law to receive service of process."[329] But Rule 4 does not stop there. Instead, it allows the plaintiff to use as equally legitimate means whatever the law of the state where the action is pending, or of the state in which the person is served, allows for serving an individual.[330] Therefore, service under any of the means outlined in Rule 4 (or by incorporation, the applicable states' law) is equally valid.

1. Personal Service: The Gold Standard—Hand-Delivering a Copy of the Summons and of the Complaint to an Individual

"Personal service is the primary method of obtaining jurisdiction over the person of a defendant."[331] Personal service: (1) "notifies the defendant of the commencement of an action against him or her" and (2) "provides the ritual that marks the court's assertion of jurisdiction over a lawsuit."[332] Personal service can be "waived by consent or agreement."[333]

Personal service does not require in-hand delivery. In the following case, a process server confronts a recalcitrant defendant. The Supreme Court of Wyoming's decision below demonstrates the test for personal service in federal courts and in state courts.

CRB v. DEPARTMENT OF FAMILY SERVICES
Supreme Court of Wyoming, 1999
974 P.2d 931

HILL, JUSTICE.

Appellant CRB appeals from an order of the district court determining paternity and setting child support payments. Appellant challenges the efficacy of the service of process and the service of a notice to appear on his attorney.

We affirm.

. . .

On June 3, 1997, the State of Wyoming, through the DFS (Department of Family Services), filed a Petition to Establish Paternity and Support in the First Judicial District Court. The Petition alleged that CRB was the putative father of the then unborn child of LS. An order was issued by the district court requiring LS and CRB to appear at an informal hearing on August 25, 1997.

At the time, CRB was residing in Lake Charles, Louisiana. Personal service of the summons,

---

[329] *See* FED. R. CIV. P. 4(e).
[330] *See id.*
[331] 62B AM. JUR. 2D Process § 179 (2017).
[332] *Id.*
[333] *Id.*

petition for paternity and the order to appear at the informal hearing was attempted on July 9, 1997. The process server tried to serve CRB at his apartment, but CRB refused to open the door to accept service. Confronted with the refusal of CRB to open his door, the process server telephoned CRB and, while observing CRB through the apartment window, advised CRB he was being served and the documents were being placed in CRB's mailbox.

. . .

CRB contends that service of process was insufficient . . . because the summons and complaint were not delivered either to him personally . . . at his dwelling house or usual place of abode. Additionally, CRB argues that even accepting the District Court's finding that "in hand" delivery is not required so long as the person to be served is in close proximity to the process server, service was still insufficient because the evidence does not conclusively demonstrate that it was CRB who was in the apartment at the time service was attempted.[334]

(d) *Personal service*— . . . Service shall be made as follows:

(1) Upon an individual . . . , by delivering a copy of the summons and of the complaint to the individual personally.

We are confronted with the question of what constitutes delivery of "a copy of the summons and of the complaint to the individual personally" in a situation where the defendant is aware that service is being attempted and seeks to avoid service by refusing to open his door to accept service.

. . .

It is the duty of a defendant to accept and submit to the service of process when he is aware of the process server's purpose. It is generally held that if the process server and the defendant are within speaking distance of each other, and such action is taken as to convince a reasonable person that personal service is being attempted, service cannot be avoided by physically refusing to accept the summons.

. . .

In this instance, CRB refused to open his apartment door to accept service. In response, the process server called CRB while still outside the apartment and informed him that he had papers to serve on him. When CRB continued to refuse to open the door, the process server informed CRB that he would deposit the summons and complaint in CRB's mailbox.

CRB engaged in conduct within the State of Wyoming which carried with it certain potential consequences, including legal obligations. CRB cannot attempt to evade those obligations by avoiding service of process. The record is clear that CRB knew service was being attempted and he deliberately attempted to avoid that service. Under these circumstances, the process server took appropriate action by informing CRB at that time that he was being served and then leaving the summons and complaint in a location where CRB was likely to find them. The rules governing service of process are intended to give a

---

[334] The requirements for personal service of process over an individual are set forth in W.R.C.P. 4(d)(1) (emphasis added).

defendant reasonable notice that an action has been brought. In this instance, despite the best efforts of CRB, he was given reasonable notice of the action against him and, therefore, service under the circumstances of this case was sufficient.

. . .

Service of process on CRB by leaving the summons and complaint in his mailbox was sufficient given that CRB had refused to accept service and CRB was told that the summons and complaint would be left in close proximity to CRB such that he could easily retrieve the documents.

Affirmed.

Follow-Up Questions and Comments

1. Under the *Erie* Doctrine, which will be addressed in depth in Chapter 14, a federal court sitting in diversity applies the substantive law of the state in which it sits. A state's choice-of-law rules are considered substantive and, therefore, the federal court must apply those. In our example above, for instance, if the tort suit was filed in the United States District Court for the District of Connecticut, the federal court could apply the traditional law of the place of tort (*lex locus delicti*) approach and choose Virginia law because the accident happened there.[335]

---

2. Substituted Service: Serving Person Residing at Defendant's Usual Place of Abode

Federal Rule of Civil Procedure 4 also allows for service as follows: "leaving a copy of each at the individual's dwelling or usual place of abode with someone of suitable age and discretion who resides there."[336] The two issues that usually arise when service is affected in this way are (1) what constitutes the defendant's "abode," and (2) whether the person on whom process was served is "suitable"?

a. Defining Abode

Rule 4 refers to serving an individual at her "dwelling or usual place of abode." State statutes and cases refer alternately to "dwelling house," "usual place of abode," or "residence." In this discussion, the term "residence" will encompass these terms. The criteria for identifying a defendant's "residence" derive from many factors, including the following:

[T]he retention of a room and storage of possessions there, the intention to return, the use of that address on official forms such as drivers' licenses and voters' registrations, the use of a telephone listing at that location, a failure to provide the post office with a forwarding address, the receipt of actual notice, and the defendant's ability to present at least some evidence that his or her abode is elsewhere.[337]

Most courts do agree that "it is the place where the person is living at the particular time when the

---

[335] *See* Klaxon Co. v. Stentor Elec. Mfg. Co., 313 U.S. 487 (1941).
[336] Fed. R. Civ. P. 4(e)(2)(b).
[337] 62B Am. Jur. 2d Process § 179 (2017).

service is made."[338] A person's place of employment, under the general rule, does not equate to an individual's residence. Serving a defendant at her business will not suffice unless delivered to the defendant personally.[339] A person's "dwelling" becomes problematic when she lives in an apartment complex or multiple dwelling unit. In such circumstances, service is not complete if left in a part of the building "in which the party to be served does not actually reside or does not exercise exclusive dominion and control."[340]

b. Serving "Person of Suitable Age and Discretion"

Under Federal Rule of Civil Procedure 4 and similar state rules, process served at an individual's residence must be left with "a person of suitable age and discretion."[341] The criteria for the suitable-age-and-discretion standard require a factual determination. Usually, a member of defendant's "family," who is at least a teenager, will weigh in favor of suitability, if the family member lives at the residence.[342] While Rule 4 does not provide a specific age that will be deemed sufficient, some state service statutes specify a threshold age for the person with whom service is left.[343] In some states, a person need not be a family member to receive service at an individual's residence if the person receiving service has been residing there.[344]

3. Service on Individual's Agent

Rule 4 provides that service on an individual can also be achieved by delivering a copy of each to an agent authorized by appointment or by law to receive service of process. It is more typical for a corporation to have a registered agent in a state—an agent whose sole purpose is to receive service of process on the defendant. Though less common, individuals can have registered agents as well. These agents can be found typically by checking with the State Corporation Commission. A more common "agent" for individuals is an agent "by operation of law" which will be discussed in more detail later in this chapter.

4. Service on Individual by Other Means Authorized by State Law

The following means of service on an individual are not described specifically as options in Rule 4. However, because Rule 4 allows service to be accomplished under the law of the state either in which the action is pending or in which the person being served is located, state laws permitting other ways of service need to be considered.

a. "Nail and Mail" Service

Some jurisdictions have so-called "nail and mail" statutes.[345] These statutes permit attaching the summons and complaint to the main door or entrance of a dwelling and, then, mailing the summons and

---

[338] *Id.*

[339] *Id.* § 187.

[340] *Id.* § 185.

[341] *Id.* § 191.

[342] *Id.* § 194.

[343] *See, e.g.,* VA. CODE ANN. § 8.01-296 (2017) (person receiving service at individual's dwelling must be 16 years old or older).

[344] *See* 62B AM. JUR. 2D Process § 178 (2017) (requirement often focuses on whether the person receiving service has been "residing" at the residence).

[345] 62B AM. JUR. 2D Process § 177 (2017).

complaint to the same address before continuing any default proceedings.[346] "Nail and mail statutes" are used "when it is impossible to serve a party personally or to deliver the process to a person of suitable age and discretion at the party's dwelling or place of abode."[347]

Such "nail and mail" service may be used only where personal service cannot be affected by the use of "due diligence." Such a statute requires affixation of the summons to the door of the defendant's residence and then a mailing of the process to the defendant. This should be accomplished by use of a nail, tack, tape, rubber band, or some other device which will ensure adherence.[348]

b. Service by Mail

Many states allow service by mail when the defendant cannot be served in the more direct ways described above.[349] Also, state long-arm statutes for serving nonresidents usually require service by mail through an official in the forum state, such as the secretary of state.[350] For mail service to be effective, a certification of the mailing (either from counsel or from the Secretary of State, depending on who actually mails the process) is always required.[351] As shown in *Miserandino v. Resort Properties, Inc.*,[352] prudent counsel will ensure that the mailing is by certified or registered mail—even if not required by the applicable statute or rule. Doing so requires little extra effort and expense and avoids the risk of a judgment later being declared void, as was the judgment in *Miserandino*, solely because the summons and complaint were mailed by first class mail and not by certified or registered mail. Many statutes and rules have already moved to requiring certified or registered mail. However, it is recommended that you always treat a statute as requiring certified or registered mail, even if it permits first-class mail, to avoid a later challenge.

c. Service by Publication

All jurisdictions contain provisions for "constructive service of process or notice of the commencement of an action by publication, in place of service of the writ or summons upon the party personally."[353] Only statutes may authorize service by publication.[354] Service by publication is an "extraordinary measure" and, therefore, may only be allowed in certain cases due to necessity when no other method of service is able to provide notice.[355]Publication statutes must only authorize such service upon residents when personal service

> is impossible or impracticable by reason of the fact that the defendant is a nonresident, or that he or she is absent from the state or not to be found therein, or that the defendant with intent to defraud his or her creditors or to avoid service of process has left the state or is concealing him-or herself within it with a like intent, and that unavailing efforts have been made to ascertain his or her whereabouts.[356]

---

[346] *See, e.g.*, N.Y. C.P.L.R. 308 (2016); VA. CODE ANN. § 8.01-296 (2017).

[347] VA. CODE ANN. § 8.01-296; *see also id.* § 8.01-204.

[348] 62B AM. JUR. 2D Process § 177 (2016).

[349] *See* 62B AM. JUR. 2D Process § 195 (2017).

[350] *See id.*

[351] See *id.*

[352] 691 A.2d 208 (Md. 1997).

[353] 62B AM. JUR. 2D Process § 206 (2017).

[354] *Id.* § 207

[355] *Id.* § 206.

[356] 62B AM. JUR. 2D Process § 216 (2016).

Most jurisdictions require filing a motion and a "due diligence" affidavit to begin service by publication.[357] The affidavit must contain the pertinent facts forming "the grounds for the issuance of an order directing publication" so that the court has "a factual basis to order service by publication."[358] The affidavit must further state that the defendant's residence is unknown.[359] This affidavit "must set forth facts indicating the serving party made a due diligent effort to locate an opposing party to effect personal service."[360] If the court deems the affidavit sufficient, it will issue "an order directing publication in a newspaper of the summons and notice and, frequently, by mailing of notice to the defendant."[361] The notice usually runs in a newspaper or other publication circulated widely for several weeks.[362]

If service by publication is to enforce rights against property in the state, service by publication may hold water. However, if a party is seeking to obtain personal jurisdiction over a defendant, the constitutionality of service by publication is suspect.[363]

5. Service on State Agent in Long-Arm Statute

Virtually every state has a long-arm statute. With the advent of long-arm statutes came the procedure in which a state official (typically the Secretary of State) is designated as the "statutory agent" of the defendant for purposes of relaying process to nonresidents once received from counsel. Thus, the Secretary of State is appointed "by law" when served by a nonresident who has satisfied one of the criteria for long-arm jurisdiction. Again, Federal Rule of Civil Procedure 4 incorporates the state law of the forum state or the state were service is accomplished as legitimate alternatives for service. Rule 4, while specifically referring to service on an agent, appears to be speaking in terms of a registered agent and not necessarily of an agent "appointed" by the law of a state. Service on the Secretary of State is not treated as the "agent" option specifically contemplated by Rule 4. Instead, the ability to serve the Secretary of State arises from the ability in Rule 4 to rely on the law of the state in which the action is pending or in which the person being served is located.

Section 8.01-329 of the Code of Virginia is a typical service statute accompanying a long-arm provision.[364] Like those in other states, this statute accompanies the Virginia's long-arm and describes how to serve a statutory agent designated for a nonresident, and the procedures the statutory agent must follow in relaying service of process to the nonresident. This particular statute provides that service can be made on the Secretary of the Commonwealth.[365] The Secretary is then required to send by certified mail to the nonresident process received from the requesting party.[366] Finally, the Secretary sends a certificate to the court in which the action is pending so that such certificate is filed in the clerk's office.[367]

---

[357] *Id.* §§ 223, 226.

[358] *Id.* § 208.

[359] *Id.* § 212.

[360] *Id.*; *see also id.* § 210.

[361] *Id.* § 207.

[362] *See id.* § 219.

[363] *See* Jennifer Lee Case, *Extra! Read All About It: Why Service by Newspaper Publication Fails to Meet Mullane's Desire-to-Inform Standard and How Modern Technology Provides a Viable Alternative*, 45 GA. L. REV. 1095 (2011).

[364] VA. CODE ANN. § 8.01-329 (2013).

[365] *Id.* § 8.01-329(C).

[366] *Id.* § 8.01-329(C) (2).

[367] VA CODE. ANN. § 8.01-329(C) (3) (2013).

It is important to note that, when service is affected by this method, the trigger date for a nonresident defendant's responsive pleading deadline may be either the date the nonresident receives mailing of process or the date on which the Secretary of State's certificate of compliance is filed in the court clerk's office. For instance, this language from the above statute makes this clear: "The time for the person to be served to respond to process sent by the Secretary shall run from the date when the certificate of compliance is filed in the office of the clerk of the court in which the action is pending."[368]

Therefore, anyone representing a nonresident defendant who has been served through the forum Secretary of State ought to determine immediately whether the trigger date for defendant's responsive pleadings is the date of receipt by the defendant or the date of filing the certificate of compliance in the trial court where the action is pending. The responsive pleading deadline will determine whether a defendant goes into default—and no lawyer wants to start a case by having to get her client out of default, particularly if that default is because the lawyer did not determine the correct deadline.

Follow-Up Questions and Comments

1. In the past, service was carried out exclusively by United States marshals in the federal system and by sheriffs in state systems. In recent years, however, the rules have been relaxed so that process can be served by anyone of a certain age (usually 18 years or older) and not a party to the case. Thus, the person carrying out service for you may have little experience. What instructions should you give the person serving process? When advising a process server, you routinely should consider various situations that the server might face, such as the defendant's absence but another person's presence at the residence. What questions should the process server ask to ensure she complies with the law of your jurisdiction? What should the process server tell the person receiving service about the contents of the process? In your jurisdiction, must the return of service be filed with the court and, if so, does the server that you employ understand that the return must be completed and filed?

2. Assume that you have met with your process server. She then goes to the defendant's residence and waits until the defendant arrives home from work. As the defendant walks to his front door, the process server asks the defendant his name. Figuring out that he's about to be served, the defendant becomes belligerent and yells at the process server to "get off his property or he'll sue for trespass." When the process server tries to hand the process to the defendant, he refuses to accept anything. The process server then tosses the process at the defendant's feet and says: "You've been served in John Smith v. Jane Doe." As she's driving off, the process server hears the process packet hit the back of her car and sees it fall into the street. In the state in which you intend to practice, would a court consider this to be proper service on an individual defendant?

Practice Problems

Practice Problem 7-1

Jefferson's car collided with Hamilton's car. Hamilton filed suit in federal court in Virginia to recover from Jefferson $25,000 for damage to Hamilton's car and $100,000 for personal injuries. A deputy

---

[368] *Id.*

sheriff attempted to serve process on Jefferson at his home in Monticello, Virginia, but Jefferson was not home to accept it. The deputy taped the summons and complaint to the front of Jefferson's curbside mailbox and told Jefferson's fourteen-year-old son, "Be sure your father sees this when he gets home." Under Rule 4, has service been properly made? Does answering the question also require you— in addition to checking what Rule 4 explicitly would allow—to check the law of the state in which the action is pending and the law of the state in which service is made, if different?

Practice Problem 7-2
John Smith was driving his automobile in Richmond, Virginia, when he struck and injured Nathanial Bacon, a pedestrian. A week later, Smith and his wife locked up their home in Richmond, leaving no one in charge, and left for a vacation in England. While the Smiths were out of the country, Bacon brought an action against Smith by filing a complaint to recover $500,000 for his injuries. A summons issued by the clerk was attached to a copy of Smith's complaint and delivered to a process server. The process server found no one present at the Smith's home and, thus, posted the papers on the front door of the residence and made his return of proof of service to the court. The process server then mailed by certified mail a summons and complaint to the address where he had posted them and mailed a signed certification to the court of both his posting and his certified mailing of process. When the Smiths returned home, they were surprised to find that Bacon had obtained judgment by default against Smith for $500,000. Under Rule 4, what do you need to know to determine whether service was proper here such that a default judgment would stand?

Practice Problem 7-3
James Bowie spent half the year working as a businessman and living in a residence in San Antonio, Texas. He spent the rest of the year, during hunting and fishing seasons, living in his cabin on a lake in a rural area in Texas. Bowie entered into a business contract with Antonio Santa Anna, a resident of New Mexico. Believing that Bowie had breached the contract, Santa Anna sued him in a U.S. district court in Texas for $100,000 and had a summons and complaint served at Bowie's cabin. Because no one was there, the process was posted on the front (and only) door to the cabin. Santa Anna soon thereafter had a certified mail version of the summons and complaint mailed to the cabin's address and filed a certificate of compliance with the court. The service was mailed at a time when Bowie ordinarily would have been at his cabin, but in this instance, he happened to be visiting an old friend, Sam Houston, in Texas. Under Rule 4, what do you need to know to determine whether service was proper here such that a default judgment would stand? Would the same hold true if Santa Anna sued in state court? Must you check the law of the state in which the action is pending and the law of the state in which service was made?

Practice Problem 7-4
Tom Jefferson sued Ethen Allen, Inc., a furniture company in New Hampshire which had contracted with Jefferson to manufacture a swivel chair Jefferson invented. Jefferson claimed the company had not paid him sufficiently and in a timely manner, but the company respectfully disagreed.

Jefferson filed suit in a United States District Court in Virginia. He relied on VA. CODE ANN. § 8.01-329 for service on the defendant by delivering to the Secretary of the Commonwealth process on December 21, 2016. The Secretary sent process by certified mail, which showed that the defendant received it on January 5, 2017, and mailed a certificate verifying its certified mailing. The clerk of the court in Virginia received the certificate and marked it filed on December 29, 2016. The applicable rule requires the defendant to respond to the process within 21 days. When must a responsive pleading be filed?

B. Serving Corporate Entities

A corporation is comprised solely of persons that act on its behalf; therefore, service of process must be made to the corporation's agents.[369] The specific language of Federal Rule of Civil Procedure 4 provides that service on a corporation can be achieved by delivering a copy of the summons and of the complaint to an officer, a managing or general agent, or any other agent authorized by appointment or by law to receive service of process and—if the agent is one authorized by statute and the statute so requires—by also mailing a copy of each to the defendant.[370]

In addition, service on corporations—as with service on individuals—can be in accordance with the method set forth in the law of the state in which the action is pending or the state in which the corporation is located.[371] The following subsections flesh out the circumstances in which service on a corporate representative will be effective.

1. Service by Delivering Process to a Managing or General Agent

The first option listed in Rule 4 is to serve a corporate officer or managing or general agent. Neither managing nor general agents need be "specifically authorized by the corporation to accept service."[372] The corporate employee's responsibilities, not her title, determine whether she qualifies as a managing or general agent.[373] For example, the title "manager" is not determinative. Instead, the key is whether the person has the type of responsibility such that she would be likely to get the process to the appropriate corporate official.[374]

2. Service by Delivering Process to a Designated State Official

As noted above, Rule 4 permits by incorporation the forum state's law concerning service on corporations, as well as the law of the state in which the corporation being served is located. One option will be service under the state's long-arm statutes because, as we have learned, virtually every state has them. These statutes do not distinguish between nonresident individuals and nonresident corporations. Thus, if the serving party provides the Secretary of State with process and other requirements under the state statute, the Secretary will follow through and serve the nonresident corporation by certified mail. For many such statutes, the date the certificate verifying service is filed with the clerk is the date on which the time to respond begins.[375]

The Secretary then mails the process by certified mail to the nonresident corporation and provides a certificate of having done so to the trial court, as done with individual nonresident defendants.

3. Service by Delivering Process to a Registered Agent

Another typical option for corporate service is on a corporation's "registered agent." Such an agent

---

[369] 62B AM. JUR. 2D Process § 222 (2017).

[370] FED. R. CIV. P. 4(h) (1) (B).

[371] *Id.* at 4(h) (1) (A).

[372] 62B AM. JUR. 2D Process § 229 (2017).

[373] *Id.* § 230.

[374] *Id.*; *see also id.* § 247 (determining whether a sales representative or distributor exercises sufficient authority over the corporation to qualify as an agent).

[375] *See, e.g.,* VA. CODE ANN.

225

is "authorized by appointment or by law to receive service of process and, if the agent is one authorized by statute to receive service and the statute so requires, by also mailing a copy to the defendant."[376] Many states have statutes constructively appointing a state officer (*e.g.*, an official of the State Corporation Commission) as an agent for the corporation if it has failed to appoint a registered agent.[377]

Remember, the fact that a corporation has a registered agent in a state does not equate to establishing personal jurisdiction in that state if that state is not the corporation's state of incorporation or principal place of business. For instance, in *Siemer v. Learjet Acquisition Corp.*,[378] the court held that the plaintiff—even when serving a corporation's registered agent in a state—needs to show that the claim arises from the corporation's actions and contacts with that state, and that such actions and contacts are sufficient to subject the corporation to specific personal jurisdiction consistent with due process.[379]

Follow-Up Questions and Comments

1. A process server will be the one effective service on the corporation. What instructions will you give the process server regarding who to serve when you send him to the headquarters of the defendant corporation? If as is likely the process server will not be able to have an office or director of the corporation come out the reception area or lobby, what should the process server do?

2. Assume that you are retained to sue a corporation incorporated outside of your jurisdiction, but which does regular business in the state in which you intend to practice. Most states require nonresident companies that do business regularly in a state to appoint a registered agent in the state for purposes of receiving service of process. Serving the registered agent, therefore, is likely to be the easiest and least expensive method of serving the corporation. Moreover, you believe that you can show the claim you are asserting arises from the corporation's activities in the state that will withstand due process scrutiny. You simply want to find the easiest way to accomplish service and believe that to be serving the registered agent. What state agency is most likely to have records of the name and address of the registered agent for a company?

Professional Identity Question: Hired Gun or Advocate?

Your client has a dispute with a corporation and asks you to handle the suit. The client wants to serve the president of the corporation in a manner best calculated to embarrass the president and to bring negative publicity to the corporation. According to your client, the corporation's president will be speaking at a local public event soon. There should be a large crowd and media coverage of the event. The client asks you whether you would be willing to have the president served in front of the crowd and media. When you ask why, your client says that his sole reason is to embarrass the president and the corporation. Would you do as the client asked? How would you respond to the client?

---

[376] 62B AM. JUR. 2D Process § 234 (2017).

[377] *See, e.g.*, VA. CODE ANN. § 13.1-836 (2016) ("Whenever a corporation fails to appoint or maintain a registered agent in the Commonwealth . . . then the clerk of the [State Corporation] Commission shall be an agent of the corporation upon whom service may be made.").

[378] 966 F. 2d 179 (5th Cir. 1992).

[379] *Id.* at 183–84.

Practice Problems

Practice Problem 7-5

Carol sued Home State Corporation, a company organized and with its principal place of business in North Carolina. Her lawyer sends a process server to the defendant's corporate office. When the process server asks the receptionist to see an officer, no officer responds. The only person who comes out to the lobby is the assistant to the corporation's public relations manager. The process server delivers the summons and complaint to this assistant. Is service valid under Rule 4)? What criteria will determine whether the assistant is a person who qualifies as one on whom service may be affected for a corporate defendant?

Practice Problem 7-6

Gotcha Insurance Company is incorporated and has its principal place of business in Tennessee. Gotcha solicited an insurance contract with your client but has refused to pay a claim for no valid reason. You search and cannot find a registered agent for Gotcha in Virginia, where your client lives and was insured by Gotcha. You have determined that you will likely have to sue Gotcha using the statute accompanying the long-arm statute for Virginia. Having concluded that both the long-arm statute and the due process principles governing exercise of personal jurisdiction would be satisfied, you file suit in federal court in Virginia. Under Rule 4, and any applicable state law incorporated by reference, what steps would you need to take to serve process on the nonresident?

C. Service on Unincorporated Entities

Similar to service of process on corporations, service of process on unincorporated associations—under Federal Rule of Civil Procedure 4 and similar state rules—may be affected when the association is subject to suit under a common name; by delivering a copy of the summons and complaint to an officer, a managing or general agent, or to any other agent authorized by appointment or by law to receive service of process; and . . . by also mailing a copy to the defendant [if the statute so requires].[380]

1. Service on Partnerships

A partnership "or other unincorporated association which is subject to suit under a common name" may be served "by delivering a copy of the summons and complaint to an officer, a managing or general agent, or to any other agent authorized by appointment or by law to receive service of process, and . . . by also mailing a copy to the defendant [if the statute so requires]."[381]

If you sue not only a partnership by serving its "general partner" or its "general manager," but also seek relief from one or more partners "in their individual capacity," service upon the general partner or manager must comply with the rules for service upon individuals.[382] Furthermore, even though partners may be liable for the torts of each other, "a vicariously liable partner" must be "individually named and served in the action."[383]

---

[380] 62B AM. JUR. 2D Process § 241 (2017).
[381] 62B AM. JUR. 2D Process § 242 (2017).
[382] *Id.*
[383] *Id.*

Follow-Up Questions and Comments

1. Traditionally, there have been two types of partnerships—general partnerships and limited partnerships. In a general partnership, each partner is liable for all liabilities of the partnership and shares in assets equally. By contrast, a limited partnership usually has one general partners (maybe more) and multiple limited partners. The limited partners' liabilities are capped at the amount of his or her contribution to the partnership.[384] In light of this difference, you can serve a single general partner but may want to serve all the general partners to ensure later, after a judgment is entered, that there are not proceedings seeking to set it aside. As to limited partnerships, however, it is not simply a matter of strategy. One must serve the general partners and not rely solely on serving one or more limited partners. Typically, the State Corporation Commission for your state will have information on entities other than corporations. This information should include what type of partnership the entity is, who the partners are (and what type of partner they are), as well as their addresses.

2. If you are suing a partnership, how can you determine the partners in the partnership? Should you serve the partners that you identify at their places of business or their personal addresses? Does your answer depend on whether you are suing the partnership, an individual partner, or both?

Practice Problem

Practice Problem 7-7

Pizza Partnership is a general partnership in Virginia. Your client, who lives in Kentucky, sues Pizza Partnership for negligence because she was seriously injured when she ate one of its pizzas that contained a piece of sharp metal under the cheese topping. You find out that there are three partners, Adam, Bob, and Carl, each of whom are businessmen with ties Virginia but who are citizens of other states (Adam in North Carolina, Bob in West Virginia, and Carl in South Carolina). After filing suit seeking compensation for your client's injuries, how should you effect service? Who would you name as a party? Where and how would you serve them? Why?

2. Service on a State, Municipal, Governmental Organizations

Plaintiffs usually accomplish service of process upon a state, municipal corporation, or other governmental organization by serving a copy of the summons and complaint personally on its chief executive officer.[385] While the chief executive officer of a state is the Governor, statutes will usually authorize serving the state's Attorney General in lieu of the Governor.[386] Typically, state laws also specify another "person or officer upon whom service of process is to be made" (*e.g.*, a city or county attorney) and that no other person may be substituted.[387] Note, however, that service by mail upon a governmental entity

---

[384] *See generally* 59A AM. JUR. 2D Partnership Summary (2017).

[385] 62B AM. JUR. 2D Process § 248 (2017).

[386] *See id.* § 249.

[387] *Id.* at § 248.

is prohibited, absent a specific state or federal statute stating otherwise.[388]

Practice Problems

Practice Problem 7-8

Gladys and her son, Ray, are both citizens of North Carolina. Ray was injured in a hallucinatory episode in Virginia and put in the Virginia Mental Hospital, which is owned and operated by Virginia. Ray is considered psychotic and represents a danger to himself without supervision. The hospital negligently failed to supervise Ray and he left the grounds. He jumped off an overpass above a passing train and was killed. Gladys brought a wrongful death action against Virginia for negligence resulting in her son's death. What are her options in serving the State?

Practice Problem 7-9

Parade City holds a parade monthly. During one of its parades, a city-owned float veered off track and hit a young boy from another state who was visiting his grandparents. The boy broke his leg and he had to wear a cast for six months. His parents retain you to sue the Parade City for negligence. What are your options in serving the city?

D. Option to Request Waiver of Service

Federal Rule of Civil Procedure 4 allows the party, in lieu of seeking service, to send a "waiver" of service form to a defendant subject to service. Please read Rule 4(d) now, as well as the sample "Notice of a Lawsuit and Request to Waive Service of Summons" accompanying the Rule 4. Be prepared to answer the follow-up questions below.

Follow-Up Questions and Comments

1. How does the party request waiver of service of process?

2. Is the party who receives the waiver form required to waive, or does she have the choice of waiving or not doing so?

3. What benefits does the Rule allow a party who signs the waiver? What penalties are imposed if the party does not sign the waiver?

4. If you are a plaintiff, when would you seek waiver of service of process?

5. If you are a party who receives a waiver of service form, when would you be willing to agree to a waiver of service?

---

[388] *Id.*

6. Notice that there is a cost-benefit analysis that goes into the decision. Can you tell from the Rule what the cost-benefit analysis involves?

_____

Practice Problem

Practice Problem 7-10

Plaintiff's counsel has been working on plaintiff's case for over a year because the client came in with enough time to do significant pretrial preparation before filing to meet the statute of limitations. The work includes information gathered by the plaintiff, experts consulted and who may testify, and work in progress on calculating damages for lost wages, etc. When the defendant is served, plaintiff can send to the defendant discovery requests that will take advantage of the superior knowledge of plaintiff's counsel and move the case along speedily, not to mention keep the defense counsel busy while he or she is playing catch-up. Plaintiff's counsel's strategy is to get the earliest possible trial date and to use the leverage she has received from being retained early enough to work on the case to be better prepared than the defense. Why would plaintiff's counsel in such a situation *not* be likely to send a request for waiver of service of process once she had filed suit and ready to engage the defendant? When would sending a waiver be appropriate? Conversely, as a defendant, if you receive a waiver, would you typically agree to it? Why?

_____

CHAPTER 8:
UNDERSTANDING THE STEPS IN A LAWSUIT, THE ROLE OF THE RULES OF CIVIL PROCEDURE, AND WHEN PARTICULAR RULES APPLY

Once the defendant or defendants have been served, civil lawsuits follow a pattern. The law at issue may change, but the stages of a civil suit do not vary much. Most law students do not know these stages. That is no one's fault. Unless you have been a party to a lawsuit or have worked in a legal office (or in a court), you ordinarily would not have been exposed to litigation as it actually occurs. Media paints a misleading picture. Someone sues another. In what seems like a week or a month, the trial is underway. In truth, a case that makes it to trial within a year of filing is considered to be on a fast track.[389] Most are not even set for trial by then and often take close to two years to be tried. That part of the litigation process is not depicted well, except in a few instances, because the media's goal is to entertain, not to teach budding lawyers the steps necessary to get a case to trial. A civil procedure course is about teaching the language of the law. It's also about the constitutional provisions that are procedural (due process, jury trial, etc.), about the federal statutes that address procedure (not just subject matter jurisdictions statutes, for instance the venue statutes on what district within a state is a proper one in which to file suit), and about the many, many Rules of Civil Procedure. Often, it is easier to see the constitutional procedural provisions as part of the checks and balances. The Framers designed to offset bias, prejudice, and other impediments to equal justice. If one looks closely enough at the federal statutes and Rules, once can see they are designed to be evenly applied regardless of a parties' race, social status, or other factors that can skew a result on the merits. The author will not pretend that the system is completely free from bias. However, the lawyer who fails to know procedure and to use it leaves the client vulnerable. In short, a lawyer who knows procedure well can level the playing field even when she represents a client with lesser resources than the adversary.

Knowing the stages of litigation, the Rules that apply, and the purposes of each stage provides valuable context to the student learning how the federal system of civil procedure works. This chapter offers an overall context for the progress of a civil case. The rest of this Casebook follows the stages of a civil case from the time it is filed and served. Each chapter will focus on the Federal Rules that apply as the stages proceed through and after trial. This chapter will describe stages of a civil action and the Rules that apply at each stage. The student needs to read the overview, review the Rules, and therefore will know what to expect in the chapters that follow. These chapters will flesh out what happens in each stage and present the Rules in action.

I. The Birth of a Lawsuit
Every lawsuit has its genesis in the events that give rise to a claim or claims asserted in the lawsuit. One driver slams into another. Someone breaches a contract. Owners of adjoining pieces of property dispute the boundary. And so on. Once the events have occurred, the party claiming to have been wronged has a period in which to sue—we call that a statute of limitations. It's not addressed a great deal here, except as one of the affirmative defenses a defendant can raise to the lawsuit but knowing the statute of limitations

---

[389] The federal judiciary's statistics show that most cases are resolved between one and three years and some a longer period. *See* Administrative Office of the United States Courts, Judicial Facts and Figures 2018, Table 4.11, at https://www.uscourts.gov/sites/default/files/data_tables/jff_4.11_0930.2018.pdf (last accessed July 1, 2019).

in practice is a big deal.

Chapters 1 through 7 of this lawsuit dealt with whether the forum—the location of the court in which suit was filed—could render an enforceable judgment. Service of process was the last piece of the enforceable-judgment puzzle. The judgment of a court that lacks subject matter jurisdiction, or personal jurisdiction, or in which the defendant has not been notified will not be enforceable. The remaining chapters—Chapters 8-18 –deal with the process by which litigation is handled after the questions of subject matter jurisdiction, personal jurisdiction, and service of process are resolved.

This chapter thus summarizes the topics of the remaining chapters in this Casebook. In so doing, it provides a sequential context for the student to understand how litigation proceeds. It also identifies the Federal Rules of Civil Procedure that apply at each stage. The Rules are in bold in this chapter to remind the student, when he or she gets to a Rule, to take time to read it and reflect on how it fits into the progress of the suit. If the student does not understand the fit, that student should seek to figure out the question. Doing so by reading related sources is one avenue. Asking one's professor is certainly another. However, the student finds the answers to her questions, she must learn that that Federal Rules are not a random series of requirements, but rather are integral parts of a system. Each Rule plays its role but may and often is supporting the same policy as other rules. Changing a Rule could, in fact, have an impact beyond the stage of the case that it appears to govern. Because cases in diversity in federal court will at times present state law that goes beyond the underlying substantive claims, the tension between state law and the Federal Rules and statutes on procedure can present challenging problems. The next section of this chapter, and the entirety of Chapter 9, will address this knotty topic.

A. What Law Applies in the Case?

Before proceeding through the stages of a lawsuit, an important issue needs to be addressed: what law will govern in the lawsuit? To question what law applies in the case may seem odd at first. One might think "The case is in federal court, so federal law must apply." Not so fast. In federal question cases, the answer to the question is clearly "yes." The underlying claim is based on federal law, typically a federal statute, and the procedure will undoubtedly be that of the Federal courts, primarily set forth in the Federal Rules of Civil Procedure but also for some procedure matters in federal statutes. The answer is less clear when the case qualifies for subject matter jurisdiction under diversity of citizenship.

In diversity cases, the only reason the parties are in federal court is because they are complete diverse and the amount in controversy exceeds $75,000 exclusive of interests and costs. The underlying claims in the case are state-law claims, such as contract, tort, or property claims. The question of whether federal procedural law applies is surprisingly knotty. In this chapter, you will learn about the now famous case of *Erie v. Thompkins*, for which the doctrine we discuss here is named—i.e., the Erie Doctrine. You may be surprised by the degree to which e Supreme Court has struggled with the question that the doctrine addresses. The Court has searched for criteria to identify when state laws *other than* the substantive law of underlying claims (e.g., the elements of a tort claim) will apply in federal diversity cases and when federal procedural law will override such state law. Chapter 9 explores the Court's search for, and the ultimate tests, for determining when federal law overrides state law, even on matters not directly related to the substantive claim, and when state law beyond the substantive claim should apply.

The *Erie* doctrine explores principles of federalism—i.e., seeking to balance the interest of the federal system with the state systems. As such one view it as philosophical. However, for the student to dismiss its significance is dangerous. The philosophical explorations lead to investigation of the role of federal procedural statutes and Federal Rules, and the role or roles that a statute or rule has in the Federal system. Thus, the wise student will recognize as the remainder of the semester proceeds through Federal Rules and statutes to pay close attention to the policy underlying a statute or rule. Doing so will often be the difference in the outcome of an *Erie* analysis. By asking how the federal system fits together, and what rule a Rule or statute plays in that system, the student comes to understand federal procedure as being highly integrated. In other words, the *Erie* analysis puts an incentive on doing more than memorizing Rules. One must know how the Rules fit together, and often how they further related policies.

B. The Complaint (Rules 8, 9, 10)

Having a handle on the law that will apply in the case, the party asserting the claim(s)—called the plaintiff—sues the defendant, the vehicle for asserting claims is a complaint. Chapter 10 will discuss the criteria provide in the Rules—specifically **Rule 8**, **Rule 9**, and **Rule 10**—for a valid complaint. A complaint is a formal pleading that, when filed, starts the lawsuit. A number is assigned to the case, and that number is used on every other pleading. A sample complaint is posted on the Course Website.[390] Federal Rule of Civil Procedure 10 provides the requirements for a complaint. It must begin with a caption identifying the court and the parties. The allegations are set forth in numbered paragraphs. Exhibits, i.e., documents referred to in and attached to the complaint, are part of the complaint.

The Complaint, with a Summons signed by the Clerk, is what must be served. And so begins the civilized resolution of a dispute between parties. Chapter 9 will discuss the components of a complaint—the pleading that begins the process. The Federal Rules governing a complaint are Rule 10, as well as Rule 8—the Rule that provides the criteria by which the sufficiency of a complaint will be measured. As discussed below, a defendant can attack a complaint that fails to meet the criteria of Rule 8. If the complaint does not set forth specific grounds on which the reader can determine that federal subject matter jurisdiction exists, the complaint is vulnerable. If the complaint fails to state enough allegations, that too can lead to dismissal. We will see that the level of allegations depends on the kind of claim. The most detailed allegations are reserved for fraud claims, as Federal Rule 9 indicates. Rule 8 governs all other claims and traditionally has required only sufficient facts showing the pleader is entitled to relief. Recent Supreme Court cases have suggested a higher level of pleading in some cases, but the concept that still prevails in our federal system is one of notice pleading. If the complaint contains sufficient facts and allegations that it puts the defendant on notice of the claim and the relief sought, then it should survive any motion.

Chapter 10 will also discuss the special requirements for a plaintiff who seeks injunctive relief at the outset of a case. **Rule 65** provides the steps a plaintiff must follow to received temporary injunctive relief. If the plaintiff would suffer irreparable harm without such relief, the court can enjoin the defending pending trial, provided the plaintiff makes a sufficient showing of need and posts a bond to protect the defendant in the event that later the court determines the injunction should not have been entered. In addition, in some cases the plaintiff will have to present pleadings sworn to by a party and signed before a notary public. If the injunction request goes to a preliminary injunction hearing, the court usually conducts an evidentiary hearing. The goal is not to try the final merits. Instead the goal of such a hearing is for the court to decide whether an injunction needs to be granted to preserve the status quo until trial.

---

[390] The Course Website is www.civpro4allstatesteachersmanual.org. The website contains materials referred to not only in this casebook, but in another casebook, CIVIL PROCEDURE FOR ALL STATES: A CONTEXT AND PRACTICE CASEBOOK (Carolina Academic Press 2010). The materials for this lawsuit are under "Federal Lawsuit."

II. Joinder of Claims, and of Multiple Defendants, in a Complaint

A. Rules Related to Joinder of Claims and Parties by Plaintiff
(Rule 18 and Rule 20)

In many if not most complaints, multiple claims will be brought against a defendant. The plaintiff can assert as many claims as the plaintiff has against the defendant, i.e. one defendant. Indeed, it is the rare complaint that contains but one claim. **Rule 18** allows a claimant to allege "as many claims as it has against an opposing party." For Rule 18 to allow joinder claims, it does not matter whether the claims arise from the same occurrences. Judicial economy dictates that a party who is suing another party ought to be able to bring all the disputes in and get them solved. However, we will see later that joinder of claims may be permitted by Rule 18 but not be within the limited jurisdiction of federal courts. One of the continuing themes of joinder will be that the rules may authorized joinder but, because federal courts are courts of limited jurisdiction, the claim must have a jurisdictional basis to be able to be in federal court. Chapter 11 will explain the analysis one must follow to (1) first determine whether a Federal Rule prohibits the type of joinder, and (2) even if so, whether there is a jurisdictional basis for the joined claim of a party in Federal Court.

In addition, the joinder rules allow suing more than one party. To add defendants—the technical term that we will use for this is "join" defendants—requires that the plaintiff meet **Rule 20's** criteria. This Rule has two requirements. First, the claims against each joined party must arise from the same transaction or occurrence or series of transactions or occurrences. Second, the claims against each joined party must have a common question of law or fact. Thus, Plaintiff can sue Defendant 1 and Defendant 2 if the claims against both arise from the same transaction or occurrence and raise common questions of fact. The fact pattern in the Course Website shows a more complicated case of joinder by an injured plaintiff of claims against a City, a State, and a manufacturer of a vehicle. The caption in such a multi-defendant complaint looks like this:

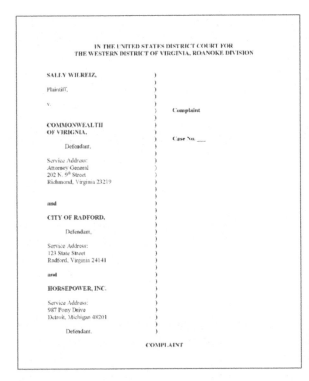

IN THE UNITED STATES DISTRICT COURT FOR
THE WESTERN DISTRICT OF VIRGINIA, ROANOKE DIVISION

SALLY WILREIZ,

Plaintiff,

v.

Complaint

COMMONWEALTH
OF VIRGINIA,

Defendant,

Case No. ___

Service Address:
Attorney General
202 N. 9th Street
Richmond, Virginia 23219

and

CITY OF RADFORD,

Defendant,

Service Address:
123 State Street
Radford, Virginia 24141

and

HORSEPOWER, INC.

Service Address:
987 Pony Drive
Detroit, Michigan 48201

Defendant.

COMPLAINT

In short, the plaintiff cannot haphazardly sue as many defendants as it wants for whatever it wants in the same suit. Look at the Course Website's description of the lawsuit there (see the facts under "Federal Lawsuit" tab). Sally Wilreiz owns the convertible that falls into a deep pothole on the border of property improperly maintained by the City and the State. In the process, the car's rollover protective device (to protect the passenger from injuries in turning over) fails. Thus, she has claims against the City for negligence, the State for negligence, and against the car manufacturer for product liability—negligence in the manufacture or design of the roll bar. The caption of a complaint in a multi-party case looks like the image on the left.

Contrast a car owner who discovers she has a claim for fraud against the seller of the car because the seller misrepresented that the car was new when it was not. Then the owner has an accident and believes the other driver was negligent. The plaintiff, defrauded car owner, could not join her claim against the seller with her claim against the other driver. The difference between Sally's ability to sue the three defendants and this car owner's inability to sue multiple defendants is whether the claims arise from the same transaction, occurrence, or series of transactions, or occurrences. Nor do the claims involve common questions of law or fact. The car owner will have to bring separate suits against each defendant.

Accomplishing joinder of defendants is not quite as easy as joining whatever claims. Rule 20's criteria is more demanding than that of Rule 18. Even more analysis will be needed because, like claims under Rule 18, satisfying the Rule is not enough. The plaintiff must show that the claims against the joined parties are supported jurisdictionally.

B. Miscellaneous Rules Requiring or Permitting Joinder if Certain Facts Exist

The joinder rules used by a plaintiff are about building a lawsuit. Rules 18 and 20 are often the only tools required to build the suit. However, other joinder rules are specialized for circumstances that either require or allow joinder under **Rules 19, 22, 23**, and **24**. Chapter 11 also address joinder under these rules. Rule 19 is designed to avoid allowing a plaintiff to fail to join a defendant o necessary for the court to grant complete relief, then the plaintiff needs to join all parties necessary to provide complete relief. An example could be disputes over property that affects plaintiff's property and two other property owners. The plaintiff needs to join both other property owners, not just one. Or, if suing on a contract to which two parties have obligated themselves to the plaintiff (called co-obligors), leaving one of those out would offend Rule 19.

Rule 22, and its statutory counterpart, 28 U.S.C. § 1335, are specialized for cases in which a plaintiff is exposed to multiple liability from various parties and needs to join these other parties to reach a resolution in one suit. The typical situation has a plaintiff as a "stakeholder," holding property (e.g. insurance proceeds) with competing claimants and seeking a binding adjudication as to the parties' rights.

Rule 23 provides the requirements in which to plead a class action. The rule allows for different types of class actions. The plaintiff chooses what type of class action to bring and then pleads the necessary allegations to satisfy that type of class action under the Rule. Rule 24 is not about drafting a complaint but rather about a party who has been left out of a suit, often a party who has an interest as a plaintiff, who wants to "intervene," i.e., be made a party to the suit after another plaintiff has filed the complaint. To intervene the intervening party needs to show that as a practical matter the suit may impair that party's ability to protect its interests. If existing parties represent the interests of the party seeking to intervene, the court might deny intervention. Thus, the Rule is simply another tool in the litigator's toolbox if a client comes to her and says a suit has been brought, she has been left out, and her rights will be impaired so that she should have a say in what happens.

Some may say, "Who cares, those are circumstances too specialized to worry about?" That kind of mentality would be akin to a builder who said all she needed was a hammer and a saw. "To heck with the rest of those tools." And these other rules are like tools known and valued by the professional craftsman that most clients hope they will get in a lawyer. If the lawyer knows all her tools, she will not miss the opportunity to use one when the circumstances warrant. A lawyer who knows only a couple of tools will inevitably fail to build a sound case.

As already suggested with Rule 18 and Rule 20, federal courts have limited jurisdiction. These miscellaneous joinder rules are likewise only the beginning, not the end, of the analysis in deciding whether claims can stay in federal court. Even if a Rule allows joinder there must be separately a jurisdictional basis for the claim or joined party. As we will see, that basis can come from the claim having an independent basis in subject matter jurisdiction. For instance, a joined claim that arises under federal question jurisdiction, 29 U.S.C. § 1331, has such an independent basis. If the joined claim or joinder party does not have an independent basis in subject matter jurisdiction, Chapter 11 will explore how the Supplemental Jurisdiction Statute, 28 U.S.C. § 1367.

III. Two Additional Issues Related to Pleading (1) Certification of Facts and Law in Pleadings and Amendment of Pleadings; and (2) Amendments to Pleadings

In addressing requirements of the complaint, Chapter 12 discusses two major issues pertinent not only to complaints, but to all other pleadings. First, the chapter will discuss the certifications that a pleader makes when signing a pleading. Among other things, the pleader certifies a good-faith basis in fact and law for allegations in a complaint and similar certifications. **Rule 11** thus requires good faith assertions, though not certainty, and carries sanctions for violating the Rule. The exception recognized in Rule 11 to the requirement of a basis in law is the ability to seek modification or reversal of existing law, but even there a party must have some basis for seeking modification or reversal of such law.

The second issue in Chapter 12 that relates to all pleadings, whenever filed in the march toward trial, is amendment of pleadings. Put aside human fallibility. Even if the party is pleading a Complaint or later, another pleading, or pleads everything that the pleader knows at that point, new facts come to light. Discovery—the longest phase of a case, discussed below—reveals facts that a party did not have. A brief period at the beginning of the case allows for amendment "of right." After that, and for most of the time a case is pending, the pleader needs leave from the court to amend. That leave is by definition "freely granted," but is not automatic. Even at trial a party can seek leave to amend, though the standard for granting leave stiffens. **Rule 15** provides the criteria for amending in the "of right" period, in the pretrial phase, and at trial. The Rule also addresses questions such as whether a claim or party added in an amended pleading will "relate back," i.e., be treated as having been in the case from the original complaint to avoid the statute of limitations.

A. Defendant's Response to Plaintiff's Complaint (Rules 8, 12)

Chapter 13 turns to the defendant's side of the case. In every lawsuit, after the plaintiff has prepared a complaint and served it, the ball is in the defendant's court. **Rule 8**, which addresses the requirements of a Complaint, also sets forth the criteria for a defendant's Answer. The defendant has options as to how to respond to the complaint, such as by a motion, or by filing a responsive pleading, i.e. an Answer that takes issue with the plaintiff's allegations and requests. The defendant must also consider whether it has claims that itself must bring or, in other circumstances, may choose to bring. To say that this part of a case is fraught with potential traps if the defense counsel does not understand the applicable rules is an understatement.

B. Options of Filing a Motion under Rule 12 or an Answer under Rule 8

Once the complaint is served, the defendant or defendants must know the options to respond. A defendant served with a lawsuit must consider several options. **Rule 12** is the fulcrum on which a defendant's options hinge. First, that Rule provides a time frame (21 days) in which the defendant must file some response. Deadlines are a big part of handling a lawsuit. Without them, the cases would hang around for years. Providing deadlines ensures that the case proceeds efficiently through the system. Left to themselves, many lawyers would not move forward with cases unless they are required to do so. Other cases, procrastination in general, would prevail. The Rules counter that tendency and ensure that parties must move forward once a case has begun. The consequences of failing to respond to a complaint once served, for instance, are that the defendant is in default. Unless allowed out of default, liability is taken as established and the plaintiff moves to a hearing on damages. Defense counsel who lets her clients go into default will not thrive in law practice.

Rule 12 allows a defendant two options to respond to the complaint and stay out of default. First, the defendant can file a motion of some kind. The first several types of motions in Rule 12 could lead to dismissal, i.e. for lack of subject matter jurisdiction, lack of personal jurisdiction, insufficient process, and/or improper service of process. Alternatively, some of the grounds for a motion will simply delay the case. For instance, Rule 12 allows the defendant to move for dismissal based on insufficient process (something wrong with the summons or complaint) or improper service of process. Typically, if a motion is granted for a reason that can be cured, the plaintiff corrects the deficiency by re-serving the defendant. One might wonder why a defendant would even bother to file motions to challenge defects that can be cured. For a defendant just hit with a lawsuit, any time gained is valuable. For the plaintiff seeking to move forward, these deficiencies are delays that should not happen but at times do because of carelessness of plaintiff's counsel or the process server.

The other option identified in Rule 12 is for the defendant to file responsive pleadings—i.e., an Answer—to the plaintiff's complaint. And, yes, Rule 8 addresses not only the criterial for a complaint in one section and the requirements of an Answer in another. The answer may be filed, if the defendant files a motion and loses, after the court denies a defendant's motion. Alternatively, the defendant can file within 21 days of being served an Answer. As Chapter 13 explains, knowing what to include in a motion—if that is the defendant's first filing—or what to include in an Answer, if that is the defendant's first pleading, can, if not understood thoroughly and followed meticulously, result in a defendant losing important defenses such as lack of personal jurisdiction or improper venue. In short, this stage of the proceedings is fraught with traps. A lawyer must know the Rules well and carefully consider all options.

IV. Defendant's Ability to Join Claims and/or Parties (Rule 13, 14, 18, 20)

Chapter 14 covers the rules and jurisdictional issues related to a defendant's joinder of claims and/or parties. The Rules also permit—and, in some cases require—the defendant to file claims. For instance, **Rule 13** provides that a defendant who has a claim arising from the same transaction or occurrence for which the plaintiff has sued that defendant "must" assert any claims the defendant has against the plaintiff. That rule is appropriately named the "compulsory" counterclaim Rule. In addition, Rule 13 allows a defendant to assert "permissive" counterclaims—i.e., claims a defendant has against the plaintiff that do not arise from the same transaction or occurrence. Yet another section of Rule 13 permits a defendant to assert "cross-claims" against a co-defendant. Finally, **Rule 14** permits a defendant who has a claim against a nonparty based on contribution or indemnity to serve that nonparty with a Third-Party Complaint and thus bring the party into the litigation. Once in, that Third Party Defendant can assert claims against the Defendant who brought it and/or against the Plaintiff. Likewise, the original Plaintiff can assert claims against the newly added Third-Party Defendant.

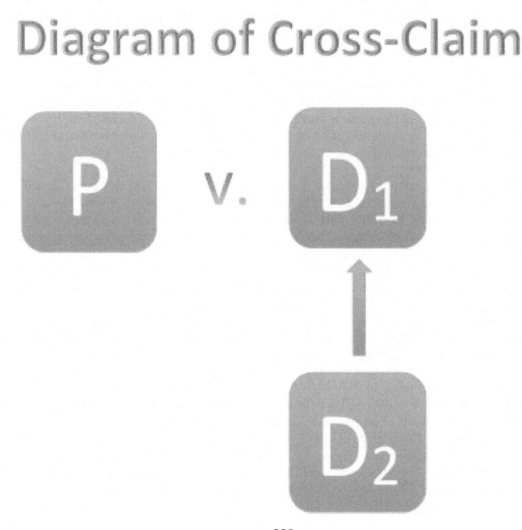

238

Diagram of Rule 14

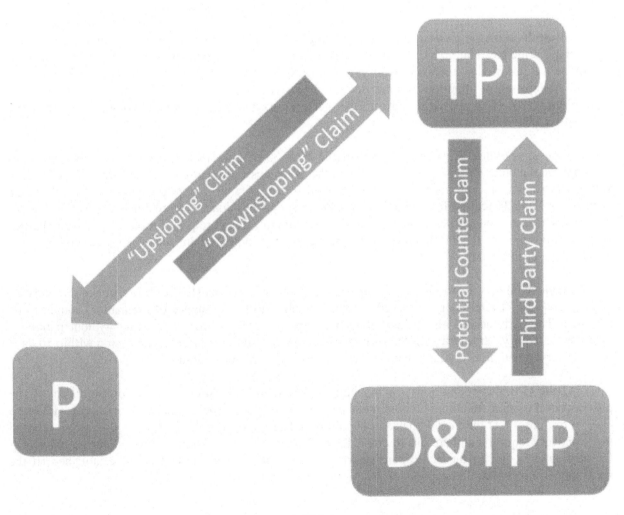

Chapter 15 builds on Chapter 14's introduction of the concept that the original defendant can go on the offensive and assert claims, just as an original plaintiff was able to join claims and parties under Rules 18 and 20, Chapter 15 also demonstrates that, whenever a joined claim is brought, even if by a defendant, the possibility exits of joining a claim and/or a party to that defendant's claim. As with the teaching of Chapter 11, however, every claim or party that is joined in federal court must be scrutinized because of the limited jurisdiction of federal courts. One cannot merely ask whether a Rule of Court allows the joinder. Instead, one must ask whether there is a jurisdictional basis for that joined claim or party. Thus, Chapter 15 emphasizes throughout that both support in a Rule and jurisdictional support are essential to join claims and/or parties.

V. The Discovery Phase of a Lawsuit (Rules 26, Rule 30, Rule 33, Rule 34, Rule 36, Rule 37, Rule 45)

A. Obtaining Information and Documents through Discovery Tools

The hallmark of modern civil litigation is discovery. As it suggests, discovery is a process in which the parties learn about the lawsuit. Of course, the lawyer for a party can learn from its own client. Discovery is designed to provide various tools by which one party can force the opponent to disclose information. Chapter 16 explores in depth the purposes, methods, and issues raised in discovery.

Rule 26 is the main discovery rule, providing criteria for the scope of discovery and other general overarching principles that govern the process. Some of the overarching principles in Rule 26 includes a section on the hallowed protection of work product, i.e. materials developed by the lawyer or the lawyer's team in anticipation of litigation. Another section discusses the primary objections to discovery that are allowed and how, if appropriate, a litigant can get a protective order to avoid production of sensitive information, or to stop harassment.

Each type of discovery tools has its own rule. **Rule 33** provides that one side (plaintiff or defendant) can serve on the other written questions that the other must answer under oath. Rule 34 provides for each side to serve on the other requests for documents or other tangible things in the possession of the other. The "cousin" of **Rule 34** request for production is **Rule 45** subpoenas "duces tecum," meaning subpoenas for documents. Because nonparties are not required to respond to Rule 34 request for production (only parties are), the Rules provide this mechanism to force nonparties to produce documents when served with a Rule 45 subpoena duces tecum.

Rule 36 allows a party to request another to admit specified facts. The Rule requires the party on whom a request for admissions is served to "fairly respond to the substance of the matter" sought to be admitted. The party served also cannot claim ignorance of whether the fact is true without making a "reasonable inquiry." In addition, if the party does not respond to the request for admission within 30 days of being served with it, everything requested to be admitted is deemed admitted.

Rule 37 deals with motions to compel and with sanctions for failure to follow discovery rules. The provisions on motions to compel require counsel to seek to resolve the dispute before filing a motion to compel responses that the movant believes should have been in provided. If a party is ordered to respond to a discovery request and then fails to do so, Rule 37 includes harsh sanctions, even so far as dismissing the other party's suit (if the nonresponsive party is a plaintiff) or deeming facts as established (if the nonresponsive party is a defendant).

VI. The Right to a Jury Trial and Motions for Summary Judgment

At the close of discovery in many cases motions for summary judgment are filed and resolved. A summary judgment motion essentially argues that the plaintiff lacks evidence on which reasonable jurors can disagree on one or more essential elements of a claim. Lawyers and judges refer to this as a "sufficiency of the evidence" question. What is usually at stake here is whether the plaintiff will receive a trial by jury or the judge will grant a motion on its own, finding the plaintiff's case cannot go forward because, if it did, the evidence would be insufficient. To understand what is at stake in summary judgment one needs to understand the right to trial by jury. Though it may seem out of order, Chapter 16 intentionally discusses the right to trial by jury first before discussing summary judgment. **Rule 38** provides the requirements for a party to demand a jury. A separate test determines whether a claim is of the kind for which a party has a constitutional right to a jury. However, even if a party has the right, it can be waived by failing to follow Rule 38. After addressing the right to a jury trial, the rules for summary judgment and the effect of summary judgment take up the rest of the chapter. A motion for summary judgment, under **Rule 56**, would be heard before a trial because it is deciding whether there will be a trial. Keep the actual chronological order in mind. However, recognize that the reason you are reading about a jury trial first is so that you can better understand what summary judgment entails.

VII. Motions at Trial and Trial Procedures

Procedural requirements continue during a trial. Chapter 18 addresses the most significant of those procedures. These include **Rule 50** and the motions allowed there. These include a motion for judgment as a matter of law (JMOL) after a party has put on its case. Thus, a defendant can move for a JMOL when the plaintiff rests, both parties can move for a JMOL at the end of the trial, and if the court allows the case to go to a verdict, a party who moved for a JMOL before may renew that motion. A related post-trial motion is a motion for a new trial under **Rule 59**. Such a motion will, as the chapter explains, be guided by different criteria than that applied in resolving a renewed JMOL. Other procedures during trial include those related to selecting a jury and the grounds for a mistrial.

VIII. Claim and Issue Preclusion

Claim and issue preclusion are a major topic that arise when some or all the parties to one suit, which had previously reached a judgment, are involved in a second suit. Chapter 18 will explain how, if claim preclusion applies, the second suit will be precluded completely. The chapter will further explain how, if claim preclusion does not apply, issue preclusion can preclude the relitigating of a second suit of an issue resolved in earlier litigation.

CHAPTER 9: THE *ERIE* DOCTRINE:
DETERMINING WHAT LAW APPLIES IN FEDERAL COURT

I. How the Topics in this Chapter Fit in the Overall Progress of a Civil Action[391]

Figure 9-1

Cause of Action (events leading to suit)	Pre-Filing Tasks (items to begin representation, interviewing, and related matters)	Choice of Forum (subject matter jurisdiction, removal, personal jurisdiction, and venue)	Notice and Service of Process (completing the process of ensuring the forum court can enter a valid judgment)	Pleading the Case and Joinder of Claims and Parties (including supplemental jurisdiction)

Responding to Claims by Motion or by Answer	Discovery (developing proof to establish claims and learn your adversary's case)	Right to Jury (pretrial motions and practice)	Final Pretrial Conference (events within last month before trial)	**Trial (procedures and motions during trial)**	Verdict	Post-Trial Motions (motions for a new trial and/or judgment as a matter of law)	Appeal

Erie[392] questions arise at any stage of the litigation process. However, litigants need to be ready to deal with the challenges of this area as soon as a diversity suit is brought to federal court. The general scenario will be the same: a case will be in federal court based on diversity of citizenship jurisdiction and there will be a question as to whether the federal way of handling something prevails over a state law. The conflict between a state provision and the federal approach can be early in a case, such as a question about when a case is deemed to be "filed," how claims should be plead, or the like. It can involve matters of what claims or parties can be joined. It can even involve differences in how the case proceeds through the system and whether something other than what is required typically in a federal case must be satisfied for the case to proceed. Although at first blush the issue here may seem a simple one, the Supreme Court has struggled mightily in this area. We will see how the pendulum swung wildly at first too far toward favoring the federal approach. Then the pendulum swung just as wildly to the position in which state law was applying in almost every case. The cases that "corrected" the imbalance—primarily *Byrd v. Blue Ridge*[393] and *Hanna v.*

---

[391] In most of the other chapters, one of the stages of the progress of a civil action is bolded to show where the topic of the chapter falls in the sequence of a suit. The Erie Doctrine is unique because the issue can arise at any stage of the progress of a civil action. Thus, no section is bolded in the chart.
[392] Erie R.R. v. Tompkins, 304 U.S. 64 (1938).
[393] Byrd v. Blue Ridge Rural Elec. Coop., 356 U.S. 525 (1958).

Plumer[394]—form the backbone of the modern analysis one would follow to determine whether federal or state law would apply today.

Experience teaches that *Erie* applies usually when two factors are present: (1) in a case based on state law brought in federal court under diversity jurisdiction; and (2) where there is a question of whether the state or federal rule or statute on point should apply. An experienced litigator will approach an *Erie* issue with not only a firm grasp on the legal precedent, but also a thorough understanding of the policies behind *Erie*. Some students find *Erie* to be a challenging concept to grasp, and that is often because it is not clear from legal precedent how to determine whether a federal rule or statute trumps a state rule. In the trickiest of *Erie* scenarios, the answer may come down to weighing the policy and purpose behind the federal rule in question against the state's interest in the state law to be enforced.

Whenever a diversity case is pending in federal court, the litigator would do well to consider whether any *Erie* conflicts arise. Moreover, the litigator needs to know the policies underlying each of the federal rule or statute implicated in a case. If the federal rule policies are strong, and if they conflict with a state provision that is not an element of the claim, the odds are that the federal rule or statute will govern. However, if the federal rule is not intended to address something that the state provision does address, and there is no conflict, then the state law can end up governing an issue even though at first blush one might think not. The only way to work through and develop the sensitivity to *Erie* issues is to practice analyzing fact patterns with the analytical framework this chapter will develop.

II. Applicable Law

A. The State of the Law Pre-*Erie*: Imbalance in Diversity Cases in Favor of Federal Courts

Erie deals with the interplay of federal and state rules alongside important federal provisions. The Supremacy Clause of the U.S. Constitution reads:

> This Constitution, and the Laws of the United States which shall be made in Pursuance thereof; and all Treaties made, or which shall be made, under the Authority of the United States, shall be the supreme Law of the Land; and the Judges in every State shall be bound thereby, any Thing in the Constitution or Laws of any State to the Contrary notwithstanding.[395]

Under the Rules of Decision Act, state law provides the underlying substantive law in cases in which no federal question is at issue (i.e., diversity cases):

> The laws of the several states, except where the Constitution or treaties of the United States or Acts of Congress otherwise require or provide, shall be regarded as rules of decision in civil actions in the courts of the United States, in cases where they apply.[396]

You will notice that it is not clear from the statute how to determine "cases where they apply." It

---

[394] Hanna v. Plumer, 380 U.S. 460 (1965).
[395] U.S. CONST. art. VI, cl. 2.
[396] 28 U.S.C. § 1652 (2017).

is also unclear what exactly is meant by "laws" of the states. Does that include common law, or statutes, or both?

In *Swift v. Tyson*, the Supreme Court construed the Rules of Decision Act to mean that the "laws of the several states" included only statutes, not court-made decisions (common law). The Court explained:

> In order to maintain the argument, it is essential, therefore, to hold, that the word 'laws,' in this section, includes within the scope of its meaning, the decisions of the local tribunals. In the ordinary use of language, it will hardly be contended, that the decisions of courts constitute laws. They are, at most, only evidence of what the laws are, and are not, of themselves, laws. They are often re-examined, reversed and qualified by the courts themselves, whenever they are found to be either defective, or ill-founded, or otherwise incorrect. The laws of a state are more usually understood to mean the rules and enactments promulgated by the legislative authority thereof, or long-established local customs having the force of laws. In all the various cases, which have hitherto come before us for decision, this court have uniformly supposed, that the true interpretation of the 34th section limited its application to state laws, strictly local, that is to say, to the positive statutes of the state, and the construction thereof adopted by the local tribunals, and to rights and titles to things having a permanent locality, such as the rights and titles to real estate, and other matters immovable and intra-territorial in their nature and character. It never has been supposed by us, that the section did apply, or was designed to apply, to questions of a more general nature, not at all dependent upon local statutes or local usages of a fixed and permanent operation. And we have not now the slightest difficulty in holding, that this section, upon its true intendment and construction, is strictly limited to local statutes and local usages of the character before stated.[397]

The Court in *Swift* thus created a distinction between matters of "general" and "local" laws in determining when a state law applied under the Rules of Decision Act. But this interpretation proved to be problematic, and *Swift* fell under increasing criticism

A visual depiction of the effect of *Swift*'s effect follows:

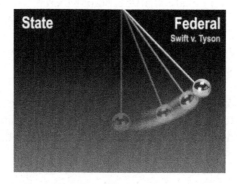

After *Swift* the pendulum fell too far on the side of federal power. By the court's erroneous reading

---

[397] Swift v. Tyson, 41 U.S. 1, 18-19 (1842) (emphasis added).

of the Rules of Decision Act, federal courts were permitted to develop their own federal com-mon law on matters that are inherently the realm of states—defining the common law of contracts, of torts, of property, and the like. When federal courts located in the same state as state courts were reaching decisions contrary to courts of the state in which the federal courts were sitting on issue of contracts, torts, property, and other common law topics, observers realized that something was very wrong. Litigants postured to get in federal or state court depending on which law favored them.

The case that best illustrated the flaw of Swift was *Black & White Taxicab Co. v. Brown & Yellow Taxicab Co.*[398] (Brown and Yellow Taxicab). There, Brown & Yellow Taxicab, a Kentucky corporation owned by Kentucky residents, and the Louisville & Nashville Railroad wanted to enter into a contract that granted Brown & Yellow exclusive rights to solicit passengers and baggage at the train station in Bowling Green, Kentucky. The only problem was that Kentucky law prohibited such anticompetitive, monopolistic contracts. Conversely, federal courts, which had developed their own "common law" on this question, deemed monopolistic contracts enforceable. Seeking federal law apply to an inevitable lawsuit, Brown & Yellow reincorporated in Tennessee so that there would be diversity between Black & White Taxicab. Despite Kentucky law's invalidation of such agreements, the federal district court in Kentucky—federal court being requires solely because Brown & Yellow was now completely diverse (Tennessee citizen from Black & Yellow (Kentucky citizen)—upheld the agreement. If litigated in in a Kentucky state court, the same agreement would have been held invalid. Due solely to its ability after reincorporating to invoke diversity jurisdiction and get into federal court, Brown & Yellow benefitted from federal law. The absurdity of such a result led an increasing number of jurists and scholars to call for the reversal of Swift. A decade after *Brown & Yellow Taxicab*, the opportunity for the Supreme Court to address the question came in *Erie v. Thompkins*, the case after which this area of law has since been named ever since.

B. The *Erie* Counterbalance: Moving Back Towards Application of State Law

Decisions such as *Brown & Yellow Taxicab* helped those who saw the flaws in *Swift v. Tyson* lead the charge to have that case overturned. These advocates had their day when the following decision was handed down.

ERIE R.R. CO. v. TOMPKINS
Supreme Court of the United States, 1938
58 S. Ct. 817

Mr. Justice BRANDEIS delivered the opinion of the Court.

The question for decision is whether the oft-challenged doctrine of *Swift v. Tyson* shall now be disapproved.

Tompkins, a citizen of Pennsylvania, was injured on a dark night by a passing freight train of the Erie Railroad Company while walking along its right of way at Hughestown in that state. He claimed that the accident occurred through negligence in the operation, or maintenance, of the train; that he was rightfully on the premises as licensee because on a commonly used beaten footpath which ran for a short distance alongside the tracks; and that he was struck by something which looked like a door projecting from one of the moving cars. To enforce that claim he brought an action in the federal court for Southern New York, which had jurisdiction because the company is a corporation of that state. It denied liability; and the

---

[398] 276 U.S. 518 (1928).

case was tried by a jury.

The Erie Railroad Company insisted that its duty to Tompkins was no greater than that owed to a trespasser. It contended, among other things, that its duty to Tompkins, and hence its liability, should be determined in accordance with the Pennsylvania law; that under the law of Pennsylvania, as declared by its highest court, persons who use pathways along the railroad right of way—that is, a longitudinal pathway as distinguished from a crossing—are to be deemed trespassers; and that the railroad is not liable for injuries to undiscovered trespassers resulting from its negligence, unless it be wanton or willful. Tompkins denied that any such rule had been established by the decisions of the Pennsylvania courts; and contended that, since there was no statute of the state on the subject, the railroad's duty and liability is to be determined in federal courts as a matter of general law.

The trial judge refused to rule that the applicable law precluded recovery. The jury brought in a verdict of $30,000; and the judgment entered thereon was affirmed by the Circuit Court of Appeals, which held that it was unnecessary to consider whether the law of Pennsylvania was as contended, because the question was one not of local, but of general, law, and that 'upon questions of general law the federal courts are free, in absence of a local statute, to exercise their independent judgment as to what the law is; and it is well settled that the question of the responsibility of a railroad for injuries caused by its servants is one of general law. . . Where the public has made open and notorious use of a railroad right of way for a long period of time and without objection, the company owes to persons on such permissive pathway a duty of care in the operation of its trains. . . . It is likewise generally recognized law that a jury may find that negligence exists toward a pedestrian using a permissive path on the railroad right of way if he is hit by some object projecting from the side of the train.'

The Erie had contended that application of the Pennsylvania rule was required, among other things, by section 34 of the Federal Judiciary Act of September 24, 1789, c. 20, 28 U.S.C. § 725, which provides: 'The laws of the several States, except where the Constitution, treaties, or statutes of the United States otherwise require or provide, shall be regarded as rules of decision in trials at common law, in the courts of the United States, in cases where they apply.'

Because of the importance of the question whether the federal court was free to disregard the alleged rule of the Pennsylvania common law, we granted certiorari.

First. *Swift v. Tyson* held that federal courts exercising jurisdiction on the ground of diversity of citizenship need not, in matters of general jurisprudence, apply the unwritten law of the state as declared by its highest court; that they are free to exercise an independent judgment as to what the common law of the state is—or should be; and that, as there stated by Mr. Justice Story, 'the true interpretation of the 34th section limited its application to state laws, strictly local, that is to say, to the positive statutes of the state, and the construction thereof adopted by the local tribunals, and to rights and titles to things having a permanent locality, such as the rights and titles to real estate, and other matters immovable and intra-territorial in their nature and character. It never has been supposed by us, that the section did apply, or was designed to apply, to questions of a more general nature, not at all dependent upon local statutes or local usages of a fixed and permanent operation, as, for example, to the construction of ordinary contracts or other written instruments, and especially to questions of general commercial law, where the state tribunals are called upon to perform the like functions as ourselves, that is, to ascertain, upon general reasoning and legal analogies, what is the true exposition of the contract or instrument, or what is the just rule furnished by the principles of commercial law to govern the case.'

The Court in applying the rule of section 34 [Rules of Decision Act] to equity cases, in *Mason v. United States* said: 'The statute, however, is merely declarative of the rule which would exist in the absence of the statute.' The federal courts assumed, in the broad field of 'general law,' the power to declare rules of decision which Congress was confessedly without power to enact as statutes. Doubt was repeatedly expressed as to the correctness of the construction given section 34, and as to the soundness of the rule which it introduced. But it was the more recent research of a competent scholar, who examined the original document, which established that the construction given to it by the Court was erroneous; and that the purpose of the section was merely to make certain that, in all matters except those in which some federal law is controlling, the federal courts exercising jurisdiction in diversity of citizenship cases would apply as their rules of decision the law of the state, unwritten as well as written.

Criticism of the doctrine became widespread after the decision of *Black & White Taxicab & Transfer Co. v. Brown & Yellow Taxicab & Transfer Co.*

Second. Experience in applying the doctrine of Swift v. Tyson, had revealed its defects, political and social; and the benefits expected to flow from the rule did not accrue. Persistence of state courts in their own opinions on questions of common law prevented uniformity; and the impossibility of discovering a satisfactory line of demarcation between the province of general law and that of local law developed a new well of uncertainties.

On the other hand, the mischievous results of the doctrine had become apparent. Diversity of citizenship jurisdiction was conferred in order to prevent apprehended discrimination in state courts against those not citizens of the state. *Swift v. Tyson* introduced grave discrimination by noncitizens against citizens. It made rights enjoyed under the unwritten 'general law' vary according to whether enforcement was sought in the state or in the federal court; and the privilege of selecting the court in which the right should be determined was conferred upon the noncitizen. Thus, the doctrine rendered impossible equal protection of the law. In attempting to promote uniformity of law throughout the United States, the doctrine had prevented uniformity in the administration of the law of the state.

The discrimination resulting became in practice far-reaching. This resulted in part from the broad province accorded to the so-called 'general law' as to which federal courts exercised an independent judgment. In addition to questions of purely commercial law, 'general law' was held to include the obligations under contracts entered into and to be performed within the state, the extent to which a carrier operating within a state may stipulate for exemption from liability for his own negligence or that of his employee; the liability for torts committed within the state upon persons resident or property located there, even where the question of liability depended upon the scope of a property right conferred by the state; and the right to exemplary or punitive damages. Furthermore, state decisions construing local deeds, mineral conveyances, and even devises of real estate, were disregarded.

In part the discrimination resulted from the wide range of persons held entitled to avail themselves of the federal rule by resort to the diversity of citizenship jurisdiction. Through this jurisdiction individual citizens willing to remove from their own state and become citizens of another might avail themselves of the federal rule. And, without even change of residence, a corporate citizen of the state could avail itself of the federal rule by reincorporating under the laws of another state, as was done in the Taxicab Case.

The injustice and confusion incident to the doctrine of *Swift v. Tyson* have been repeatedly urged as reasons for abolishing or limiting diversity of citizenship jurisdiction. Other legislative relief has been proposed. If only a question of statutory construction were involved, we should not be prepared to abandon a doctrine so widely applied throughout nearly a century. But the unconstitutionality of the course pursued has now been made clear, and compels us to do so.

Third. Except in matters governed by the Federal Constitution or by acts of Congress, the law to be applied in any case is the law of the state. And whether the law of the state shall be declared by its Legislature in a statute or by its highest court in a decision is not a matter of federal concern. There is no federal general common law. Congress has no power to declare substantive rules of common law applicable in a state whether they be local in their nature or 'general,' be they commercial law or a part of the law of torts. And no clause in the Constitution purports to confer such a power upon the federal courts. As stated by Mr. Justice Field when protesting in *Baltimore & Ohio R.R. Co. v. Baugh*, against ignoring the Ohio common law of fellow-servant liability:

'I am aware that what has been termed the general law of the country— which is often little less than what the judge advancing the doctrine thinks at the time should be the general law on a particular subject—has been often advanced in judicial opinions of this court to control a conflicting law of a state. I admit that learned judges have fallen into the habit of repeating this doctrine as a convenient mode of brushing aside the law of a state in conflict with their views. And I confess that, moved and governed by the authority of the great names of those judges, I have, myself, in many instances, unhesitatingly and confidently, but I think now erroneously, repeated the same doctrine. But, notwithstanding the great names which may be cited in favor of the doctrine, and notwithstanding the frequency with which the doctrine has been reiterated, there stands, as a perpetual protest against its repetition, the constitution of the United States, which recognizes and preserves the autonomy and independence of the states,—independence in their legislative and independence in their judicial departments. Supervision over either the legislative or the judicial action of the states is in no case permissible except as to matters by the constitution specifically authorized or delegated to the United States. Any interference with either, except as thus permitted, is an invasion of the authority of the state, and, to that extent, a denial of its independence.'

The fallacy underlying the rule declared in *Swift v. Tyson* is made clear by Mr. Justice Holmes. The doctrine rests upon the assumption that there is 'a transcendental body of law outside of any particular State but obligatory within it unless and until changed by statute,' that federal courts have the power to use their judgment as to what the rules of common law are; and that in the federal courts 'the parties are entitled to an independent judgment on matters of general law':

'But law in the sense in which courts speak of it today does not exist with-out some definite authority behind it. The common law so far as it is enforced in a State, whether called common law or not, is not the common law generally but the law of that State existing by the authority of that State without regard to what it may have been in England or anywhere else.

'The authority and only authority is the State, and if that be so, the voice adopted by the State as its own (whether it be of its Legislature or of its Supreme Court) should utter the last word.' Thus[,] the doctrine of *Swift v. Tyson* is, as Mr. Justice Holmes said, 'an unconstitutional assumption of powers by the Courts of the United States which no lapse of time or respectable array of opinion should make us hesitate to correct.' In disapproving that doctrine we do not hold unconstitutional section 34 of the Federal Judiciary Act of 1789 or any other act of Congress. We merely declare that in applying the doctrine this Court and the lower courts have invaded rights which in our opinion are reserved by the Constitution to the several states.

Fourth. The defendant contended that by the common law of Pennsylvania as declared by its highest court in *Falchetti v. Pennsylvania R.R. Co.*,[399] the only duty owed to the plaintiff was to refrain from willful or wanton injury. The plaintiff denied that such is the Pennsylvania law. In support of their respective contentions the parties discussed and cited many decisions of the Supreme Court of the state. The Circuit Court of Appeals ruled that the question of liability is one of general law; and on that ground declined to decide the issue of state law. As we hold this was error, the judgment is reversed and the case remanded to it for further proceedings in conformity with our opinion.

Reversed.

Mr. Justice REED (concurring in part).

I concur in the conclusion reached in this case, in the disapproval of the doctrine of Swift v. Tyson, and in the reasoning of the majority opinion, except in so far as it relies upon the unconstitutionality of the 'course pursued' by the federal courts.

The 'doctrine of *Swift v. Tyson*,' as I understand it, is that the words 'the laws,' as used in § 34, line 1, of the Federal Judiciary Act of September 24, 1789, 28 U.S.C.A. § 725, do not included in their meaning 'the decisions of the local tribunals.' Mr. Justice Story, in deciding that point, said, 'Undoubtedly, the decisions of the local tribunals upon such subjects are entitled to, and will receive, the most deliberate attention and respect of this court; but they cannot furnish positive rules, or conclusive authority, by which our own judgments are to be bound up and governed.'

To decide the case now before us and to 'disapprove' the doctrine of *Swift v. Tyson* requires only that we say that the words 'the laws' include in their meaning the decisions of the local tribunals. As the majority opinion shows, by its reference to Mr. Warren's researches and the first quotation from Mr. Justice Holmes, that this Court is now of the view that 'laws' includes 'decisions,' it is unnecessary to go further and declare that the 'course pursued 'was 'unconstitutional,' instead of merely erroneous.

The 'unconstitutional' course referred to in the majority opinion is apparently the ruling in Swift v. Tyson that the supposed omission of Congress to legislate as to the effect of decisions leaves federal courts free to interpret general law for themselves. I am not at all sure whether, in the absence of federal statutory direction, federal courts would be compelled to follow state decisions. There was enough doubt about the matter in 1789 to induce the first Congress to legislate. No former opinions of this Court have passed upon it. Mr. Justice Holmes evidently saw nothing 'unconstitutional' which required the overruling of Swift v. Tyson, for he said in the very opinion quoted by the majority, 'I should leave *Swift v. Tyson* undisturbed, as I indicated in *Kuhn v. Fairmont Coal Co.*, but I would not allow it to spread the assumed dominion into new fields.' *Black & White Taxicab Co. v. Brown & Yellow Taxicab Co.* If the opinion commits this Court to the position that the Congress is without power to declare what rules of substantive law shall govern the federal courts, that conclusion also seems questionable. The line between procedural and substantive law is hazy, but no one doubts federal power over procedure. The Judiciary Article, 3, and the 'necessary and proper' clause of article 1, § 8, may fully authorize legislation, such as this section of the Judiciary Act.

In this Court, stare decisis, in statutory construction, is a useful rule, not an inexorable command. It seems preferable to overturn an established construction of an act of Congress, rather than, in the circumstances of this case, to interpret the Constitution.

---

[399] 307 Pa. 203 (1932).

There is no occasion to discuss further the range or soundness of these few phrases of the opinion. It is sufficient now to call attention to them and express my own non-acquiescence.

Follow-Up Questions and Comments

1. What would the result in *Erie* have been if the approach of *Swift v. Tyson* had been followed? What change in the interpretation of the Rules of Decision Act did the Court make so that state law governed the underlying claim?

2. What "mischievous results" did the Court identify as flowing from *Swift v. Tyson*? The Court saw an element in which *Swift v. Tyson* was unconstitutional. What did the Court in *Erie* suggest was unconstitutional about *Swift*'s approach?

3. Felix Frankfurter, before he ascended to the Supreme Court, was a professor who corresponded with President Franklin Roosevelt. Although many did not realize at the time that *Erie* marked a major correction in constitutional balance between state and federal governments, the decision was not lost on Frankfurter. In a letter to Roosevelt, he wrote: "I certainly didn't expect to live to see the day when the Court would announce, as they did Monday, that it itself has usurped power for nearly a hundred years. And think not a single New York paper—at least none that I saw—having a nose for the significance of such a decision."[400]

4. The state in which Mr. Thompkins was injured was Pennsylvania. Thompkins, however, filed suit in New York. In *Erie*, the Court ruled that the railroad's standard of care derived from state law, not federal law. However, the Court did not indicate which state's law would apply in a scenario such as this. The court assumed Pennsylvania law would apply but did not explain the basis by which he reached that state's law as applicable in a federal court in New York. Later, in *Klaxon Company v. Stentor Electric Manufacturing Company*,[401] the Court held that in diversity cases the federal court should apply the conflict of law rules of the state in which the federal court is located. Thus, if that approach had been followed in *Erie*, the New York federal court would have applied New York's conflicts of law rules. Those rules likely would have pointed to Pennsylvania because the accident occurred there. In short, the Court's assumption in *Erie* that Pennsylvania law applied was accurate, but it did not explain the means by which courts in states other than the one where an accident happened can end up applying another state's law.

5. Justice Reed's concurring opinion could be the source of the "substance" versus "procedure" approach that is so alluring in, but which ultimately is not the ideal approach to resolving, situations where federal law and state law are in tension, which law should govern. We will see the further struggles below, after *Erie*, to deal with questions that were not clearly related to the underlying claim and thus required more analysis. In other words, one cannot simply use labels "substance" or "procedure" without providing analysis to support the conclusion.

---

[400] Roosevelt and Frankfurter: Their Correspondence 1928-45, 456 (Max Freedman ed., 1967).
[401] 313 U.S. 487 (1941).

A prior diagram showed the imbalance in the equilibrium between federal and state powers resulting from *Swift v. Tyson*. Following is a visual depiction of the "correction" to the imbalance achieved by *Erie v. Thompkins*:

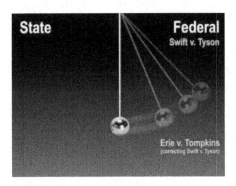

C. *Erie* and the Outcome-Determinative Test

Although *Erie* corrected the balance of state verses federal law in diversity cases, it left for future cases some key questions. For instance, on what issues must federal courts apply state laws? In his concurrence in *Erie*, Justice Reed suggested it came down to whether the issue was one of "substance" or "procedure." However, the Court revisited this issue in *Guaranty Trust Co. v. York*[402] and established instead an analysis based on how the rule at issue would affect the outcome of the case. It helps to think of this test as the "outcome-determinative test." In Guaranty Trust, the Court faced the question of whether the doctrine of laches (a form of the statute of limitations applied in equity) would bar the plaintiff's suit. Under state law, the case would clearly have been barred. Under federal law, it was not clear that the case would be barred. Applying its "outcome-determinative" test, the Court held that applying federal law would change the outcome. Thus, to correct for that, the Court's outcome-determinative test required state law to apply. The Court in *Guaranty Trust* explained the test as follows:

Here, we are dealing with a right to recover derived not from the United States but from one of the States. When, because the plaintiff happens to be a nonresident, such a right is enforceable in a federal as well as in a State court, the forms and mode of enforcing the right may at times, naturally enough, vary because the two judicial systems are not identic [sic]. But since a federal court adjudicating a state-created right solely because of the diversity of citizenship of the parties is for that purpose, in effect, only another court of the State, it cannot afford recovery if the right to recover is made unavailable by the State nor can it substantially affect the enforcement of the right as given by the State. And so [,] the question is not whether a statute of limitations is deemed a matter of "procedure" in some sense. The question is whether such a statute concerns merely the manner and the means by which a right to recover, as recognized by the State, is enforced, or whether such statutory limitation is a matter of substance in the aspect that alone is relevant to our problem, namely, does it significantly affect the result of a litigation for a federal court to disregard a law of a State that would be controlling in an action upon the same claim by the same parties in a State court?

It is therefore immaterial whether statutes of limitation are characterized either as "substantive" or "procedural" in State court opinions in any use of those terms unrelated to the specific issue before us. *Erie*

---

[402] Guaranty Trust Co. v. York, 326 U.S. 99 (1945).

Railroad Company v. Tompkins was not an endeavor to formulate scientific legal terminology. It expressed a policy that touches vitally the proper distribution of judicial power between State and federal courts. In essence, the intent of that decision was to insure . . . where a federal court is exercising jurisdiction solely because of the diversity of citizenship of the parties, the outcome of the litigation in the federal court should be substantially the same, so far as legal rules determine the outcome of a litigation, as it would be if tried in a State court. The nub of the policy that underlies *Erie*[] is that for the same transaction the accident of a suit by a non-resident litigant in a federal court instead of in a State court a block away, should not lead to a substantially different result. . . . Plainly enough, a statute that would completely bar recovery in a suit if brought in a State court bears on a State created right vitally and not merely formally or negligibly. As to consequences that so intimately affect recovery or non-recovery a federal court in a diversity case should follow State law.[403]

The problem with the *Guaranty Trust* outcome-determinative approach was that it proved too much. In other words, if there was any difference between federal and state law, it almost always could be said to affect the outcome. An example of the degree to which this threw the balance far in the direction of state law is *Cohen v. Beneficial Industrial Loan Corp.*,[404] a case involving Federal Rule of Civil Procedure 23.1. That Rule set forth the procedures for a derivative action—a suit in which shareholders in a corporation seek to enforce the rights of the corporation when they believe the management has not done so—and did not require a bond to be posted by the plaintiffs. By contrast, New Jersey law—the state in which the federal suit in Cohen was pending—required shareholders to post a significant bond to bring a derivative action. Applying Guaranty Trust, the Court in Cohen ruled that New Jersey's requirement of a significant bond must apply because, otherwise, the lack of a bond requirement under the Federal Rule could affect the outcome.

The real problem with a test that focused on the difference in outcome-based outcome-under-state-law state versus outcome-under-federal-law is that it failed to recognize the Constitution's authorization of Congress and the Supreme Court to adopt procedures and rules for handling cases in federal courts. The Rules Enabling Act, 28 U.S.C. § 2072, carries out the constitutional grant for Congress to make rules for the handling of federal court cases. That Act permits the Supreme Court to propose rules of procedure, which Congress ultimately allows, modifies, or disallows. These are the source for the Federal Rules of Civil Procedure. During the Guaranty Trust era, the Court was ignoring Congress' constitutional power to enact rules to govern the means by which federal courts operate. Such power arose from the grant of authority in both Article I, Section 8 and in Article III to create tribunals inferior to the United States Supreme Court.[405]

That the federal courts had their own constitutional authority, in diversity cases, to run their courts as permitted under the Rules, thus seemed to have been lost on the Court in the period in which Guaranty Trust held sway. The new imbalance, this time far to the side of state power, is shown below:

---

[403] Guaranty Trust Co. of N.Y. v. York, 326 U.S. 99, 108–10 (1945) (emphasis added).
[404] 337 U.S. 541 (1949).
[405] *See* 19 CHARLES ALAN WRIGHT & ARTHUR R. MILLER, FEDERAL PRACTICE AND PROCEDURE § 4505 (2d ed. 2018).

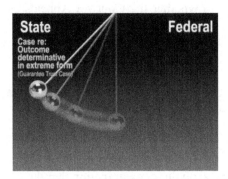

D. Fixing the Flaws in the Outcome-Determinative Test

As already suggested, it became apparent that under the outcome-determinative test an argument could be made that the difference between state and federal law is determinative in most scenarios. This reality suggested that, under the Guaranty outcome-determinative test, federal courts would have to follow state law on even the smallest matters. Such an approach cast doubt on the strength and legitimacy of the Federal Rules. But the Court addresses this problem to some extent in the following case decided less than a decade after Guaranty Trust. By reducing the outcome-determinative test to one of three factors (adding state-interest factor and federal-interest factor), the decision in *Byrd v. Blue Ridge* began a "correction" in the analysis.

BYRD v. BLUE RIDGE RURAL ELECTRIC COOPERATIVE, INC.
Supreme Court of the United States, 1958
356 U.S. 525

Mr. Justice BRENNAN delivered the opinion of the Court.

This case was brought in the District Court for the Western District of South Carolina. Jurisdiction was based on diversity of citizenship. 28 U.S.C. §1332, 28 U.S.C.A. § 1332. The petitioner, a resident of North Carolina, sued respondent, a South Carolina corporation, for damages for injuries allegedly caused by the respondent's negligence. He had judgment on a jury verdict. The Court of Appeals for the Fourth Circuit reversed and directed the entry of judgment for the respondent. We granted certiorari, and subsequently ordered reargument.

The respondent is in the business of selling electric power to subscribers in rural sections of South Carolina. The petitioner was employed as a lineman in the construction crew of a construction contractor. The contractor, R. H. Bouligny, Inc., held a contract with the respondent in the amount of $334,300 for the building of some 24 miles of new power lines, the reconversion to higher capacities of about 88 miles of existing lines, and the construction of 2 new substations and a breaker station. The petitioner was injured while connecting power lines to one of the new substations.

One of respondent's affirmative defenses was that under the South Carolina Workmen's Compensation Act, the petitioner—because the work contracted to be done by his employer was work of the kind also done by the respondent's own construction and maintenance crews—had the status of a statutory employee of the respondent and was therefore barred from suing the respondent at law because obliged to accept statutory compensation benefits as the exclusive remedy for his injuries. Two questions concerning this defense are before us: (1) whether the Court of Appeals erred in directing judgment for respondent without a remand to give petitioner an opportunity to introduce further evidence; and (2) whether petitioner, state practice notwithstanding, is entitled to a jury determination of the factual issues raised by this defense.

I

The Supreme Court of South Carolina has held that there is no particular formula by which to determine whether an owner is a statutory employer under § 72—111.[406]

. . .

The respondent's manager testified on direct examination that three of its substations were built by the respondent's own construction and maintenance crews. When pressed on cross-examination, however, his answers left his testimony in such doubt as to lead the trial judge to say, 'I understood he changed his testimony, that they had not built three.' But the credibility of the manager's testimony, and the general question whether the evidence in support of the affirmative defense presented a jury issue, became irrelevant because of the interpretation given § 72—111 by the trial judge. In striking respondent's affirmative defense at the close of all the evidence he ruled that the respondent was the statutory employer of the petitioner only if the construction work done by respondent's crews was done for somebody else, and was not the statutory employer if, as the proofs showed, the crews built facilities only for the respondent's own use. 'My idea of engaging in the business is to do something for somebody else. What they (the respondent) are doing—and everything they do about repairing lines and building substations, they do it for themselves.' On this view of the meaning of the statute, the evidence, even accepting the manager's testimony on direct examination as true, lacked proof of an essential element of the affirmative defense, and there was thus nothing for the petitioner to meet with proof of his own.

The Court of Appeals disagreed with the District Court's construction of § 72—111. Relying on the decisions of the Supreme Court of South Carolina, . . . the Court of Appeals held that the statute granted respondent immunity from the action if the proofs established that the respondent's own crews had constructed lines and substations which, like the work contracted to the petitioner's employer, were necessary for the distribution of the electric power which the respondent was in the business of selling. We ordinarily accept the interpretation of local law by the Court of Appeals and do so readily here since neither party now disputes the interpretation.

However, instead of ordering a new trial at which the petitioner might offer his own proof pertinent to a determination according to the correct interpretation, the Court of Appeals made its own determination on the record and directed a judgment for the respondent.

We believe that the Court of Appeals erred. Although the respondent's evidence was sufficient to withstand the motion under the meaning given the statute by the Court of Appeals, it presented a fact question, which, in the circumstances of this case to be discussed infra, is properly to be decided by a jury. This is clear not only because of the issue of the credibility of the manager's vital testimony, but also because, even should the jury resolve that issue as did the Court of Appeals, the jury on the entire record—consistent with the view of the South Carolina cases that this question is in each case largely one of degree

---

[406] The Worker's Compensation "bar" prevents an employee from suing his or her employer for injuries sustained on the job. The sole source of relief is through the Workers' Compensation Commission, not through the courts. If someone who might otherwise be considered an independent contractor is doing the work of an employee, such a person is deemed to be hired by the "statutory employer" and be a "statutory employee"—i.e., will be barred from suing the employer as if he or she were an actual employee.

254

and of fact—might reasonably reach an opposite conclusion from the Court of Appeals as to the ultimate fact whether the respondent was a statutory employer.

. . .

II

A question is also presented as to whether on remand the factual issue is to be decided by the judge or by the jury. The respondent argues on the basis of the decision of the Supreme Court of South Carolina in *Adams v. Davison-Paxon Co.*,[407] that the issue of immunity should be decided by the judge and not by the jury. That was a negligence action brought in the state trial court against a store owner by an employee of an independent contractor who operated the store's millinery department. The trial judge denied the store owner's motion for a directed verdict made upon the ground that § 72—111 barred the plaintiff's action. The jury returned a verdict for the plaintiff. The South Carolina Supreme Court reversed, holding that it was for the judge and not the jury to decide on the evidence whether the owner was a statutory employer, and that the store owner had sustained his defense. The court rested its holding on decisions, listed in footnote 8, infra, involving judicial review of the Industrial Commission and said:

> Thus the trial court should have in this case resolved the conflicts in the evidence and determined the fact of whether (the independent contractor) was performing a part of the 'trade, business or occupation' of the department store-appellant and, therefore, whether (the employee's) remedy is exclusively under the Workmen's Compensation Law.

The respondent argues that this state-court decision governs the present diversity case and 'divests the jury of its normal function' to decide the disputed fact question of the respondent's immunity under § 72—111. This is to contend that the federal court is bound under *Erie Railroad Company v. Tompkins*, to follow the state court's holding to secure uniform enforcement of the immunity created by the State.

First. It was decided in *Erie []* that the federal courts in diversity cases must respect the definition of state-created rights and obligations by the state courts. We must, therefore, first examine the rule in Adams v. Davison-Paxon Co. to determine whether it is bound up with these rights and obligations in such a way that its application in the federal court is required.

The Workmen's Compensation Act is administered in South Carolina by its Industrial Commission. The South Carolina courts hold that, on judicial review of actions of the Commission under § 72—111, the question whether the claim of an injured workman is within the Commission's jurisdiction is a matter of law for decision by the court, which makes its own findings of fact relating to that jurisdiction. The South Carolina Supreme Court states no reasons in *Adams v. Davison-Paxon Co[mpany]* why, although the jury decides all other factual issues raised by the cause of action and defenses, the jury is displaced as to the factual issue raised by the affirmative defense under § 72—111. The decisions cited to support the holding are those listed in footnote 8, which are concerned solely with defining the scope and method of judicial review of the Industrial Commission. A State may, of course, distribute the functions of its judicial machinery as it sees fit. The decisions relied upon, however, furnish no reason for selecting the judge rather than the jury to decide this single affirmative defense in the negligence action. They simply reflect a policy . . . that administrative determination of 'jurisdictional facts' should not be final but subject to judicial review. The conclusion is inescapable that the [South Carolina approach of having judges, not juries, find

---

[407] 96 S.E.2d 566 (1957).

facts on whether the Workers' Compensation bar applies] is grounded in the practical consideration that the question had theretofore come before the South Carolina courts from the Industrial Commission and the courts had become accustomed to deciding the factual issue of immunity without the aid of juries. We find nothing to suggest that this rule was announced as an integral part of the special relationship created by the statute. Thus[,] the requirement appears to be merely a form and mode of enforcing the immunity . . . and not a rule intended to be bound up with the definition of the rights and obligations of the parties.

Second. But cases following Erie have evinced a broader policy to the effect that the federal courts should conform as near as may be—in the absence of other considerations—to state rules even of form and mode where the state rules may bear substantially on the question whether the litigation would come out one way in the federal court and another way in the state court if the federal court failed to apply a particular local rule.[408] Concededly the nature of the tribunal which tries issues may be important in the enforcement of the parcel of rights making up a cause of action or defense, and bear significantly upon achievement of uniform enforcement of the right. It may well be that in the instant personal-injury case the outcome would be substantially affected by whether the issue of immunity is decided by a judge or a jury. Therefore, were 'outcome' the only consideration, a strong case might appear for saying that the federal court should follow the state practice.

But there are affirmative countervailing considerations at work here. The federal system is an independent system for administering justice to litigants who properly invoke its jurisdiction. An essential characteristic of that system is the manner in which, in civil common-law actions, it distributes trial functions between judge and jury and, under the influence—if not the command—of the Seventh Amendment, assigns the decisions of disputed questions of fact to the jury. The policy of uniform enforcement of state-created rights and obligations,[409] cannot in every case exact compliance with a state rule—not bound up with rights and obligations—which disrupts the federal system of allocating functions between judge and jury. Thus[,] the inquiry here is whether the federal policy favoring jury decisions of disputed fact questions should yield to the state rule in the interest of furthering the objective that the litigation should not come out one way in the federal court and another way in the state court.

We think that in the circumstances of this case the federal court should not follow the state rule. It cannot be gainsaid that there is a strong federal policy against allowing state rules to disrupt the judge-jury relationship in the federal courts. In *Herron v. Southern Pacific Co[mpany]*, the trial judge in a personal-injury negligence action brought in the District Court for Arizona on diversity grounds directed a verdict for the defendant when it appeared as a matter of law that the plaintiff was guilty of contributory negligence. The federal judge refused to be bound by a provision of the Arizona Constitution which made the jury the sole arbiter of the question of contributory negligence. This Court sustained the action of the trial judge, holding that 'state laws cannot alter the essential character or function of a federal court' because that function 'is not in any sense a local matter, and state statutes which would interfere with the appropriate performance of that function are not binding upon the federal court under either the Conformity Act or the 'Rules of Decision' Act.' Perhaps even more clearly in light of the influence of the Seventh Amendment, the function assigned to the jury 'is an essential factor in the process for which the Federal Constitution provides.'

Third. We have discussed the problem upon the assumption that the outcome of the litigation may be substantially affected by whether the issue of immunity is decided by a judge or a jury. But clearly there

---

[408] *E.g.*, Guaranty Trust Co. of New York v. York, 326 U.S. 99 (1945).
[409] *Id*,

is not present here the certainty that a different result would follow,[410] or even the strong possibility that this would be the case. There are factors present here which might reduce that possibility. The trial judge in the federal system has powers denied the judges of many States to comment on the weight of evidence and credibility of witnesses, and discretion to grant a new trial if the verdict appears to him to be against the weight of the evidence. We do not think the likelihood of a different result is so strong as to require the federal practice of jury determination of disputed factual issues to yield to the state rule in the interest of uniformity of outcome.

The Court of Appeals did not consider other grounds of appeal raised by the respondent because the ground taken disposed of the case. We accordingly remand the case to the Court of Appeals for the decision of the other questions, with instructions that, if not made unnecessary by the decision of such questions, the Court of Appeals shall remand the case to the District Court for a new trial of such issues as the Court of Appeals may direct.

Reversed and remanded.

Follow-Up Questions and Comments

1. The worker's compensation bar is a prevalent defense. The notion is that, if an employer pays workers' compensation insurance, then an injured employee ought to be able to proceed for job-related injuries solely in the worker's compensation claim system, not in regular court proceedings. The twist that we see here is that even if the employee is technically not on the payroll of a company, if the party is doing the work an employee of the company would ordinarily do, then that person is deemed a "statutory employee." If a plaintiff is deemed such, she must use the worker's compensation system as her exclusive injury for job related compensation. The question of whether an independent contractor is a "statutory employee," and thus subject to the worker's compensation bar, involves factual questions that must be resolved.

2. What factfinder (judge or jury) did South Carolina have resolve the fact question of whether a person was a "statutory employee"?

3. What is the federal system's approach to resolving factual disputes in general, as best you can tell from *Byrd*?

4. What factors did the *Byrd* decision suggest should be accounted for before deciding whether state law or federal law applied under *Erie*?

5. Did the approach include as part of the analysis the outcome-determinative factor other factors separate from the outcome-determinative analysis? If so, was the outcome-determinative test at least diminished in *Byrd* by the focus on federal interests and on state interests as significant factors apart from the outcome-determinative test? was it different, however, from the approach of *Guaranty Trust*? The key to *Byrd* may be found here—how it considered outcome determination but also considered the other factors as equal considerations in a balancing test.

---

[410] *Cf. id.*

The diagram below shows the partial correction achieved by the *Byrd* case.

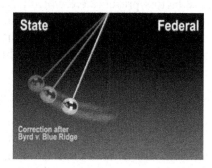

E. Completing the "Correction": *Hanna* and the Rules Enabling Act

In *Hanna*, the Court finished the last leg of the modern *Erie* doctrine. But before moving on to *Hanna*, take a moment to carefully read the following text from the Rules Enabling Act and an important case interpreting that Act. The Rules Enabling Act is crucial to the *Hanna/Erie* analysis.

§ 2072. Rules of procedure and evidence; power to prescribe

> The Supreme Court shall have the power to prescribe general rules of practice and procedure and rules of evidence for cases in the United States district courts (including proceedings before magistrate judges thereof) and courts of appeals. Such rules shall not abridge, enlarge or modify any substantive right. All laws in conflict with such rules shall be of no further force or effect after such rules have taken effect.[411]

If a Federal Rule is "valid" as adopted under the Rules Enabling Act (REA), the Rule will, under the Constitution's Supremacy clause and the reasoning of *Hanna v. Plumer*, trump any state law inconsistent with the valid Federal Rule. A Federal Rule will be valid so long as (1) it deals with management of a lawsuit, such that it can in some way be deemed "procedural"; and (2) does not "abridge, enlarge or modify" substantive rights. The second criteria seems like it might be one that could be a problem in some cases. Because of the manner in which the "abridge, enlarge, or modify" language has been interpreted, Federal Rules will inevitably pass the REA test. In *Sibbach v. Wilson & Company*,[412] for instance, the state whose law applied had a statute ensuring citizens of the state the ability to refuse medical examinations against their consent as an absolute right. The defendant in *Sibbach*, however, pointed to Rule 35—the Federal Rule that allows a defendant to move for a medical examination, and for the federal court to require one—whenever the plaintiff in a case puts his or her medical condition at issue by suing for injuries. If ever one could have argued that a Federal Rule "abridged . . . or modified" substantive law, this case would have been the one to qualify. However, the Court held that so long as the Rule is in some way procedural, it can have a great incidental impact on one's substantive rights and still be a valid Rule under the REA.[413] In short, the *Sibbach* and later rulings apply an extremely generous test for validity of a Federal Rule leave one wondering what it would take for a Federal Rule to ever be held invalid. In fact, to date no

---

[411] 28 U.S.C. § 2072 (2015).
[412] 312 U.S. 1 (1941).
[413] *See also* Mississippi Pub. Corp. v. Murphree, 326 U.S. 438, 445 (1946) (citing *Sibbach* as establishing an "incidental impact" test in which the Federal Rule would be valid, as suggested, if in any way procedure despite an incidental impact on substantive rights).

Federal Rule has been held invalid under this test.

Follow-Up Questions and Comments

1. Please see 28 U.S.C. § 2072, the modern version of the REA, which essentially is the same as that examined in *Sibbach*. Subsection (1) provides that the Supreme Court can prescribe rules of procedure. Moreover, subsection (2) provides that the rules "shall not abridge, enlarge or modify any substantive rights." What test did the *Sibbach* case state as the key criteria for determining whether a rule will be deemed valid and not abridging, enlarging, or modifying any substantive right? Commentators, though not all in favor of such a forgiving test, agree that the test in *Sibbach* will mean a Rule is valid so long as it seeks to effect procedure, even if the incidental impact on substantive rights is significant.[414]

III. No Federal Rule of Civil Procedure has yet been held invalid under *Sibbach*.

As we will now see in *Hanna*, when dealing with an *Erie* issue where a Federal Rule of Civil Procedure is involved, analysis should begin with examination of the validity of the Rule in question. There will be an additional aspect of the analysis explained in *Hanna*: is the Rule applicable or "on point" so that it conflicts with the state law or can the Federal Rule or Statute and state law coexist because the Federal Rule's policy is not intended to deal with whatever the state law in question requires? When there is no Federal Rule or Statute on point, then the analysis should proceed under the Rules of Decision Act discussed at the beginning of this chapter—essentially a *Byrd* analysis with a twist added by *Hanna*.

HANNA v. PLUMER
Supreme Court of the United States, 1965
380 U.S. 460

Mr. Chief Justice WARREN delivered the opinion of the Court.

The question to be decided is whether, in a civil action where the jurisdiction of the United States district court is based upon diversity of citizenship between the parties, service of process shall be made in the manner prescribed by state law or that set forth in Rule 4(d) (1) of the Federal Rules of Civil Procedure.

On February 6, 1963, petitioner, a citizen of Ohio, filed her complaint in the District Court for the District of Massachusetts, claiming damages in excess of $10,000 for personal injuries resulting from an automobile accident in South Carolina, allegedly caused by the negligence of one Louise Plumer Osgood, a Massachusetts citizen deceased at the time of the filing of the complaint. Respondent, Mrs. Osgood's executor and also a Massachusetts citizen, was named as defendant. On February 8, service was made by leaving copies of the summons and the complaint with respondent's wife at his residence, concededly in compliance with Rule 4(d) (1), which provides:

> The summons and complaint shall be served together. The plaintiff shall furnish
> the person making service with such copies as are necessary. Service shall be made

---

[414] *See, e.g.,* Kevin M. Clermont, *The Repressible Myth of Shady Grove*, 86 NORTE DAME L. REV. 987, 1004–05 (2011).

as follows:

(1) Upon an individual other than an infant or an incompetent person, by delivering a copy of the summons and of the complaint to him personally or by leaving copies thereof at his dwelling house or usual place of abode with some person of suitable age and discretion then residing therein.

Respondent filed his answer on February 26, alleging, inter alia, that the action could not be maintained because it had been brought 'contrary to and in violation of the provisions of Massachusetts General Laws (Ter. Ed.) Chapter 197, Section 9.' That section provides:

Except as provided in this chapter, an executor or administrator shall not be held to answer to an action by a creditor of the deceased which is not commenced within one year from the time of his giving bond for the performance of his trust, or to such an action which is commenced within said year unless before the expiration thereof the writ in such action has been served by delivery in hand upon such executor or administrator or service thereof accepted by him or a notice stating the name of the estate, the name and address of the creditor, the amount of the claim and the court in which the action has been brought has been filed in the proper registry of probate.[415]

On October 17, 1963, the District Court granted respondent's motion for summary judgment, citing . . . *Guaranty Trust Co. of New York v. York*,[416] in support of its conclusion that the adequacy of the service was to be measured by § 9, with which, the court held, petitioner had not complied. On appeal, petitioner admitted noncompliance with § 9, but argued that Rule 4(d) (1) defines the method by which service of process is to be affected in diversity actions. The Court of Appeals for the First Circuit, finding that '[r]elatively recent amendments (to § 9) evince a clear legislative purpose to require personal notification within the year,' concluded that the conflict of state and federal rules was over 'a substantive rather than a procedural matter,' and unanimously affirmed.[417] Because of the threat to the goal of uniformity of federal procedure posed by the decision below, we granted certiorari.

We conclude that the adoption of Rule 4(d) (1), designed to control service of process in diversity actions, neither exceeded the congressional mandate embodied in the Rules Enabling Act nor transgressed constitutional bounds, and that the Rule is therefore the standard against which the District Court should have measured the adequacy of the service. Accordingly, we reverse the decision of the Court of Appeals.

The Rules Enabling Act,[418] provides, in pertinent part:

The Supreme Court shall have the power to prescribe, by general rules, the forms of process, writs, pleadings, and motions, and the practice and procedure of the district courts of the United States in civil actions. Such rules shall not abridge, enlarge or modify any substantive right and shall preserve the right of trial by jury.

Under the cases construing the scope of the Enabling Act, Rule 4(d) (1) clearly passes muster.

---

[415] MASS. GEN. LAWS ANN., c. 197, sec. 9 (1958).
[416] 326 U.S. 99
[417] 331 F.2d 157.
[418] 28 U.S.C. s 2072 (1958 ed.).

Prescribing the manner in which a defendant is to be notified that a suit has been instituted against him, it relates to the 'practice and procedure of the district courts.'

The test must be whether a rule really regulates procedure,—the judicial process for enforcing rights and duties recognized by substantive law and for justly administering remedy and redress for disregard or infraction of them.'[419]

In *Mississippi Pub. Corp. v. Murphree*,[420] this Court upheld Rule 4(f), which permits service of a summons anywhere within the State (and not merely the district) in which a district court sits:

'We think that Rule 4(f) is in harmony with the Enabling Act. . . . Undoubtedly most alterations of the rules of practice and procedure may and often do affect the rights of litigants. Congress' prohibition of any alteration of substantive rights of litigants was obviously not addressed to such incidental effects as necessarily attend the adoption of the prescribed new rules of procedure upon the rights of litigants who, agreeably to rules of practice and procedure, have been brought before a court authorized to determine their rights.[421] The fact that the application of Rule 4(f) will operate to subject petitioner's rights to adjudication by the district court for northern Mississippi will undoubtedly affect those rights. But it does not operate to abridge, enlarge or modify the rules of decision by which that court will adjudicate its rights.'[422]

Thus[,] were there no conflicting state procedure, Rule 4(d) (1) would clearly control. However, respondent, focusing on the contrary Massachusetts rule, calls to the Court's attention another line of cases, a line which—like the Federal Rules—had its birth in 1938. *Erie []* held that federal courts sitting in diversity cases, when deciding questions of 'substantive' law, are bound by state court decisions as well as state statutes. The broad command of Erie was therefore identical to that of the Enabling Act: federal courts are to apply state substantive law and federal procedural law. However, as subsequent cases sharpened the distinction between substance and procedure, the line of cases following Erie diverged markedly from the line construing the Enabling Act. *Guaranty Trust Co[mpany]. of New York v. York* . . . made it clear that *Erie*-type problems were not to be solved by reference to any traditional or common-sense substance-procedure distinction:

> And so the question is not whether a statute of limitations is deemed a matter of
> 'procedure' in some sense. The question is . . . does it significantly affect the result
> of a litigation for a federal court to disregard a law of a State that would be
> controlling in an action upon the same claim by the same parties in a State court?

Respondent . . . suggests that the *Erie* doctrine acts as a check on the Federal Rules of Civil Procedure, that despite the clear command of Rule 4(d) (1), *Erie* and its progeny demand the application of the Massachusetts rule. Reduced to essentials, the argument is: (1) *Erie*, as refined in *York*, demands that federal courts apply state law whenever application of federal law in its stead will alter the outcome of the case. (2) In this case, a determination that the Massachusetts service requirements obtain will result in immediate victory for respondent. If, on the other hand, it should be held that Rule 4(d) (1) is applicable, the litigation will continue, with possible victory for petitioner. (3) Therefore, *Erie* demands application of the Massachusetts rule. The syllogism possesses an appealing simplicity, but is for several reasons invalid.

---

[419] Sibbach v. Wilson & Co., 312 U.S. 1 (1941).
[420] 326 U.S. 438 (1946).
[421] *Sibbach*, 312 U.S. at 12.
[422] *Id.*

In the first place, it is doubtful that, even if there were no Federal Rule making it clear that in-hand service is not required in diversity actions, the *Erie* rule would have obligated the District Court to follow the Massachusetts procedure. 'Outcome-determination' analysis was never intended to serve as a talisman.[423] Indeed, the message of York itself is that choices between state and federal law are to be made not by application of any automatic, 'litmus paper' criterion, but rather by reference to the policies underlying the *Erie* rule.

The *Erie* rule is rooted in part in a realization that it would be unfair for the character of result of a litigation materially to differ because the suit had been brought in a federal court.

'Diversity of citizenship jurisdiction was conferred in order to prevent apprehended discrimination in state courts against those not citizens of the state. *Swift v. Tyson* . . . introduced grave discrimination by noncitizens against citizens. It made rights enjoyed under the unwritten 'general law' vary according to whether enforcement was sought in the state or in the federal court; and the privilege of selecting the court in which the right should be determined was conferred upon the noncitizen. Thus, the doctrine rendered impossible equal protection of the law.'[424]

The decision was also in part a reaction to the practice of 'forum-shopping' which had grown up in response to the rule of *Swift v. Tyson*. That the York test was an attempt to effectuate these policies is demonstrated by the fact that the opinion framed the inquiry in terms of 'substantial' variations between state and federal litigation. Not only are non(*sic*)substantial, or trivial, variations not likely to raise the sort of equal protection problems which troubled the Court in *Erie*; they are also unlikely to influence the choice of a forum. The 'outcome-determination' test therefore cannot be read without reference to the twin aims of the Erie rule: discouragement of forum-shopping and avoidance of inequitable administration of the laws.

The difference between the conclusion that the Massachusetts rule is applicable, and the conclusion that it is not, is of course at this point 'outcome-determinative' in the sense that if we hold the state rule to apply, respondent prevails, whereas if we hold that Rule 4(d) (1) governs, the litigation will continue. But in this sense every procedural variation is 'outcome-determinative.' For example, having brought suit in a federal court, a plaintiff cannot then insist on the right to file subsequent pleadings in accord with the time limits applicable in state courts, even though enforcement of the federal timetable will, if he continues to insist that he must meet only the state time limit, result in determination of the controversy against him. So it is here. Though choice of the federal or state rule will at this point have a marked effect upon the outcome of the litigation, the difference between the two rules would be of scant, if any, relevance to the choice of a forum. Petitioner, in choosing her forum, was not presented with a situation where application of the state rule would wholly bar recovery; rather, adherence to the state rule would have resulted only in altering the way in which process was served. Moreover, it is difficult to argue that permitting service of defendant's wife to take the place of in hand service of defendant himself alters the mode of enforcement of state-created rights in a fashion sufficiently 'substantial' to raise the sort of equal protection problems to which the Erie opinion alluded.

There is, however, a more fundamental flaw in respondent's syllogism: the incorrect assumption that the rule of *Erie R. Co. v. Tompkins* constitutes the appropriate test of the validity and therefore the applicability of a Federal Rule of Civil Procedure. The *Erie* rule has never been invoked to void a Federal Rule. It is true that there have been cases where this Court has held applicable a state rule in the face of an

---

[423] Byrd v. Blue Ridge Rural Elec. Cooperative, 356 U.S. 525 (1958).
[424] Erie R.R. Co. v. Tompkins, 304 U.S. 64 (1938).

argument that the situation was governed by one of the Federal Rules. But the holding of each such case was not that *Erie* commanded displacement of a Federal Rule by an inconsistent state rule, but rather that the scope of the Federal Rule was not as broad as the losing party urged, and there-fore, there being no Federal Rule which covered the point in dispute, *Erie* commanded the enforcement of state law. . . .(Here, of course, the clash is unavoidable; Rule 4(d) (1) says—implicitly, but with unmistakable clarity—that in hand service is not required in federal courts.) At the same time, in cases adjudicating the validity of Federal Rules, we have not applied the York rule or other refinements of *Erie* but have to this day continued to decide questions concerning the scope of the Enabling Act and the constitutionality of specific Federal Rules in light of the distinction set forth in *Sibbach*.

Nor has the development of two separate lines of cases been inadvertent. The line between 'substance 'and 'procedure' shifts as the legal context changes. 'Each implies different variables depending upon the particular problem for which it is used.' It is true that both the Enabling Act and the *Erie* rule say, roughly, that federal courts are to apply state 'substantive' law and federal 'procedural' law, but from that it need not follow that the tests are identical. For they were designed to control very different sorts of decisions. When a situation is covered by one of the Federal Rules, the question facing the court is a far cry from the typical, relatively unguided *Erie* Choice: the court has been instructed to apply the Federal Rule, and can refuse to do so only if the Advisory Committee, this Court, and Congress erred in their prima facie judgment that the Rule in question transgresses neither the terms of the Enabling Act nor constitutional restrictions.

We are reminded by the *Erie* opinion that neither Congress nor the federal courts can, under the guise of formulating rules of decision for federal courts, fashion rules which are not supported by a grant of federal authority contained in Article I or some other section of the Constitution; in such areas state law must govern because there can be no other law. But the opinion in *Erie*, which involved no Federal Rule and dealt with a question which was 'substantive' in every traditional sense (whether the railroad owed a duty of care to Tompkins as a trespasser or a licensee), surely neither said nor implied that measures like Rule 4(d) (1) are unconstitutional. For the constitutional provision for a federal court system (augmented by the Necessary and Proper Clause) carries with it congressional power to make rules governing the practice and pleading in those courts, which in turn includes a power to regulate matters which, though falling within the uncertain area between substance and procedure, are rationally capable of classification as either. . . Neither York nor the cases following it ever suggested that the rule there laid down for coping with situations where no Federal Rule applies is coextensive with the limitation on Congress to which Erie had adverted. Although this Court has never before been confronted with a case where the applicable Federal Rule is in direct collision with the law of the relevant State, courts of appeals faced with such clashes have rightly discerned the implications of our decisions.

'One of the shaping purposes of the Federal Rules is to bring about uniformity in the federal courts by getting away from local rules. This is especially true of matters which relate to the administration of legal proceedings, an area in which federal courts have traditionally exerted strong inherent power, completely aside from the powers Congress expressly conferred in the Rules. The purpose of the Erie doctrine . . . was never to bottle up federal courts with 'outcome-determinative' and 'integral-relations' stoppers—when there are 'affirmative countervailing (federal) considerations' and when there is a Congressional mandate (the Rules) supported by constitutional authority.'

Erie and its offspring cast no doubt on the long-recognized power of Congress to prescribe housekeeping rules for federal courts even though some of those rules will inevitably differ from comparable state rules. 'When, because the plaintiff happens to be a non-resident, such a right is enforceable in a federal as well as in a State court, the forms and mode of enforcing the right may at times, naturally enough, vary because the two judicial systems are not identical.' Thus, though a court, in measuring a Federal Rule against the standards contained in the Enabling Act and the Constitution, need not wholly blind itself to the degree to which the Rule makes the character and result of the federal litigation stray from the course it would follow in state courts,[425] it cannot be forgotten that the *Erie* rule, and the guidelines suggested in York, were created to serve another purpose altogether. To hold that a Federal Rule of Civil Procedure must cease to function whenever it alters the mode of enforcing state-created rights would be to disembowel either the Constitution's grant of power over federal procedure or Congress' attempt to exercise that power in the Enabling Act. Rule 4(d) (1) is valid and controls the instant case.

Reversed.

Follow-Up Questions and Comments

1. *Hanna* recognized that a Federal Rule of Civil Procedure was applicable or, to put it another way, "was on point." What analysis did the Court perform once it recognized that—before declaring that the Federal Rule would thus have to govern in the federal court proceedings even in a diversity case?

2. Although the analysis of a governing Federal Rule does not make it explicit, the Court is relying on Article VI of the Constitution, which states that federal law shall be the "supreme law of the land." The so-called Supremacy Clause, provided at the beginning of this chapter, is in place so that, when federal law and state law conflict, federal law will prevail. It is, for instance, the reason that Federal Rule of Civil Procedure 4 in *Hanna* governed despite a state law that required an executor to be served in person. Federal Rules, enacted under the REA, are considered federal law. Thus, Rule 4 trumped the state statute.

3. *Hanna* also discussed how to analyze an *Erie* question when no Federal Rule is on point. This discussion is dicta, but it has turned out to be persuasive dicta. What does the Court suggest is the appropriate analysis in such cases? In this part of the opinion the Court discusses the ills that the *Erie* doctrine was designed to address—at other times referred to as "mischievous results." What does the Court mean when it suggests that the "outcome-determinative" test must be applied with the goals of preventing these evils in mind? This is what we will call the "modified outcome-determinative test"—*Hanna*'s "twist" on that test that has since become the norm.

4. *Erie* thus finished the correction that *Byrd* started. It provides, as will be explained more fully below, a two-part analysis for *Erie* questions. It incorporates many of the concepts included in prior cases but tweaks them so that they work more effectively. In short, *Hanna* restored balance to the distribution of power between the federal system and state systems, as the image below depicts.

---

[425] Sibbach v. Wilson & Co., 312 U.S. 1 (1941).

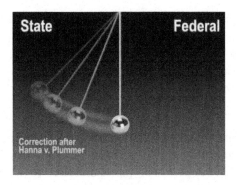

Correction after Hanna v. Plummer

A. Logical Extension of *Hanna*: Federal Rules Governing Procedure Trump State Laws Too

If Federal Rules of Civil Procedure which is directly in conflict with state law will govern under the Supremacy Clause, it is logical that federal statutes addressing procedural matters would—if state law conflicted with the federal statute in a diversity case—also trump inconsistent state law. Following is a Supreme Court case confirming that, if such a conflict exists, then the federal statute on a procedural matter will govern in diversity in federal court. At issue in the following case was an Alabama law that invalidated clauses in contracts that chose a forum outside of Alabama versus 28 U.S.C. § 1404, which allows the federal district court discretion to transfer a case to a more convenient forum and accounts for any choice-of-forum clause in the parties' contract.

STEWART ORGANIZATION, INC. v. RICOH CORP.
Supreme Court of the United States, 1988
487 U.S. 22

MARSHALL, J., delivered the opinion of the Court, in which REHNQUIST, C.J., and BRENNAN, WHITE, BLACKMUN, STEVENS, O'CONNOR, and KENNEDY, JJ., joined. KENNEDY, J., filed a concurring opinion, in which O'CONNOR, J., joined, post, p. ——. SCALIA, J., filed a dissenting opinion, post, p. ——.

. . .

This case presents the issue whether a federal court sitting in diversity should apply state or federal law in adjudicating a motion to transfer a case to a venue provided in a contractual forum-selection clause.

I

The dispute underlying this case grew out of a dealership agreement that obligated petitioner company, an Alabama corporation, to market copier products of respondent, a nationwide manufacturer with its principal place of business in New Jersey. The agreement contained a forum-selection clause providing that any dispute arising out of the contract could be brought only in a court located in Manhattan. Business relations between the parties soured under circumstances that are not relevant here. In September 1984, petitioner brought a complaint in the United States District Court for the Northern District of Alabama. The core of the complaint was an allegation that respondent had breached the dealership agreement, but petitioner also included claims for breach of warranty, fraud, and antitrust violations.

Relying on the contractual forum-selection clause, respondent moved the District Court either to transfer the case to the Southern District of New York under 28 U.S.C. § 1404(a) or to dismiss the case for improper venue under 28 U.S.C. § 1406. The District Court denied the motion. It reasoned that the transfer motion was controlled by Alabama law and that Alabama looks unfavorably upon contractual forum-selection clauses. The court certified its ruling for interlocutory appeal . . . and the Court of Appeals for the Eleventh Circuit accepted jurisdiction.

On appeal, a divided panel of the Eleventh Circuit reversed the District Court. The panel concluded that questions of venue in diversity actions are governed by federal law, and that the parties' forum-selection clause was enforceable as a matter of federal law. The panel therefore reversed the order of the District Court and remanded with instructions to transfer the case to a Manhattan court. After petitioner successfully moved for rehearing en banc . . . the full Court of Appeals proceeded to adopt the result, and much of the reasoning, of the panel opinion. The en banc court, citing Congress' enactment or approval of several rules to govern venue determinations in diversity actions, first deter-mined that "[v]enue is a matter of federal procedure." . . . The Court of Appeals then applied the standards articulated in the admiralty case of *The Bremen v. Zapata Off–Shore Company*,[426] to conclude that "the choice of forum clause in this contract is in all respects enforceable generally as a matter of federal law" . . . We now affirm under somewhat different reasoning.

II

Both the panel opinion and the opinion of the full Court of Appeals referred to the difficulties that often attend "the sticky question of which law, state or federal, will govern various aspects of the decisions of federal courts sitting in diversity." . . . A district court's decision whether to apply a federal statute such as § 1404(a) in a diversity action, however, involves a considerably less intricate analysis than that which governs the "relatively unguided *Erie* choice."[427] Our cases indicate that when the federal law sought to be applied is a congressional statute, the first and chief question for the district court's determination is whether the statute is "sufficiently broad to control the issue before the Court."[428] This question involves a straightforward exercise in statutory interpretation to determine if the statute covers the point in dispute. . .

If the district court determines that a federal statute covers the point in dispute, it proceeds to inquire whether the statute represents a valid exercise of Congress' authority under the Constitution.[429] If Congress intended to reach the issue before the District Court, and if it enacted its intention into law in a manner that abides with the Constitution, that is the end of the matter; "[f]ederal courts are bound to apply rules enacted by Congress with respect to matters . . . over which it has legislative power."[430] Thus, a district court sitting in diversity must apply a federal statute that controls the issue before the court and that represents a valid exercise of Congress' constitutional powers.

III

Applying the above analysis to this case persuades us that federal law, specifically 28 U.S.C. § 1404(a), governs the parties' venue dispute.

---

[426] 407 U.S. 1 (1972).

[427] Hanna v. Plumer, 380 U.S. 460, 471 (1965) (referring to Erie R.R. Co. v. Tompkins, 304 U.S. 64 (1938)).

[428] Walker v. Armco Steel Corp., 446 U.S. 740, 749–50 (1980).

[429] *See* Hanna Plumer, supra, 380 U.S., at 471 (citing Erie R. Co. v. Tompkins, 304 U.S., at 7779.

[430] Prima Paint Corp. v. Flood & Conklin Mfg. Co., 388 U.S. 395, 406 (1967); *cf.* Hanna v. Plumer, supra, 380 U.S., at 471 ("When a situation is covered by one of the Federal Rules . . .the court has been instructed to apply the Federal Rule, and can refuse to do so only if the Advisory Committee, this Court, and Congress erred in their prima facie judgment that the Rule in question transgresses neither the terms of the Enabling Act nor constitutional restrictions").

A

At the outset we underscore a methodological difference in our approach to the question from that taken by the Court of Appeals. The en banc court determined that federal law controlled the issue based on a survey of different statutes and judicial decisions that together revealed a significant federal interest in questions of venue in general, and in choice-of-forum clauses in particular. The Court of Appeals then proceeded to apply the standards announced in our opinion in *The Bremen v. Zapata Off–Shore Company*,[431] to determine that the forum-selection clause in this case was enforceable. But the immediate issue before the District Court was whether to grant respondent's motion to transfer the action under § 1404(a), and as Judge Tjoflat properly noted in his special concurrence below, the immediate issue before the Court of Appeals was whether the District Court's denial of the § 1404(a) motion constituted an abuse of discretion. Although we agree with the Court of Appeals that the Bremen case may prove "instructive" in resolving the parties' dispute . . . the first question for consideration should have been whether § 1404(a) itself controls respondent's request to give effect to the parties' contractual choice of venue and transfer this case to a Manhattan court. For the reasons that follow, we hold that it does.

B

Section 1404(a) provides: "For the convenience of parties and witnesses, in the interest of justice, a district court may transfer any civil action to any other district or division where it might have been brought." Under the analysis outlined above, we first consider whether this provision is sufficiently broad to control the issue before the court. That issue is whether to transfer the case to a court in Manhattan in accordance with the forum-selection clause. We believe that the statute, fairly construed, does cover the point in dispute.

Section 1404(a) is intended to place discretion in the district court to adjudicate motions for transfer according to an "individualized, case-by-case consideration of convenience and fairness."[432] A motion to transfer under § 1404(a) thus calls on the district court to weigh in the balance a number of case-specific factors. The presence of a forum-selection clause such as the parties entered into in this case will be a significant factor that figures centrally in the district court's calculus. In its resolution of the § 1404(a) motion in this case, for example, the District Court will be called on to address such issues as the convenience of a Manhattan forum given the parties' expressed preference for that venue, and the fairness of transfer in light of the forum-selection clause and the parties' relative bargaining power. The flexible and individualized analysis Congress prescribed in § 1404(a) thus encompasses consideration of the parties' private expression of their venue preferences.

Section 1404(a) may not be the only potential source of guidance for the District Court to consult in weighing the parties' private designation of a suitable forum. The premise of the dispute between the parties is that Alabama law may refuse to enforce forum-selection clauses providing for out-of-state venues as a matter of state public policy. If that is so, the District Court will have either to integrate the factor of the forum-selection clause into its weighing of considerations as prescribed by Congress, or else to apply, as it did in this case, Alabama's categorical policy disfavoring forum-selection clauses. Our cases make clear that, as between these two choices . . . the instructions of Congress are supreme.

. . .

---

[431] 407 U.S. 1 (1972).
[432] Van Dusen v. Barrack, 376 U.S. 612, 622 (1964).

It is true that § 1404(a) and Alabama's putative policy regarding forum-selection clauses are not perfectly coextensive. Section 1404(a) directs a district court to take account of factors other than those that bear solely on the parties' private ordering of their affairs. The district court also must weigh in the balance the convenience of the witnesses and those public-interest factors of systemic integrity and fairness that, in addition to private concerns, come under the heading of "the interest of justice." It is conceivable in a particular case, for example, that because of these factors a district court acting under § 1404(a) would refuse to transfer a case notwithstanding the counterweight of a forum-selection clause, whereas the coordinate state rule might dictate the opposite result. . . . But this potential conflict in fact frames an additional argument for the supremacy of federal law. Congress has directed that multiple considerations govern transfer within the federal court system, and a state policy focusing on a single concern or a subset of the factors identified in § 1404(a) would defeat that command. Its application would impoverish the flexible and multifaceted analysis that Congress intended to govern motions to transfer within the federal system. The forum-selection clause, which represents the parties' agreement as to the most proper forum, should receive neither dispositive consideration (as respondent might have it) nor no consideration (as Alabama law might have it), but rather the consideration for which Congress provided in § 1404(a).[433] This is thus not a case in which state and federal rules "can exist side by side . . .each controlling its own intended sphere of coverage without conflict."[434]

Because § 1404(a) controls the issue before the District Court, it must be applied if it represents a valid exercise of Congress' authority under the Constitution. The constitutional authority of Congress to enact § 1404(a) is not subject to serious question. As the Court made plain in Hanna, "the constitutional provision for a federal court system . . .carries with it congressional power to make rules governing the practice and pleading in those courts, which in turn includes a power to regulate matters which, though falling within the uncertain area between substance and procedure, are rationally capable of classification as either."[435] Section 1404(a) is doubtless capable of classification as a procedural rule, and indeed, we have so classified it in holding that a transfer pursuant to § 1404(a) does not carry with it a change in the applicable law.[436] It therefore falls comfortably within Congress' powers under Article III as augmented by the Necessary and Proper Clause. . . .

We hold that federal law, specifically 28 U.S.C. § 1404(a), governs the District Court's decision whether to give effect to the parties' forum-selection clause and transfer this case to a court in Manhattan. We therefore affirm the Eleventh Circuit order reversing the District Court's application of Alabama law. The case is remanded so that the District Court may determine in the first instance the appropriate effect under federal law of the parties' forum-selection clause on respondent's § 1404(a) motion.

It is so ordered.

---

[433] *Cf.* Norwood v. Kirkpatrick, 349 U.S. 29, 32 (1955) (§ 1404(a) accords broad discretion to district court, and plaintiff's choice of forum is only one relevant factor for its consideration).

[434] Walker v. Armco Steel Corp., 446 U.S. 740, 752 (1980).

[435] 380 U.S. at 472. *See also id.* at 473 ("*Erie* and its offspring cast no doubt on the long-recognized power of Congress to prescribe housekeeping rules for federal courts").

[436] *See Van Dusen*, 376 U.S. at 636–37 ("[B]oth the history and purposes of § 1404(a) indicate that it should be regarded as a federal judicial house-keeping measure").

Follow-Up Questions and Comments

1. In addition to Federal Statutes and Federal Rules, the U.S. Constitution to the extent it applies, would trump any contrary state law. The issue of such a conflict does not arise frequently. An example could be, however, a diversity case in a state that allows jury verdicts to be less than unanimous. Although the U.S. Supreme Court has never ruled on the matter, the prevailing assumption is that the Seventh Amendment requires unanimity in a jury verdict.[437] If in a diversity case in which state law governed under *Erie* the state allowed non-unanimous jury verdicts, the Seventh Amendment would trump state law, just as a Federal Statute or a Federal Rule would.

IV. The Analytical Framework Derived from *Hanna* and *Stewart*

Hanna and *Stewart* provide a blueprint for analyzing any *Erie* question. The opinion alternates between its discussion of the "Federal-Rule/Statute-On-Point" and "No-Federal-Rule/Statute-On-Point" analyses. (Although *Hanna* discussed a Federal Rule of Civil Procedure, rather than a federal statute governing a procedural issue, the same result will follow if a federal statute governing procedure conflicts with state law on procedure. The federal statute will govern under the Supremacy Clause.) Thus, the following offers the logical sequence in which to analyze an *Erie* question. First, recognize that the issue arises only when a case is in federal court based on diversity and there is tension between a Federal Rule/Statute (or interest) and a state law. If so, you would want to do both of the following analyses. If you reach a conclusion under the "Federal Rules/Statute on Point" analysis, go ahead and state your conclusion and then proceed to analyze under the "No Federal Rule/Statute on Point (or arguably not on point)" so that you do a full *Erie* analysis. It is important to get into the habit of making alternative arguments. You may be wrong in your first analysis, or in real life, the Judge may not find it persuasive. If you only perform what you think is the required analysis, and do not analyze the alter-native approach, you will lose an opportunity to show you know the subject (or in real life, an opportunity to persuade with a second argument when the first did not do it).

The following is a step-by-step approach to analyzing any *Erie* question:

I.   The initial inquiry, according to *Hanna*, must be: Is there a Federal Rule of Civil Procedure or Federal Statute on point/applicable? If the Federal provision is a rule, is that Rule valid under the Rules Enabling Act? To be valid, the Rule must deal with procedure and not enlarge, abridge or modify substantive law. Here, the *Sibbach* case we covered before *Hanna* is critical because it gives a test—and the test is a generous one. The case holds that if a Rule is procedural, i.e. deals with management of a case, then it can have a significant incidental impact on substantive rights. The temptation here is to skip this part and say, "No Federal Rule has been held invalid." Avoid that temptation, state the Rules Enabling Act's language and *Sibbach* test, and analogize your factual situation to *Sibbach*. A federal statute will not have the same validity analysis as a Federal Rule because, unlike the Rule which must conform to a statute (the Rules Enabling Act), the federal statute will be presumptively valid.

---

[437] *See* 9B Charles Alan Wright & Arthur R. Miller, Federal Practice And Procedure (2018).

A. Does the Rule/Statute conflict with the state law? Here is when the degree to which the policy supported by the Rule is integral to the Federal system can make a difference. If a Rule implicates an important federal policy, then there is an argument that, even if the state "procedural" law does not appear to directly conflict, if it would produce different results from the policy furthered by the Rule, one may argue for a conflict. The weightier the policy supported by the Rule, the broader one may consider its "influence." If, however, the Federal Rule/Statute (1) is valid, and (2) conflicts with the state law, meaning that they cannot coexist because to allow the state law to operate would undercut the policy of the Federal Rule/Statute—then, under the Supremacy Clause, you should conclude that the Federal Rule governs and will control.

B. Remember at this point to state your conclusion as to the first part of the analysis. There is a Federal Rule of Civil Procedure or Federal Statute on point, or arguably on point. It is valid. Either its policy is such that the state law in question cannot coexist with the Rule/Statute, or the policy is such that the state law is aimed at something different and the Rule/Statute and the state law can coexist.

II. Assuming for purposes of argument, however, that the Rule/Statute is not dispositive, the analysis under the traditional *Erie* approach will reveal another basis on which the court can conclude whether the state law should apply or not apply. We here assume that there is no Federal Rule/Statute on Point, that the Federal Rule/Statute arguably is invalid, and/or that the Federal Rule/Statute can coexist with the state law. We thus go into the more flexible *Erie* analysis *Hanna* urged courts to apply to further the aims of *Erie*.

A. Federal courts consistently find state law to be substantive and thus controlling for certain types of issues. These issues are (1) the elements of a substantive claim; (2) statutes of limitations for state-law claims; (3) rules on accrual of such statutes of limitations and for when a case is deemed to have been "filed" so as to satisfy the statute of limitations; and (4) choice-of-law rules that determine what substantive law applies (recognizing that a case may be pending in a forum but, under choice-of-law principles, the substantive law of another state may govern).

B. If one is dealing with any other area, the analysis is quite simply unpredictable. However, the three-part balancing test of *Byrd v. Blue Ridge* can guide someone who wishes to reach a principled result. It is an analysis that seeks to see what result, as guided by the factors discussed, most clearly accomplishes the aims of *Erie*. No one factor necessarily dominates. It is the convergence of the conclusions you reach that should lead you to see whether allowing the state law to apply will undermine the goals of *Erie* or will undercut them.

1. What is the federal interest at stake? Is the federal interest as strong as in *Byrd*, for instance, or less so? What is the state interest at stake? Is it stronger than in *Byrd*, more tied to the underlying claims or elements of the claims than in *Byrd*? The more a state interest is somehow linked to the underlying cause of action in the case (e.g., breach of contract, tort, property right, etc.) the stronger the state interest will be. This is the territory where *Erie* made clear that the rules of decision—i.e. the substantive law being applied—needed to be that of the state.

2. As part of the No-Federal-Rule/Statute-On-Point analysis, what does the "modified out-come-determinative test" as developed in *Hanna* do to change that part of the analysis? Here, *Hanna* puts a brilliant "spin" on outcome determination. It says that "[t]he 'out-come-determination'

test therefore cannot be read without reference to the twin aims of the *Erie* rule: discouragement of forum-shopping and avoidance of the inequitable administration of justice."[438] Whereas the flaw in the old outcome-determinative test was that it made virtually any difference between state and federal law outcome determinative, the Court in *Hanna* took a different approach.

3. It encouraged looking at the difference between the Federal Rules/Statute or interest and the state law and ask: Would a plaintiff have an incentive to file in federal court because of the difference in law? You can analogize here to *Brown & Yellow Taxicab*, where the incentive was so strong to get to federal court and federal law that the party reincorporated. By contrast, you could also analogize to the Federal Rule at issue in *Hanna*. The Federal Rule on service of process allows several alternatives, which someone might think would motivate a party to sue in federal court rather than state where the service statute in Massachusetts required serving the executor in person. However, *Hanna* suggests that such a difference would not be likely to provide the kind of incentive with which *Erie* is concerned. In other words, at this stage, one must ask: "Is the difference between the law that will apply in federal court and that in state court really so significantly an advantage in federal court that the plaintiff will be drawn there?" We know that in a diversity case, it will no longer be a difference in the underlying rights and duties. *Erie* made that clear. The federal court will apply state law to the claims in a diversity case. The question is whether there is something else, such as perhaps the availability of a jury in federal court or some other major difference that would draw litigants to federal court for reasons other than having an independent claim. If you have that, then you could have a situation in which the "modified out-come-determinative" test would apply. The inequitable administration of law would flow from such forum shopping—e.g., something like the inequity that we saw in *Brown & Yellow Taxicab*, where state courts would be ruling one way in a state in which the federal courts in diversity would on the same claims be ruling another solely because of the difference in law.

III. If you concluded that there was a Federal Rule/Statute that was valid and on point such that it would govern under the Supremacy Clause, it would be wise at this point to refer to that. If you have a Federal Rule/Statute that is valid and applicable, the federal provision will govern. If you follow the analytical framework suggested above, you will also have done the alternative analysis to be thorough, but you will return to the conclusion that federal law governs under the Supremacy Clause if indeed there is an applicable Federal Rule or Statute. If it is not clear that Federal Rule or Statute is/are applicable because there is no Federal Rule or Statute squarely on point, you would say that but argue that the policy of Rule(s) can still be sufficient to suggest the federal interest should win out, especially if the "modified" outcome-determinative test does not show a great risk of litigants seeking federal court solely to get an advantage in the particular procedure at issue. . Alternatively, if you are confident that there is not a Federal Rule or Statute on point and that the policy of any Rule or Statute is not strong enough to force a conflict, and that the state law ought to be able to coexist in the federal system, then say that.

---

[438] 380 U.S. 460, 468 (1965).

Practice Problems

Practice Problem 9-1

The State of Calisota recognizes negligent infliction of emotional distress as a cause of action. The elements of the claim are (1) person observes (2) conduct that would be considered outrageous to the ordinary person, and (3) no actual injury is required if the conduct is such that an ordinary person would be extremely upset by such conduct. Yani, a citizen of California, witnessed Tex, a citizen of Texafornia, beating his six-year-old son with a belt on the sidewalk. Yani said she could not stop flashbacks of the image of the poor child being whipped and it had ruined her life. She sued Tex for negligent infliction of emotional distress in a Calistota Federal Court. For the majority of states that recognize negligent infliction of emotional distress, and a majority of federal courts in those states, the negligent infliction of emotional distress claim requires not only that the person observe conduct that would be deemed outrageous to the ordinary person, but also that the plaintiff demonstrate some physical effects from the events such as loss of weight, vomiting, etc. Whose law should the Calisota Federal Court apply—the State of Calisota's elements for negligent infliction of emotional distress or the majority standard?

Practice Problem 9-2

Pete, a citizen of Virginia, was defrauded by Sleazy, Inc., which was incorporated and had its principal place of business in Illinois. Pete sued for $500,000 in Federal Court in Virginia. Virginia follows the choice-of-law rules set forth in the *Restatement (First) of Conflicts*. For tort like fraud, the *Restatement (First)* dictates that the court apply the law of the state in which the fraudulent acts or omissions occurred. Here, that was Illinois. In non-diversity cases in which choice of law is an issue, assume that most federal courts choose to follow the *Restatement (Second) of Conflicts*. Under the *Restatement (Second)*, the law of the place where the defrauded person lives is more likely to apply. What state's law should the federal court apply here?

Practice Problem 9-3

Fred Walker, a citizen of Oklahoma, struck a nail that fragmented and went into his eye. He sued Armco Steel Corporation (Armco), a Pennsylvania corporation with its principal place of business in Pennsylvania, in the U.S. District Court for the Western District of Oklahoma. He sought $500,000 in damages for being blinded by a nail that his expert concluded as defective. Oklahoma law provides that product manufacturers owe a duty to persons to manufacture their products in accordance with a standard of reasonable care. Failure to comply with this standard constitutes a breach, such that if the breach caused a person's injuries, the manufacturer will be liable for damages. The statute of limitations on this type of claim is two-years. Unlike most states, which provide that the statute of limitations is met on "commencement of the action" and that "commencement" occurred on filing the complaint in court, Oklahoma provided that commencement of an action to stop the statute of limitations did not occur on filing the complaint in court, but rather occurred on serving the defendant by any of the permissible means of service—i.e., not on commencement of the action but rather when after commencement process is actually served on the defendant.

Fred filed his complaint in the U.S. district court barely within two-years of the accident. However, he did not achieve service on Armco until two months later, by which time the statute of limitations had run. Federal Rule of Civil Procedure 3 provides as follows: "A civil action is commenced by filing a complaint with the court." The history related to the adoption of Rule 3 states that the sole reason for defining the "commencement of the action" in the Federal Rules of Civil Procedure is so that, when another Federal Rule refers to a time frame running from "commencement of the action," it would be clear what date the time would run from. For instance, certain other rules provide that there must be conferences with

272

the court within [specified] days of "commencement of the action." The history states that Rule 3 is not intended to have any effect beyond an internal frame of reference for deadlines identified within the Federal Rule of Civil Procedure themselves and which used "commencement of the action" as an internal reference point.

Armco Steel moved to dismiss the case as untimely. Armco pointed out that Oklahoma law required the action to be commenced within two years of the accident and specifically defined "commencement" as not simply filing the complaint but actually serving the defendant. Armco also cited significant authority that statutes of limitation are considered to be a part of the state's allowance of claims because the state not only specifies the basis for liability but places limits on how long it will allow someone to be sued. In other words, courts have traditionally considered statutes of limitations to be intertwined with substantive rights. You can assume the validity of Armco's authority on the treatment of statute of limitations as being intertwined with the substantive law of a claim for which a limitation is stated. Fred argued that Rule 3 governed because the case was filed in Federal Court and Rule 3 provided that "commencement of the action" was filing of the complaint. Conduct a thorough *Erie* analysis to determine whether the state rule on commencement of the action for purposes of the statute of limitations applies or whether Federal Rule of Civil Procedure 3 applies.

Practice Problem 9-4

Calisota adopted legislation purporting to invalidate arbitration agreements contracts between car purchasers and the manufacturer of the cars. The sales contract between Paul and Venus, Inc. nevertheless had an arbitration clause requiring mandatory arbitration to be pursued before a party files suit. Paul sued in United States District Court in Calisota. Venus filed a motion to compel arbitration under the Federal Arbitration Act, 9 U.S.C. § 2 (2018), which expressly holds ineffective any state laws that seek to invalidate arbitration agreements. The court held that the federal law governed and not Calisota law. Was the court correct and, if so, why?

Practice Problem 9-5

The State of Texafonia adopted a rule that in malpractice cases, if the plaintiff was suing more than one defendant for negligence resulting from the same transaction or occurrence, or series of transactions or occurrences, then the plaintiff was required to sue each defendant in separate suits. (The concern was that one defendant may be prejudiced by the actions of another defendant. Texafonia had experienced several high-profile cases in which defendants joined with other defendants had been held liable for judgments that seemed disproportionate to the defendant's role in the suit.) Paula Plaintiff sues Dandy Doctor and Happy Hospital for malpractice in that, during her stay there, the hospital gave the doctor the wrong X-rays (which belonged to another patient) and the doctor failed to follow protocols accepted in the profession that would have notified him that he had the wrong X-rays. As a result, the doctor operated on a healthy organ before realizing the one that needed to be operated on was elsewhere. Paula, a model, claims that the extra fifteen inches of scars not only caused her unnecessary pain and suffering but would cause major damage to her career. She thus seeks $1 million in damages. Paula sued Dandy Doctor and Happy Hospital in Federal Court based on diversity (she's a citizen of Louisiana, the Doctor is a citizen of Texafonia and the Hospital is a citizen of Texafonia). The defendants challenge the suit on the ground that Texafonia law, which gives rise to the substantive malpractice claims, requires the two defendants to be sued separately. How should the Court rule on this challenge?

Practice Problem 9-6

The Commonwealth of Massachusetts observed many suits for claims of abuse brought against churches and members of their clergy. The Massachusetts Legislature decided to step into the arena. In particular, the Legislature was concerned about the impact of subjecting plaintiffs in such cases to discovery. The Legislature thus passed the following statute:

Title of Statute: This statute shall be known as the "Limitations on Defendants' Discovery in Suits Asserting Claims of Abuse against Churches, Clergy, or Church Employees."

Findings: It being hereby found:

(1) that victims of abuse by clergy, particularly children, suffer lasting consequences;

(2) the litigation process, particularly the process of discovery, places stresses on parties and, in the case of abuse victims, the stress likely will cause them to relive painful experiences;

(3) as a result of the stress and pain just mentioned, some per-sons who could bring lawsuits never file them;

(4) although one cannot presume that a plaintiff in fact suffered abuse until a judge or jury reaches a verdict, the number of verdicts to date suggests that at least some percentage of plaintiffs asserting such claims are in fact victims; and

(5) limitations on discovery procedures as set forth in this statute are likely to lessen the pain to actual victims of abuse while still allowing defendants sufficient opportunity not only to determine the grounds on which the plaintiff is basing his or her suit but also to develop any defenses to such suits.

Be It Hereby Enacted: In all suits in which the plaintiff alleges a claim of abuse under Massachusetts common law against a clergy or other person employed by a church, including but not limited to clergy, discovery of the plaintiff by the defendant shall be limited as follows:

Interrogatories: 25 in number including parts and subparts;

Requests for Production of Documents: Unlimited, subject to any reasonable limitation imposed by the court on a case-by-case basis;

Requests for Admissions: Unlimited, subject to any reasonable limitation imposed by the court on a case-by-case basis;

Depositions of the Plaintiff: Only upon moving the court for leave to do so, specifying with reasonable particularity the subjects in which the defendant proposes to question the plaintiff, and demonstrating good cause for the taking of a deposition, but in no event— even when the court finds good cause and orders a deposition— shall the deposition exceed one hour; and

Deposition of persons other than the Plaintiff: Unlimited but subject to the maximum number permitted in the Federal Rules of Civil Procedure.

Paul Plaintiff, a citizen of Massachusetts, sued Cal Clergyman, a citizen of New York, alleging that

Paul was abused as a minor while a parishioner of the church in Massachusetts where Cal was then serving as pastor. Paul filed his complaint in the United States District Court for the District of Massachusetts. He sought $10 million in damages for his abuse claim. A Massachusetts common law abuse claim is a tort claim requiring the plaintiff to show a duty, breach, and proximate cause of harm (even if solely emotional harm) to the plaintiff.

After Cal answered, and discovery began on a date approved by the Court, Cal's counsel served interrogatories seeking limited information because, as he had been taught, interrogatories should be used for limited purposes and the remaining questions saved for a deposition of the party. Cal's counsel also served a request for production of documents. Paul's counsel served answers to the interrogatories and responses to request for production of documents.

Cal's counsel then sent a notice of deposition requiring Paul to appear before a court reporter in the offices of Cal's counsel to answer questions under oath by deposition "for the time permitted for any and all depositions in cases in the federal system." Paul's counsel interpreted the deposition notice to suggest Cal's counsel did not intend to abide by the limitations in the Massachusetts statute. In a follow-up telephone call, Cal's counsel confirmed as much. Paul's counsel thus filed an objection to the deposition and moved to require Cal, in any deposition of Paul, to comply with the limitations in the Massachusetts statute. After conferring with Paul's counsel and determining that Paul's counsel insisted on compliance with the Massachusetts statute, Cal's counsel filed a motion to compel the production of Paul pursuant to the deposition notice and argued that the deposition should not be limited in any way by the Massachusetts statute. Cal argued that the Massachusetts statute was inapplicable and, therefore, Paul's objection and motion should be overruled and Cal's motion to compel Paul to appear for a deposition should be granted. How should the Court rule on the question raised by the competing motions made by Paul and Cal? Explain your analysis.

CHAPTER 10: PLEADING ESSENTIALS AND SEEKING INJUNCTIVE RELIEF WHILE A SUIT IS PENDING

I. How the Topics in this Chapter Fit in the Overall Progress of a Civil Action

Here is where the topic of this chapter fits in the progress of a civil action:

Figure 10-1

Cause of Action (events leading to suit)	Pre-Filing Tasks (items to begin representation, interviewing, and related matters)	Choice of Forum (subject matter jurisdiction, removal, personal jurisdiction, and venue)	Notice and Service of Process (completing the process of ensuring the forum court can enter a valid judgment)	**Pleading the Case and Joinder of Claims and Parties (including supplemental jurisdiction)**

Responding to Claims by Motion or by Answer	Discovery (developing proof to establish claims and learn your adversary's case)	Right to Jury (pretrial motions and practice)	Final Pretrial Conference (events within last month before trial)	Trial (procedures and motions during trial)	Verdict	Post-Trial Motions (motions for a new trial and/or judgment as a matter of law)	Appeal

This chapter discusses two overarching subjects. First, it addresses the fundamentals of pleading. The fundamentals include the format of the pleading such as a complaint. Fundamental principles also include the way in which claims are alleged. That includes how the caption of a case begins a pleading, the title of the pleading (e.g., Complaint), the necessity form breaking allegations into units and numbering them. Fundamentals of pleading also include the degree of specificity with which claims must be pled. Finally, the basics address how a pleading concludes with a request for the relief sought.

The second topic of this chapter, included at the end, addresses the steps a party must follow if she is seeking injunctive relief during the pendency of the lawsuit. The requirements under Federal Rule of Civil Procedure 65 for a temporary restraining order and for a preliminary injunction are de-tailed. A lawyer needs to know that she must not only prepare a complaint adhering to the fundamentals of pleading, but also file a motion and provide either affidavits or testimony supporting the request for injunctive relief. Thus, the conclusion of this chapter outlines the steps, in addition to filing a complaint, that a party facing irreparable harm must take to achieve preliminary injunctive relief.

II. Requirements for Adequate Pleading

A. Formal Requirements

All pleadings must conform to Federal Rule of Civil Procedure 10. Please read that Rule now. The "caption" referred to in Rule 10 is the heading of the document that identifies the court in which it is filed, the names of the parties, and the addresses of all defendants. The title of the pleading, e.g., "COMPLAINT," should go in or directly under the caption, depending on the rule of the court in which you will be filing. A jury demand typically should be included in the complaint.[439] Of course, doing so assumes you have told your client you believe that demanding a jury is wise. The rest of the complaint will be devoted to the business of pleading the allegations that will get the suit underway. Rule 10 requires these allegations to be in numbered paragraphs. Refer to the sample complaint at the end of this chapter to see both an example of a caption and how allegations are organized in segments by consecutive numbers.

B. Sufficiency of Pleadings

Federal Rule of Civil Procedure 8(a) governs sufficiency of claims. Please read that Rule now. Notice that Rule 8(a) (1) requires allegations of the basis for jurisdiction. Why do the Rules require a party to allege the basis for the federal court's jurisdiction?

Rule 8(a) (3) deals with the relief to be requested. This part of the pleading typically comes after all other allegations and is introduced in a paragraph that begins with "WHEREFORE, for the reasons set forth above, John Doe respectfully requests the following relief: [then in numbered para-graphs, the party sets forth all relief requested]." Typically, a party will know whether she is requesting damages, injunctive or other equitable relief, or both. The issues arise, for instance, in situations where a federal statute on which the suit's claim is based allows for attorney's fees. If the complaint does not request such fees, then they will not be awarded. Likewise, if the plaintiff is seeking damages beyond compensatory damages, such as punitive damages, she must allege a basis for the punitive damages in the pleadings and then request such damages in the request for relief. A foundation for punitive damages typically requires allegations of an intentional tort, or in some jurisdictions, gross negligence or reckless conduct. You will need to research the required foundation for such damages in your jurisdiction and be sure to allege what is necessary and to request punitive damages specifically.

Whereas the requirements of Rule 8(a) (1) and 8(a) (3) are straightforward, those of Rule 8(a) (2) are far more involved. The criteria identifying sufficient specificity in pleading allegations has become an oft-litigated issue because of Supreme Court decisions that have created uncertainty about the requirements imposed by Rule 8(a) (2). This part of the pleading rule deals with the level of allegations (facts and law) that must be pled to be sufficient. To appreciate the significance of the requirements on the degree of allegations to plead a sufficient complaint, a brief review of the history of pleadings is pertinent here. In the eighteenth-century English and early American law, so-called "writ pleading" prevailed. Under that form of pleading, a party had to make extremely detailed allegations, in just the right form, or fail to get into court.[440]

---

[439] One way to demand a jury trial is to "endorse" the pleading by including in in the caption or after the Request for Relief at the end: "Plaintiff demands trial by jury on all issues triable of right by jury.

"Although including a jury demand in the pleading is not a requirement under Rule 10, Rule 38 permits parties to endorse the request on a pleading to avoid the risk of accidently waiving your client's constitutional right. *See* FED. R. CIV. P. 10, 38; *cf. also* FED. R. CIV. P. 81 (jury demand on removal of case).

[440] *See, e.g.*, Spangler v. Pugh, 21 Ill. 85, 86 (1859) ("However much the right to a jury trial is discussed later in

Recognizing that the writ system glorified form over justice, pleading in the Code drafted by David Dudley Field became the norm in the latter part of the nineteenth century in America. In pleading under the Field Code, parties were required to plead sufficient "facts" to allow their claims to proceed and summary judgment was introduced as a mechanism that, after a party had the opportunity to pursue discovery and develop evidence for her claims, would weed out those claims on which the evidence was insufficient to go to trial.

Because judges who were trained in the writ system interpreted "facts" too strictly and as a result many cases were being dismissed, the modern form of pleading, called "notice pleading," evolved with the adoption of the Federal Rules of Civil Procedure in 1938. Notice pleading asks that a pleader allege a short and plain statement of the claim showing the pleader is entitled to relief. For half a century, the United States Supreme Court's decision in *Conley v. Gibson*,[441] guided courts on interpreting Rule 8's modest pleading criteria. The Court's guidance was generous to claim-ants:

In appraising the sufficiency of the complaint[,] we follow, of course, the accepted rule that a complaint should not be dismissed for failure to state a claim unless it appears beyond doubt that the plaintiff can prove no set of facts in support of his claim which would entitle him to relief.[442]

Conley went on to elaborate, in a similar vein:

> The respondents also argue that the complaint failed to set forth specific facts to support its general allegation of discrimination and that its dismissal is therefore proper. The decisive answer to this is that the Federal Rules of Civil Procedure do not require a claimant to set out in detail the facts upon which he bases his claim. To the contrary, all the Rules require is "a short and plain statement of the claim that will give the defendant fair notice of what plaintiff's claim is and the grounds upon which it rests." The illustrative forms appended to the Rules plainly demonstrate this. Such simplified "notice pleading" is made possible by the liberal opportunity for discovery and the other pretrial procedures established by the Rules to disclose more precisely the basis of both the claim and defense and to define more narrowly the disputed facts and issues.[443]

In two decisions, however, the Supreme Court has provided a basis for many to question whether notice pleading is being replaced by a pleading standard requiring something more than that traditionally deemed acceptable. The first of these decisions is *Bell Atlantic Corp. v. Twombly*. Following is this decision:

Chapter 15. The point here is, even if a party has the kind of case that qualifies for a jury trial, that party will fail to have a jury if one is not requested courts may regret that a slip in pleading should delay the party in the administration of justice, the rules of law must be observed.").

[441] 355 U.S. 41 (1957).

[442]Conley v. Gibson, 355 U.S. 41, 45–46 (1957), *overruled in part by* Bell Atl. Corp. v. Twombly, 550 U.S 544, 127

[443] *Id.* at 47–48.

BELL ATLANTIC CORP. v. TWOMBLY
Supreme Court of the United States, 2007
50 U.S. 544

SOUTER, J., delivered the opinion of the Court, in which ROBERTS, C. J., and SCALIA, KENNEDY, THOMAS, BREYER, and ALITO, JJ., joined. STEVENS, J., filed a dissenting opinion, in which GINSBURG, J., joined, except as to Part IV, post, p. 1974.

Justice SOUTER delivered the opinion of the Court.

Liability under § 1 of the Sherman Act, 15 U.S.C. § 1, requires a "contract, combination, or conspiracy, in restraint of trade or commerce." The question in this putative class action is whether a § 1 complaint can survive a motion to dismiss when it alleges that major telecommunications providers engaged in certain parallel conduct unfavorable to competition, absent some factual context suggesting agreement, as distinct from identical, independent action. We hold that such a complaint should be dismissed.

I

The upshot of the 1984 divestiture of the American Telephone & Telegraph Company's (AT & T) local telephone business was a system of regional service monopolies (variously called "Regional Bell Operating Companies," "Baby Bells," or "Incumbent Local Exchange Carriers" (ILECs)), and a separate, competitive market for long-distance service from which the ILECs were excluded. More than a decade later, Congress withdrew approval of the ILECs' monopolies by enacting the Telecommunications Act of 1996 (1996 Act), 110 Stat. 56, which "fundamentally restructure[d] local telephone markets" and "subject[ed] [ILECs] to a host of duties intended to facilitate market entry." In recompense, the 1996 Act set conditions for authorizing ILECs to enter the long-distance market.[444]

"Central to the [new] scheme [was each ILEC's] obligation . . .to share its network with competitors,". . . which came to be known as "competitive local exchange carriers" (CLECs) . . . . A CLEC could make use of an ILEC's network in any of three ways: by (1) "purchas[ing] local telephone services at wholesale rates for resale to end users," (2) "leas[ing] elements of the [ILEC's] network 'on an unbundled basis,'" or (3) "interconnect[ing] its own facilities with the [ILEC's] network." Owing to the "considerable expense and effort" required to make unbundled network elements available to rivals at wholesale prices. . . . the ILECs vigorously litigated the scope of the sharing obligation imposed by the 1996 Act, with the result that the Federal Communications Commission (FCC) three times revised its regulations to narrow the range of network elements to be shared with the CLECs.

Respondents William Twombly and Lawrence Marcus (hereinafter plaintiffs) represent a putative class consisting of all "subscribers of local telephone and/or highspeed internet services . . .from February 8, 1996 to present." In this action against petitioners, a group of ILECs, plaintiffs seek treble damages and declaratory and injunctive relief for claimed violations of § 1 of the Sherman Act . . . which prohibits "[e]very contract, combination in the form of trust or otherwise, or conspiracy, in restraint of trade or commerce among the several States, or with foreign nations."

The complaint alleges that the ILECs conspired to restrain trade in two ways, each supposedly

---

[444] *See* 47 U.S.C. § 271.

inflating charges for local telephone and high-speed Internet services. Plaintiffs say, first, that the ILECs "engaged in parallel conduct" in their respective service areas to inhibit the growth of upstart CLECs. Their actions allegedly included making unfair agreements with the CLECs for access to ILEC networks, providing inferior connections to the networks, overcharging, and billing in ways designed to sabotage the CLECs' relations with their own customers. Ibid. According to the complaint, the ILECs' "compelling common motivatio[n]" to thwart the CLECs' competitive efforts naturally led them to form a conspiracy; "[h]ad any one [ILEC] not sought to prevent CLECs . . .from competing effectively ..., the resulting greater competitive inroads into that [ILEC's] territory would have revealed the degree to which competitive entry by CLECs would have been successful in the other territories in the absence of such conduct."

Second, the complaint charges agreements by the ILECs to refrain from competing against one another. These are to be inferred from the ILECs' common failure "meaningfully [to] pursu[e]" "attractive business opportunit[ies]" in contiguous markets where they possessed "substantial competitive advantages," . . . and from a statement of Richard Notebaert, chief executive officer (CEO) of the ILEC Qwest, that competing in the territory of another ILEC "might be a good way to turn a quick dollar but that doesn't make it right" . . .

The complaint couches its ultimate allegations this way:

> In the absence of any meaningful competition between the [ILECs] in one another's markets, and in light of the parallel course of conduct that each engaged in to prevent competition from CLECs within their respective local telephone and/or high speed internet services markets and the other facts and market circumstances alleged above, Plaintiffs allege upon information and belief that [the ILECs] have entered into a contract, combination or conspiracy to prevent competitive entry in their respective local telephone and/or high speed internet services markets and have agreed not to compete with one another and otherwise allocated customers and markets to one another.

[The district court dismissed the case for failing to state a sufficient claim under pleading standards. The Court of Appeals reversed, and the Supreme Court granted certiorari]

. . .

B

This case presents the antecedent question of what a plaintiff must plead in order to state a claim under § 1 of the Sherman Act. Federal Rule of Civil Procedure 8(a) (2) requires only "a short and plain statement of the claim showing that the pleader is entitled to relief," in order to "give the defendant fair notice of what the . . .claim is and the grounds upon which it rests,"[445] While a complaint attacked by a Rule 12(b) (6) motion to dismiss does not need detailed factual allegations . . . a plaintiff's obligation to provide the "grounds" of his "entitle[ment] to relief" requires more than labels and conclusions, and a formulaic recitation of the elements of a cause of action will not do . . . . Factual allegations must be enough to raise a right to relief above the speculative level.[446]

---

[445] Conley v. Gibson, 355 U.S. 41 (1957).

[446] *See* 5 C. WRIGHT & A. MILLER, FEDERAL PRACTICE AND PROCEDURE § 1216, pp. 235–36 (3d ed.2004) (hereinafter Wright & Miller) ("[T]he pleading must contain something more . . . than . . . a statement of facts that merely creates a suspicion [of] a legally cognizable right of action"), on the assumption that all the allegations in the complaint are true (even if doubtful in fact), *see, e.g.*, Swierkiewicz v. Sorema N. A., 534 U.S. 506 (2002); Neitzke v. Williams, 490

In applying these general standards to a § 1 claim, we hold that stating such a claim requires a complaint with enough factual matter (taken as true) to suggest that an agreement was made. Asking for plausible grounds to infer an agreement does not impose a probability requirement at the pleading stage; it simply calls for enough fact to raise a reasonable expectation that discovery will reveal evidence of illegal agreement. And, of course, a well-pleaded complaint may proceed even if it strikes a savvy judge that actual proof of those facts is improbable, and "that a recovery is very remote and unlikely." In identifying facts that are suggestive enough to render a § 1 conspiracy plausible, we have the benefit of the prior rulings and considered views of leading commentators, already quoted, that lawful parallel conduct fails to bespeak unlawful agreement. It makes sense to say, therefore, that an allegation of parallel conduct and a bare assertion of conspiracy will not suffice. Without more, parallel conduct does not suggest conspiracy, and a conclusory allegation of agreement at some unidentified point does not supply facts adequate to show illegality. Hence, when allegations of parallel conduct are set out in order to make a § 1 claim, they must be placed in a context that raises a suggestion of a preceding agreement, not merely parallel conduct that could just as well be independent action.

The need at the pleading stage for allegations plausibly suggesting (not merely consistent with) agreement reflects the threshold requirement of Rule 8 (a) (2) that the "plain statement" possess enough heft to "sho[w] that the pleader is entitled to relief." A statement of parallel conduct, even conduct consciously undertaken, needs some setting suggesting the agreement necessary to make out a § 1 claim; without that further circumstance pointing toward a meeting of the minds, an account of a defendant's commercial efforts stays in neutral territory. An allegation of parallel conduct is thus much like a naked assertion of conspiracy in a § 1 complaint: it gets the complaint close to stating a claim, but without some further factual enhancement it stops short of the line between possibility and plausibility of "entitle[ment] to relief."[447]

We alluded to the practical significance of the Rule 8 entitlement requirement in *Dura Pharmaceuticals, Inc. v. Broudo*,[448] when we explained that something beyond the mere possibility of loss causation must be alleged, lest a plaintiff with "'a largely groundless claim'" be allowed to "'take up the time of a number of other people, with the right to do so representing an *in terrorem* increment of the settlement value.'" So, when the allegations in a complaint, however true, could not raise a claim of entitlement to relief, "'this basic deficiency should . . .be exposed at the point of minimum expenditure of time and money by the parties and the court.'"[449]

It is no answer to say that a claim just shy of a plausible entitlement to relief can, if groundless, be weeded out early in the discovery process through "careful case management," . . . given the common lament that the success of judicial supervision in checking discovery abuse has been on the modest side.[450]

U.S. 319, 327 (1989) ("Rule 12(b) (6) does not countenance . . . dismissals based on a judge's disbelief of a complaint's factual allegations"); Scheuer v. Rhodes, 416 U.S. 232, 236 (1974) (a well-pleaded complaint may proceed even if it appears "that a recovery is very remote and unlikely").

[447] *Cf.* DM Research, Inc. v. College of Am. Pathologists, 170 F.3d 53, 56 (C.A.1 1999) ("[T]erms like 'conspiracy,' or even 'agreement,' are border-line: they might well be sufficient in conjunction with a more specific allegation, for example, identifying a written agreement or even a basis for inferring a tacit agreement . . .but a court is not required to accept such terms as a sufficient basis for a complaint").

[448] 544 U.S. 336 (2005).

[449] 5 WRIGHT & MILLER § 1216, at 233–234 ("[S]ome threshold of plausibility must be crossed at the outset before a patent antitrust case should be permitted to go into its inevitably costly and protracted discovery phase").

[450] *See, e.g.*, Easterbrook, *Discovery as Abuse*, 69 B.U.L. REV. 635, 638 (1989) ("Judges can do little about

And it is self-evident that the problem of discovery abuse cannot be solved by "careful scrutiny of evidence at the summary judgment stage," much less "lucid instructions to juries," post, at 1975; the threat of discovery expense will push cost-conscious defendants to settle even anemic cases before reaching those proceedings. Probably, then, it is only by taking care to require allegations that reach the level suggesting conspiracy that we can hope to avoid the potentially enormous expense of discovery in cases with no "'reasonably founded hope that the [discovery] process will reveal relevant evidence'" to support a § 1 claim.

Plaintiffs do not, of course, dispute the requirement of plausibility and the need for something more than merely parallel behavior explained in Theatre Enterprises, Monsanto, and Matsushita, and their main argument against the plausibility standard at the pleading stage is its ostensible conflict with an early statement of ours construing Rule 8. Justice Black's opinion for the Court in *Conley v. Gibson* spoke not only of the need for fair notice of the grounds for entitlement to relief but of "the accepted rule that a complaint should not be dismissed for failure to state a claim unless it appears beyond doubt that the plaintiff can prove no set of facts in support of his claim which would entitle him to relief."[451] This "no set of facts" language can be read in isolation as saying that any statement revealing the theory of the claim will suffice unless its factual impossibility may be shown from the face of the pleadings; and the Court of Appeals appears to have read *Conley* in some such way when formulating its understanding of the proper pleading standard.[452]

On such a focused and literal reading of *Conley*'s "no set of facts," a wholly conclusory statement of claim would survive a motion to dismiss whenever the pleadings left open the possibility that a plaintiff might later establish some "set of [undisclosed] facts" to support recovery. So here, the Court of Appeals specifically found the prospect of unearthing direct evidence of conspiracy sufficient to preclude dismissal, even though the complaint does not set forth a single fact in a context that suggests an agreement.[453] It seems fair to say that this approach to pleading would dispense with any showing of a "'reasonably founded hope'" that a plaintiff would be able to make a case .

We could go on, but there is no need to pile up further citations to show that *Conley*'s "no set of facts" language has been questioned, criticized, and explained away long enough. To be fair to the *Conley* Court, the passage should be understood in light of the opinion's preceding summary of the complaint's concrete allegations, which the Court quite reasonably understood as amply stating a claim for relief. But the passage so often quoted fails to mention this understanding on the part of the Court, and after puzzling the profession for 50 years, this famous observation has earned its retirement. The phrase is best forgotten as an incomplete, negative gloss on an accepted pleading standard: once a claim has been stated adequately, it may be supported by showing any set of facts consistent with the allegations in the complaint.[454] *Conley*, then, described the breadth of opportunity to prove what an adequate complaint claims, not the minimum standard of adequate pleading to govern a complaint's survival.

III

When we look for plausibility in this complaint, we agree with the District Court that plaintiffs' claim of conspiracy in restraint of trade comes up short. To begin with, the complaint leaves no doubt that

---

impositional discovery when parties control the legal claims to be presented and conduct the discovery themselves").
[451] 355 U.S., at 45–46.
[452] *See* 425 F.3d, at 106, 114 (invoking *Conley*'s "no set of facts" language in describing the standard for dismissal).
[453] 425 F.3d at 106, 114.
[454] *See Sanjuan*, 40 F.3d, at 251 (once a claim for relief has been stated, a plaintiff "receives the benefit of imagination, so long as the hypotheses are consistent with the complaint").

plaintiffs rest their § 1 claim on descriptions of parallel conduct and not on any independent allegation of actual agreement among the ILECs. Although in form a few stray statements speak directly of agreement, on fair reading these are merely legal conclusions resting on the prior allegations. Thus, the complaint first takes account of the alleged "absence of any meaningful competition between [the ILECs] in one another's markets," "the parallel course of conduct that each [ILEC] engaged in to prevent competition from CLECs," "and the other facts and market circumstances alleged [earlier]"; "in light of" these, the complaint concludes "that [the ILECs] have entered into a contract, combination or conspiracy to prevent competitive entry into their . . .markets and have agreed not to compete with one another." . . . The nub of the complaint, then, is the ILECs' parallel behavior, consisting of steps to keep the CLECs out and manifest disinterest in becoming CLECs themselves, and its sufficiency turns on the suggestions raised by this conduct when viewed in light of common economic experience.

We think that nothing contained in the complaint invests either the action or inaction alleged with a plausible suggestion of conspiracy. As to the ILECs' supposed agreement to disobey the 1996 Act and thwart the CLECs' attempts to compete, we agree with the District Court that nothing in the complaint intimates that the resistance to the upstarts was anything more than the natural, unilateral reaction of each ILEC intent on keeping its regional dominance. The 1996 Act did more than just subject the ILECs to competition; it obliged them to subsidize their competitors with their own equipment at wholesale rates. The economic incentive to resist was powerful, but resisting competition is routine market conduct, and even if the ILECs flouted the 1996 Act in all the ways the plaintiffs allege, . . . there is no reason to infer that the companies had agreed among themselves to do what was only natural anyway; so natural, in fact, that if alleging parallel decisions to resist competition were enough to imply an antitrust conspiracy, pleading a § 1 violation against almost any group of competing businesses would be a sure thing.

The complaint makes its closest pass at a predicate for conspiracy with the claim that collusion was necessary because success by even one CLEC in an ILEC's territory "would have revealed the degree to which competitive entry by CLECs would have been successful in the other territories." But, its logic aside, this general premise still fails to answer the point that there was just no need for joint encouragement to resist the 1996 Act; as the District Court said, "each ILEC has reason to want to avoid dealing with CLECs" and "each ILEC would attempt to keep CLECs out, regardless of the actions of the other ILECs."[455]

. . .

Plaintiffs' second conspiracy theory rests on the competitive reticence among the ILECs themselves in the wake of the 1996 Act, which was supposedly passed in the "'hop[e] that the large incumbent local monopoly companies . . .might attack their neighbors' service areas, as they are the best situated to do so.'" Contrary to hope, the ILECs declined "'to enter each other's service territories in any significant way,'" . . . and the local telephone and high–speed Internet market remains highly compartmentalized geographically, with minimal competition. Based on this state of affairs and perceiving the ILECs to be blessed with "especially attractive business opportunities" in surrounding markets dominated by other ILECs, the plaintiffs assert that the ILECs' parallel conduct was "strongly suggestive of conspiracy."

But it was not suggestive of conspiracy, not if history teaches anything. In a traditionally unregulated industry with low barriers to entry, sparse competition among large firms dominating separate geographical segments of the market could very well signify illegal agreement, but here we have an obvious

---

[455] 313 F.Supp.2d at 184.

alternative explanation. In the decade preceding the 1996 Act and well before that, monopoly was the norm in telecommunications, not the exception.[456] The ILECs were born in that world, doubtless liked the world the way it was, and surely knew the adage about him who lives by the sword. Hence, a natural explanation for the noncompetition alleged is that the former Government-sanctioned monopolists were sitting tight, expecting their neighbors to do the same thing.

In fact, the complaint itself gives reasons to believe that the ILECs would see their best interests in keeping to their old turf. Although the complaint says generally that the ILECs passed up "especially attractive business opportunit[ies]" by declining to compete as CLECs against other ILECs . . . it does not allege that competition as CLECs was potentially any more lucrative than other opportunities being pursued by the ILECs during the same period, and the complaint is replete with indications that any CLEC faced nearly insurmountable barriers to profitability owing to the ILECs' flagrant resistance to the network sharing requirements of the 1996 Act. . . . Not only that, but even without a monopolistic tradition and the peculiar difficulty of mandating shared networks, "[f]irms do not expand without limit and none of them enters every market that an outside observer might regard as profitable, or even a small portion of such markets." The upshot is that Congress may have expected some ILECs to become CLECs in the legacy territories of other ILECs, but the disappointment does not make conspiracy plausible. We agree with the District Court's assessment that antitrust conspiracy was not suggested by the facts adduced under either theory of the complaint, which thus fails to state a valid
§ 1 claim.

. . .

Here, in contrast, we do not require heightened fact pleading of specifics, but only enough facts to state a claim to relief that is plausible on its face. Because the plaintiffs here have not nudged their claims across the line from conceivable to plausible, their complaint must be dismissed.

. . .

The judgment of the Court of Appeals for the Second Circuit is reversed, and the case is remanded for further proceedings consistent with this opinion.

It is so ordered.

Follow-Up Questions and Comments

1. In a decision after *Twombly*, the Supreme Court in *Ashcroft v. Iqbal*,[457] seemed to confirm a philosophical shift that will demand more than notice pleading as set forth in Conley. *Iqbal*, a Pakistani Muslim, was detained in a maximum-security facility in New York after the 9/11 terrorist attacks. Afterward, he sued several federal officials, including John Ashcroft, the former Attorney General, and Robert Mueller, the Director of the Federal Bureau of Investigation. According to the complaint, these government officials designated him a person of high interest based on his race, religion, or national origin. The complaint further alleged a policy of indiscriminately detaining

---

[456] *See* Verizon Communications Inc. v. FCC, 535 U.S. 467, 477–78 (2002) (describing telephone service providers as traditional public monopolies).
[457] 556 U.S. 662 (2009).

persons for such reasons after the 9/11 attacks. The complaint ultimately alleged that the defendants "willfully and maliciously" agreed to subject him to harsh confinement solely due to his race, religion, or national origin. Attorney General Ashcroft and Director Mueller were alleged to be the prime architects of a policy that violated the First and Fifth Amendments. Citing *Twombly*, the Court held the complaint insufficient to state a claim under Rule 8.[458] The Court observed that "labels," "conclusions," "formulaic recitation of the elements of a cause of action," and "naked assertions" without factual support would not suffice.[459] Instead, the Court observed:

2. To survive a motion to dismiss, a complaint must contain sufficient factual matter, accepted as true, to "state a claim to relief that is plausible on its face." A claim has facial plausibility when the plaintiff pleads factual content that allows the court to draw the reasonable inference that the defendant is liable for the conduct alleged. The plausibility standard is not akin to a "probability requirement," but it asks for more than a sheer possibility that a defendant has acted unlawfully. Where a complaint pleads facts that are "merely consistent with" a defendant's liability, it "stops short of the line between possibility and plausibility of 'entitlement to relief.'"[460]

3. Some fear that *Twombly* and *Iqbal* harbor a return to the old, pre-1938 "code pleading" standards that required detailed facts to support a claim. The decisions, however, more likely represent a shift to some point in between the code pleading standard of old and the "anything goes" standard of *Conley*. In these decisions, the Court has sent a message that it interprets Rule 8 as requiring facts, not conclusions, to be pled on each element of each claim. Most good lawyers already followed the practice of identifying the elements of a claim and pleading not just conclusions (e.g., the defendant committed an assault), but also facts to support each element (e.g., the defendant walked up on January 1, 2009, acted as if he was going to punch the plaintiff, but stopped within inches of the plaintiff's face). Requiring some facts to support each element of a claim usually is not burdensome.

4. An influential decision of the United States Court of Appeals for the Seventh Circuit has provided valuable guidance on the degree to which traditional notice pleading still applies and when *Iqbal* and *Twombly* ought to be considered. Following is that decision:

SWANSON v. CITIBANK, N.A.
United States Court of Appeals for the Seventh Circuit, 2010
614 F.3d 400

WOOD, Circuit Judge.

Gloria Swanson sued Citibank, Andre Lanier, and Lanier's employer, PCI Appraisal Services, because she believed that all three had discriminated against her on the basis of her race (African-American) when Citibank turned down her application for a home-equity loan. . . . [W]e proceed solely with respect to Swanson's part of the case. She was unsuccessful in the district court, which dismissed in response to the defendants' motion under Fed. R. Civ. P. 12(b) (6).

---

[458] *Id.* at 677.
[459] *Id.*
[460] *Iqbal*, 552 U.S. at 677 (2009), (quoting *Twombly*, 550 U.S. at 556–57, 570) (internal citation omitted).

Swanson based her complaint on the following set of events, which we accept as true for purposes of this appeal. In February 2009 Citibank announced a plan to make loans using funds that it had received from the federal government's Troubled Assets Relief Program. Encouraged by this prospect, Swanson went to a Citibank branch to apply for a home-equity loan. A representative named Skertich told Swanson that she could not apply alone, because she owned her home jointly with her husband; he had to be present as well. Swanson was skeptical, suspecting that Skertich's demand was a ploy to discourage loan applications from African-Americans. She therefore asked to speak to a manager. When the manager joined the group, Swanson disclosed to both Skertich and the manager that Washington Mutual Bank previously had denied her a home-equity loan. The manager warned Swanson that, although she did not want to discourage Swanson from applying for the loan, Citibank's loan criteria were more stringent than those of other banks.

Still interested, Swanson took a loan application home and returned the next day with the necessary information. She was again assisted by Skertich, who entered the information that Swanson had furnished into the computer. When he reached a question regarding race, Skertich told Swanson that she was not required to respond. At some point during this exchange, Skertich pointed to a photograph on his desk and commented that his wife and son were part African-American.

A few days later Citibank conditionally approved Swanson for a home-equity loan of $50,000. It hired Andre Lanier, who worked for PCI Appraisal Services, to visit Swanson's home for an onsite appraisal. Although Swanson had estimated in her loan application that her house was worth $270,000, Lanier appraised it at only $170,000. The difference was critical: Citibank turned down the loan and explained that its conditional approval had been based on the higher valuation. Two months later Swanson paid for and obtained an appraisal from Midwest Valuations, which thought her home was worth $240,000.

Swanson saw coordinated action in this chain of events, and so she filed a complaint (later amended) charging that Citibank, Lanier, and PCI disfavor providing home-equity loans to African-Americans, and so they deliberately lowered the appraised value of her home far below its actual market value, so that they would have an excuse to deny her the loan. She charges that in so doing, they violated the Fair Housing Act, 42 U.S.C. § 3605, and the Equal Credit Opportunity Act, 15 U.S.C. § 1691(a) (1). The district court granted the defendants' motions to dismiss both theories. It relied heavily on *Latimore Citibank Fed. Savings Bank*,[461] a case in which this court described the evidence required to defeat a defense motion for summary judgment on a credit discrimination claim. Initially, the court liberally construed Swanson's complaint to include a common-law fraud claim and declined to dismiss that aspect of the case. Later, however, the defendants moved to dismiss the fraud claim as well, and the district court granted the motion on the grounds that the statements on which Swanson relied were too indefinite and her reliance was unreasonable. This appeal followed.

Before turning to the particulars of Swanson's case, a brief review of the standards that apply to dismissals for failure to state a claim is in order. It is by now well established that a plaintiff must do better than putting a few words on paper that, in the hands of an imaginative reader, might suggest that something has happened to her that might be redressed by the law.[462] The question with which courts are still struggling is how much higher the Supreme Court meant to set the bar, when it decided not only *Twombly*, but also

---

[461] 151 F.3d 712 (7th Cir. 1998).

[462] *Cf.* Conley v. Gibson, 355 U.S. 41, 45–46 (1957), disapproved by Bell Atlantic Corp. v. Twombly, 550 U.S. 544, 563 (2007) ("after puzzling the profession for 50 years, this famous observation [the 'no set of facts' language] has earned its retirement").

Erickson v. Pardus,[463] and *Ashcroft v. Iqbal*.[464] This is not an easy question to answer, as the thoughtful dissent from this opinion demonstrates. On the one hand, the Supreme Court has adopted a "plausibility" standard, but on the other hand, it has insisted that it is not requiring fact pleading, nor is it adopting a single pleading standard to replace Rule 8, Rule 9, and specialized regimes like the one in the Private Securities Litigation Reform Act ("PSLRA").[465]

Critically, in none of the three recent decisions—*Twombly*, *Erickson*, or *Iqbal*—did the Court cast any doubt on the validity of Rule 8 of the Federal Rules of Civil Procedure. To the contrary: at all times it has said that it is interpreting Rule 8, not tossing it out the window. It is therefore useful to begin with a look at the language of the rule:

Claim for Relief. A pleading that states a claim for relief must contain: . . . a short and plain statement of the claim showing that the pleader is entitled to relief.

As one respected treatise put it in 2004, all that is necessary is that the claim for relief be stated with brevity, conciseness, and clarity. . . . [T]his portion of Rule 8 indicates that a basic objective of the rules is to avoid civil cases turning on technicalities and to require that the pleading discharge the function of giving the opposing party fair notice of the nature and basis or grounds of the pleader's claim and a general indication of the type of litigation that is involved.[466]

Nothing in the recent trio of cases has undermined these broad principles. As *Erickson* underscored, "[s]pecific facts are not necessary."[467] The Court was not engaged in a sub rosa campaign to reinstate the old fact-pleading system called for by the Field Code or even more modern codes. We know that because it said so in *Erickson*: "the statement need only give the defendant fair notice of what the . . . claim is and the grounds upon which it rests."[468] Instead, the Court has called for more careful attention to be given to several key questions: what, exactly, does it take to give the opposing party "fair notice"; how much detail realistically can be given, and should be given, about the nature and basis or grounds of the claim; and in what way is the pleader expected to signal the type of litigation that is being put before the court?

This is the light in which the Court's references in *Twombly*, repeated in *Iqbal*, to the pleader's responsibility to "state a claim to relief that is plausible on its face" must be understood.[469] "Plausibility" in this context does not imply that the district court should decide whose version to believe, or which version is more likely than not. Indeed, the Court expressly distanced itself from the latter approach in *Iqbal*, "the plausibility standard is not akin to a probability requirement."[470] As we understand it, the Court is saying instead that the plaintiff must give enough details about the subject-matter of the case to present a story that holds together. In other words, the court will ask itself could these things have happened, not did they happen. For cases governed only by Rule 8, it is not necessary to stack up inferences side by side and allow the case to go forward only if the plaintiff's inferences seem more compelling than the opposing inferences.

---

[463] 551 U.S. 89 (2007).

[464] 551 U.S. 89 (2007).

[465] 15 U.S.C. § 78u-4(b) (2).

[466] CHARLES ALAN WRIGHT & ARTHUR R. MILLER, FEDERAL PRACTICE AND PROCEDURE, 165–73 (3d ed. 2004).

[467] 551 U.S. at 93.

[468] *Id.*

[469] *See Twombly*, 550 U.S. at 570; *Iqbal*, 552 U.S. at 677.

[470] 552 U.S. at 677(internal quotation marks omitted).

The Supreme Court's explicit decision to reaffirm the validity of *Swierkiewicz v. Sorema N.A.*,[471] which was cited with approval in *Twombly*, indicates that in many straightforward cases, it will not be any more difficult today for a plaintiff to meet that burden than it was before the Court's recent decisions. A plaintiff who believes that she has been passed over for a promotion because of her sex will be able to plead that she was employed by Company X, that a promotion was offered, that she applied and was qualified for it, and that the job went to someone else. That is an entirely plausible scenario, whether or not it describes what "really" went on in this plaintiff's case. A more complex case involving financial derivatives, or tax fraud that the parties tried hard to conceal, or antitrust violations, will require more detail, both to give the opposing party notice of what the case is all about and to show how, in the plaintiff's mind at least, the dots should be connected. Finally, as the Supreme Court warned in *Iqbal* and as we acknowledged later in *Brooks v. Ross*,[472] "abstract recitations of the elements of a cause of action or conclusory legal statements,"[473] do nothing to distinguish the particular case that is before the court from every other hypothetically possible case in that field of law. Such statements therefore do not add to the notice that Rule 8 demands.

We realize that one powerful reason that lies behind the Supreme Court's concern about pleading standards is the cost of the discovery that will follow in any case that survives a motion to dismiss on the pleadings. The costs of discovery are often asymmetric, as the dissent points out, and one way to rein them in would be to make it more difficult to earn the right to engage in discovery. That is just what the Court did, by interring the rule that a complaint could go forward if any set of facts at all could be imagined, consistent with the statements in the complaint that would permit the pleader to obtain relief. Too much chaff was moving ahead with the wheat. But, in other contexts, the Supreme Court has drawn a careful line between those things that can be accomplished by judicial interpretation and those that should be handled through the procedures set up in the Rules Enabling Act.[474]

Returning to Swanson's case, we must analyze her allegations defendant-by-defendant. We begin with Citibank. On appeal, Swanson challenges only the dismissal of her Fair Housing Act and fraud claims. The Fair Housing Act prohibits businesses engaged in residential real estate transactions, including "[t]he making … of loans or providing other financial assistance . . . secured by residential real estate," from discriminating against any person on account of race.[475] Swanson's complaint identifies the type of discrimination that she thinks occurs (racial), by whom (Citibank, through Skertich, the manager, and the outside appraisers it used), and when (in connection with her effort in early 2009 to obtain a home-equity loan). This is all that she needed to put in the complaint.

The fact that Swanson included other, largely extraneous facts in her complaint does not undermine the soundness of her pleading. She points to Citibank's announced plan to use federal money to make more loans, its refusal to follow through in her case, and Skertich's comment that he has a mixed-race family. She has not pleaded herself out of court by mentioning these facts; whether they are particularly helpful for proving her case or not is another matter that can safely be put off for another day. It was therefore error for the district court to dismiss Swanson's Fair Housing Act claim against Citibank.

. . .

We now turn to Swanson's claims against Lanier and PCI. Here again, she pursues only her Fair

---

[471] 534 U.S. 506 (2002).

[472] 578 F.3d 574 (7th Cir. 2009).

[473] *Id.* at 581.

[474] 28 U.S.C. §§ 2071 et seq.

[475] 42 U.S.C. § 3605(a), (b) (1) (B).

Housing Act and fraud claims. (The appraisal defendants point out that they do not extend credit, and thus their actions are not covered in any event by the Equal Credit Opportunity Act, 15 § 1691a(e).) The Fair Housing Act makes it "unlawful for any person or other entity whose business includes engaging in residential real estate-related transactions to discriminate against any person in making available such a transaction, or in the terms or conditions of such a transaction, because of race . . . ."[476] The statute goes on to define the term "residential real estate-related transaction" to include "the selling, brokering, or appraising of residential real property." [477] There is an appraisal exemption also, found in § 3605(c), but it provides only that nothing in the statute prohibits appraisers from taking into consideration factors other than race or the other protected characteristics.

Swanson accuses the appraisal defendants of skewing their assessment of her home because of her race. It is unclear whether she believes that they did so as part of a conspiracy with Citibank, or if she thinks that they deliberately undervalued her property on their own initiative. Once again, we find that she has pleaded enough to survive a motion under Rule 12(b) (6). The appraisal defendants knew her race, and she accuses them of discriminating against her in the specific business transaction that they had with her. When it comes to proving her case, she will need to come up with more evidence than the mere fact that PCI (through Lanier) placed a far lower value on her house than Midwest Valuations did.[478] All we hold now is that she is entitled to take the next step in this litigation.

This does not, however, save her common-law fraud claim against Lanier and PCI. She has not adequately alleged that she relied on their appraisal, nor has she pointed to any out-of-pocket losses that she suffered because of it.

We therefore REVERSE the judgment of the district court insofar as it dismissed Swanson's Fair Housing Act claims against all three defendants, and we AFFIRM insofar as it dismissed the common-law fraud claims against all three. Each side will bear its own costs on appeal.

Follow-Up Questions and Comments

1. In line with the balanced assessment of *Iqbal* and *Twombly* set forth in Swanson, one can also point to a decision of the U.S. Supreme Court after both *Twombly* and *Iqbal*.[479] In addition, the Court more recently, in Skinner v. Switzer,[480] reversed the dismissal of a complaint and stated: "[Plaintiff]'s complaint is not a model of the careful drafter's art, but under the Federal Rules of Civil Procedure, a complaint need not pin plaintiff's claim for relief to a precise legal theory. Rule 8(a) (2) of the Federal Rules of Civil Procedure generally requires only a 'short and plain' statement of the plaintiff's claim, not an exposition of his legal argument."). Some lower court decisions suggest that the *Twombly* and *Iqbal* decisions change the standard for pleading sufficiency.[481]

---

[476] 42 U.S.C. § 3605(a).

[477] 42 U.S.C. § 3605(b) (2).

[478] *See* Latimore, 151 F.3d at 715 (need more at the summary judgment stage than evidence of a discrepancy between appraisals).

[479] *See* Erickson v. Pardus, 551 U.S. 89, 93 (2007) (reversing lower courts' dismissal of claim by prisoner of deliberate indifference and stating, "Federal Rule of Civil Procedure 8(a) (2) requires only a 'short and plain statement of the claim showing the pleader is entitled to relief.' specific facts are not necessary.").

[480] 562 U.S. 521, 530 (2011).

[481] *See, e.g.*, Fowler v. UPMC Shadyside, 578 F.3d 203, 210 (3d Cir. 2009) ("[P]leading standards have seemingly shifted from simple notice pleading to a more heightened form of pleading."), called into question by *In re Ins.*

2. A respected authority suggests, as the above discussions suggests, that effect of the decision is to require more factual detail to the extent the case is more complex than most cases.[482]

3. Although you must research the law of the jurisdiction in which you are litigating to determine the impact of *Iqbal* and *Twombly* in that jurisdiction, the author's view is consistent with Swanson. The *Twombly* and *Iqbal* cases will likely have the most impact in more complex cases, such as antitrust cases, while for most cases the notice pleading standard should remain in place.

Brokerage Antitrust Litig., 618 F.3d 300, 319 n.17 (3d Cir. 2010); Francis v. Giacomelli, 588 F.3d 186,192 n.1 (4th Cir. 2009) (suggesting *Twombly* and *Iqbal* have changed pleading standard).

[482] *See* 2 JEFFREY A. PARNESS & JERRY E. SMITH, MOORE'S FEDERAL PRACTICE – CIVIL § 8.04 (2019).

Figure 10-2 below illustrates a possible flow chart for evaluating how to plead claims:

Figure 10-2

```
┌─────────────────────┐         ┌──────────┐         ┌────────────────────────────────────┐
│ Is this a Rule 9    │         │          │         │ Must plead with particularity:     │
│ (fraud or           │────────▶│   YES    │────────▶│  • code pleading on steroids       │
│ mistake) claim?     │         │          │         │  • do not generalize               │
└─────────────────────┘         └──────────┘         │  • specific paragraphs for 5 W's   │
         │                                            └────────────────────────────────────┘
         ▼
   ┌──────────┐
   │    NO    │
   └──────────┘
         │
         ▼
┌──────────────────────────────────┐
│ Refer to Rule 8                  │
│ 8(a) Complaint must contain:     │
│   • grounds for jurisdiction     │
│   • short and plain statement of │
│     claim                        │
│   • grounds for relief           │
└──────────────────────────────────┘
         │
         ▼
┌──────────────────────────────────┐
│ 1. Grounds for jurisdiction      │
└──────────────────────────────────┘
         │
         ▼
┌──────────────────────────────────────────────────────────────┐
│ 2. Short and Plain Statement                                 │
│                                                              │
│ Complicated Cases such as RICO claims:                       │
│   • more facts required to support specific claim (*Iqbal*   │
│     and *Twombly*)                                           │
│   • remember to provide basis for punitive damages (e.g.     │
│     willful and wanton conduct, intentional or at least      │
│     recklessness                                             │
│                                                              │
│ Run of the Mill Cases:                                       │
│   • enough facts and details to form a cohesive story        │
│     (*Swanson*)                                              │
└──────────────────────────────────────────────────────────────┘
         │
         ▼
┌──────────────────────────────────┐
│ 3. Ground for relief             │
│   • potential sources of relief  │
│   • demand a jury trial          │
└──────────────────────────────────┘
```

291

Practice Problems

Practice Problem 10-1

In order to plead facts in support of a prima facie case for age discrimination under the Federal Age Discrimination in Employment Act (ADEA), 29 U.S.C. § 621 et seq., plaintiffs must allege that (1) they are members of a protected class; (2) they were qualified for the positions; they suffered adverse employment actions based on age; and (4) the beneficiaries of the adverse employment action were younger. Plaintiffs at Salt Mines, Inc. alleged:

This Court has Jurisdiction under the Federal Age Discrimination in Employment Act (ADEA), a federal statute, and thus the Court has federal question jurisdiction under 28 U.S.C. § 1331. The plaintiffs are members of the class of persons protected by the ADEA. Ranging in age from 66 to 69, plaintiffs had worked at Salt Mines, Inc. for over two decades (beginning in early 2000 to present), without being terminated or reprimanded. That they had suffered adverse employment when persons younger than them, specifically persons ranging in age from 34 years old to 44 years old, were given supervisory jobs, rather than the plaintiffs, at Salt Mines, Inc. (specific names and approximate time of such events provided). Salt Mines, Inc. discriminated against the plaintiffs and in favor of the younger employees because the younger employees would have longer careers with the company and, thus, would result in more profitability to the company.

WHEREFORE, the plaintiffs seek damages, back pay, promotions, and such other relief as the ADEA permits, including attorney's fees.

Is the above complaint sufficient under Rule 8(a)? Why or why not? Please explain the reasoning supporting your answer.

Practice Problem 10-2

The Racketeering Influenced and Corrupt Organization Act ("RICO"). 18 U.S.C. § 1961 et seq. includes a civil remedy providing for triple damages if a defendant engages in a pattern of racketeering activity. Racketeering activity includes, but is not limited to, making misrepresentations by use of mail (considered mail fraud) or telephone (considered wire fraud). The Dentists Association of America sued DentaInsur Corp., an insurer of patients who sought care of dentists in the Dental Association. Plaintiff's Complaint alleged:

This Court has Jurisdiction under the Racketeering Influenced and Corrupt Organizations Act, 18 U.S.C. § 1961 et seq. which as a federal statute provides jurisdiction under federal jurisdiction, including 28 U.S.C. § 1331. The plaintiff is a dental association whose members all treat patients insured by Defendant for dental care and procedures. DentaInsur represented to the patients and to the members of the dental association that it would cover the cost of a wide range of procedures, including taking x-rays, filling cavities, installing crowns, and making mouth guards for patients whose bite at night was wearing down their teeth. DentaInsur sent such representations in materials in the mail and in conversations with patients and members of the dental association over the phone. Contrary to their representations, DentaInsur automatically down-coded claims for taking x-rays, filling cavities, installing crowns, and making mouth guards for patients whose bite at night was wearing down their teeth, such that the provider of services did not receive the full cost that they would receive if they were treating a patient without insurance.

DentaInsur's pattern of paying less to the members of the dental association than what the members charged patients able to self-pay reflected a pattern of fraudulent behavior. The pattern of fraudulent behavior resulted in damages to the members of the dental association. WHEREFORE, the plaintiffs seek damages of $1 million, including treble damages, and attorney's fees and costs.

Is the above complaint sufficient under Rule 8(a)? Why or why not? Please explain the reasoning supporting your answer.

---

1. Pleading Special Claims

Please read Federal Rule of Civil Procedure 9(b). By comparing Rule 8(a) and Rule 9(b) can you determine when one needs to plead matters with more specificity and what kinds of matters those are? Following is a case on the requirement of pleading under Rule 9(b).

HAYNES v. JPMORGAN CHASE BANK
United States Court of Appeals for the Eleventh Circuit, 2012
466 F. App'x. 763

Before WILSON, PRYOR, and KRAVITCH, Circuit Judges.

Darryl Haynes appeals pro se the district court's grant of summary judgment in favor of JPMorgan Chase Bank, N.A. ("Chase") on Haynes's action for declaratory and injunctive relief to stay foreclosure of his property. . . . [The district court dismissed his complaint and, on considering his proposed amended complaint, refused to grant leave to amend because the complaint failed to plead the fraud claim it alleged with the particularity required by Federal Rule of Civil Procedure 9(b).]

. . .

Hanes's proposed amended complaint made allegations of fraud and asserted that Chase lacked legal standing to foreclose. In order to plead fraud sufficiently, a claimant must state with particularity the circumstances constituting the fraud.[483] "The particularity rule serves an important purpose in fraud actions by alerting defendants to the precise misconduct with which they are charged and protecting defendants against spurious charges of immoral and fraudulent behavior." In order to satisfy the particularity rule, a complaint of fraud must set forth:

(1) precisely what statements were made in what documents or oral representations or what omissions were made, and (2) the time and place of each such statement and the person responsible for making (or, in the case of omissions, not making) same, and (3) the content of such statements and the manner in which they misled the plaintiff, and (4) what the defendants obtained as a consequence of the fraud.[484]

Haynes's proposed amended complaint did not satisfy these requirements, nor did it state any other legal claims supported by factual allegations. As such, amendment of his original complaint would have been futile and thus the denial of Haynes's motion was not an abuse of discretion.

---

[483] FED. R. CIV. P. 9(b).
[484] Brooks v. Blue Cross & Blue Shield of Fla., Inc., 116 F.3d 1364, 1371 (11th Cir.1997).

. . .

Affirmed.

Follow- Up Questions and Comments

1. A useful rule of thumb in pleading a matter requiring particularized pleading is to ask the five "W's": Who, What, When, Where, and Why? Pleading with particularity, in other words, ought to answer these questions: Who was involved in the event(s)? What happened in the event(s) and/or by what means (e.g., in person, by mail, by facsimile, etc.)? When did the event(s) in question happen? Where did the event(s) occur? Why do/does the event/events matter causally? Thus, in pleading a fraud claim, one should include as to all allegedly fraudulent communications or nondisclosures: (1) the names of all parties involved; (2) the precise content of the allegedly fraudulent communications and not only what was communicated—or, in the case of fraudulent nondisclosure, what of significance was not disclosed—but also the means by which the communications occurred (in person, by mail, etc.); (3) the exact date(s) of all such communications/nondisclosures, including date(s) sent and date(s) received; (4) where the communication(s) happened; and (5) why the communications/nondisclosures led the plaintiff to rely on them (i.e., why the communications were ones reasonably relied on by the person asserting the claim—typically referred to as the "materiality" element).[485]

Practice Problem

Practice Problem 10-3

Plaintiffs, home purchasers, sue the real estate agent that led them to buy a house. The house had a basement and plaintiffs asked whether there had ever been any flooding in the basement. Plaintiffs alleged that defendant did not acknowledge that there had been flooding in the basement, something they discovered after they had bought the property. Plaintiffs sue the defendant for fraud and assert the above facts as their allegations. Defendant challenges the complaint as failing to allege fraud in accordance with Rule 9(b). How should the court rule? Why?

---

2. Additional Requirements for Injunctive Relief during Pendency of Case

In addition to filing a complaint that satisfies all the formal requirement described earlier in this chapter, a plaintiff seeking injunctive relief during the pendency of the lawsuit must do more. How much "more" the plaintiff needs to provide depends on whether she is seeking a motion for a temporary restraining order (TRO), which can last only 14 days, or a preliminary injunction, which can last the entirety of the time a case is pending and until the final judgment.

---

[485] *See* Barney J. Finberg, *Construction and Application of Provision of Rule 9(b)*, 27 A.L.R. FED. 407 (1976).

C. Motions for Temporary and Preliminary Injunctive Relief

In some cases, filing a complaint will not be enough to begin the process of resolving a dispute. Cases take time to get to trial. In that time—often called the "pendency of the case"—some plaintiffs need an interim ruling to maintain the status quo until the case is resolved. Otherwise, the plaintiff can suffer irreparable harm—i.e., harm that cannot be quantified or compensated. Examples of scenarios justifying a TRO and a preliminary injunctive relief are many. For instance, someone who is repeatedly trespassing or threatening to exercise power over another's property (e.g., to cut down trees), would need interim relief prior the final resolution of the case. The law considers the right to avoid trespasses as something that, even if someone could calculate damages in some fashion, cannot be fully compensated by money.

In the same vein intellectual property cases take up a fair amount of the federal court's docket. A plaintiff whose trademark is arguably being infringed in violation of the Federal Lanham Act,[486] a copyright owner whose copyrighted material is being used without permission in violation of the Copyright Act, 17 U.S.C. §§ 101, and/or a patent owner whose invention is being copied and sold without the owner's permission in violation of the Patent Act,[487] each of these plaintiffs would suffer irreparable harm if the defendant was able to continue to violate the intellectual property owner's rights during the pendency of the suit. Moreover, the need for preliminary injunction extends to many other situations. These forms of injunctive relief are appropriate whenever, absent such relief, irreparable harm would occur. That could take the form of damage to one's property, disclosure of trade secrets, and any number of other scenarios in which the effect of the defendant's act (or failure to act) would lead to consequences that could not be compensated by money damages.

Federal Rule of Civil Procedure 65 provides such a party the opportunity to protect her interests during the pendency of the suit. These scenarios range from matters that are ordinary, such as the enforcement of an employee's covenant not to compete against an employer after leaving, to the protection of constitutional rights. Indeed, anyone familiar with the history of desegregation following Brown v. Board of Education, realizes that the implementation of that decision could not have occurred without both preliminary and permanent injunctive relief.

1. Temporary Restraining Orders

Please read Rule 65. Although the Rule mentions preliminary injunctions before temporary restraining orders (TROs), the logical sequence in which to discuss these different types of interim injunction is first to address TROs. TROs are designed to allow for immediate relief. Rule 65 contemplates that a TRO can be issued—if the conditions specified in Rule 65(b) (1) are met—without notice. This provision requires an affidavit stating not only grounds for emergency relief but "the reason why [notice] should not be required. It takes a rare case to justify not providing notice. If, for instance, the affidavit can set forth reasons that, if notice is provided, the defendant would remove trade secrets or take action that the plaintiff seeks to be enjoined, then the plaintiff may be able to satisfy the requirement.[488] However, these circumstances are rare and typically the plaintiff should plan to provide notice to a defendant, even on a TRO. In practice, courts are more likely to grant a TRO if the defendant has received notice and participates in the hearing.

---

[486] 5 U.S.C. §§ 1051 et seq.
[487] 35 U.S.C. §§ 1051 et seq.
[488] 13 JOSEPH T. MCLAUGHLIN & ANTHONY J. SCIRICA, MOORE'S FEDERAL PRACTICE-CIVIL § 65.32 (2018).

A TRO, by rule, last no more than 14 days unless "for good cause" the TRO is extended. If after a TRO has been issued the enjoined party wishes to move to dissolve the TRO, the party can move for such dissolution. Again, that would be more likely to happen if the defendant were not provided notice. If the defendant received notice and participated in the TRO hearing, the more likely result is for the court to set a hearing on a motion for a preliminary injunction.

2. Preliminary Injunction

A preliminary injunction provides relief through the pendency of the case. Thus, if a plaintiff is seeking injunctive relief at trial, the plaintiff need not wait. Indeed, as already suggested, in waiting such a plaintiff would often suffer irreparable harm. A preliminary injunction can preserve the status quo, enjoin the defendant to do or refrain from doing matters that would cause irreparable harm during the pendency of the suit. Indeed, the court can consolidate a hearing on the preliminary injunction with the trial on the merits. Rule 65(a) (2) permits such expediting of the hearing on a matter such that, if a hearing on the preliminary injunction is consolidated with a trial on the merits, the ultimate resolution of the case will be far sooner than most cases that go to trial.

A court facing the decision of whether to grant a TRO or a preliminary injunction evaluates the evidence in light of a four-part test. The following case provides an example of the four-part test and the way in which it applies.

PAISLEY PARK ENTERPRISES, INC., v. GEORGE IAN BOXILL
United States District Court for the District of Minnesota, 2017
253 F. Supp. 3d 1037

ORDER GRANTING IN PART AND DENYING IN PART MOTION FOR PRELIMINARY INJUNCTION

Wilhelmina M. Wright, United States District Judge

This lawsuit involves a dispute over the ownership of previously unreleased recordings of five songs by the internationally known recording artist Prince Rogers Nelson (Prince). Defendant George Ian Boxill is a sound engineer who worked with Prince during Prince's lifetime to record and edit the five songs at issue. After Prince's death in 2016, Boxill worked with Defendants Rogue Music Alliance, LLC, and Deliverance, LLC, on a commercial release of the disputed Prince recordings in Boxill's possession. Plaintiffs Paisley Park Enterprises, Inc., and Comerica Bank & Trust, N.A., as Personal Representative of the Estate of Prince Rogers Nelson, initiated this lawsuit to enjoin Defendants from promoting and distributing the disputed recordings and to secure the return of those recordings to Prince's estate.

Plaintiffs moved for a temporary restraining order, which the Court issued on April 19, 2017. Thereafter, Defendants filed a motion to modify the temporary restraining order and for early discovery.

Plaintiffs also filed a motion for a preliminary injunction. The Court extended the temporary restraining order in a May 3, 2017 Order, which effectively granted some of the relief sought by Defendants' motion to modify the temporary restraining order. For the reasons addressed below, the Court grants Plaintiffs' motion for a preliminary injunction and denies as moot Defendants' motion to modify the temporary restraining order and for early discovery.

296

BACKGROUND

Boxill is a sound engineer who worked with Prince on several music recordings between 2004 and 2008. Plaintiff Paisley Park Enterprises, Inc., is a Minnesota corporation that Prince owned during his lifetime and is now owned by his estate. Plaintiff Comerica Bank & Trust, N.A., is the personal representative of Prince's estate.

In early 2004, Boxill was engaged as a consultant to assist in selecting and testing recording equipment for the recording studios at Prince's residence in Chanhassen, Minnesota, known as Paisley Park. Boxill executed a Confidentiality Agreement with Paisley Park Enterprises in March 2004. That Confidentiality Agreement provides that recordings and other physical materials that resulted from Boxill's work with Prince "shall remain Paisley's sole and exclusive property, shall not be used by [Boxill] in any way whatsoever, and shall be returned to Paisley immediately upon request."

Boxill began recording music with Prince in 2004 and is credited as a sound engineer on Prince's album titled 3121, which was released in 2006. In 2006, Boxill worked with Prince to record the five songs at issue in this lawsuit: "Deliverance," "No One Else," "I Am," "Touch Me," and "Sunrise Sunset." Between 2006 and 2008, Boxill edited these five recordings and communicated with Prince regarding their progress. These recordings were not released during Prince's lifetime. Boxill and Prince stopped working together regularly in December 2008.

After Prince's death in April 2016, and ten years after Boxill worked with Prince to record the songs, Boxill mixed and edited "Deliverance," "No One Else," "I Am," "Touch Me," and "Sunrise Sunset." Boxill negotiated with representatives of Prince's estate regarding the release of these songs, but Boxill and the estate were unable to reach an agreement. In September 2016, attorneys for Boxill and for Prince's estate also jointly attempted to reach a negotiated agreement with Atlantic Records to include "Deliverance" on the movie soundtrack for Birth of a Nation. But the parties also were unable to reach an agreement on that contract.

In March 2017, representatives of Prince's estate learned that Boxill was planning an independent re-lease of "Deliverance" and demanded the immediate return of any recordings of Prince in Boxill's possession. Boxill refused. Plaintiffs subsequently initiated this lawsuit in Minnesota state court, seeking possession of the disputed recordings. Plaintiffs filed a motion for a temporary restraining order in the state-court proceeding on April 14, 2017.

On April 18, 2017, Rogue Music Alliance, LLC, issued a press release announcing the April 21, 2017 nationwide release of an EP2 titled DELIVERANCE that includes six previously unreleased songs featuring Prince—the five songs described above plus an extended version of the song titled "I Am." At the time of the press release, DELIVERANCE was available for pre-order through several online retailers, and the song "Deliverance" was available for purchase in advance of DELIVERANCE's release.

Also, on April 18, 2017, Boxill removed the state-court action to this Court. The next day, Plaintiffs again filed a motion for a temporary restraining order to prevent the release of DELIVERANCE and to secure possession of the masters and all copies of any unreleased recordings. The Court held a hearing and issued a temporary restraining order the same day. The temporary restraining order permitted Boxill and others acting in concert with him to continue distributing the song "Deliverance" but enjoined the release of the remaining songs on the DELIVERANCE EP, citing the Confidentiality Agreement be-tween

297

Boxill and Paisley Park Enterprises. The temporary restraining order also required Boxill to de-liver all of the Prince recordings in his possession to Plaintiffs.

Boxill moved to modify the temporary restraining order and for expedited discovery. Plaintiffs filed an amended complaint, which added two defendants—Rogue Music Alliance, LLC, and Deliverance, LLC—and a variety of claims, including copyright and trademark violations. Plaintiffs also moved for a preliminary injunction to enjoin Defendants from selling or promoting any of the songs on the DE-LIVERANCE EP.

The Court held a consolidated hearing on the parties' pending motions. After the hearing, the Court extended the duration of the temporary restraining order, modified the temporary restraining order to require the disputed recordings to be retained by counsel for each party for use only in this litigation, and ordered Plaintiffs to post a bond.

ANALYSIS

Plaintiffs' Motion for Preliminary Injunction

Legal Standard

When determining whether a preliminary injunction is warranted, a district court considers four factors:

> (1) the probability that the movant will succeed on the merits, (2) the threat of irreparable harm to the movant, (3) the balance between this harm and the injury that the injunction will inflict on other parties, and (4) the public interest.[489] "While the absence of a likelihood of success on the merits strongly suggests that preliminary injunctive relief should be denied, a finding of a likelihood of success on the merits only justifies preliminary relief if there is a risk of irreparable harm and the balance of the factors support an injunction."[490] The burden to establish the propriety of injunctive relief rests with the movant. . . . The purpose of a preliminary injunction is to "preserve the relative positions of the parties until a trial on the merits can be held."

. . .

Likelihood of Success on the Merits

The Court first considers the probability that Plaintiffs will succeed on the merits of their claims. To demonstrate that a preliminary injunction is warranted, Plaintiffs "need only show a reasonable probability of success, that is, a fair chance of prevailing" on the merits. This factor does not require a party seeking preliminary injunctive relief to prove a greater than fifty percent chance that the party will prevail on the merits. Although no single Dataphase factor is determinative, "the probability of success factor is the most significant.

In support of their motion for a preliminary injunction, Plaintiffs assert that they are likely to

---

[489] Dataphase Sys., Inc. v. C L Sys., Inc., 640 F.2d 109, 114 (8th Cir. 1981) (en banc).
[490] CDI Energy Servs., Inc. v. W. River Pumps, Inc., 567 F.3d 398, 402 (8th Cir. 2009).

succeed on the merits of five of their legal claims—breach of contract, conversion, misappropriation of trade secrets, copyright infringement, and trademark infringement. The Court addresses Plaintiffs' likelihood of success as to each of these claims.

Breach of Contract

As to the breach-of-contract claim, Plaintiffs contend that Boxill breached the Confidentiality Agreement by retaining recordings, refusing to return those recordings to Paisley Park Enterprises on demand, and attempting to exploit those recordings for his own gain at the expense of Prince's estate. Boxill counters that Plaintiffs are not likely to succeed on the merits of their breach-of-contract claim because the Confidentiality Agreement does not apply to Boxill's work with Prince as a sound engineer.

To prevail on a breach-of-contract claim under Minnesota law, Plaintiffs must prove formation of a contract, performance of any conditions precedent to the right to demand performance by the defendant, and breach of the contract by the defendant. Here, the Confidentiality Agreement signed by Boxill establishes the formation of a contract. Boxill's affidavit establishes that he was engaged to render services to Paisley Park Enterprises and permitted to enter Prince's homes at Paisley Park and in Holly-wood, California. Paisley Park Enterprises performed its obligations under the Confidentiality Agreement when it provided Boxill the opportunity to work with Prince. In paragraph 2 of the Confidentiality Agreement, Boxill disclaims any property interest in materials connected to his work with Paisley Park Enterprises. Yet Boxill undisputedly refused to return recordings of Prince in Boxill's possession de-spite a demand pursuant to the Confidentiality Agreement. In addition, Boxill has released publicly and facilitated the distribution of the song "Deliverance."

Boxill argues that the plain language of the Confidentiality Agreement demonstrates that the parties could not have intended the Confidentiality Agreement to apply to Boxill's work as a sound engineer. The Confidentiality Agreement expressly provides that Boxill "shall not photograph, tape, film or otherwise record any likenesses, performances or activities of [Prince]," yet Boxill argues that he could not have performed his work as a sound engineer without violating this provision of the Confidentiality Agreement. Boxill contends that when the Confidentiality Agreement was signed, the parties did not contemplate that Boxill would ever record music with Prince. Because of the inherent inconsistencies between Boxill's work as a sound engineer and the terms of the Confidentiality Agreement, Boxill asserts, the only reasonable interpretation of the Confidentiality Agreement is that it applied only to Boxill's work as a consultant on the remodeling of the recording studios at Paisley Park in 2004.

Plaintiffs dispute Boxill's interpretation of the Confidentiality Agreement and assert that it applies, without limitation, to all of the work that Boxill performed for Prince. At the hearing on the pending motions, Plaintiffs' counsel conceded that Paisley Park Enterprises had waived the provision of the Confidentiality Agreement prohibiting Boxill from recording Prince when Boxill was hired as a sound engineer whose job was to record Prince. Despite that concession, Plaintiffs assert that the remainder of the Confidentiality Agreement continued to apply to Boxill's sound engineering work with Prince because the terms of the Confidentiality Agreement are not limited to Boxill's work as a consultant on the remodeling of Paisley Park's recording studios. Although Boxill offers a plausible interpretation of the Confidentiality Agreement, the Court cannot finally resolve the meaning of the Confidentiality Agreement on the limited record presented at this stage of the proceedings. Plaintiffs' interpretation of the Confidentiality Agreement also is plausible and gives them "a fair chance of prevailing" on the merits.

Conversion

Plaintiffs also assert that they are likely to prevail on their common-law conversion claim because Boxill has deprived Paisley Park Enterprises of use and possession of the disputed recordings. Minnesota law defines conversion as "an act of willful interference with [the personal property of another], done, without lawful justification, by which any person entitled thereto is deprived of use and possession" or "the exercise of dominion and control over goods inconsistent with, and in repudiation of, the owner's rights in those goods." . . . Plaintiffs' theory as to conversion appears to be that the disputed recordings were created at Paisley Park, subject to the Confidentiality Agreement, and Boxill, therefore, had no legal right to take the recordings from the premises in the first instance. But through his sworn declarations with attached emails from Prince, Boxill presents testimony that his work with Prince required Boxill to take the original recordings from the studio and that Prince knew Boxill possessed the recordings. To the extent that Plaintiffs' claim to lawful ownership of the recordings is based on the Confidentiality Agreement, the likelihood that Plaintiffs can succeed on their conversion claim is closely tied to Plaintiffs' likelihood of success on their breach-of-contract claim. Based on the record presented at this early stage of the proceedings, Plaintiffs have a fair chance of prevailing on their conversion claim because Plaintiffs also have a fair chance of prevailing on their claim that the Confidentiality Agreement makes them the sole owners of the disputed recordings.

Misappropriation of Trade Secrets

Plaintiffs contend that they also are likely to succeed on the merits of their misappropriation-of-trade-secrets claim. Minnesota law requires that a party seeking protection under the Minnesota Uniform Trade Secrets Act "show both the existence and the misappropriation of a trade secret." . . . A trade secret is defined as information, including a formula, pattern, compilation, program, device, method, technique, or process that:

derives independent economic value, actual or potential, from not being generally known to, and not being readily ascertainable by proper means by, other persons who can obtain economic value from its disclosure or use, and is the subject of efforts that are reasonable under the circumstances to maintain its secrecy.[491]

The statutory requirement that a trade secret must derive independent economic value from secrecy "carries forward the common law requirement of competitive advantage."[492] Information creates a competitive advantage if a prospective competitor could use the information to obtain a valuable share of the market.[493]

At this stage, Plaintiffs have not demonstrated that the disputed recordings are a trade secret. Instead, Plaintiffs ask the Court to accept at face value the proposition that the recordings are a "trade secret" because they are secret. Although, as Plaintiffs suggest, the economic value of the disputed recordings might increase as those recordings are kept secret as a result of pent-up demand for unreleased Prince music. Paisley Park Enterprises does not derive any competitive advantage in the marketplace from the secrecy of the unreleased Prince recordings. The recordings differ fundamentally from the type of information that is subject to trade-secret protection to permit a party in possession of the information to produce a superior product. No other artist or record company could take market share from Paisley Park

---

[491] Minn. Stat. § 325C.01, subd. 5 (2016).
[492] Electro–Craft Corp. v. Controlled Motion, Inc., 332 N.W.2d 890, 900 (Minn. 1983).
[493] *Id.* at 900–01.

Enterprises by discovering the contents of the disputed recordings. The only economic value of the recordings derives from the right to sell the recordings to the public. Certainly, the timing of any sale might affect the value of the recordings, but Plaintiffs cannot realize any independent economic value by keeping the contents of the recordings secret. Because Plaintiffs have not demonstrated that the disputed recordings are a trade secret within the meaning of the statute, Plaintiffs at this stage have not demonstrated a likelihood of succeeding on the merits of their trade-secret claim.

Copyright Infringement

Plaintiffs also assert that a preliminary injunction is warranted because they are likely to succeed on the merits of their copyright-infringement claim against each defendant. As a threshold matter, Defendants assert that Plaintiffs' copyright-infringement claim is premature because Plaintiffs have applied for copyright registrations in the disputed recordings[,] but the Copyright Office has not yet rendered a decision on those applications. Section 411(a) of the Copyright Act provides, in relevant part: [N]o civil action for infringement of the copyright in any United States work shall be instituted until . . . registration of the copyright claim has been made in accordance with this title. In any case, however, where the deposit, application, and fee required for registration have been delivered to the Copyright Office in proper form and registration has been refused, the applicant is entitled to institute a civil action for infringement if notice thereof, with a copy of the complaint, is served on the Register of Copyrights.

17 U.S.C. § 411(a). The United States Court of Appeals for the Eighth Circuit has not directly addressed whether a plaintiff can institute an action for infringement under the Copyright Act once the plaintiff has filed an application for copyright registration. Other circuits are divided as to whether the application for copyright registration satisfies the statutory requirement of registration of the copyright claim as a prerequisite to filing a copyright-infringement lawsuit. At least one other court in this District has concluded that an application for copyright registration does not satisfy the statutory requirement of registration as a prerequisite to filing an infringement lawsuit.

The Court need not resolve the question of whether an application for copyright registration is sufficient to permit a plaintiff to institute a civil action for copyright infringement because, based on the present record, the Court cannot conclude that Plaintiffs have any likelihood of succeeding on the merits of their copyright-infringement claim. A certificate of copyright registration is "prima facie evidence of the validity of the copyright and of the facts stated in the certificate."[494] Authors who create a joint work are co-owners of the copyright in that work.[495] "A co-owner of a copyright cannot be liable to another co-owner for infringement of the copyright."[496] Although Plaintiffs have presented evidence that they filed applications for copyright registrations in the disputed recordings, Boxill possesses certificates of copyright registration for the disputed recordings that list Boxill and Prince as co-authors. Plaintiffs dispute that Prince intended to create joint works with Boxill. But at this stage of the proceedings, the Court cannot conclude that the facts stated in the certificates of copyright registration are erroneous. As a result, the Court also cannot conclude that Plaintiffs have even a "fair chance of prevailing" on the merits of their copyright-infringement claim.

---

[494] 17 U.S.C. § 410(c).
[495] 17 U.S.C. § 201(a).
[496] Oddo v. Ries, 743 F.2d 630, 632–33 (9th Cir. 1984).

Trademark Infringement

Plaintiffs also contend that a preliminary injunction is warranted because they are likely to succeed on their trademark-infringement claims against Defendants Rogue Music Alliance, LLC, and Deliverance, LLC. To prevail on a trademark-infringement claim, a plaintiff must prove that the plaintiff owns a valid trademark and that a likelihood of confusion exists between the registered mark and the alleged infringing use by the defendant.[497] When determining whether the use of a trademark is likely to cause confusion among consumers as to the source of an allegedly infringing product, a district court considers six non-exclusive factors: (1) the strength of the plaintiff's mark; (2) the similarity between the plaintiff's mark and the alleged infringer's mark; (3) the degree of competition between the products; (4) the alleged infringer's intent to "pass off" its product as that of the plaintiff; (5) incidents of actual confusion; and (6) the type of product, the product's cost, and the conditions of purchase.[498] Plaintiffs have presented evidence that Plaintiffs own the trademark "PRINCE®" for use with recordings of musical performances and that the promotional materials for the song "Deliverance" use the PRINCE® trademark. According to Plaintiffs, based on Defendants' use of the PRINCE® trademark, consumers could believe that the release of "Deliverance" was authorized by Prince's estate.

Defendants argue that Plaintiffs cannot demonstrate a likelihood of success on the merits of the trade-mark-infringement claim because Defendants' use of Plaintiffs' trademarks in the promotion and distribution of the song "Deliverance" are nominative "fair use." But Defendants' arguments as to fair use, like their arguments regarding the interpretation of the Confidentiality Agreement, seek a decision on the merits of the parties' dispute without a fully developed factual record. Plaintiffs have established that they have a "fair chance of prevailing" on the merits of their trademark-infringement claim, which is all that is required to demonstrate a likelihood of success on the merits. That Defendants also have a colorable defense to Plaintiffs' allegations does not undermine this conclusion.

The Court's conclusion that Plaintiffs have demonstrated a likelihood of success on the merits with respect to their breach-of-contract, conversion, and trademark-infringement claims does not mean that Plaintiffs "will ultimately win." . . . Likewise, the Court's conclusion that Plaintiffs cannot demonstrate a likelihood of success on the merits of their misappropriation-of-trade-secret and copyright-infringement claims does not mean that Defendants ultimately will prevail on those claims. At this stage of the proceedings, however, this factor weighs in favor of granting in part Plaintiffs' motion for a preliminary injunction.

Threat of Irreparable Harm

A party seeking a preliminary injunction also must establish that the party faces a threat of irreparable harm. A possibility of irreparable harm in the absence of an injunction is not sufficient; rather, a plaintiff seeking a preliminary injunction must "demonstrate that irreparable injury is likely in the absence of an injunction." . . . An alleged harm that can be remedied through damages is not irreparable.

. . .

Here, many of the harms alleged by Plaintiffs address the monetary value of the disputed recordings. Although harms that are compensable in damages generally are not grounds for injunctive relief,

---

[497] Davis v. Walt Disney Co., 393 F. Supp. 2d 839, 843 (D. Minn. 2005).
[498] Everest Capital Ltd. v. Everest Funds Mgmt., L.L.C., 393 F.3d 755, 759–60 (8th Cir. 2005).

Plaintiffs argue that injunctive relief is warranted because Defendants would be unable to satisfy an award of adequate damages. A preliminary injunction "may issue to protect plaintiff's remedy" when "the plaintiff has demonstrated sufficient evidence to support the claim that it will be unable to recover absent a preliminary injunction." . . . Plaintiffs have stated only that the "damages in this case will be millions of dollars" and that it would be beyond the means of most individuals to satisfy a damages award of that magnitude. Although based on these assertions, it may be unlikely that Defendants would be able to satisfy a damages award in this case, this circumstance does not satisfy Plaintiffs' burden to "demonstrate[ ] a clear probability that defendants will not be able to satisfy an award of adequate damages." . . . The record does not include any evidence as to Defendants' assets or their ability to satisfy a judgment if Plaintiffs prevail.

To the extent Plaintiffs have alleged that the publication of previously unreleased recordings of Prince violates the Confidentiality Agreement, however, the disclosure of such confidential information can-not be adequately compensated in damages. Plaintiffs assert that the right to decide whether and when to release songs that Prince recorded, but did not release during his lifetime, belongs solely to the estate. If Defendants are not enjoined from further publication and dissemination of the disputed recordings, Plaintiffs will be permanently deprived of the right to decide whether, when and in what manner the release of the disputed songs will benefit Prince's public image and reputation. Because any further disclosure of confidential information protected by the Confidentiality Agreement threatens to irreparably damage Plaintiffs' right to control Prince's confidential information, reputation and public persona, this factor weighs in favor of granting Plaintiffs' motion for a preliminary injunction. However, because the song "Deliverance" already has been released, Plaintiffs can be compensated in damages for any ongoing harm resulting from that distribution. For this reason, injunctive relief as to the continued sale of the song "Deliverance" based on the Confidentiality Agreement is not warranted.

Plaintiffs offer two additional arguments in support of their contention that Defendants should be enjoined from continuing to promote or distribute the song "Deliverance." First, Plaintiffs assert that their business relationship with Universal Music Group will be irreparably damaged because the release of an unauthorized song "greatly devalues the rest of the catalog." In turn, Plaintiffs contend that damage to their business relationship with Universal Music Group will irreparably damage Plaintiffs' reputation in the marketplace. But to the extent that the release of an unauthorized song has caused a loss in value of other Prince music or damaged Plaintiffs' relationship with Universal Music Group, those harms already have occurred. Plaintiffs offer no reason why the continued sale of the song "Deliverance," which has been available for sale online for weeks, will cause additional irreparable harm for which damages are not an adequate remedy.

Second, Plaintiffs argue that Defendants are using Plaintiffs' PRINCE® trademark to promote the disputed recordings, which causes customer confusion as to whether "Deliverance" was released by Plaintiffs and may damage both public perception of the disputed recordings and the consumer goodwill associated with the PRINCE® trademark. The Court agrees that Defendants' use of Plaintiffs' trademark without authorization to sell Prince's music, when Plaintiffs are not involved in the production, promotion, or distribution of that music, risks damaging Plaintiffs' reputation. But this reasoning supports only an injunction prohibiting Defendants from continuing to use Plaintiffs' trademark to sell the song "Deliverance."

Defendants contend that Plaintiffs' decision to negotiate with Boxill and Warner Brothers as to the inclusion of "Deliverance" on a movie soundtrack without disputing Boxill's co-ownership weakens Plaintiffs' claim that Prince's reputation or Plaintiffs' business relationship with Universal Music Group will be irreparably damaged in the absence of an injunction. But this argument does not undermine the

303

Court's conclusion that an injunction is warranted to prevent Defendants' continued use of Plaintiffs' trademark or the disclosure of additional material that arguably is subject to the Confidentiality Agreement. Neither Plaintiffs' negotiations with Boxill nor Boxill's assertions that he is a co-owner of the disputed recordings give Defendants the right to use Plaintiffs' trademarks. Furthermore, nothing about Plaintiffs' negotiations with Boxill impairs whatever rights Plaintiffs have under the Confidentiality Agreement. And Boxill's claim of co-ownership, despite the Confidentiality Agreement, goes to the merits of the parties' dispute and does not undermine Plaintiffs' assertion that they will be irreparably damaged if the unreleased recordings are released but later found to be subject to the terms of the Confidentiality Agreement.

For these reasons, this factor weighs in favor of granting Plaintiffs' motion for a preliminary injunction to the extent the relief sought is based on legal claims on which Plaintiffs have established a likelihood of success on the merits.

Balance of the Equities

When deciding whether a preliminary injunction should issue, a district court also weighs the threat of irreparable harm to the movant against the injury the injunction would inflict on other parties. Boxill asserts that he is a co-author and co-owner of the copyright in the disputed recordings and, for that reason, he has a right to publish the recordings so long as he compensates the estate for its share of the royalties. Boxill also asserts that the Confidentiality Agreement does not apply to the disputed recordings and, therefore, does not bar Defendants from distributing the recordings. But if Boxill is correct, monetary damages can compensate Boxill for any lost sales or profits. The Court has ordered Plaintiffs to post a bond, so as to compensate Defendants for any damages resulting from the injunction if later it is determined that the injunction should not have issued. If the disputed recordings are released and Plaintiffs prevail on the merits, however, Plaintiffs will have irretrievably lost the right to decide not to publish—or to be the first to publish—these songs. Consequently, the threat of irreparable harm to Plaintiffs outweighs the risk that Defendants will suffer a compensable financial loss as a result of an injunction. This factor weighs in favor of issuing a preliminary injunction.

Public Interest

Finally, when deciding whether a preliminary injunction should issue, the Court considers the interests of the public. The public has a strong interest in preserving the ability to enter contracts and in the availability of a forum for the enforcement of contract and property rights. Although the competing interests at stake in this case are predominately private economic interests, because Plaintiffs have demonstrated a likelihood of success on their breach-of-contract claim, this factor weighs in favor of issuing a preliminary injunction to preserve the availability of a meaningful remedy pending the resolution of the merits of the dispute.

Conclusion

On balance, the Dataphase factors weigh in favor of granting Plaintiffs' motion for a preliminary in-junction. However, the scope of a preliminary injunction should not be greater than necessary to protect the movant until the dispute can be resolved on the merits. As such, the Court will not issue an injunction broader than necessary to protect Plaintiffs from irreparable harm that likely would result from additional breaches of the Confidentiality Agreement or infringement of Plaintiffs' trademark.

The Court enjoins Boxill, Rogue Music Alliance, LLC, Deliverance, LLC, and others acting in

304

concert with them, from publishing or disseminating any previously unreleased recordings that comprise the work of Prince, including but not limited to the four-part medley titled "Man Opera" and the extended version of the track titled "I Am." The Court further enjoins Boxill, Rogue Music Alliance, LLC, Deliverance, LLC, and others acting in concert with them, from using the PRINCE® trademark in connection with the promotion and sale of the song "Deliverance." Because the Court concludes that Plaintiffs have not demonstrated a likelihood of success on the merits of misappropriation-of-trade-secret and copyright-infringement claims, a preliminary injunction is not warranted to prevent any alleged irreparable harm related to those claims. This Order preserves the parties' respective positions pending the resolution of the merits of this dispute.

Bond Requirement

Rule 65(c), Fed. R. Civ. P., provides that a district court "may issue a preliminary injunction . . . only if the movant gives security in an amount that the court considers proper to pay the costs and damages sustained by any party found to have been wrongfully enjoined or restrained." The amount of the bond required by Rule 65(c) is in the discretion of the district court. Defendants assert that, if Plaintiffs' motion for a preliminary injunction is granted, Plaintiffs should be required to post a bond in the amount of $1 million. Plaintiffs do not take a position on the appropriate amount of the bond but suggest that a bond in the amount that Defendants have invested in the promotion of DELIVERANCE—$378,000— would be adequate. But Plaintiffs' position that its damages are likely to be millions of dollars strongly suggests that a bond in the amount of $378,000 would not be sufficient to compensate Defendants if Defendants are later found to have been wrongfully enjoined. Accordingly, the May 3, 2017 Order extending the temporary restraining order required Plaintiffs to post a bond in the amount of $1 million by May 12, 2017, and Plaintiffs did so. This preliminary injunction similarly shall be secured by a bond in the amount of $1 million.

Boxill's Motion to Modify the Temporary Restraining Order and for Early Discovery

After the Court issued its order granting Plaintiffs' motion for a temporary restraining order, Boxill moved to modify the temporary restraining order and for early discovery. Specifically, Boxill sought modification of the temporary restraining order to permit him to deposit the disputed recordings with the Court, a third-party escrow agent, or Plaintiffs' counsel, rather than with Plaintiffs. Boxill also sought early discovery of five categories of materials for use in responding to Plaintiffs' motion for a preliminary injunction.

To the extent Boxill's motion sought a modification of the temporary restraining order to require the disputed recordings to be deposited with Plaintiffs' counsel, rather than with Plaintiffs, pending resolution of the parties' dispute over ownership of the recordings, the motion was addressed in the Court's May 3, 2017 Order extending and modifying the temporary restraining order. The May 3, 2017 Order directed Boxill to deposit the copies of the disputed recordings in his possession with Plaintiffs' counsel for use only in this litigation and permitted defense counsel to retain a copy of the recordings for this limited purpose. This Order, which supersedes the temporary restraining order, imposes the same requirement. But because the temporary restraining order is no longer in effect upon the issuance of this Order, Boxill's motion to modify the temporary restraining order is denied as moot.

To the extent Boxill's motion seeks expedited discovery to support his response to Plaintiffs' motion for a preliminary injunction, the motion is denied as moot. Boxill sought discovery to respond to Plaintiffs' motion for a preliminary injunction, but in light of the expedited briefing schedule, it was not

305

practical to require Plaintiffs to produce documents in time for Boxill to rely on them in his response. If any party believes that early discovery is warranted in this case for another purpose, that party may raise the issue by separate motion.

ORDER

Based on the foregoing analysis and all the files, records and proceedings herein, IT IS HEREBY OR-DERED:

The motion to modify the temporary restraining order and for early discovery filed by Defendant George Ian Boxill . . . is DENIED AS MOOT, as outlined herein.

The motion for a preliminary injunction filed by Plaintiffs Paisley Park Enterprises, Inc., and Comerica Bank & Trust, N.A., as Personal Representative of the Estate of Prince Rogers Nelson . . . is GRANTED to the extent outlined herein.

Defendants George Ian Boxill, Rogue Music Alliance, LLC, Deliverance, LLC, and others acting in concert with them, shall not publish or otherwise disseminate any unreleased recordings that comprise the work of Prince Rogers Nelson that are alleged to be within the scope of the Confidentiality Agreement between Boxill and Paisley Park Enterprises, Inc.

Defendants George Ian Boxill, Rogue Music Alliance, LLC, Deliverance, LLC, and others acting in concert with them, shall deliver all recordings acquired through Boxill's work with Paisley Park Enterprises, Inc., including original recordings, analog and digital copies, and any derivative works, to Plaintiffs' counsel—not Plaintiffs—for use only in this litigation. Counsel for Defendants may retain a copy of any recordings deposited with Plaintiffs' counsel for use only in this litigation.

Defendants George Ian Boxill, Rogue Music Alliance, LLC, Deliverance, LLC, and others acting in concert with them, shall cease the use of the trademark PRINCE® in connection with the promotion, sale, and distribution of the song "Deliverance."

The preliminary injunction issued by this Order shall be secured by a bond in the amount of $1,000,000 posted by Plaintiffs Paisley Park Enterprises, Inc., and Comerica Bank & Trust, N.A., as Personal Representative of the Estate of Prince Rogers Nelson.

Follow-Up Questions and Comments

1. The four-part test relied on by the Eighth Circuit by which the court decided whether to grant a preliminary injunction represents the test applied in every circuit court of appeals. Notice how the court explains that the strength of one or two factors allows for less of a showing on other factors, and vice versa. In Paisley Park Enterprises, how did the court apply the four-factor test to reach the conclusion that it should grant the preliminary injunction?

2. Read Federal Rule of Civil Procedure 65(c). A sample injunction bond is located at: www.cod.uscourts.gov/Portals/0/Documents/Forms/CivilForms/temp_res_ord_bond_sur.pdf.

3. What is the purpose of "security," as required by Rule 65(c)? How will such security protect an enjoined party? Federal Rule of Civil Procedure 65.1 establishes procedures by which a party who is protected by a surety bond may file a motion for recovery on the bond if, for instance, the injunction is found to have been wrongfully issued. The movant, however, must prove damages to recover on the bond.[499]

4. Periodically, the issue arises over who is bound by an injunction. Clearly, the parties enjoined are bound. Moreover, Rule 65(d) (2) provides that, in addition, a party's "officers, agents, servants, employees, and attorneys" are bound, as are "other persons who are in active concert or participation" with the parties or their agents.

Practice Problems

Practice Problem 10-4

Four oncologists, Dr. Able, Dr. Best, Dr. Can, and Dr. Dew, signed contracts with Centura Healthcare, Inc. The contracts provide for compensation and support to the doctors in their practice with cancer patients, but also included covenants not to compete. Specifically, these covenants provided as follows: "Upon [Doctor's] departure from Centura, whether termination for cause or by election of the Doctor, Doctor shall not practice medicine within 100 miles of Centura's headquarters for a period of one year." After working for Centura for a few years, the four doctors decided to go out on their own, convinced that Centura was more concerned with money than with patients.

The Doctors provided Centura written notice of their planned departure and of their intention to continue treating the cancer patients with whom they had become close over the course of treatment, in an office within 100 miles of Centura's headquarters. The doctors advised Centura that they were sending letters to patients advising the patients of their relocation, offering patients the option of staying with Centura and switching to a new oncologist, or of seeing the Doctors at their new location. The Doctors further advised that all patients had decided to stay with the Doctors and see them at their new location. Centura sought a preliminary injunction against the Doctors seeking the court bind them to the covenant not to compete. The law governing enforceability of covenants not to compete holds that they are enforceable so long as they are not unreasonable in geographic scope, or in length of time, or for some other reason. No precedent in the jurisdiction had yet dealt with enforcement of a covenant not to compete involving physicians who would be barred from ongoing treatment of patients. Using the four-factor test, analyze whether a preliminary injunction should be granted here.

---

[499] *See* 11A CHARLES ALAN WRIGHT & ARTHUR R. MILLER, FEDERAL PRACTICE AND PROCEDURE § 2973 (3d ed. 2018).

CHAPTER 11: JOINDER OF CLAIMS
AND PARTIES BY PLAINTIFFS

I. How the Topics in this Chapter Fit in the Overall Progress of a Civil Action

Below is a diagram of the stages of a civil action showing in bold where in the progress of the case this chapter discusses.

Figure 11-1

Cause of Action (events leading to suit)	Pre-Filing Tasks (items to begin representation, interviewing, and related matters)	Choice of Forum (subject matter jurisdiction, removal, personal jurisdiction, and venue)	Notice and Service of Process (completing the process of ensuring the forum court can enter a valid judgment)	**Pleading the Case and Joinder of Claims and Parties (including supplemental jurisdiction)**

Responding to Claims by Motion or by Answer	Discovery (developing proof to establish claims and learn your adversary's case)	Right to Jury (pretrial motions and practice)	Final Pretrial Conference (events within last month before trial)	Trial (procedures and motions during trial)	Verdict	Post-Trial Motions (motions for a new trial and/or judgment as a matter of law)	Appeal

The lawyer drafting a pleading for the plaintiff seeking relief from a defendant or defendants must evaluate several questions. First, the lawyer considers the basics of what a lawyer asserting a claim must consider—the format of the pleading, the degree of specificity required in the allegations of each claim, and the relief requested. Chapter 10 explained those requirements. However, the lawyer sculpting a lawsuit does not stop there. She asks what claims her client can assert against an opposing party. She also asks whether multiple parties need to be or should be joined.

If the lawyer asserting the claims is joining more than one defendant to the claims,129 she must have a basis for doing so. Even if there is a basis in the substantive law and the Rules would permit joinder, you nevertheless should consider whether it is strategically wise to have multiple defendants in a case. Sometimes it is. Defendants pointing fingers at one another usually inures to the plaintiff's benefit. If, however, multiple defendants create enhanced resources for defendants to work together to defeat a plaintiff, it may not be so wise to add every potential defendant. These are the judgment calls you must make. However, what we will cover in this chapter presumes that the plaintiff is bringing as many claims as possible against as many defendants as possible.

A. Joinder of Claims by Plaintiff Against Defendant

Typically, a plaintiff brings more than one claim. Thus, the plaintiff joins claims in one suit. Here's a diagram of what this will look like:

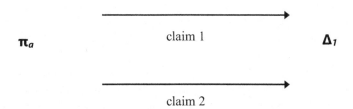

Does it matter whether the claims differ in nature, such as some being torts and others being contractual? Does it matter that they differ in the kind of proof necessary to sustain them? Must they all arise from the same transaction or occurrence?

B. Rule 18's Requirements

Please read Federal Rule of Civil Procedure 18(a). What does the Rule suggest about the answer to the above questions?

Practice Problems

Practice Problem 11-1

Pete Plaintiff, now 60 years old, had worked as an employee of Happy Homes, Inc., for thirty years, before the company fired him and immediately hired a younger person to fill his job. Pete sued under the Federal Age Discrimination in Employment Act. He added a claim for negligence because he had fallen on his last visit to Happy Homemakers headquarters due to a broken step that the employer had neglected to fix or warn him that it was broke. Does Rule 18 allow Pete to join the negligence claim to his Federal Age Discrimination in Employment Act claim? Is there jurisdiction over the joined claim such that the claim can be brought in federal court with the Age Discrimination claim?

C. Jurisdictional Requirements

Before answering the last question in Practice Problem 11-1, please consider the following case:

UNITED MINE WORKERS v. GIBBS
Supreme Court of the United States, 1966
383 U.S. 715

MR. JUSTICE BRENNAN delivered the opinion of the Court.

Respondent Paul Gibbs was awarded compensatory and punitive damages in this action against petitioner United Mine Workers of America (UMW) for alleged violations of § 303 of the Labor

Management Relations Act, 1947, as amended, and of the common law of Tennessee. The case grew out of the rivalry between the United Mine Workers and the Southern Labor Union over representation of workers in the southern Appalachian coal fields. Tennessee Consolidated Coal Company, not a party here, laid off 100 miners of the UMW's Local 5881 when it closed one of its mines in southern Tennessee during the spring of 1960. Late that summer, Grundy Company, a wholly owned subsidiary of Consolidated, hired respondent as mine superintendent to attempt to open a new mine on Consolidated's property at nearby Gray's Creek through use of members of the Southern Labor Union. As part of the arrangement, Grundy also gave respondent a contract to haul the mine's coal to the nearest railroad loading point.

On August 15 and 16, 1960, armed members of Local 5881 forcibly prevented the opening of the mine, threatening respondent and beating an organizer for the rival union. The members of the local believed Consolidated had promised them the jobs at the new mine; they insisted that if anyone would do the work, they would. At this time, no representative of the UMW, their international union, was present. George Gilbert, the UMW's field representative for the area including Local 5881, was away at Middlesboro, Kentucky, attending an Executive Board meeting when the members of the local discovered Grundy's plan; he did not return to the area until late in the day of August 16. There was uncontradicted testimony that he first learned of the violence while at the meeting and returned with explicit instructions from his international union superiors to establish a limited picket line, to prevent any further violence, and to see to it that the strike did not spread to neighboring mines. There was no further violence at the mine site; a picket line was maintained there for nine months; and no further attempts were made to open the mine during that period.

Respondent lost his job as superintendent, and never entered into performance of his haulage contract. He testified that he soon began to lose other trucking contracts and mine leases he held in nearby areas. Claiming these effects to be the result of a concerted union plan against him, he sought recovery not against Local 5881 or its members, but only against petitioner, the international union. The suit was brought in the United States District Court for the Eastern District of Tennessee, and jurisdiction was premised on allegations of secondary boycotts under § 303. The state law claim, for which jurisdiction was based upon the doctrine of pendent jurisdiction, asserted "an unlawful conspiracy and an unlawful boycott aimed at him and [Grundy] to maliciously, wantonly and willfully interfere with his contract of employment and with his contract of haulage." [Author's Note: At the time of this case, "pendent jurisdiction" and "ancillary jurisdiction" were terms used to describe what is now known as "supplemental jurisdiction;" hence, do not get caught up in the older terminology.]

The trial judge refused to submit to the jury the claims of pressure intended to cause mining firms other than Grundy to cease doing business with Gibbs; he found those claims unsupported by the evidence. The jury's verdict was that the UMW had violated both § 303 and state law. Gibbs was awarded $60,000 as damages under the employment contract and $14,500 under the haulage contract; he was also awarded $100,000 punitive damages. On motion, the trial court set aside the award of damages with respect to the haulage contract on the ground that damage was unproved. It also held that union pressure on Grundy to discharge respondent as supervisor would constitute only a primary dispute with Grundy, as respondent's employer, and hence was not cognizable as a claim under § 303. Interference with the employment relationship was cognizable as a state claim, however, and a remitted award was sustained on the state law claim. The Court of Appeals for the Sixth Circuit affirmed. We granted certiorari. We reverse.

A threshold question is whether the District Court properly entertained jurisdiction of the claim based on Tennessee law.

310

. . .

Pendent jurisdiction, in the sense of judicial power, exists whenever there is a claim "arising under [the] Constitution, the Laws of the United States, and Treaties made, or which shall be made, under their Authority ,"[500] and the relationship between that claim and the state claim permits the conclusion that the entire action before the court comprises but one constitutional "case." The state and federal claims must derive from a common nucleus of operative fact. But if, considered without regard to their federal or state character, a plaintiff's claims are such that he would ordinarily be expected to try them all in one judicial proceeding, then, assuming substantiality of the federal issues, there is power in federal courts to hear the whole.

That power need not be exercised in every case in which it is found to exist. It has consistently been recognized that pendent jurisdiction is a doctrine of discretion, not of plaintiff's right. Its justification lies in considerations of judicial economy, convenience and fairness to litigants; if these are not present a federal court should hesitate to exercise jurisdiction over state claims, even though bound to apply state law to them. Needless decisions of state law should be avoided both as a matter of comity and to promote justice between the parties, by procuring for them a surer-footed reading of applicable law. Certainly, if the federal claims are dismissed before trial, even though not insubstantial in a jurisdictional sense, the state claims should be dismissed as well. Similarly, if it appears that the state issues substantially predominate, whether in terms of proof, of the scope of the issues raised, or of the comprehensiveness of the remedy sought, the state claims may be dismissed without prejudice and left for resolution to state tribunals. There may, on the other hand, be situations in which the state claim is so closely tied to questions of federal policy that the argument for exercise of pendent jurisdiction is particularly strong. Finally, there may be reasons independent of jurisdictional considerations, such as the likelihood of jury confusion in treating divergent legal theories of relief, that would justify separating state and federal claims for trial, Fed. Rule Civ. Proc. 42 (b). If so, jurisdiction should ordinarily be refused.

The question of power will ordinarily be resolved on the pleadings. But the issue whether pendent jurisdiction has been properly assumed is one which remains open throughout the litigation. Pretrial procedures or even the trial itself may reveal a substantial hegemony of state law claims, or likelihood of jury confusion, which could not have been anticipated at the pleading stage. Although it will of course be appropriate to take account in this circumstance of the already completed course of the litigation, dismissal of the state claim might even then be merited. For example, it may appear that the plaintiff was well aware of the nature of his proofs and the relative importance of his claims; recognition of a federal court's wide latitude to decide ancillary questions of state law does not imply that it must tolerate a litigant's effort to impose upon it what is in effect only a state law case. Once it appears that a state claim constitutes the real body of a case, to which the federal claim is only an appendage, the state claim may fairly be dismissed.

We are not prepared to say that in the present case the District Court exceeded its discretion in proceeding to judgment on the state claim. We may assume for purposes of decision that the District Court was correct in its holding that the claim of pressure on Grundy to terminate the employment contract was outside the purview of § 303. Even so, the § 303 claims based on secondary pressures on Grundy relative to the haulage contract and on other coal operators generally were substantial. Although § 303 limited recovery to compensatory damages based on secondary pressures, *Teamsters Union v. Morton*, and state law allowed both compensatory and punitive dam-ages and allowed such damages as to both secondary and primary activity, the state and federal claims arose from the same nucleus of operative fact and reflected

---

[500] U.S. CONST., Art. III, § 2.

alternative remedies. Indeed, the verdict sheet sent to the jury authorized only one award of damages, so that recovery could not be given separately on the federal and state claims.

It is true that the § 303 claims ultimately failed and that the only recovery allowed respondent was on the state claim. We cannot confidently say, however, that the federal issues were so remote or played such a minor role at the trial that in effect the state claim only was tried. Although the District Court dismissed as unproved the § 303 claims that petitioner's secondary activities included attempts to induce coal operators other than Grundy to cease doing business with respondent, the court submitted the § 303 claims relating to Grundy to the jury. The jury returned verdicts against petitioner on those § 303 claims, and it was only on petitioner's motion for a directed verdict and a judgment n. o. v. that the verdicts on those claims were set aside. The District Judge considered the claim as to the haulage contract proved as to liability, and held it failed only for lack of proof of damages. Although there was some risk of confusing the jury in joining the state and federal claims—especially since, as will be developed, differing standards of proof of UMW involvement applied—the possibility of confusion could be lessened by employing a special verdict form, as the District Court did. Moreover, the question whether the permissible scope of the state claim was limited by the doctrine of pre-emption afforded a special reason for the exercise of pendent jurisdiction; the federal courts are particularly appropriate bodies for the application of pre-emption principles. We thus conclude that although it may be that the District Court might, in its sound discretion, have dismissed the state claim, the circumstances show no error in refusing to do so.

. . .

Reversed.

See Figure 11-2 below for a diagram of the claims in *Gibbs*. Note, the state law claim was not supported independently by federal law and was not among diverse citizens. Therefore, this was not a joined claim.

Figure 11-2

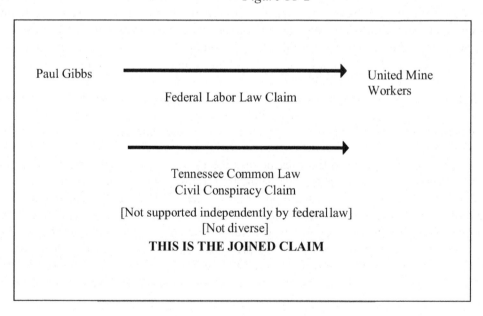

312

Follow-Up Questions and Comments

1. The main claim, the one that got this case into federal court, is the Federal Labor Law claim concerning secondary boycotts. The joined claim, the one that would never have made it into federal court if it were not hitched to the Labor Law Claim, is Gibbs' Tennessee state-law civil conspiracy claim. What is the issue presented by this case?

2. What part of Article III, Section 2 does the United States Supreme Court rely on to find a constitutional basis for supplemental jurisdiction of claims, like the state claim here, that are tied up with the facts of the federal claim?

3. What phrase does the Court use to describe a situation where a federal claim and a state claim arise from interwoven facts? This phrase signifies the now-established test for determining, after this case, whether supplemental jurisdiction exists over joined claims/parties.

4. The Court relied on eminently practical criteria by which any court (or student) viewing a federal and state claim can ask some simple questions that will lead to answer of whether the claims are so close together that joinder is appropriate and constitutional. What practical questions does the Court identify as helpful keys to determining whether the original case and the joined claim are appropriately tried together?

5. The Court went on to describe how a federal court, in its discretion, could decide not to exercise jurisdiction over a joined claim even though the federal court had the power to do so. What circumstances did the Court suggest might support the exercise of discretion not to exercise jurisdiction over state claims?

II. The Supplemental Jurisdiction Statute

The *Gibbs* test has been codified in the supplemental jurisdiction statute, 28 U.S.C. § 1367, which provides as follows:

(a) Except as provided in subsections (b) and (c) or as expressly provided otherwise by Federal statute, in any civil action of which the district courts have original jurisdiction, the district courts shall have supple-mental jurisdiction over all other claims that are so related to claims in the action within such original jurisdiction that they form part of the same case or controversy under Article III of the United States Constitution. Such supplemental jurisdiction shall include claims that involve the join-der or intervention of additional parties.

(b) In any civil action of which the district courts have original jurisdiction founded solely on section 1332 of this title, the district courts shall not have supplemental jurisdiction under subsection (a) over claims by plaintiffs against persons made parties under Rule 14, 19, 20, or 24 of the Federal Rules of Civil Procedure, or over claims by persons proposed to be joined as plaintiffs under Rule 19 of such rules, or seeking to intervene as plaintiffs under Rule 24 of such rules, when exercising supplemental jurisdiction over such claims would be inconsistent with the jurisdictional requirements of section 1332.

(c) The district courts may decline to exercise supplemental jurisdiction over a claim under subsection (a) if the claim raises a novel or complex issue of State law, the claim substantially predominates over the claim or claims over which the district court has original jurisdiction, the district court has dismissed all claims over which it has original jurisdiction, or in exceptional circumstances, there are other compelling reasons for declining jurisdiction.

Follow-Up Questions and Comments

1. In what ways does subsection (a) of the supplemental jurisdiction statute incorporate *Gibbs*? Remember the practical test derived from *Gibbs* in determining whether claims are intertwined such that they are so connected that they form one case. Would that test also answer the question, derived from subsection (a), whether "claims that are so related to claims in the action within such original jurisdiction that they form part of the same case or controversy under Article III of the United States Constitution"?

2. If you are analyzing a claim and whether it satisfies subsection (a) of the supplemental jurisdiction statute, and you determine that the answer is "no," that the main claim and the supplemental claim are not so related as to satisfy the statute, do you stop your analysis?

3. If you are analyzing a claim and whether it satisfies subsection (a) of the supplemental jurisdiction statute, and you determine that the answer is "yes," is that the end of your analysis? If you think so, read subsection (b) of the supplemental jurisdiction statute. Then you will realize that subsection (a) is only the threshold phase of a joined claim or joined party's being deemed appropriately within supplemental jurisdiction.

4. Subsection (b) of 28 U.S.C. § 1367 only applies to claims brought solely under the diversity statute. As you will see, this subsection will—despite subsection (a) being met, exclude certain claim if they meet the criteria in subsection (b). One of the main criteria of subsection (b) is that the original action, or main claim, be based solely on diversity of citizenship. By implication, subsection (b) will not remove supplemental jurisdiction when joinder is based on a federal question claim. If the exclusions in sub-section (b) were not there, would the supplemental jurisdiction statute enable parties to circumvent fundamental requirements of diversity of citizenship jurisdiction? In other words, can you see why Congress thought it necessary to have the exclusions in subsection (b) to preserve the integrity of diversity of citizenship jurisdiction?

Now return to Practice Problem 11-1. In the light of *Gibbs* and the Supplemental Jurisdiction statute, what is the answer to the question posed there? Why?

III. Plaintiff's Joinder of Parties as Defendants

Joinder of parties typically involves rules similar to but more demanding than the rules for joinder of claims. Please read Federal Rule of Civil Procedure 20. However, instead of joining claims against the same party, this Rule deals with joining another party against whom the claim is directed along with the other parties which are sued on the claim. Here is a diagram of what the scenario looks like:

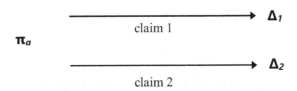

How does this Rule compare to Rule 18? Does it require the same showing, less, or more? To explore the implications of Rule 20, please read the following fact pattern, after which potential claims will be explored.

Fact Pattern as a Basis for Joinder Analysis

On the evening of January 18, 2018, Brad T. Rex was riding a motorcycle that he had borrowed from his friend, Harley Davidson. Assume for this fact pattern and the pleadings below that motorcycle airbag jackets had become standard equipment purchased as part of the sale of a motorcycle, and Rex was wearing one. The motorcycle airbag jacket in question was manufactured by Kagasaki, Inc., and was supposed to deploy whenever the bike driver was thrown off the bike.

On this sunny, cold day, Rex was driving the motorcycle on a public, single-lane road called Easy Street in the City of Arcadia, State of Illyria, at around 4:00 p.m. He was driving between 15 miles per hour (the minimum speed limit) and 35 miles per hour (the maximum speed limit). Rex was proceeding on Easy Street where it intersected with Dangerous Drive (the "Intersection"), and the Intersection was controlled by a stoplight. Rex, the plaintiff in the pleadings below, was traveling west on Easy Street. Other vehicles traveling west on Easy Street proceeded through the Intersection, as did Rex. Although Rex cannot now recall whether he saw a green light, he at least inferred from the other vehicles' entering the Intersection that he "must have" had a green light.

At the same time and on the same day, the Defendant, Ena Hurry, was driving her car north on Dangerous Drive in the right-hand lane of the two-lane road. Hurry, late for an appointment, was traveling well above the posted speed limit. As she approached the Intersection, she did not pay attention to the traffic light. Instead, Hurry proceeded into the Intersection. Rex and the motorcycle slammed into the side of Hurry's car. The collision catapulted Rex over Hurry's car and he landed on the asphalt. The state-of-the-art motorcycle airbag jacket did not inflate, and Rex sustained serious injuries throughout his body. Rex's injuries required—and will continue to require—medical attention. Additionally, the accident caused significant pain, discomfort, and suffering, all of which required him to miss several months working as the head chef of a popular restaurant.

As Rex struggled to stand after being tossed to the pavement, and was feeling a bit woozy, Hurry approached Rex in a threatening manner and shoved Rex with both hands. Rex, who had had enough by this time, began to scream at Hurry, calling her "a syphilis-ridden criminal." He pushed her back with such great force that Hurry tumbled to the ground, doing two backward somersaults and landing facedown. Hurry suffered cuts, bruises, and severe pain.

Immediately following the collision, at least one person stopped at the scene of the crash and heard

Rex call Hurry "a syphilis-ridden criminal." Hurry neither has syphilis, nor is she a criminal. The witness called for the police and an ambulance.

Following is a sample complaint that serves both as an example and the basis for questions later in this chapter:

Sample Complaint

PLAINTIFF DEMANDS TRIAL BY JURY

IN THE UNITED STATES DISTRICT COURT
FOR THE EASTERN DISTRICT OF ILLYRIA

BRAD T. REX	)	
Plaintiff(s)	)	
v.	)	**Case No.** 2016cv10
ENA HURRY & KAGASAKI, INC.	)	
Defendant(s)		

COMPLAINT

The Plaintiff, Brad T. Rex, by counsel, for his Complaint against defendants, Ena Hurry and Kagasaki, Inc., states as follows:

Parties

The Plaintiff, Brad T. Rex, is a citizen of the State of Illyria and the Defendant, Ena Hurry, is a citizen of the State of Elysium. Defendant, Kagasaki, Inc., is incorporated in Delaware and has its principal place of business in Michigan. All plaintiffs are therefore of diverse citizenship from all defendants. Moreover, Plaintiff is suing for more than $75,000 exclusive of interests and costs. Thus, the requirements of 28 U.S.C. § 1332 have been satisfied so that there is jurisdiction in federal court.

Negligence Claim Against Hurry

The preceding allegations are hereby restated and incorporated as if set forth herein.

(1) The Defendant Hurry had a duty at the time of the events which occurred on or about January 18, 2018, to use ordinary care to avoid injury to others and to the property of others. The Defendant Hurry breached her duty to use ordinary care in a variety of ways, including but not limited to driving at an unsafe speed and/or failing to follow the traffic signals at the Intersection.

The Defendant Hurry's breach is described in the preceding paragraph.

(2) As a proximate result of the Defendant Hurry's breach of her duty, the Plaintiff suffered a

316

concussion, cuts, and bruises; suffered great pain of body and mind; incurred expenses for medical attention and hospitalization; and has lost income from being unable to work at the restaurant where he is employed as head chef.

Assault Claim Against Hurry

The preceding allegations are hereby restated and incorporated as if set forth herein.

(3) When the Defendant Hurry intentionally approached the Plaintiff after the collision in a physically threatening manner, she created a reasonable apprehension of immediate, offensive bodily contact. The Defendant Hurry had the apparent ability to carry out the threatened offensive bodily contact. The Defendant Hurry's actions constituted an assault for which she is liable to the Plaintiff for both compensatory and punitive damages.

Battery Claim Against Hurry

The preceding allegations are hereby restated and incorporated as if set forth herein.

(4) The Defendant Hurry intentionally touched the Plaintiff in a manner offensive to a reasonable person. The Defendant Hurry's actions constitute a battery for which she is liable to the Plaintiff for both compensatory and punitive damages.

Negligence (Product Liability) Claim Against Kagasaki

The preceding allegations are hereby restated and incorporated as if set forth herein.

(5) A manufacturer has a duty to make products that are reasonably safe and, in particular, when the product is designed to operate in a manner to safeguard someone, the manufacturer has a duty to ensure the product is manufactured in a manner such that it will perform its safety function.

(6) A manufacturer breaches its duty of due care when it manufactures a product designed and represented as a safety product that fails to perform.

(7) A manufacturer's duty to manufacture a safety product that performs as represented is breached when the product fails to function at all, much less to deploy in an accident, and is a proximate cause of injuries resulting from an accident in which the safety product was supposed to provide protection but failed to operate at all.

(8) A person injured by the failure of a manufacturer's safety product to operate as represented has a negligence (or product liability) claim against the manufacturer, along with which any other person causing the accident shall be considered a joint tortfeasor with such manufacturer.

(9) Defendant Kagasaki's airbag, designed to deploy in an accident, failed to deploy at all in the Plaintiff's accident with the Defendant Hurry, resulting in aggravation of his injuries.

(10) Defendant Kagasaki breached its duty to manufacture a safety product that would perform as designed to do—i.e., inflate in an accident and minimize injury to the motorcycle rider.

(11) Defendant Kagasaki's breach proximately caused injuries to the Plaintiff, specifically by

317

failing to operate to minimize the injuries to his body as a result of the collision.

(12) The Plaintiff relied on the motorcycle airbag in choosing to ride the motorcycle and would not have done so had he known the airbag was defective.

(13) The defect in Defendant Kagasaki's airbag proximately caused the Plaintiff's injuries and/or aggravated his injuries by failing to provide the safety that it was held out to provide.

WHEREFORE, the Plaintiff demands the following relief against the Defendants:

Compensatory damages in a sum exceeding $1 million against Ena Hurry, exclusive of interest and costs, the complete amount to be determined at trial; and

Compensatory damages in a sum exceeding $1 million against Kagasaki, Inc., exclusive of interest and costs, the complete amount to be determined at trial.

BRAD T. REX
By /s/ Jim Justice
Of Counsel

The Law Offices of Jim Justice, Esq.
111 Liberty Street
Arcadia, Illyria 23464
757-222-3333/jim@justice.com
Counsel for Plaintiff

IV. Analyzing Whether Rule 20 is Satisfied

Are the requirements of Rule 20 met in the above complaint? Why or why not?
What does the "same transaction or occurrence, or series of transactions occurrences" mean? Consider the following discussion from a leading treatise:

> For purposes of that rule, all logically related events entitling a person to institute a legal action against another generally are regarded as comprising a transaction or occurrence. The logical-relationship test is consistent with the philosophy underlying the passage in Rule 20 that allows joinder of parties whenever the claims arise out of "the same series of transactions or occurrences." Moreover, the flexibility of this standard enables the federal courts to promote judicial economy by permitting all reasonably related claims for relief by or against different parties to be tried in a single proceeding under the provisions of Rule 20. Illustrative of the liberal approach to the concept of same transaction or occurrence employed by many federal courts are cases in which the court permits an injured plaintiff to join both the original tortfeasor and a second tortfeasor whose subsequent negligence aggravated plaintiff's original injuries. In a similar vein, language in a number of decisions suggests that the courts are inclined to find that claims arise out of the same transaction or occurrence when the likelihood of overlapping proof and duplication in testimony indicates that separate trials would result in delay, inconvenience, and added expense to the parties and to the court.

A. Analyzing whether a Jurisdictional Basis exists even if Rule Allows Joinder

Here we see a pattern that will become familiar. When analyzing joinder under any Rule, one must analyze first whether the Rule permits joinder of the claim or party. The next question, however, is crucial. Is there a jurisdictional basis for the joined claim or joined party? Federal Rules cannot expand the Constitutional basis for the limited jurisdiction of federal courts.

Of course, it does not expand the Constitution if the joinder involves a claim or party joined under an independent basis in subject matter jurisdiction. In those situations, the main claim has a basis in subject matter jurisdiction and the joined claim meets either diversity of citizenship or federal question jurisdiction. If that is true, there will be a jurisdictional basis for the joined claim or party.

But what if the Rule allows a joined claim or party and there is not an independent basis in subject matter jurisdiction supporting the joined claim or party. Yet again, we then turn to the *Gibbs* case to understand how joined claims can be within the limited jurisdiction of federal courts. One word— "case"— or the phrase "case or controversy"—explains how the Court in *Gibbs* justified certain joined claims and/or parties being within the limited jurisdiction of federal courts. If the joined claim or party relates to claims or parties that are part of the same common nucleus of operative facts, then the claims/parties are part of the same "case" or "case or controversy" over which the court has subject matter jurisdiction already. Hence, joinder her does not violate the limited jurisdiction of federal courts.

Practice Problem

Practice Problem 11-2

Behemoth, Inc. is incorporated and has its principal place of business in New York. Ed, a New Jersey citizen, left Behemoth, Inc. and started his own company that used as its trademark a name remarkably similar to Behemoth. Behemoth thus sued Ed in the United States District Court for the Southern District of New York for trademark infringement under the federal Lanham Act. Behemoth also sued in the same action Lou Smith, a New York citizen and former employee of Behemoth who had worked with Ed in the same department at Behemoth, claiming $20,000 in damages for the office supplies Lou allegedly took from Behemoth with him to Ed's office, where Lou works as an employee with Ed in making products that compete with Behemoth, Inc.

Does Rule 20 support joinder of Lou? If so, is there an independent basis in subject matter jurisdiction to support having the claim in federal court? If not, does the supplemental jurisdiction statute support joinder of Lou in the lawsuit?

Follow-Up Questions and Comments

1. How is Practice Problem 11-2's scenario different from the *Rex v. Hurry* scenario? What part of the analytical process does this Practice Problem require to reach an answer that is not required by *Rex v. Hurry*?

V. Miscellaneous Joinder Rules that Arise in Specific Circumstances

This section deals with a variety of rules that either require joinder or permit it in specific circumstances. They are joinder scenarios, like Rule 18 and Rule 20 in the sense that they follow the same analytical framework. One first asks whether a Federal Rule requires and/or allows joinder. Then one asks whether, even if a Rule requires or permits joinder, is there jurisdiction over the joined claims or parties. That jurisdiction, as we learned above, may come from an independent basis in subject matter jurisdiction, independently supporting the joined claim/party. Alternatively, the Supplemental Jurisdiction statute may provide a basis for jurisdiction. If neither of these grounds for jurisdiction exist, however, the joined claim or party cannot proceed.

A. Joinder of Necessary Parties

Please read Federal Rule of Civil Procedure 19. Notice that the Rule, in subpart (a) outlines when a party fits the category of a necessary party—i.e., a party that "must be joined." The first example of a necessary party is when in the absence of a party, the court cannot provide "complete relief." For instance, if a landowner sues a defendant who owns adjoining land but includes and serves only one of two owners of the property. Without all owners of jointly owned property, the court cannot provide complete relief. An owner left out of the suit, and who was not sued and notified of the suit, could come along later to challenge any judgment because he was not made a party.

Rule 19 offers also, as an instance of a necessary party, a situation when someone claims an interest relating to the subject matter of the action and, practically speaking, proceeding without that party would impair that party's ability to protect his or her interest. Suppose Plaintiff entered into a contract with a closely held corporation (Close, Inc.) owned equally by Don and Dianne. Plaintiff sues Close, Inc. and Don but not Dianne. Because owners of a closely held corporation's interests will be affected by litigation involving that corporation, leaving Dianne out would, as a practical matter, impair Diane's ability to protect her interests.

Rule 19's other example of a problematic scenario is where the plaintiff is seeking to resolve a matter and, leaving out a party from the litigation would subject a party to a substantial risk of facing claims from strangers to the first suit. In other words, Rule 19 here seeks to avoid exposure to multiple liability. For instance, suppose Polly has an insurance policy payable on her death to a named beneficiary. She dies, and the person named in the policy is her son Bob. Her daughter, Debbie, believes that Bob exercised undue influence to have Polly, who was mentally unstable in her later years, to change the named beneficiary from Debbie to Bob. Debbie informs the insurance company in writing of her claim of undue influence and entitlement to the policy proceeds. The insurance company refuses to pay Bob who then sues the insurance company but does not name Debbie as a party. Here, the insurance company faces the risk of multiple liability on the same policy if Debbie is not part of the suit.

We now turn to subsection (b) of Rule 19. This provision assumes that a necessary party as defined under subsection (a) has been identified but that it is not feasible to join that party, usually because it would destroy subject matter jurisdiction or because there is a lack of personal jurisdiction over the non-party. The Rule provides in subsection (b) that, if a necessary party has been identified, the court must decide whether "in equity and good conscience" the suit can proceed or should be dis-missed.

The following case provides an example of a court analyzing both subsections (a) and (b) of Rule 19 and deciding the case must be dismissed.

TORRINGTON CO. v. YOST
United States District Court, D. South Carolina, Greenville Division, 1991
139 F.R.D. 91

HERLONG, District Judge.

This is a trade secrets case. From 1982 to 1990, the defendant, Mark Yost ("Yost"), worked for the plaintiff, The Torrington Company ("Torrington"), manufacturing various types of bearings. While at Torrington, Yost signed an agreement not to divulge any secret or confidential information of Torrington. After leaving Torrington, Yost went to work for INA Bearing Company, Inc. ("INA") which pro-duces the same type of bearings as Torrington. On June 4, 1991, Torrington filed suit against Yost seeking, among other things, an injunction limiting Yost's employment at INA for eighteen (18) months, and actual damages from the alleged use of Torrington's trade secrets. Yost moved to dismiss under Rule 19 of the Federal Rules of Civil Procedure for failure to join Yost's new employer, INA, as an indispensable party. Yost contends that INA's absence will prejudice him and impair INA's interests.

The issue before this court is whether INA is an indispensable party to this action under Rule 19. For the reasons set forth below, the court concludes that INA, Yost's new employer, is an indispensable party whose joinder would deny the court of diversity jurisdiction. Therefore, this case must be dis-missed.

Fed. R. Civ. P. 19 requires a two-step analysis. The first part of the rule, subdivision (a), identifies the persons who should be joined if feasible. If joinder is not feasible, then subdivision (b) is applied to decide whether the case should be dismissed.

Under subdivision (a), a person should be joined when feasible if nonjoinder would under (a) (1) deny complete relief to the parties present, or under (a) (2), impair the absent person's interest or prejudice the persons already parties by subjecting them to a risk of multiple or inconsistent obligations.

In the matter *sub judice*, 19(a) (2) is the pertinent subsection. Clearly subsection (a) (2) applies, and INA should be joined if feasible. INA has an employment contract with Yost, and its interest in his fulfilling that contract would be adversely affected if Torrington were granted an injunction preventing Yost from continuing to work for INA in his current position. In addition, there is a real possibility that if INA were not joined, Yost may be subject to inconsistent obligations. In order to obey a court order enjoining him from working for INA (or enjoining him from working on certain projects at INA), Yost may have to breach his employment contract with INA. Because Yost may be prejudiced if INA is not joined and INA has an interest which may be impaired in its absence, under Rule 19(a) the court is required to join INA as a party if feasible.

The sole basis for federal court jurisdiction in this action is diversity of citizenship. 28 U.S.C. § 1332. Both INA and Torrington are Delaware corporations. Joinder of INA would destroy diversity jurisdiction. Therefore, it is not feasible to join INA, and the court must consider Rule 19(b) to determine whether the action should proceed with the parties before it or should be dismissed.

Rule 19(b) contains four factors which must be considered when deciding whether to dismiss the action: (1) to what extent a judgment rendered in the person's absence may be prejudicial to the person or those already parties; (2) the extent to which, by protective provisions in the judgment, the prejudice can be lessened or avoided; (3) whether a judgment rendered in the person's absence will be adequate; and (4) whether the plaintiff will have an adequate remedy if the action is dismissed for nonjoinder.

The first factor weighs heavily in favor of dismissal. Torrington contends that INA is not an indispensable party and is at most a joint tortfeasor who would not be prejudiced by not being joined. In the case at bar, Torrington is seeking to enjoin Yost from "working or consulting for INA for a period of eighteen (18) months, at any plant which makes thrust bearings or any supplier or subcontractor or tool designer involved with thrust bearings." Torrington is also asking the court to compel Yost "and those in privity with him, and those who became aware of any such injunction: . . . To return to Torrington, all documents, computerized and non-verbal disclosures, and physical embodiments of Torrington's trade secrets and confidential information." . . . In addition, the risk that Yost would be subjected to inconsistent obligations is significant. As already discussed, if the court limits the type of work Yost may do for INA, Yost may have inconsistent obligations to an order of the court and to INA.

The second factor requires the court to consider the feasibility of protective provisions. The drastic remedy of dismissal need not be invoked if the court can fashion relief so that neither the parties nor the person not joined is prejudiced. Torrington contends that if the court merely enjoins Yost from working at INA plants which manufacture the bearings in question, Yost could still work for INA. There is no evidence before the court, however, that such a protective provision would protect Yost from breaching his employment contract. Even if such a provision protects Yost, it would not protect INA. INA would be limited in the way it could use its employee. There is no reasonable means of protecting Yost and INA from the prejudice they would suffer if INA were not a party.

322

Third, it is doubtful that any judgment Torrington receives would be adequate if INA were not made a party. Torrington's complaint is replete with references to INA. If Yost has revealed trade secrets to INA as Torrington fears, INA will be able to continue profiting from them if INA is not a party in this action. Even if Torrington is completely successful in this suit, if INA is not a party, INA cannot be prevented from using Torrington's trade secrets information.

Finally, another forum exists for the plaintiff. Torrington will not be left without a remedy if this action is dismissed. Torrington can sue both Yost and INA in state court.

The grounds for dismissal in this case are overwhelming. INA is clearly an indispensable party. Each of the four factors of Rule 19(b) indicates that dismissal is appropriate. If Torrington wishes to continue with this suit, it must do so in state court and join INA. For the foregoing reasons, this case is dismissed pursuant to Rule 19, Fed. R. Civ. P.

IT IS SO ORDERED.

Follow-Up Questions and Comments

1. Rule 19 and necessary parties covered by it will not always be considered by the plaintiff's lawyer in choosing whom to join. A plaintiff's lawyer could anticipate that, unless the plaintiff joins a party that could qualify as necessary under Rule 19, the court could grant a defendant's motion to dismiss under Federal Rule of Civil Procedure 12(b) (7). Questions about whether a party fits under Rule 19 are more often raised by a defendant's Rule 12 motion challenging the plaintiff's failure to join a party. In Chapter 11, we will cover Rule 12, which deals with the defendant's options in responding to a complaint. Rule 12(b) (7) allows a motion to dismiss for failure to join a party under Rule 19. Thus, keep Rule 19 in mind so that, when we explore Rule 12 motions, you will recall that one such motion is based on Rule 19 and the analysis we have just addressed.

Practice Problem

Practice Problem 11-3

Ted, a citizen of Colorado, owns massive amounts of real property. He leased property in Texas to John, a citizen of Georgia. The lease from Ted required Ted's permission for John to sublet the premises. John entered into a franchise agreement with Big Burger, Inc., a fast food franchise incorporated and with its principal place of business in Dallas, Texas. John wanted to sublease the property on which his Burger franchise was operated to his son, Junior, a citizen of Texas. Big Burger, Inc. had no problem with Junior taking over the franchise because he had been running it for years for his father and made it a success. When Ted refused to grant permission to the sublease, Big Burger, Inc. and John brought a declaratory judgment suit against Ted seeking to show that the withholding of permission to sublease had to rest on some rational basis. Junior was not a party to the suit. Under Federal Rule of Civil Procedure 19(a), is Junior a necessary party? If so, under Rule 19(b) what must the court decide about the suit and what do you think the result should be? Would there be jurisdiction over the joinder of Junior.

B. Intervention

Read Federal Rule of Civil Procedure 24. Rule 24 distinguishes between intervention "of right" and "permissive intervention." In both scenarios you will see the same posture: some person or entity will not be a party named in a lawsuit but will want to be brought into the lawsuit as a party. If someone is not in a lawsuit, why would they want to be brought in? Well, sometimes litigation has begun and a person or entity that is so interested in the outcome of the litigation that it wants to take part and to help shape the result.

Here is where we need to distinguish between intervention "of right" and "permissive intervention." The court addressing a motion to intervene has limited discretion to deny an "of right" motion to intervene, whereas the court has wide discretion to deny permissive intervention.

1. Intervention "of Right"

Rule 24(a) addresses intervention of right. As noted, some statutes specifically allow a right to intervene. The most significant of these is the statute that allows the U.S. to intervene to protect the government's interest in a case.[501] However, the more common form of intervention of right is one in which the party seeking to intervene "claims an interest relating to the property or transaction that is the subject matter of the action and is so situated that disposing of the action may as a practical matter impair or impede the movant's ability to protect its interest, unless existing parties adequately represent that interest."[502]

If the language of Rule 24(a) (2) seems familiar, it should. It's virtually identical to the language in Rule 19(a) (1) (B) (i). The party moving to intervene as "of right" must show (1) she has an interest in the property or transaction that is the subject matter of the action; (2) that interest could as a practical matter be harmed by the lawsuit; and (3) the parties named in the suit would not adequately represent the interests of the party moving to intervene. The interest necessary to intervene has generally been interpreted broadly to include economic interest, injury to reputation, or similar interests.[503] Likewise, the second element requires only that the harm be in practical terms.[504] The adequacy of representation typically depends on whether the interests of the would-be intervenor are identical to those of a party, or instead are not fully aligned with a party.[505]

A good example of the potential scope of Rule 24 was illustrated in *United States v. Alisal Water Corp.*.[506] There, the government sued a water provider under the Safe Drinking Water Act. A judgment creditor of the defendant water provider sought to intervene on the grounds that the fines sought by the government were such that, if sustained, would leave the water provider unable to pay the $1.7 million judgment owed to the intervening party. Thus, the interest of the intervenor could be harmed, and the parties did not represent the judgment creditor's interests. The court allowed intervention under Rule 24(a).

---

[501] *See* 28 U.S.C. § 2403.
[502] FED. R. CIV. P. 24(a)(2) (emphasis added).
[503] *See* 7C CHARLES ALAN WRIGHT & ARTHUR R. MILLER, FEDERAL PRACTICE AND PROCEDURE § 1908.1 (3d. ed. 2018).
[504] *See id.* §1908.2.
[505] *See id.* § 1909.
[506] 370 F.3d 915 (9th Cir. 2004).

2. Permissive Intervention

Unlike intervention under Rule 24(a), which must be allowed if the three conditions are met, the decision of whether to grant a motion to intervene under Rule 24(b) is within the trial court's discretion. To even be in the ballpark (absent a statute permitting intervention), the absent party moving to intervene must show she has a claim or defense that "shares with the main action a common question of law or fact." An example of a court's allowing permissive intervention can be seen in *Kootenay Tribe of Idaho v. Veneman,*[507] where U.S. and environmental groups aligned together in defending the U.S. Forest Service's Roadless Area Conservation Rule.

Follow-Up Questions and Comments

1. You should recognize that a motion to intervene does not mean that the moving party is always seeking to be added as a plaintiff. In fact, at least as often motions to intervene are to be added as a defendant so that the absentee can become part of the litigation and defend claims brought against the original plaintiff when a ruling on such claims will affect the intervenors' rights.

Practice Problem

Practice Problem 11-4

Love Your Mother, Inc., a conservation group incorporated and with its principal place of business in Louisiana sued the Unites States Secretary of Agriculture and asserted that cutting trees in national forests located in Texas violated federal laws. Timber-4-U Trade Association, a citizen of Arkansas, who represented purchasers of timber from the national forests in question, moved to intervene as defendants, to argue that the tree cutting in question complied with federal law. The trial court granted the motion to intervene and found that Timber-4-U had legally protected property interests in the dispute because the current contracts and future contracts to harvest timber in the forests would be affected by the litigation.[508] Why is this intervention an example of intervention of right under Rule 24(a) rather than permissive intervention under Rule 24(b)? Is there jurisdiction over the joinder of the intervening party, Timber-4-U Trade Association?

C. Statutory and Rule Interpleader

Interpleader is a unique but important means of joining parties to a suit in a particular scenario. At times a party is the holder of funds or property, such as a life insurance company holding the proceeds of a policy after the insured has died. Competing claimants to the funds want them. The holder does not care who gets the funds. However, the holder does not want to be subject to multiple liability. Thus, the holder of the funds or property wants to put the money or property into court and file a suit engaging all claimants and then let the court decide who gets the funds or property.

Oddly, Congress has provided for interpleader both by a statute *and* in a rule. As we will see the statute is broader in application than the Rule.

---

[507] 313 F.3d 1094 (10th Cir. 2002).
[508] *See* Sierra Club v. Espy, 18 F.3d 1202 (5th Cir. 1994).

325

1. Statutory Interpleader

The interpleader statute, 28 U.S.C. § 1335, provides as follows:

> The district courts shall have original jurisdiction of any civil action of interpleader or in the nature of interpleader filed by any person, firm, or corporation, association, or society having in his or its custody or possession money or property of the value of $500 or more, or having issued a note, bond, certificate, policy of insurance, or other instrument of value or amount of $500 or more, or providing for the delivery or payment or the loan of money or property of such amount or value, or being under any obligation written or unwritten to the amount of $500 or more, if

> Two or more adverse claimants, of diverse citizenship as defined in subsection (a) or (d) of section 1332 of this title, are claiming or may claim to be entitled to such money or property, or to any one or more of the benefits arising by virtue of any note, bond, certificate, policy or other instrument, or arising by virtue of any such obligation; and if (2) the plaintiff has deposited such money or property or has paid the amount of or the loan or other value of such instrument or the amount due under such obligation into the registry of the court, there to abide the judgment of the court, or has given bond payable to the clerk of the court in such amount and with such surety as the court or judge may deem proper, conditioned upon the compliance by the plaintiff with the future order or judgment of the court with respect to the subject matter of the controversy.

> Such an action may be entertained although the titles or claims of the conflicting claimants do not have a common origin or are not identical but are adverse to and independent of one another.

The above statute, called the Federal Interpleader Statute, allows a party to file an action under the statute in federal court if (1) the plaintiff holds money or property worth more than $500; (2) there are two or more adverse claimants to the money or property; and (3) the plaintiff has deposited the money or property in the court or given a bond that assures the plaintiff will comply with the court's ultimate order as to whom the money or property should be paid.

You might wonder how a suit can be brought in federal court based on diversity jurisdiction when there is a lack of complete diversity. If you go back to Chapter 3, you will see in the discussion of complete diversity that the concept is contrasted there with minimal diversity.[509] The discussion there makes clear that the mandate of the Constitution in Article III, section 2 is that there must be "minimal diversity" between the adverse parties. The requirement of complete diversity is a requirement based on the Supreme Court's interpretation of the general diversity statute, 28 U.S.C. § 1332, not based on the Constitution. The Supreme Court interpreted the scope of the constitutional grant of "citizens of different states" in an interpleader action where there was minimal diversity—there was at least one claimant to the stakeholder's fund that was of diverse citizenship from another stakeholder.[510] The Court held in *Tashire* that subject matter jurisdiction existed in interpleader actions based on the constitutional grant and the interpleader statute, 28 U.S.C. § 1335, which requires only minimal diversity.

---

[509] *See* supra Ch. 3.
[510] *See* State Farm Fire & Cas. Co. v. Tashire, 386 U.S. 523 (1926).

Now read Federal Rule of Civil Procedure 22. That rule provides a procedural mechanism by which a stakeholder of property of funds can sue competing claimants to the property or funds. Thus, it serves the same purpose as statutory interpleader if one can supply a basis in subject matter jurisdiction. Rule 22 cannot supply an independent basis in subject matter jurisdiction for an interpleader action. Thus, while the stakeholder can put the property or funds in the court, as in an interpleader action under 28 U.S.C. § 1335, a suit based on Rule 22 must rely on traditional grounds of subject matter jurisdiction—i.e., either federal question jurisdiction, or general diversity of citizenship jurisdiction. As such, a Rule interpleader suit, if it rests on diversity, must rest on complete diversity of citizenship between the plaintiff stakeholder and every defendant who the stakeholder joins as a claimant.

Practice Problems

The following Practice Problems will demonstrate the difference between Statutory Inter-pleader and Rule Interpleader.

Practice Problem 11-5

Trustus Insurance Company, incorporated in Delaware and with its principal place of business in New York, has $500,000 that after filing suit in federal court it places in the court while suing three beneficiaries who each claim entitlement to all the funds. Two of those claimants brought into the suit are from Louisiana and one is from New York. Why could the above suit be brought in federal court under the federal interpleader statute, 28 U.S.C. § 1335, but not be brought under Federal Rule 22 based on the general diversity statute for subject matter jurisdiction?

Practice Problem 11-6

An art gallery held, during the life of the deceased, possession of a painting that is authenticated as an early painting of Vincent Van Gogh worth $300,0000. The art gallery is incorporated and has its principal place of business in Texas. On the death of the deceased, four claimants, all citizens of Arkansas, assert the right to inherit the painting. Why could the above suit not be brought under 28 U.S.C. § 1335? Why could the suit be brought as an interpleader action in federal court under Rule 22 and the complete diversity statute, 28 U.S.C. § 1332?

D. Class Actions

Class actions are perhaps the most extraordinary form of joinder. Although class actions could comprise an entire book, this section introduces the basics.

A class action is the joinder (or aggregation) of multiple claims against a defendant or defend-ants. In several ways, the joinder achieved by a class action is markedly different form the joinder described in the other methods in this chapter. First, the class is far larger than the number of parties typically joined. Second, a small group—parties designated "class representatives"—represents the interests of the entire class. Third, lawyer(s) designated "class counsel" litigate the case on behalf of the class but typically deal only with the class representatives. Fourth, the class representatives after suit is filed must move for certification of the class. That certification order will recognize the named plaintiffs as representatives of the class, will define the class represented by these plaintiffs, and will appoint class counsel as well as other details.

The purpose of a class action is to promote judicial efficiency, ease of proving a case, for the defendant or defendants, the protection of knowing that all claims have been resolved once the case comes to a resolution. Another value—i.e., due process for both all class members and for defendants— is another strong theme in Rule 23. Keep these purposes in mind as you consider the requirements, discussed below, for proceeding as a class action.

Now read Federal Rule of Civil Procedure 23. It may help you, as you read, to pretend you are a lawyer who has been asked by a client to pursue a class action against a large company over a claim that, if brought by itself, would not justify the expense or litigating. Consider whether, if your imaginary client had a defective product, and thousands of other consumers had the same defective product, the requirements in Rule 23 make more sense in providing a mechanism to make it possible (and desirable) for parties who have the same or highly similar claims against a defendant to join those together so as to make it economical to pursue.

As you read Rule 23, ask yourself:

What are the four prerequisites a court must find to certify a class action? If the four prerequisites for any type of class action are met, how can one know what kind of class action for which to seek certification? Are potential class members given notice of the class action and, if so, are they permitted to choose to "opt out" and pursue one's individual claim? What must the certification order, if granted, include?
What procedures does the Rule include to protect class members in the conduct of the litigation?
What are the criteria for being appointed "class counsel"?

1. Four Prerequisites for a Class Action Under Federal Rule of Civil Procedure 23(a)

The four prerequisites that any class action must satisfy are: (a) numerosity of the class; (b) commonality of questions of law or fact for the class; (c) that the claims or defenses of the representative parties are typical of the claims and defenses of the class; and (d) that the representative parties will fairly and adequately protect the class members' interests.

The following explain in a bit more detail what satisfying these requirements usually involves.

Numerosity requires that the class be sufficiently numerous that joinder of the members as individual parties asserting each's own claim in one action would be inefficient and difficult. A good rule of thumb is about 50 members, perhaps a bit less, would be the range at which one could start to satisfy the numerosity requirement. (b) The commonality requirement simply requires that there be a question of fact or of law common to the class. (c) The typicality requirement will be satisfied when the claims and defenses of the named party typify those of the class and that the named party lacks distinctive vulnerabilities. (d) The adequacy requirement demands that the named parties, and their lawyers demonstrate they will competently (meaning experience necessary), fairly, diligently and without conflict with class members protect the members of the class.

Lawyers who bring class actions do not do so unless they have sufficiently numerous class members. Moreover, such lawyers typically are experienced in class action cases and can satisfy the adequacy of representation requirement. The commonality requirement had been one that traditionally had been applied permissively. However, the United States Supreme Court's recent decision in *Wal-Mart*

Stores, Inc. v. Dukes,[511] suggested that the "commonality" requirement re-quires that the class members rest the claims on a common contention and that the claims of the class members will be able to be decided on a class-wide basis. In Dukes, a class of 1.5 million female employees claimed gender discrimination in violation of Title VII of the Civil Rights Act of 1964. The Supreme Court held that the class lacked commonality because each of the plaintiffs had been discriminated against in separate employment decisions and suffered different injuries. Although the impact of the Court's ruling on commonality in Dukes needs further exposition, the reality is that in many other scenarios the class members can demonstrate that their claims involve common contentions and the resolution of these in a class action will resolve all the claims. For instance, stockholders defrauded by a fraudulent proxy statement should have little difficulty showing that the commonality of their being defrauded and relying to their detriment on a fraudulent proxy satisfies the commonality requirement.

Finally, the typicality requirement has generally been read broadly. The class members' claims and the representative parties' claims need not be identical. Instead, if they raise issues that the class members will litigate, even if they do not raise all aspects of a claim, the named plaintiffs will still be adequately representing the class. The typicality requirement is thus designed to bolster the adequacy of representation requirement.[512]

2. The Additional Requirement—Depends on What Kind of Class Action

Assume that all four requirements of Rule 23(a) have been met. Even so, the court must also find— for the case to be certified to proceed as a class action—that the action satisfies at least one of the added requirements in Rule 23(b). That rule splits class actions into three kinds of class action.

Rule 23, First Kind of Class Action: The court can certify under Rule 23(b) (1) a class action if independent suits by the individual class members creates a risk of prejudice, either to the class members or to whomever opposes the class. Such a class action, sometimes called a "prejudice" class action rests on the same issues we saw in interpleader and intervention. For instance, as is true with inter-pleader, the party opposing the class may be at risk of being exposed to multiple and competing findings and judgments. If the defendant, for instance, has limited assets (or a fund). If these assets (or fund) could be depleted by separate suits. If there are too many claimants to handle such a case by inter-pleader, this kind of class action works well. The other scenario is where multiple lawsuits deplete the assets such that all claimants would not recover unless this type of class action was certified.

Rule 23, Second Kind of Class Action: The court can certify under Rule 23(b) (2) a class action that seeks primarily equitable relief, such as an injunction, rather than monetary relief. Employment discrimination class actions and civil rights class actions often fall into this category.

Rule 23, Third Kind of Class Action: The court can certify under Rule 23(b) (3) class actions seeking monetary damages. Such class actions far exceed the other two kinds. And here is an important point: If the class action seeks monetary damages, the court must make two other findings before certifying the class. First, the common issues of fact or law must predominate over individual issues. Second, the class action must be "superior to other available methods for fairly and efficiently adjudicating the controversy." Thus, the court here compares a class action approach to suits by individual class members. Although each

---

[511] 564 U.S. 338 (2011).

[512] *See* 7A Charles Alan Wright & Arthur R. Miller, Federal Practice and Procedure § 1764 (3d. ed. 2018).

potential class action hinges on its circumstances, some general observations can be made. If the claimants have claims for limited amounts that would not make independent actions economical, then the court would see a class action as superior because it would be achieving what class actions are in part designed to do. Moreover, if the court has already found that the initial requirement in Rule 23(a) of implacability of joinder of separate suits, then typically the court will also find that a class action is a superior method for adjudicating the controversy.

Following is a case in which the court granted the motion for class certification. In the opinion, the court succinctly but persuasively concludes that the requirements of Rule 23(a) have been met and, in addition, that the requirements of Rule 23(b) (3) were met.

KLEIN v. O'NEAL, INC.
United States District Court, N.D. Texas, Wichita Falls Division, 2004
222 F.R.D. 564

MEMORANDUM OPINION; CLASS CERTIFICATION

BUCHMEYER, Senior District Judge.

Before this Court is PLAINTIFFS'MOTION FOR CLASS CERTIFICATION. . . After considering the motion, response, and reply, the evidence presented at the hearing, applicable authorities, and the arguments of counsel, the motion is GRANTED. The court certifies the following class:

> All persons in the United States, including any estate representatives or heirs of deceased persons, who, during the period from November 1, 1983, until April 30, 1984, were administered E–Ferol. Included in the class are parents, spouses, children, guardians, and legal representatives of such persons with direct or derivative claims. This Opinion will address, in turn, each of the requirements for class certification.

Class Certification

Under Federal Rule of Civil Procedure 23(a), this Court may certify a class if Plaintiffs prove that the class meets four requirements: numerosity, commonality, typicality, and adequacy. In addition to the Rule 23(a) requirements, the proposed class must also fit within one of the categories outlined in Federal Rule of Civil Procedure 23(b). In this case, Plaintiffs make a claim for certification under Rule 23(b) (3), which requires that "questions of law or fact pre-dominate over any questions affecting only individual members, and that a class action is superior to other available methods for the fair and efficient adjudication of the controversy." As explained below, Plaintiffs have satisfied each of the requirements for class certification.

Numerosity

The certified class consists of all persons who were administered E–Ferol between November 1, 1983, and April 30, 1984. The class is contained to persons within the borders of the continental United States. Parties agree, based on Food and Drug Administration ("FDA") data, that approximately 1,008 premature infants received the drug in the relevant time period. Excluding persons who have filed claims over injuries due to E–Ferol receipt, the potential class numbers approximately 866. The potential class membership exceeds the number of claimants who could practicably be joined as individual plaintiffs, and class treatment of these claimants pro-vides a more convenient and manageable process for the fair and efficient resolution of their claims.

Commonality

To meet the commonality requirement, the court must find issues of law or fact common to the class. . . . . The Court finds, pursuant to Fed. R. Civ. P. 23(a) (2), that the complaints of the Plaintiffs raise questions of fact common to the class. While a single common issue is sufficient to satisfy Rule 23(a) (2), this case presents numerous important common questions upon which each class member's ultimate right to recover will depend.

Common questions of fact exist regarding the development, manufacturing, distribution, testing, and sale of the drug. Common fact questions also exist regarding the drug and its effects, and Defendants' role in curing the harms or warning infants who received E–Ferol. Common questions include factual issues related to liability of the Defendants for placing into commerce a drug determined by the FDA to have not been properly presented to the FDA and for misrepresenting or mislabeling the drug. The facts relating to product liability negligence, breach of warranty, and misrepresentation and fraud are substantially the same for all class members. To the extent that individual causation and damages questions arise with regard to individual class members, such issues may be given individual treatment. The appropriate procedure for structuring and organizing a trial of common issues as well as procedures for adjudicating any individual issues are not decided [now] but await further discovery and clarification.

Typicality

The claims of Victoria Klein and Ashley Swadley are typical of the claims of the class members as required by Fed. R. Civ. P. 23(a) (3). Plaintiff Victoria Klein was born on March 23, 1984 at Wichita Falls General Hospital. She was administered 16 doses of E–Ferol intravenously at Cook Children's Medical Center, formerly known as Fort Worth Children's Hospital, between March 23, 1984, and April 9, 1984. Plaintiff Ashley Swadley was born on February 18, 1984, at Baylor University Medical Center. She received four doses of E–Ferol between February 18, 1984, and February 28, 1984. These hospitals failed to notify patients who had received E–Ferol that it had been administered to them and further, failed to notify parents of these infants, some of whom died from E–Ferol, that they had been so exposed. These acts occurred despite findings that showed E–Ferol as the cause of death in some instances.

Typicality exists when the class representatives' claims arise from the same event or course of conduct and are based on the same legal or remedial theories as those of the class. Individual variations among class members' claims with respect to individual causation, medical history, general health, extent of injury, or damages, do not defeat typicality, provided that the claims arise from the same events or course of conduct and are based on the same legal theories. Here, all claims arise in the same course of conduct placing in commerce for use as an intravenous drug a substance that did not have FDA clearance and for which the Defendants were convicted of criminal violations, including fraud and misrepresentation. Common liability questions apply to each and every member of the class with regard to the testing, manufacturing, marketing, and sale of the product, and hence all arise from the same course of conduct. The typicality requirement is satisfied.

Adequacy of Representation

The proposed named Plaintiffs will fairly and adequately protect and pursue the interest of the class. No conflict of interest exists between Plaintiffs and the proposed class. Furthermore, Plaintiffs' attorneys have demonstrated to this Court that they are qualified, experienced, and able to conduct this litigation.

Rule 23(b) (3) Requirements

To maintain a class action under Rule 23(b) (3), the questions common to the class must predominate over the questions affecting individual members, and a class action must be superior to other available methods of adjudication.

Common questions predominate over questions affecting individual class members. While there may be variations in the amounts of damages, each class member was injured by a sin-gular course of action by Defendants. Individual damage amounts may involve proof of the individual circumstances of each class member, but many of the same facts will apply to each class member's damage claims, and the elements of damages for each individual plaintiff will involve proof of common questions.

As this case involves tort law as it applies in many different states, Plaintiffs have thoroughly reviewed the applicable products liability laws. Through their review and briefing, this Court is satisfied that Plaintiffs correctly urge that the differences in state laws do not present insurmountable obstacles to class certification. The relevant states recognize causes of action under (or substantially similar to) Restatement (Second) of Torts §§ 402A and 402B. The factual proof required to establish claims will be substantially similar for all class members. Further-more, without class certification, parties will litigate the same core facts regarding the development, manufacturing, distribution, testing, and sale of the drug, as well as facts relating to the drug and its effects and Defendants' role in curing the harms or warning infants who received E–Ferol.

Certification of this litigation as a voluntary ("opt-out") class action is superior to individual actions or other available methods for the fair and efficient adjudication of this controversy. Joinder is impracticable due to the number of potential claimants, and individual cases would first require the resolution of issues that could be better resolved on a class basis. Resolution of the common issues of fact in this case will further the resolution of individual damages claims. Alternative methods of adjudication fail to offer the efficient resolution of factual is-sues offered by class certification, and the interests of judicial economy and justice require that this Court certify a class of Plaintiffs as proposed.

Conclusion

For the reasons stated in this Opinion, Plaintiffs' Motion for Class Certification is GRANTED. The Court certifies a class as defined above. Plaintiffs' attorney shall submit a class certification order pursuant to this Opinion. Each and every hospital or medical provider that administered E–Ferol during the applicable period are hereby ordered to produce, pursuant to this Court's order attached hereto as Exhibit A, the information contained in that order to Plaintiffs' counsel so that personal notification to each class member can be made.

The parties shall meet forthwith and prepare and submit an agreed proposed scheduling order to the Court for its consideration.

It is so ORDERED.

Follow-Up Questions and Comments

1. Rule 23(b) (3) class actions raise concerns about fairness to different class members. Claimants in a Rule 23(b) (3) class action have claims that often are more independent of one another than in the other two kinds of class action. However, the emphasis on packaging litigation along transactional

lines—a recurring theme in joinder—plays a role here. Rule 23(b) (3) class actions are likely the most efficient way to determine factually related claims all together.

2. Because class members in a Rule 23(b) class action have claims that are not as closely related as in the other two kinds of class actions, courts are aware of the adequacy of reputation. Moreover, the Rule itself provides for different treatment of prospective class members in such a class action. Rule 23(c) (2) (B) re-quires notice to individual class members that the certified Rule 23(b) (3) class action is pending. Moreover, the Rule allows members of a Rule 23(b) (30 class to respond to the notice that they choose not to be part of the class, and thus to retain their ability to sue separately. Such a decision is known colloquially as "opting out" of a class. If a class member opts out, she is not bound by the judgment in the class action.

3. Because the decision whether to certify a class is so significant, and to otherwise follow the usual path of waiting until the final judgment to appeal any prior decisions. Rule 23(f) allows parties to seek interlocutory appellate review of the certification decision before the class action proceed too far, and the appellate court has the discretion to accept or deny review. Rule 23(d) provides that courts, in certifying a class action, can define the scope of the class, to appoint class counsel, to determine the notice to be sent, and in general to handle with great discretion the way to the class action is managed.

4. Rule 23(e) provides that the court must approve any settlement, voluntary dismissal, or compromise of a class action. In deciding whether to approve a settlement, voluntary dismissal, or compromise, the court must under Rule 23(e) (1) give notice to all class members "who would be bound by" the action. Such notice is required in all types of class actions, not just Rule 23(b) (3) actions. On other matters, notice to class members is something the court "may" require in prejudice and class actions seeking equitable relief. The requirement reflects the desire to have the fullest opportunity for those interested to weigh in on the appropriateness of a settlement or dismissal.

---

3. Jurisdiction over Class Actions

In class actions based on diversity of citizenship, the citizenship of named class representatives is all that is compared to the citizenship of a defendant to determine if complete diversity exists.[513] Moreover, the Class Action Fairness Act, 28 U.S.C. §1332(d), 1453, established that in multistate class actions based on diversity, only minimal diversity is required. As to the amount in controversy, the Court has held that only one named class member need meet the amount in controversy requirement and that other members can rely on supplemental jurisdiction to support their claims.[514]

Practice Problems

Practice Problem 11-7

Cal, the Class Action Specialist, had learned that Truckster Motors, Inc. incorporated and with its principal place of business in Michigan. Truck Motors, Inc. manufactured both station wagons and trucks, had sold 8,000 of its large pickups, Total Trucksers, but the truck had been designed with a center of gravity

---

[513] *See, e.g.,* Snyder v. Haris, 394 U.S. 332, 340 (1969).
[514] *See* Exxon Mobil Corp. v. Allapattah Serv., Inc., 545 U.S. 546 (2005).

that led it to flip even when traveling at acceptable speed limits if the truck rounded a curve. Cal had located over 200 persons injured in rollovers, each with damages exceeding $75,000 in personal injuries, not to mention each truck owner being left with totaled vehicles (total loss of $25,000 per truck). He picked ten of the members who agreed to serve as named parties are not citizens of Michigan. The ten named class representatives filed the action in the U.S. District Court for the Eastern District of Michigan as a putative class action and moved for certification of the class action as a Rule 23(b) (3) class action. What would the court have to find in order to certify this action as a class action under Rule 23(b) (3)? What obstacles would this scenario present for class action treatment? If the court ended up certifying the case as a class action, what steps would have to be taken to notify class members? Why if the requirements of Rule 23 are met would jurisdiction exist (even if some of the class members are citizens of Michigan)?

CHAPTER 12: ADDITIONAL PLEADING ISSUES: CERTIFICATIONS OF PLEADINGS, SANCTIONS FOR IMPROPER PLEADINGS OR REPRESENTATIONS, AND ABILITY TO AMEND PLEADINGS

I. How the Topics in this Chapter Fit into the Overall Progress of a Civil Action

Below is a diagram of the stages of a civil action showing where the topics discussed in this chapter fall in the progress of a case.

Figure 12-1

Cause of Action (events Leading to suit)	Pre-Filing Tasks (items to begin representation, interviewing, and related matters)	Choice of Forum (subject matter jurisdiction, removal, personal jurisdiction, and venue)	Notice and Service of Process (completing the process of ensuring the forum court can enter a valid judgment)	**Pleading the Case and Joinder of Claims and Parties (including supplemental jurisdiction)**

Responding to Claims by Motion or by Answer	Discovery (developing proof to establish claims and learn your adversary's case)	Right to Jury (pretrial motions and practice)	Final Pretrial Conference (events within last month before trial)	Trial (procedures and motions during trial)	Verdict	Post-Trial Motions (motions for a new trial and/or judgment as a matter of law)	Appeal

We are in the pleading stage of the case when we discuss certifications made by the one who signs a pleading. The "Rule 11 certifications," as they are known, apply to both plaintiff and defense counsel. Any "offensive" pleading—a complaint by a plaintiff, a counterclaim by a defendant, a cross-claim or third-party claim—will, when signed by counsel, carry certifications of that counsel. If the certifications are not true, the opposing party can take steps to seek sanctions or other relief. The same applies to defensive pleadings—an answer by a defendant, a plaintiff's answer to a counter-claim, answer to a cross-claim or third-party claim. Pleadings are thus prepared and filed in the shadow of Federal Rule of Civil Procedure 11. As we will see, the nature of the certifications encourages counsel to only plead facts and claims that she can justify.

We will also address in this chapter the amendment of pleadings after initial filing. The amendment process, as will be described below, can occur at any of three phases: (1) amendment-of-right for a very short period at the beginning of the case; (2) amendments prior to trial after the "of right" stage and before trial begins—thus, the longest period we will discuss; and (3) amendments at trial. Federal Rule of Civil

Procedure 15 governs amendments and encourages liberal amendments. We will see, however, that courts are less willing to allow amendments as trial nears. Even then, however, amending pleadings is possible.

The law of certifications on signing pleadings and of amending pleadings may seem to be distinct areas. However, they are combined here because the two are more closely linked than may at first appear. Counsel preparing and signing a pleading must bear in mind the effect of her signature— that when the lawyer signs the pleadings, that is telling the court that the pleadings are not purposely designed to delay the case, that the lawyer has a good faith basis in the circumstances for facts and claims asserted, etc. Amendment of pleadings goes hand in hand with the careful approach to pleading that Rule 11 incentivizes. Parties may believe that the first version of a pleading filed will be the only opportunity to plead a claim, plead defenses, or the like. To the contrary, effective counsel make it a practice to review their pleadings after the case has progressed and to move for leave to amend pleadings to bring them into line with what the lawyer has learned. Because a lawyer may only have a case for a brief period before filing, factual allegations made (and reasonably certified) in the beginning may need to be removed or amended as the case proceeds and the lawyer's understanding of the case develops.

Just as significantly, lawyers need to help their clients' claims (or defenses) by adding to them key allegations or even new claims that grow out of the same events. Often in litigation, discovery will reveal new grounds on which a lawyer can plead a claim for relief not originally requested. A practice of reviewing and updating one's pleadings can make the difference between prevailing on such additional claims (and relief) and being barred from presenting evidence on the claim or seeking relief based on it. Generally, if the party has not pled a claim or a defense, the opposing party can object to introduction of evidence at trial that is not included in the pleading. As we will see, there is a possibility of conforming the pleadings to the evidence by amendment during trial. Such a practice, however, is risky because the opposing party can make a stronger case for prejudice when she did not have the opportunity to perform discovery on such claims. If the lawyer can remove that argument by moving for leave to amend before trial (and while discovery is still possible), the movant will typically prevail.

Ideally, the lawyer has a firm grasp on her client's case. She knows as much of the facts as possible, or at least enough to seek discovery. She also knows that she has a good faith basis in law for the claims sought. She has a reminder system in place to remind her as litigation proceeds whether her pleadings need to be amended. If she uncovers facts that support a new claim and does not seek leave to amend in order to plead it, the client will not be able to recover on the claim. On the other hand, if counsel knows facts stated in discovery are untrue, she has an obligation to supplement and correct the matter.

II. Applicable Law

A. Certifications Upon Signing a Pleading--Rule 11

Please read Federal Rule of Civil Procedure 11. Signing a pleading under Rule 11 triggers several certifications by the signing lawyer. What are they? Rule 11(b) also states that the certification attaches to every "presenting" of any "pleading, written motion, or other paper." When does such a "presenting" occur and what duty does that place on counsel as the signing party (or member of the firm of the signing party)?

To beef up Rule 11, amendments in 1983 provided that sanctions "shall" be imposed on violation of a certification. The result was a spike in Rule 11 motions and "satellite litigation"— litigation not focused on the merits but rather on attempting to recover monetary sanctions against the other side. Moreover, some used the motions as tactical tools. In 1993, the Rule was amended again, this time to remove the mandatory nature of sanctions and to move the emphasis away from awarding money from one side to another and toward deterrence of certification violations. Where do you see indications of these amendments in the current version of Rule 11?

A represented party cannot be sanctioned with monetary sanctions for violating one of the certifications. Which certification is that? Why does this approach make sense?

The 1993 amendments added another addition—some would say the most important amendment—known as the "safe harbor" provision. Prior to the 1993 amendment, a party could file a Rule 11 motion with the court without giving notice to the opposing party or lawyer(s) against whom the movant was seeking sanctions. Is this still possible? Why or why not? What does it mean in Rule 11(c) (2) that the motion must be served "under Rule 5"?[515] If a motion is served on an attorney in this way, is there anything filed with the court at the time of service on the attorney? Where in Rule 11(c) (2) is there language clarifying service of the Rule 11 motion and not requiring anything be filed with the court?

Practice Problems
Practice Problem 12-1
In Rule 11(b), it states that the signing of a pleading is a certification "that to the best of the person's knowledge, information, and belief, formed after an inquiry reasonable in the circumstances," the four items in Rule 11(b) (1)-(4) are true. What is "reasonable under the circumstances?" Take the *Rex v. Hurry* case from Chapter 11. What if, in your first interview, Rex told you that he assumed the light had turned green because other traffic adjacent to him started moving toward it? You also know the accident report noted witnesses, but you have not been able to talk to them yet before you must file the complaint (the statute of limitations is running out). If you signed a complaint by Rex against Hurry, alleging that "Rex entered an intersection lawfully," would that allegation be reasonable under the circumstances?

Practice Problem 12-2
In Rule 11(b) (2), the certification provides that the claims, defenses, and other legal contentions "are warranted by existing law or by a non-frivolous argument for extending, modifying, or reversing existing law or for establishing new law." What if the applicable law sued on in a diversity case in federal court is whether a host of a party owes "social host" liability to someone who was injured when a person, inebriated from the party, left and drove drunk into an accident? Assume that just the prior year the highest court in the state ruled against imposing social host liability, with one justice dissenting. If you are currently faced with the prospect of pleading a claim for social host liability, could you, in these circumstances, file a complaint that would fall under the non-frivolous provision?

Practice Problem 12-3
Paul is a trespasser on Denny's wooded property without permission. Denny has a hazardous condition on his property—a pit that's hard to see until one is on it and that has rocks at the bottom. While hunting, Paul is confused about whose property he is on and falls into the pit and breaks his leg. He sues Denny for premises liability for maintaining a hazardous condition on his property that presents a risk of deadly harm or death to others. Although the parties are in federal court because of diversity, the law governing is the state's law on premises liability. The last decision of the highest court of the state, which is over 100 years old, holds that a landowner owes no duty, even for hazardous conditions, to trespassers.

---

[515] FED. R. CIV. P. 5(b)(1).

However, many states around the country have changed their rule in such cases over time, with a majority now holding that a landowner can be liable to even a trespasser for hazardous conditions. Moreover, the state whose law is in question in this diversity case had made other reforms in tort law, such as providing that a lessor or landlord owed a duty of care to anyone on their property from unsafe conditions, even if the injured person is not the lessee or tenant. Paul asks you to sue Denny. If you were counsel for Paul, could you file a complaint that would not violate the certifications of Rule 11(b)(2)?

Practice Problem 12-4

Patty, who is over 60-years-old, sues Zydeco Corporation. In one of her claims, Patty alleges that Zydeco fired her based on age discrimination. She alleges "on information and belief" that Zydeco fired her based on her age, and that this allegation is "likely to have evidentiary support after a reasonable opportunity for further investigation or discovery." When she files the complaint, Patty's counsel has performed a preliminary investigation and has some basis for believing that the allegation against Zydeco is true but anticipates developing evidence through discovery from Zydeco. After completing discovery, Patty is unable to show that Zydeco fired her based on age. Has Patty violated Rule 11? Why or why not? Say that Zydeco Corporation's counsel is inept. He neither serves a Rule 11 motion on Patty nor moves for summary judgment. Patty proceeds to trial and based on the original complaint's allegations contends that her client is a "discrimination victim" deserving justice. Are Patty's oral representations, based on her pleadings, violations of Rule 11 certifications?

Practice Problem 12-5

Horace sues Harry, who is diverse, for nuisance based on sewage that Harry is allowing to be stored on Harry's property. He claims $300,000 in damages. The sewage is creating an intolerable smell. Harry files a pleading stating only: "I have the right to use my property as I wish, and thus, Horace's case should be thrown out." Horace files a Rule 11 motion with the court and serves Harry. Horace asserts that Harry violates all the certifications of Rule 11(b)(1)(4) and, because he signed the pleading pro se (i.e. himself), money sanctions should be imposed. Can the court grant Horace's motion?

Follow-Up Questions and Comments

1. Can a court issue Rule 11 sanctions "sua sponte," i.e., on its own motion? If so, what procedures must the court follow?

2. Please read Federal Rule of Civil Procedure 11(d). We will discuss the discovery process in Chapter 13, but for now, what does this provision tell you about Rule 11's ability to govern sanctions for failure to abide by the discovery rules? If not, what Rules govern?

3. Judges determine Rule 11 violations using the "objective," reasonable-attorney standard. "Pleading in the alternative" is not strictly a violation of Rule 11, so long as there is a good faith basis.

4. Completely independent of the Rules, State Bar Associations that license attorneys have adopted variations of the ABA Model Code of Professional Responsibility. These standards are not designed to provide for sanctions in a case, but rather are a basis on which lawyers can be disciplined. Judges can, and often do, refer to State Bar Associations incidents in litigation that they believe should be addressed by the Bar. The lawyer will then have to go through a disciplinary process, the results of which can affect her license. Federal courts refer to the State Bar of the state

in which the U.S. District Court is located. Following is ABA Model Rule 3.1 ("Meritorious Claims and Contentions"):

5. A lawyer shall not bring or defend a proceeding, or assert or controvert an issue therein, unless there is a basis in law and fact for doing so that is not frivolous, which includes a good faith argument for an extension, modification or reversal of existing law. A lawyer for the defendant in a criminal proceeding, or the respondent in a proceeding that could result in incarceration, may nevertheless so defend the proceeding as to require that every element of the case be established.[516]

B. Examples of Instances in Which Rule 11 Sanctions Imposed and When Not Imposed

Many students and new associates are often interested (and uncertain) about the extent to which a pleader will be considered to lack a good faith basis for changing or extending existing law or creating new law. The following are samples of findings determining whether a good faith basis exists for a claim or whether the claim sought was frivolous.

Goldstein v. Malcolm G. Fries & Assoc., Inc., 72 F. Supp. 2d 620 (E.D. Va. 1999) (legal contention is not warranted by existing law if it is based on legal theories plainly foreclosed by well-established legal principles and authoritative precedent, unless advocate plainly states argument for reversal or change of law and provides non-frivolous argument to support position).

Cancer Found., Inc. v. Cerberus Capital Mgmt., L.P., No. 07-cv-4120, 2008 WL 927989 (N.D. Ill. Apr. 4, 2008) (clearly time barred claims were not sanctioned because there is no monetary sanction under Rule 11(b) (2) and there was no improper purpose because, despite clarity of statute of limitations, age of allegations, and warnings from attorneys, there was no evidence suggesting alternative purpose other than legal relief for perceived injury).

Kesler v. Auto-Owners Ins., No. 3:06–cv–79, 2007 WL 4233173 (D.N.D. Nov. 28, 2007) (granting more tolerance to an argument to reverse existing law if identified as such and considering support gained in law review articles, consultation with other attorneys, and minority opinions; held argument nonfrivolous because plaintiff cited North Dakota case law and case law from other jurisdictions).

Bader v. Electronics for Imaging, Inc., 195 F.R.D. 659 (N.D. Cal. 2000) (sanctions were not appropriate because issues in cases were on border of state and federal jurisdiction and thus it was difficult for plaintiff to predict development of federal and state statutory and case law, and action was filed in good faith).

HSBC Bank USA Nat. Ass'n v. Crowe, No. 08–cv–00685–WDM–CBS, 2008 WL 1699758 (D. Colo. Apr. 9, 2008) (show cause order regarding why court should not sanction party for removing case that court previously remanded).

Vanover v. Cook, 77 F. Supp. 2d 1176 (D.C. Kan.1999) (although plaintiff's claim was dismissed, it was not unreasonable because state case law was unclear, and plaintiff's interpretation was supported by decisions in other jurisdictions).

Bautista v. Star Cruises, 696 F. Supp. 2d 1274 (S.D. Fla. 2010) (sanctioning warranted because counsel

---

[516] Model Rules of Prof'l Conduct r. 3.1 (Am. Bar Ass'n 2016).

failed to cite controlling law in attempt to mislead court and counsel and failed to do basic legal research that would have shown plaintiff's claim was frivolous).

Feingold v. Budner, No. 08-80539-CIV, 2010 WL 917314, *4 (S.D. Fla. Mar. 11, 2010) ("Courts are hesitant to impose Rule 11 sanctions where the argument advanced is not directly precluded by controlling case law.").

Kolfenbach v. Mansour, 36 F. Supp. 2d 1351 (S.D. Fla. 1999) (advancing claims subject to disputed interpretations of law is not enough to warrant imposition of sanctions on either plaintiff or plaintiff's counsel).

New Life Homecare, Inc. v. Blue Cross of Northeastern Pennsylvania, No. 3:06-CV-2485, 2008 WL 534472, *2 (M.D. Pa. Feb. 20, 2008) ("A court may consider such factors as: (1) the amount of time available to the signer for conducting the factual and legal investigation; (2) the necessity of relying on a client for the underlying factual information; (3) the plausibility of the legal position advocated; and (4) whether the case was referred to the signer by another member of the Bar.").

Fishoff v. Coty, Inc., 634 F.3d 647 (2d Cir. 2011) (plaintiff's argument that stock options were "securities" under Securities and Exchange Act of 1934 did not warrant sanctions because it was not frivolous, it was not foreclosed by binding precedent, and it included non-binding support).

Adams v. IntraLinks, Inc., No. 03 Civ. 5384 (SAS), 2005 WL 1863829 (S.D.N.Y. Aug. 5, 2005) (argument identified as seeking change of law should be viewed with greater tolerance).

Neighborhood Research Inst. v. Campus Partners for Cmty. Urban Dev., 212 F.R.D. 374 (E. D. Oh. 2002) (court will not impose sanctions on the plaintiffs for asserting claims contrary to existing law when the only existing law comes from jurisdictions whose precedent is not binding on the court).

Hartmax Corp. v. Abboud, 326 F.3d 862 (7th Cir. 2003) (parties were arguing over the construction and interpretation of a new rule, the court of appeals found it improper to impose sanctions on the defendant when the district court sided with the plaintiff's interpretation; moreover, in the defendant's drive to convince the court to interpret the new rule favorably, it did not "flip-flop" blatantly—and thereby violate Rule 11—by proposing three legally plausible positions).

Sidell v. CRF First Choice, Inc., No. 1:09–cv–0607–TWP–TAB, 2010 WL 2732913, *3 (S.D. Ind. July 7, 2010) (plaintiff's legal theory was not frivolous because "of the historically heavy state involvement in the delivery of care to the mentally handicapped in Indiana and the rather complicated legal determination of when a private entity has assumed a role which is traditionally that of the government").

Wright v. Metropolitan Life Ins., 74 F. Supp. 2d 1150 (D. Al. 1979) (no sanctions warranted despite state precedent that poses significant obstacle to plaintiff's claims because precedent is relatively recent and not fully developed, and breadth of precedent is uncertain).

Virgin Islands Daily News v. Government of Virgin Islands, No. Civ. 593/2002, 2002 WL 31956031 (Terr. V. I. Dec. 19, 2002) (an attorney must cite some legal authority for her argument; otherwise, she has failed to argue for the extension, modification, or reversal of existing law).

Knipe v. Skinner, 19 F.3d 72 (2d Cir. 1994) (merely raising legal theories rejected in other circuits is not

340

enough to be sanctioned; however, counsel must be candid about the legal theories' prior lack of success and have good faith arguments for their adoption).

Nisenbaum v. Milwaukee, 333 F.3d 804, 809 (7th Cir. 2003) (Easterbrook, J.) ("Burying one's head in the sand, in the hope that a judge will disregard an adverse decision by the Supreme Court, is a paradigm of frivolous litigation. ... [C]ourts do not penalize litigants who try to distinguish adverse precedents, argue for the modification of existing law, or preserve positions for presentation to the Supreme Court. [The plaintiff], however, did none of these things.").

What themes do you identify in the cases cited above? When are courts more likely to find an argument frivolous? When are they more likely to find a legal argument not frivolous? Can you present legal arguments to improve your chances of a claim being deemed not frivolous, a good-faith argument for the extension or reversal of existing law, etc.? How?

C. Certifications Apply to Later Pleadings and Representations but Do Not Apply to Discovery Motions, Papers, Etc.

To this point, you might have the impression that Federal Rule of Civil Procedure 11 applies solely to pleadings at the outset—e.g., the plaintiff's complaint and the defendant's answer. Pleadings, motions, briefs, and other such filings are filed throughout a case. Rule 11 applies to all of them. Moreover, when a lawyer relies in an argument on a previously filed pleading, that represents a "presentment"—again governed by Rule 11.

However, Rule 11(d) provides that "[t]his rule does not apply to disclosures and discovery requests, responses, objections, and motions under Rules 26 through 37." The rationale for excluding discovery related filings is sound. The process of serving a notice of Rule 11 sanctions and allowing the party time to withdraw would, if it were the required approach in discovery, slow down the discovery process. The discovery phase of a case already slows down the progress to trial more than any other. Allowing parties to move to compel proper responses to discovery requests, without having to wait, allows the parties to keep the process moving as fast as possible. Moreover, the discovery rules have their own sanctions for failure to play fair, as will be seen below in Chapter 13, the one dealing with discovery.

III. Amendments to Pleadings

We now address another key subject related to pleading. Parties often must amend pleadings after suit is filed. It could be either the plaintiff amending a Complaint, or a defendant amending an Answer. Good lawyers keep their pleadings up to date with what they learn as a case proceeds. By doing so, the plaintiff's lawyer will go to trial with a Complaint that contains accurate allegations. Moreover, many plaintiff's lawyer will tell you that discovery has uncovered facts that allowed the plaintiff to plead claims—and seek relief—that was not apparent earlier in the case.

Good defense counsel also amend pleadings. An Answer may require an affirmative defense that was not originally raised. If defense counsel is not in the habit of checking her pleadings to ensure all legitimate defenses are raised, her client may not be allowed to assert a defense at trial that she could otherwise advance.

Please read Federal Rule of Civil Procedure 15. If the theme of Rule 11 and sanctions is punishment, the theme of amendments is mercy. The modern system of civil procedure is premised on the opportunity, if the party seeking to amend does so sufficiently far ahead of trial to avoid prejudice, to allow amendments.

Rule 15 contemplates three timeframes in which parties (plaintiffs or defendants) can either amend or seek amendments. First, in the "of right" phase early in a case, the party can amend without leave of court.[517] Second, a party can move for leave to amend after the "of right" phase and before the trial begins. See id. 15(a) (2). Third, a party can even move for leave to amend at trial. See id. 15(b). The text will now deal with each of these time frames and the different criteria applicable to each.

1. First Timeframe: Amendment "Of Right" Phase

Please read Rule 15(a) (1). What does amending "as a matter of course" mean? Why allow for such amendments even without court approval? If the period in which one could make amendments of right were longer, what problems, if any, could result?

Practice Problems
Practice Problem 12-6
Plaintiff has filed in federal court a complaint against Defendant. One of the claims is based on a statute that requires the plaintiff to have given notice of the claim by letter to the Defendant within a certain time period. Plaintiff gave such notice but did not plead in her complaint that she had given notice that would satisfy the statute. Moreover, Plaintiff's counsel has thought of a claim that was not included in the complaint that counsel believes would be one on which Plaintiff could recover. The complaint was served seven days ago, on a weekday. Can the plaintiff "as a matter of course" file an amended complaint without leave of court adding (a) the allegation about giving notice and (b) the new claim? What part of Rule 15(a) allows such amendment? How long does plaintiff have to file the amended complaint before the time will have passed when she can do it without leave of court?

Practice Problem 12-7
Defendant is a nonresident of the state in which she was sued in federal court. Defense counsel timely filed an answer as her response to the complaint. Counsel realizes that she left out of the answer the defense of "lack of personal jurisdiction." What part of Rule 15(a) allows the defendant to file an amended complaint that includes this defense? Within how much time from the filing of the original answer does the defendant have to file the amended complaint? If defense counsel exceeds the time permitted by Rule 15(a), is the defense of lack of personal jurisdiction lost, even if the court later allows an amendment to add that defense?

---

[517] *See* FED. R. CIV. P. 15(a) (1).

The period in which parties most frequently move for leave to amend is after the "of right" period and prior to trial. However, the court's willingness to grant leave to amend may well be affected by whether the motion for leave to amend simply seeks to add a claim to the plaintiff's case or whether, by comparison, it seeks to add a completely new party. In either scenario, the amendment often will need to "relate back" to the date of the original complaint's filing to avoid a statute of limitations problem.

a. Amendments Not Needing to "Relate Back" to the Original Filing Date for Purposes of the Statute of Limitations

Rarely should the plaintiff's initial complaint, or the defendant's answer, go to trial without an amended version being filed. As we will see in the discussion of amendments at trial below, a party can move for leave to conform the proof she is offering at trial and her pleadings. The need there is because the pleadings do not make an allegation, or assert a claim, on which the party is presenting evidence and seeking relief. Likewise, a defendant can seek leave to amend her answer to add defenses if she is offering evidence on a defense not pled. Alternatively, the plaintiff or defendant offering evidence on allegations, claims, or defenses not pled can cross her fingers and hope that the opposing party does not object. If that happens, the evidence is deemed to come in "by consent." However, relying on the other side not to object is a huge risk.

The principle you ought to follow is this: if you plan to offer evidence on a claim, or offer evidence on a defense, you should make sure that the applicable pleading offers a basis on which you can show that the evidence is pertinent. Many litigators recognize that, to accomplish the goal of being able to offer evidence on matters they have pled, they will need to amend the complaint after pursuing discovery to bolster the allegations. The parties exchange information and documents through discovery. Counsel takes depositions of witnesses and learns a great deal more about cases. Often experts become involved and that adds issues a party needs to consider in terms of proving a claim or defending a claim. Thus, the prudent counsel regularly reviews her pleadings in light of discovery and considers what amendments need to be made.

Please read Federal Rule of Civil Procedure 15(a) (2). What does the Rule require, in this time frame, for a party to be able to amend a pleading? What are the criteria stated in this provision by which the court will be guided in deciding whether to grant leave to amend? As the language of Rule 15(a) (2) suggests, amendments can be significant and introduce substantial variations on what has been asserted. Essentially the only check on a courts' granting leave to amend in the pretrial phase derives from the following passage from the influential Supreme Court case of *Foman v. Davis*:[518]

> If the underlying facts or circumstances relied upon by a plaintiff may be a proper subject of relief, he ought to be afforded an opportunity to test his claim on the merits. In the absence of any apparent or declared reason—such as undue delay, bad faith or dilatory motive on the part of the movant, repeated failure to cure deficiencies by amendments previously allowed, undue prejudice to the opposing party by virtue of allowance of the amendment, futility of amendment, etc.—the leave

---

[518] 371 U.S. 178 (1962).

This last question presumes that the court's allowance of the amendment beyond the time frame will be over plaintiff's objection and that the ultimate ruling on whether the trial court can allow the defense to be raised in this way will be made by the appellate court. sought should, as the rules require, be 'freely given.' Of course, the grant or denial of an opportunity to amend is within the discretion of the District Court, but outright refusal to grant the leave without any justifying reason appearing for the denial is not an exercise of discretion; it is merely abuse of that discretion and inconsistent with the spirit of the Federal Rules.[519]

You should know, as context, that the court holds an initial pretrial conference at which it sets a trial date, and then provides deadlines preceding the trial for cutoff of discovery, for a pretrial conference, and other key deadlines.[520] With that in mind, what would represent the "undue delay" that *Foman* suggests would justify denying leave to amend? What are circumstances that would represent "bad faith or dilatory motive" on behalf of the one moving for leave to amend? What would be an example of "repeated failures to cure deficiencies?" What would represent "undue prejudice" to the party opposing the amendment? What would be an example of a futile amendment?

Practice Problems

Practice Problem 12-8
Plaintiff files a complaint for breach of contract and alleges damages of $200,000. Defendant files an answer. The case is set to be tried a year from the date of the initial pretrial conference, with the discovery cutoffs occurring two months before trial. Suppose plaintiff learns, in the first round of written discovery responses and depositions of witnesses, that plaintiff has a basis for amending the complaint to assert business tort claims. Whereas with contract claims the plaintiff cannot recover punitive damages, the plaintiff can recover both compensatory and punitive damages if the factfinder rules that the defendant committed intentional torts. Suppose plaintiff waits several months and then, one month before the discovery cutoff, moves for leave to amend to add the business tort claims. Which, if any, *Foman* factors could the defendant argue in support of denying leave to amend?

Practice Problem 12-9
Suppose plaintiff brings a claim against a company for exposing plaintiffs to toxic chemicals with knowledge of the dangers. Plaintiff alleges that the corporation is incorporated in Delaware and has its "main office" in Charlotte, North Carolina. The court grants defendant's Rule 12(b) (6) motion on the grounds that the plaintiff has failed to allege the principal place of business of the corporation to satisfy the jurisdictional allegations required by Federal Rule 8(a). In its order, the court grants leave to plaintiff to amend to allege the principal place of business of defendant. Plaintiff refiles the complaint and repeats the language stating only that the "main office" of the defendant is in Charlotte. The court again grants a motion to dismiss and gives leave to amend to correct the failure to state the principal place of business. Believing the court to be overly particular, plaintiff's counsel refiles the same complaint as its amended complaint yet again. In granting the motion to dismiss, the court refuses to grant leave to amend further. Would the court be justified in so doing? On what basis?

---

[519] *Id.* at 182.
[520] *See* FED. R. CIV. P. 16 (addressing the primary rule for pretrial deadlines).

3. Amendments that Need to "Relate Back" to the Original Filing Date for Purposes of the Statute of Limitations

Two scenarios arise with amended complaints in which the plaintiff, if stuck with the date of the filing of the amended complaint, which is typically months or even over a year into the case, would be barred by the applicable statute of limitations (i.e., the time in which to bring the claim) unless the amended complaint is deemed to "relate back" to the date of the original complaint. First, a plaintiff can seek to add a new claim or claims against the same defendant in an amended complaint. Second, a plaintiff can seek to add, in an amended complaint, a new party defendant.

a. "Relation Back" of the New Claim(s) to the Original Complaint

Please read Federal Rule of Civil Procedure Rule 15(c) (1) (B). We skip Federal Rule 15(c) (1) (A) because it deals with the peculiarities of a state's law that in a special case provides that an amended claim will "relate back" for that type of case. The specific-state-law situation of Rule 15(c) (1) (A) is rare. If it does arise, it would override the far more common scenario presented by Rule 15(c) (1) (B). However, we are presuming here that the more common scenario exists in our discussion below. As you can see, the determination of whether an amended claim or claims will "relate back" to the date of the complaint's original filing date—and thus the claims in the amended complaint will be timely—depends largely on whether the new claims relate to the same transaction, occurrence, or series of transactions or occurrences as were sued on in the original complaint. Consider the following case as an example of the Rule in operation.

JONES v. GREENSPAN
United States District Court for the District of Columbia, 2006
445 F. Supp. 2d 53

URBINA, District Judge

INTRODUCTION
This employment discrimination case comes before the court on the plaintiff's motion to amend the complaint. The plaintiff alleges that the defendant, the Federal Reserve System, retaliated against him after he filed charges of age and gender discrimination with the Equal Employment Opportunity Commission ("EEOC"). The plaintiff now moves the court for leave to add claims of age and gender discrimination to the complaint. Because the amendment relates back to the original complaint and because the proposed amendment is not futile, the court finds no reason to depart from the traditional practice that motions to amend be freely given. Accordingly, the court grants the plaintiff's motion.

BACKGROUND
Factual Background

The plaintiff, a certified public accountant, was born on May 30, 1948. *Jones v. Greenspan*, 402 F. Supp. 2d 294, 296 (2005). He began working at the defendant's Division of Reserve Bank Operations and Payment Systems in April 1991. In July 1993, the plaintiff transferred to the Division of Banking Supervision and Regulation at grade level FR–27.

The plaintiff alleges that in March 1998, Michael Martinson, his then-supervisor, denied him a promotion to a managerial position at the FR–29 grade level, and instead selected Heidi Richards, "a woman in her early thirties." Id. Concerned that his supervisor was "effectuating [d]efendant's policy of promoting young women to positions of management," the plaintiff approached Martinson after Richards' selection. Id. In response to the plaintiff's concerns, in May 1998, Martinson allegedly "assured" the plaintiff that he would receive a promotion to grade level FR–28.

"Having not received the promised promotion by September 1998," the plaintiff approached Martinson to inquire about the status of the promotion to the FR–28 grade level. Martinson "assured" the plaintiff that "he would be promoted with the next group of promotions." The plaintiff alleges that during this time period, Martinson "effectively demoted [him] by stripping him of his primary job duties and reassigning them to Mrs. Richards."

"Based on Mr. Martinson's assurances that a promotion was forthcoming, [the plaintiff] did not pursue the matter with the [d]efendant's EEOC office." On October 7, 1999, Martinson promoted a group of individuals. The plaintiff, however, was not one of those individuals. Martinson explained that he could not justify the plaintiff's promotion "because of his recently truncated work responsibilities." Soon afterwards, in November 1999, the plaintiff filed an informal charge with the defendant's EEOC office alleging age and gender discrimination. The plaintiff filed a formal discrimination charge in January 2000.

PROCEDURAL BACKGROUND

On July 9, 2004, the plaintiff received a Notice of Final Agency Action dismissing his EEOC discrimination charges as untimely. The plaintiff filed a complaint in this court on October 4, 2004. The complaint alleged that his supervisor unlawfully retaliated against him by lowering his performance ratings in 2000, 2001, 2002, and 2003, in violation of Title VII, 42 U.S.C. § 2000e–1 et seq. and the Age Discrimination in Employment Act ("ADEA"), 29 U.S.C. § 633a et seq.

On June 14, 2005, the defendant filed a motion to dismiss and for summary judgment. While awaiting the court's summary judgment ruling, the plaintiff filed a motion to amend the complaint. On December 13, 2005, the court granted summary judgment for the defendant on all of the counts except the count alleging that the plaintiff's 2000 performance evaluation was retaliatory. The court now turns to the plaintiff's motion.

ANALYSIS

Because the plaintiff's complaint only contains claims for retaliation, he now moves the court to add the "underlying complaints of age and gender discrimination that led to the retaliatory acts discussed in the complaint." Specifically, the plaintiff moves to add claims of age and gender discrimination to his claim that his March 1998 non-promotion to the FR–29 managerial position was retaliatory. The defendant makes two arguments in opposition to the plaintiff's motion. First, the defendant argues that the amended complaint is time-barred because the plaintiff did not file a suit alleging age and gender discrimination within ninety days of receiving the Notice of Final Agency Action. The plaintiff concedes that he did not file a suit alleging age and gender discrimination within ninety days of receiving the Notice of Final Agency Action but argues that the amended complaint is timely because the age and gender discrimination claims relate back to the original retaliation complaint, which he timely filed. Second, the defendant argues that the amended complaint is futile because the plaintiff did not contact an EEOC counselor within forty-five days of the allegedly discriminatory incident. The plaintiff, however, contends that "the 45–day time limit should not apply because it was the Defendant's own misconduct that prevented [him] from timely

346

complaining of the discrimination." Because the amended complaint relates back to the original complaint, and because the amended complaint is not futile, the court grants the plaintiff's motion to amend the complaint.

A. Legal Standard to Amend the Complaint Pursuant to Rule 15(a) and 15(c)

Under Federal Rule of Civil Procedure 15(a), a party may amend his complaint once as a matter of course at any time before a responsive pleading is served. Once a responsive pleading is filed, a party may amend the complaint only by leave of the court or by written consent of the adverse party.[521] The grant or denial of leave is committed to the discretion of the district court. The court must heed Rule 15's mandate that leave is to be "freely given when justice so requires."[522] "If the underlying facts or circumstances relied upon by a plaintiff may be a proper subject of relief, he ought to be afforded an opportunity to test his claims on the merits."[523] Denial of leave to amend therefore constitutes an abuse of discretion unless the court gives sufficient reason, such as futility of amendment, undue delay, bad faith, dilatory motive, undue prejudice, or repeated failure to cure deficiencies by previous amendments.[524]

Rule 15(c) allows a plaintiff to amend his complaint to add a claim or defense when that claim or defense "arose out of the conduct, transaction, or occurrence" set forth in the original pleading.[525] But "those that significantly alter the nature of a proceeding by injecting new and unanticipated claims are treated far more cautiously."[526] Courts inquire into whether the opposing party has been put on notice regarding the claim.[527] If the alteration is "so substantial that it cannot be said that defendant was given adequate notice . . .then the amendment will not relate back and will be time barred if the limitations period has expired."

The Amended Complaint Relates Back to the Original Complaint

The amended complaint relates back to original complaint because it "ar[i]ses out of the conduct, transaction, or occurrence set forth or attempted to be set forth in the original complaint."[528]
The allegedly discriminatory non-promotion to the FR–29 position occurred in March 1998.[529] In November 1999, the plaintiff filed an EEOC charge alleging age and gender discrimination based on Martinson's failure to promote him to the FR–29 position. Thereafter, Martinson allegedly gave the plaintiff diminished performance evaluations in retaliation for filing the EEOC charge. The plaintiff's suit in this court alleges that the defendant retaliated against the plaintiff for filing the EEOC charge.

The defendant argues that the allegedly discriminatory acts that led the plaintiff to file the EEOC charge are not related to the acts of retaliation that took place after the plaintiff filed the EEOC charge. The close relationship between the allegations of discriminatory non-promotion and the alleged retaliation,

---

[521] Foman v. Davis, 371 U.S. 178, 182 (1962).

[522] FED. R. CIV. P. 15(a); *Foman*, 371 U.S. at 182.

[523] *Foman*, 371 U.S. at 182.

[524] *Id.*

[525] FED. R. CIV. P. 15(c); United States v. Hicks, 283 F.3d 380, 388 (D.C. Cir. 2002) (discussing the relation-back doctrine). Typically, amendments that build on previously alleged facts relate back. *Hicks*, 283 F.3d at 388.

[526] *Id.*

[527] 6A FED. PRAC. & PROC. CIV. 2d § 1497.

[528] FED. R. CIV. 15(c) (2).

[529] *Jones*, 402 F.Supp.2d at 296.

however, make them part of a "common core of operative facts."[530] In particular, the amended complaint "expands upon" and "clarifies" facts alleged in the original complaint.[531] For example, the original complaint states that . . . the plaintiff filed a charge with the EEOC office raising "claims of age discrimination, gender discrimination, and retaliation." The proposed amended complaint expands upon the allegations of discrimination by describing them in more detail. Thus, the plaintiff's proposed amended complaint relates back to the complaint because the allegations of discrimination and the discrimination claims arise from facts set out in the initial complaint.[532]

The defendant, moreover, was on notice of the age and gender discrimination allegations. The plaintiff informed the defendant that he "intends to pursue all of the claims that he raised before the EEOC, including, but not limited to, his claims of age discrimination." Additionally, the complaint contains numerous references to the alleged discriminatory activity and put the defendant on notice of potential discrimination claims.[533] Because the amended complaint builds on previously alleged facts and because the defendant had notice of the discrimination claims, the amended complaint relates back to the original complaint.

B. The Amended Complaint is Not Futile
The defendant also argues that the amendment is futile because the plaintiff did not timely exhaust his administrative remedies. In particular, the defendant points out that the plaintiff did not contact an EEOC counselor until November 1999, more than forty-five days after the March 1998 non-promotion. The plaintiff admits that he did not present his concerns to an EEOC counselor with the 45–day limit required under the rules of the Board and the EEOC. He argues, however, that Martinson "mislead" and "dissuaded" him from contacting an EEOC counselor by falsely promising future promotions.

Like a statute of limitations, the requirement of filing a timely administrative complaint is "subject to waiver, estoppel, and equitable tolling."[534] Equitable estoppel "prevents a defendant from asserting untimeliness where the defendant has taken active steps to prevent the plaintiff from litigating in time." Additionally, "an employer's affirmatively misleading statements that a grievance will be resolved in the employee's favor can establish equitable estoppel." The reasoning behind this is that "[u]nder those circumstances, an employee understandably would be reluctant to file a complaint with the EEOC for fear he would jeopardize his chances to gain relief voluntarily."

According to the plaintiff, Martinson's promises to recommend him to a promotion to the FR–28 level dissuaded him from pursuing his claims of non-selection to the FR–29 position. Immediately following the plaintiff's non-promotion to the FR–29 position in March 1998, Martinson allegedly assured

---

[530] Mayle v. Felix, 545 U.S. 644 (2005) (reaffirming that "[s]o long as the original and amended petitions state claims that are tied to a common core of operative facts, relation back will be in order").

[531] *Hicks*, 283 F.3d at 388 (stating that "amendments that expand upon or clarify facts previously alleged will typically relate back").

[532] Dean v. United States, 278 F.3d 1218, 1222 (11th Cir. 2002) (noting that "[o]ne purpose of an amended claim is to fill in facts missing from the original claim").

[533] Baldwin County Welcome Ctr. v. Brown, 466 U.S. 147, 150 n. 3 (1984) (stating that "[t]he rationale of Rule 15(c) is that a party who has been notified of litigation concerning a particular occurrence has been given all the notice that statutes of limitations were intended to provide"); *see also Hicks,* 283 F.3d at 388 (reasoning that "in cases in which notice has been afforded, for example where the amendment seeks merely to elaborate upon his earlier claims, this effort should not generally be barred by the statute of limitations").

[534] Zipes v. Trans World Airlines, Inc., 455 U.S. 385 (1982).

the plaintiff that he had "recommended [him] for a FR–28 promotion."[535] Later that year, Martinson allegedly assured the plaintiff that "he would be promoted within the next group of promotions." In both May and June of 1999, Martinson again allegedly assured the plaintiff that he would be promoted within the next promotion group.

The defendant counters that a promise of a promotion to a Grade 28 position would not "have changed the alleged discriminatory selection of a younger woman to a Grade 29 position." While a promotion to an FR–28 position may not have remedied the plaintiff's non-selection to the FR–29 position, an employee in the plaintiff's position would understandably be reluctant to bring an EEOC charge for fear of jeopardizing the promised promotion, even if the promised promotion was not the one he desired. Thus, the supervisor's alleged promises are "affirmatively misleading statements" suggesting that the non-promotion would be resolved in the plaintiff's favor.[536] Accordingly, the court concludes that the amended complaint is not futile.

CONCLUSION

For the foregoing reasons, the court grants the plaintiff's motion to amend the complaint.

Practice Problem

Practice Problem 12-10

Greg runs a car dealership. He buys cars from several wholesalers, including Jeff. Greg buys 20 Porsches from Jeff on September 15, 2010, under a contract specifying not only the amount Greg would pay, but also that the Porsches would be new ones. On December 15, 2010, Greg buys 60 Toyota Corollas from Jeff under a contract specifying not only the amount Jeff would pay, but also that the cars would be delivered with undercarriage protection already added. On September 1, 2013, Greg sues Jeff in federal court. (Greg and Jeff are of diverse citizenship and the amount in controversy requirement is met.) Relying on breach of contract, Greg claims that the Porsches were not new as required by the parties' contract. The relevant statute of limitations on contract claims is three years. Over six months after initiating the above suit and before trial, on March 15, 2015, Greg filed a motion for leave to file an amended complaint. In addition to the breach-of-contract claim over the Porsches already filed, the amended complaint would add a claim for breach of contract concerning the Toyota Corollas on the basis that they were not delivered with undercarriage protection as specified in the contract for them, and Greg had to incur expenses in providing undercarriage protection. Assume that Jeff opposes the motion. How should the Court rule on Greg's motion? Explain your answer.

Follow-Up Questions and Comments

1. What distinguishing factors or criteria show that a claim arises from the same transaction or occurrence, or series of transactions or occurrences, from claims that do not arise from the same transaction or occurrence, or series of transactions or occurrences?

2. Can you rely on the criteria you learned in joinder analysis—in which the same transaction or occurrence test is applied—to perform an analysis of whether claims relate back?

---

[535] *Jones*, 402 F. Supp. 2d at 296.
[536] *Currier*, 159 F.3d at 1368; *see also* Sanders v. Veneman, 131 F. Supp. 2d 225, 230 (D.D.C. 2001) (tolling the timely filing requirement where the plaintiff's supervisor made repeated promises of an eventual promotion).

3. What seems to be the purpose of the relation-back rule?

b. "Relation Back" of New Parties Added by Amendment

An amended complaint that changes the name of the defendant is much more problematic. What is the scenario that will exist so that you know you are dealing with this issue? In the above relation back scenario, the plaintiff and defendant in the original complaint were the same, and the only difference was the addition of new claims in the amended complaint. Here, the plaintiff will be the same, but the defendant will be a newly named party because the plaintiff has likely realized she made a mistake in who she named as defendant. Thus, the defendant in the amended complaint is for the first-time defending claims.

Of the criteria required in Federal Rule of Civil Procedure 15(c), what is the most difficult for a plaintiff to show in arguing that the complaint against a newly named defendant "relates back" to the filing date of the original complaint? It is probably not Rule 15(c) (1) (B)—the requirement that the claim in the amended complaint arise from the same transaction or occurrence as the original complaint. Yes, the same requirement as is imposed on a plaintiff adding a new claim is put on a plaintiff adding a new defendant in an amended complaint. But there is more. Specifically, Rule 15(c) (1) (C)'s requirement that the newly named defendant in the amended complaint, within the 90 days after filing of the original complaint required by Federal Rule of Civil Procedure 4(m), received notice of the action or knew or should have known that the action would have been brought against the newly named party but for the mistaken identity of the defendant. The United States Supreme Court's decision in *Schiavone v. Fortune*,[537] illustrates the great hurdle a plaintiff faces in achieving relation back of an amended complaint naming a new defendant. There, within a month of the one-year statute of limitations, the plaintiff sued "Fortune" as the named defendant. Plaintiff intended to sue Fortune magazine, but did not realize that it was a trademark of Time, Inc. A couple of months later, plaintiff sought to file an amended complaint against Time, Inc., the correct defendant. The Court held, however, that the amended complaint was time-barred because it did not relate back to the original complaint. The reason: the plaintiff had not shown that Time, Inc., knew, within the relatively short period under Federal Rule of Civil Procedure 4(m), that Time, Inc. had received notice of the action or knew, or should have known, that the plaintiff made a mistake in filing the suit against Fortune.

4. Third Timeframe: Amendments at Trial

Please read Federal Rule 15(b) (1) and (2). When you read subsection (b) (2), do you understand why, in your analysis of evidence offered at trial that varies from the pleadings (typically called a "variance") you will want to ask first whether the defendant objected to the introduction of the evidence and pointed out the variance? Can one also infer a prerequisite from subsection (b) (1)'s prefatory "If . . . a party objects" language? If the party against whom such evidence was offered does not object, what does Rule 15(b) (2) provide about how the variance should be treated?

Okay, let's say that the party objects to evidence offered at trial as not having been pled. Thus, Rule 15(b) (2)'s trial "by consent" is not applicable. What are the criteria in subsection (b) (1) that the court should apply in deciding whether to grant leave to amend at trial? Who has the burden of showing that the "evidence would prejudice that party's action or defense?" Why should the party against whom evidence that has not been pled have such a burden?

---

[537] 477 U.S. 21 (1986).

The following case offers some insight into Rule 15(b) (1)'s focus on prejudice:

ROBBINS v. JORDAN
United States Court of Appeals for the District Columbia Circuit, 1950
181 F.2d 793

CLARK, Circuit Judge.

The court below directed a verdict in favor of the defendant at the close of the plaintiffs' case. The plaintiffs have prosecuted this appeal to test the validity of that judgment.

The action sounds in tort for malpractice. The plaintiffs claim negligence on the part of Dr. Jordan in that he failed to take pelvic measurements of Mrs. Robbins at the proper time and as a result a normal birth was attempted when timely measurements would have indicated to a practitioner of average skill and knowledge in this locality that a Caesarean operation was necessary. The husband asks damages for loss of services and consortium while Mrs. Robbins asks compensation for certain resulting injuries including pain and suffering.

The principal error assigned by the appellants to the proceedings below involves the failure of the trial judge to allow them to amend their pleadings in order to introduce evidence to the effect that the defendant held himself out to them as a specialist in obstetrics.

The complaint alleged that the defendant was a 'duly licensed physician practicing medicine in the District of Columbia and holding himself out to the general public, including the plaintiffs, as a practicing physician, and a doctor of medicine, and one well qualified in the treatment of disorders and diseases of women.' But the court rules that these allegations were not broad enough to permit proof that the defendant had represented himself to the plaintiffs as an obstetrician. After this ruling the appellants sought permission to amend their complaint so as to enable them to introduce the evidence, but the court again ruled against them and disallowed the amendment.

There can be no question that the plaintiffs were prejudiced by these rulings. Instead of being able to proceed on the theory that the defendant was a specialist and was therefore held to a standard of care and skill normally exercised by such specialists, they were compelled to try their case on the theory that the duty owed them by the defendant was to be measured by that standard of skill and knowledge required of a general practitioner. That the standard of care and skill required of the specialist in obstetrics is stricter than that required of the general practitioner is demonstrable from the record. Take for example the testimony of the roentgenologist who examined Mrs. Robbins with reference to the anticipated delivery of her second child. He stated on cross-examination that in his experience, since 1930, no general practitioner had resorted to the use of pelvimetry. And yet since he testified that he had made a great many thousand of such measurements, it is reasonable to suppose that they were made at the behest of specialists.

Having found that the court's refusal to grant the plaintiffs leave to amend their complaint worked to their prejudice, the only other problem for us to decide, therefore, is whether or not the learned trial judge exceeded the limits of his discretion in so refusing. Rule 15(b) of the Federal Rules of Civil Procedure, 28 U.S.C.A., provides in part: 'If evidence is objected to at the trial on the ground that it is not within the issues made by the pleadings, the court may allow the pleadings to be amended and shall do so freely when the presentation of the merits of the action will be subserved thereby and the objecting party fails to satisfy the

351

court that the admission of such evidence would prejudice him in maintaining his action or defense on the merits. The court may grant a continuance to enable the objecting party to meet such evidence.'

As was said in International *Ladies' Garment Workers' Union v. Donnelly Garment Company*:[538] 'The Supreme Court of the United States has fixed the limits of permissible amendment with increasing liberality and has ruled that a change of the legal theory of the action is no longer accepted as a test of the propriety of a proposed amendment . . . Rule 15 of the Rules of Civil Procedure . . . expresses the same liberality with respect to the amendment of pleadings.'

. . .

In the instant case the amendment proposed by the plaintiffs did not state a new cause of action. It simply altered theory of their case. The only reason for denying the proposed amendment was stated by the lower court in the following discussion which was had at the beginning of the trial.

'The Court: Well, I think that would come too late, because that prejudices the defendant in his defense.

'Mr. Quimby: The case has not started.

'The Court: I know, but I am assuming that, being the type of lawyer that I know Mr. Daily is, he has prepared his defense. If the plaintiff is going to change his theory of the case, then he is in a position where he ought to be protected from going forward on a change of theory.' There can be no question that a defendant should be protected from surprise resulting from a change of theory; but it is our opinion that the court erred in the method it chose to protect him. The proper procedure would have been to grant the defendant a continuance in order to meet the new evidence. But it was beyond the limits of its judicial discretion to refuse to allow the amendment.

. . . This is a question on which the trial court should pass initially.

Reversed and remanded.

Follow-Up Questions and Comments

(1) First, what were the threshold events that led the court in Robbins to evaluate prejudice to the defendant of an amendment at trial? Nevertheless, many if not most instances in which amendments are sought at trial result in granting leave to amend or result in a continuance.[539] Due to the cost of litigation, however, courts have in recent years become less willing to grant continuances. Thus, if a defendant can truly show prejudice, she ought to have a better chance at having evidence that is beyond the matters pled excluded at trial.

---

[538] 8 Cir., 1941, 121 F.2d 561, 563.
[539] *See, e.g., See* 6A CHARLES ALAN WRIGHT & ARTHUR R. MILLER, FEDERAL PRACTICE AND PROCEDURE § 1493 (3d. ed. 2018).

Practice Problem

Practice Problem 12-11

Patty files a claim for breach of contract. Dirk answers, and the parties go through discovery to trial. At trial, Patty starts putting on evidence of the tort of intentional interference with contractual relations (that Dirk interfered with contracts Patty had entered with a third party). Tort law generally allows for a broader range of damages than contract claims. Intentional torts also provide a basis for punitive damages. What if Dirk makes no objection at trial? Does the evidence on the intentional tort claim go to the jury and get resolved by verdict? Why or why not? What part of Rule 15(b) would you point to?

If Dirk objects to the tortious interference evidence, claiming a variance between pleadings and proof, what standard will the court use to determine whether to allow the tort if Patty moves for leave to amend at trial? If you represented Patty, what arguments would you make? If you represented Dirk, what arguments would you make?

B. Amendment to Pleadings Are Different from Amendments to Discovery Responses

The following chapter addresses discovery. A party usually will have answers to interrogatories, responses to requests for admission, and other such discovery responses. If the party who has served such discovery responses learns that some or all the information is inaccurate or incomplete, she is obligated to amend or supplement her responses. Please do not confuse amendments or supplementation of discovery responses with amendments to pleadings. Federal Rule of Civil Procedure 26(e) governs correcting and supplementing responses to discovery. It leaves no doubt that, on learning a discovery response is in accurate or incomplete, the party must serve corrected responses.

CHAPTER 13:
THE DEFENDANT'S OPTIONS IN RESPONSE

I. How the Topics in this Chapter Fit in the Overall Progress of a Civil Action

Below is a diagram of the stages of a civil action showing in bold where the topics in this chapter fall in the progress of a case.

Figure 13-1

Cause of Action (events leading to suit)	Pre-Filing Tasks (items to begin representation, interviewing, and related matters)	Choice of Forum (subject matter jurisdiction, removal, personal jurisdiction, and venue)	Notice and Service of Process (completing the process of ensuring the forum court can enter a valid judgment)	Pleading the Case and Joinder of Claims and Parties (including supplemental jurisdiction)

Responding to Claims by Motion or by Answer	Discovery (developing proof to establish claims and learn your adversary's case)	Right to Jury (pretrial motions and practice)	Final Pretrial Conference (events within last month before trial)	Trial (procedures and motions during trial)	Verdict	Post-Trial Motions (motions for a new trial and/or judgment as a matter of law)	Appeal

Here is a question only a litigator could appreciate: when is a party in litigation a "defendant?" If you answer, "Well, of course, when you're the party sued by the plaintiff who brings a case," you have fallen for the trick question. The question was not whether the party is an *original plaintiff* or an *original defendant*. A party is a defendant whenever that party has claims brought against her. These may be original claims by a plaintiff or counterclaims in which the original plaintiff is a "defendant," and so on. Whenever a party has claims asserted against her, she must go through the process of deciding how to respond as outlined below.

This chapter, addresses the options of an original defendant, named a defendant at the outset of a case. Such options, however, are the same as those of a plaintiff/counterclaim defendant responding to a counterclaim. This chapter will, nevertheless, for the purpose of clarity, refer to the defendant in the classic sense—the party or parties named at the outset in litigation as a defendant on the right side of the "v.". Despite the chapter using "defendant" in the classic sense, you should realize that anything discussed regarding such a defendant will apply to any other party who defends a claim.

As defense counsel, you may start at a disadvantage. The plaintiff's lawyer has had the case for a longer period and, if she is worth her salt, has made valuable use of that time. In the pre-suit stage, plaintiff's counsel should have researched the law of each potential claim, the statute of limitations on each claim, and all possible defenses. Moreover, plaintiff's counsel should have performed a thorough investigation, preserved evidence, and should generally be in command of the case by the time of filing a complaint.

The reality is that most plaintiffs' lawyers do not take advantage of what they could achieve by pre-filing preparation. Effective lawyers do, but they are in the minority. Even when facing an effective plaintiff's lawyer who has a strong command of the case, a defendant's lawyer can always catch up. She just must be willing to work. The order of decisions and tasks will hinge on priorities. First and foremost, defense counsel must determine the best means to respond to the complaint in time to avoid default. That in turn requires her to determine the deadline for responding to the complaint. More strategically, defense counsel must help her client decide on the optimal pleading to file in response to a complaint.

II. Applicable Law

A. Calculating the Response Deadline Under Rule 6

Federal Rule of Civil Procedure 12 allows a defendant to file a response to a complaint within 21 days after service of process. Defense counsel must look to Federal Rule of Civil Procedure 6 to determine how to count the 21 days. Please read Rule 6 now. What day does it say should be Day 1 of the 21-day period? If Day 21 falls on a weekend or holiday, what does Rule 6 say about when the responsive pleading will be due? An area of frequent confusion is whether to include weekends and holidays that fall within the 21-day period but are not at Day 21. Do you exclude these in the calculation of response time?

Practice Problem

Practice Problem 13-1

Sunday	Monday	Tuesday	Wednesday	Thursday	Friday	Saturday
January 2016					1	2
3	4	5	6	7	8	9
10	11	12	13	14	15	16
17	18	19	20	21	22	23
24	25	26	27	28	29	30
31	Notes					

On July 1, 2014, Doug Defendant (Virginia citizen) slammed into Polly Plaintiff (Maryland citizen) while she was stopped at a red light. On January 4, 2016, Polly filed a suit seeking recovery for personal injuries resulting from Doug's negligence exceeding $75,000, exclusive of interests and costs. Above is a

355

calendar for January 2016. Using the calculation rules of Rule 6, determine when Doug's responsive pleading under Rule 12 is due.

B. Deciding How to Respond to a Complaint Under Rule 12

Please read Federal Rule of Civil Procedure 12. The Rule states early on in subsection (a) (1) (A) that a "defendant must serve an answer" within the 21-day deadline already discussed. That statement sounds as if the defendant has no choice but to file an answer. An answer, as we will see later in this chapter, is a responsive pleading that, if filed, effectively means the case will proceed beyond the initial motions phase and into discovery. In other words, if the answer were the only pleading a defendant could file, she would have no chance of having the case dismissed. But keep reading in Rule 12. Notice subsection (a) (4), entitled "Effect of a Motion." Although it is anything but explicit, the entirety of the Rule—reading subsection (a) (1(A), and subsection (a) (4), together—means that a defendant has options at the outset. She can file an answer, as suggested, but that is conceding the case will continue. Alternatively, she can file a motion. By filing a motion, she is not conceding that the case will proceed beyond the initial phases.

1. Waivable Defenses Under Rule 12

The most common motions under Rule 12 are those set forth in subsection (b). Rule 12(b) states:

> **How to Present Defenses.** Every defense to a claim for relief in any pleading must be asserted in the responsive pleading if one is required. But a party may assert the following defenses by motion:
>
> - lack of subject-matter jurisdiction;
> - **lack of personal jurisdiction;**
> - **improper venue;**
> - **insufficient process;**
> - **insufficient service of process;**
> - failure to state a claim upon which relief can be granted; and
> - failure to join a party under Rule 19.[540]

The four defenses in bold are "highly waivable defenses," as this text will refer to them. Rule 12 provides that these defenses must be raised in a defendant's initial response—specifically, in a pre-answer motion, as an affirmative defense in the answer within the time period allowed for responding to the complaint. If the defendant does not raise every available highly waivable defense in the initial response, the defendant waives the defense permanently.[541]

Requiring the defendant to raise these defenses in her initial response promotes both judicial efficiency and fairness to the opposing party. Otherwise, a defendant could strategically save one of these defenses until she saw whether the litigation was, in her opinion, going favorably. If not, and the case was going poorly on the merits for the defendant, she could press for a ruling on one of these defenses. By holding such an ace, and obtaining dismissal or transfer of venue, the defendant could waste substantial

---

[540] *See* FED. R. CIV. P. 12(b).
[541] *Id.*

time and resources. Unlike other defenses that a defendant may not discover until later in the litigation process, waivable defenses are ones of which the defendant should be aware at the outset of litigation. To illustrate, a defendant knows the hoe she was served and can determine whether service was "proper." She also knows the degree of contacts she has with a state and can challenge personal jurisdiction at the outset of the case if the contacts are insufficient.

But there is even more to understand about this waiver trap. Under Rule 12, a defendant can waive defenses in two ways. The first way is by making a pre-trial motion that does not include one of the highly waivable defenses. The second is, if the defendant foregoes a pre-answer motion, by failing to include the defense in an answer or an amendment to it. The importance of the waiver provisions derives from subsections (g) and (h), which follow:

2. Joining Motions

Right to Join. A motion under this rule may be joined with any other motion allowed by this rule. Limitation on Further Motions. Except as provided in Rule 12(h)(2) or (3), a party that makes a motion under this rule must not make another motion under this rule raising a defense or objection that was available to the party but omitted from its earlier motion.

(h) Waiving and Preserving Certain Defenses

(1) **When Some Are Waived**. A party waives any defense listed in Rule 12(b) (2)-(5) by: omitting it from a motion in the circumstances described in Rule 12(g) (2); or failing to either: make it by motion under this rule; or include it in a responsive pleading or in an amendment allowed by Rule 15(a) (1) as a matter of course.

(2) **When to Raise Others**. Failure to state a claim upon which relief can be granted, to join a person required by Rule 19(b), or to state a legal defense to a claim may be raised: in any pleading allowed or ordered under Rule 7(a); by a motion under Rule 12(c); or at trial. Lack of Subject-Matter Jurisdiction. If the court determines at any time that it lacks subject-matter jurisdiction, the court must dismiss the action.[542]

Even the best of lawyers must read and re-read Federal Rules of Civil Procedure 12(g) and 12(h) to remember the waiver traps they present. The goal here is to introduce you to these traps so that you are familiar with them. However, you too would benefit by checking the rules to ensure each time your client is served with a complaint so that the traps are fresh in your mind. We may be able to better appreciate the intricacies of Rule 12 by pretending that we are listening to an experienced litigator explaining the Rule. The lawyer begins with the subdivision that refers to "waiving" defenses, subdivision (h). That section speaks to a party who has filed a motion under Rule 12. The lawyer would have to know whether the defendant answered first or filed a pre-answer motion. We will assume here that the defendant filed a pre-answer motion and we will deal with the "answer scenario" next. The seasoned lawyer would then read the first part of subdivision (h), which provides that the moving party waives a defense by failing to "make it by motion under this rule."[543]

---

[542] FED. R. CIV. P. 12(g)-(h).
[543] FED. R. CIV. P. 12(h)(1)(B)(i).

However, if the defendant did file a motion, what is the problem? "Well," our seasoned lawyer would say, "you must go back up to Rule 12(g) to see what kind of failure this is referring to." Specifically, Rule 12(g) precludes a party who has filed a Rule 12 motion from filing "another motion under this rule raising a defense or objection that was available to the party but omitted from its earlier motion." This scenario involves one party filing a pre-answer motion but leaving out one of the following specified defenses—12(b)(2) (personal jurisdiction), 12(b) (3) (venue), 12(b) (4) (improper process), and/or 12(b) (5) (insufficient service of process)—one or more of which were available under Rule 12 and could have been included in the first motion. According to subdivision (g) of Rule 12, leaving out one or more defense in this way means that a "party waives any of the defenses in Rule 12(b) (2)-(5). . . ."

C. First Waiver Scenario: Defendant Chooses to File a Motion as the First Response to a Complaint

The following is a case that illustrates a pre-trial motion that omits one of the highly waivable defenses:

TIERNAN v. DUNN
United States District Court for the District of Rhode Island, 1969
295 F. Supp. 1253

PETTINE, District Judge.

This is a diversity action in which the plaintiff, the administrator of the estate of the decedent, James Tiernan, seeks recovery of damages for the allegedly wrongful death of the decedent. The plaintiff alleges that the plaintiff's decedent was riding in the car of the defendant's decedent and was killed in an automobile-tractor-trailer collision in Plainville, Massachusetts on April 10, 1964 due to the negligence of the defendant's decedent. The plaintiff commenced action against the defendant on March 25, 1965. The record shows that service of process was made on the defendant personally on April 7, 1965 in Attleboro, Massachusetts by the United States Marshal for the District of Massachusetts and on the defendant as administratrix of her husband's estate by service on the clerk of the Westchester Surrogate's Court in White Plains, New York by the United States Marshal for the Southern District of New York on April 8, 1965. Thereafter, on May 7, 1965, the defendant . . . moved to dismiss counts 1 and 2. The motion to dismiss was granted and an order was entered on July 22, 1965. . . . The defendant has now moved to dismiss this action under Fed. R. Civ. P. 12(b) (5) for lack of in personam jurisdiction and improper service of process. The defendant contends that she was never in Rhode Island but was a citizen and resident of New York at the time of the happening of the accident and a citizen and resident of Massachusetts at the time of the commencement of this action. She concludes that she never was nor could have been either personally subject to this court's jurisdiction or properly served with process within the territorial limits of this district, as required by Fed. R. Civ. P. 4(f). Plaintiff argues that jurisdiction over the person exists under the R.I. 'minimum contacts' statute, § 9-5-33 R.I.G.L.1956, as amended, which is applicable in the federal courts by operation of Fed. R. Civ. P. 4(f) & 4(d) (7), and that service was also therefore proper, and finally that, in any case, defendant has waived these defenses under Fed. R. Civ. P. 12(g) & (h).

In his argument concerning satisfaction of the minimum contacts statute the plaintiff refers to the allegedly numerous and various contacts of the defendant's decedent with Rhode Island as shown by certain of the answers and statements in certain of the pre-trial materials in the case. The court is not inclined at this juncture of the proceedings to maintain a factual hearing on minimum contacts; nor is it disposed to treat this motion as one for summary judgment. Instead, the court prefers to treat this motion on the basis of the waiver arguments. Fed.R.Civ.P. 12(g) concerns consolidation of defenses in one motion and states in pertinent part:

A party who makes a motion under this rule may join with it any other motions herein provided for and then available to him. If a party makes a motion under this rule but omits therefrom any defense or objection then available to him which this rule permits to be raised by motion, he shall not thereafter make a motion based on the defense or objection so omitted.

. . .

As applied to the facts of this case, Rule 12(g) would seem to have required the defendant to have included her motions to dismiss for insufficient service of process and lack of in personam jurisdiction in her motion to dismiss for failure to state a claim. Specifically, under the second sentence of Rule 12(g) the defendant moved under Rule 12 (12(b)(6) motion to dismiss for failure to state claim) but omitted from the motion defenses then available to her (insufficient service of process; lack of in personam jurisdiction), which defenses Rule 12 permits to be raised by motion (Rule 12(b)(2), (b)(5)). Accordingly[,] under the latter part of the second sentence of Rule 12(g) the defendant cannot now make a motion based on the omitted defenses. Fed.R.Civ.P. 12(h) deals with waiver and states in pertinent part:

A defense of lack of jurisdiction over the person . . . or insufficiency of service of process is waived . . . if omitted from a motion in the circumstances described in subdivision (g).

As applied to the facts of this case, Rule 12(h) requires that the defendant's assertions of lack of in personam jurisdiction and insufficiency of service of process be deemed to have been waived, because, as previously described, those assertions were omitted when the defendant made her Rule 12(b)(6) motion.

. . .

One final point requires some consideration. The defendant has argued in its memorandum that no waiver should be effectuated here because the certainty that the motion to dismiss for failure to state a claim would be granted was so great, as of the time of the making of that motion, that the defendant felt no need to raise any other defense. Defendant argues further that the grant of the plaintiff's motion to vacate the dismissal puts the case back to the time of the dismissal, at least for the purpose of making additional defenses. Whatever may have been the defendant's reason for not raising her additional defenses on her initial motion, the fact remains that she did not do so. She could have saved all her grounds by making a consolidated motion and still have obtained the expeditious dismissal on the 12(b)(6) basis she now claims to have been seeking. To permit this defense to be raised now would undermine the very purpose of Rule 12(g), (h), which is the avoidance of time-consuming, piece-meal litigation of pre-trial motions.

Accordingly, the motion to dismiss is denied.

Practice Problem

Practice Problem 13-2
Peppy Plaintiff and Dierdre Defendant are citizens of different states. Peppy brings a personal injury claim seeking damages arising out of a car accident that occurred while he was visiting family in the

state of which Dierdre is a citizen. Claiming $100,000 in damages, Peppy files suit in the state where he lives to minimize litigation expenses. The only time that Dierdre has ever set foot in Peppy's home state was 10 years earlier when she temporarily worked on a job assignment there. Peppy serves Dierdre but, in the process of mailing by the appropriate state official, the summons is damaged by water. On receiving the summons and complaint, Dierdre can read the response deadline but cannot make out the clerk's signature.

Dierdre files a motion to dismiss based solely on insufficiency of process. The court denies the motion. Dierdre files a second motion to dismiss, including this time a challenge to personal jurisdiction. Plaintiff opposes the motion on the ground that the defendant has waived any challenge to personal jurisdiction. What is the correct result?

D. Second Waiver Scenario: Defendant Chooses to File an Answer as the First Response to a Complaint

The second way to waive a defense occurs when the defendant chooses not to file a pre-answer motion and then fails to include a highly waivable defense in the answer. Federal Rule of Civil Procedure 12 mandates waiver of highly waivable defenses here, as well. Again, we would benefit from observing the thought process of a seasoned lawyer as she reads through the rest of Rule 12. As she notes, Rule 12(h) specifically singles out—after it refers to waiver by a motion that omits one of these defenses—another way to waive the four highly waivable defenses.[544] Rule 12(h) provides, as she observes, that these four defenses will be waived "by . . . failing to either make a motion under this rule; or include it in a responsive pleading or in an amendment allowed by Rule 15(a) (1) as a matter of course." The lawyer recognizes that the first part of the quoted language describes waiver by omission from a Rule 12 motion (the same waiver scenario she analyzed above and which was discussed in the Tiernan case).

The following is a case addressing the second form of waiver contemplated by Rule 12:

RENFRO v. SPARTAN COMPUTER SERVICES, INC.
United States District Court for the District of Kansas, 2008
No. 06-2284-KHV, 2008 U.S. Dist. LEXIS 29715

VRATIL, United States District Judge.

Plaintiffs bring suit against Spartan Computer Services, Inc., Jack Steenhausen and Terry Connorton seeking recovery of unpaid overtime under the Fair Labor Standards Act of 1938 ("FLSA"), 29 U.S.C. § 201 et seq. On April 20, 2007, plaintiffs filed their amended complaint, which for the first time named Steenhausen and Connorton as defendants. On June 18, 2007, defendants—without having filed any pre-answer motions—answered the complaint. This matter comes before the Court on Defendants'Jack Steenhausen And Terry Connorton's Motion to Dismiss For Lack Of Personal Jurisdiction filed December 28, 2007. For reasons stated below, the Court overrules the motion.

In their motion to dismiss, Steenhausen and Connorton argue that the Court lacks personal

---

[544] Recall, the highly waivable defenses under Rule 12 include the defenses of lack of personal jurisdiction (Rule 12(b)(2)), improper venue (Rule 12(b)(3)), insufficient process (Rule 12(b)(4)), and insufficient service of process (Rule 12(b)(5)).

jurisdiction over them because they have no substantial contacts with the State of Kansas. Plaintiffs respond in part that Steenhausen and Connorton have waived their personal jurisdiction defense. The Court agrees.

A defect in the district court's jurisdiction over a party is a personal defense which may be asserted or waived. Fed. Deposit Ins. Corp. v. Oaklawn Apartments, 959 F.2d 170, 174–75 (10th Cir.1992). Rule 12(b), provides that "[a] motion asserting [lack of personal jurisdiction] must be made before pleading if a responsive pleading is allowed." Under Rule 12(b), objections to personal jurisdiction must be asserted in the answer or in a pre-answer motion. . . . The failure to assert lack of personal jurisdiction in the answer or pre-answer motion constitutes a waiver of the defense.

As noted above, the record is clear that defendants did not file any pre-answer motion in this case. Steenhausen and Connorton argue that they preserved their personal jurisdiction defense by raising it in their answer. They do not, however, specifically identify any portion of the answer which asserts a lack of personal jurisdiction. Having reviewed the answer, the Court finds no indication that Steenhausen and Connorton raised lack of personal jurisdiction as a defense to plaintiffs' claims. Because Steenhausen and Connorton have not raised lack of personal jurisdiction in their answer or by way of pre-answer motion, they have waived the defense.

IT IS THEREFORE ORDERED that Defendants'. . . Motion to Dismiss for Lack of Personal Jurisdiction . . . be and hereby is *OVERRULED*.

Practice Problem

Practice Problem 13-3
Alice, a citizen of Rhode Island, sues Dean, a citizen of New Hampshire, over a car accident in New Hampshire. Alice sues in the U.S. District Court for the District of Rhode Island, alleging diversity of citizenship and seeking $300,000 in damages. Defendant responds within 21 days with an Answer. The Answer denies allegations of negligence and includes as the sole additional "affirmative" defense that Alice was herself negligent. Two months later, Dean files a motion to dismiss the case on the ground that the court lacks personal jurisdiction because the accident happened in New Hampshire and that he has never been to Rhode Island. How should the court rule?

E. Third Waiver Scenario: Defendant Fails to Raise a Highly Waivable Defense Within the Amendment "Of Right" Period

The third way in which a defendant can waive a highly waivable defense is by filing an answer that does not include a highly waivable defense, and then by trying to raise the highly waivable defense after the amendment-of-right period has run out. Unlike the second scenario, the defendant at least tries to raise the defense here. Yet, we see the strict nature in which courts view the necessity to raise the highly waivable defenses early, if at all. Federal Rule of Civil Procedure 12(h) anticipates waiver when one of these four defenses is not raised "in a responsive pleading or in an amendment allowed by Rule 15(a) (1) as a matter of course." Because the language allows for an exception—the amendment as a matter of course—one must turn to Rule 15(a) (1) (B), which states that a party may amend its pleading (i.e., answer) once as a matter of course "within 21 days after serving the pleading if a responsive pleading is not allowed and the action is not yet on the trial calendar." Thus, the third way in which a party can waive one of the four waivable defenses is by failing to include the defense in her answer or to amend that answer in the brief period permitted "of right" after a responsive pleading is filed.

The following is a case illustrating this third form of waiver:

KONIGSBERG v. SHUTE
United States Court of Appeals for the Third Circuit, 1970
435 F.2d 551

OPINION OF THE COURT PER CURIAM:

We are reversing a summary judgment of the district court which dismissed a complaint filed in the district of New Jersey served on a defendant in the state of Missouri on the ground that ["]the defendant has not had sufficient minimum contact with the state of New Jersey to make him amenable to process under F.R.C.P. 4(e).["] We hold that appellee waived his right to assert the defense of lack of jurisdiction over the person or insufficiency of process.

A complaint based on diversity was filed August 19, 1969, in the district of New Jersey. After being served with process in the state of Missouri, the defendant moved for a change of venue to which the plaintiff filed a reply opposing the change. Thereafter, on September 11 defendant filed an answer denying the allegations on the merits.

On October 9, 1969, the defendant moved for leave to file an amended answer which for the first time asserted the defense that the court lacked jurisdiction over the person of the defendant. An amended answer was then filed on December 18, pursuant to a court order dated December 15, 1969, granting leave.

Rule 12(h)(1) provides that 'a defense of lack of jurisdiction over the person, improper venue, insufficiency of process, or insufficiency of service of process is waived . . . if it is neither made by motion under this rule nor included in a responsive pleading or an amendment thereof permitted by Rule 15(a) to be made as a matter of course.'

Rule 15(a) provides that 'a party may amend his pleading once as a matter of course at any time before a responsive pleading is served or, if the pleading is one to which no responsive pleading is permitted and the action has not been placed upon the trial calendar, he may so amend it at any time within 20 days after it is served. Otherwise a party may amend his pleading only by leave of court or by written consent of the adverse party; and leave shall be freely given when justice so requires.'[Author's Note: The current version of Rule 15(a) is stricter, allowing 21 days from filing the pleading (i.e., answer) to file an amendment of right.]

Defendant-appellee's original answer was served by mailing to his adversary on September 9, and was filed September 11. Under Rule 15(a) he had 20 days after service upon plaintiff-appellant to file an amendment as of course. This period expired before October 9, 1969, when application was made to the court for leave to file an amended answer; a fortiori the time period had long expired before December, when the amended answer was in fact filed. He therefore was no longer entitled to file an amended answer as a matter of course. He required leave of court, which he sought and received.

His court-authorized amended answer did not qualify as one described in waiver Rule 12(h) (1) as

362

'an amendment thereof permitted by Rule 15(a) to be made as a matter of course.' *In Orange Theatre Corp. v. Rayherstz Amusement Corp.*,[545] this court, speaking through Judge Maris stated:

> If the defense of lack of jurisdiction of the person is not raised by motion before answer or in the answer itself it is by the express terms of paragraph (h) of Civil Procedure Rule 12 to be treated as waived, not because of the defendant's voluntary appearance but because of his failure to assert the defense within the time prescribed by the rules.

The judgment of the district court in favor of the defendant will be reversed and the cause remanded for further proceedings.

Practice Problem

Practice Problem 13-4

Plaintiff, Cardservice International, Inc. ("CSI") is incorporated in Texafornia and has its principal place of business there. CSI is the owner of certain trade secrets by which it has been able to provide credit and debit card processing services less expensively than competitors. WRM Associates, Inc. ("WRM") is a company with its principal place of business in a state other than CSI. WRM has set up an Internet website offering card processing services and calls itself "The Cardservice Company." A former officer of CSI set up WRM and used CSI's trade secrets to accomplish card processing in the less expensive manner only CSI had accomplished to date. CSI has had some business activity in the state in which you intend to practice, but its main connection with the state is the location of its preferred outside counsel (you). A couple of businesses in the state in which you intend to practice have seen the WRM website, but there is no evidence of a person or business in that state using WRM's card processing services.

CSI sues WRM in federal court in your state alleging misappropriation of trade secrets. WRM files an answer denying the allegations in CSI's complaint. Two months after filing its answer, WRM moves for leave to file an amended answer raising lack of personal jurisdiction and improper venue as defenses. CSI opposes the motion on the grounds that WRM has waived these defenses. How should the court rule?

F. Synthesis of Waiver Provisions

The federal system is sending a clear message through the waiver rules. What is that message? Put aside immediate reactions such as, "Wow, that's harsh!" Ask yourself why the system would consider it necessary to force the kinds of defenses that are highly waivable to be raised at the outset of a case? That, after all, is the result of having such waiver provisions in place for these defenses. Indeed, why can one even argue that it is fair to require such defenses to be raised early or not at all?

G. Other Defenses and Relief Under Rule 12

The scenarios we just covered were to highlight the danger of waiving certain defenses. However,

---

[545] 139 F.2d 871, 874 (3 Cir. 1944).

there is much more to Federal Rule of Civil Procedure 12 than those scenarios alone. Rule 12 offers several other valuable options for a defendant.

III. Motion to Dismiss: Rule 12(b)(6)

The most common defense motion is a motion to dismiss for failure to state a claim upon which relief may be granted, often referred to in federal practice as a "Rule 12(b) (6) motion," or in some state jurisdictions as a "motion for failure to state a claim." 61 AM. JUR. 2d Pleading § 330 (2017). Unlike the highly waivable defenses, a motion to dismiss for failure to state a claim upon which relief can be granted can be raised as late as trial. See FED. R. CIV. P. 12(h) (2). This motion tends to fall into two types of motions to dismiss for failure to state a claim— (1) motions challenging pleadings that fail to make enough allegations to support claims, and (2) motions challenging pleadings that allege claims that are not actionable. If the defect is an insufficient pleading that the plaintiff can fix, the court will generally grant the motion with leave to amend. If the defect is not something that can be fixed, the court will not grant leave to amend because it would be futile to do so.

When reviewing the complaint, defense counsel should ask these questions: Has the plaintiff alleged enough facts on each element of a claim so that my client knows why she is being sued? Are the claims actionable in my jurisdiction? If the answer to both questions is "yes," filing a motion to dismiss for failure to state a claim makes little sense. The most likely result is that you will waste your client's time and money. Even if the court grants the motion, the plaintiff will receive leave to amend and can correct a deficiency. If the answer to either question is a resounding "no," a motion to dismiss for failure to state a claim is appropriate. Knowing when to file, and when not to file, takes sound judgment.

The complaint may leave out a key allegation, which is sometimes the case where the plaintiff sues an employer based on vicarious liability for the negligence of the employee. If the complaint does not allege that the employee's acts were within the scope of employment, the claim ought to be dismissed because such an allegation is essential. Moreover, it may not be purely technical. What if the plaintiff cannot allege that the employee was acting within the scope of employment because that is not true? By insisting on the allegation, the defendant has smoked out a vulnerability in the plaintiff's case at the earliest possible stage. A less careful defense lawyer simply answers and realizes only later, perhaps at trial, the hole in the plaintiff's case. By then, a great deal of time (and expenses to the client) have been expended. Thus, insisting on essential allegations for a claim can ensure your client does not face claims and incur litigation expenses unnecessarily.

Another common scenario is where the complaint alleges fraud, mistake, or some other matter that requires particularized pleading. In such cases, the defendant may file a motion to dismiss (or demurrer) if the complaint is not sufficiently specific.[546] For example, in a fraud claim, the plaintiff must plead each element of fraud and the specific facts relied upon to satisfy each element.[547] Typically, the plaintiff must allege the specific communications, the parties to these, the dates of any such communications, the manner in which they are fraudulent, and why the plaintiff could reasonably rely on the statements.[548] One reason for requiring particularity in certain types of claims is that the claims involve matters that are more difficult to defend without specifics, so the defendant needs to be properly put on notice of the specifics of the claim in order to prepare a defense.[549] Another reason for the requirement is that a fraud claim implicates a

---

[546] *See* 37 AM. JUR. 2d Fraud and Deceit § 441 (2017).

[547] *Id.* § 454; *see, e.g.*, FED. R. CIV. P. 9.

[548] 37 AM. JUR. 2d Fraud and Deceit § 444 (2017).

[549] *Id.* § 445.

person's reputation—something that the law does not want plaintiffs to be able to do casually.[550] Also, if the plaintiff is asserting other claims in which the defendant's reputation could suffer from the complaint's allegations, a jurisdiction may require particularized pleadings, just as with fraud or mistake.[551]

Practice Problems

Practice Problem 13-5

Patty Plaintiff files a complaint against Defendant Yard Works, Inc. for $150,000 in federal court because the parties are diverse. The complaint alleges the following: (1) that Patty was injured as she tripped over a shovel that Simple Simon had negligently left on the street in front of Plaintiff's home; (2) that Simple Simon was an employee of Yard Works, Inc.; and (3) that Patty suffered damages as the result of her injury exceeding $75,000. Recalling tort and agency principles, you determine that Yard Works, Inc. can file a motion to dismiss for failure to state a claim. Why?

Practice Problem 13-6

Pam (CA) witnessed Doug (NV) swinging a chain around his head in increasingly large con-centric circles. Doug did not see a ten-year-old girl approaching from behind, but Pam observed the whole series of events and could not yell because, as she put it, she was frozen with fear. The chain knocked the girl out and left a gash across her face. Pam was not related to the girl but was deeply disturbed at witnessing the incident. She continued to dream of it and could not shake its effects. She has been seeing a psychiatrist for over a year and will have to continue to do so, due to her flashbacks to the incident. Pam sues Doug for negligent infliction of emotional distress and seeks, $100,000. However, the applicable law does not recognize tort liability for negligent infliction of emotion distress. On a motion to dismiss under Rule 12(b)(6), how should the court rule? Should the court, if it grants the motion, allow Pam to amend her complaint if it agrees that no such claim is actionable in that state?

IV. Motion for a More Definite Statement-Rule 12(e)

Federal Rule of Civil Procedure 12 also allows a defendant to file a motion for a more definite statement if the complaint "is so vague or ambiguous that the party cannot reasonably prepare a response."[552] Motions for more definite statements are not favored. The ability of defendants to respond that the defendant lacks information sufficient to form a belief as to the truth of the allegations makes some response to a complaint typically available. The defendant should only use this motion if the ambiguous complaint was one that, if clarified, would still fail to state a claim.[553]

V. The Alternative to a Motion (or What You Do if a Motion is Denied): Answer the Complaint

Rule 12 makes clear that one of the primary options of a defendant in responding to a complaint within 21 days is to answer it. Federal Rule of Civil Procedure 8 in turn governs answers. Please read Rule

---

[550] See id.

[551] Id.

[552] FED. R. CIV. P. 12(e).

[553] See 5C CHARLES ALAN WRIGHT & ARTHUR R. MILLER, FEDERAL PRACTICE AND PROCEDURE § 1378 (3d. ed. 2018).

8(b) and 8(c) now.

If a defendant does not have a basis for filing a pre-answer motion, or strategically chooses to save certain defenses for later in the litigation, the defendant must file an answer. The answer is one of the most important pleadings in a case. Too often it is treated casually as a perfunctory step to get the case moving.

In the answer, the defendant must respond to each of the allegations in the complaint. The applicable rule in most jurisdictions is that the defendant must "fairly admit or deny the allegations in the complaint."[554] Defense counsel must categorize a complaint's allegations. One important category to identify first includes the allegations for which the defendant's counsel, who typically is new to the case, lacks a sufficient basis to determine the accuracy of allegations. Often, a defendant who has just been sued does not have sufficient facts to admit or deny a factual allegation. Recognizing this reality, almost every state allows a defendant to respond that it *lacks information sufficient to form a belief as to the accuracy of the allegation.*[555] As Rule 8 provides, such a statement has the effect of a denial. If the state in which you intend to practice does not make clear that such a response serves as a denial, then the safer course is to state that "the defendant lacks information sufficient to form a belief as to [the specific allegation] and therefore denies the allegation." Why be careful? Because Rule 8 provides that the failure to respond to an allegation operates as an admission, whereas responding that the responding party lacks information sufficient to form a belief on which to respond operates as a denial. Especially when one is early in litigation and has not had the opportunity to investigate thoroughly, counsel should beware of such an "admission." The effect of an admission is that the facts and allegations admitted must be treated as a judicial admission accepted as true for all purposes—meaning that no proof need be offered on the matter at trial. Following is a case that illustrates the effect of failing to respond to all the allegations in a complaint. Do not be concerned that it is a Rhode Island case. Because that state's rules mirror the Federal Rules of Civil Procedure on the point in question, the decision shows how the same case would turn out in federal court.

MARTIN v. LILLY
Supreme Court of Rhode Island, 1986
505 A.2d 1156

WEISBERGER, J., delivered the opinion of the Court.

. . .

This appeal raises three issues (two of which were raised by counsel): (1) whether [Defendant/Appellant] Dean's appeal of the action brought by [Plaintiff/Appellee] George for property damage is properly before this court; (2) whether the trial justice's denial of the motion to amend Dean's answers to add the defenses of lack of consent and ownership was proper; and (3) whether the trial justice's denial of the motion for directed verdict was proper. We answer the first issue in the negative and the second and third issues in the affirmative.

After plaintiffs had rested and after the defense had presented two witnesses, Dean filed a motion to amend its answer to assert the defenses of lack of ownership and lack of consent. The trial justice denied this motion, and Dean appealed. Before reaching the merits on this issue, we think it is necessary to discuss briefly the operation of [R.I. Gen. Laws] §§ 31-33-6 and 31-33-7 so as to clarify the manner in which these statutes operate.

---

[554] *See* FED. R. CIV. P. 8(b).
[555] 61A AM. JUR. 2d Pleading § 292 (2017).

[General Laws 1956 (1968 Reenactment) § 31-33-6 provides:

Owner's liability for acts of others. Whenever any motor vehicle shall be used, operated, or caused to be operated upon any public highway of this state with the consent of the owner, or lessee, or bailee, thereof, expressed or implied, the driver thereof, if other than such owner, or lessee, or bailee, shall in case of accident be deemed to be the agent of the owner or lessee, or bailee, of such motor vehicle unless such driver shall have furnished proof of financial responsibility in the amount set forth in chapter 32 of this title, prior to such accident; and for the purposes of this section the term 'owner' shall include any person, firm, copartner-ship, association or corporation having the lawful possession or control of a motor vehicle under a written sale agreement.

General Laws 1956 (1968 Reenactment) § 31-33-7 provides:

Prima facie evidence of consent of owner. In all civil proceedings, evidence that at the time of the accident or collision the motor vehicle was registered in the name of the defendant, shall be prima facie evidence that it was being operated with the consent of the defendant, and the absence of consent shall be an affirmative defense to be set up in the answer and proved by the defendant.]

The actions against Dean were based on § 31-33-6. There was no allegation of the application of § 31-33-7 in the complaint, and the judge did not instruct the jury concerning § 31-33-7.

Having not alleged § 31-33-7 in their complaint, plaintiffs did not raise § 31-33-7 and were not entitled to its benefits. Because the complaint did not assert the application of § 31-33-7, Dean was not required to plead affirmatively lack of consent. If the complaints had alleged the application of § 31-33-7, Dean would have been required to plead affirmatively lack of consent. However, even if § 31-33-7 had been invoked, Dean would not have been required to plead affirmatively lack of ownership or registration. An answer denying plaintiffs' allegations would have sufficed. To achieve the benefits of § 31-33-7, plaintiffs would have first to prove registration,[556] and defendants could traverse the fact of registration without the necessity of an affirmative plea.

As we have stated, the case against Dean was premised solely on § 31-33-6. Without question, plaintiffs must prove each essential element of their action to recover. . . . To recover under this statute, plaintiffs were required to prove four elements: (1) that the driver (Maria) was negligent; (2) that the car was being operated on a public highway; (3) that the car was owned by defendant; and (4) that the car was driven with the owner's (Dean's) consent.

To oppose any of these elements, all a defendant must do is file an answer disputing the essential facts asserted in the complaint. . . . Therefore, we conclude that an answer denying plaintiffs' claim based on § 31-33-6 would entitle defendant to produce evidence challenging plaintiffs' allegations on any essential elements. However, if a plaintiff alleges that the defendant is the registered owner, then § 31-33-7 would be applicable and defendant would be required to plead affirmatively absence of consent. In the case at bar, an answer that denied ownership and consent would have sufficed to meet the allegations of this complaint.

---

[556] Gemma v. Rotondo, 5 A.2d 297, 299 (1939).

Rule 8(b) of the Superior and District Court Rules of Civil Procedure requires a party to "admit or deny the averments upon which the adverse party relies." Under Rule 12(a) of the Superior and District Court Rules of Civil Procedure, the answer must be filed within twenty days of service of the complaint. Failure to deny an averment results in a judicial admission of the alleged fact.[557] A judicially admitted fact is conclusively established . . . that is, removed from the area of controversy, obviating the need of the plaintiff to produce evidence on the fact and precluding the defendant from challenging the fact. By not answering the allegations of ownership and consent, Dean admitted these facts and every other allegation relating to liability in the complaint. The trial justice therefore properly precluded Dean from introducing evidence to challenge the facts of ownership and consent.

For the reasons stated above, we affirm the trial justice's denial of the motion to "amend" the answer. Further, although Dean's motion with respect to No. 74-749 was not a Rule 15(b) motion because no answer existed to amend, the trial justice's denial of Dean's motion to amend a nonexistent answer and preclusion of evidence challenging lack of ownership and lack of consent was correct. The trial justice had determined that to allow Dean to challenge ownership and consent at that juncture would severely prejudice plaintiffs because of the impossibility of obtaining registry records to verify ownership. As the trial justice pointed out, trial by ambush is no longer allowed under our modern view of pleadings. The purpose of modern pleadings is "to define with clearness and reasonable certainty the issue to be tried." . . . Dean's attempt to challenge ownership, raised for the first time after plaintiffs had rested and at a time when plaintiffs could no longer obtain registry records, would constitute trial by ambush, and the motion to amend was properly denied.

. . .

The final issue under review is whether the trial justice properly denied Dean's motion for a directed verdict. Dean claims that he was entitled to a directed verdict because the only evidence produced by plaintiffs to show Dean's ownership of the car was inadmissible hearsay and, therefore, plaintiffs failed to make out a prima facie case.

In the ordinary case, as we stated in *Young v. Park*,[558] in reviewing a trial justice's decision on a motion for directed verdict, "we have the same duty as the trial justice to view the evidence and the inferences to which it is reasonably susceptible in the light most favorable to [the plaintiff]. We do this without weighing the evidence or assessing the credibility of witnesses. Instead, we decide whether the evidence is sufficient in law to support a verdict for the plaintiff." In the case at bar the trial justice could have reached only one conclusion.

In the instant case all allegations in respect to liability, ownership, and consent had been admitted by the failure of Dean to file an answer denying the essential averments of the complaint. Consequently, any evidence purportedly admitted in support of these allegations was mere surplusage. Therefore, we need not reach the issue of the admissibility of Maria's hearsay declaration. In light of Dean's judicial admissions, the only issue remaining to be resolved was damages. 1 Kent, § 8.5 at 86 (averments of damages are not admitted if not denied). Since an entry of appearance had been made on Dean's behalf, it was entitled to an evidentiary hearing on the issue of damages just as it would have been in the case of the entry of a formal default.[559] Since no default had been entered, the case was submitted to a jury. No error inhered in

---

[557] FED. R. CIV. P. 8(d); DIST. R. CIV. P. 8(d); 1 KENT, R.I. CIV. PRAC. § 8.5 at 86 (1969); MCCORMICK, EVIDENCE § 262 at 776 (3d ed. Cleary 1984).
[558] 417 A.2d 889, 893 (R.I. 1980).
[559] *See* FED. R. CIV. P. 55(b)(2).

this procedure.

For the reasons stated, the purported appeal from civil action No. 76-747 is not properly before us and is dismissed pro forma; the appeal from civil action No. 76-749 is denied and dismissed. The judgment of the Superior Court is affirmed, and the papers in the case may be remanded to the Superior Court.

. . .

To avoid results such as those illustrated in the above case, one which applies the same rule as is applied in federal courts, the careful attorney will compare the complaint's allegations with the defendant's answer to ensure that the answer responds to each of the complaint's allegations. In addition, the defendant should add affirmative defenses to the answer. Federal Rule of Civil Procedure 8(c) provides a non-exhaustive list of affirmative defenses. In the writ pleading days of old, the matters now listed as affirmative defenses would have been considered issues of "confession and avoidance." Affirmative defenses are not denials; they are a way for the defendant to "avoid" liability for the plaintiff's claim.[560] An affirmative defense asserts a legal point, for which the defendant bears the burden of proof that, if true, will allow the defendant to escape liability in whole or in part even though the plaintiff could otherwise prove all elements of a claim to hold the defendant liable.[561] The defendant can raise an affirmative defense (such as statute of limitations) and take on the task of proving the defense. In other words, even if the plaintiff's allegations are true, the defendant can avoid liability by proving to the factfinder that the grounds for her defense are true.[562] For example, the defendant could show that the statute of limitations accrued (i.e., began running) at a point in time which, by the time suit was filed, was later than the time for such a claim to be brought. Even though the plaintiff may be able to prove every element of the claim, bringing the claim beyond the limitations period will "avoid" judgment against the defendant if she proves that the statute of limitations has run on the claim.[563] Counsel's failure to raise an affirmative defense typically results in waiver of the defense.[564]

The following is a chart comparing the *Rex v. Hurry* complaint with a sample answer to that complaint. The complaint is in the left column, and responses typically seen in an answer appear in the right column. A comparison such as this will help to ensure that the answer responds to every allegation in the complaint. Note that most of the responses in the answer column below are of the "without information to respond and therefore denies the allegations" variety. Such responses are legitimate in most cases because, at the outset of a case, defense counsel usually has limited facts. Defense counsel, in good faith, can give such a response. Because it serves effectively as a denial,[565] it provides a safe way for a party to respond without making a costly admission.

---

[560] 61A AM. JUR. 2d Pleading § 271 (2017).

[561] *Id.*

[562] *Id.* § 272.

[563] For a discussion of the analysis for determining whether the statute of limitations period has run on a claim, see Chapter 2.

[564] *Id.* § 274.

[565] *See* FED. R. CIV. P. 8(b)(5).

Figure 13-2

Comparison of Sample Complaint and Answer

Sample Complaint	Sample Answer
IN THE UNITED STATES DISTRICT COURT FOR THE EASTERN DISTRICT OF ILLYRIA **BRAD T. REX,** Plaintiff, <div align="right">**Case No.**</div><div align="center">**2016cv10**</div>v. **ENA HURRY,** Defendant.	**IN THE UNITED STATES DISTRICT COURT FOR THE EASTERN DISTRICT OF ILLYRIA** **BRAD T. REX,** Plaintiff, <div align="right">**Case No.**</div>**2016cv10** v. **ENA HURRY,** Defendant.
<div align="center">**COMPLAINT**</div>	<div align="center">**ANSWER**</div>
The Plaintiff, Brad T. Rex, by counsel, for his Complaint against defendants, Ena Hurry and Kagasaki, Inc., states as follows:	The Defendant, Ena Hurry, by counsel, for her Answer to Plaintiff's Complaint, states as follows:
Parties (1) The Plaintiff, Brad T. Rex, is a citizen of the State of Illyria and the Defendant, Ena Hurry, is a citizen of the State of Elysium. Defendant, Kagasaki, Inc., is incorporated in Delaware and has its principal place of business in Michigan.	**Parties** (1) The Defendant, Ena Hurry, admits only that she is a citizen of the State of Illyria. Hurry lacks information sufficient to form a belief as to the truth of the remaining allegations in paragraph 1 of the Complaint and therefore denies them.

Facts Common to All Counts

(2) On or about January 18, 2018, Rex was driving a motorcycle owed by a friend, Harley Davidson, who had given Rex permission to ride the bike with Rex's motorcycle was in the shop for repairs.

(3) Rex was driving Davidson's motorcycle between the minimum speed limit of 15 miles per hour and the maximum speed limit of 35 miles per hour. He was driving the motorcycle during daylight at around 4:00 p.m. on a public, single-lane road called Easy Street in Arcadia, Illyria, which intersects with Dangerous Drive (the "Intersection"). The intersection is controlled by a traffic light. Rex, who was traveling west on Easy Street, entered the Intersection immediately after other vehicles traveling in the same direction had done so.

(4) At the same time and on the same day Hurry was driving her car north on Dangerous Drive in the right-hand lane of the two-lane road. Hurry proceeded through the intersection negligently despite the lack of a green light

(5) Hurry, who was traveling at a high rate of speed that exceeded the speed limited, proceeded through the Intersection at an unsafe speed and/or despite traffic signals indicating she should have stopped.

(6) Rex and the motorcycle collided with the side of Hurry's car. Rex was thrown over Hurry's car onto the asphalt and received numerous and serious injuries throughout his body, for which he has received—and continues to receive—medical care. Rex has experienced significant pain, suffering, discomfort, and significant disruption to his life. The collision and aftermath damaged Davidson's motorcycle in the amount that will likely exceed $50,000 or more to repair.

Facts Common to All Counts

(2) Hurry lacks information sufficient to form a belief as to the truth of the remaining allegations in paragraph 2 of the Complaint and therefore denies them.

(3) Hurry admits only that Easy Street and Dangerous Drive intersect in the City of Arcadia. Hurry lacks information sufficient to form a belief as to the truth of the remaining allegations in paragraph 3 of the Complaint and therefore denies them.

(4) Hurry admits only that, on the day alleged, she was operating her car on Dangerous Drive at the intersection with Easy Street. Hurry denies the remaining allegations in paragraph 4 of the Complaint.

(5) Hurry admits only that, on the day alleged, she was operating her car on Dangerous Drive. Hurry denies the remaining allegations in paragraph 5 of the Complaint.

(6) Hurry admits only that her vehicle and Rex's motorcycle collided. Hurry is without information sufficient to form a belief as to the truth of the remaining allegations in paragraph 6 of the Complaint and therefore denies them.

(7) Rex was wearing a new state-of-the-art motorcycle airbag jacket manufactured by Kagasaki, Inc. Kagasaki advertises the jacket as an essential safety device that will inflate immediately when a rider is thrown from a motorcycle and protect him from serious trauma. The air bag jacket that Rex was wearing did not inflate when Rex was thrown from the motorcycle.	(7) Hurry is without information sufficient to form a belief as to the truth of the allegations in paragraph 7 of the Complaint and therefore denies them.
(8) Stunned by all these events, Rex stood up after a great effort—only to have Hurry approach him in a threatening matter and push him with both of her hands on his shoulders	(8) Hurry denies the allegations in paragraph 8 of the Complaint

Negligence Claim	Negligence Claim
(9) The preceding allegations are hereby restated and incorporated as if set forth herein.	(9) Hurry incorporates her responses to the allegations preceding paragraph 9 of the Complaint as set forth herein.
(10) Hurry had a duty at the time of the events which occurred on or about January 18, 2018, to use ordinary care to avoid injury to others and to the property of others.	(10) Hurry states that the allegation in paragraph 10 of the Complaint set forth conclusions of law to which she is not required to respond. To the extent any factual allegations are implicit in this paragraph, Hurry denies them
(11) Hurry breached her duty to use ordinary care in a variety of ways, including but not limited to driving at an unsafe speed and/or failing to follow the traffic signals at the Intersection, and/or observing a traffic signal indicating she should stop and proceeding through the Intersection anyway.	(11) Hurry denies the allegations in paragraph 11 of the Complaint.
(12) Hurry's breach is described in the preceding paragraph.	(12) Hurry denies the allegations in paragraph 12 of the Complaint
(13) As a proximate result of Hurry's breach of her duty, Rex suffered severe injuries to his cervical spine and neck among other severe injuries, was prevented from attending school and/or transacting business, suffered great pain of the body and mind, and incurred expenses for medical attention and hospitalization.	(13) Hurry denies the allegation that she breached any duty to Rex and denies any factual allegations implicit in such allegation. As to the remaining allegations in paragraph 13 of the Complaint, Hurry is without information sufficient to form a belief as to the truth of the allegations and therefore denies them.

Assault Claim	Assault Claim
(14) The preceding allegations are hereby restated and incorporated as if set forth herein.	(14) Hurry incorporates her responses to the allegations preceding paragraph 14 of the Complaint as set forth herein.
(15) When Hurry intentionally approached Rex after the collision in a physically threatening manner, she created a reasonable apprehension of immediate, offensive bodily contact.	(15) Hurry denies the allegations in paragraph 15 of the Complaint.
(16) Hurry had the apparent ability to carry out the threatened offensive bodily contact.	(16) Hurry denies the allegations in paragraph 16 of the Complaint.
(17) Hurry's actions constituted an assault for which she is liable to the Plaintiff for both compensatory and punitive damages.	(17) Hurry states the allegations in paragraph 17 of the Complaint set forth conclusions of law to which she is not required to respond. To the extent any factual allegations are implicit in this paragraph, Hurry denies them.
Battery Claim	**Battery Claim**
(18) The preceding allegations are hereby restated and incorporated as if set forth herein.	(18) Hurry incorporates her responses to the allegations preceding paragraph 18 of the Complaint as set forth herein.
(19) Hurry intentionally touched Rex in a manner offensive to a reasonable person.	(19) Hurry denies allegations as to paragraph 19 of the Complaint.
(20) Hurry's actions constitute a battery.	(20) Hurry denies the allegations in paragraph 20 of the Complaint.
	(21) To the extent that the Plaintiff's Complaint states any facts that are not otherwise responded to in this Answer, such facts are hereby denied."
	AFFIRMATIVE DEFENSES Defendant, Ena Hurry, hereby alleges the following defenses: (21) Negligence of the Plaintiff, Brad T. Rex, proximately caused any or all his injuries.

374

	(22) Any other defense that under applicable law represents an affirmative defense— i.e., a defense that, if proved, will avoid liability of the Defendant even if the Plaintiff's allegations are true, or at least lessen liability such as where the duty to mitigate damages applies.[566]
WHEREFORE, the Plaintiff demands the following relief against the Defendants: • Compensatory damages in a sum exceeding $1 million against Defendant, Ena Hurry, exclusive of interests and costs, the complete amount to be determined at trial; • Punitive damages in a sum exceeding $5 million, the true and complete amount to be determined at trial against Defendant, Ena Hurry.	WHEREFORE, having fully answered, the Defendant respectfully requests that the Plaintiff's actions be dismissed with prejudice.
BRAD T. REX By: /s/ Jim Justice Of Counsel (Plaintiff) The Law Offices of Jim Justice, Esq. 111 Liberty Street Arcadia, Illyria 23464 757-222-3333 jim@justice.com	ENA HURRY By: /s/ Dee Fender Of Counsel (Def.) Dee Fender, Esq. 1000 Liberty Street Arcadia, Illyria 23464 757-625-5000 deefender@yahoo.com

The key to filing effective answers is both research (facts and law) and painstaking care in drafting. The list of affirmative defenses provided by Federal Rule of Civil Procedure 8 (and its state counterparts) is not exhaustive. Therefore, defense counsel must research the applicable juris-diction's law to see what affirmative defenses apply. For a list of defenses that courts have recognized as affirmative defenses beyond the scope of Rule 8.[567] Furthermore, a practitioner must continue the research process as a case moves forward. As already stated, an affirmative defense may only become apparent after conducting discovery and learning more facts. Only by continued research in light of facts as they become known in discovery can an attorney be sure that she has protected her client by raising affirmative defenses that may avoid liability, or at least lessen the damages a client may face.

---

[566] The first paragraph of Affirmative Defenses is included because contributory negligence states will bar recovery to a negligent Plaintiff; in comparative negligence states, you would state that any recovery by a Plaintiff must be reduced by the percentage of negligence contributable to the Plaintiff.
[567] *See* 61A AM. JUR. 2D § 271 (2017).

Follow-Up Questions and Comments

1. How will you decide whether, in a given case, your client's interests are best served by filing a dispositive motion (such as a motion to dismiss), or alternatively, (b) filing an answer preserving defenses and waiting until you have sufficient factual support to assert the defense?

2. You may have noticed that Rule 12(c) allows a party to move for judgment on the pleadings. As is noted above, the motion to dismiss for failure to state a claim is not waived until after trial. Thus, a Rule 12(b) (6) motion, if made later in a case, would often be a motion for judgment on the pleadings. Motions for judgment on the pleadings cannot go beyond the allegations in the complaint into consideration of facts. If the moving party (and the court) relies on anything beyond what is alleged in the pleadings, the motion is converted into a motion for summary judgment and must abide by the rules applicable to such motions.[568]

---

[568] *See* 2-12 JAMES WM.. MOORE ET. AL, MOORE'S FEDERAL PRACTICE-CIVIL § 12.38 (2018).

CHAPTER 14:
DEFENDANTS' JOINDER OF CLAIMS

I. How the Topics in this Chapter Fit in the Overall Progress of a Civil Action

Below is a diagram of the stages of a civil action showing where the topics addressed in this chapter fall in the progress of a case.

Figure 14-1

Cause of Action (events leading to suit)	Pre-Filing Tasks (items to begin representation, interviewing, and related matters)	Choice of Forum (subject matter jurisdiction, removal, personal jurisdiction, and venue)	Notice and Service of Process (completing the process of ensuring the forum court can enter a valid judgment)	Pleading the Case and Joinder of Claims and Parties (including supplemental jurisdiction)

Responding to Claims by Motion or by Answer	Discovery (developing proof to establish claims and learn your adversary's case)	Right to Jury (pretrial motions and practice)	Final Pretrial Conference (events within last month before trial)	Trial (procedures and motions during trial)	Verdict	Post-Trial Motions (motions for a new trial and/or judgment as a matter of law)	Appeal

II. Joinder of Claims and/or Parties by Original Defendants

Defense counsel not only has to consider whether to bring a motion or answer in response to a complaint, but also to consider (a) whether an original defendant must bring a counterclaim, or (b) whether such a defendant or defendants can join claims or parties under other provisions of the Rules. Being a defense counsel at the point of dealing with a complaint is not an easy job.

When we discussed joinder by plaintiffs of claims under Rule 18 and of parties under Rule 20, we did not focus on the language of these rules—in particular, how the rules avoid the use of the terms "plaintiff" or "defendant." Rather than referring to "plaintiffs" and "defendants," the Rules are careful to refer instead to "opposing parties." The reason is simple. If the Rules used "plaintiffs" and "defendants," they would be overlooking the realities of litigation. A plaintiff can quickly become a defendant. All it takes is for the defendant to assert a counterclaim against the plaintiff. For all practical purposes, a defendant who asserts a claim has two hats: (1) that of defendant on the claim in which he or she has been sued, and

(2) that of plaintiff on the claim brought by that defendant against another. Hence, the caption of cases often lists parties as "Defendant and Counterclaim Plaintiff," "Defendant and Cross-Claim Plaintiff," or "Defendant and Third-Party Plaintiff," as a couple of examples of parties who wear both the plaintiff's and the defendant's hats.

Thus, referring to the parties who asserted a claim and who had a claim asserted against them as "opposing parties"—the approach of the Federal Rules—avoids confusion. The Rules allow "opposing parties" to assert (and in some cases, require the opposing party to assert) that party's own claims. Thus, a skilled lawyer thinks in terms of "claimants" and "opponents" to claims. If you are inclined to label parties solely as plaintiffs and defendants, you can get confused once the fur starts flying—i.e., when defendants assert their own claims, including at times claims against plaintiffs, thus making the plaintiffs in effect defendants as to those claims. Of course, any party against whom a claim has been asserted needs to file some responsive pleading to stay out of default. A responsive pleading typically is either an answer to the claims (taking issue with the allegations) or a motion seeking to challenge the complaint on some ground. Fear not. Chapter 13 thoroughly addressed the options in responding to a complaint and the traps inherent in Rule 12. The point here is that a "defendant" may be any party, e.g., the original plaintiff if the original defendant asserts a counterclaim. The moment one's client has a claim asserted against her, that is when one must consider the options (and traps) in Rule 12.

This chapter now introduces the reader to joinder of claims by a party who has had a claim asserted against him, most typically the original plaintiff. Motivated by judicial economy, the Federal Rules allow broad joinder of such claims, with certain outside limits within the Rules. In addition, this chapter emphasizes that permission by a rule to assert a claim is not enough. The new claims asserted, or the new parties added by these rules, must have a basis in subject matter jurisdiction. That basis may be that the claim has an independent basis in subject matter jurisdiction, typically the federal question statute or the diversity statute. Alternatively, the claim can be supported by the Supplemental Jurisdiction statute, 28 U.S.C. § 1367.

A. Counterclaims

Please read Federal Rules of Civil Procedure 13(a) and 13(b). What is the difference between a Rule 13(a) counterclaim and a Rule 13(b) counterclaim? A single word in each rule conveys a great deal about the difference between each provision. What is that word?

1. Compulsory Counterclaims

The effect of failing to bring a compulsory counterclaim may not be immediately apparent. The following case should clarify that effect.

TWIN DISC, INC. v. LOWELL
United States District Court for the Eastern District of Wisconsin, 1975
69 F.R.D. 64

WARREN, District Judge.

Counsel for the defendant named above has filed a motion to dismiss this action. He contends that the issues presented in the complaint are barred by the provisions of Rule 13(a) of the Federal Rules of Civil Procedure (Rule 13(a)) because, in accordance with that rule, it was necessary that said issues be raised and resolved as compulsory counterclaims in a prior action in the United States District Court for the Eastern District of New York. The plaintiff here was the defendant there and the defendant here was the plaintiff.[569]

. . .

I

From a reading of the pleadings, briefs, and other written documents that constitute the record in this case, it appears that the following facts constitute the background to this litigation:

Sometime during the year 1967, plaintiff Twin Disc, Incorporated (Twin Disc) entered into negotiations with the defendant Frank Lowell for the sale of stock of Lem Instruments Corporation (Lem). Lowell and one Robert Everett, not a party here, were the sole stockholders of Lem. As a result of these negotiations, certain written agreements were signed on or about July 3, 1968. By virtue of these agreements, Twin Disc agreed to purchase the Lem stock then held by Lowell and Everett, and permit Lowell to acquire stock in Twin Disc; Lem agreed to hire Lowell for a period of seven years beginning July 3, 1968; and Twin Disc agreed to guarantee performance by Lem under the terms of the aforementioned contract of employment.

In accordance with their respective commitments, Twin Disc acquired the outstanding stock of Lem, and Lowell acquired stock in Twin Disc and became President and General Manager of Lem. It is apparent that this relationship was found to be unsatisfactory because, on October 8, 1972, Lowell was discharged. Subsequent to that discharge, three suits were commenced, including the action at issue here.

The first of the suits described above was filed by Lowell against Twin Disc in the Supreme Court of Suffolk County, New York. It was subsequently removed to the United States District Court for the Eastern District of New York. The complaint in that action charged that Lem had breached its employment agreement with Lowell and sought damages from Twin Disc as the guarantor of that contract.

A second suit was commenced by Lowell in the Supreme Court of Suffolk County, New York, against Lem. The complaint in that action essentially asserted the allegations raised in the original action against Twin Disc but sought damages from Lem in connection with the breach of the employment contract.

The third suit was brought in this Court by Twin Disc against Lowell. The complaint, filed February 27, 1973, asserts in Count I that damages are due as a result of conduct of the defendant that is alleged to be in violation of 15 U.S.C. § 77q, the Securities Exchange Act of 1934, and Rule 10b–5 of the Rules of the Securities and Exchange Commission promulgated thereunder. Count II charges the defendant with breach of the employment contract with Lem by virtue of certain intentional and negligent conduct, and seeks additional damages as a result thereof.

After the commencement of the three actions described above, it appears that the following events took place:

On March 30, 1973, counsel for defendant Lowell filed a motion to dismiss the Wisconsin federal suit, or for summary judgment therein, on the ground that all matters presented were barred by the provisions of Rule 13(a).

---

[569] *See* Lowell v. Twin Disc, Inc., Case No. 72–C– 1582 (E.D.N.Y., Order entered March 28, 1975).

An amended complaint was filed in the action pending in the Eastern District of New York, apparently in response to the motion to dismiss. In essence, the breach of contract claim raised by Twin Disc in Count II of the complaint in this Court was added as a counterclaim there.

On April 1, 1975, judgment was entered on the merits of Lowell's claims in the New York federal action; plaintiff Lowell was thereby denied leave to amend his complaint, and defendant Twin Disc was granted summary judgment. The complaint was ordered . . . barred because Twin Disc was in privity with [Author's note: "privity" is legal term for standing in the shoes of another, hence having the same claims or defenses] Lem and because a jury in the New York state suit had determined that Lem was not liable to Lowell for any breach of the contract of employment.[570]

By letter dated July 31, 1975, counsel for Twin Disc informed this Court that leave had been granted to withdraw the counterclaim from the New York federal suit. By letter dated August 18, 1975, counsel for Lowell informed this Court that the decision in the New York action was being vigorously appealed to the United States Court of Appeals for the Second Circuit.

To summarize the foregoing, it appears that both of the two suits commenced by Lowell in New York have passed their respective trial stages. The issues confronting this Court thus concern the question of whether Twin Disc may now proceed with either or both of the two counts of the complaint pending here. Counsel for defendant Lowell stands on his motion to dismiss the action: he claims that each issue raised in this Court is barred by the provisions of Rule 13(a) in that, as compulsory counter-claims, they could be heard, if at all, only in the New York federal suit. Counsel for plaintiff Twin Disc disputes these arguments and urges that this Court proceed to deny the motions to dismiss and for summary judgment and hear the case on the merits. For reasons to be articulated in this opinion, the Court finds that dismissal is appropriate at this time.

II

Rule 13(a) of the Federal Rules of Civil Procedure reads in pertinent part as follows:

> Compulsory Counterclaims. A pleading shall state as a counterclaim any claim which at the time of serving the pleading the pleader has against any opposing party, if it arises out of the transaction or occurrence that is the subject matter of the opposing party's claim and does not require for its adjudication the presence of third parties of whom the court cannot acquire jurisdiction.

Simply stated, the problem before the Court at this time is whether the claims in the complaint at issue here arose out of the same transactions or occurrences as those with which the New York federal suit was concerned. This Court finds that they do.

Prior to the enactment of Rule 13(a) in its present form, the United States Supreme Court held the word 'transaction' to be one of a flexible meaning which, for purposes of compulsory counterclaims, could encompass a series of occurrences with a logical connection. *Moore v. New York Cotton Exchange*,[571] It appears that this is the general rule to be followed in construing Rule 13(a) at this time.

---

[570] *See* Lowell v. Twin Disc, Inc., 527 F.2d 767 (1975).
[571] 270 593 (1926).

While a variety of standards have been utilized to define the terms 'transaction or occurrence' for purposes of Rule 13(a), it is generally thought that a compulsory counterclaim is any claim that a party has against an opposing party that is 'logically related' to the claims being asserted by said opposing party and is not within an exception listed in the text of Rule 13(a) itself.[572]

In accordance with the foregoing, this Court must proceed to determine whether the issues raised in the complaint in this action logically relate to those presented by Lowell in his New York federal suit by virtue of their common origin. There is no claim that the issues raised by Twin Disc were not mature when the New York federal suit was pending; no party suggests that any exception listed in the text of Rule 13(a) is applicable.

III

The Court would first deal with Count II of the instant complaint; as noted above, it charges that damages are due as a result of certain negligent and intentional conduct on the part of Lowell during the course of his employment at Lem.

A review of the claims presented by Lowell in the suit removed to federal court in New York reveals that said claims were directly concerned with the particulars of his conduct at Lem and the propriety of his termination. See, Lowell v. Twin Disc, Inc., supra. Because Count II of this complaint concerns those same occurrences, and is logically related thereto, it may not be litigated here. By the dictates of Rule 13(a), such issues were to be determined, if at all, in the suit brought to the United States District Court for the Eastern District of New York. Counsel for Twin Disc appears to have acknowledged this fact when an amended answer was filed to present what is Count II here as a counterclaim there. Counsel should not have requested that said counterclaim be withdrawn.

IV

The Court would next deal with Count I. As noted above, it charges that defendant Lowell violated certain anti-fraud provisions of the Securities Exchange Act of 1934 by virtue of his statements and conduct in connection with the sale of securities affected in 1968. The Court finds that the issues raised by these allegations concern transactions and occurrences that were before the Court in the Eastern District of New York. For this reason, this portion of the complaint must be dismissed as well.

A reading of the six paragraphs that constitute Count I demonstrates that certain material misrepresentations are alleged to have been perpetrated during the course of the negotiations leading to the contracts signed in July of 1968. These misrepresentations allegedly include statements regarding past and future profit figures and sales projections of Lem, as well as statements regarding the capability of the defendant in particular to develop additional products and markets for Lem, yet all are concerned with the negotiations leading to the contracts that were later consummated. It seems apparent that these are the very negotiations that were at issue in the Eastern District of New York.

It nowhere appears that the negotiations that were conducted by these parties were in any way bifurcated; the complaint itself asserts at paragraph 11 that the employment contract at issue in New York was 'part and parcel of the [stock] acquisition agreement . . .' The Court cannot hold that the transactions and occurrences upon which these two federal suits were based are so logically or factually divergent as to require that defendant's motion for dismissal be denied. In addition, because the capabilities of defendant Lowell as an individual are challenged in the charges listed in Count I, his activities during the course of

---

[572] *See* 6 WRIGHT & MILLER, FEDERAL PRACTICE AND PROCEDURE: CIVIL § 1410 (1971 ed.).

his employment at Lem may very well come into question. In this circumstance, the action in this Court would take on even more of the characteristics of the one that has been litigated in the Eastern District of New York. Such would appear to lend further support to a decision to order dismissal.

After thorough review of the written record in this matter, and for the reasons stated above, the Court concludes that the charges made by Twin Disc in Count I of the complaint currently at issue were logically related to the transactions and occurrences at issue in the prior New York federal suit such as to warrant a ruling that they were compulsory counterclaims there. As a matter of waiver and estoppel, such claims may not be litigated now.[573]

It is clear that the fragmentation of litigation and multiplicity of suits illustrated by the course of conduct undertaken by Twin Disc here are principal targets at which the provisions of Rule 13(a) are aimed.

V

For the reasons set out in the foregoing memorandum opinion, the motion to dismiss the complaint, filed on behalf of defendant Lowell, is hereby granted.

Follow-Up Questions and Comments

1. Would the court in *Twin Disc* have held any differently if the counterclaim in the New York litigation had not been withdrawn? Was the withdrawal of the counterclaim even relevant to the court's holding?

2. When a party is barred from bringing a claim because of Rule 13(a), called the "Rule bar?" The significance will become clearer later in latter chapters when we deal with the question of preclusion of claims, known as "bar by claim preclusion," or "bar by issue preclusion"—principles distinct from Rule 13's bar.

3. So, what will the analysis likely be if you are presented with a Rule 13 compulsory counterclaim issue? More specifically, what criteria can you draw from the above case to help you decide whether a claim brought in the second suit is one that arose from the same transaction or occurrence, or series of transactions or occurrences, as the first suit?

Practice Problems

Practice Problem 14-1

Paula (VA citizen) and Deb (NC citizen) have a car collision at an intersection. Paula sues Deb for negligence, seeking damages of $100,000 for her injuries. Deb defends on the ground that it was Paula who was negligent. The jury returns a verdict for Deb and the court enters a judgment that becomes final. Later, Deb sues Paula for negligence, seeking damages for her injuries in the collision. Paula moved to dismiss on the ground that Deb is barred by Rule 13(a)'s compulsory counterclaim rule. How should the court rule? If Deb argued that she could not have brought a counterclaim in the earlier suit because there was not a jurisdictional basis, why would she be wrong?

---

[573] *See* 6 WRIGHT & MILLER, CIVIL § 1417 at 96.

IN THE UNITED STATES DISTRICT COURT
FOR THE EASTERN DISTRICT OF ILLYRIA

Norfolk Division

BRAD T. REX, **Plaintiff/Counterclaim Defendant,**	)))	
v.	))	Counterclaim
ENA HURRY, **Defendant/Counterclaim Plaintiff,**	)))	Case No. 2018cv10
and	))	
KAGASAKI, INC., **Defendant.**	))	

COUNTERCLAIM

The Defendant and Counterclaim Plaintiff, Ena Hurry ("Hurry"), by counsel, for her Counterclaim against Plaintiff and Counterclaim Defendant, Brad T. Rex ("Rex"), states as follows:

Facts Common to All Counts

(1) On or about January 18, 2018, Rex was driving a motorcycle and collided with Hurry's vehicle during daylight at around 4:00 p.m. on a public, single-lane road called Easy Street in Arcadia, Illyria, which intersects with Dangerous Drive (the "Intersection").

(2) Rex then responded by screaming loudly at Hurry that she was "a syphilis-ridden criminal." He proceeded to push her so hard that she went backwards and did two somersaults, landing face down. As a result of the fall, Hurry suffered cuts, bruises, and severe pain.

(3) At least one third-party witness, and possibly others, heard Rex's statement described in the preceding paragraph.

(4) Hurry has neither syphilis nor any other communicable diseases. She is not a criminal and has never been convicted of even a traffic offense, much less a more serious crime.

Slander

(5) The preceding allegations are hereby restated and incorporated as if set forth here.

(6) The words screamed after the accident by Rex at Hurry, described above, constitute slander per se because they accuse Hurry of having a communicable disease.

(7) The words were published because a third person, and possibly others, heard them.

(8) The words are false.

(9) The events constitute slander per se for which Hurry is entitled to both compensatory and punitive damages.

Assault

(10) The preceding allegations are hereby restated and incorporated as if set forth here.

(11) Rex intentionally approached Hurry after the collision in a physically threatening manner and created reasonable apprehension of immediate, offensive bodily contact.

(12) Rex had the apparent ability to carry out the threatened offensive bodily contact.

(13) These actions constitute an assault for which Hurry is entitled to both compensatory and punitive damages.

Battery

(14) The preceding allegations are hereby restated and incorporated as if set forth here.

(15) Rex intentionally touched Hurry in a manner offensive to a reasonable person.

(16) These actions constitute battery for which Hurry is entitled to both compensatory and punitive damages.

WHEREFORE, Hurry demands the following relief against Rex:

- Compensatory damages of $100,000 or such greater amount as shall be proved at trial;

- Punitive damages in an amount to be determined at trial; and

- Such other relief as the Court deems just.

ENA HURRY

By /s/_____
Dee Fender, Esq.

Ena Hurry, Esq.
1000 Liberty Street
Arcadia, Illyria, 23464
757-625-5000
deefender@gmail.com
Counsel for Ena Hurry

CERTIFICATE OF SERVICE

I, Dee Fender, hereby certify that on this 8th day of February, 2019, I mailed by first-class United States mail this Counterclaim to counsel for Plaintiff and Counterclaim Defendant, Jim Justice, Esq., 111 Liberty Street, Arcadia, Illyria 23464.

/s/_____
Dee Fender, Counsel for Ena Hurry

Follow-Up Questions and Comments

1. Are the claims in Hurry's counterclaim related to the same transaction and occurrence or series of transactions and occurrences, on which Rex based his claims against Hurry? Why or why not?

2. You are now familiar with the concept of whether claims arise "from the same transaction or occurrence, or series of transactions or occurrences." Do the claims in Hurry's counterclaim fall within the same transaction and occurrence or series of transactions and occurrences? Does the reality that these occurred as a closely related series of events nevertheless suggest they meet the transaction-or-occurrence test?

3. The claims in Harry's counterclaim are very different in terms of legal concepts and proof from the ones in the plaintiff's complaint. For instance, slander is very different from negligence. Does that preclude a slander claim from being part of the same transaction or occurrence? Or are there other factors that must be accounted for when applying the compulsory counterclaim bar?

4. If there is any doubt about whether a claim is part of the same transaction or occurrence, or series of transactions or occurrences, why would a party not assert the claim in the first suit (e.g., here in a counterclaim) to ensure it is not barred later in litigation?

2. Permissive Counterclaims

Please read Federal Rule of Civil Procedure 13(b). How will one know if a claim is not part of the same transaction or occurrence and, thus, a permissive counterclaim?

Practice Problems

Practice Problem 14-2

Creditor (TN) sues Debtor (NC) for failing to pay a debt of $100,000. Debtor has on another occasion been harassed by the same Creditor because the Creditor called the Debtor at home repeatedly in the evenings and on the weekends seeking repayment of the debt, all in violation of the Federal Fair Debt Collections Act. When Creditor sues Debtor, Debtor brings a counterclaim for the Fair Debit Collections Act violation. Is this a proper permissive counterclaim? Although Defendant here is not required but rather may choose whether to bring the counterclaim, why if plaintiff objected on grounds that jurisdiction did not exist over the permissive counterclaim would plaintiff be wrong?

Practice Problem 14-3

Debtor (NC) sues Creditor (TN) for trespassing on Debtor's property and demands nominal damages. Creditor brings a counterclaim for nonpayment of a $100,000 loan. Why would such a permissive counterclaim lack a jurisdictional basis?

Please read Federal Rule of Civil Procedure 13(g). What will be the posture of a case in which a cross-claim will be made? In other words, what will the parties to the cross-claim have in common? The key to answering this question is understanding what it means for one defendant and another to be "co-parties."

Are cross-claims compulsory? Does Rule 13(g) have language allowing you to reach a conclusion on the question? Must cross-claims relate to the same transaction or occurrence as stated in the original action or a counterclaim? Do you see any language about permissive cross-claims? If not, why might the Rules limit the joined claims that are compulsory—require compulsory counterclaims but not compulsory cross-claims?

Practice Problems

Practice Problem 14-4

Deanne (VA citizen) was driving a car owned by Don (NC citizen), who had been warned of a defect in the brakes but has failed to have it fixed. When the brakes failed, Deanne ran into Peg (TN citizen) and injured her. Peg sues Deanne seeking $100,000 for negligence in following her car too closely and Don for negligence in failing to maintain his vehicle properly. Deanne, who was also injured, sues Don for $100,000 for negligence in failing to maintain his vehicle and failing to warn her of the defect, seeking recovery for her injuries. Is this a proper cross-claim under Rule 13(g)? What, if any, jurisdictional basis supports the cross-claim?

Practice Problem 14-5

Incorporate all the facts from the previous Practice Problem. In addition to the first claim, Deanne asserts a claim against Don on the grounds that, if Deanne is liable to Peg for all or part of her claim, then Don is liable to Deanne to pay all or part of any amount for which Peg secures a judgment against Deanne. Such a claim is referred to as a contribution claim because it is by one tortfeasor whose allegedly negligent acts joined with another to cause a single injury to the plaintiff, giving rise to a right among the joint tortfeasors to sue other tortfeasors whose negligence caused the injuries for that tortfeasor's share. (The *Marvickca* case, set forth below in this chapter, describes that kind of claim). Note the last sentence of Rule 13(g) concerning claims such as this one. Would Deanne thus be able to bring this additional claim against Don? Would there be a jurisdictional basis for the claim?

C. Impleader (also known as Third-Party Claims)

Please read Federal Rule of Civil Procedure 14. Notice that such a claim would be against a person or entity not named in the suit originally. In an impleader/Rule 14 scenario, the defendant and third-party plaintiff serves a party who was not originally in the lawsuit. By so doing, the defendant/third-party plaintiff serves the third-party defendant with process in the same way that a plaintiff serves a defendant at the outset of litigation. What is the predicate for bringing a third-party claim under Rule 14?

MARKVICKA v. BRODHEAD-GARRETT CO.
United States District Court for the District of Nebraska, 1977
76 F.R.D. 205

DENNEY, District Judge.

This matter is before the Court upon the motion of third-party defendant, the School District of Ralston, to dismiss the third-party complaint against it filed by defendant and third-party plaintiff, Brodhead-Garrett Company. This action was brought on behalf of a minor child who suffered severe injuries while using a jointer machine manufactured by the defendant. Plaintiff attributes his injuries to the defective design and condition of the jointer machine.

The defendant's third-party complaint against the School District of Ralston alleges that the accident occurred in the course of a woodworking class held by the third-party defendant and charges that the School District's improper maintenance of the machine and inadequate supervision of the students caused plaintiff's injuries.

The third-party complaint alleges a right to indemnity from the School District. However, the Court finds that the third-party complaint more accurately states a claim for contribution.

Contribution and indemnity are two separate remedies which may be available to a tortfeasor who seeks to place all or part of the burden of a judgment upon his fellow tortfeasor. Contribution is based upon the common, though not necessarily identical, liability of two or more actors for the same injury. It equalizes the burden on the wrongdoers by requiring each to pay his own proportionate share of damages. Indemnity, on the other hand, enables one tortfeasor to shift the entire burden of the judgment to another. It tempers the harshness of the doctrines of respondeat superior and vicarious liability since it allows one who has been compelled to pay solely because of a certain legal relationship to shift the ultimate burden of the judgment to the actual culprit.

. . .

In sum, Nebraska law seems to permit indemnity when it has been provided for in a specifically drawn contract or when liability has been imposed upon a party simply because of his legal relationship to the negligent party. It appears, however, that indemnity will not be allowed when both parties have been negligent to a certain degree.

In *Royal Indem. Co. v. Aetna Cas. & Sur. Co.*,[574] the Nebraska Supreme Court clarified the law of contribution among negligent joint tortfeasors in Nebraska.

We, therefore, hold that in this jurisdiction there is no absolute bar to contribution among negligent joint tortfeasors; and also, as in this case, that a right to equitable contribution exists among judgment debtors jointly liable in tort for damages negligently caused, which right becomes enforceable on behalf of any party when he discharges more than his proportionate share of the judgment.

Thus[,] it is now clear that as between defendants against whom a joint judgment in tort has been rendered, contribution is allowed. The court did not directly rule as to contribution between negligent joint

---

[574] 193 Nev. 752 (1975).

tortfeasors against whom judgments have not yet been rendered. However, the statement that 'there is no absolute bar to contribution among negligent joint tortfeasors' would seem to envision contribution not only among those against whom a plaintiff has successfully obtained judgments but also among those whose liability remains to be fixed either in a third-party claim in the original plaintiff's suit or in an independent action for contribution by the original defendant.

The third-party complaint alleges a factual basis for contribution from the School District of Ralston should Brodhead-Garrett be found liable to the plaintiff. If the defendant's allegations are true, the School District's negligence was a concurrent cause of the plaintiff's injury.

Fed. R. Civ. P. 14(a) permits the joinder of a party who 'is or may be liable' to the defending party for all or part of the plaintiff's claim. Where state law creates a right to contribution or indemnity among tortfeasors, the wrongdoer who has been sued by an injured party may implead his co-wrongdoers before the plaintiff successfully obtains a judgment. 'The fact that contribution may not actually be obtained until the original defendant has been cast in judgment and has paid does not prevent impleader; the impleader judgment may be so fashioned as to protect the rights of the other tortfeasors, so that defendant's judgment over against them may not be enforced until the defendant has paid plaintiff's judgment or more than his proportionate share, whichever the law may require.'[575]

The defendant has alleged that if it was at fault in the design or construction of the jointer machine, so was the School District in its maintenance of the machine and supervision of the students. Both owed the plaintiff a duty of care.

Therefore, as the School District 'may be liable' for contribution, it may be joined as third-party defendant in this action in order to determine its accountability. The fact that the defendant erroneously defined its claim as 'indemnity' does not alter this conclusion. . . . At this stage of the proceedings, the Court will grant the defendant leave to amend the third-party complaint to state the correct theory for its cause of action.

IT IS ORDERED that the motion of third-party defendant, the School District of Ralston, to dismiss the third-party complaint will be denied if, within ten (10) days hereof, the defendant, Broadhead-Garrett Company, amends its third-party complaint against the School District to allege a claim for contribution.

Follow-Up Questions and Comments

1. What are the two kinds of claims that the above case identifies as proper ones under the so-called "impleader" provisions of Rule 14?

2. Why will such claims always be related to the original action brought by the plaintiff against the original defendant? As such, contribution and indemnity claims are known as "derivative claims"—claims that derive from the claim asserted by the original plaintiff against one or more defendants who can seek contribution or indemnity against another party.

3. What does Rule 14 state that the third-party defendant "must" do after being brought into the case? What does the Rule state that the third-party defendant "may" do after being brought into the case?

---

[575] 3 MOORE'S FED. PRACTICE § 14.11 at 14-322 (1976) et seq.

After the third-party is brought into the case, what does the Rule state that the original plaintiff can do?

_____

Please review the following sample third-party complaint from the Rex v. Hurry case. Assume as the procedural posture that Rex only brought claims against Defendant Ena Hurry in his initial suit. Hurry, then, brought the following third-party complaint against Kagasaki, Inc. and had that defendant served.

IN THE UNITED STATES DISTRICT COURT
FOR THE EASTERN DISTRICT OF ILLYRIA

BRAD T. REX, **Plaintiff,**	)))	
v.	))	Complaint
ENA HURRY, **Defendant/Third-Party Plaintiff,**	)))	Case No. 2016cv10
And	))	
KAGASAKI, INC., Service Address: 112 Main Street Detroit Michigan 48201 **Defendant**.	))))))	

THIRD-PARTY COMPLAINT

Pursuant to Federal Rule of Civil Procedure 14, Defendant and Third-Party Plaintiff, Ena Hurry ("Hurry"), files this Third-Party Complaint against Kagasaki, Inc. ("Kagasaki"), the Third-Party Defendant.

General Facts

(1) On or about January 18, 2018, the Plaintiff was driving a motorcycle owned by a friend, Harley Davidson, who had given the Plaintiff permission to ride the motorcycle for over a month while the Plaintiff's motorcycle was in the shop for repairs. Motorcycle airbag jackets had become avail-able by this point, and Plaintiff was wearing one. The motorcycle airbag jacket in question was manufactured by Kagasaki. The jacket was attached by a pin to the motorcycle and designed so that, whenever the rider was thrown, the pin would detach. The jacket was designed so that, when the pin detached, the jacket would inflate and prevent serious injuries to the person wearing it.

(2) The Plaintiff was driving Davidson's motorcycle within the minimum speed limit of 15 miles per hour and the maximum speed limit of 35 miles per hour. He was driving the motorcycle during daylight at around 4:00 p.m. on a public, single-lane road called Easy Street in the City of Arcadia, State of Illyria, which intersects with Dangerous Drive ("The Intersection"). The Intersection is controlled by a traffic light. On the same day and at the same time described in the preceding paragraph, Hurry was operating her car on Dangerous Drive in the right-hand lane of the two lanes heading north. Plaintiff Rex file suit on

391

February 15, 2019, and served Defendant Hurry a week prior to the filing of the Third-Party Claim herein. Plaintiff Rex alleges negligence of Hurry in the collision, which Hurry has denied in an Answer filed contemporaneously with this Third-Party Claim.

(3) The Plaintiff and his motorcycle collided with the side of Hurry's car. The Plaintiff was thrown over the car onto the asphalt. Plaintiff was wearing a new state-of-the-art motorcycle airbag jacket sold with the motorcycle as standard equipment. The manufacturer of the airbag jacket was Kagasaki. It advertises the jacket as an essential safety device that will inflate immediately when a rider is thrown from a motorcycle and protect him from serious trauma. The motorcycle jacket worn by Plaintiff did not inflate even though he was thrown from the bike and the pin detached from the motorcycle.

Hurry's Contribution Claim Against Kagasaki

(4) Hurry incorporates and realleges the previous allegations by reference.

(5) Kagasaki, advertises that its motorcycle airbag jacket is the only state-of-the art motorcycle safety device designed to inflate, without any action taken by the rider, whenever the rider is thrown from the bike. According to the Kagasaki, the airbag jacket is designed to prevent the rider from incurring significant injuries during an accident. The airbag jacket did not inflate when Plaintiff was thrown from the bike.

(6) Kagasaki has a duty to use ordinary care in the manufacture of its motorcycle airbag jacket, including but not limited to manufacturing the jackets in a manner to prevent bodily injury.

(7) Kagasaki breached its duty either by failing to design the airbag jacket so that it would inflate when the rider was ejected and/or by defectively manufacturing this jacket so that the air bag jacket did not operate properly. Kagasaki's breach of duty proximately resulted in the injuries to Plaintiff for which he has sued Hurry. Therefore, Kagasaki is a tortfeasor responsible for Plaintiff's injuries.

Contribution

(8) Hurry incorporates and realleges the previous allegations by reference.

(9) Although Hurry has denied liability to the Plaintiff, to the extent that Hurry is nevertheless held liable to the Plaintiff, then Kagasaki is liable to Hurry for all or part of any judgment entered for Plaintiff against Hurry. Although Hurry has denied liability to Plaintiff, if she is found to be liable as a tortfeasor to Plaintiff, Kagasaki is a joint tortfeasor jointly and severally responsible for any injuries to Plaintiff, under principles of contribution.

WHEREFORE, Hurry moves the Court to enter judgment against Kagasaki, Inc. for all or part of any damages awarded to Brad T. Rex to the extent that Ena Hurry is held liable to Brad T. Rex and enter a judgment against Kagasaki for its proportional share of the judgment; award such other costs, prejudgment interests, and other relief as the Court deems appropriate; and such other relief as the Court deems just.

/s/_____

Of Counsel

392

Dee Fender, Esq.
1000 Liberty Street
Arcadia, Illyria, 23464
757-625-5000
deefender@gmail.com
Counsel for Ena Hurry

CERTIFICATE OF SERVICE

I, Dee Fender, hereby certify that on this 8th day of February, 2019, I mailed appropriate copies of the Third-Party Summons and Complaint to the Secretary of State of Illyria, with all required fees and charges and papers, so as to be sent by the Secretary under applicable law by certified mail to Third-Party Defendant, Kagasaki Motors, Inc. at the address in the caption of this Complaint, and mailed by first-class United States mail this Third-Party Complaint to counsel for Plaintiff, Jim Justice, Esq., 111 Liberty Street, Arcadia, Illyria 23464.

/s/ _____
Of Counsel

Follow-Up Questions and Comments

1. Is the above third-party complaint a proper one? Why or why not?

2. What authorizes Hurry to sue Kagasaki, Inc.? Should not it be Rex, if anyone, who sues Kagasaki, Inc.?

3. What does Hurry's counsel need to do to make Kagasaki, Inc. a party?

4. What are the deadlines for her to effectively bring Kagasaki into the suit.?

Practice Problems

Practice Problem 14-6
Mel (VA Citizen) sues PowerU, Inc. (NC Citizen), an electrical utility serving the local area, after a crane in which Mel was operating came into contact with high voltage lines that were, according to Mel, not sufficiently high and distant enough from the building on the work site. After responding to Mel's complaint, PowerU brought a third-party claim against Steel-N-Motion, Inc. (NC Citizen), the crane manufacturer involved in the accident, contending that its negligent design created higher risks of contact with utility lines and that, if PowerU is found liable to Mel for all or part of the damages he seeks, then Steel-N-Motion is liable to PowerU for all or part of any amount for which PowerU is held liable to Mel. Is PowerU's claim a proper third-party claim under Rule 14? What type of third-party claim is PowerU bringing here? Is there a jurisdictional basis for this third-party claim?

Practice Problem 14-7
Ed Employee was an independent contractor asked by Woody, Inc., a lumber company, to cut timber in a certain area. Ed signed a contract in which Woody, Inc. agreed to indemnify him and hold him

harmless if the timber he cut turned out to belong to someone else and led to a suit. Part of the timber Ed ended up cutting was on Larry Landowner's property. Larry sued Ed for compensation for the loss of such timber. Ed in turn brought a third-party claim against Woody, Inc. on the ground that, if Ed was liable to Larry for all or part of any amount it sued him on, then Woody, Inc. was liable to Ed for any such amounts. Is this a proper third-party claim under Rule 14? What type of claim is Ed bringing here?

Practice Problem 14-8

Dave (NC Citizen) told Bruce (TX citizen) that he ought to contract with Amory's Auction House, Inc. (VA citizen). According to Dave, Bruce could make a lot of money supplying second-hand furniture and other items to the company, especially because Amory's Auction House was not too picky about what it would sell.

Bruce entered an agreement with Amory's Auction House that required him to provide a certain quota of items each month. Bruce should have read the agreement more carefully because it gave Amory's Auction House the discretion to accept or refuse whatever Bruce provided. Bruce believed a great deal of the items he offered were just fine, while the Auction House disagreed. Bruce failed to meet his quota and the Auction House lost money because it had switched to Bruce rather than another provider. The Auction House sued Bruce for breach of contract. Bruce brought a third-party claim against Dave on the ground that Dave had misled him and ought to pay all or part of any amount for which Bruce is held liable. Is this a proper third-party claim under Rule 14? If so, is there a jurisdictional basis for the claim?

D. Ability of Defendants as Claimants to Use Rule 18 and Rule 20

When we first addressed Rule 18 joinder of claims and Rule 20 joinder of parties in Chapter 14, we did so in the context of plaintiffs joining claims against a defendant (Rule 18) and plaintiffs joining two or more parties as defendants (Rule 20). Recall now what was emphasized at the outset of *the present* chapter. The Federal Rules are written in such a way that, so long as a litigant becomes a claimant, that litigant can rely on Rule 18 and Rule 20.

Thus, if a defendant has a counterclaim or cross-claim, for instance, the defendant can join "as many claims as he has against the opposing party." Thus, a defendant asserting a cross-claim who has other claims against the cross-claim defendant, can join such claims under Rule 18.

Likewise, Rule 20 allows a defendant to join in one action any defendants to the defendant's claim (counterclaim, cross-claim, etc.) if the right to relief arises from the same transaction or occurrence or series of transactions or occurrences.

Practice Problem

Practice Problem 14-9

Creditor (TN citizen) sues Debtor (North Carolina citizen) for failing to pay a debt of $90,000. Debtor has on another occasion been harassed by the same Creditor because the Creditor called the Debtor at home repeatedly in the evenings and on the weekends seeking repayment of the debt, all in violation of the Federal Fair Debt Collections Act. When Creditor sues Debtor, Debtor brings a counterclaim for the Fair Debt Collections Act violation. We know that this is a legitimate cross-claim, supported by jurisdiction. What if the Creditor tells a third party that Debtor engaged in criminal activity, causing damage to debtor's reputation of at least $100,000? Could Debtor bring that additional claim under Rule 18? What would be the jurisdictional basis?

Practice Problem 14-10

Deanne (Virginia citizen) was driving a car owned by Don (North Carolina citizen), who had been warned of a defect in the brakes but had failed to have the breaks fixed. When the brakes failed, Deanne ran into Peg (Tennessee citizen) and injured her. Peg sues Deanne seeking $100,000 for negligence in following her car too closely and Don for negligence in failing to maintain his vehicle properly. Deanne, who was also injured, sues Don (South Carolina citizen) for $100,000 for negligence in failing to maintain his vehicle and failing to warn her of the defect, seeking recovery for her injuries. She also sues Mike Mechanic (South Carolina citizen), for negligence in Mike's work on Don's car. Because Don said he took the car in to have the brakes worked on, and Deanne asserts the brakes failed, Deanne can plausibly allege a claim that the mechanic was a joint tortfeasor from whom she can claim damages for her injuries and, potentially, contribution if she is held liable to Peg. Can Deanne join the mechanic under Rule 20? Is there a jurisdictional basis for this joined party?

CHAPTER 15:
DISCOVERY—THE BATTLE FOR INFORMATION

I. How the Topics in this Chapter Fit in the Overall Progress of a Civil Action

Below is a diagram of the stages of a civil action showing where the topics addressed in this chapter fall in the progress of a case.

Figure 15-1

Cause of Action (events leading to suit)	Pre-Filing Tasks (items to begin representation, interviewing, and related matters)	Choice of Forum (subject matter jurisdiction, removal, personal jurisdiction, and venue)	Notice and Service of Process (completing the process of ensuring the forum court can enter a valid judgment)	Pleading the Case and Joinder of Claims and Parties (including supplemental jurisdiction)

Responding to Claims by Motion or by Answer	**Discovery (developing proof to establish claims and learn your adversary's case)**	Right to Jury (pretrial motions and practice)	Final Pretrial Conference (events within last month before trial)	Trial (procedures and motions during trial)	Verdict	Post-Trial Motions (motions for a new trial and/or judgment as a matter of law)	Appeal

At this stage of the litigation, the parties are "at issue." Those asserting claims, including the plaintiff and, possibly, the defendant in a counterclaim, cross-claim, or third-party claim, have received answers that take issue with the allegations seeking relief on a claim. Only a factfinder can resolve the issues—i.e., determine whether the claims are proved, whether and what relief is appropriate, and make decisions reflecting such determinations. However, a case does not go to trial until the parties have had their opportunity to develop their case by gathering information to prepare for trial.

The tools of discovery are the means by which a party collects information and documents, pins down witness' testimony, and otherwise prepares for trial. While each party will have their own testimony they can offer, or perhaps testimony from an expert witness or another source other than the discoverable materials of the opponent, she still needs to rely on the tools of discovery to obtain information from the opposing party and other non-party witnesses. The litigant who knows how to use the discovery tools well can learn everything she needs to know about the opponent's case: the facts the opponent will rely on, the documents the opponent will offer at trial, and the witnesses the opponent will call. This chapter will explain how each party can use the tools of discovery to obtain the information she needs about an opposing party's case. Once armed with the opponent's discovery responses, she can object if the opponent tries to offer evidence, documents, or witnesses at trial that were not disclosed in response to discovery. In short, the first goal of discovery is to gather evidence to support one's claims or defenses— indeed, discovery is where claims and defenses are built. However, the second and equally important goal is building a record of your opponent's responses in order to protect yourself and your client from surprise at trial.

"You cannot win cases in discovery, but you sure can lose them there," many seasoned trial lawyers like to say. That is because attorneys must gather information and facts with the goal of successfully winning over a judge or jury should the case go to trial. However, because a claim cannot prevail until trial, discovery is a necessary (though not sufficient) means to that end. If a lawyer fails to develop sufficient evidence in the course of discovery to support each element of the client's claims, an opponent's summary judgment motion will expose those flaws. "A chain is only as strong as its weakest link" is another refrain of experienced litigators. A party could have great evidence on three elements of a claim, but if the claim requires four elements to be proven, that fourth element may be the weak link that breaks the chain if not properly shown.

Your plan must be to both evaluate your case and to determine how to build it. Typically, the burden of proof in civil cases is proof by a preponderance of the evidence.[576] Thus, your client's evidence must convince the factfinder that each of the elements of her claim is, more likely than not, true. Or, simply put, if the plaintiffs' evidence sits on one side of the scale, and the defendants' evidence sits on the other side, the scale must tip (even if only slightly) in your client's favor to win. Defenses raised by the opponent must also be considered. Although a party asserting a defense bears the burden of proving that defense, your client will want to develop evidence showing that the opponent's defenses lack merit.

Although discovery may seem tedious, it is anything but tedious in the hands of a skillful lawyer. An experienced and proficient lawyer intentionally evaluates the case at the outset, determines the proof needed to prevail, and then goes after that proof. Such a lawyer anticipates at the outset of her case what discovery she will need to prove it. The lawyer may rely on some of her own witnesses or documents, but she will pursue discovery to, at minimum, determine whether she can bolster her case with evidence from the opponent, such as documents only within the opponent's possession or witnesses identified by the opponent that otherwise would not have been known. The strategic use of discovery lies in knowing what one wants—in having a plan—before even beginning the discovery process. Moreover, the skillful advocate knows that there are advantages and disadvantages to each discovery tool. She will know that there is an optimal sequence in which to pursue discovery. She will know not only how to develop her case but how to obtain discovery responses that require the opponent to identify all facts, documents, and witnesses on which she will rely.

In addition, appreciating the strategic value of discovery, the best lawyers also show persistence. Discovery will test a lawyer's resolve as much as any other part of the case—probably more. A new lawyer would be well-advised to cultivate tenacity and a determination to get from one's opponent everything sought in discovery. Opposing counsel often will not answer discovery requests in a timely manner. Ask yourself: *Will you be someone who calls opposing counsel the day after you should have received responses and ask where the responses are? Will you confer with opposing counsel promptly (as you are required to do before moving to compel responses) and then follow through with a motion to compel on anything the opposing counsel has not agreed to provide? Will you file your motion to compel as early as possible, brief the motion, and get a hearing date?*

If you've decided you will handle discovery in this manner and will not accept "I'll get back to

---

[576] While the burden of proof in most civil cases is by a preponderance of the evidence, some unique civil claims, such as fraud, requires proof by clear and convincing evidence.

you" responses, or permit other delay tactics, you will most likely to be the kind of lawyer clients want to handle their case.

Facing an opponent's delays in responding to discovery, a lawyer can take the easy approach of letting inadequate responses sit. The lawyer who issued the discovery requests sooner or later gets around to moving to compel, but the delay itself is a problem. The client is entitled to resolution of her case as soon as possible. Letting an opponent get away with unresponsive discovery only encourages an opponent to hold out. By contrast, keeping pressure on the party and pressuring for full and timely responses will send a message to the opponent that the case is serious. Moreover, because your case will likely have a discovery schedule with a cutoff, delays can put you in the position of not being able to get all the discovery you need by the deadline. Once you get a response, that often prompts additional discovery requests. If you have a relentless mindset, however, you will do your client a great service. Discovery is responsible for delay, continuances, and frustration of case development more than anything else in the legal system. You will be introduced to tools below that you can use to prevent such delays. Timely and complete discovery responses are no less than what litigants are entitled to. The practice of keeping pressure on your opponent to do what she is supposed to do, and to avoid procrastination, separates the run-of-the-mill lawyers from true advocates. Overreaching, unnecessary criticism, name-calling, and other acts to denigrate a fellow attorney are not necessary in seeking your goals here. While opposing counsel may find an advocate who pressures her to comply with discovery obligations, such pressure sends a message. The lawyer seeking discovery is on top of her case and will be insisting that opposing counsel be timely and thorough in responding. We are not talking her about being overly aggressive, just about insisting on what a party is entitled to receive. Over the course of a case, the lawyer who shows that she is on top of deadlines and insisting on responses will gain leverage. That is not to say a lawyer can take a case with weak facts. Yet she can, simply by insisting that the opponent stick to the rules, become an adversary that opposing counsel would just as soon not have on the other side. In this way, the persistent and competent lawyer at times achieves settlements that limit her clients' liability or that compensate her client more than the value of the case.

II. The Scope of Discovery

Traditionally, the scope of discovery has been very broad. Parties could seek information from an opponent so long as the discovering party could make a credible argument that the information or documents could help the party in developing her case. Such unfettered discovery led to long delays in cases and significant expense. To limit the scope of discovery, Federal Rule of Civil Procedure 26 was amended in 2000 to read "[P]arties may obtain discovery regarding any non-privileged matter that is relevant to any party's claim or defense."[577] However, even in federal courts, this change has had little impact on narrowing the scope of discovery.[578] Recent amendments changed the scope-of-discovery definition—now called the "proportionality provision."

---

[577] FED. R. CIV. P. 26(b)(1). Prior to its amendment in 2000, Rule 26(b) (1) previously allowed discovery "of any matter relevant to the subject matter of the pending action."

[578] *See, e.g.*, Equal Employment Opportunity Comm'n v. Caesar's Entm't, Inc., 237 F.R.D. 428 (D. Nev. 2006) ("There seems to be a general consensus that the [2000] Amendments to Rule 26(b) 'do not dramatically alter the scope of discovery'. . . . Most courts that have addressed the issue find that the amendments to Rule 26 still contemplate liberal discovery, and that relevancy under Rule 26 is still extremely broad."); *see also* 8 CHARLES ALAN WRIGHT & ARTHUR R. MILLER, FEDERAL PRACTICE AND PROCEDURE § 2008 n.31 (2018) (collecting cases reaching the same conclusion as the Caesar's Entertainment decision).

A. Rule 26. Duty to Disclose; General Provisions Governing Discovery

1. Discovery Scope and Limits.

Scope in General. Unless otherwise limited by court order, the scope of discovery is as follows: Parties may obtain discovery regarding any nonprivileged matter that is relevant to any party's claim or defense and proportional to the needs of the case, considering the importance of the issues at stake in the action, the amount in controversy, the parties' relative access to relevant information, the parties' resources, the importance of the discovery in resolving the issues, and whether the burden or expense of the proposed discovery outweighs its likely benefit. Information within this scope of discovery need not be admissible in evidence to be discoverable.[579]

The "proportionality" concept included above has been a part of Rule 26 for some time, though not previously as prominently located in the Rules. The prior version of Federal Rule of Civil Procedure 26 concerning objections read, in relevant part:

(b) **Discovery Scope and Limits.**

Limitations on Frequency and Extent.

. . .

When Required. On motion or on its own, the court must limit the frequency or extent of discovery otherwise allowed by these rules or by local rule if it determines that:

the burden or expense of the proposed discovery outweighs its likely benefit, considering the needs of the case, the amount in controversy, the parties' resources, the importance of the issues at stake in the action, and the importance of the discovery in resolving the issues.[580]

Because proportionality has already been a part of the Rules for some time, we have precedent on how courts may interpret proportionality under the December 2015 amendment. The Judicial Conference Committee's notes accompanying the recent amendments do not provide much guidance in the practical application of proportionality. Until case law interpreting the new scope-of-discovery provision has developed, litigants can rely on cases interpreting Federal Rule 26(b) (2) (C) (iii)—the previous location of the proportionality concept. Because that provision already included limits on discovery similar to the new proportionality amendment, cases decided under this longstanding language in the Rule ought to help in advancing arguments for proportionality that limits discovery. Because some of the language in Rule 26(b) (2(C) (iii) is identical to the amended scope of discovery provisions, courts will likely be willing to follow limits on discovery imposed under the prior language of Rule 26(b) (2) (C) (iii).

---

[579] Order of the Supreme Court of the United States, April 29, 2015, transmitting Amendments to Congress.
[580] FED. R. CIV. P. 26(b) (2) (C) (iii) (effective until December 1, 2015).

In *Witt v. GC Services Limited Partnership*,[581] for instance, the United States District Court for the District of Colorado invoked "proportionality" in applying Rule 26(b) (2) (C) (iii) in ruling against the defendant in a Fair Debt Collection Practices Act suit. The court granted the plaintiff's motion to compel, but only in part, based on the principle of proportionality and the resources of the parties.[582] Specifically, the court applied one of the proportionality factors listed in Rule 26, the "importance of the issues at stake in the action," when it discussed the importance of public policy and the plaintiff "counsel's role in vindicating his client's interest" pursuant to the Fair Debt Collection Practices Act.[583] By characterizing Rule 26(b) (2) (C) (iii) as embodying proportionality even before the amendment adding proportionality to Rule 26(b), the court signaled its recognition that the principle has been in the Rules for some time now, and that the amendment simply emphasizes its significance.

Similarly, in *Tucker v. American International Group, Inc.*,[584] the United States District Court for the District of Connecticut sustained a motion to quash an overly broad subpoena served on a party with limited resources. In so ruling, the court relied on Rule 26(c) (b) (2) (C) and, like the District Court for Colorado in Witt, referred to a proportionality principle even before that term had been added.[585] The court's discussion of proportionality echoes two factors that have long been part of Rule 26's "limitations" on discovery: (a) "the parties' resources" and (b) "whether the burden or expense of the proposed discovery outweighs its likely benefit."[586] The court in Tucker weighed the high cost that the third party would have to bear in complying with the subpoena against the relative importance of the information.[587]. Other cases and resources are available to further illustrate proportionality principles in application.[588] In addition to these cases, a party seeking to avoid discovery could refer to the following Judicial Conference Committee Report, which states:

[T]hree previous Civil Rules Committees in three different decades have reached the same conclusion as the current Committee – that proportionality is an important and necessary feature of civil litigation in federal courts. And yet . . . proportionality is still lacking in too many cases. The Committee's purpose in returning the proportionality factors to Rule 26(b) (1) is to make them an explicit component of the scope of discovery, requiring parties and courts alike to consider them when pursuing discovery and resolving discovery disputes.[589]

Nevertheless, you should realize that discovery is not restricted to the search for evidence that will be admissible at trial. Even if the information or documents sought would not be admissible under the rules

---

[581] 90 Fed. R. Serv. 3d (Callaghan) 801 (D. Colo. 2014).

[582] *See id.* at 815 (refusing to "condone discovery requests that ignore principles of proportionality, reasonableness, convenience, and common sense.").

[583] *Id.*

[584] 281 F.R.D. 85 (D. Conn. 2012).

[585] *See id.* at 91 ("Under Rule 26(b) (2) (C), courts impose a proportionality test to weigh the interests of the parties to determine whether discovery, even if relevant, should be allowed to proceed. Thus, pursuant to Rule 26(b) (2) (C), the court may limit or deny discovery.").

[586] *Id.* at 91, n.14.

[587] *Id.* at 98–99

[588] *See, e.g.*, Chen-Oster v. Goldman, Sachs & Co., 285 F.R.D. 294 (2012) (applying proportionality to overly broad requests for electronic sources of information); see also John L. Carroll, *Proportionality in Discovery: A Cautionary Tale*, 32 CAMPBELL REV. 455 (2010) (providing helpful analysis of proportionality tools and how to use them); SEDONA CONFERENCE, COMMENTARY ON PROPORTIONALITY IN ELECTRONIC DISCOVERY, 11 SEDONA CONF. J. 289 (2010) (discussing best practices in proportionality for electronic discovery issues).

[589] JUDICIAL CONFERENCE OF THE U.D., REP. OF THE JUDICIAL CONFERENCE COMMITTEE ON RULES OF PRACTICE AND PROCEDURE, App. B at 8 (Sept. 2014).

of evidence, a discovering party can obtain such information or documents. Unless the courts radically change the approach to discovery, the discovering party need only show that the information or documents could reasonably lead to admissible evidence. Also, because a primary purpose of discovery is to narrow the issues in the case, the parties can pursue discovery on matters beyond the pleadings. In other words, while the 2015 amendment may limit more effectively than in the past parties who engage in extensive discovery, courts are unlikely to redefine the scope of that which is discoverable.

Following is a decision that reflects the approach courts to date have been taking with the new version of Rule 26.

STATE FARM MUTUAL AUTOMOBILE INSURANCE CO. v. FAYDA
United States District Court for the Southern District of New York, 2015
No. 14CIV9792WHPJCF, 2015 WL 7871037

JAMES C. FRANCIS IV, United States Magistrate Judge

In this action, plaintiff State Farm Mutual Automobile Insurance Company ("State Farm") alleges that various healthcare providers, including defendants Arkady Kiner and Contemporary Acupuncture P.C. (together, the "Kiner Defendants"), submitted fraudulent insurance claims for services that were not medically necessary. State Farm has filed a motion to compel the Kiner Defendants to produce financial records as well as documents from other acupuncture practices he controls. The motion is granted.
BACKGROUND

New York law requires an automobile insurer, like State Farm, to provide its insureds with certain personal injury protection benefits, known as "no-fault benefits," which include up to $50,000 in coverage for various healthcare expenses. An insured may assign his right to such benefits to a healthcare provider, who then submits claims directly to the appropriate insurer to collect payment. Here, State Farm alleges a racketeering enterprise operated out of a shared medical facility at 100 Dyckman Street in Manhattan in which the defendants, including the Kiner Defendants, submitted bills for services that either were not performed or were not medically necessary. The allegedly fraudulent conduct "was the product of an alleged 'predetermined treatment protocol'" pursuant to which patients were not legitimately "examined, diagnosed, or treated in accord with legitimate medical standards." The Kiner Defendants are named in counts alleging fraud; violation of the Racketeering Influenced Corrupt Organizations Act ("RICO"),[590] based on mail fraud; RICO conspiracy; and unjust enrichment.

The complaint explains that the defendant healthcare providers gained access to patients by paying kickbacks, sometimes disguised as rent for the subleasing of space at the facility, to non-physicians, including defendant Stanislav Lentsi, who actually controlled the facility and its main tenants' medical practice. Discovery already produced indicates that Contemporary Acupuncture paid the entities from which it rented space an amount far in excess of the purported rent, made payments to certain business entities at the direction of Mr. Lentsi, and wrote checks totaling over $160,000 to a check-cashing outfit that "was at the center of multiple indictments concerning the avoidance of currency reporting requirements and unlawful laundering of proceeds from healthcare fraud. In addition, there is evidence that Mr. Kiner provided an interest-free loan of $30,000—which has not been re-paid—to a co-defendant to start the medical practice from which Contemporary Acupuncture allegedly leases space. Finally, at his deposition,

---

[590] 18 U.S.C. § 1961 et seq..

Mr. Lentsi asserted his Fifth Amendment privilege in response to questions regarding whether Mr. Kiner paid kickbacks and whether Mr. Lentsi shared in the proceeds of Contemporary Acupuncture.

State Farm seeks bank records for bank accounts in Mr. Kiner's name, Mr. Kiner's tax returns for the years 2009 through the present, and information related to professional corporations and healthcare practices other than Contemporary Acupuncture, including "(a) agreements, including leases regarding activities at [these other practices]; (b) documents reflecting or relating to payments relating to such agreements; and (c) transcripts of testimony" from examinations under oath. The Kiner Defendants object, arguing that the information is both irrelevant and private.

DISCUSSION

Legal Standard

The 2015 amendments to the Federal Rules of Civil Procedure "govern in all proceedings in civil cases" commenced after December 1, 2015, and, "insofar as just and practicable, all proceedings [ ] pending" on that date. Order re: Amendments to Federal Rules of Civil Procedure (April 29, 2015). No party has argued that the application of the amended rules to this dispute is unfair or impracticable, and I find no reason that they should not be applied to this dispute.

The amendments to Rule 26(b) (1) allow discovery of any nonprivileged matter that is relevant to any party's claim or defense and proportional to the needs of the case, considering the importance of the issues at stake in the action, the amount in controversy, the parties' relative access to relevant information, the parties' resources, the importance of the discovery in resolving the issues, and whether the burden or expense of the proposed discovery outweighs its likely benefit.

As the advisory committee notes, the proportionality factors have been restored to their former position in the subsection "defining the scope of discovery," where they had been located prior to the 1993 amendments to the rules. Relevance is still to be "construed broadly to encompass any matter that bears on, or that reasonably could lead to other matter that could bear on" any party's claim or defense. However, the amended rule is intended to "encourage judges to be more aggressive in identifying and discouraging discovery overuse"[591] by emphasizing the need to analyze proportionality before ordering production of relevant information. The burden of demonstrating relevance remains on the party seeking discovery, and the newly-revised rule "does not place on the party seeking discovery the burden of addressing all proportionality considerations." In general, when disputes are brought before the court, "the parties' responsibilities [ ] remain the same" as they were under the previous iteration of the rules, so that the party resisting discovery has the burden of showing undue burden or expense.

The July 21, 2015 Order

State Farm repeatedly contends I have already found this information to be discoverable and that therefore the law of the case doctrine requires its production. Previously, State Farm requested similar information from defendants Yuri Fayda, M.D., Dyckman Neighborhood Medical, P.C., and Hadassah Orenstein, M.D. I found that tax records of Dr. Orenstein, bank records of Dr. Orenstein and Dr. Fayda, and information regarding health care practices by defendants at locations other than 100 Dyckman Street were relevant and discoverable. However, State Farm argued in part that the information was relevant to show that Dyckman Neighborhood Medical was not owned by either Dr. Fayda or Dr. Orenstein, but, rather, by Mr. Lentsi, who is not a physician. This would assertedly establish that the medical practice was

---

[591] FED. R. CIV. P. 26(b)(1) advisory committee's notes to 2015 amendment.

"illegally incorporated and ineligible to bill for services, and every bill it submitted to State Farm representing that its services were reimbursable was false."

As the Kiner Defendants point out, State Farm does not allege that Contemporary Acupuncture is similarly illegally incorporated. Thus, the Kiner Defendants are not situated similarly to Dr. Orenstein and Dr. Fayda, so that the July 21 Order does not mandate the outcome here.

Bank Records and Tax Returns

State Farm argues that the bank records and tax returns are "crucial" to showing that the medical providers at the facility "paid kickbacks for access to patients, and that treatment was not provided because it was medically necessary but because money was paid to the people who controlled the patients." According to the plaintiff, the financial records sought will enable them to show that the Kiner Defendants were financially dependent on the individuals who referred the patients to the practice by demonstrating that the amount the Kiner Defendants earned by treating these patients "represented a significant portion of [their] overall annual compensation." This, in turn, would provide a motive for their participation in the alleged scheme to submit fraudulent bills for medically-unnecessary treatment.

Case law indicates that evidence of a defendant's motive for participation in a fraudulent medical billing scheme is relevant to such claims and that financial documents like these are discoverable to establish that motive.[592] The Kiner Defendants, however, argue that this argument is "inane. The motive for fraud is money. It is a given. There is no need to look at money in Kiner['s] and his family's financial records and say, in effect, 'hey I see money—that is the motive for fraud.'" The concession that money can be a motive for participation in fraud is well-taken. Having admitted this, however, it is unclear why the Kiner Defendants would imagine that discovery tending to establish such motive—that is, discovery revealing sources and amounts of the Kiner Defendants' profits—is irrelevant. It would be an unlikely trial strategy for the plaintiff to argue to the fact-finder that the Kiner Defendants participated in the fraud and RICO enterprise for financial gain but then fail to put on evidence of such gain.

In addition, the plaintiff asserts it has uncovered evidence of complex financial transactions that may have been used "to conceal assets or income." As State Farm argues, such evidence could be used to show consciousness of guilt. Consciousness of guilt, in turn, could be used to establish the Kiner Defendants' intent to defraud (an element of a fraud claim under New York law . . . and an element of mail fraud . . ., which is the predicate offense for State Farm's civil RICO claim. Thus, the requested financial records are relevant.

The Kiner Defendants also argue that they should not be required to produce the records because the discovery is disproportionate to the needs of the case and because the records are private. Neither objection succeeds.

Rule 26(b) (1) instructs parties and courts to evaluate whether the benefit of the discovery sought is proportional to the burden of producing it, taking into account issues like access, importance, and available resources.[593] The Kiner Defendants allege that State Farm paid them approximately $12,000 and

---

[592] *See, e.g.*, State Farm Mutual Automobile Insurance Co. v. CPT Medical Services, P.C., 375 F. Supp. 2d 141, 155-56 (E.D.N.Y. 2005) (financial records "may be relevant to establishing that defendants profited from their willingness" to order medically-unnecessary test.).

[593] FED. R. CIV. P. 26(b) (1); *see also* In re Weatherford International Securities Litigation, No. 11 Civ. 1646, 2013 WL 2355451, at *5 (S.D.N.Y. May 28, 2013) ("A proportionality analysis requires the court to balance the value of the requested discovery against the cost of its production.").

that the discovery requested is therefor of little value to the case. However, they have failed to rebut State Farm's showing that the financial records are relevant and material to its case against them. Nor have they established that the plaintiff has an alternative source for the information or that producing it would be particularly burdensome.[594] Therefore, their proportionality argument fails.

Federal courts regularly entertain objections to discovery requests based on a "constitutionally-based right of privacy." . . . Nevertheless, a court will order tax returns and other sensitive financial information produced where it is relevant to the action and there is a compelling need for the documents because the information is not otherwise readily available. . . . "[T]he party resisting disclosure should bear the burden of establishing alternative sources for the information."

State Farm has demonstrated the relevance of this information. As noted above, however, the Kiner Defendants have not attempted to show that there are alternative sources for the information. Rather, they, through their counsel, merely insist that the information is sensitive:

Let me be straight—I would not want an organization like State Farm and its buff [sic] investigators and cadre of attorneys and the [National Insurance Crime Bureau] looking at my personal finances. The lingerie I may have purchased for my wife; my liquor store purchases; the possible purchases of other romantic enhancements — even Viagra, etc. Even the football equipment I purchase for my son—I do not want an organization like State Farm soiling my family. The Kiner family feels the same way.

They are also concerned because among the accounts for which bank records are sought are a joint account held by Mr. Kiner and his parents and a joint account held by Mr. Kiner, his wife, and their son. Neither of these objections constitutes a reason to wall off this relevant information, especially since it will be designated confidential pursuant to the protective order entered in this case.

Information About Other Practices

State Farm asserts it is entitled to production of "(a) agreements, including leases, regarding activities at [Mr.] Kiner's other practices; (b) documents reflecting or relating to payments relating to such agreements; and (c) transcripts of testimony." It argues that the testimony sought is relevant to whether unnecessary medical treatment like that alleged in the complaint was provided at other practices. As to the agreements and financial documents, State Farm notes that if they reveal financial arrangements similar to those at the 100 Dyckman Street facility it would tend to show that [Mr.] Kiner did not provide care because it was medically necessary, but because of the financial relationships he had with lay 'gatekeepers' who controlled the locations. Conversely, if the financial arrangements were different at other locations because reimbursement was paid by a source other than No-Fault benefits—or the care patients received at other locations was different—this would also support State Farm's theory, that the scheme at 100 Dyckman was designed to take full advantage of the No-Fault system.

The Kiner Defendants again contend that this information is not relevant because the fraud alleged against them deals only with whether treatment they performed at the 100 Dyckman Street facility was medically necessary. However, as noted, State Farm argues that comparing the treatment and financial

---

[594] See FED. R. CIV. P. 26(b)(1) advisory committee's notes to 2015 amendment (noting that "the [2015 amendments] do[ ] not place on the party seeking discovery the burden of addressing all proportionality considerations" because, for example, "a party requesting discovery . . .may have little information about the burden or expense of responding"); see also In re Weatherford, 2013 WL 2355451, at *5 (ordering discovery where parties opposing production "have not shown that the information sought is not sufficiently germane, nor, on the other side of the scale, have they provided any specific evidence of burden").

arrangements at other facilities with those at 100 Dyckman Street may provide evidence as to the fraud alleged against the Kiner Defendants in the complaint. The Kiner Defendants further object to production of transcripts of "examinations under oath." According to them, these examinations are specific between the insurance company that insured the patient and the applicant for benefits. [They] involve[ ] patient information and confidentiality since [they are] compelled. It is generally understood that insurance companies after taking [an examination under oath] are not free to send the transcript . . .to another insurance company. That would be grounds for sanction by the Department of Finance. The Kiner Defendants cite no authority for this proposition. However, even assuming that it is true, patient confidentiality can be preserved by redacting patient names and by designating the records as confidential pursuant to the protective order.

Future Cooperation

Counsel for the Kiner Defendants states that his working relationship with counsel for the plaintiff "has grown quite contentious." There is disheartening evidence in the submissions made in connection with this motion that the relationship between counsel has eroded. The rhetoric of the Kiner Defendants opposition brief is overblown and intemperate, characterizing State Farm's arguments as "duplicitous and deceitful," "desperate," "obtuse," "delusional," and "inane," and accusing the plaintiff, its investigators, and its attorneys of attempting to "soil[]" Mr. Kiner's family. For its part, State Farm asserts that because the Kiner Defendants are "willing to produce medical records from [o]ther [p]ractices," they have "implicitly conced[ed]" that treatment at other locations is relevant." Treating as a "concession" an opponent's cooperation in resolving a discovery dispute, while not an ethical violation as the Kiner Defendants imply is both a losing argument and a short-sighted strategy that is likely to curtail cooperation among counsel. Indeed, counsel for the Kiner Defendants asserts that this conduct is "unprofessional" and that he is "well within [his] rights to never negotiate with [the] [p]laintiff's counsel about any and every dispute that may arise." Of course, counsel is mistaken. The federal rules require, and this Court expects, that counsel will cooperate to resolve any future disputes and will behave respectfully toward each other and toward the Court.

CONCLUSION

For the foregoing reasons, State Farm's motion to compel is granted. The Kiner Defendants' request for oral argument is denied. The requested documents shall be produced within fourteen days of the date of this order.

So Ordered.

Follow-Up Questions and Comments

1. You may have noticed that a "United States Magistrate Judge" wrote the decision in State Farm Mutual Automobile Insurance Company v. Fayda. Since the Federal Magistrates Act of 1968,[595] Magistrate Judges have become a major part of federal practice, particularly in dealing with pretrial matters such as discovery disputes and motions. Since the Magistrate Act, several Rules have been adopted dealing with Magistrates, each of which is designed to implement the authority provided by the Magistrate Act. Such authority is crucial because United States Judges are typically nominated by the President of the United States and confirmed by the Senate. These are called "Article III judges." United States Magistrate judges are not Article III judges. They are appointed

---

[595] 18 U.S.C.A. §§ 3401 to 3402, 3060; 28 U.S.C.A. §§ 604, 631–39.

by the judges in the district court in which they serve. If the statute and rules did not ensure review by Article III judges of rulings on matters referred to a Magistrate Judge, a constitutional violation would likely occur. Thus, Federal Rule of Civil Procedure 71 allows parties to file objections to any ruling on a matter referred to a Magistrate Judge within 14 days of the Magistrate Judge's order. If such objections are filed, then a United States Judge will review the Magistrate Judge's rulings on a clearly erroneous basis. Litigants should know that, if they wish a Magistrate Judge to make the final decision on any matter, or to hear the entirety of a case, all parties must consent to Magistrate Judge jurisdiction. Note, as a practical matter, always address a Magistrate Judge, as "Judge" not "Magistrate Judge." If ever in doubt, your safest course is to refer to any judge or magistrate as "Your Honor."

2. How does the court determine whether the documents sought is discoverable by the plaintiff?

3. How does the court evaluate proportionality?

4. Although the opinion is not as clear as it could be, each defendant is at best a moderately sized business, e.g. an acupuncture facility. Could each defendant have done a better job of arguing lack of proportional resources—specifically, that each had significantly fewer financial resources than State Farm—to preclude or limit discovery?

5. In the section of the opinion entitled "Future Cooperation," you read the court's characterization of the way counsel handled discovery. What lessons can you learn from the court's reaction to the way plaintiffs' counsel presented their client's position? Ill-informed laypersons and lawyers would consider the kind of aggressive stances and language that plaintiffs' counsel used to be "zealous advocacy." How did the advocacy affect the court's rulings?

Practice Problem

Practice Problem 15-1

Say that a plaintiff is injured in a wreck caused by a hazardous condition created by the State. Plaintiff sues under the State's Tort Claims Act. Assume the plaintiff's request for production of documents to the State includes the following request.

"Please produce all documents showing the addresses of persons who live on Route 3 (the site of the accident) and who may use Route 3 and have observed the hazardous condition prior to the accident."

How do you think a court would handle it under the proportionality test now applied? The information could certainly lead to information on which the plaintiff could develop evidence. What if you were applying the new Rule 26(b) (1) standard? What criteria would you consider in determining whether this request would be proportionate to the needs of the case? Would you need to see whether the plaintiff could obtain the same information through less cumbersome, time-consuming efforts? Would not questions such as the following need to be answered just to get a handle on the scope of the request (a) how many persons are we talking about?; (b) is Route 3 one mile or 50 miles long? In short, a discovery request may seem harmless and one to which you can respond—until you must do the hard work of gathering the information or documents. That's when you will wish, if you did not, you objected to the discovery in a timely fashion. Only then can you argue that the request is not proportional to the needs of the case and other objections that are permitted if true (e.g., unduly broad requests, overly burdensome requests, easier ways for the requesting party to gain the information).

---

2. Specific Tools of Discovery

We will now explore the specific means of discovery under the Federal Rules of Civil Procedure. Most requests must be initiated by one party serving on the other a discovery request, such as a request for production of documents. The exceptions are the so-called automatic disclosures required by Rule 26.

3. Automatic Disclosures

a. Initial Automatic Disclosures

Please read Federal Rule of Civil Procedure 26(a) (1). Adopted in 2000, the automatic disclosure provisions are designed to get the process of exchanging information underway without delay.[596] The four initial automatic disclosures are: (1) a computation of damages, (2) any insurance agreement that may be liable to satisfy judgment, (3) supporting witnesses, and (4) supporting documents.[597] Requiring a party to provide a computation of damages, and documents upon which the computation is based, is a valuable requirement. Although parties are supposed to produce the best damages calculations of which they are capable at the outset of litigation, the Rule does not require a party asserting a claim to have detailed damage calculations, and parties are permitted to amend.[598] Moreover, the requirement of early production of any insurance agreements that may be liable to satisfy a judgment likely helps to promote settlement. If a party has limited insurance coverage, the claimant may be less inclined to seek damages to the same degree as otherwise.

The two other automatic disclosures, of witnesses and of documents, allow counsel to see what a party considers significant to her case. Note, however, that both Rule 26(a) (1) (A) and 26(a) (1) (B) qualify the witnesses and documents that must be produced if the party "may use them to support its claims or defenses."[599] In other words, a disclosing party can know of witnesses or documents crucial to the case but which it deems to be unhelpful to its claims or defenses. If so, the party has no obligation to disclose them under the automatic disclosure provisions. That major hole in these automatic disclosure provisions requires a litigant to count on the traditional discovery tools discussed below—interrogatories, requests for production of documents, requests for admission, and depositions. If worded correctly by the party sending the written discovery request, or by asking the question at a deposition, the opponent must respond even if the witnesses identified or the documents produced hurt the opponent's case. In other words, formal discovery should identify the witnesses and the documents that the opponent both will and will not rely upon. An attorney wants all the witnesses identified and all potentially relevant documents produced, especially those that do not support an opponent's case. The reason is obvious: these are the witnesses and documents that have the most potential to support your client's case. In traditional discovery, an attorney can uncover a "smoking gun"—a litigator's phrase for a piece of evidence of great value to her client (and damaging to an opponent). Automatic disclosures, due to the phrase limiting them to witnesses or documents that "may support" a litigant's case, assure that smoking guns will not be produced through that form of discovery. Hence, formal discovery must seek all facts, witnesses, and documents related to the case.

---

[596] See FED. R. CIV. P. 26 advisory committee's note to 2000 amendment.
[597] See FED. R. CIV. P. 26(a) (1) (A).
[598] See 6-26 PATRICK E. HIGGINBOTHAM, MOORE'S FEDERAL PRACTICE AND PROCEDURE § 26.22 (2018).
[599] Id. (emphasis added).

b. Automatic Disclosures Regarding Experts

Please read Federal Rule of Civil Procedure 26(a) (2). What different types of experts does the Rule describe? What is required of an expert who is "retained or specially employed to provide expert testimony?" What is required of witnesses who, though they will provide testimony that qualifies as expert testimony, are not retained or specially employed to provide expert testimony?

You should not rely solely on Rule 26(a) (2) expert disclosures. Instead, you should make it a routine to include in interrogatories,[600] an "expert interrogatory" that effectively will get almost as much information as in an expert report. The key point to recognize is that witnesses who offer expert testimony or facts on which expert testimony is based who are not "retained or specially employed to provide expert testimony" need only provide a summary disclosure and not a full expert report. Given that, you take an unnecessary risk if you rely on automatic disclosures. Thus, you will want to serve an interrogatory asking at least for the following: (a) For all persons who will provide testimony under Federal Rules of Civil Procedure 702, 703, and 705 and/or otherwise related to matters of expert testimony, (b) the facts and/or opinions to which such witnesses may testify, and (c) and the number of times the person has testified in depositions and/or trials.

c. Automatic Final Pretrial Disclosures

Finally, please read Federal Rule of Civil Procedure 26(a) (3) which provides for so-called "final automatic pretrial disclosures." Notice that the final pretrial disclosures require a party to identify persons that the party "expects to present or those it may call if the need arises."[601] Similarly, a party has to identify documents if "the party expects to offer" them. Why do these disclosures have the same disadvantages as Rule 26(a) (1) initial disclosures? What, then, would be the safest means to ensure you had all facts, documents, and witnesses related to the case?

4. The Primary Written Forms of Discovery

After ensuring that you have a pretrial schedule that benefits your client, and that you have preserved electronic data as far as possible, an intelligent discovery plan will begin with written discovery requests.

a. Requests for Production of Documents to Parties

Please read Federal Rules of Civil Procedure 34. This Rule addresses, among other things, how to request documents or enter another's land for purposes of inspection when the request is to a party to the case. What is the procedure for making a request under this Rule? Is there any limit on the number of requests you can make here? When must the party served with the request for production respond?

Even if you cannot (or choose not to) respond to each request by the deadline, you must serve all objections to those requests by the applicable deadline. In addition, you should know that every U.S. district court has local rules. Local rules often set deadlines to object to discovery requests. Typically, the deadline for objecting imposed by local rules is before the deadline for producing documents, answering

---

[600] Interrogatories, discussed more fully below, are essentially a written question to the opponent that must be answered and signed by the answering party under oath.

[601] FED. R. CIV. P. 26(a) (3) (A) (i).

interrogatories, etc.[602] As an illustration, Local Rule 26(c) of the U.S. District Court for the Eastern District of Virginia requires objections to be served within 15 days of service of requests for production.[603] If the attorney fails to object by the applicable deadline, a party's objections will be deemed waived. That party can then be subjected to enormous burden and expense due to the simple failure to object. Why would courts, in local rules, move the objection deadline up from 30 days to 15 days? What purpose will that serve?

b. Subpoenas Duces Tecum to Nonparties

Now please read Federal Rule of Civil Procedure 45. On whom are Rule 45 subpoenas served? Why will a thorough search for documents typically involve both a request for production of documents to opposing parties and one or more subpoenas to nonparties for documents? What is the difference in the manner of serving requests for production of documents and subpoenas for documents?

By serving a subpoena for documents under Rule 45, counsel is invoking the subpoena power of the court to aid in gathering information for purposes of litigating the case. However, because that person or entity is not a party, the person or entity must be served with the subpoena duces tecum as if that person or entity were being sued.[604] In other words, counsel must serve the subpoena duces tecum through a process server. If the party fails to respond, counsel then can bring that party before the court to answer why she should not be held in contempt. More often, if the request is a broad one, the person or party served may move to quash the subpoena duces tecum and schedule a hearing. Out of that usually comes some resolution requiring the nonparty to produce at least some of what has been included in the subpoena duces tecum, though the nonparty may not be required to produce everything. Often, when such a motion to quash is filed, counsel for the nonparty and counsel issuing the subpoena can reach an agreement limiting the scope to the documents that the requesting party really needs.

---

[602] *See, e.g.*, E.D. VA., LOC. R. 26(c) (2017), http://www.vaed.uscourts.gov/localrules/Local RulesEDVA.pdf.
[603] *See id.*
[604] "Subpoena duces tecum" is the colloquial term for a subpoena requesting production of documents.

Sample Subpoena Duces Tecum

UNITED STATES DISTRICT COURT
FOR THE EASTERN DISTRICT OF VIRGINIA

Norfolk Division

[NAME]	)	
Plaintiff	)	
v.	)	Civil Action No. _____
	)	
[NAME]	)	(If action is pending in another district
Defendant	)	District of _____)
	)	

SUBPOENA TO PRODUCE DOCUMENTS, INFORMATION, OR OBJECTS OR TO PERMIT INSPECTION OF PREMISES IN A CIVIL ACTION

To: _____

Production: YOU ARE COMMANDED to produce at the time, date, and place set forth below the following documents, electronically stored information, or objects, and permit their inspection, copying, testing, or sampling of the material:

Place: _____ Date and Time:_____

Inspection of Premises: YOU ARE COMMANDED to permit entry onto the designated premises, land, or other property possessed or controlled by you at the time, date, and location set forth below, so that the requesting party may inspect, measure, survey, photograph, test, or sample the property or any designated object or operation on it.

Place: _____ Date and Time:_____

The provision of Fed. R. Civ. P. 45(c), relating to your protection as a person subject to subpoena, and Rule 45(d) and (e), relating to your duty to respond to this subpoena and the potential consequences of not doing so, are attached.

Date: _____

CLERK OF COURT
OR

_____   _____
Signature of Clerk or Deputy Clerk   Attorney's signature

The name, address, e-mail, and telephone number of the attorney representing [name of party], who issues or requests this subpoena, are: _____.[605]

---

[605] You can access the document reproduced in the text, fill in information online, and print it from the Federal Judiciary's website. *See* AO 88B-Subpoena to Produce Documents, Information, or Objects or to Permit Inspection of Premises in a Civil Action, (Feb. 1, 2014), USCOURTS.GOV,

Electronic discovery is becoming increasingly prominent in practically every type of lawsuit. Although entire texts are written on handling Electronically Stored Information (or "ESI"), and a full treatment is beyond the scope of an introductory text, some major points are worth observing. First, the protection of electronic data must be among the first items an attorney considers after filing suit (or having a suit filed against a client). The prudent lawyer will write opposing counsel at the very beginning of a case, especially if the defendant is a corporate, governmental, or similar entity that deletes e-mail on a regular basis and seek what is known as a "discovery hold." You can also request the court to issue an order preventing the destruction of electronic data or ask opposing counsel to agree to a cessation of data destruction—something typically called a "litigation hold order." You should memorialize the agreement with opposing counsel in an order and, if opposing counsel will not consent, file a motion to require a litigation hold order.

"A duty to preserve evidence exists when a party has notice that the evidence is relevant to litigation or when a party should know that the evidence may be relevant to future litigation."[606] The intentional destruction of evidence is termed "spoliation," and is recognized in some jurisdictions as a separate cause of action.[607] Most jurisdictions follow the Federal Rules, which allow for the court to impose sanctions including but not limited to dismissal of the case, default judgment, or monetary sanctions.[608] In *United States v. Phillip Morris Inc.*,[609] the court ordered Phillip Morris to pay $2,750,000.00 in sanctions for the "reckless disregard and gross indifference displayed" toward the company's duty to preserve documents for discovery.

The modern lawyer must also be familiar with "metadata"—embedded data automatically created by software that, unless the user is knowledgeable, will often go unnoticed. "Most metadata is not visible on the computer screen, does not appear on the electronic file when a copy is printed, and is often completely unknown to the person who generates the file."[610] The information stored within an electronically created document usually includes not only the identity of authors, but also dates of creation and revision, the parts that a particular author worked on, etc. See id. Such embedded information could be privileged, such as communications between an attorney and client about a contract, lease, or other document. A recent ethics opinion interpreting the American Bar Association Model Code of Professional Responsibility concluded that a party who received documents containing metadata can, unless she is aware that it was produced unintentionally, use such data freely.[611] The opinion notes that a party producing electronic data can "scrub" the data from the document or produce the document in a form that does not contain the metadata. See id. The "scrubbing" of metadata involves using a program, such as Adobe Acrobat®, to remove metadata from an electronic file. As noted below, however, the party responding to discovery typically will have to put an opponent on notice of data "withheld," such as by scrubbing.

---

http://www.uscourts.gov/sites/default/files/ao088b.pdf.

[606] Maria Perez Crist, *Preserving the Duty to Preserve: The Increasing Vulnerability of Electronic Information*, 58 S.C.L. Rev. 7, 9 (2006).

[607] *See generally* Martha J. Dawson, Electronic Discovery Today, 716 P.L.I. 7, 32–44 (2004); *cf. also* RSC Quality Measurement Co. v. IPSOS-ASI, Inc., 196 F. Supp. 2d 609, 615 (S.D. Ohio 2002) (explaining that Indiana and Ohio recognize spoliation of evidence as an intentional tort and a separate cause of action).

[608] Donald G. Gifford, *Market Share Liability Beyond Des Cases: The Solution to the Causation Dilemma in Lead Paint Litigation*, 58 S.C. L. Rev. 7, 10–11 (2007).

[609] 327 F. Supp. 2d 21, 26 (D.D.C. 2004).

[610] John K. Rabiej, *Rabieji on Native File Format and Metadata*, Emerging Issues, Aug. 4, 2008.

[611] *See* ABA Comm'n On Ethics And Prof'l Responsibility, Formal Op. 06-442 (2006).

Although this discussion is but an introduction, the significance of electronic data, its preservation, and avoiding production of privileged information in metadata are some of the issues that you should be familiar with. A good argument can be made that an attorney is not competent if she does not have sufficient information about electronic information to protect her client.

Follow-Up Questions and Comments

1. If your client allows documents to be deleted, as happens automatically in most companies' information systems, it can have significant consequences. The doctrine of "spoliation of evidence" can lead to the court's giving instructions that your client had documents that were relevant but destroyed them, and, thus, that the jury should presume the documents would have established something the opposing party needs to prove.[612] Louisiana, Florida, Montana, New Jersey, and West Virginia also recognize spoliation as an intentional tort.

2. For an interesting discussion regarding discovery of deleted electronic records, see the authorities cited in the footnote below.[613]

B. Interrogatories

You may wonder why requests for production of documents and subpoenas for documents are suggested as initial tools to use before interrogatories. The lawyer seeking discovery needs to remember that there is an optimal sequence of seeking information. Interrogatories can be among the first formal discovery, but even if interrogatories are asked, requests for production of documents and subpoenas should go out simultaneously. The goal is to use these tools intelligently to gather information to prepare for depositions. Although document requests and subpoenas are discussed first, they may be served simultaneously with interrogatories.

Please read Federal Rule of Civil Procedure 33. What is the limit on number of interrogatories? On whom are interrogatories served? Look at the sample Interrogatories below. What do you observe about how they are constructed and what they seek? According to Rule 33, how long does the party on whom interrogatories have been served have to answer? What does it mean that the answers must be "under oath"? What consequences does a party face if she answers falsely under oath?

As with requests for production of documents, objections to interrogatories must be filed either within 30 days or, if local rules require less time, then by whatever earlier date is required. In a document that combines interrogatory answers with objections to certain interrogatories, an attorney must sign as to the objections. However, she can sign the interrogatories "as to objections only," to protect herself by limiting the scope of her signature to objections, leaving to the client the job of signing to verify answers.

---

[612] *See generally* MARTHA J. DAWSON, ELECTRONIC DISCOVERY TODAY, 716 P.L.I. 7, 32–44 (2004); *cf. also* RSC Quality Measurement Co. v. IPSOS-ASI, Inc., 196 F. Supp. 2d 609, 615 (S.D. Ohio 2002) (explaining that Indiana and Ohio recognize spoliation of evidence as an intentional tort and a separate cause of action).

[613] *See* Marjorie A. Shields, Discovery of Deleted E-mail and Other Deleted Electronic Records, 27 A.L.R. 6th 565 (2007). *See also* MARTHA J. DAWSON, ELECTRONIC DISCOVERY TODAY, 716 P.L.I. 7, 32–44 (2004); STANLEY M. GIBSON, LITIGATION HOLDS: TURNING ON—AND OFF—THE SWITCH TO AVOID SANCTIONS AND COSTLY E-DISCOVERY BLUNDERS, 766 P.L.I. 151 (2007).

Just as with responses, you must serve objections to interrogatories by the deadline imposed by the applicable jurisdiction. Failure to observe a deadline to serve an objection typically results in waiver of one's right to object.

Below is the beginning of a sample set of interrogatories on behalf of a plaintiff:

Sample Interrogatories

IN THE UNITED STATES DISTRICT COURT
FOR THE DISTRICT OF ILLYRIA

[PARTY NAME], Plaintiff,	)))	
v.	))	Case No. 123456
[PARTY NAME], Defendant,	)))	

INTERROGATORIES

Pursuant to Federal Rule of Civil Procedure 33, Plaintiff requests the Defendant to answer the following interrogatories.

Definitions[614]

. . .

"Document(s)" means all materials within the full scope of Fed. R. Civ. P. 34 including but not limited to: all writings and recordings, including the originals and all non-identical copies, whether different from the original by reason of any notation made on such copies or otherwise (including but without limitation to, emails and attachments, correspondence, memoranda, notes, diaries, minutes, statistics, letters, telegrams, contracts, reports, studies, checks, statements, tags, labels, invoices, brochures, periodicals, telegrams, receipts, returns, summaries, pamphlets, books, interoffice and intraoffice communications, offers,

---

[614] Here, as with a request for production of documents or other tangible things, the drafting party should define "documents" or "tangible things" as broadly as possible. Many believe definitional sections of discovery requests have gotten out of hand. Some definitional sections go on for pages. The point is to ensure that the key terms used in the interrogatories, most often the term "document," comprise every kind of document that might exist— originals, copies, handwritten documents, typed documents, electronic documents of all varieties, etc. So long as the definitional section of your jurisdiction is broad enough to ensure a responding party cannot avoid responding because the interrogatory does not define the requested materials broadly enough, you should be safe. This section should also define terms such as "you" or "your" to refer to include the opposing party, any agent of the opposing party, or anyone acting on behalf of the opposing party. Likewise, the facts of the case will dictate terms that would be used repetitively in the interrogatories if you did not define them. For instance, in a personal injury case over a vehicular accident, counsel would do well to define "accident" to mean the accident on [insert date] at [insert location] involving plaintiff and defendant.].

notations of any sort of conversations, working papers, applications, permits, file papers, indices, telephone calls, meetings or printouts, teletypes, telefax, invoices, worksheets, and all drafts, alterations, modifications, changes and amendments of any of the foregoing), graphic or aural representations of any kind (including without limitation, photographs, charts, microfiche, microfilm, videotape, recordings, motion pictures, plans, drawings, surveys), and electronic, mechanical, magnetic, optical or electric records or representations of any kind (including without limitation, computer files and programs, tapes, cassettes, discs, recordings), including metadata.

Request for Production

(1) Identify any and all expert witnesses you may call at the trial of this case, regardless of whether such witnesses are persons retained by you to testify and describe the information to which each such expert has been exposed (oral communications, documents, etc.), any opinions such expert has formed, the basis or bases for any such opinions, and any reports produced by such experts. In addition, please identify (a) all documents or other materials reviewed by the expert, (b) any information provided to the expert from any person or from observation of objects, site visits, etc., (c) all tests or simulations the expert has performed and any document related to such, (d) the experts curriculum vitae, and (e) the courts in which the person has been identified as either a potential expert or testifying expert, the captions of any such lawsuits, and any reports prepared or interrogatory answers identifying her/his opinions and the basis therefor.

(2) Identify all facts supporting your allegations in paragraphs through of the Complaint, under the title "Facts Common to All Counts." Also identify all documents related to such facts and all persons with knowledge of such facts.

(3) Identify all facts supporting your allegations in paragraphs through of the Complaint, under the title "Count One." Also identify all documents related to such facts and all persons with knowledge of such facts.

(4) Identify all facts supporting your allegations in paragraphs through of the Complaint, under the title "Count Two." Also identify all documents related to such facts and all persons with knowledge of such facts.

(5) Identify all facts supporting your allegations in paragraphs through of the Complaint, under the title "Count Three." Also identify all documents related to such facts and all persons with knowledge of such facts.

(6) Identify all facts supporting your allegations in paragraphs through of the Complaint, under the title "Affirmative Defenses." Also identify all documents related to such facts and all persons with knowledge of such facts and related to such facts and all per-sons with knowledge of such facts.

[NAME OF PARTY]
/s/_____
Of Counsel

[Name of Counsel for Party][615]
Address of Counsel Tele. No., E-Mail
(and in some States, State Bar No.)

CERTIFICATE OF SERVICE

I certify that on this day of ___ , 20____ , a true copy of the foregoing INTERROGATORIES were served by first-class mail on the following:

[Insert names and addresses of all other counsel in the case]

By_____
Of Counsel

Follow-Up Questions and Comments

1. When pressed for time, attorneys sometimes sign *answers* to interrogatories for their client. Such a shortcut presents the opportunity for embarrassment, not to mention potential sanctions from the court. Notice that Federal Rule of Civil Procedure requires the party on whom Interrogatories are served to answer them under oath. If the lawyer for a client attests to the accuracy of facts, opposing counsel may even be allowed to question the lawyer in a deposition. Indeed, if it turns out that facts provided by a client but sworn by her lawyer are not true, the lawyer could be prosecuted. Therefore, the client always should be the person to swear to the accuracy of answers.

2. Unlike requests for production of documents, which are not limited in number, Rule 33 places a limit on interrogatories of 25 "including all discrete subparts."[616] How many subparts are there to Interrogatory No. 1 above? How about Interrogatory Nos. 2 through 7? Can you make an argument that the above interrogatories exceed the number of interrogatories permitted?

3. You will need to know the way the court in which you are litigating handles parts and subparts of interrogatories. In any event, a party should not send all that party's allotted interrogatories in the first set. If questions come up in discovery on which you believe a follow-up interrogatory would be appropriate, you will want to have the ability to send a supplemental interrogatory. Moreover, as noted below, interrogatories have value for limited and very specific purposes. After reading the next section on "Contention Interrogatories," ask yourself whether you can identify the information that is best uncovered through interrogatories.

---

[615] Note that counsel for a party sends interrogatories and signs them. However, answers to interrogatories are supposed to be signed by the party answering the interrogatories under oath. Counsel can only sign answers to interrogatories "as to objections only." If a lawyer signs interrogatory answers, she opens the door to opposing counsel

[616] FED R. CIV. P. 33 (a)(1).

1. Contention Interrogatories

Please return to Federal Rule of Civil Procedure 33 and now focus on section (a) (2). Interrogatory Nos. 2 through 7 in the Sample Interrogatories above are called "contention interrogatories" that are clearly permitted by the Rule. They are so dubbed because they ask an opponent to reveal facts, persons with knowledge (i.e., witnesses), and documents concerning a contention that the opposing party has made. When a plaintiff asserts allegations or a claim set forth in a series of paragraphs in a complaint, such denials represent the defendant's contention or contentions. Why would identifying all facts, witnesses, and documents related to such contentions be important?

In the same way that a plaintiff can ask contention interrogatories, a defendant can ask interrogatories of the plaintiff seeking facts, documents, and witnesses supporting the allegations in the complaint. For instance, a defendant could ask: "state all facts, persons with knowledge of, and documents related to your contention in paragraphs of the [fill in the paragraph numbers of the pleading, "Complaint" if you are representing the defendant seeking to know the contentions of the plaintiff, or "Answer" if you are representing the plaintiff seeking to know the basis on which the defendant is defending the suit) of the complaint that defendant was negligent.]" Then the plaintiff would have to identify all facts upon which she based the allegations, all persons with knowledge of such factual allegations, and all documents related to such factual allegations. Note, if the defendant simultaneously serves a request for production of documents that seeks all documents identified in response to interrogatory answers, the plaintiff will have to produce all documents related to the contentions supporting his claim. Can you see the value of contention interrogatories? Will they assist in determining which persons to depose, what documents to focus on, etc.?

Another advantage of contention interrogatories is that there should be no surprise. You should, if you ask correctly, force the opposing party to name every potential witness, identify every fact on which that party relies, and provide the identity of every witness. If, however, the party comes up with a new fact, witness, or document at a final pretrial conference or at trial, and if you have asked contention interrogatories on every one of your opponent's contentions, you will be able to object and argue persuasively for exclusion of any "new" fact, witness, or document that your opponent failed to previously identify.

C. Requests for Admission

Please read Federal Rule of Civil Procedure 36. Requests for admission remove uncontested factual issues before trial, promoting efficiency of the trial process. Below is a sample request for admissions sent on behalf of a plaintiff:

IN THE UNITED STATES DISTRICT COURT
FOR THE EASTERN DISTRICT OF VIRGINIA

Norfolk Division

[PARTY NAME], Plaintiff,	)))	
v.	))	Case No. 123456
[PARTY NAME], Defendant,	)))	

REQUEST FOR ADMISSIONS

Pursuant to Rule 36, Plaintiff requests [Opposing Party's Name] to admit the following.

1. Admit that the accident report dated [date of accident] is a genuine copy of the report filled out and signed by Officer_____after the accident.

2. Admit that you ingested six beers within hours before the accident.

3. Admit that you have 20-40 vision and a restricted driver's license requiring corrective lenses.

4. Admit that you were not wearing the corrective lenses at the time of the accident.

. . . .

[PARTY's NAME]
By /s/_____
Of Counsel

Name of Counsel for Party
Address of Counsel
Tele. No.
E-Mail (and in some States, State Bar No.)

CERTIFICATE OF SERVICE

I certify that on this day of ____, 20___, a true copy of the foregoing REQUEST FOR ADMISSIONS was served by first-class mail on the following:

[Insert names and addresses of all other counsel in the case]

By_____
Of Counsel

Follow-Up Questions and Comments

1. What is the scope of matters for which admissions may be sought under Federal Rule of Civil Procedure 36? What is the procedure for seeking them?

2. What is the deadline for responding to requests for admission? As with other written discovery, when would objections have to be made?

3. What is the effect of a responding party's failure to respond within the allotted time?

4. What is the effect of an admission according to Rule 36(a)(6)?

5. What does Rule 36 state about a responding party's obligations in responding to the requests? Can the party serving requests challenge the sufficiency of a responding party's response and, if so, how?

6. Can a party who has served responses to Requests for Admission withdraw a response admitting a Request for Admissions? If so, what is the criteria the court applies in deciding whether to allow that?

III. The Optimal Sequence of Discovery: How Best to Employ the Above Discovery Tools Before Taking Depositions

Lawyers who think strategically recognize the logical sequence in which discovery should be pursued. They will issue the written discovery requests outlined above so that they have sufficient time to follow up with depositions of the "persons with knowledge" identified in the discovery. They realize that interrogatories are not the best means of asking some questions because of the ability of the lawyer to script answers with a client. Yes, the typical process of developing an interrogatory answer has the lawyer serving as drafter for the client. The practice may seem artificial, but it is well accepted. If anyone complains, the answer received is something like: "If you want to ask spontaneous questions without the lawyer's intervention in the process of answering, take a deposition. That's what they're designed to allow." Having recognized the weakness of interrogatories, we should acknowledge how they are valuable. Interrogatories are highly useful for identifying preliminary facts, documents related to the case, and persons with knowledge of the facts.

As valuable as depositions are, one must choose the persons to depose thoughtfully. Federal Rule of Civil Procedure 30 limits discovery to ten depositions without requiring a motion for leave to take more. Moreover, in most cases, a party's litigation budget effectively limits the number of persons deposed.[617] Again, contention interrogatories—ones that force an opponent to identify persons who support key contentions—help to prioritize the persons to be deposed. Such interrogatories reveal the persons who know the facts on which the opponent is basing her claims or defenses. If counsel's opponent lists dozens of witnesses in response to a contention interrogatory, counsel may have to move to compel answers that separate the persons who know detailed facts from those who may have superficial or limited factual knowledge and are thrown into the mix in order to make counsel's job harder.

Requests for production of documents and subpoena duces tecum are usually the first tools on which an attorney relies. Responses to requests for production of documents allow the attorney to gather and review documents prior to the depositions. The limited interrogatories (expert interrogatory and contention interrogatory) ought to also be sent early in discovery, if not simultaneously with the requests for production of documents and subpoena duces tecum to third parties. After reviewing the documents, the lawyer selects the witnesses to be questioned. The reality of discovery, however, is that you will rarely get all of the documents that you need without moving to compel the opponent, to have the court overrule objections, and to ensure you have all or at least most of the key documents. The strategy discussion near the beginning of this chapter stresses you ought to anticipate the need to put pressure on an opponent to respond promptly to discovery requests. As soon as you receive responses from interrogatory answers, responses to request for production of documents, etc., discuss with opposing counsel the documents that have not been produced based on objections. If counsel cannot agree on production (and that is usually the case), then the quicker the discovering party moves to compel, the better. Persistence, relentlessness, and thoroughness are the characteristics of an effective litigator in discovery.

Requests for admission are less useful at early stages of litigation unless you wish to determine whether your opponent will challenge the authenticity of certain documents. Thus, you will typically take depositions before sending out requests for admissions. Your opponent will almost always, in responses, skirt damaging admissions of fact. Furthermore, even if an admission of fact is conceded, the admission can be withdrawn later if the opponent realizes there were grounds for denial (although the court will have to allow it, and it is not always easy to convince a court to do so).

The most valuable use of requests for admissions is to request the opponent to admit that documents are genuine. Doing so helps considerably with providing the evidentiary foundation for documents to be offered into evidence. In some cases, the responses will negate the need to subpoena custodians for trial to come and provide mind-numbing testimony that the document is what it appears to be (e.g., a hospital record). The part of Federal Rule of Civil Procedure 36 that allows a party to seek attorney's fees if an opponent denies requests that require counsel to expend resources to prove a matter that should have been admitted often encourages parties to admit this kind of request for admission. If you are seeking an admission that a document is genuine, you can remind an opponent that Rule 36 is designed to avoid needless disputes. You can ask your opponent whether she will have a good response in the final pretrial conference when you tell the court of the witnesses necessary solely due to the opponent's refusal to admit authenticity. When pressed, opposing counsel typically will agree to such requests. If you do not make the requests, however, you will end up having to bring such witnesses and spend valuable time and effort when you could otherwise be focusing on the substance of the facts you need to prove.

---

[617] Depositions can cost thousands of dollars in light of the court reporter's fee, transcription costs, witness fees, etc. In addition, if your client is paying you on an hourly basis, the time for you to prepare for and take the deposition will be added to the client's bill.

A. Depositions: The Most Powerful Discovery Tool

Please read Federal Rule of Civil Procedure 30. Depositions are by far the most powerful discovery tool. They offer the opportunity to ask spontaneous questions of an opposing party or witness, to follow up on answers, and to get unscripted responses to the questions. Depositions are an area in which more seasoned lawyers can take advantage of less experienced ones. Thus, it is imperative to know not only how to prepare for a deposition, but also the rules by which they operate. If well-prepared, any lawyer, even in her first deposition, can effectively represent her client.

Preparation is the key to success in depositions. An attorney should have studied interrogatory answers and all potential documents prior to the deposition. Having the court reporter mark the documents with exhibit stickers before the deposition begins makes the deposition proceed more smoothly. If an attorney moves from one pre-marked exhibit to the next, the witness will be more likely to follow along at the pace the attorney sets. If the attorney is searching around for documents during the deposition, handing them back and forth to the witness and court reporter, the deposition will not only take longer, but she will find that the witness begins to offer spontaneous clarifications to her testimony during pauses. Often these spontaneous responses are ones that dilute the deponent's testimony. Again, if the attorney is setting the pace, and not taking long pauses, she cuts out these opportunities for the opponent to volunteer information and editorialize answers.

Next, an attorney will want to know who will be attending the deposition. The court reporter, who is trained in stenographic transcription (so that he or she can take down everything that is said and reproduce it), will be present. The reporter is the closest to a court representative at the deposition. He or she will administer the oath to the person answering questions (the "deponent"), who may be a party or a nonparty witness. In addition, the counsel for both parties, the deponent, the parties, and, at times, expert witnesses, will also be there.

Follow-Up Questions and Comments

1. What must the lawyer do to take a deposition? What must be included in the document the lawyer prepares and serves? If the person being deposed is a non-party, what additional step must counsel noticing the deposition take?

2. Under Rule 30(b) (6), if the deposition is of an organization or entity, how does the notice let the organization or entity know whom to produce for the deposition?

3. What are the steps in a deposition, from the time it starts through the end?

4. How are objections severely limited by Rule 30? When may a lawyer instruct a witness not to answer? What is the duration permitted for a deposition? Can a deposition be terminated or limited? If so, how? Can the court impose a sanction for interference with the conduct of the deposition?

B. Objections at Depositions: A Problem Area

As with discovery in general, the scope of questions permitted at a deposition is relatively broad, so long as counsel is asking questions that are relevant to the cause of action or a defense at hand.[618] If questions can arguably lead to admissible evidence regarding the case in controversy, they are usually permitted.[619]

Objections allowed at depositions are limited. The only objections that truly need to be made, other than objections protecting a privilege, are ones "as to the form of the question."[620] This limited role for objections is clearer upon reading both Federal Rules of Civil Procedure 30 and 32 together. Rule 32(b) states that a party may object to admissibility of matters addressed in a deposition at trial. However, the only objections that are waived if not made at a deposition are those of "form."[621]

Objections to the Form of the Question

An objection to the form of the question presumes that the question, as stated, cannot be answered. For instance, some attorneys will ask long, compound questions that cannot be answered effectively because they pack too much into the question. For example: "Didn't you get in the car, turn on the ignition, put the car in gear, back up, start to drive, stop at the stop sign, travel some distance up Stingray Street, and then slam into the rear of my client's convertible?" The question asks so many separate questions that a witness cannot possibly answer it with one response. Opposing counsel properly may state: "Objection. Compound question." Such an objection does not prevent the witness from answering the questions. If the witness has any common sense, however, she will realize that the question is too confusing and, in some parts, vague (e.g., "traveled some distance"). A witness who has been counseled on the unique challenges of a deposition should be sensitive to the difference between everyday communication and the precision required of answers to questions in depositions. Such a witness will be cautious of questions that cannot be answered precisely and accurately and will let the questioning lawyer know that she has difficulty with the question. The lawyer will then have to break the question into parts, as the lawyer should have done to begin with. The value of objecting to form is that, if the questioning lawyer does not rephrase the question, and then attempts to use the deposition testimony at trial, the objecting lawyer can rely on her objection to form. Then the court can rule at trial that the question was inappropriate and, thus, the deposition testimony cannot be used.

1. Objections Based on Admissibility

Objections to relevance, hearsay, and other grounds of admissibility at trial of testimony or exhibits are preserved in every jurisdiction until trial, even if the attorney never objects at the deposition.[622] Thus, a new lawyer should realize that most questions will be answered at a deposition. Even if a deposing attorney asks a question in a manner that violates the proper form, opposing counsel may register an objection, but the question will still be answered so long as the witness is able to answer it.

---

[618] 27 C.J.S. DISCOVERY § 72 (2017).

[619] *Id.* § 68.

[620] 23 AM. JUR. 2d Depositions and Discovery § 112 (2017).

[621] FED. R. CIV. P. 32(c).

[622] FED. R. CIV. P. 30(c)(1); *see also* FED. R. CIV. P. 32(b).

The area in which inexperienced counsel ought to be most on guard is the practice of "speaking objections." Some attorneys will object and include in their objection signals to the witness of whether to answer a question and what problems might lie in doing so. For example, interrogating counsel asks, "Please identify all facts surrounding the accident leading to this case." What if opposing counsel then states: "Objection, overly broad and vague. The witness cannot possibly identify all facts surrounding any instance." A witness, hearing this objection, may then say, "I cannot recall all of the facts." Such a response suggests that the lawyer's statement of her objection is influencing the witness's response. Some lawyers are more strategic and save their speaking objections for questions that are pivotal to the case. The best way to spot speaking objections is that they generally involve clues to the witness on how the witness should answer the question. Federal Rule of Civil Procedure 30(c) provides a strong statement against the practice of speaking objections:

> An objection must be stated concisely in a nonargumentative and nonsuggestive manner. A person may instruct a deponent not to answer only when necessary to preserve a privilege, to enforce a limitation ordered by the court, or to present a motion under Rule 30(d) (3) [concerning motions to limit or suspend a deposition when confronted with bad faith or oppressive conduct in the taking of a deposition].[623]

Quite simply, an attorney should not direct her client how to answer a question. A representative opinion reflecting the views of most judges on speaking objections follows. *Figure 13-2*, at the conclusion of this chapter, summarizes the types of objections that must be made a depositions (very few, designed to ensure a confusing question is made clear on the spot), to the unique nature of objections to questions on the attorney-client privilege or work-product doctrine (which if answered would waive the privilege or work-product protections), to the objections that typically ought to be saved and not made at the deposition because the court later rules on most questions of admissibility.

Following is a notorious case in which plaintiff's counsel breaks virtually every rule on objections in a deposition, not to mention civil behavior. Ask yourself how defendant's counsel could have better dealt with such conduct.

PARAMOUNT COMMUNICATIONS v. QVC NETWORK
Supreme Court of Delaware, 1994
637 A.2d 34

VEASEY, Chief Justice.

In this appeal we review an order of the Court of Chancery dated November 24, 1993 (the "November 24 Order"), preliminarily enjoining certain defensive measures designed to facilitate a so-called strategic alliance between Viacom Inc. ("Viacom") and Paramount Communications Inc. ("Paramount") approved by the board of directors of Paramount (the "Paramount Board" or the "Paramount directors") and to thwart an unsolicited, more valuable, tender offer by QVC Network Inc. ("QVC"). In affirming, we hold that the sale of control in this case, which is at the heart of the proposed strategic alliance, implicates enhanced judicial scrutiny of the conduct of the Paramount Board. We further hold that the conduct of the Paramount Board was not reasonable as to process or result.

---

[623] FED. R. CIV. P. 30(c) (2).

QVC and certain stockholders of Paramount commenced separate actions (later consolidated) in the Court of Chancery seeking preliminary and permanent injunctive relief against Paramount, certain members of the Paramount Board, and Viacom. This action arises out of a proposed acquisition of Paramount by Viacom through a tender offer followed by a second-step merger (the "Paramount-Viacom transaction"), and a competing unsolicited tender offer by QVC. The Court of Chancery granted a preliminary injunction.

The Court of Chancery found that the Paramount directors violated their fiduciary duties by favoring the Paramount-Viacom transaction over the more valuable unsolicited offer of QVC. The Court of Chancery preliminarily enjoined Paramount and the individual defendants (the "Paramount defendants") from amending or modifying Paramount's stockholder rights agreement (the "Rights Agreement"), including the redemption of the Rights, or taking other action to facilitate the consummation of the pending tender offer by Viacom or any proposed second-step merger, including the Merger Agreement between Paramount and Viacom dated September 12, 1993 (the "Original Merger Agreement"), as amended on October 24, 1993 (the "Amended Merger Agreement"). Viacom and the Paramount defendants were enjoined from taking any action to exercise any provision of the Stock Option Agreement between Paramount and Viacom dated September 12, 1993 (the "Stock Option Agreement"), as amended on October 24, 1993. The Court of Chancery did not grant preliminary injunctive relief as to the termination fee provided for the benefit of Viacom in Section 8.05 of the Original Merger Agreement and the Amended Merger Agreement (the "Termination Fee").

Under the circumstances of this case, the pending sale of control implicated in the Paramount-Viacom transaction required the Paramount Board to act on an informed basis to secure the best value reasonably available to the stockholders. Since we agree with the Court of Chancery that the Paramount directors violated their fiduciary duties, we have AFFIRMED the entry of the order of the Vice Chancellor granting the preliminary injunction and have REMANDED these proceedings to the Court of Chancery for proceedings consistent herewith.

We also . . . [address] serious deposition misconduct by counsel who appeared on behalf of a Paramount director at the time that director's deposition was taken by a lawyer representing QVC.

. . .

The issue of discovery abuse, including lack of civility and professional misconduct during depositions, is a matter of considerable concern to Delaware courts and courts around the nation. One particular instance of misconduct during a deposition in this case demonstrates such an astonishing lack of professionalism and civility that it is worthy of special note here as a lesson for the future — a lesson of conduct not to be tolerated or repeated.

On November 10, 1993, an expedited deposition of Paramount, through one of its directors, J. Hugh Liedtke, was taken in the state of Texas. The deposition was taken by Delaware counsel for QVC. Mr. Liedtke was individually represented at this deposition by Joseph D. Jamail, Esquire, of the Texas Bar. Peter C. Thomas, Esquire, of the New York Bar appeared and defended on behalf of the Paramount defendants. It does not appear that any member of the Delaware bar was present at the deposition representing any of the defendants or the stockholder plaintiffs.

Mr. Jamail did not otherwise appear in this Delaware proceeding representing any party, and he was not admitted pro hac vice. Under the rules of the Court of Chancery and this Court, lawyers who are admitted pro hac vice to represent a party in Delaware proceedings are subject to Delaware Disciplinary Rules and are required to review the Delaware State Bar Association Statement of Principles of Lawyer Conduct (the "Statement of Principles"). During the Liedtke deposition, Mr. Jamail abused the privilege of representing a witness in a Delaware proceeding, in that he: (a) improperly directed the witness not to answer certain questions; (b) was extraordinarily rude, uncivil, and vulgar; and (c) obstructed the ability of the questioner to elicit testimony to assist the Court in this matter.

To illustrate, a few excerpts from the latter stages of the Liedtke deposition follow:

> (By Mr. Johnston [Delaware counsel for QVC], hereafter MR. JOHNSTON) Okay. Do you have any idea why Mr. Oresman was calling that material to your attention?
>
> MR. JAMAIL: Don't answer that.
> How would he know what was going on in Mr. Oresman's mind? Don't answer it. Go on to your next question.
> MR. JOHNSTON: No, Joe —
> MR. JAMAIL: He's not going to answer that. Certify it. I'm going to shut it down if you don't go to your next question.
> MR. JOHNSTON: No. Joe, Joe —
> MR. JAMAIL: Don't "Joe" me, [ass****].[624] You can ask some questions, but get off of that. I'm tired of you. You could gag a maggot off a meat wagon. Now, we've helped you every way we can.
> MR. JOHNSTON: Let's just take it easy.
> MR. JAMAIL: No, we're not going to take it easy. Get done with this. MR. JOHNSTON: We will go on to the next question.
> MR. JAMAIL: Do it now.
> MR. JOHNSTON: We will go on to the next question. We're not trying to excite anyone.
> MR. JAMAIL: Come on. Quit talking. Ask the question. Nobody wants to socialize with you.
> MR. JOHNSTON: I'm not trying to socialize. We'll go on to another question. We're continuing the deposition.
> MR. JAMAIL: Well, go on and shut up. MR. JOHNSTON: Are you finished?
> MR. JAMAIL: Yeah, you —
> MR. JOHNSTON: Are you finished?
> MR. JAMAIL: I may be and you may be. Now, you want to sit here and talk to me, fine. This deposition is going to be over with. You don't know what you're doing. Obviously someone wrote out a long outline of stuff for you to ask. You have no concept of what you're doing.
> Now, I've tolerated you for three hours. If you've got another question, get on with it. This is going to stop one hour from now, period. Go.
> MR. JOHNSTON: Are you finished?
> MR. THOMAS: Come on, Mr. Johnston, move it. MR. JOHNSTON: I don't need this kind of abuse. MR. THOMAS: Then just ask the next question.

---

[624] Mr. Jamail actually used the full seven-letter word in the deposition.

Q. (By Mr. Johnston) All right. To try to move forward, Mr. Liedtke, . . . I'll show you what's been marked as Liedtke 14 and it is a covering letter dated October 29 from Steven Cohen of Wachtell, Lipton, Rosen & Katz including QVC's Amendment Number 1 to its Schedule 14D-1, and my question —

A. No.

Q. — to you, sir, is whether you've seen that?

A. No. Look, I don't know what your intent in asking all these questions is, but, my God, I am not going to play boy lawyer.

Q. Mr. Liedtke —

A. Okay. Go ahead and ask your question.

— I'm trying to move forward in this deposition that we are entitled to take. I'm trying to streamline it.

MR. JAMAIL: Come on with your next question. Don't even talk with this witness.

MR. JOHNSTON: I'm trying to move forward with it.

MR. JAMAIL: You understand me? Don't talk to this witness except by question. Did you hear me? MR. JOHNSTON: I heard you fine.

MR. JAMAIL: You fee makers think you can come here and sit in somebody's office, get your meter running, get your full day's fee by asking stupid questions. Let's go with it.

. . .

Staunch advocacy on behalf of a client is proper and fully consistent with the finest effectuation of skill and professionalism. Indeed, it is a mark of professionalism, not weakness, for a lawyer zealously and firmly to protect and pursue a client's legitimate interests by a professional, courteous, and civil attitude toward all persons involved in the litigation process. A lawyer who engages in the type of behavior exemplified by Mr. Jamail on the record of the Liedtke deposition is not properly representing his client, and the client's cause is not advanced by a lawyer who engages in unprofessional conduct of this nature. It happens that in this case there was no application to the court, and the parties and the witness do not appear to have been prejudiced by this misconduct.

Nevertheless, the Court finds this unprofessional behavior to be outrageous and unacceptable. If a Delaware lawyer had engaged in the kind of misconduct committed by Mr. Jamail on this record, that lawyer would have been subject to censure or more serious sanctions. While the specter of disciplinary proceedings should not be used by the parties as a litigation tactic, conduct such as that involved here goes to the heart of the trial court proceedings themselves. As such, it cries out for relief under the trial court's rules . . . . Under some circumstances, the use of the trial court's inherent summary contempt powers may be appropriate.

Although busy and overburdened, Delaware trial courts are "but a phone call away" and would be responsive to the plight of a party and its counsel bearing the brunt of such misconduct.

[Depositions are the factual battleground where the vast majority of litigation actually takes place. . . Thus, it is particularly important that this discovery device not be abused. Counsel should never forget that even though the deposition may be taking place far from a real courtroom, with no black-robed overseer peering down upon them, as long as the deposition is conducted under the caption of this court and proceeding under the authority of the rules of this court, counsel are operating as officers of this court. They

425

should comport themselves accordingly; should they be tempted to stray, they should remember that this judge is but a phone call away.]

It is not appropriate for this Court to prescribe in the abstract any particular remedy or to provide an exclusive list of remedies under such circumstances. We assume that the trial courts of this State would consider protective orders and the sanctions permitted by the discovery rules. Sanctions could include exclusion of obstreperous counsel from attending the deposition (whether or not he or she has been admitted pro hac vice), ordering the deposition recessed and reconvened promptly in Delaware, or the appointment of a master to preside at the deposition. Costs and counsel fees should follow.

. . .

Counsel attending the Liedtke deposition on behalf of the Paramount defendants had an obligation to ensure the integrity of that proceeding. The record of the deposition as a whole . . . demonstrates that, not only Mr. Jamail, but also Mr. Thomas (representing the Paramount defendants), continually interrupted the questioning, engaged in colloquies and objections which sometimes suggested answers to questions, and constantly pressed the questioner for time throughout the deposition. . . . As to Mr. Jamail's tactics quoted above, Mr. Thomas passively let matters proceed as they did, and at times even added his own voice to support the behavior of Mr. Jamail. A Delaware lawyer or a lawyer admitted pro hac vice would have been expected to put an end to the misconduct in the Liedtke deposition.

[Rule 30 (d) (1) of the revised Federal Rules of Civil Procedure, which became effective on December 1, 1993, requires objections during depositions to be "stated concisely and in a non-argumentative and non-suggestive manner." The Delaware trial courts and this Court are evaluating the desirability of adopting certain of the new Federal Rules, or modifications thereof, and other possible rule changes.

[W]e share [the trial court's] view not only of the impropriety of coaching witnesses on and off the record of the deposition . . . but also the impropriety of objections and colloquy which "tend to disrupt the question-and-answer rhythm of a deposition and obstruct the witness's testimony." . . . To be sure, there are also occasions when the questioner is abusive or otherwise acts improperly and should be sanctioned. . . . Although the questioning in the Liedtke deposition could have proceeded more crisply, this was not a case where it was the questioner who abused the process.]

This kind of misconduct is not to be tolerated in any Delaware court proceeding, including depositions taken in other states in which witnesses appear represented by their own counsel other than counsel for a party in the proceeding. Yet, there is no clear mechanism for this Court to deal with this matter in terms of sanctions or disciplinary remedies at this time in the context of this case. Nevertheless, consideration will be given to the following issues for the future: (a) whether or not it is appropriate and fair to take into account the behavior of Mr. Jamail in this case in the event application is made by him in the future to appear pro hac vice in any Delaware proceeding; and (b) what rules or standards should be adopted to deal effectively with misconduct by out-of-state lawyers in depositions in proceedings pending in Delaware courts.

As to (a), this Court will welcome a voluntary appearance by Mr. Jamail if a request is received from him by the Clerk of this Court within thirty days of the date of this Opinion and Addendum. The purpose of such voluntary appearance will be to explain the questioned conduct and to show cause why such conduct should not be considered as a bar to any future appearance by Mr. Jamail in a Delaware proceeding. As to (b), this Court and the trial courts of this State will undertake to strengthen the existing mechanisms for dealing with the type of misconduct referred to in this Addendum and the practices relating to admissions pro hac vice.

[Conclusion of opinion.]

Follow-Up Comments and Questions

1. What should Mr. Johnston have done during the deposition? If he could not get through on the phone to a judge in the court in which the case was pending, what would be the next best option? Sooner or later, you will run into a lawyer who, if not as offensive as Mr. Jamail, will test whether you know how to handle improper intervention affecting the deposition. The most important thing an inexperienced lawyer can do before a deposition is to prepare. You should always make sure you have thorough knowledge of the rules of what can, and cannot, be objected to in a deposition. Be sure that you bring the court's telephone number to the deposition. Counsel should call the trial court to deal with inappropriate deposition conduct. If you are questioning a witness and opposing counsel begins to make inappropriate speaking objections, you should ask the court reporter to "mark in the record the questions and objections that counsel has been making." Then, the interrogating attorney should state for the record that the objection is inappropriate and why. If opposing counsel continues to make speaking objections, call the court and ask for a judge to resolve the deposition dispute. If you must call the court, you can have the court reporter at that point read back questions, objections, whatever the witness says, etc. If the attorney cannot reach a judge at that time, suspend the deposition and move for a protective order directing counsel to cease speaking objections. You can also seek fees and expenses associated with the motion.[625] Before suspending a deposition and filing a motion, the attorney would be wise to have several questions on the record to which opposing counsel makes speaking objections. In that way, the chances increase of a judge's ruling in favor of the protective order, granting a request for fees and expenses, and probably censuring opposing counsel.

2. The interrogating counsel should keep her poise throughout this process and avoid getting into arguments with opposing counsel. Again, knowing the rules, showing opposing counsel that you know them, and seeking the court's intervention if opposing counsel interferes in the deposition all go a long way to keeping you in charge of your deposition and the opposing counsel in her proper place. In addition, another technique some lawyers use—particularly for lawyers with a reputation for being obstreperous—is to include in the notice of the deposition (which always must be sent ahead of the deposition) that the deposition will be taken down by the court reporter and videotaped. Lawyers are far less likely to misbehave when they know that a court (or bar disciplinary committee) could end up seeing them? Recall that arguments with another lawyer are fruitless; the only one to whom you should argue is the court.

3. What about opposing counsel deposing your client and asking questions that would require the client to disclose privileged information? Objections to questions that invade privilege are exceptions to the rule that most objections cannot be made at a deposition. Counsel "defending" a deposition—i.e., not interrogating, but rather representing a client while that client or another witness is being deposed—must remain alert for questions that invade the attorney-client privilege

---

[625] 23 AM. JUR. 2D Depositions and Discovery § 213 (2017).

or work product doctrine.[626] These types of questions, and others that invade other privileges recognized by law, are the kind of deposition questions that an attorney can instruct a witness not to answer, in addition to objecting for the record.[627]

4. Either party may want to offer the testimony of a witness "unavailable" to testify at trial.[628] For such witnesses, you can subpoena the witness through the U.S. District Court where the witness is located. Such a deposition is called a "trial deposition" or a *de bene esse deposition*." Both counsel need to approach such a deposition as if the witness is testifying at trial. The deponent's testimony will be read to the factfinder or shown by video. For obvious reasons, counsel needs to review the ground rules for such a deposition before taking (or defending) one.[629]

5. At trial, such depositions of witnesses who otherwise would not be available are read as if the witness was in court. The opposing party can object on grounds like hearsay, relevance, etc. just as that party can to any testimony. The author's suggestion is that, if a witness whose deposition is taken to be presented at trial is important enough, you should consider taking the deposition both stenographically and by videotape. The rules allow for videotape depositions and the jury (or judge in a bench trial) will have a better sense of the witness' credibility if they can observe the witness. Typically, the parties would resolve any objections prior to trial and edit the videotape according to the court's rulings.

IV. Attorney-Client Privilege and Work-Product Doctrine

A. Attorney-Client Privilege

The attorney-client privilege is one of the most sacred in the law. Other privileges exist as well, such as the priest-penitent privilege, doctor-patient privilege, and many others. We address the attorney-client privilege here because it is fundamental and typically not covered in-depth in evidence courses. However, if any privilege applies, it could be a basis for objecting to questions asked in a deposition or to written discovery requests, or for that matter to questions asked in court.

The difference between privileges like the attorney-client privilege and the work-product doctrine are that the attorney client privilege can apply to information not in documentary form and to documents, whereas the work-product doctrine will apply solely to documents. The criteria for attorney-client privilege are (1) whether there was a communication (oral or written) between a client and an attorney, (2) for purposes of rendering legal advice or representation. If someone asks a lawyer at a party what the lawyer thinks about a case, that probably is not attorney client privileged information. The person is not a client and the information is not for legal advice. Conversely, if that person took the lawyer aside and told the lawyer she needed legal advice, and the attorney showed indications of representing the person, the information shared would likely be privileged. If in doubt, the lawyer should be wary of offering opinions or advice until it is clear whether an attorney-client relationship exists.

---

[626] MARILYN J. BERGER ET AL., PRETRIAL ADVOCACY 339 (2d ed. 2007). *See generally* 27 C.J.S. DISCOVERY § 42 (2016).

[627] *Id.*

[628] *See* FED. R. CIV. P. 32(a) (4) (defining "unavailable witness").

[629] *See* JAY E. GRENNING & JEFFERY S. KINSLER, HANDBOOK OF FEDERAL CIVIL DISCOVERY & DISCLOSURE § 7.13 (4th ed. 2016).

There are some limited exceptions to the attorney-client privilege. If a party shows the "crime fraud exception" (where the attorney is participating in a crime or fraudulent activity that can only be revealed by piercing the attorney-client privilege), then that party may pierce the attorney-client privilege and force disclosure of attorney-client communications.[630] Note, however, that even though you ordinarily will be able to withhold materials that fall within the attorney-client privilege, states, like the federal system, require a listing of any documents that are withheld under the privilege.[631] An attorney should always specify the documents that are being withheld based on the attorney-client privilege or the work-product doctrine (a separate type of privilege discussed below) in the privilege log that she provides to opposing counsel. The privilege log should be produced at the time counsel serves her response to a request for production of documents.161 More often than not, counsel will seek production of documents withheld under the work-product doctrine rather than attempt to overcome the attorney-client privilege. If the opposing counsel can show substantial need and inability to obtain the substantial equivalent to the withheld documents, she can force production of the documents withheld under the work-product doctrine.[632] It is for this reason that the work-product doctrine is more easily pierced than the attorney-client privilege.

Follow-Up Questions and Comments

1. As discussed, if one is objecting to the items under either the attorney-client privilege or the work-product doctrine, the party must not only object but prepare a list of the items withheld. Please visit the Federal Rules of Civil Procedure Rule 26(b)(5).

2. What does Rule 26(b)(5) require? What does it say about items protected by a privilege or the work-product doctrine that are inadvertently produced? Can the materials be recovered without waiving the protection of the privilege or work-product doctrine? What must the party who inadvertently produced the material do?

3. Each federal district court can have its own local rules that, though they cannot be inconsistent with the Federal Rules, can be more demanding (e.g, require objections within fifteen days of service rather than 30 days). If local rules or the applicable request for production rules require a party to object, and virtually every request for production rule requires responding "or objecting" within a specified time, it is imperative that counsel object on attorney-client and/or work product grounds or risk waiving these privileges. If one is litigating in a court with local rules that accelerate the time for objections, one had better follow those rules. Otherwise, objections to production will be waived.

B. Work Product

Work product refers to the information and materials an attorney (or other agent of a party) gathers for a party in anticipation of litigation. Work product can be categorized as both "non-documentary" work product and "documentary" work product. Many do not think of work product protection in non-

---

[630] 24 CHARLES ALAN WRIGHT & ARTHUR R. MILLER, FEDERAL PRACTICE AND PROCEDURE § 5501 (1st ed. 2018).
[631] FED. R. CIV. P. 26(b) (5).
[632] FED. R. CIV. P. 26(b) (5).

documentary terms. However, the Hickman case, following below, dealt with precisely that issue: interrogatory questions to a lawyer who gathered information in anticipation of litigation and was later asked to provide that information in discovery.

1. The Common-Law Version of Work Product

In the justly famous decision that follows, the U.S. Supreme Court held for the first time that there was a work-product basis for refusing to produce documents or information gathered by an attorney in anticipation of litigation.

HICKMAN v. TAYLOR
Supreme Court of the United States, 1947
329 U.S. 495

Mr. Justice MURPHY delivered the opinion of the Court.

This case presents an important problem under the Federal Rules of Civil Procedure as to the extent to which a party may inquire into oral and written statements of witnesses, or other information, secured by an adverse party's counsel in the course of preparation for possible litigation after a claim has arisen. Examination into a person's files and records, including those resulting from the professional activities of an attorney, must be judged with care. It is not without reason that various safeguards have been established to preclude unwarranted excursions into the privacy of a man's work. At the same time, public policy supports reasonable and necessary inquiries. Properly to balance these competing interests is a delicate and difficult task.

On February 7, 1943, the tug 'J. M. Taylor' sank while engaged in helping to tow a car float of the Baltimore & Ohio Railroad across the Delaware River at Philadelphia. The accident was apparently unusual in nature, the cause of it still being unknown. Five of the nine crew members were drowned. Three days later the tug owners and the underwriters employed a law firm, of which respondent Fortenbaugh is a member, to defend them against potential suits by representatives of the deceased crew members and to sue the railroad for damages to the tug.

A public hearing was held on March 4, 1943, before the United States Steamboat Inspectors, at which the four survivors were examined. This testimony was recorded and made available to all interested parties. Shortly thereafter, Fortenbaugh privately interviewed the survivors and took statements from them with an eye toward the anticipated litigation; the survivors signed these statements on March 29. Fortenbaugh also interviewed other persons believed to have some information relating to the accident and in some cases[,] he made memoranda of what they told him. At the time when Fortenbaugh secured the statements of the survivors, representatives of two of the deceased crew members had been in communication with him. Ultimately claims were presented by representatives of all five of the deceased; four of the claims, however, were settled without litigation. The fifth claimant, petitioner herein, brought suit in a federal court under the Jones Act on November 26, 1943, naming as defendants the two tug owners, individually and as partners, and the railroad.

One year later, petitioner filed 39 interrogatories directed to the tug owners. The 38th interrogatory read: 'state whether any statements of the members of the crews of the Tugs 'J. M. Taylor' and 'Philadelphia' or of any other vessel were taken in connection with the towing of the car float and the sinking of the Tug 'John M. Taylor'. Attach hereto exact copies of all such statements if in writing, and if oral, set forth in detail the exact provisions of any such oral statements or reports.' supplemental interrogatories asked whether any oral or written statements, records, reports or other memoranda had been made concerning any matter relative to the towing operation, the sinking of the tug, the salvaging and repair of the tug, and the death of the deceased. If the answer was in the affirmative, the tug owners were then requested to set forth the nature of all such records, reports, statements or other memoranda.

The tug owners, through Fortenbaugh, answered all of the interrogatories except No. 38 and the supplemental ones just described. While admitting that statements of the survivors had been taken, they declined to summarize or set forth the contents. They did so on the ground that such requests called 'for privileged matter obtained in preparation for litigation' and constituted 'an attempt to obtain indirectly counsel's private files.' It was claimed that answering these requests 'would involve practically turning over not only the complete files, but also the telephone records and, almost, the thoughts of counsel.'

In connection with the hearing on these objections, Fortenbaugh made a written statement and gave an informal oral deposition explaining the circumstances under which he had taken the statements. But he was not expressly asked in the deposition to produce the statements. The District Court for the Eastern District of Pennsylvania, sitting en banc, held that the requested matters were not privileged. 4 F.R.D. 479. The court then decreed that the tug owners and Fortenbaugh, as counsel and agent for the tug owners forthwith 'Answer Plaintiff's 38th interrogatory and supplemental interrogatories; produce all written statements of witnesses obtained by Mr. Fortenbaugh, as counsel and agent for Defendants; state in substance any fact concerning this case which Defendants learned through oral statements made by witnesses to Mr. Fortenbaugh whether or not included in his private memoranda and produce Mr. Fortenbaugh's memoranda containing statements of fact by witnesses or to submit these memoranda to the Court for determination of those portions which should be revealed to Plaintiff.' Upon their refusal, the court adjudged them in contempt and ordered them imprisoned until they complied.

The Third Circuit Court of Appeals, also sitting en banc, reversed the judgment of the District Court. It held that the information here sought was part of the 'work product of the lawyer' and hence privileged from discovery under the Federal Rules of Civil Procedure. The importance of the problem, which has engendered a great divergence of views among district courts, led us to grant certiorari.

The pre-trial deposition-discovery mechanism established by Rules 26 to 37 is one of the most significant innovations of the Federal Rules of Civil Procedure. Under the prior federal practice, the pre-trial functions of notice-giving issue-formulation and fact-revelation were performed primarily and inadequately by the pleadings. Inquiry into the issues and the facts before trial was narrowly confined and was often cumbersome in method. The new rules, however, restrict the pleadings to the task of general notice-giving and invest the deposition-discovery process with a vital role in the preparation for trial. The various instruments of discovery now serve (1) as a device, along with the pre-trial hearing under Rule 16, to narrow and clarify the basic issues between the parties, and (2) as a device for ascertaining the facts, or information as to the existence or whereabouts of facts, relative to those issues. Thus[,] civil trials in the federal courts no longer need be carried on in the dark. The way is now clear, consistent with recognized privileges, for the parties to obtain the fullest possible knowledge of the issues and facts before trial.

There is an initial question as to which of the deposition-discovery rules is involved in this case. Petitioner, in filing his interrogatories, thought that he was proceeding under Rule 33. That rule provides that a party may serve upon any adverse party written interrogatories to be answered by the party served. The District Court proceeded on the same assumption in its opinion, although its order to produce and its contempt order stated that both Rules 33 and 34 were involved. Rule 34 establishes a procedure whereby, upon motion of any party showing good cause therefor and upon notice to all other parties, the court may order any party to produce and permit the inspection and copying or photographing of any designated documents, etc., not privileged, which constitute or contain evidence material to any matter involved in the action and which are in his possession, custody or control.

The Circuit Court of Appeals, however, felt that Rule 26 was the crucial one. Petitioner, it said, was proceeding by interrogatories and, in connection with those interrogatories, wanted copies of memoranda and statements secured from witnesses. While the court believed that Rule 33 was involved, at least as to the defending tug owners, it stated that this rule could not be used as the basis for condemning Fortenbaugh's failure to disclose or produce the memoranda and statements, since the rule applies only to interrogatories addressed to adverse parties, not to their agents or counsel. And Rule 34 was said to be inapplicable since petitioner was not trying to see an original document and to copy or photograph it, within the scope of that rule. The court then concluded that Rule 26 must be the one really involved. That provides that the testimony of any person, whether a party or not, may be taken by any party by deposition upon oral examination or written interrogatories for the purpose of discovery or for use as evidence; and that the deponent may be examined regarding any matter, not privileged, which is relevant to the subject matter involved in the pending action, whether relating to the claim or defense of the examining party or of any other party, including the existence, description, nature, custody, condition and location of any books, documents or other tangible things.

The matter is not without difficulty in light of the events that transpired below. We believe, however, that petitioner was proceeding primarily under Rule 33. He addressed simple interrogatories solely to the individual tug owners, the adverse parties, as contemplated by that rule. He did not, and could not under Rule 33, address such interrogatories to their counsel, Fortenbaugh. Nor did he direct these interrogatories either to the tug owners or to Fortenbaugh by way of deposition; Rule 26 thus could not come into operation. And it does not appear from the record that petitioner filed a motion under Rule 34 for a court order directing the production of the documents in question. Indeed, such an order could not have been entered as to Fortenbaugh since Rule 34, like Rule 33, is limited to parties to the proceeding, thereby excluding their counsel or agents.

Thus[,] to the extent that petitioner was seeking the production of the memoranda and statements gathered by Fortenbaugh in the course of his activities as counsel, petitioner misconceived his remedy. Rule 33 did not permit him to obtain such memoranda and statements as adjuncts to the interrogatories addressed to the individual tug owners. A party clearly cannot refuse to answer interrogatories on the ground that the information sought is solely within the knowledge of his attorney. But that is not this case. Here production was sought of documents prepared by a party's attorney after the claim has arisen. Rule 33 does not make provision for such production, even when sought in connection with permissible interrogatories. Moreover, since petitioner was also foreclosed from securing them through an order under Rule 34, his only recourse was to take Fortenbaugh's deposition under Rule 26 and to attempt to force Fortenbaugh to produce the materials by use of a subpoena duces tecum in accordance with Rule 45. But despite petitioner's faulty choice of action, the District Court entered an order, apparently under Rule 34, commanding the tug owners and Fortenbaugh, as their agent and counsel, to produce the materials in question. Their refusal led to the anomalous result of holding the tug owners in contempt for failure to produce that which was in the possession of their counsel and of holding Fortenbaugh in contempt for failure to produce that which he could not be compelled to produce under either Rule 33 or Rule 34.

But under the circumstances we deem it unnecessary and unwise to rest our decision upon this procedural irregularity, an irregularity which is not strongly urged upon us and which was disregarded in

432

the two courts below. It matters little at this later stage whether Fortenbaugh fails to answer interrogatories filed under Rule 26 or under Rule 33 or whether he refuses to produce the memoranda and statements pursuant to a subpoena under Rule 45 or a court order under Rule 34. The deposition-discovery rules create integrated procedural devices. And the basic question at stake is whether any of those devices may be used to inquire into materials collected by an adverse party's counsel in the course of preparation for possible litigation. The fact that the petitioner may have used the wrong method does not destroy the main thrust of his attempt. Nor does it relieve us of the responsibility of dealing with the problem raised by that attempt. It would be inconsistent with the liberal atmosphere surrounding these rules to insist that petitioner now go through the empty formality of pursuing the right procedural device only to reestablish precisely the same basic problem now confronting us. We do not mean to say, however, that there may not be situations in which the failure to proceed in accordance with a specific rule would be important or decisive. But in the present circumstances, for the purposes of this decision, the procedural irregularity is not material. Having noted the proper procedure, we may accordingly turn our attention to the substance of the underlying problem.

In urging that he has a right to inquire into the materials secured and prepared by Fortenbaugh, petitioner emphasizes that the deposition-discovery portions of the Federal Rules of Civil Procedure are designed to enable the parties to discover the true facts and to compel their disclosure wherever they may be found. It is said that inquiry may be made under these rules, epitomized by Rule 26, as to any relevant matter which is not privileged; and since the discovery provisions are to be applied as broadly and liberally as possible, the privilege limitation must be restricted to its narrowest bounds. On the premise that the attorney-client privilege is the one involved in this case, petitioner argues that it must be strictly confined to confidential communications made by a client to his attorney. And since the materials here in issue were secured by Fortenbaugh from third persons rather than from his clients, the tug owners, the conclusion is reached that these materials are proper subjects for discovery under Rule 26.

As additional support for this result, petitioner claims that to prohibit discovery under these circumstances would give a corporate defendant a tremendous advantage in a suit by an individual plaintiff. Thus[,] in a suit by an injured employee against a railroad or in a suit by an insured person against an insurance company the corporate defendant could pull a dark veil of secrecy over all the pertinent facts it can collect after the claim arises merely on the assertion that such facts were gathered by its large staff of attorneys and claim agents. At the same time, the individual plaintiff, who often has direct knowledge of the matter in issue and has no counsel until sometime after his claim arises could be compelled to disclose all the intimate details of his case. By endowing with immunity from disclosure all that a lawyer discovers in the course of his duties, it is said, the rights of individual litigants in such cases are drained of vitality and the lawsuit becomes more of a battle of deception than a search for truth.

But framing the problem in terms of assisting individual plaintiffs in their suits against corporate defendants is unsatisfactory. Discovery concededly may work to the disadvantage as well as to the advantage of individual plaintiffs. Discovery, in other words, is not a one-way proposition. It is available in all types of cases at the behest of any party, individual or corporate, plaintiff or defendant. The problem thus far transcends the situation confronting this petitioner. And we must view that problem in light of the limitless situations where the particular kind of discovery sought by petitioner might be used.

We agree, of course, that the deposition-discovery rules are to be accorded a broad and liberal treatment. No longer can the time-honored cry of 'fishing expedition' serve to preclude a party from inquiring into the facts underlying his opponent's case. Mutual knowledge of all the relevant facts gathered by both parties is essential to proper litigation. To that end, either party may compel the other to disgorge whatever facts he has in his possession. The deposition-discovery procedure simply advances the stage at which the disclosure can be compelled from the time of trial to the period preceding it, thus reducing the possibility of surprise. But discovery, like all matters of procedure, has ultimate and necessary boundaries. As indicated by Rules 30(b) and (d) and 31(d), limitations inevitably arise when it can be shown that the examination is being conducted in bad faith or in such a manner as to annoy, embarrass or oppress the person subject to the inquiry. And as Rule 26(b) provides, further limitations come into existence when the inquiry touches upon the irrelevant or encroaches upon the recognized domains of privilege.

We also agree that the memoranda, statements and mental impressions in issue in this case fall outside the scope of the attorney-client privilege and hence are not protected from discovery on that basis. It is unnecessary here to delineate the content and scope of that privilege as recognized in the federal courts. For present purposes, it suffices to note that the protective cloak of this privilege does not extend to information which an attorney secures from a witness while acting for his client in anticipation of litigation. Nor does this privilege concern the memoranda, briefs, communications and other writings prepared by counsel for his own use in prosecuting his client's case; and it is equally unrelated to writings which reflect an attorney's mental impressions, conclusions, opinions or legal theories.

But the impropriety of invoking that privilege does not provide an answer to the problem before us. Petitioner has made more than an ordinary request for relevant, non-privileged facts in the possession of his adversaries or their counsel. He has sought discovery as of right of oral and written statements of witnesses whose identity is well known and whose availability to petitioner appears unimpaired. He has sought production of these matters after making the most searching inquiries of his opponents as to the circumstances surrounding the fatal accident, which inquiries were sworn to have been answered to the best of their information and belief. Interrogatories were directed toward all the events prior to, during and subsequent to the sinking of the tug. Full and honest answers to such broad inquiries would necessarily have included all pertinent information gleaned by Fortenbaugh through his interviews with the witnesses. Petitioner makes no suggestion, and we cannot assume, that the tug owners or Fortenbaugh were incomplete or dishonest in the framing of their answers. In addition, petitioner was free to examine the public testimony of the witnesses taken before the United States Steamboat Inspectors. We are thus dealing with an attempt to secure the production of written statements and mental impressions contained in the files and the mind of the attorney Fortenbaugh without any showing of necessity or any indication or claim that denial of such production would unduly prejudice the preparation of petitioner's case or cause him any hardship or injustice. For aught that appears, the essence of what petitioner seeks either has been revealed to him already through the interrogatories or is readily available to him direct from the witnesses for the asking.

The District Court, after hearing objections to petitioner's request, commanded Fortenbaugh to produce all written statements of witnesses and to state in substance any facts learned through oral statements of witnesses to him. Fortenbaugh was to submit any memoranda he had made of the oral statements so that the court might determine what portions should be revealed to petitioner. All of this was ordered without any showing by petitioner, or any requirement that he make a proper showing, of the necessity for the production of any of this material or any demonstration that denial of production would cause hardship or injustice. The court simply ordered production on the theory that the facts sought were material and were not privileged as constituting attorney-client communications.

In our opinion, neither Rule 26 nor any other rule dealing with discovery contemplates production under such circumstances. That is not because the subject matter is privileged or irrelevant, as those concepts are used in these rules. Here is simply an attempt, without purported necessity or justification, to secure written statements, private memoranda and personal recollections prepared or formed by an adverse party's counsel in the course of his legal duties. As such, it falls outside the arena of discovery and contravenes the public policy underlying the orderly prosecution and defense of legal claims. Not even the most liberal of discovery theories can justify unwarranted inquiries into the files and the mental impressions of an attorney.

Historically, a lawyer is an officer of the court and is bound to work for the advancement of justice while faithfully protecting the rightful interests of his clients. In performing his various duties, however, it is essential that a lawyer work with a certain degree of privacy, free from unnecessary intrusion by opposing parties and their counsel. Proper preparation of a client's case demands that he assemble information, sift what he considers to be the relevant from the irrelevant facts, prepare his legal theories and plan his strategy without undue and needless interference. That is the historical and the necessary way in which lawyers act within the framework of our system of jurisprudence to promote justice and to protect their clients' interests. This work is reflected, of course, in interviews, statements, memoranda, correspondence, briefs, mental impressions, personal beliefs, and countless other tangible and intangible ways—aptly though roughly termed by the Circuit Court of Appeals in this case . . . as the 'Work product of the lawyer.' Were such materials open to opposing counsel on mere demand, much of what is now put down in writing would remain unwritten. An attorney's thoughts, heretofore inviolate, would not be his own. Inefficiency, unfairness and sharp practices would inevitably develop in the giving of legal advice and in the preparation of cases for trial. The effect on the legal profession would be demoralizing. And the interests of the clients and the cause of justice would be poorly served.

We do not mean to say that all written materials obtained or prepared by an adversary's counsel with an eye toward litigation are necessarily free from discovery in all cases. Where relevant and non-privileged facts remain hidden in an attorney's file and where production of those facts is essential to the preparation of one's case, discovery may properly be had. Such written statements and documents might, under certain circumstances, be admissible in evidence or give clues as to the existence or location of relevant facts. Or they might be useful for purposes of impeachment or corroboration. And production might be justified where the witnesses are no longer available or can be reached only with difficulty. Were production of written statements and documents to be precluded under such circumstances, the liberal ideals of the deposition-discovery portions of the Federal Rules of Civil Procedure would be stripped of much of their meaning. But the general policy against invading the privacy of an attorney's course of preparation is so well recognized and so essential to an orderly working of our system of legal procedure that a burden rests on the one who would invade that privacy to establish adequate reasons to justify production through a subpoena or court order. That burden, we believe, is necessarily implicit in the rules as now constituted.

Rule 30(b), as presently written, gives the trial judge the requisite discretion to make a judgment as to whether discovery should be allowed as to written statements secured from witnesses. But in the instant case there was no room for that discretion to operate in favor of the petitioner. No attempt was made to establish any reason why Fortenbaugh should be forced to produce the written statements. There was only a naked, general demand for these materials as of right and a finding by the District Court that no recognizable privilege was involved. That was insufficient to justify discovery under these circumstances and the court should have sustained the refusal of the tug owners and Fortenbaugh to produce.

But as to oral statements made by witnesses to Fortenbaugh, whether presently in the form of his mental impressions or memoranda, we do not believe that any showing of necessity can be made under the circumstances of this case so as to justify production. Under ordinary conditions, forcing an attorney to repeat or write out all that witnesses have told him and to deliver the account to his adversary gives rise to grave dangers of inaccuracy and untrustworthiness. No legitimate purpose is served by such production.

435

The practice forces the attorney to testify as to what he remembers or what he saw fit to write down regarding witnesses' remarks. Such testimony could not qualify as evidence; and to use it for impeachment or corroborative purposes would make the attorney much less an officer of the court and much more an ordinary witness. The standards of the profession would thereby suffer.

Denial of production of this nature does not mean that any material, non-privileged facts can be hidden from the petitioner in this case. He need not be unduly hindered in the preparation of his case, in the discovery of facts or in his anticipation of his opponents' position. Searching interrogatories directed to Fortenbaugh and the tug owners, production of written documents and statements upon a proper showing and direct interviews with the witnesses themselves all serve to reveal the facts in Fortenbaugh's possession to the fullest possible extent consistent with public policy. Petitioner's counsel frankly admits that he wants the oral statements only to help prepare himself to examine witnesses and to make sure that he has overlooked nothing. That is insufficient under the circumstances to permit him an exception to the policy underlying the privacy of Fortenbaugh's professional activities. If there should be a rare situation justifying production of these matters, petitioner's case is not of that type.

We fully appreciate the wide-spread controversy among the members of the legal profession over the problem raised by this case. It is a problem that rests on what has been one of the most hazy frontiers of the discovery process. But until some rule or statute definitely prescribes otherwise, we are not justified in permitting discovery in a situation of this nature as a matter of unqualified right. When Rule 26 and the other discovery rules were adopted, this Court and the members of the bar in general certainly did not believe or contemplate that all the files and mental processes of lawyers were thereby opened to the free scrutiny of their adversaries. And we refuse to interpret the rules at this time so as to reach so harsh and unwarranted a result.

We therefore affirm the judgment of the Circuit Court of Appeals.

Affirmed.

Mr. Justice JACKSON, concurring.

The narrow question in this case concerns only one of thirty-nine interrogatories which defendants and their counsel refused to answer. As there was persistence in refusal after the court ordered them to answer it, counsel and clients were committed to jail by the district court until they should purge themselves of contempt.

The interrogatory asked whether statements were taken from the crews of the tugs involved in the accident, or of any other vessel, and demanded 'Attach hereto exact copies of all such statements if in writing, and if oral, set forth in detail the exact provisions of any such oral statements or reports.' The question is simply whether such a demand is authorized by the rules relating to various aspects of 'discovery'.

The primary effect of the practice advocated here would be on the legal profession itself. But it too often is overlooked that the lawyer and the law office are indispensable parts of our administration of justice. Law-abiding people can go nowhere else to learn the ever changing and constantly multiplying rules by which they must behave and to obtain redress for their wrongs. The welfare and tone of the legal profession is therefore of prime consequence to society, which would feel the consequences of such a practice as petitioner urges secondarily but certainly.

'Discovery' is one of the working tools of the legal profession. It traces back to the equity bill of discovery in English Chancery practice and seems to have had a forerunner in Continental practice . . . Since 1848 when the draftsmen of New York's Code of Procedure recognized the importance of a better system of discovery, the impetus to extend and expand discovery, as well as the opposition to it, has come from within the Bar itself. It happens in this case that it is the plaintiff's attorney who demands such unprecedented latitude of discovery and, strangely enough, amicus briefs in his support have been filed by several labor unions representing plaintiffs as a class. It is the history of the movement for broader discovery, however, that in actual experience the chief opposition to its extension has come from lawyers who specialize in representing plaintiffs because defendants have made liberal use of it to force plaintiffs to disclose their cases in advance. Discovery is a two-edged sword and we cannot decide this problem on any doctrine of extending help to one class of litigants.

It seems clear and long has been recognized that discovery should provide a party access to anything that is evidence in his case. It seems equally clear that discovery should not nullify the privilege of confidential communication between attorney and client. But those principles give us no real assistance here because what is being sought is neither evidence nor is it a privileged communication between attorney and client.

To consider first the most extreme aspect of the requirement in litigation here, we find it calls upon counsel, if he has had any conversations with any of the crews of the vessels in question or of any other, to 'set forth in detail the exact provision of any such oral statements or reports.' Thus[,] the demand is not for the production of a transcript in existence but calls for the creation of a written statement not in being. But the statement by counsel of what a witness told him is not evidence when written plaintiff could not introduce it to prove his case. What, then, is the purpose sought to be served by demanding this of adverse counsel?

Counsel for the petitioner candidly said on argument that he wanted this information to help prepare himself to examine witnesses, to make sure he overlooked nothing. He bases his claim to it in his brief on the view that the Rules were to do away with the old situation where a law suit developed into 'a battle of wits between counsel.' But a common law trial is and always should be an adversary proceeding. Discovery was hardly intended to enable a learned profession to perform its functions either without wits or on wits borrowed from the adversary.

The real purpose and the probable effect of the practice ordered by the district court would be to put trials on a level even lower than a 'battle of wits.' I can conceive of no practice more demoralizing to the Bar than to require a lawyer to write out and deliver to his adversary an account of what witnesses have told him. Even if his recollection were perfect, the statement would be his language permeated with his inferences. Everyone who has tried it knows that it is almost impossible so fairly to record the expressions and emphasis of a witness that when he testifies in the environment of the court and under the influence of the leading question there will not be departures in some respects. Whenever the testimony of the witness would differ from the 'exact' statement the lawyer had delivered, the lawyer's statement would be whipped out to impeach the witness. Counsel producing his adversary's 'inexact' statement could lose nothing by saying, 'Here is a contradiction, gentlemen of the jury. I do not know whether it is my adversary or his witness who is not telling the truth, but one is not.' Of course, if this practice were adopted, that scene would be repeated over and over again. The lawyer who delivers such statements often would find himself branded a deceiver afraid to take the stand to support his own version of the witness's conversation with him, or else he will have to go on the stand to defend his own credibility—perhaps against that of his chief witness, or possibly even his client.

Every lawyer dislikes to take the witness stand and will do so only for grave reasons. This is partly because it is not his role; he is almost invariably a poor witness. But he steps out of professional character to do it. He regrets it; the profession discourages it. But the practice advocated here is one which would force him to be a witness, not as to what he has seen or done but as to other witnesses' stories, and not because he wants to do so but in self-defense.

And what is the lawyer to do who has interviewed one whom he believes to be a biased, lying or hostile witness to get his unfavorable statements and know what to meet? He must record and deliver such statements even though he would not vouch for the credibility of the witness by calling him. Perhaps the other side would not want to call him either, but the attorney is open to the charge of suppressing evidence at the trial if he fails to call such a hostile witness even though he never regarded him as reliable or truthful.

Having been supplied the names of the witnesses, petitioner's lawyer gives no reason why he cannot interview them himself. If an employee-witness refuses to tell his story, he, too, may be examined under the Rules. He may be compelled on discovery as fully as on the trial to disclose his version of the facts. But that is his own disclosure—it can be used to impeach him if he contradicts it and such a deposition is not useful to promote an unseemly disagreement between the witness and the counsel in the case.

It is true that the literal language of the Rules would admit of an interpretation that would sustain the district court's order. So[,] the literal language of the Act of Congress which makes 'Any writing or record. . . made as a memorandum or record of any . . . occurrence, or event,'[633] admissible as evidence, would have allowed the railroad company to put its engineer's accident statements in evidence. . . . But all such procedural measures have a background of custom and practice which was assumed by those who wrote and should be by those who apply them. We reviewed the background of the Act and the consequences on the trial of negligence cases of allowing railroads and others to put in their statements and thus to shield the crew from cross-examination. We said, 'such a major change which opens wide the door to avoidance of cross-examination should not be left to implication.' We pointed out that there, as here, the 'several hundred years of history behind the Act . . . indicate the nature of the reforms which it was designed to effect.' We refused to apply it beyond that point. We should follow the same course of reasoning here. Certainly nothing in the tradition or practice of discovery up to the time of these Rules would have suggested that they would authorize such a practice as here proposed.

The question remains as to signed statements or those written by witnesses. Such statements are not evidence for the defendant.[634]. Nor should I think they ordinarily could be evidence for the plaintiff. But such a statement might be useful for impeachment of the witness who signed it, if he is called and if he departs from the statement. There might be circumstances, too, where impossibility or difficulty of access to the witness or his refusal to respond to requests for information or other facts would show that the interests of justice require that such statements be made available. Production of such statements are governed by Rule 34 and on 'showing good cause therefor' the court may order their inspection, copying or photographing. No such application has here been made; the demand is made on the basis of right, not on showing of cause.

I agree to the affirmance of the judgment of the Circuit Court of Appeals which reversed the district court.

---

[633] 28 U.S.C. § 695.
[634] Palmer v. Hoffman, 318 U.S. 109 (1943).

Mr. Justice FRANKFURTER joins in this opinion.

Follow-Up Comments and Questions

1. What is the difference between that which is protected by attorney-client communications and that which is protected by the work-product doctrine (or privilege) recognized for the first time in this case?

2. The trial court held Fortenbaugh and his partners in contempt and ordered them imprisoned upon their refusal to produce the witness statements. Why could Fortenbaugh and his partners not produce these statements and avoid jail? If they had produced the statements, and appealed at the end of the case the trial court's order to produce them, would the damage of revealing of the protected materials already have been done? Lest you glamorize the lawyers here, you should realize that the trial court and the lawyers knew that the only way to get an appeal heard before the end of the case would be to hold the lawyers in contempt. Lest you fear for the poor lawyer, be assured that trial courts typically certify that such an order should be heard by the appellate court immediately. Thus, lawyers in these circumstances are rarely held in jail while an appeal is under way. In this sense, the trial court's holding Fortenbaugh and his partners in contempt helped them.[635]

3. Did the Court simply ignore that the request for the statements had been made by interrogatories (the wrong way to seek documents such as the statements) and treat the discovery request "as if" they had been made under Rule 34 request for production?

4. What rule did the Court develop in this case for determining whether items qualified as attorney work product?

5. Did the Court rule that, even if the criteria for considering items work product had been met, that the privilege could be overcome by the discovering party's making certain showings? If so, what showings?

6. Did the Court recognize that there is a class of attorney work product that is immune and would have to be protected even if other privileged items were produced? Typically, in such situations a party makes the showings necessary to overcome the work-product privilege, but the documents contain such absolutely protected information, the protected information is redacted from the document.

7. Justice Robert Jackson took a leave of absence from the Supreme Court to be the lead prosecutor in the Nuremburg trials of Nazi officials. There, the governing law allowed lawyers to obtain statements and other materials gathered by the opposing attorney. Justice Jackson had returned to the Court when Hickman was decided. Some believe his experiences in the Nuremburg trials influenced his views. In his well-written concurring opinion, what arguments does Justice Jackson develop in favor of protecting work product?

---

[635] *See, e.g.*, RICHARD L. MARCUS, THE STORY OF HICKMAN: PRESERVING ADVERSARIAL INCENTIVES WHILE EMBRACING BROAD DISCOVERY, IN CIVIL PROCEDURE STORIES 307, 320 (Kevin M. Clermont ed., 2004).

2. The Codification of Hickman—Rule 26(b)(3)

The Federal Rules of Civil Procedure eventually codified the work-product doctrine, as stated in *Hickman* (along with the basis for overcoming the privilege and the immunity of attorney work product). Please review Rule 26(b) (3).

Follow-Up Questions and Comments

1. Do you see the rule for identifying items protected from discovery by the work-product doctrine included in Rule 26(b) (3)? In which part?

2. In what way does the Rule expand the scope of protected items beyond those gathered by an attorney—the common-law work product rule form *Hickman*—to others who may be considered part of the "litigation team"?

3. Does the Rule recognize the ability of the party seeking production of work-product items to make the showing recognized in *Hickman* that would overcome work-product protection? Where do you see in the Rule language allowing a party to overcome the work-product doctrine?

4. Do you also see a provision that provides, when work product is produced, there is a class of work product that is immune and ought to be redacted? What part of the Rule recognizes that?

5. What does Rule 26(b)(5) provide? What does it say about items protected by a privilege or the work-product doctrine that are inadvertently produced? Can the materials be recovered without waiving the protection of the privilege or work-product doctrine? What must the party who inadvertently produced the material do?

C. Discovery of Expert Witnesses

Experts are persons who have knowledge beyond that of the ordinary person on a topic pertinent to the case.[636] A party may serve an interrogatory seeking the identification of any experts who may testify, an explanation of such experts' opinions, the information reviewed in forming such opinions, and an explanation of the grounds for the experts' opinions.[637] Indeed, the sample interrogatories above (Figure 15-2 below) illustrate just such an interrogatory. Furthermore, a party may take depositions of an opponent's testifying experts.[638]

Although an attorney is wise to include an expert interrogatory in the first round of interrogatories, counsel ordinarily would not want to depose the other side's experts until after depositions of fact witnesses. The reason is simple: experts may rely on the testimony of fact witnesses, and counsel would want to know—at the time the expert is deposed—everything on which he or she relies. Typically, the party taking an expert's deposition is responsible for paying that expert's fee for the time during which the expert is

---

[636] *See* FED. R. EVID. 701.
[637] *See, e.g.*, FED. R. CIV. P. 26(b)(4)(B).
[638] *Id.*

440

being deposed.[639] For some experts, the fee can be quite large. Therefore, counsel should ensure that she takes the expert's deposition once and once only, to avoid unnecessary trouble and expense.

A party may retain non-testifying experts, usually referred to as "consulting" experts. Generally, counsel cannot ask discovery questions of such an expert because the Rules state that discovery may only be had from an expert who may testify at trial.[640] They are treated as part of the trial team and, thus, communications with them are comparable to "work product" and should not ordinarily be discoverable. In cases where the subject matter is technical or complicated and the attorney needs assistance in order to understand the subject matter, a consulting expert can be invaluable in the attorney's preparation. However, counsel should be sure that her consulting expert and testifying expert do not exchange information. If so, that could expose the consulting expert to being deposed. The testifying expert often will have to disclose any such communications because generally any information a testifying expert is exposed to will be fair game in discovery.

A final category of experts are those persons with specialized knowledge but who happen to be involved in the facts of the case. For instance, a physician who treated the plaintiff in a personal injury case may be one of the most effective experts in a case. Others, such as a mechanic who worked on a car that malfunctioned or an equipment operator would fall into this category. These experts should be identified in response to interrogatory answers. Because the expert often is not allied with any party, sometimes the expert will offer helpful information for your side of the case. In any event, an attorney ought not to overlook the experts who happen to be part of the history of a case. If you plan to rely on the testimony of such a witness, be sure you identify them under the automatic disclosures of Federal Rule of Civil Procedure 26(a) (2) discussed above and any interrogatory served on your client asking for identification and testimony of experts. Just because you do not pay the witness does not mean you can ignore these requirements. If you fail to treat such witnesses as experts and to provide disclosures and/or interrogatory answers, you may well find that on an objection the court prevents you from eliciting expert testimony from them.

Experts are permitted to require parties who either consult with counsel and/or who testify to charge the client that the attorney represents at a rate commensurate with what the expert is paid in her field. Expert testimony can become quite expensive. Be warned, moreover, that in deposing an opposing party's expert, the party who id initiating the deposition is expected to pay for the expert's time. One would be wise to discuss what the amount will be before embarking on lengthy depositions.

D. Objections to Discovery and Protective Orders

Courts know that attorneys tend to be overly zealous in discovery. Some lawyers practice a "scorched earth" method of discovery designed to require so much work and resources of an opponent that the opposing party gives in and settles more favorably to the discovering party than necessary. Effective attorneys do not permit such tactics to affect a client's case. The system allows for objections to discovery and issuance of protective orders to prevent abusive practices such as these. Indeed, objections can even account for the different level or resources of opposing litigants. Because too few attorneys are aware of their ability to shield a client from abusive discovery, some with legitimate claims do in fact give up pursuing a person or entity that has enough resources to wear down the prospective claimant. Realistically, some litigants will find litigating against an opponent with considerable resources requires them to either settle or end the litigation. However, a client with lesser resources should never have to do so because her

---

[639] 23 AM. JUR. 2d Depositions and Discovery § 51 (2017).
[640] *See id.* § 49; *see, e.g.*, FED. R. CIV. P. 26(b)(4).

lawyer failed to seek protection under the Rules. In other words, inequitable resources will likely always play a part in denying justice to some, but that happens far more than necessary because lawyers simply fail to protect their clients.

1. Objections

Some objections derive directly from a discovery rule. For instance, most interrogatory rules limit the number of interrogatories to 25 including parts and subparts.[641] If a party exceeds that number, the party on whom the interrogatories are served can object based Federal Rule of Civil Procedure 26. Objections to discovery found in Rule 26(b) (2) (C) include: (1) that the discovery sought is unreasonably cumulative or duplicative, or can be obtained from some other source that is more convenient, less burdensome, or less expensive; (2) the party seeking discovery has had ample opportunity to obtain the information by discovery in the action; and (3) that the burden or expense of the proposed discovery outweighs its likely benefit, considering the needs of the case, the amount in controversy, the parties' resources, the importance of the issues at stake in the action, and the importance of the discovery in resolving the issues.

2. Protective Orders

In addition to objecting to discovery, a party may also move for a protective order. Protective orders are a flexible, powerful tool by which the court can hold parties in check and prevent abuse. Most jurisdictions have a rule modeled on Rule 26(c), which is reprinted below. The rule permits courts, upon motion and for good cause, to issue an order to protect a party or person from annoyance, embarrassment, oppression, or undue burden and expense, including one or more of the following:

Protective Orders

> In general . . . . [a protective order may be entered] forbidding the . . . discovery; specifying terms, including time and place, for the . . . discovery; prescribing a discovery method other than the one selected by the party seeking discovery; forbidding inquiry into certain matters, or limiting the scope of . . . discovery to certain matters; designating the persons who may be present while the discovery is conducted; requiring that a deposition be sealed and opened only on court order; requiring that a trade secret or other confidential research, development, or commercial information not be revealed or be revealed only in a specified way; and requiring that the parties simultaneously file specified documents or information in sealed envelopes, to be opened as the court directs.[642]

E. Discovery Motions and Sanctions

Few attorneys will get through a case without filing a motion to compel discovery. This unfortunate fact likely results from the mindset that is fostered by an adversarial system of justice. Lawyers who receive discovery requests commonly look for a way to interpret them to justify providing less information (or materials) than an objective reading of the request would call for.

---

[641] 23 AM. JUR. 2d Depositions and Discovery § 119 (2017).
[642] FED. R. CIV. P. 26(c).

The introduction of broad discovery into American civil litigation was intended to foster cooperative exchange of information, avoid surprises, and foster settlements.[643] To some extent, broad discovery probably has achieved those goals. A high percentage of cases settle before trial, and a major contributing factor is the exchange of information that allows parties to see how their case is likely to turn out. Id. Unfortunately, the reality in our modern adversarial system is that a litigant will have to fight for much of the information to which she is fairly entitled. Rarely will an attorney receive responses to interrogatories or requests for production without some objections upon which the opponent may very well be withholding valuable information. Even attorneys who seek to maintain a level of professionalism will justify withholding discoverable information that could be produced upon a fair reading of a discovery request. They rationalize that the adversarial system dictates that if they have any arguable objection to responding (especially with a document that is harmful to their party's case), that they should raise the objection and withhold the requested information with the knowledge that opposing counsel can move to compel, and the court will rule on whether the information must be submitted. Although the goals of avoiding surprises and fostering settlements seem to have been somewhat furthered, the goal of cooperation has not been advanced to the same extent.

An attorney should enter discovery with her eyes wide open, expecting to relentlessly pursue her discovery requests until they are fully answered. Then and only then can an attorney be confident that she has all the information (or documents) to which her client is entitled. Additionally, through thorough discovery the attorney can gain whatever leverage is appropriate to the strength of her client's claims or defenses. Counsel will need to be persistent in discovery to ensure she gains that leverage appropriate to her client's position so that, if there is a settlement, it is based on full disclosure of the facts—providing an accurate picture of the likely outcome of the trial—rather than a settlement based on an incomplete view of the facts and likely outcome.

Federal Rule of Civil Procedure 37, the federal sanctions rule, is the one under which one would seek to compel production and/or sanctions in federal court. A significant difference between Rule 37 and Rule 11 is that the moving party need not serve her motion on opposing counsel and wait. She can bring the motion immediately, without providing the "safe harbor" allowed under Rule 11 for non-discovery filings. Nevertheless, an attorney seeking discovery should realize that she will first have to move to compel discovery responses, schedule a hearing, and receive an order compelling the responses desired. Rule 37 is designed to require such an order as a prerequisite to sanctions—i.e., the party ordered to produce responses after a motion to compel fails to do so and, thus, violates the court's order.

A healthy trend in discovery has been to require the moving party to certify that she has attempted to resolve the discovery dispute with opposing counsel prior to filing a motion to compel. When attorneys take the time to discuss the objections that have been made (by either side) they can often reach an agreement concerning the discovery that is being sought. If not, they will at least narrow the controversy that the court must resolve. Rule 37 (a) (1) requires a motion to compel to contain a certification of a good faith attempt to resolve the discovery dispute.

If counsel has attempted to resolve a discovery dispute and cannot, a motion to compel would follow. Unlike pleadings and motions, discovery requests and responses are not filed with the court. Instead, they are served on counsel for the parties. Thus, the only way the court will learn of a discovery request or response, what objections were made, or what was provided is when the moving party files a motion to compel, explaining these facts and attaching pertinent documents. After obtaining the dates on which the

---

[643] 23 AM. JUR. 2D Depositions and Discovery § 1 (2017)

opposing counsel is available for a hearing, an attorney filing a motion to compel would then schedule a hearing with the court. Rule 37, moreover, allows for imposition of attorney's fees and costs upon the litigant who wrongfully forces her opponent compel or block discovery, though courts do not always impose these sanctions.[644] Thus, the party responding to a discovery request has less incentive to respond fully in the first response. Again, the party seeking discovery should acknowledge this fact and expect to be required to move to compel more than once. In balance, how-ever, an attorney that shows her opponent that she is unwilling to permit an adversary to withhold information or documents sets a strong tone for the remainder of the litigation. Aggressive discovery can even force the opponent's hand, often leading to earlier settlement discussions.

Sanctions in discovery generally come in two forms. First, a recalcitrant party can face sanctions for failure to comply with an order compelling discovery. If the court has granted an order compelling discovery or otherwise ordered a party to produce information or make a witness available, the failure of such a party to comply with the order justifies sanctions.[645] The possible sanctions a court can order in this situation typically include: (a) having the matter sought to be discovered taken as established for the purposes of trial; (b) prohibiting the party who failed to comply with the court's order from supporting claims or defenses or from introducing certain evidence; (c) striking pleadings, in whole or in part; (d) staying the case until the order is obeyed; (e) dismissing the suit in whole or in part; (f) entering a default judgment against the party who failed to comply, and/or holding the party who failed to comply in contempt of court.[646] Second, a party may be sanctioned for certain failures even without a prior court order, including (1) failure to appear for a deposition properly noticed by the opposing party, or (2) failure to provide any answers to interrogatories, or any responses to requests for production of documents, or otherwise respond at all to discovery requests.[647]

Practice Problem
Practice Problem 15-1
D.W. piloted an AERO, Inc. plane that left the airport in Atlanta, Georgia but started to experience mechanical failures not long after taking off. The landing gear on the plane would not deploy to allow D.W. to make an emergency landing. Thus, D.W. made the unprecedented maneuver of flipping the plane and landing it in a field upside down. By doing so, D.W. saved most of the passengers on the plane. AERO immediately sent an investigative team to the site. The investigative team is led by AERO's General Counsel. The team includes lawyers other than the General Counsel, airplane experts on various parts of the plane, and photographers. The team is instructed to inspect the site and the plane, interview D.W. and the witnesses, and write a report for the AERO Board of Directors on its findings as to the cause of the crash, whether D.W. had any part in it, and the exposure to the company from the accident.

The survivors of those who were killed in the landing sued AERO for damages based on wrongful death. In the course of discovery, plaintiffs make a request for production of documents seeking (a) a copy of the Report to the Board of AERO; (b) all photos or videos of the accident site taken by the investigative team; (c) all photos or videos of the accident site taken by witnesses or other non-parties and given to or sold to AERO; (d) all signed statements given by witnesses; (e) all audiotapes or videotapes of interviews with witnesses; (f) all notes and memoranda concerning the investigation; (g) the results of all tests the investigative team performed on any parts of the plane; (h) names of everyone inter-viewed as part of the

---

[644] *See* FED. R. CIV. P. 37; 23 AM. JUR. 2D Depositions and Discovery § 208 (2017).

[645] *See* 23 AM. JUR. 2d Depositions and Discovery § 210 (2015).

[646] *See* FED. R. CIV. P. 37(b).

[647] *See, e.g.*, FED. R. CIV. P. 37(c)(d).

investigation; and (i) a summary of each witness interviewed.

Follow-Up Questions and Comments

1. Which, if any, of these items are discoverable?

2. Would any of the items listed above have to be disclosed if AERO decided to call as an expert witness at trial one of the experts who participated in the investigation and gathering the materials described?

3. The plaintiffs' interrogatories also request detailed information on why the plane's landing gear failed, and the plane crashed. Can AERO refuse to answer on the grounds that the information was learned as part of the work-product investigation?

4. Suppose that D.W., in a moment of guilt-induced confession after the accident, admitted he drank approximately seven beers late in the evening before the early morning flight and that he had taken Adderall that was not prescribed for him, but which he had received from a friend so that he could get "cleared up and alert" when he was feeling the effects of the night before. In addition, D.W. gave the names and addresses of the crew members that were with him in the bar where he was drinking. In discovery, the plaintiff's interrogatories ask:

    a. For the 24-hour period immediately prior to the takeoff of the AERO flight, state whether Captain D.W. ingested any alcohol or drugs of any kind.

    b. If Captain D.W. did consume alcohol or drugs of any kind during the 24 hours prior to the takeoff of the flight, state when and where the alcohol was consumed, the quantity consumed, and for the drugs ingested, the amount ingested, and the time(s) ingested.

5. Must AERO answer the interrogatories? If so, why?

Figure 15-2

Brief Overview Deposition Objections[648]

Objection	Example	Purpose	Waivable?
Privilege	"I am instructing my client not to answer this question pursuant to his fifth amendment privilege."	To prevent disclosure of privileged information.	Disclosure of privileged information to a non-privileged third party waives the privilege as to the information already disclosed.
Work Product	"Objection – that information is attorney work product."	To prevent disclosure of information protected by the work-product doctrine.	Yes.
Form of the Question	"Objection – Compound question."	To prevent the deponent's answers from admission at trial, and from potential out-of-context use.	Yes.
Violation of a Limiting Order	"Objection – this information is undiscoverable pursuant to a court or-der."	To prevent disclosure of information previously excluded from discovery by court order.	No. This information can still be excluded at trial, but may lead to other discovery, or waste of litigants' time and resources.
Admissibility (Frivolous)	"Objection – Hearsay."	To prevent disclosure of inadmissible information.	No. Issues of admissibility are preserved for trial, and such objections may be frivolous in a deposition.
Speaking Objections (Prohibited)	"Objection, overly broad and vague. The witness cannot possibly identify all facts surrounding any instance."	To identify and communicate to the deponent a problem with the form of the question.	Yes. The underlying form of the question objection may be waived. However, these objections violate Rule 30(d) by intention-ally giving clues to the deponent about how she should answer.

---

[648] Ultimately, Federal Rules of Civil Procedure Rules 30 and 32 govern objections at a deposition and should be reviewed to ensure understanding of the scope permitted at a deposition.

CHAPTER 16: THE RIGHT TO A JURY TRIAL AND SUMMARY JUDGMENT

I. How the Topics in this Chapter Fit in the Overall Progress of a Civil Action

Below is a diagram of the stages of a civil action showing in bold where the topics in this chapter fall in the progress of a case.

Figure 16-1

Cause of Action (events leading to suit)	Pre-Filing Tasks (items to begin representation, interviewing, and related matters)	Choice of Forum (subject matter jurisdiction, removal, personal jurisdiction, and venue)	Notice and Service of Process (completing the process of ensuring the forum court can enter a valid judgment)	Pleading the Case and Joinder of Claims and Parties (including supplemental jurisdiction)

Responding to Claims by Motion or by Answer	Discovery (developing proof to establish claims and learn your adversary's case)	**Right to Jury (pretrial motions and practice)**	Final Pretrial Conference (events within last month before trial)	Trial (procedures and motions during trial)	Verdict	Post-Trial Motions (motions for a new trial and/or judgment as a matter of law)	Appeal

We will assume that the lawyers in the case know the procedure for demanding a jury in cases that qualify for a jury trial. If they do, they know that the jury demand must be early in the case (no later than 14 days after the answer or, if the case is removed from state court to federal court, 14 days from the notice of removal). The requirements of a jury demand, and how to determine whether the case is one to which a jury trial right attaches, are discussed below.

For those who do not demand a jury in the time required, their client's ability to have a jury trial will be waived even if the case otherwise would be one that is within a party's right to a jury trial. Thus, the demand is crucial. It will also be important that the case be within the category of cases for which a party is entitled to a jury trial. The first part of this chapter will explore these topics because they are foundational. However, as will be shown, the real battle over whether the case will go to a jury trial, will be at the summary judgment stage.

The lawyer can develop her own philosophy on what she advises clients about whether to demand juries. Consider the following. Some believe that a lawyer seeking damages for a plaintiff should err on the side of requesting a jury trial. Juries historically do award greater damage awards than judges, regardless

447

of the type of case. But the preference for juries as the ultimate decision-maker goes beyond that rationale. A group of individuals, though admittedly flawed as human beings (as are all of us), collectively offset the prejudice that can flow from one person's bias. A judge is one person, no matter how smart, and a group of jurors stand the best chance of reaching a fair decision.[649]

Former Supreme Court Justice, Sandra Day O'Connor, spent many years as a trial judge before ascending to the high court. The following observation by Justice O'Connor, therefore, is telling: "As a trial judge, I presided over many jury trials in both civil and criminal trials. In all but two or three cases, I felt the jury reached an entirely appropriate verdict and the jurors were almost always conscientious and sincere in trying to do a proper job."[650] Stories about what jurors talk about and consider in the jury room, told after the fact by former jurors, do not inspire confidence. Yet what is lost is exactly what Justice O'Connor observed from the bench: jurors have a knack for getting to the right result.

Some believe that defense lawyers should avoid juries and prefer judges. That may be true because judges do tend to award less in damages. However, if as a defense lawyer you believe you have a good case against liability, you would do well to consider a jury. The instances in which a lawyer ought to avoid a jury are less than some suggest. If one's client is truly unsympathetic, perhaps choosing a judge—who deals with many unsympathetic people—could be better than a jury. The other scenario that urges caution is when a defendant has a highly technical defense, probably based on legal technicalities, and the opponent has fairness on her side. Judges are more apt to apply the law, even if technical, rather than be swayed by passion. We cannot forget, however, that judges are people too and will be influenced by equity. While, there are no easy answers to the question of whether to demand a jury, at a minimum, the lawyer should talk through with the client the pros and cons of a jury and come to a resolution.

This discussion assumes that (1) a party has a right to a jury trial on one or more claims, and (2) has timely demanded the right to a jury trial. Summary judgment typically follows the close of all discovery. Courts will have in a pretrial order, after the close of discovery, a deadline for dispositive motions. Nevertheless, the prudent plaintiff's lawyer will assume that, as soon as a case goes into the discovery phase, the opponent will move summary judgment at the close of discovery. If that is the lawyer's mindset, she will keep her eye on developing enough evidence, from her own client, from experts, and from the tools of discovery previously discussed in Chapter 13. Then, if the opponent moves for summary judgment, a plaintiff's counsel can show facts on each of the elements of the client's claims on which reasonable jurors can disagree. That, after all, is all that plaintiff's counsel need show to avoid summary judgment. If by chance the opponent does not file a summary judgment motion, the work done in developing the claim will pay off at trial. The point is that the lawyer must anticipate the likely course of proceedings from the very beginning of the case. If she does, she will almost always be thinking ahead of opposing counsel and preparing to meet any challenges. As a plaintiff's counsel, being prepared to meet the challenge of summary judgment means that the lawyer has considered the key evidence that will be necessary to show that reasonable jurors can differ on whether the plaintiff should prevail. As defense counsel, being prepared for summary judgment means to evaluate the weak spots in the plaintiff's case and prepare to show that the plaintiff's evidence is so weak, or would require such speculation, that reasonable jurors could not disagree on plaintiff's claim.

---

[649] *See* Benjamin V. Madison, III, *Trial by Jury or by Military Tribunal for Accused Terrorist Detainees Facing the Death Penalty? An Examination of Principles that Transcend the Constitution*, 17 U. FLA J.L. & PUB. POL'Y 347, 391–97 (2006)(examining the extent to which juries reflect principles consistent with biblical and natural law principles).
[650] Sandra Day O'Connor, *Juries: They May Be Broken, But We Can Fix Them*, 44 June FED. LAWYER 20 (1997).

The prudent defense lawyer also keeps summary judgment in mind from the outset. If the defense lawyer spots weaknesses in the plaintiff's chain of proof, she can prepare to offer to the court facts that show the plaintiff cannot even show, on a required element of proof, sufficient evidence on which reasonable jurors can disagree. The classic example that will resonate with experienced negligence lawyers is the element of proximate cause. In many cases, particularly product defect cases, the plaintiff will have ample facts of duty, breach of duty, and injuries. Nevertheless, the plaintiff often lacks sufficient facts on which reasonable jurors can disagree about whether the defendant's breach of duty was the proximate cause of the injuries.

Again, the strategic challenge thus needs to be thought through early in litigation. Lawyers who do so can often find just enough evidence to get past summary judgment (if representing a plaintiff). Those who wait until the end of discovery, when summary judgment is upon them, are the ones who see their clients' claims dismissed because they did not plan ahead and develop evidence to present such that the lawyer could argue that reasonable jurors could disagree on whether the plaintiff could prove her claim.

Figure 16-2

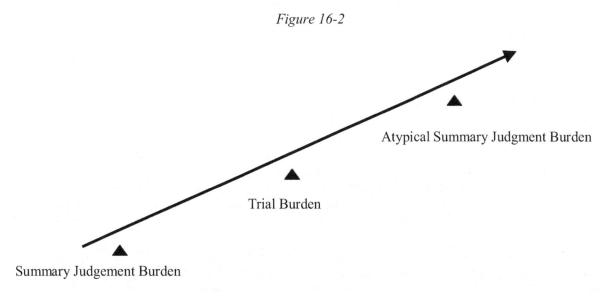

Atypical Summary Judgment Burden

Trial Burden

Summary Judgement Burden

II. Summary Judgment Burden

Figure 16-2 illustrates that the required showing to get the case to a jury is not all that difficult. All that one must do is satisfy the court that there is sufficient evidence to get past the triangle on the far left. That triangle on the far left is called the "summary judgment burden" here because we are discussing a pretrial effort, under Rule 56, to dismiss a case on summary judgment. As we will see in the chapter on motions at trial, the same triangle is all that a plaintiff need get past to show he or she has sufficient evidence on which reasonable jurors could disagree. Thus, the threshold for "sufficiency of the evidence" is the same before trial (if challenged on summary judgment) or at trial (if challenged by a motion for judgment as a matter of law). All a party seeking a jury trial must show is that reasonable jurors could disagree on each of the required elements of the claim. If so, then the judge is not to take away a jury trial even though she may think the case is weak. The burden in the middle, however, shows that the burden at trial on which the jury will be instructed is a higher burden than at summary judgment. The standard at trial—which the jury will decide when it deliberates and weighs the evidence, including determining credibility of witnesses— is typically the "preponderance of the evidence" standard. Proving something by a preponderance of the evidence means the party convinces the jury that "more likely than not" has been proved. The point to remember, however, is that the preponderance-of-the-evidence standard does not apply when the court determines a summary judgment motion. Rather, the court is supposed to consider whether the evidence presented (in affidavits, depositions, etc.) shows sufficient evidence on which the claim can proceed. For the party with the jury right, such a standard is a friendly one. Often counsel in pretrial hearings mix up the standards and argue that a claim "cannot be proved." Well-informed counsel will not make that mistake. If defending one's right to a jury trial, counsel will correct any such argument by pointing out that sufficiency of evidence is far different from satisfying the preponderance of evidence standard at trial. Thus, the plaintiff need not prove anything; she merely needs to offer sufficient evidence showing that reasonable jurors could disagree on her ability to prove her claim.

In the last half of this chapter, we will explore both the procedures for bringing a summary judgment motion under Federal Rule of Civil Procedure 56 and the standard the court applies in deciding whether to grant summary judgment. It is helpful, however, to first see what is at stake—the right to a jury trial— before addressing summary judgment. After all, summary judgment motions are made in the shadow of the right to a jury trial. Thus, it helps for one to explore the procedure for demanding a jury, so that one knows whether a jury trial is even possible, and then how the court determines whether the claim or claims in the case are of the kind in which one has a right to jury trial. Some claims, we will see, are not ones for which the jury right extends. Therefore, applying the test for determining to which claims a jury trial right attaches is a threshold question.

III. The Right to a Jury Trial

The right to a jury trial and motions for summary judgment are highly interrelated. When a party demands a jury trial, she seeks a group of laypersons from the community to decide the disputed facts and apply the law to the facts. Usually, a major disputed fact will be the amount of damages necessary to compensate the plaintiff if the defendant is found liable. A summary judgment motion seeks to take the decision from the jury and place it in the hands of a judge. The rationale of a motion for summary judgment is that the party who bears the burden of proving her claim must show that her case is worthy of a jury trial.

Why, then, are the right to jury trial and summary judgment motions related? The standard for granting summary judgment has been crafted to preserve a party's right to a jury trial. The reasonable-persons-can-differ standard is a generous one and reflects the preference under American law favors cases being resolved by juries when possible. The judge intervenes in two general categories of cases. The first category includes cases in which the plaintiff asserts a claim that the jurisdiction does not recognize as actionable (e.g., a claim against a social host for allowing a guest to become intoxicated at the guest's behest, and then allowing the inebriated guest to drive off and injure or kill someone). The second category of cases in which the judge intervenes is when the claimant, usually the plaintiff, but sometimes a counterclaimant—fails to show that she has sufficient evidence such that reasonable jurors can disagree about the evidence supporting the claim. In the second category of cases, a judge will short-circuit the litigation process because the claimant can do no better at trial than at summary judgment. The judge here rules that the case is not worthy of the time and effort involved in a jury trial. The judge can see from the summary judgment materials that judgment will have to be granted as a matter of law at trial due to the lack of sufficient evidence. American jurisprudence favors giving parties an opportunity to have their day in court. However, it does not guarantee the right to have every case heard in a court of law regardless of whether a party can show that there is a dispute to be tried.

To get a jury trial, the party demanding a jury must show that the matter is one in which juries traditionally decide the facts and verdict. If the case falls in the category of those for which jury trials are

450

allowed, the other challenge is for the demanding party to show sufficient evidence such that reasonable jurors could disagree on whether facts should be found for that party and relief granted.

A. Demand for Jury Trial

Please read Federal Rule of Civil Procedure 38. When does a jury demand need to be made? What happens if a party fails to make the demand within the required time? Please read Federal Rule of Civil Procedure 81 (regarding cases removed from state court to federal court). In cases removed from state court to federal court in which no jury demand has yet been made, how long does a party must make a demand? What happens if no party makes a demand within that time frame?

B. Claims to Which Jury Trial Right Attaches

In American law, few rights are held as precious as the right to a trial by jury. The right for an American citizen to have her claims decided by a group of her equals is fundamental to the American judicial system. Parties can point to support for this right not only in the U.S. Constitution, but also in the constitutions of the states, the statutes of the states, and/or state procedural rules.[651] The foundation of the right to trial by jury can be traced back to the Magna Carta, the famous charter resulting from the revolt of English barons against their tyrannical king. Led by Archbishop Stephen Langton, the barons forced King John to sign the Magna Carta on June 15, 1215. Among the rights that the King recognized were the following:

> No free man shall be seized or imprisoned, or stripped of his rights or possessions, or outlawed or exiled, or deprived of his standing in any other way, nor will we proceed with force against him, or send others to do so, except by the lawful judgment of his equals.[652]

Magna Carta decreased the centralized power of the king of England and is generally considered one of the foundations for English and American constitutional government.[653] Originally, the right to trial by jury afforded protection only to certain members of English society. Eventually, English common law and later American common law recognized this right as one owed to every member of society.[654]

Nevertheless, the right to a jury trial has never extended to all claims. Recall from Chapter One that in the English courts the Court of Common Pleas was the traditional place of cases "at common law" and juries were the norm in cases "at law." However, the English court system also developed a Court of Chancery. Chancery, in which the judges were called "chancellors," arose to allow for equitable, more flexible relief when remedies at law were absent. Juries were not part of the Chancery courts. Thus, if a case presents purely equitable claims, neither party can demand a jury. A chancellor would find the facts and make the decision on whether to grant equitable relief, such as issue an injunction, rescind a contract, or any of the other flexible remedies that arose in equity.

The test for determining whether a party is entitled to a jury trial derives from the above historical background. The following case incorporates that background in providing the Supreme Court's view on the appropriate test for determining when a party gets a jury.

---

[651] 47 AM. JUR. 2d Jury § 3 (2009).

[652] MAGNA CARTA § 39 (1215).

[653] *See, e.g.*, MD. CONST., art. 24 (2014) (quoting the MAGNA CARTA).

[654] RUSSELL KIRK, THE ROOTS OF AMERICAN ORDER, 185–86 (2004).

CHAUFFEURS LOCAL 391 v. TERRY
Supreme Court of the United States, 1990
494 U.S. 558

JUSTICE MARSHALL delivered the opinion of the Court, except as to Part III-A.

This case presents the question whether an employee who seeks relief in the form of backpay for a union's alleged breach of its duty of fair representation has a right to trial by jury. We hold that the Seventh Amendment entitles such a plaintiff to a jury trial.

I

McLean Trucking Company and the Chauffeurs, Teamsters and Helpers Local No. 391 (Union) were parties to a collective-bargaining agreement that governed the terms and conditions of employment at McLean's terminals. The 27 respondents were employed by McLean as truckdrivers in bargaining units covered by the agreement, and all were members of the Union. In 1982 McLean implemented a change in operations that resulted in the elimination of some of its terminals and the reorganization of others. As part of that change, McLean transferred respondents to the terminal located in Winston-Salem and agreed to give them special seniority rights in relation to "inactive" employees in Winston-Salem who had been laid off temporarily.

After working in Winston-Salem for approximately six weeks, respondents were alternately laid off and recalled several times. Respondents filed a grievance with the Union, contesting the order of the layoffs and recalls. Respondents also challenged McLean's policy of stripping any driver who was laid off of his special seniority rights. Respondents claimed that McLean breached the collective-bargaining agreement by giving inactive drivers preference over respondents. After these proceedings, the grievance committee ordered McLean to recall any respondent who was then laid off and to lay off any inactive driver who had been recalled; in addition, the committee ordered McLean to recognize respondents' special seniority rights until the inactive employees were properly recalled.

On the basis of this decision, McLean recalled respondents and laid off the drivers who had been on the inactive list when respondents transferred to Winston-Salem. Soon after this, though, McLean recalled the inactive employees, thereby allowing them to regain seniority rights over respondents. In the next round of layoffs, then, respondents had lower priority than inactive drivers and were laid off first. Accordingly, respondents filed another grievance, alleging that McLean's actions were designed to circumvent the initial decision of the grievance committee. The Union representative appeared before the grievance committee and presented the contentions of respondents and those of the inactive truckdrivers. At the conclusion of the hearing, the committee held that McLean had not violated the committee's first decision.

McLean continued to engage in periodic layoffs and recalls of the workers at the Winston-Salem terminal. Respondents filed a third grievance with the Union, but the Union declined to refer the charges to a grievance committee on the ground that the relevant issues had been determined in the prior proceedings.

In July 1983, respondents filed an action in District Court, alleging that McLean had breached the collective-bargaining agreement in violation of § 301 of the Labor Management Relations Act,[655] and that

---

[655] 1947, 29 U. S. C. § 185 (1982 ed.).

the Union had violated its duty of fair representation. Respondents requested a permanent injunction requiring the defendants to cease their illegal acts and to reinstate them to their proper seniority status; in addition, they sought, inter alia, compensatory damages for lost wages and health benefits. In 1986 [,] McLean filed for bankruptcy; subsequently, the action against it was voluntarily dismissed, along with all claims for injunctive relief.

Respondents had requested a jury trial in their pleadings. The Union moved to strike the jury demand on the ground that no right to a jury trial exists in a duty of fair representation suit. The District Court denied the motion to strike. After an interlocutory appeal, the Fourth Circuit affirmed the trial court, holding that the Seventh Amendment entitled respondents to a jury trial of their claim for monetary relief. We granted the petition for certiorari to resolve a Circuit conflict on this issue,[656] and now affirm the judgment of the Fourth Circuit.

II

The duty of fair representation is inferred from unions' exclusive authority under the National Labor Relations Act (NLRA),[657] to represent all employees in a bargaining unit. The duty requires a union "to serve the interests of all members without hostility or discrimination toward any, to exercise its discretion with complete good faith and honesty, and to avoid arbitrary conduct." A union must discharge its duty both in bargaining with the employer and in its enforcement of the resulting collective-bargaining agreement. Thus, the Union here was required to pursue respondents' grievances in a manner consistent with the principles of fair representation.

Because most collective-bargaining agreements accord finality to grievance or arbitration procedures established by the collective-bargaining agreement, an employee normally cannot bring a § 301 action against an employer unless he can show that the union breached its duty of fair representation in its handling of his grievance. Whether the employee sues both the labor union and the employer or only one of those entities, he must prove the same two facts to recover money damages: that the employer's action violated the terms of the collective-bargaining agreement and that the union breached its duty of fair representation.

III

We turn now to the constitutional issue presented in this case--whether respondents are entitled to a jury trial. The Seventh Amendment provides that "[i]n Suits at common law, where the value in controversy shall exceed twenty dollars, the right of trial by jury shall be preserved." The right to a jury trial includes more than the common-law forms of action recognized in 1791; the phrase "Suits at common law" refers to "suits in which legal rights [are] to be ascertained and determined, in contradistinction to those where equitable rights alone [are] recognized, and equitable remedies [are] administered."[658] The right extends to causes of action created by Congress. Since the merger of the systems of law and equity,[659] this Court has carefully preserved the right to trial by jury where legal rights are at stake. As the Court noted in *Beacon Theatres, Inc. v. Westover*,[660] "'Maintenance of the jury as a fact-finding body is of such importance and occupies so firm a place in our history and jurisprudence that any seeming curtailment of the right to a

---

[656] 491 U.S. 903 (1989).

[657] 29 U. S. C. § 159(a) (1982 ed.).

[658] Parsons v. Bedford, 3 Pet. 433, 447 (1830) ("[T]he amendment then may well be construed to embrace all suits which are not of equity and admiralty jurisdiction, whatever may be the peculiar form which they may assume to settle legal rights.").

[659] FED. R. CIV. P. 2

[660] 359 U.S. 500, 501 (1959) (quoting Dimick v. Schiedt, 293 U.S. 474, 486 (1935).

jury trial should be scrutinized with the utmost care'"

To determine whether a particular action will resolve legal rights, we examine both the nature of the issues involved and the remedy sought. "First, we compare the statutory action to 18th-century actions brought in the courts of England prior to the merger of the courts of law and equity. Second, we examine the remedy sought and determine whether it is legal or equitable in nature." The second inquiry is the more important in our analysis.

A

An action for breach of a union's duty of fair representation was unknown in 18th-century England; in fact, collective bargaining was unlawful. We must therefore look for an analogous cause of action that existed in the 18th century to determine whether the nature of this duty of fair representation suit is legal or equitable.

The Union contends that this duty of fair representation action resembles a suit brought to vacate an arbitration award because respondents seek to set aside the result of the grievance process. In the 18th century, an action to set aside an arbitration award was considered equitable.[661] In support of its characterization of the duty of fair representation claim, the Union cites *United Parcel Service, Incorporated v. Mitchell*,[662] in which we held that, for purposes of selecting from various state statutes an appropriate limitations period for a § 301 suit against an employer, such a suit was more analogous to a suit to vacate an arbitration award than to a breach of contract action.

The arbitration analogy is inapposite, however, to the Seventh Amendment question posed in this case. No grievance committee has considered respondents' claim that the Union violated its duty of fair representation; the grievance process was concerned only with the employer's alleged breach of the collective-bargaining agreement. Thus, respondents' claim against the Union cannot be characterized as an action to vacate an arbitration award because "'[t]he arbitration proceeding did not, and indeed, could not, resolve the employee's claim against the union. . . . Because no arbitrator has decided the primary issue presented by this claim, no arbitration award need be undone, even if the employee ultimately prevails.'"[663]

The Union next argues that respondents' duty of fair representation action is comparable to an action by a trust beneficiary against a trustee for breach of fiduciary duty. Such actions were within the exclusive jurisdiction of courts of equity. This analogy is far more persuasive than the arbitration analogy. Just as a trustee must act in the best interests of the beneficiaries . . . a union, as the exclusive representative of the workers, must exercise its power to act on behalf of the employees in good faith. Moreover, just as a beneficiary does not directly control the actions of a trustee . . . an individual employee lacks direct control over a union's actions taken on his behalf.

. . .

Respondents contend that their duty of fair representation suit is less like a trust action than an attorney malpractice action, which was historically an action at law. In determining the appropriate statute of limitations for a hybrid § 301/duty of fair representation action, this Court in *DelCostello* noted in dictum

---

[661] 2 J. STORY, COMMENTARIES ON EQUITY JURISPRUDENCE § 1452, pp. 789–90 (13th ed. 1886) (equity courts had jurisdiction over claims that an award should be set aside on the ground of "mistake of the arbitrators"); *see, e.g.,* Burchell v. Marsh, 17 How. 344 (1855) (reviewing bill in equity to vacate an arbitration award).
[662] 451 U.S. 56 (1981).
[663] *DelCostello*, 462 U.S. at 167.

454

that an attorney malpractice action is "the closest state-law analogy for the claim against the union." The Court in *DelCostello* did not consider the trust analogy, however. Presented with a more complete range of alternatives, we find that, in the context of the Seventh Amendment inquiry, the attorney malpractice analogy does not capture the relationship between the union and the represented employees as fully as the trust analogy does.

The attorney malpractice analogy is inadequate in several respects. Although an attorney malpractice suit is in some ways similar to a suit alleging a union's breach of its fiduciary duty, the two actions are fundamentally different. The nature of an action is in large part controlled by the nature of the underlying relationship between the parties. Unlike employees represented by a union, a client controls the significant decisions concerning his representation. Moreover, a client can fire his attorney if he is dissatisfied with his attorney's performance. This option is not available to an individual employee who is unhappy with a union's representation, unless a majority of the members of the bargaining unit share his dissatisfaction. Thus, we find the malpractice analogy less convincing than the trust analogy.

Nevertheless, the trust analogy does not persuade us to characterize respondents' claim as wholly equitable. The Union's argument mischaracterizes the nature of our comparison of the action before us to 18th-century forms of action. As we observed in *Ross v. Bernhard*,[664] "The Seventh Amendment question depends on the nature of the issue to be tried rather than the character of the overall action." [665] (emphasis added) (finding a right to jury trial in a shareholder's derivative suit, a type of suit traditionally brought in courts of equity, because plaintiffs' case presented legal issues of breach of contract and negligence). As discussed above . . . to recover from the Union here, respondents must prove both that McLean violated § 301 by breaching the collective-bargaining agreement and that the Union breached its duty of fair representation. When viewed in isolation, the duty of fair representation issue is analogous to a claim against a trustee for breach of fiduciary duty. The § 301 issue, however, is comparable to a breach of contract claim—a legal issue.

Respondents' action against the Union thus encompasses both equitable and legal issues. The first part of our Seventh Amendment inquiry, then, leaves us in equipoise as to whether respondents are entitled to a jury trial.

B

Our determination under the first part of the Seventh Amendment analysis is only preliminary. In this case, the only remedy sought is a request for compensatory damages representing backpay and benefits. Generally, an action for money damages was "the traditional form of relief offered in the courts of law." This Court has not, however, held that "any award of monetary relief must necessarily be 'legal' relief." Nonetheless, because we conclude that the remedy respondents seek has none of the attributes that must be present before we will find an exception to the general rule and characterize damages as equitable, we find that the remedy sought by respondents is legal.

First, we have characterized damages as equitable where they are restitutionary, such as in "action[s] for disgorgement of improper profits[.]" The backpay sought by respondents is not money wrongfully held by the Union, but wages and benefits they would have received from McLean had the Union processed the employees' grievances properly. Such relief is not restitutionary.

Second, a monetary award "incidental to or intertwined with injunctive relief" may be equitable.[666]

---

[664] 396 U.S. 531 (1970).
[665] *Id.* at 538
[666] *Tull*, at 424. *See, e. g.*, Mitchell v. Robert DeMario Jewelry, Inc., 361 U.S. 288, 291–92 (1960) (District Court had

Because respondents seek only money damages, this characteristic is clearly absent from the case.

The Union argues that the backpay relief sought here must nonetheless be considered equitable because this Court has labeled backpay awarded under Title VII of the Civil Rights Act of 1964,[667] as equitable.[668] It contends that the Title VII analogy is compelling in the context of the duty of fair representation because the Title VII backpay provision was based on the NLRA provision governing backpay awards for unfair labor practices.[669] We are not convinced.

The Court has never held that a plaintiff seeking backpay under Title VII has a right to a jury trial. Assuming, without deciding, that such a Title VII plaintiff has no right to a jury trial, the Union's argument does not persuade us that respondents are not entitled to a jury trial here. Congress specifically characterized backpay under Title VII as a form of "equitable relief."[670] Congress made no similar pronouncement regarding the duty of fair representation. Furthermore, the Court has noted that backpay sought from an employer under Title VII would generally be restitutionary in nature,[671] in contrast to the damages sought here from the Union. Thus, the remedy sought in this duty of fair representation case is clearly different from backpay sought for violations of Title VII.

Moreover, the fact that Title VII's backpay provision may have been modeled on a provision in the NLRA concerning remedies for unfair labor practices does not require that the backpay remedy available here be considered equitable. The Union apparently reasons that if Title VII is comparable to one labor law remedy it is comparable to all remedies available in the NLRA context. Although both the duty of fair representation and the unfair labor practice provisions of the NLRA are components of national labor policy, their purposes are not identical. Unlike the unfair labor practice provisions of the NLRA, which are concerned primarily with the public interest in effecting federal labor policy, the duty of fair representation targets "'the wrong done the individual employee.'" Thus, the remedies appropriate for unfair labor practices may differ from the remedies for a breach of the duty of fair representation, given the need to vindicate different goals. Certainly, the connection between backpay under Title VII and damages under the unfair labor practice provision of the NLRA does not require us to find a parallel connection between Title VII backpay and money damages for breach of the duty of fair representation.

We hold, then, that the remedy of backpay sought in this duty of fair representation action is legal in nature. Considering both parts of the Seventh Amendment inquiry, we find that respondents are entitled to a jury trial on all issues presented in their suit.

IV

---

power, incident to its injunctive powers, to award backpay under the Fair Labor Standards Act; also backpay in that case was restitutionary).

[667] 42 U.S.C. § 2000e et seq. (1982 ed.).

[668] *See* Albemarle Paper Co. v. Moody, 422 U.S. 405, 415–18 (1975) (characterizing backpay awarded against employer under Title VII as equitable in context of assessing whether judge erred in refusing to award such relief).

[669] 29 U.S C. § 160(c) (1982 ed.) ("[W]here an order directs reinstatement of an employee, back pay may be required of the employer or labor organization").

[670] 42 U. S. C. § 2000e-5(g) (1982 ed.) ("[T]he court may . . . order such affirmative action as may be appropriate, which may include, but is not limited to, reinstatement or hiring of employees, with or without back pay . . ., or any other equitable relief as the court deems appropriate"; *see also* Curtis v. Loether, 415 U.S. 189, 196–97 (1974)(distinguishing backpay under Title VII from damages under Title VIII, the fair housing provision of the Civil Right Act, 42 U. S. C. §§ 3601–19 (1982 ed.), which the Court characterized as "legal" for Seventh Amendment purposes).

[671] *See Loether*, 415 U.S. at 197

456

On balance, our analysis of the nature of respondents' duty of fair representation action and the remedy they seek convinces us that this action is a legal one. Although the search for an adequate 18th-century analog revealed that the claim includes both legal and equitable issues, the money damages respondents seek are the type of relief traditionally awarded by courts of law. Thus, the Seventh Amendment entitles respondents to a jury trial, and we therefore affirm the judgment of the Court of Appeals.

It is so ordered.

Practice Problems

Practice Problem 16-1

Fun University, a state university, entered into a contract with Band-Jo, a popular musical band to perform on campus. Contracts with bands typically include an amount for which the musicians will be paid to perform at an appointed day and time, half before the concert and the rest after it. The contract in turn typically includes conditions requiring that the venue be secure, that the stage be safe, and other such requirements. Band-Jo had received $250,000 as the first half of its payment. On the day Band-Jo was to perform, Band-Jo's manager went to the venue. The manager observed a stage that he said was structurally unsafe. The manager notified the University that it had failed to provide a stage that was secure, and Band-Jo flew home to Los Angeles. A month later, the University sued Band-Jo for breach of contract and claimed damages of $250,000—the money it had paid up front before the scheduled performance. Band-Jo filed an answer denying allegations of breach and asserted a counterclaim for breach of contract by the University for the $250,000 that was due under the contract. The University requested a judge, but Band-Jo in its answer and counterclaim included, in a short phrase at the conclusion of the pleading "Defendant hereby demands trial by jury." Is the demand as made by Band-Jo sufficient? Will Band-Jo prevail? Will the University's request to have a judge decide its claim be respected?

Practice Problem 16-2

A.H. and Ida Zimmer owned a 471-acre tract and home known as Ferguson Farms in Dinwiddie County, Virginia. The Zimmers were citizens of Virginia. After his famous exploration, Meriwether Lewis, originally a Virginian who had become a citizen of the District of Columbia, wanted to return to his native state. He kept after the Zimmers about buying their farm, but the Zimmers balked. Then at a bar one evening Lewis offered Zimmer $1 million for the farm. Zimmer, who had had a couple of drinks but was not intoxicated, did not believe Lewis would pay $1 million for the farm. So, he thought to himself, "I'll call his bluff," and wrote on a napkin: "A.H. and Ida Zimmer hereby sell for the purchase price of $1 million Ferguson Farms, title satisfactory to buyer." Lewis asked Mr. Zimmer to have Mrs. Zimmer sign the napkin, too. Because she was there, Mr. Zimmer went to her and asked her sign. She hesitated but ended up signing. The next day Lewis tendered $1million into escrow and told the Zimmers they needed to move out of the Farm. Mr. Zimmer said, "You cannot be serious. I signed that napkin only to call your bluff. You cannot be serious in thinking I intended to sell the Farm to you." Lewis brought an action for specific performance in the U.S. District Court for the Eastern District of Virginia. Lewis sought one remedy, specific performance of the sale of the farm. Is this a case that would be heard by a jury? Why or why not?

Practice Problem 16-3

Jefferson, a great inventor, was a citizen of the District of Columbia, but loved Virginia and bought property directly adjacent to Ferguson Farms discussed in Practice Problem 16-2 above. Jefferson had invented a number of modern forms of entertainment, such as a huge seesaw, a dunking device, and "zip" lines by which one could glide on a line hung between trees at a high rate of speed. Jefferson planned to open a park with these devices for profit, expecting that customers would flock to the attractions. His workers staked off where they planned to cut trees. Lewis saw that the marked area came more than twenty acres into Ferguson Farms, in an area with some of the oldest oak trees in Virginia. He protested to the workers and ultimately to Jefferson, pointing to a survey done less than a year before that supported Lewis' claim to ownership. Jefferson told him he was going ahead anyway. Lewis filed an action in the United States District Court for the Eastern District of Virginia seeking a preliminary injunction and ultimately a permanent injunction against entry on Ferguson Farms or the cutting of any trees. Jefferson answered the complaint and demanded a jury. Under Federal Rule of Civil Procedure 65, would the preliminary injunction be heard by a judge? Would the permanent injunction at trial be heard by a jury or a judge?

---

1. Claims Merged in Law and Equity

Before the adoption of the Federal Rules of Civil Procedure in 1938, law cases were brought separately from equity cases. Law cases and equity cases were filed as separate actions in the same federal court. However, in law cases, the judge acted in the tradition of judges "at law," and juries were available if demanded. In equity cases, the judge acted as chancellors in the tradition of the English Chancery Court and juries were not available. The Federal Rules merged law and equity by allowing parties to bring law claims and equity claims in one unified case. Interestingly, the issue of whether a jury would hear legal claims, and if so what impact that would have on equity claims, was not fully addressed until over three decades after the adoption of the modern Federal Rules in 1938. The following decision in a Pennsylvania mandamus[672] proceeding explains the Court's rationale in merged cases for protecting the right of any party who has the right to a jury trial on any issue or claim.

DAIRY QUEEN, INC. v. WOOD
Supreme Court of the United States, 1962
369 U.S. 469

Mr. Justice BLACK delivered the opinion of the Court.

The United States District Court for the Eastern District of Pennsylvania granted a motion to strike petitioner's demand for a trial by jury in an action now pending before it on the alternative grounds that either the action was 'purely equitable' or, if not purely equitable, whatever legal issues that were raised were 'incidental' to equitable issues, and, in either case, no right to trial by jury existed. The petitioner then sought mandamus in the Court of Appeals for the Third Circuit to compel the district judge to vacate this order. When that court denied this request without opinion, we granted certiorari because the action of the Court of Appeals seemed inconsistent with protections already clearly recognized for the important constitutional right to trial by jury in our previous decisions.

At the outset, we may dispose of one of the grounds upon which the trial court acted in striking the demand for trial by jury—that based upon the view that the right to trial by jury may be lost as to legal

---

[672] Mandamus is an extraordinary remedy sought of an appellate court to order a lower court to perform an action for which the lower court has no discretion to ignore. In particular, mandamus proceedings have a long history as a means of protecting the right to a trial by jury when a lower court judge rules that a jury trial will not be had. In mandamus proceedings, the trial judge is named as a defendant, hence the Defendant here is Judge Wood, the judge in the U.S. District Court for the Eastern District of Pennsylvania who had ruled no jury trial would be allowed. The focus of this case for our purposes is not on the mandamus procedure, but rather on the right to a jury trial in a case with merged law and equity claims.

issues where those issues are characterized as 'incidental' to equitable issues—for our previous decisions make it plain that no such rule may be applied in the federal courts. In *Scott v. Neely*, decided in 1891, this Court held that a court of equity could not even take jurisdiction of a suit 'in which a claim properly cognizable only at law is united in the same pleadings with a claim for equitable relief.' That holding, which was based upon both the historical separation between law and equity and the duty of the Court to insure 'that the right to a trial by a jury in the legal action may be preserved intact,' created considerable inconvenience in that it necessitated two separate trials in the same case whenever that case contained both legal and equitable claims. Consequently, when the procedure in the federal courts was modernized by the adoption of the Federal Rules of Civil Procedure in 1938, it was deemed advisable to abandon that part of the holding of Scott v. Neely which rested upon the separation of law and equity and to permit the joinder of legal and equitable claims in a single action. Thus Rule 18(a) provides that a plaintiff 'may join either as independent or as alternate claims as many claims either legal or equitable or both as he may have against an opposing party.' And Rule 18(b) provides: 'Whenever a claim is one heretofore cognizable only after another claim has been prosecuted to a conclusion, the two claims may be joined in a single action; but the court shall grant relief in that action only in accordance with the relative substantive rights of the parties. A plaintiff may state a claim for money and a claim to have set aside a conveyance fraudulent as to him, without first having obtained a judgment establishing the claim for money.'

The Federal Rules did not, however, purport to change the basic holding of *Scott v. Neely*[,] that the right to trial by jury of legal claims must be preserved. Quite the contrary, Rule 38(a) expressly reaffirms that constitutional principle, declaring: 'The right of trial by jury as declared by the Seventh Amendment to the Constitution or as given by a statute of the United States shall be preserved to the parties inviolate.' Nonetheless, after the adoption of the Federal Rules, attempts were made indirectly to undercut that right by having federal courts in which cases involving both legal and equitable claims were filed decide the equitable claim first. The result of this procedure in those cases in which it was followed was that any issue common to both the legal and equitable claims was finally determined by the court and the party seeking trial by jury on the legal claim was deprived of that right as to these common issues. This procedure finally came before us in *Beacon Theatres, Inc. v. Westover*, a case which, like this one, arose from the denial of a petition for mandamus to compel a district judge to vacate his order striking a demand for trial by jury.

Our decision reversing that case not only emphasizes the responsibility of the Federal Courts of Appeals to grant mandamus where necessary to protect the constitutional right to trial by jury but also limits the issues open for determination here by defining the protection to which that right is entitled in cases involving both legal and equitable claims. The holding in *Beacon Theatres* was that where both legal and equitable issues are presented in a single case, "only under the most imperative circumstances, circumstances which in view of the flexible procedures of the Federal Rules we cannot now anticipate, can the right to a jury trial of legal issues be lost through prior determination of equitable claims." That holding, of course, applies whether the trial judge chooses to characterize the legal issues presented as "incidental" to equitable issues or not. Consequently, in a case such as this where there cannot even be a contention of such "imperative circumstances," *Beacon Theatres* requires that any legal issues for which a trial by jury is timely and properly demanded be submitted to a jury. There being no question of the timeliness or correctness of the demand involved here, the sole question which we must decide is whether the action now pending before the District Court contains legal issues.

The District Court proceeding arises out of a controversy between petitioner and the respondent owners of the trademark "DAIRY QUEEN" with regard to a written licensing contract made by them in December 1949, under which petitioner agreed to pay some $150,000 for the exclusive right to use that trademark in certain portions of Pennsylvania. The terms of the contract provided for a small initial payment with the remaining payments to be made at the rate of 50% of all amounts received by petitioner on sales and franchises to deal with the trademark and, in order to make certain that the $150,000 payment would be completed within a specified period of time, further provided for minimum annual payments regardless of petitioner's receipts. In August 1960, the respondents wrote petitioner a letter in which they claimed that petitioner had committed 'a material breach of that contract' by defaulting on the contract's payment provisions and notified petitioner of the termination of the contract and the cancellation of petitioner's right to use the trademark unless this claimed default was remedied immediately.10 When petitioner continued to deal with the trademark despite the notice of termination, the respondents brought an action based upon their view that a material breach of contract had occurred.

The complaint filed in the District Court alleged, among other things, that petitioner had "ceased paying . . . as required in the contract;" that the default "under the said contract . . . (was) in excess of $60,000.000;" that this default constituted a "material breach" of that contract; that petitioner had been notified by letter that its failure to pay as alleged made it guilty of a material breach of contract which if not "cured" would result in an immediate cancellation of the contract; that the breach had not been cured but that petitioner was contesting the cancellation and continuing to conduct business as an authorized dealer; that to continue such business after the cancellation of the contract constituted an infringement of the respondents' trademark; that petitioner's financial condition was unstable; and that because of the foregoing allegations, respondents were threatened with irreparable injury for which they had no adequate remedy at law. The complaint then prayed for both temporary and permanent relief, including: (1) temporary and permanent injunctions to restrain petitioner from any future use of or dealing in the franchise and the trademark; (2) an accounting to determine the exact amount of money owing by petitioner and a judgment for that amount; and (3) an injunction pending accounting to prevent petitioner from collecting any money from "Dairy Queen" stores in the territory.

In its answer to this complaint, petitioner raised a number of defenses, including: (1) a denial that there had been any breach of contract, apparently based chiefly upon its allegation that in January 1955 the parties had entered into an oral agreement modifying the original written contract by removing the provision requiring minimum annual payments regardless of petitioner's receipts thus leaving petitioner's only obligation that of turning over 50% of all its receipts; (2) laches and estoppel arising from respondents' failure to assert their claim promptly, thus permitting petitioner to expend large amounts of money in the development of its right to use the trademark; and (3) alleged violations of the antitrust laws by respondents in connection with their dealings with the trademark. Petitioner indorsed upon this answer a demand for trial by jury in accordance with Rule 38(b) of the Federal Rules of Civil Procedure.

Petitioner's contention, as set forth in its petition for mandamus to the Court of Appeals and reiterated in its briefs before this Court, is that insofar as the complaint requests a money judgment it presents a claim which is unquestionably legal. We agree with that contention. The most natural construction of the respondents' claim for a money judgment would seem to be that it is a claim that they are entitled to recover whatever was owed them under the contract as of the date of its purported termination plus damages for infringement of their trademark since that date. Alternatively, the complaint could be construed to set forth a full claim based upon both of these theories—that is, a claim that the respondents were entitled to recover both the debt due under the contract and damages for trademark infringement for the entire period of the alleged breach including that before the termination of the contract. Or it might possibly be construed to set forth a claim for recovery based completely on either one of these two theories—that is, a claim based solely upon the contract for the entire period both before and after the attempted termination on the theory that the termination, having been ignored, was of no consequence, or a claim based solely upon the charge of infringement on the theory that the contract, having been breached,

460

could not be used as a defense to an infringement action even for the period prior to its termination. We find it unnecessary to resolve this ambiguity in the respondents' complaint because we think it plain that their claim for a money judgment is a claim wholly legal in its nature however the complaint is construed. As an action on a debt allegedly due under a contract, it would be difficult to conceive of an action of a more traditionally legal character. And as an action for damages based upon a charge of trademark infringement, it would be no less subject to cognizance by a court of law.

The respondents' contention that this money claim is "purely equitable" is based primarily upon the fact that their complaint is cast in terms of an "accounting," rather than in terms of an action for "debt" or "damages." But the constitutional right to trial by jury cannot be made to depend upon the choice of words used in the pleadings. The prerequisite to the right to maintain a suit for an equitable accounting, like all other equitable remedies, is, as we pointed out in Beacon Theatres, the absence of an adequate remedy at law. Consequently, in order to maintain such a suit on a cause of action cognizable at law, as this one is, the plaintiff must be able to show that the "accounts between the parties" are of such a "complicated nature" that only a court of equity can satisfactorily unravel them. In view of the powers given to District Courts by Federal Rule of Civil Procedure 53(b) to appoint masters to assist the jury in those exceptional cases where the legal issues are too complicated for the jury adequately to handle alone, the burden of such a showing is considerably increased and it will indeed be a rare case in which it can be met. But be that as it may, this is certainly not such a case. A jury, under proper instructions from the court, could readily determine the recovery, if any, to be had here, whether the theory finally settled upon is that of breach of contract, that of trademark infringement, or any combination of the two. The legal remedy cannot be characterized as inadequate merely because the measure of damages may necessitate a look into petitioner's business records.

Nor is the legal claim here rendered "purely equitable" by the nature of the defenses interposed by petitioner. Petitioner's primary defense to the charge of breach of contract—that is, that the contract was modified by a subsequent oral agreement—presents a purely legal question having nothing whatever to do either with novation, as the district judge suggested, or reformation, as suggested by the respondents here. Such a defense goes to the question of just what, under the law, the contract between the respondents and petitioner is and, in an action to collect a debt for breach of a contract between these parties, petitioner has a right to have the jury determine not only whether the contract has been breached and the extent of the damages if any but also just what the contract is.

We conclude therefore that the district judge erred in refusing to grant petitioner's demand for a trial by jury on the factual issues related to the question of whether there has been a breach of contract. Since these issues are common with those upon which respondents' claim to equitable relief is based, the legal claims involved in the action must be determined prior to any final court determination of respondents' equitable claims. The Court of Appeals should have corrected the error of the district judge by granting the petition for mandamus. The judgment is therefore reversed[,] and the cause remanded for further proceedings consistent with this opinion.

Reversed and remanded.

Follow-Up Questions and Comments

1. What were the legal claims in *Dairy Queen*? Under the *Terry* test, would a party demanding a jury be entitled to a jury trial on the claims and issue raised in *Dairy Queen*?

2. What are the equitable claims in *Dairy Queen*? Would a jury decide these claims? In deciding the legal claims, will the jury not only decide the amount to be awarded, if any, but also be the factfinder on what has been proved in terms of the elements of the claim underlying the law claim? Once the jury decides the facts and the amount to be awarded, how if at all does that affect the court's decision of the equitable matters? The Court held that the "legal claims involved in the action must be determined prior to any final court determination of respondents' equitable claims." With that said, is the court bound by the jury's finding of facts on the legal claim?

3. In *Dairy Queen*, the Court referred to *Beacon Theaters v. Westover*,[673] There, the plaintiff was a movie theater in San Bernardino, California, which claimed the exclusive right to show first-run movies in that region. The defendant was a theater in the same region that had informed the plaintiff theater that it considered that theater's claim of exclusive rights to violate antitrust laws. The plaintiff brought a declaratory judgment act proceeding and sought both a declaration that its agreement with distributors was not a violation of the antitrust laws and sought an injunction against the defendant from showing first-run movies in the region. The defendant not only answered, but brought a counterclaim asserting antitrust violations and seeking damages. Because the counterclaim sought damages, the Court considered it to be a claim at law for which the defendant/counterclaimant had a right to a jury trial. The Court suggested that the legal claims needed to be resolved by a jury first and only then should the court address the equitable claims.

Practice Problems

Practice Problem 16-4

A restaurant and museum business, Restaurant and Museum, Inc., ("RMI") operates near a coal terminal operated by Carbon Coal Co. RMI claims that coal from the terminal is interfering with its business, causing it expenses such as repeated cleaning of facilities, lost restaurant and museum business, and the like. RMI sues Carbon Coal and seeks injunctive relief to prevent alleged repeated trespasses (coal particles invading RMI's property) and nuisance. In addition, RMI seeks damages based on the same legal theories for damages up to the date of the suit, including lost business, cleaning expenses, etc. RMI timely demands trial by jury. Should it receive a jury trial in light of its claims? Will the jury consider the equitable claims? If not, when will the judge consider them? Even if the jury considers the claims for damages first, factual findings on those claims will overlap with factual findings affecting the equitable claims. How should the court treat such factual findings?

Practice Problem 16-5

PetCo Inc., a large gas company, not only sold petroleum products but owned certain gas stations that it allowed to be leased and used under a franchise agreement. PetCo entered into a franchise agreement allowing the Smiths to lease one of its gas stations and use the PetCo name in selling gas. The Smiths fell

---

[673] 359 U.S. 500 (1959).

on financial hard times and could not continue. J. Paul Getty heard of the situation and approached PetCo about the lease and franchise agreement. Getty arranged with PetCo to assume the franchise agreement between the Smiths and PetCo, but the parties never entered into a final agreement. The parties engaged in several months of negotiations, and Getty operated the station during this time despite the lack of a signed agreement. PetCo maintained that Getty's operation of the station during this time was not a waiver of its standard requirement that any party operating its station do so under a signed franchise agreement. Finally, it became clear that the parties could not agree on terms, and that Getty would not sign the franchise agreement substituting him for the Smiths. PetCo instructed Getty orally and then in writing to vacate the gas station, but Getty refused.

PetCo sued Getty and, in its complaint, sought an injunction under a state unfair trade practices statute that authorizes injunctive relief when someone has used the trade name of another without written permission. Getty counterclaimed against PetCo and sought damages for the time when Getty operated the station without a franchise agreement and, according to them, did not get paid sufficiently. Getty timely demanded a jury trial. Assume that PetCo opposes the demand for a jury trial, and the court must rule on whether the Getty has the right to a jury trial. How should the court rule? If the court finds that there is a right to jury trial on at least some issues, what issues will be resolved by the jury? What issues, if any, will be resolved by the judge? In what order should the issues be resolved?

III. Motions for Summary Judgment

A. Purpose of Summary Judgment

Summary judgment motions are the primary means by which cases are dismissed when they are not "trial worthy." A case is not "worthy" of a jury trial when there are no genuine issues of material fact. In other words, if the court can tell prior to trial that—even if a jury ruled for a party, that ruling would have to be set aside as insufficient—there is no point in letting the case go to a jury. Federal Rule of Civil Procedure 56 is the Rule governing summary judgment. It states that judgment must be entered as a matter of law if the movant "show[s] that there is no genuine issue as to any material fact and that the movant is entitled to judgment as a matter of law." [674]

We should consider the role that the pretrial summary judgment process plays in the modern system of civil procedure. The adoption of pleading Codes, such as the Field Code, and later in 1938 the Federal Rules of Civil Procedure, represented a major shift in the philosophy of the stage at which cases should be weeded out as not worthy of trial.[675] Previously, the pleading stage had been significant and often a thicket the plaintiff could not penetrate. The Field Code, and even more so the Federal Rules, removed pleading as a primary barrier for litigating claims. See id. However, the modern system of procedure contemplates that after a party has pled enough of a case to get to discovery and has had her opportunity to develop facts to show her case is "worthy" of a jury trial, summary judgment would serve as the threshing floor on which cases lacking sufficient evidence are weeded out.

Please read Rule 56. Rule 56(c) states that a summary judgment motion may be brought "at any time until 30 days after discovery." That may sound as if one can move for summary judgment whenever one feels ready. A summary judgment motion before the close of discovery is likely to be met with an

---

[674] FED. R. CIV. P. 56(a).
[675] 5 CHARLES ALAN WRIGHT & ARTHUR R. MILLER, FEDERAL PRACTICE AND PROCEDURE § 1202 (3d ed. 2018).

affidavit of the opponent under Rule 56(d) contending that the non-moving party has not had been given enough time to take discovery. As suggested above, the place of summary judgment in the larger scheme of the handling of a case is after discovery and before trial. If you are contemplating summary judgment, you will want to begin preparing for your motion even before discovery is completed to be able to move within 30 days of the close of discovery.

In ruling on a summary judgment motion, the court will review what is called the "paper record." This record consists of all documents presented with the motion (including electronic documents), such as transcribed deposition testimony, interrogatory answers, party admissions, letters, memoranda, affidavits, etc. Following is a sample affidavit. The affidavit will include facts that are pertinent to the case at hand. In addition, the court can consider summary judgment stipulations—where the parties agree on certain facts and so certify to the court.

Sample Affidavit

IN THE UNITED STATES DISTRICT COURT
FOR THE DISTRICT OF

[PARTY NAME],	)	
Plaintiff,	)	
	)	
v.	)	Case No. _____
	)	
[PARTY NAME],	)	
Defendant,	)	

AFFIDAVIT OF

, being duly sworn, swears the following under oath:

I am_____and have person knowledge of the facts stated below:
1.
2.
3.
4.
5.

I swear under oath that the above is true and correct on_____[date] at_____[city, state].

<u>[signature]</u>
[typed name]

SUBSCRIBED AND SWORN TO BEFORE ME
on_____[date] at_____[city, state].

<u>[Notary's signature]</u>
[Notary's seal]
[typed name]

After the moving party submits documents supporting summary judgment, the opposing party will submit documents in opposition. Typically, summary judgment submissions will be comprised of a motion accompanied by a brief that includes, as attachments, any supporting documentation such as interrogatory answers, deposition testimony, admissions, and sworn affidavits. Live testimony is not something the court would consider. That would be reserved for trial if the case gets beyond the summary judgment stage. As already noted, the record before the court is comprised of the materials just described. Thinking of summary judgment as a preview of the trial—in paper submissions—should help in understanding the nature of this motion.

One potential objection could be that this procedure is not fair because the court does not hear witnesses to judge credibility. The point of keeping summary judgment to a paper record, however, is to avoid having judges make credibility determinations when the real question is simply: Does the party with the claim have sufficient evidence on which reasonable jurors could disagree? The procedure would only be unfair if the required showing to survive a summary judgment motion required the claimant to prove her case by the same burden of proof she will have at trial. The standard at summary judgment is not, however, the standard applied by the judge to determine whether a case proceeds to trial. Indeed, the standard is a much less demanding one. If the claimant produced evidence—in the form permitted by Rule 56—on the claim upon which reasonable jurors could disagree, then she will overcome summary judgment and proceed to trial. The following diagram is a helpful way to understand the process at work in a summary judgment decision:

Figure 16-3

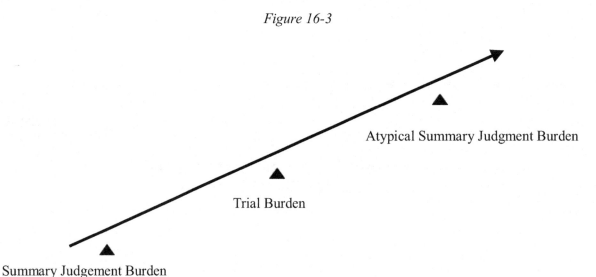

Atypical Summary Judgment Burden

Trial Burden

Summary Judgement Burden

As discussed above, the burden on the far left ("Summary Judgment Burden") depicts the typical threshold for a party opposing summary judgment and seeking trial. To survive summary judgment, the opposing party must produce sufficient evidence to show that her case is beyond that benchmark. If the evidence on any one required element of her claim is insufficient, reasonable jurors could not decide for her at trial. The court should then grant summary judgment because the plaintiff cannot win. However, the burden on the far right ("Atypical Summary Judgment Burden") is representative of the scenario in which— if the claimant produces sufficient evidence to go beyond that benchmark—reasonable jurors would have to find for the plaintiff. Occasionally a plaintiff's case is so compelling (and the defendant's position is so weak) that there is no other reasonable result to reach than finding for the plaintiff. Between the typical summary judgment and atypical summary judgment benchmarks, however, is the broad area in which reasonable jurors can disagree about the evidence. Most cases fall within this area.

466

The middle of the diagram ("Trial Burden") represents a threshold that is the key to the burden of proof at trial, not at the summary judgment stage. In deciding summary judgment, a judge should not consider whether a party has met her trial burden on evidence. The trial burden for a claim or defense can vary but in the great majority of cases it is the preponderance-of-the-evidence trial burden—whether something tips the scale to make the fact or element more likely than not. For the purposes of summary judgment, the judge only considers whether the parties have produced sufficient evidence such that reasonable jurors could disagree as to whether a party will prove her claim at trial. The judge does not decide whether the party shows in her summary judgment submissions that something is more likely than not true. That decision is for the jury to decide after trial.

Because the burden at summary judgment is far less demanding than the burden at trial, the mechanism by which Federal Rule of Civil Procedure 56 allows the court to see a preview of the trial is fair. Because the judge is not observing witnesses as they testify, the judge cannot make credibility decisions at this stage. On summary judgment, the judge must review only the facts in the materials allowed to be considered.

1. Typical Scenario in Which Summary Judgment Arises

Following is a typical case in which the existence of disputed facts requires that summary judgment be denied.

CARTER v. ENTERPRISE RENT–A–CAR CO.
United States District Court for the Northern District of Illinois, 2002
No. 01 CV 4494, 2002 WL 1759821

COAR, J.

Before this court is defendant's, Enterprise Rent–A–Car Company a/k/a Enterprise Rent–A–Car Company–Midwest ("Enterprise"), motion for summary judgement, pursuant to Fed. R. Civ. P. 56., against plaintiff's, Lawanda Carter ("Carter"), complaint containing allegations of discriminatory retaliation under the Family and Medical Leave Act ("FMLA"), 29 U.S.C. § 2601, et seq. For the following reasons the defendant's motion is DENIED.

Statement of Facts

Carter was employed by Enterprise which rents automobiles to individuals and businesses through its various branches in the Chicagoland area. Enterprise's rental branches are small, ordinarily employing between three and five individuals.

In 2001, Carter was an Assistant Manager at Enterprise's South Shore branch, located on 75th Street in Chicago. As Assistant Manager, Carter was responsible for, in part, general operation of the South Shore branch, including servicing customer, completing financial paperwork, making sales calls and training more junior employees.

The South Shore branch employed three other employees: Rubin Vasquez (car porter) ("Vasquez"), Eric McAtee (Management Trainee) ("McAtee"), and Stacey Cole (Branch Manager) ("Cole").

Carter reported directly to Branch Manager Cole. Cole, in turn, reported to the South Chicago area Manager Jason Roof ("Roof"). Roof supervised three branches in the South Chicago area. Roof reported to Regional

Vice President Charlie Petrolia ("Petrolia"). Petrolia oversaw all of the branches in the South Chicagoland Region, including the South Shore branch. Human Resources Generalist Manager Sarah Ruiz ("Ruiz") supported the South Chicagoland Region in 2001. Ruiz reported directly to Petrolia.

Responsibilities shared by all branch employees included putting gas in a customer's car or in the car being used the branch manager. To facilitate this process, Enterprise enlists an outside vendor, Wright Express, to issue gasoline cards to Enterprise's branches. These cards allow branch employees to use these gas cards to purchase fuel at local filling stations. Wright Express then collects the charge data from the various filling stations and collectively bills Enterprise for the gasoline. The South Shore facility was issued two gas cards: one assigned to Cole and one for general branch use. Enterprise issues a personal identification number ("PIN") to each employee using a gas card in order to identify when and where an employee used the gas card.

Cole was permitted to use a company car to get her home and back to the office. Employees generally, including Cole, were not allowed to put gas in a car for their personal benefit. Roof admits that prior to the investigation incriminating Carter he knew that several employees were taking gas cards home. Roof states that he believed that the repeated disappearance of the South Shore gas card was a cause for concern. And Cole admits that she sometimes would put in half a tank so that she could pick up and drop off her daughter.

In late 2000 or early 2001, Carter informed Cole that she would need to take two months leave in order to care of her ill son. According to Carter, Cole allowed Carter one or two days of leave but no more. Soon thereafter, Carter spoke to Ruiz who was visiting the South Shore Branch. Ruiz agreed to send Carter FMLA forms to fill out and submit. A week later, Carter had not yet received the forms so she called Ruiz again. Carter advised Cole that she would be submitting the FMLA application.

According to Carter, she sent the completed FMLA paperwork to Ruiz on February 16, 2001, via inter-office mail. The paperwork requested leave from March 16, 2001 to May 31, 2001. Ruiz testifies, however, that she never received Carter's completed FMLA paperwork.

On February 15, 2001, for the first time in Carter's employment, Cole sent Carter home for the day. The next morning, February 16, Carter was sent to Hobart, Indiana to respond to questions by Ruiz and Petrolia who were conducting an investigation about an employee's misuse of a gas card. According to Carter, this was the first investigation of this type ever conducted in the South Chicagoland Region. In the meeting that occurred on February 16, both Petrolia and Ruiz asked Carter general questions about Carter's use of the company gas card on February 13, 2001 after closing. Carter told Petrolia that she left work on February 13, 2001 between 6:30 and 6:45 p.m. Carter does not deny that she used the gas card at 6:31 pm on February 13. Carter told Petrolia that on that day, she used the gas card to fuel a company car while taking customers to their destinations. Carter also confirmed Ruiz's receipt and completion of the FMLA documents. When the meeting concluded, Carter was sent home for the second day in a row.

On February 21, six days after filing her FMLA claim, Petrolia, Ruiz and Carter met at the Enterprise's Chicago Heights Branch. Petrolia asked Carter further questions about her use of the gas card on February 13, including whether she could identify the customers she helped after closing that day. According the Petrolia, in that meeting Carter was unable to provide any other information that supported her previous statements that she was assisting customers. Petrolia testifies that based on this investigation, he concluded that Carter's 6:31 gas charge was for personal use and a terminable work rule violation. Petrolia and Ruiz signed Carter's termination memorandum and presented it to Carter at the meeting.

Enterprise moves for summary judgement against Carter's complaint of retaliatory discharge.

Standard of Review

Summary judgment may only be granted when no material question of fact is in dispute. The party moving for summary judgment bears the burden of identifying the evidence that demonstrates the absence of a disputed material issue of fact and establishes that the moving party is entitled to judgment as a matter of law.[676] The evidence must be viewed in the light most favorable to the party opposing the motion, with doubts resolved and all reasonable inferences drawn in favor of the nonmoving party. Further, "the inquiry involved in a ruling on a motion for summary judgment or for a directed verdict necessarily implicates the substantive evidentiary standard of proof that would apply at the trial level on the merits."

Analysis

Defendant argues that plaintiff is unable to establish prima facie case of retaliation under the FMLA. This court disagrees.

. . .

While the FMLA provides certain substantive guarantees, "the FMLA also affords employees protection in the event they are discriminated against for exercising their rights under the Act."

In a case where an employee is alleging discrimination based on the FMLA, "[t]he issue becomes whether the employer's actions were motivated by an impermissible retaliatory or discriminatory animus." Because Carter alleges retaliatory discharge under the FMLA, she must establish that the parties involved engaged in intentional discrimination. Since Carter has not provided this court with any direct evidence of discrimination, we will apply the McDonnell Douglas burden-shifting framework to her claim.

To prove a prima facie case of retaliatory discharge under the FMLA, Carter must show that: (1) she engaged in a protected activity; (2) she suffered an adverse employment action; and (3) there is a causal connection between her protected activity and the defendants' adverse employment action. If she makes that showing, the burden of producing a legitimate, nondiscriminatory reason for her discharge shifts to Enterprise, and once it does so, Carter bears the burden of showing that Enterprise's proffered reasons are pretextual and that its actual reason was discriminatory.

Defendant argues that Carter is unable to establish a prima facie case of retaliatory discharge because she cannot establish a causal connection between her request for FMLA leave and her termination. Carter argues that she has established the requisite causal connection.

Generally, a plaintiff may establish such a link through evidence that the discharge took place on the heels of protected activity. The Appellate Courts agree, however, that there can be no causal link between protected activity and an adverse employment action if the employer remained unaware of the protected activity.

In this case, viewing the evidence in a light most favorable to the plaintiff, a genuine issue of material fact exists as to whether Carter has established a prima facie case of retaliatory discrimination. According to Carter, she was subject to an internal investigation and termination only subsequent to her

---

[676] Celotex Corp. v. Catrett, 477 U.S. 317, 323 (1986).

469

request for leave under the FMLA. She, in fact, was terminated only six days after she submitted the completed FMLA documentation. Enterprise contends that a causal connection is impossible to establish because Carter cannot prove that Petrolia had knowledge that Carter had requested FMLA leave prior to launching an investigation of Carter's alleged fraudulent use of the Enterprise gas card.

Carter, however, is not required to demonstrate by direct evidence that Roof and Petrolia were aware of her request for FMLA leave. A Title VII plaintiff may rely on circumstantial evidence to establish her employer's awareness of protected expression. Moreover, Carter need not prove by a preponderance of the evidence at the summary judgment stage that Petrolia was aware of her request for leave under the FMLA; she must only produce evidence that would support an inference that he was so aware.

Summary judgment generally is improper where the plaintiff can show that an employee with discriminatory animus provided factual information or other input that may have affected the adverse employment action. *See Shager v. Upjohn Co.*, 913 F.2d 398, 405 (7th Cir.1990) (even where the plaintiff's supervisor may not have passed along discriminatory animus to the ultimate decisionmaker, that animus tainted his assessment of the plaintiff's performance, on which the decisionmaker did rely); *Jardien v. Winston Network, Inc.*, 888 F.2d 1151, 1155 (7th Cir.1989) (relevant to jury's determination in age discrimination case that decisionmaker accepted input from supervisor who had discriminatory motive); *see also Robinson v. PPG Indus., Inc.*, 23 F.3d 1159, 1165–66 (7th Cir.1994) (summary judgment improper where supervisor who allegedly made age-related remarks participated in ranking the performance of company employees and in the eventual decision to terminate the plaintiff's employment); *Gusman v. Unisys Corp.*, 986 F.2d 1146, 1147 (7th Cir.1993) (reasonable jurors could conclude that a supervisor intent on purging the workforce of older employees lied to his superiors about the quality of the plaintiff's job skills); *Stacks v. Southwestern Bell Yellow Pages, Inc.*, 27 F.3d 1316 (8th Cir.1994) (employers cannot escape responsibility for sex discrimination "when the facts on which the reviewers rely have been filtered by a manager determined to purge the labor force of women."); *Kientzy v. McDonnell Douglas Corp.*, 990 F.2d 1051, 1057–60 (8th Cir.1993) (evidence sufficient to support sex discrimination claim where superior's discriminatory animus was reflected in the information he provided to ultimate decisionmakers); *cf. Wilson v. Stroh Cos.*, 952 F.2d 942, 945–46 (6th Cir.1992) (Title VII plaintiff failed to show that lower level employee with discriminatory animus infected superiors' independent decision to terminate plaintiff's employment).

Accepting Carter's facts as true for the purposes of this summary judgement motion, Carter has sufficiently supported an inference that Cole's animus may have informed and/or "tainted" Petrolia's decision to investigate and terminate Carter. For example, according to Carter, Cole threatened her when she initially requested a two month leave. In addition, Carter's assertions are supported by the fact that Cole had never reported anyone for taking a gas card home, and only reported Carter after Carter had asked Cole for leave under the FMLA. Finally, according to Carter and Cole, Cole spoke to Petrolia and discussed Cole's belief that Carter had taken the gas card, again, only after Carter had mentioned that she wanted an extended leave.

This court finds that the above creates a viable inference that the investigation of Carter's fraudulent gas card usage and her subsequent termination occurred in retaliation to her request for FMLA leave. Enterprise disagrees with this inference, arguing that the investigation itself, as well as its consequences, were independent decisions made by Petrolia. This, therefore, is a genuine issue of material fact. Viewing the evidence in a light most favorable to the plaintiff, this court then assumes for the purposes of this summary judgement motion that Carter has established the requisite causal connection. Under the McDonnel–Douglas test, Enterprise must now produce a legitimate, nondiscriminatory reason for Carter's discharge; if it does so Carter bears the burden of showing that Enterprise's proffered reasons are pretextual and that its actual reason was discriminatory.[677] In this court's opinion, there is a genuine issue of material fact with respect whether Enterprise's proffered reason is pretextual and that its actual reason was discriminatory.

Enterprise contends that Carter was terminated due to her misuse of a company gas card. Carter argues that Carter's reason for terminating is pretextual because Enterprise only became concerned about the fraudulent use of the gas card around the time that Carter requested leave under the FMLA, and further, that Carter was alone punished for her usage of the card despite the fact that others were found to have engaged in the same behavior.

A plaintiff may establish that her employer's non-discriminatory reason for the adverse employment actions is pretextual by showing that the reason "(1) had no basis in fact, (2) did not actually motivate [her] discharge, or (3) [was] insufficient to motivate the discharge."

The plaintiff supports her contention of pretext primarily by demonstrating that discrepancies in testimony exist between those who propagated the gas card investigation, and subsequently Carter's termination, and other employees of Enterprise. For example, Area Manager Roof's concern for misuse of the South Shore gas card as well as his conversations with Cole and McAtee with respect to the gas card are not corroborated by other employees at Enterprise or even testimony by Cole or McAtee. In addition, Roof admits that prior to the investigation implicating Carter he knew that several employees had taken a gas card home. The record does not indicate, however, that Roof believed it was a matter of concern. Carter further supports her assertions by demonstrating the possibility that the investigation of fraudulent gas card use began the day before she submitted her FMLA claim and throughout the investigation she was singled out for disparate treatment. For the three[-]month period from Cole's arrival as manager in November 2000 until Carter termination, there were twenty-five after-hours gasoline purchases for the branch. Of these purchases, 13 were by Cole, 7 were by Junea Buford (car porter) and the remaining 5 were by Carter. In fact, there are two instances in which Cole made two gas purchases within five minutes of one another, and no investigation was conducted in those instances.

Enterprise contends that no reasonable fact-finder could find in favor of chain of events as construed by Carter. Enterprise does not, however, provide evidence to contradict the discrepancies pointed out by Carter. Instead, it argues that those discrepancies are irrelevant. This court disagrees.

Ultimately the question for the trier of fact is whether the reason why Carter was terminated was her invocation of the FMLA. A[t] this point, this court cannot answer that question as a matter of law.

. . .

Conclusion

For the foregoing reasons, the defendant's motion for summary judgement is *DENIED*.

---

[677] *See, e.g.*, McDonnell Douglas Corp. v. Green, 411 U.S. 792 (1973).

In *Carter*, the Defendant supported its summary judgment motion with the variety of items permitted to be considered on summary judgment—affidavits of witnesses signed under oath, deposition testimony, documents produced in discovery. Thus, the Defendant offered the materials identified in Rule 56 as available for consideration on summary judgment to have the court rule that reasonable jurors could not disagree about whether Carter had been discriminated against. Such a motion is the typical way summary judgment motions are presented.

However, another way of having the court decide whether a case ought to be dismissed on summary judgment is to rely creatively on the discovery tools already discussed. Then, if the plaintiff for instance has failed to identify facts, witnesses, or documents supporting the plaintiff's claim, the defendant can simply offer to the court these discovery responses on summary judgment. The difference in approach is subtle but important to understand. In this second type of summary judgment motion, the defendant is not offering its own affidavits asserting certain facts, or other documents to establish facts. Instead, the defendant is saying (1) the plaintiff has to prove certain elements; (2) the defendant asked in discovery for facts, witnesses, and documents that the plaintiff will use to prove each element, and (3) the plaintiff failed to identify any facts, witnesses, or documents on at least one required element. Therefore, the defendant can argue successfully that there is no point in going to a trial because, even if the case went to trial, the plaintiff would lack proof on a key element. The following case is one of the most famous examples of the ability to receive summary judgment by showing, through an opponent's discovery responses, the opponent's inability to prove something.

CELOTEX CORP. v. CATRETT
Supreme Court of the United States, 1986
477 U.S. 317

Justice REHNQUIST delivered the opinion of the Court.

The United States District Court for the District of Columbia granted the motion of petitioner Celotex Corporation for summary judgment against respondent Catrett because the latter was unable to produce evidence in support of her allegation in her wrongful-death complaint that the decedent had been exposed to petitioner's asbestos products. A divided panel of the Court of Appeals for the District of Columbia Circuit reversed, however, holding that petitioner's failure to support its motion with evidence tending to negate such exposure precluded the entry of summary judgment in its favor. We granted certiorari to resolve the conflict . . . and now reverse the decision of the District of Columbia Circuit.

Respondent commenced this lawsuit in September 1980, alleging that the death in 1979 of her husband, Louis H. Catrett, resulted from his exposure to products containing asbestos manufactured or distributed by 15 named corporations. Respondent's complaint sounded in negligence, breach of warranty, and strict liability. Two of the defendants filed motions challenging the District Court's in personam jurisdiction, and the remaining 13, including petitioner, filed motions for summary judgment. Petitioner's motion, which was first filed in September 1981, argued that summary judgment was proper because respondent had "failed to produce evidence that any [Celotex] product . . .was the proximate cause of the injuries alleged within the jurisdictional limits of [the District] Court." In particular, petitioner noted that respondent had failed to identify, in answering interrogatories specifically requesting such information, any witnesses who could testify about the decedent's exposure to petitioner's asbestos products. In response to petitioner's summary judgment motion, respondent then produced three documents which she claimed "demonstrate that there is a genuine material factual dispute" as to whether the decedent had ever been exposed to petitioner's asbestos products. The three documents included a transcript of a deposition of the decedent, a letter from an official of one of the decedent's former employers whom petitioner planned to call as a trial witness, and a letter from an insurance company to respondent's attorney, all tending to establish that the decedent had been exposed to petitioner's asbestos products in Chicago during 1970– 1971. Petitioner, in turn, argued that the three documents were inadmissible hearsay and thus could not be considered in opposition to the summary judgment motion.

In July 1982, almost two years after the commencement of the lawsuit, the District Court granted all of the motions filed by the various defendants. The court explained that it was granting petitioner's summary judgment motion because "there [was] no showing that the plaintiff was exposed to the defendant Celotex's product in the District of Columbia or elsewhere within the statutory period." Respondent appealed only the grant of summary judgment in favor of petitioner, and a divided panel of the District of Columbia Circuit reversed. The majority of the Court of Appeals held that petitioner's summary judgment motion was rendered "fatally defective" by the fact that petitioner "made no effort to adduce any evidence, in the form of affidavits or otherwise, to support its motion." According to the majority, Rule 56(e) of the Federal Rules of Civil Procedure, and this Court's decision in *Adickes v. S.H. Kress & Co.*,[678] establish that "the party opposing the motion for summary judgment bears the burden of responding only after the moving party has met its burden of coming forward with proof of the absence of any genuine issues of material fact." The majority therefore declined to consider petitioner's argument that none of the evidence produced by respondent in opposition to the motion for summary judgment would have been admissible at trial. The dissenting judge argued that "[t]he majority errs in supposing that a party seeking summary judgment must always make an affirmative evidentiary showing, even in cases where there is not a triable, factual dispute." According to the dissenting judge, the majority's decision "undermines the traditional authority of trial judges to grant summary judgment in meritless cases."

We think that the position taken by the majority of the Court of Appeals is inconsistent with the standard for summary judgment set forth in Rule 56(c) of the Federal Rules of Civil Procedure. Under Rule 56(c), summary judgment is proper "if the pleadings, depositions, answers to interrogatories, and admissions on file, together with the affidavits, if any, show that there is no genuine issue as to any material fact and that the moving party is entitled to a judgment as a matter of law." In our view, the plain language of Rule 56(c) mandates the entry of summary judgment, after adequate time for discovery and upon motion, against a party who fails to make a showing sufficient to establish the existence of an element essential to that party's case, and on which that party will bear the burden of proof at trial. In such a situation, there can be "no genuine issue as to any material fact," since a complete failure of proof concerning an essential element of the nonmoving party's case necessarily renders all other facts immaterial. The moving party is "entitled to a judgment as a matter of law" because the nonmoving party has failed to make a sufficient showing on an essential element of her case with respect to which she has the burden of proof. "[T]h[e] standard [for granting summary judgment] mirrors the standard for a directed verdict under Federal Rule of Civil Procedure 50(a). . . ."

Of course, a party seeking summary judgment always bears the initial responsibility of informing the district court of the basis for its motion, and identifying those portions of "the pleadings, depositions, answers to interrogatories, and admissions on file, together with the affidavits, if any," which it believes demonstrate the absence of a genuine issue of material fact. But unlike the Court of Appeals, we find no express or implied requirement in Rule 56 that the moving party support its motion with affidavits or other

---

[678] 398 U.S. 144, 159 (1970).

473

similar materials negating the opponent's claim. On the contrary, Rule 56(c), which refers to "the affidavits, if any" . . . suggests the absence of such a requirement. And if there were any doubt about the meaning of Rule 56(c) in this regard, such doubt is clearly removed by Rules 56(a) and (b), which provide that claimants and defendants, respectively, may move for summary judgment "with or without supporting affidavits" The import of these subsections is that, regardless of whether the moving party accompanies its summary judgment motion with affidavits, the motion may, and should, be granted so long as whatever is before the district court demonstrates that the standard for the entry of summary judgment, as set forth in Rule 56(c), is satisfied. One of the principal purposes of the summary judgment rule is to isolate and dispose of factually unsupported claims or defenses, and we think it should be interpreted in a way that allows it to accomplish this purpose.

Respondent argues, however, that Rule 56(e), by its terms, places on the nonmoving party the burden of coming forward with rebuttal affidavits, or other specified kinds of materials, only in response to a motion for summary judgment "made and supported as provided in this rule." According to respondent's argument, since petitioner did not "support" its motion with affidavits, summary judgment was improper in this case. But as we have already explained, a motion for summary judgment may be made pursuant to Rule 56 "with or without supporting affidavits." In cases like the instant one, where the nonmoving party will bear the burden of proof at trial on a dispositive issue, a summary judgment motion may properly be made in reliance solely on the "pleadings, depositions, answers to interrogatories, and admissions on file." Such a motion, whether or not accompanied by affidavits, will be "made and supported as provided in this rule," and Rule 56(e) therefore requires the nonmoving party to go beyond the pleadings and by her own affidavits, or by the "depositions, answers to interrogatories, and admissions on file," designate "specific facts showing that there is a genuine issue for trial."

We do not mean that the nonmoving party must produce evidence in a form that would be admissible at trial in order to avoid summary judgment. Obviously, Rule 56 does not require the nonmoving party to depose her own witnesses. Rule 56(e) permits a proper summary judgment motion to be opposed by any of the kinds of evidentiary materials listed in Rule 56(c), except the mere pleadings themselves, and it is from this list that one would normally expect the nonmoving party to make the showing to which we have referred.

The Court of Appeals in this case felt itself constrained, however, by language in our decision in *Adickes*. There we held that summary judgment had been improperly entered in favor of the defendant restaurant in an action brought under 42 U.S.C. § 1983. In the course of its opinion, the *Adickes* Court said that "both the commentary on and the background of the 1963 amendment conclusively show that it was not intended to modify the burden of the moving party . . .to show initially the absence of a genuine issue concerning any material fact." We think that this statement is accurate in a literal sense, since we fully agree with the *Adickes* Court that the 1963 amendment to Rule 56(e) was not designed to modify the burden of making the showing generally required by Rule 56(c). It also appears to us that, on the basis of the showing before the Court in *Adickes*, the motion for summary judgment in that case should have been denied. But we do not think the *Adickes* language quoted above should be construed to mean that the burden is on the party moving for summary judgment to produce evidence showing the absence of a genuine issue of material fact, even with respect to an issue on which the nonmoving party bears the burden of proof. Instead, as we have explained, the burden on the moving party may be discharged by "showing"—that is, pointing out to the district court—that there is an absence of evidence to support the nonmoving party's case.

The last two sentences of Rule 56(e) were added, as this Court indicated in *Adickes*, to disapprove a line of cases allowing a party opposing summary judgment to resist a properly made motion by reference only to its pleadings. While the *Adickes* Court was undoubtedly correct in concluding that these two sentences were not intended to reduce the burden of the moving party, it is also obvious that they were not adopted to add to that burden. Yet that is exactly the result which the reasoning of the Court of Appeals would produce; in effect, an amendment to Rule 56(e) designed to facilitate the granting of motions for summary judgment would be interpreted to make it more difficult to grant such motions. Nothing in the two sentences themselves requires this result, for the reasons we have previously indicated, and we now put to rest any inference that they do so.

Our conclusion is bolstered by the fact that district courts are widely acknowledged to possess the power to enter summary judgments sua sponte, so long as the losing party was on notice that she had to come forward with all of her evidence. It would surely defy common sense to hold that the District Court could have entered summary judgment sua sponte in favor of petitioner in the instant case, but that petitioner's filing of a motion requesting such a disposition precluded the District Court from ordering it.

Respondent commenced this action in September 1980, and petitioner's motion was filed in September 1981. The parties had conducted discovery, and no serious claim can be made that respondent was in any sense "railroaded" by a premature motion for summary judgment. Any potential problem with such premature motions can be adequately dealt with under Rule 56(f), which allows a summary judgment motion to be denied, or the hearing on the motion to be continued, if the nonmoving party has not had an opportunity to make full discovery.

In this Court, respondent's brief and oral argument have been devoted as much to the proposition that an adequate showing of exposure to petitioner's asbestos products was made as to the proposition that no such showing should have been required. But the Court of Appeals declined to address either the adequacy of the showing made by respondent in opposition to petitioner's motion for summary judgment, or the question whether such a showing, if reduced to admissible evidence, would be sufficient to carry respondent's burden of proof at trial. We think the Court of Appeals with its superior knowledge of local law is better suited than we are to make these determinations in the first instance.

The Federal Rules of Civil Procedure have for almost 50 years authorized motions for summary judgment upon proper showings of the lack of a genuine, triable issue of material fact. Summary judgment procedure is properly regarded not as a disfavored procedural shortcut, but rather as an integral part of the Federal Rules as a whole, which are designed "to secure the just, speedy and inexpensive determination of every action." Before the shift to "notice pleading" accomplished by the Federal Rules, motions to dismiss a complaint or to strike a defense were the principal tools by which factually insufficient claims or defenses could be isolated and prevented from going to trial with the attendant unwarranted consumption of public and private resources. But with the advent of "notice pleading," the motion to dismiss seldom fulfills this function any more, and its place has been taken by the motion for summary judgment. Rule 56 must be construed with due regard not only for the rights of persons asserting claims and defenses that are adequately based in fact to have those claims and defenses tried to a jury, but also for the rights of persons opposing such claims and defenses to demonstrate in the manner provided by the Rule, prior to trial, that the claims and defenses have no factual basis.

The judgment of the Court of Appeals is accordingly reversed, and the case is remanded for further proceedings consistent with this opinion.

It is so ordered.

Follow-Up Questions and Comments

1. What was the claim at issue in *Celotex*?

2. What forms of discovery did the defendant use to ask the plaintiff for evidence on the claim?

3. How did the defendant in *Celotex* then demonstrate that there was no genuine issue of material fact?

4. How had the court of appeals, in the Supreme Court's view as stated in *Celotex*, misconstrued the Supreme Court's prior *Adickes* decision in a way to preclude the type of summary judgment the Court considered appropriate?

B. Comparison of Traditional Summary Judgment Scenarios with the *Celotex* Method

Recall that a defendant may bring a summary judgment motion in at least two scenarios.[679] First, she can gather evidence on one or more of the elements of a plaintiff's claim that tends to prove that the plaintiff is unable to carry her burden of proof. In this first scenario, the defendant files her motion, attaches the proof she has gathered in discovery disproving the plaintiff's case, after which the plaintiff must respond or suffer summary judgment.[680] At this point, the plaintiff will typically answer with a brief in opposition to the summary judgment motion and attach discovery and affidavits attempting to show she can prove the matter at issue.[681]

In the second kind of summary judgment motion, the moving party does not produce affirmative evidence seeking to demonstrate facts, such as by an affidavit or deposition testimony. Instead, the party will have already sought from the opposing party in discovery identification of facts, witness, or documents supporting various elements of a claim. For instance, a defendant may propound an interrogatory to the plaintiff seeking persons with knowledge of, or documents supporting, a key element of a claim. The party who asked for information through discovery then takes the depositions of all persons identified in the opponent's responses. If neither the discovery responses nor the persons identified provide evidence on which reasonable jurors can disagree about a required element, then a *Celotex* motion for summary judgment is appropriate. The movant argues (a) that her opponent bears the burden of proof at trial on material facts, (b) that discovery has revealed the plaintiff cannot even produce evidence on which reasonable jurors could disagree, and (c) thus no genuine issue of material facts exists.[682]

For the party opposing a summary judgment motion, she cannot simply rest on denials contained in her pleadings, or on conclusory allegations.[683] Instead, she must provide a response that is supported by whatever materials are permitted to be considered, such as deposition testimony, affidavits, discovery responses, and the like to show the court that there is a genuine issue of material fact to be tried.[684]

---

[679] *See* 73 AM. JUR. 2D Summary Judgment § 17 (2017).

[680] 49 C.J.S. JUDGMENTS § 308 (2017).

[681] *Id.*

[682] *See* Celotex Corp. v. Catrett, 477 U.S. 317–27 (1986).

[683] 73 AM. JUR. 2D Summary Judgment § 31 (2017).

[684] FED. R. CIV. P. 56(e).

The goal of the party opposing summary judgment is simple: to show a genuine issue of material fact, that reasonable jurors can disagree over the findings that should be made from the evidence. Thus, the opposing party needs to know the elements of the claim to determine what issues are material to the case. A case will often have myriad facts. However, those facts that relate to the elements of a claim or defense that have the capability to change the outcome of a lawsuit are the ones that are "material."[685] Moreover, the dispute over these facts needs to be a genuine, real, or triable issue that is supported by evidence and not merely non-essential details that parties are quibbling over.[686] Needless to say, if counsel has been following the advice of the earlier chapters, strategically considering the elements of the case from the outset, and developing evidence through a variety of means, then she should be able to overcome a motion for summary judgment motion.

Practice Problems

Practice Problem 16-6

Marge, the beneficiary of a life insurance policy owned by Mal, sues Insurance Company to collect the policy's proceeds. Insurance Company denies liability and asserts that Mal committed suicide. If true, Insurance Company would not have to pay under the policy. Insurance Company moves for summary judgment, attaching an affidavit that Mal had left a note saying he "did not see any reason to keep going on," also attaches an affidavit of the person who found Mal on the ground next to the side of his house with the roof directly above him. Marge files a brief in opposition to the summary judgment motion and attaches an affidavit in which she states under oath that "Mal would never commit suicide and did not do so here." How should the trial court rule on the summary judgment motion? What if Marge offered, instead, an affidavit affirming that a ladder was against the roof on a part that allowed access to the roof gutters, and that on the roof was a bucket with debris, mud, and other materials exactly like that in the gutter?

Practice Problem 16-7

Roddy Runner has a Ferrari of which he is very fond. He backs the Ferrari out of the garage and, as he is about to drive away, remembers he has forgotten his wallet. He parks the car along the street and runs inside. When he came back out, he was shocked to see the side of his car. Still parked, the Ferrari had circular-shaped scrapes along the side. Roddy looked in the distance and saw a truck with wheels so large that they are at about the same height as the side of his Ferrari and with spokes extending out. Roddy saw "Dan the Man's Painting" on the back of the truck before it turned. He later found out that a neighbor down the street had Dan the Man's Painting do a paint job on the day in question. Roddy sued Dan the Man's Painting who denied scraping the Ferrari. On defendant's summary judgment motion, Roddy offered, with his brief in opposition, an affidavit testifying (1) that the car was parked legally on the street, (2) the circular-shaped scrapes were not on the car when he went inside but were there when he came out of his house, and (3) Roddy saw the Defendant's truck down the street traveling on the street where his car had been parked. Roddy also offers an affidavit verifying measurements that place the extended spokes on the truck at the exact same height as the scrapes on his car. Finally, Roddy submitted the neighbor's affidavit that Dan the Man's Painting was painting at the neighbor's house before the incident. Defendant offered an affidavit of a metallurgist expert stating that the spokes on the truck have no more tensile strength than the metal on Roddy's Ferrari. How should the court rule on the motion?

---

[685] 73 AM. JUR. 2D Summary Judgment § 48 (2017).
[686] Id. § 47.

Practice Problem 16-8

Bee Jones owned property on the waterfront near Cape Henry in Virginia Beach, Virginia. Cape Henry is believed to be where John Smith's expedition to America first landed. Every year a gentleman named Charles Smith, who lives in North Carolina, travels to Virginia and sets up a tent on Bee's property. When she challenged his right to do so, he claimed to be the descendant of John Smith and to have the right to camp anywhere he likes in that area. Bee finally gets fed up and sues Smith. In his deposition when asked the basis for his continuing to return to Bee's property, Charles repeats that he is descended from John Smith and as such ought to be able to camp anywhere near where the great explorer landed. He admitted that no deed provided him ownership rights to Bee's property. Bee provides an affidavit confirming she is the fee owner of the property and it is not on any historical register. Bee moved for summary judgment based on her submissions. Charles responded by offering pages copies from a book about John Smith's landing at Cape Henry. Charles offered handwritten notes that he claimed were records he had searched that helped to show he was a descendant of John Smith. Should the court grant summary judgment to Bee on her claim seeking a permanent injunction barring Charles from entering her property?

Practice Problem 16-9

Plaintiff, To Your Health, Inc. ("TYH"), a medical center incorporated and with its principal place of business in North Carolina, had a contract with Dr. Hippocrates ("Dr. Hip") containing a covenant not to compete (also known as a non-competition agreement) that precluded the doctor from treating patients within a twenty-five-mile radius of TYH's headquarters for one year from the date he leaves TYH. Dr. Hip left TYH and begins treating patients through Southern Medical Center, Inc. ("SMC"), incorporated and with its principal place of business in Virginia. Instead of suing Dr. Hip (because of a concern about bad publicity in preventing a doctor from continuing to care for patients), TYH sued SMC for the tort of intentional interference with contractual relations. The tort's requirements, in virtually every state, require a third party to know of a contract between two parties, to intentionally engage in conduct to induce a party to breach that contract, and to cause damages thereby. SMC served interrogatories on TYH seeking the identity of all persons with knowledge of TYH's contentions that SMC knew of the contract or engaged in intentional interference with the contract to induce a breach. SMC also served a request for production of documents seeking documents supporting these contentions. The plaintiff responded to the document requests that it lacked responsive documents. SMC deposed the witnesses that TYH identified. The best testimony these witnesses could offer was that SMC "must have known" that Dr. Hip had a contract with TYH containing a noncompetition agreement in it. Accordingly, SMC filed a summary judgment motion attaching the relevant deposition testimony and the document requests, along with plaintiff's response indicating it lacked responsive documents. How should the court rule on SMC's motion? How does this summary judgment motion take an approach different from that in the summary judgment motions described in Practice Problems 16-6 through 16-8?

CHAPTER 17:
MOTIONS AND OTHER PROCEDURES AT TRIAL

I. How the Topics in this Chapter Fit in the Overall Progress of a Civil Action

Below is a diagram of the stages of a civil action showing in bold where the topics in this chapter fall in the progress of a case.

Figure 17-1

Cause of Action (events leading to suit)	Pre-Filing Tasks (items to begin representation, interviewing, and related matters)	Choice of Forum (subject matter jurisdiction, removal, personal jurisdiction, and venue)	Notice and Service of Process (completing the process of ensuring the forum court can enter a valid judgment)	Pleading the Case and Joinder of Claims and Parties (including supplemental jurisdiction)

Responding to Claims by Motion or by Answer	Discovery (developing proof to establish claims and learn your adversary's case)	Right to Jury (pretrial motions and practice)	Final Pretrial Conference (events within last month before trial)	**Trial (procedures and motions during trial)**	Verdict	Post-Trial Motions (motions for a new trial and/or judgment as a matter of law)	Appeal

Assume at this point you have represented your client throughout the pretrial process— pleadings, discovery, pretrial motions, and more. You evaluated her case and were prepared when the judge asked whether you had explored settlement. The defendants refused to respond to settlement inquires. They told the judge that their client simply cannot settle because the precedent of doing so here would be too damaging. That makes your job easier because you can now focus on the trial and representing your client when she has her day in court.

This chapter will discuss certain procedures that arise at trial. It will not attempt to teach trial advocacy or to address each aspect of the handling of a trial. Those procedures are beyond the scope of a first-year course. Instead, it will focus on the procedural aspects of a trial, such as jury selection and motions during trial—in particular, motions for judgment as a matter of law under Federal Rule of Civil Procedure 50 and motions for a new trial under Federal Rule of Civil Procedure 59.

The goal of a plaintiff's counsel who demanded a jury trial is to get the case to the jury. No lawyer will win every case. However, if the case is one over which litigation goes into discovery, the lawyer ought to be able to develop facts to show that reasonable jurors can disagree. Then, if the case does not settle, the lawyer can do her best for the client at trial. The plaintiff's lawyer needs to rely on the fact that each of the motions the defendant can make at trial (e.g., a motion for judgment as a matter of law) favors a jury trial so long as a claimant gives the judge something to rely on. If counsel puts on her client's case, and avoids judgment prior to verdict, the lawyer has given her client a chance to succeed. However, whether you win or lose will often depend more on the facts of the case than it will on the lawyer's presentation.

II. Judgment as a Matter of Law (JMOL)

The terminology of Rule 50, which governs motions for JMOL, does not conform to traditional terminology. The defendant can move when the plaintiff rests her case for a motion that asks the court to throw the case out because it lacks sufficient evidence to go to a jury. Historically, judges and lawyers referred to that motion as a "motion for a directed verdict." Rule 50 now calls that motion a "motion for judgment as a matter of law." At the end of the case, a party can motion again to have the case thrown out. Such a motion is nothing more, under Rule 50, than another JMOL motion during trial. Do not assume that because it is the second time a party has made the JMOL it qualifies as a "renewed" JMOL. Rule 50(b) has a special category for "renewed" JMOLs. A "renewed" JMOL occurs after trial when a party seeks to set aside a jury verdict. This historically would have been called a "motion for judgment notwithstanding the verdict," or a "motion for judgment n.o.v." However, Rule 50's new terminology refers to such a motion after verdict as a "renewed" JMOL. As we will discuss below, renewed JMOLs have a significant condition attached.

A. The Mechanics of Rule 50

Federal Rule of Civil Procedure 50 must be read carefully to understand the procedural traps it contains. If one does not understand these traps, the lawyer can forfeit the right to bring a motion for JMOL altogether. Thus, we will first consider the overall progress of a typical trial, the points at which a JMOL can be made, and answer questions based on Rule 50. If you understand the answers to these questions, you will be able to avoid the traps in Rule 50. Then we can address how a JMOL motion should be treated and the extent to which it is both different from and similar to a pretrial summary judgment motion under Federal Rule of Civil Procedure 56.

As the diagram below shows, Rule 50 deals with motions for JMOL at three points. The first point is after the plaintiff has rested her case. A defendant can move for JMOL then. The second point at which a motion for JMOL can be made is after the defendant has put on her case in chief and rested. At the end of trial, the plaintiff can again move for judgment as a matter of law. Moreover, at this point, the defendant can also move for judgment as a matter of law. The third point at which parties can move for JMOL is after the verdict if that party has moved during the trial for JMOL. This third point is called the "renewed" motion for JMOL. As that suggests, one must have already made the motion earlier. Hence, trial counsel needs to ensure at some point in the trial the initial motion for JMOL is on the record. Otherwise, once a verdict comes in, that party will be unable to ask for the verdict to be set aside. She can move for a new trial if there was a serious error or the verdict is, for instance, excessive. However, a motion for JMOL will not be an option if counsel has not moved for judgment as a matter of law during the trial. Following, in Figure 17-2, is a diagram of the three points in trial in which the motion for JMOL arises followed by a series of questions. If you can answer the questions, you likely have gained an understanding of Fed. R. Civ. P. 50.

Figure 17-2

Plaintiff Rests   **Rule50(a)**   Defendant Rests   **Rule50(a)**   Verdict ⟶ **Rule 50 (b)**
Case in ⟶ **JMOL**   Case in Chief ⟶ **JMOL**   **Renewed**
Chief   **JMOL**

Follow-Up Questions and Comments

Please read Federal Rule of Civil Procedure 50 and answer the following questions:

1. Plaintiff presents overwhelming evidence supporting her claims. At the close of the presentation of Plaintiff's evidence, she moves for JMOL. Can the Court grant JMOL under Rule 50? Why or why not?

2. Plaintiff and Defendant both present their evidence. Neither Plaintiff nor Defendant moves for JMOL. After the case has gone to the jury for deliberations but before a verdict has been rendered, Defendant moves for JMOL. Can the Court grant JMOL under Rule 50? Why or why not?

3. At the close of all the evidence, Defendant's counsel moves for JMOL and states the following: "Respectfully, Your Honor, the Court should enter judgment as a matter of law for the Defendant because the Plaintiff just has not proved her case." Should the Court grant JMOL under Rule 50? Why or why not?

4. Both Plaintiff and Defendant present their evidence. Neither party moves for JMOL. Following a jury verdict for the Plaintiff, the judge on her own decides that there was not sufficient evidence for the verdict and enters JMOL setting aside the verdict. Can the Court do so under Rule 50? Why or why not?

5. Defendant moves for JMOL at the close of all the evidence. After a jury verdict for the Plaintiff, the Court enters judgment and Defendant immediately makes an oral motion for JMOL. Defendant does not file a written motion for JMOL until more than thirty days after entry of judgment. Can the Court grant JMOL under Rule 50? Why or why not?

6. After Plaintiff rests her case in chief, Defendant moves for JMOL. The Defendant does not move for JMOL after resting. The jury returns a verdict for the Plaintiff. Within 28 days of the Court's judgment on that verdict, Defendant files a motion for a renewed JMOL. Can the Court grant the renewed JMOL? Why or why not?

B. The Standard by Which a Court Should Decide Whether to Grant a JMOL

Assume you have avoided the traps in Federal Rule of Civil Procedure 50 and have a Rule 50 JMOL motion before the court. What is the standard that the trial court should apply in deciding whether to grant your JMOL? Following are two leading cases on the standard that courts have applied to motions for a directed verdict. As we have learned, "motions for directed verdicts" are the same as motions for JMOLs. Therefore, these cases are sound precedent for modern JMOLs.

LAVENDER v. KURN
Supreme Court of the United States, 1946
327 U.S. 645

MR. JUSTICE MURPHY delivered the opinion of the Court.

The Federal Employers' Liability Act permits recovery for personal injuries to an employee of a railroad engaged in interstate commerce if such injuries result "in whole or in part from the negligence of any of the officers, agents, or employees of such carrier, or by reason of any defect or insufficiency, due to its negligence, in its cars, engines, appliances, machinery, track, roadbed, works, boats, wharves, or other equipment."[687]

Petitioner, the administrator of the estate of L.E. Haney, brought this suit under the Act against the respondent trustees of the St. Louis-San Francisco Railway Company (Frisco) and the respondent Illinois Central Railroad Company. It was charged that Haney, while employed as a switch-tender by the respondents in the switchyard of the Grand Central Station in Memphis, Tennessee, was killed as a result of respondents' negligence. Following a trial in the Circuit Court of the City of St. Louis, Missouri, the jury returned a verdict in favor of petitioner and awarded damages in the amount of $30,000. Judgment was entered accordingly. On appeal, however, the Supreme Court of Missouri reversed the judgment, holding that there was no substantial evidence of negligence to support the submission of the case to the jury. We granted certiorari to review the propriety of the Supreme Court's action under the circumstances of this case.

It was admitted that Haney was employed by the Illinois Central, or a subsidiary corporation thereof, as a switch-tender in the railroad yards near the Grand Central Station, which was owned by the Illinois Central. His duties included the throwing of switches for the Illinois Central as well as for the Frisco and other railroads using that station. For these services, the trustees of Frisco paid the Illinois Central two-twelfths of Haney's wages; they also paid two-twelfths of the wages of two other switch-tenders who worked at the same switches. In addition, the trustees paid Illinois Central $1.87 1/2 for each passenger car switched into Grand Central Station, which included all the cars in the Frisco train being switched into the station at the time Haney was killed.

The Illinois Central tracks run north and south directly past and into the Grand Central Station. About 2,700 feet south of the station the Frisco tracks cross at right angles to the Illinois Central tracks. A west-bound Frisco train wishing to use the station must stop some 250 feet or more west of this crossing and back into the station over a switch line curving east and north. The events in issue center about the switch several feet north of the main Frisco tracks at the point where the switch line branches off. This switch controls the tracks at this point.

It was very dark on the evening of December 21, 1939. At about 7:30 p. m. a west-bound interstate Frisco passenger train stopped on the Frisco main line, its rear some 20 or 30 feet west of the switch. Haney, in the performance of his duties, threw or opened the switch to permit the train to back into the station. The respondents claimed that Haney was then required to cross to the south side of the track before the train passed the switch; and the conductor of the train testified that he saw Haney so cross. But there was also

---

[687] 45 U.S.C. § 51.

evidence that Haney's duties required him to wait at the switch north of the track until the train had cleared, close the switch, return to his shanty near the crossing and change the signals from red to green to permit trains on the Illinois Central tracks to use the crossing. The Frisco train cleared the switch, backing at the rate of 8 or 10 miles per hour. But the switch remained open and the signals still were red. Upon investigation Haney was found north of the track near the switch lying face down on the ground, unconscious. An ambulance was called, but he was dead upon arrival at the hospital.

Haney had been struck in the back of the head, causing a fractured skull from which he died. There were no known eyewitnesses to the fatal blow. Although it is not clear, there is evidence that his body was extended north and south, the head to the south. Apparently[,] he had fallen forward to the south; his face was bruised on the left side from hitting the ground and there were marks indicating that his toes had dragged a few inches southward as he fell. His head was about 5 1/2 feet north of the Frisco tracks. Estimates ranged from 2 feet to 14 feet as to how far west of the switch he lay.

The injury to Haney's head was evidenced by a gash about two inches long from which blood flowed. The back of Haney's white cap had a corresponding black mark about an inch and a half long and an inch wide, running at an angle downward to the right of the center of the back of the head. A spot of blood was later found at a point 3 or 4 feet north of the tracks. The conclusion following an autopsy was that Haney's skull was fractured by "some fast moving small round object." One of the examining doctors testified that such an object might have been attached to a train backing at the rate of 8 or 10 miles per hour. But he also admitted that the fracture might have resulted from a blow from a pipe or club or some similar round object in the hands of an individual.

Petitioner's theory is that Haney was struck by the curled end or tip of a mail hook hanging down loosely on the outside of the mail car of the backing train. This curled end was 73 inches above the top of the rail, which was 7 inches high. The overhang of the mail car in relation to the rails was about 2 to 2 1/2 feet. The evidence indicated that when the mail car swayed or moved around a curve the mail hook might pivot, its curled end swinging out as much as 12 to 14 inches. The curled end could thus be swung out to a point 3 to 3 1/2 feet from the rail and about 73 inches above the top of the rail. Both east and west of the switch, however, was an uneven mound of cinders and dirt rising at its highest points 18 to 24 inches above the top of the rails. Witnesses differed as to how close the mound approached the rails, the estimates varying from 3 to 15 feet. But taking the figures most favorable to the petitioner, the mound extended to a point 6 to 12 inches north of the overhanging side of the mail car. If the mail hook end swung out 12 to 14 inches it would be 49 to 55 inches above the highest parts of the mound. Haney was 67 1/2 inches tall. If he had been standing on the mound about a foot from the side of the mail car he could have been hit by the end of the mail hook, the exact point of contact depending upon the height of the mound at the particular point. His wound was about 4 inches below the top of his head, or 63 1/2 inches above the point where he stood on the mound--well within the possible range of the mail hook end.

Respondents' theory is that Haney was murdered. They point to the estimates that the mound was 10 to 15 feet north of the rail, making it impossible for the mail hook end to reach a point of contact with Haney's head. Photographs were placed in the record to support the claim that the ground was level north of the rail for at least 10 feet. Moreover, it appears that the area immediately surrounding the switch was quite dark. Witnesses stated that it was so dark that it was impossible to see a 3-inch pipe 25 feet away. It also appears that many hoboes and tramps frequented the area at night in order to get rides on freight trains. Haney carried a pistol to protect himself. This pistol was found loose under his body by those who came to his rescue. It was testified, however, that the pistol had apparently slipped out of his pocket or scabbard as he fell. Haney's clothes were not disarranged and there was no evidence of a struggle or fight. No rods, pipes or weapons of any kind, except Haney's own pistol, were found near the scene. Moreover, his gold watch and diamond ring were still on him after he was struck. Six days later his unsoiled billfold was found on a high board fence about a block from the place where Haney was struck and near the point where he had been placed in an ambulance. It contained his social security card and other effects, but no money. His wife testified that he "never carried very much money, not very much more than $10." Such were the facts in relation to respondents' theory of murder.

Finally, one of the Frisco foremen testified that he arrived at the scene shortly after Haney was found injured. He later examined the fireman's side of the train very carefully and found nothing sticking out or in disorder. In explaining why he examined this side of the train so carefully he stated that while he was at the scene of the accident "someone said they thought that train No. 106 backing into Grand Central Station is what struck this man" and that Haney "was supposed to have been struck by something protruding on the side of this train." The foreman testified that these statements were made by an unknown Illinois Central switchman standing near the fallen body of Haney. The foreman admitted that the switchman "didn't see the accident . . ." This testimony was admitted by the trial court over the strenuous objections of respondents' counsel that it was mere hearsay falling outside the res gestae rule.

The jury was instructed that Frisco's trustees were liable if it was found that they negligently permitted a rod or other object to extend out from the side of the train as it backed past Haney and that Haney was killed as the direct result of such negligence, if any. The jury was further told that Illinois Central was liable if it was found that the company negligently maintained an unsafe and dangerous place for Haney to work, in that the ground was high and uneven and the light insufficient and inadequate, and that Haney was injured and killed as a direct result of the said place being unsafe and dangerous. This latter instruction as to Illinois Central did not require the jury to find that Haney was killed by something protruding from the train.

The Supreme Court, in upsetting the jury's verdict against both the Frisco trustees and the Illinois Central, admitted that "It could be inferred from the facts that Haney could have been struck by the mail hook knob if he were standing on the south side of the mound and the mail hook extended out as far as 12 or 14 inches." But it held that "all reasonable minds would agree that it would be mere speculation and conjecture to say that Haney was struck by the mail hook" and that "plaintiff failed to make a submissible[sic] case on that question." It also ruled that there "was no substantial evidence that the uneven ground and insufficient light were causes or contributing causes of the death of Haney." Finally, the Supreme Court held that the testimony of the foreman as to the statement made to him by the unknown switchman was inadmissible under the res gestae rule since the switchman spoke from what he had heard rather than from his own knowledge.

We hold, however, that there was sufficient evidence of negligence on the part of both the Frisco trustees and the Illinois Central to justify the submission of the case to the jury and to require appellate courts to abide by the verdict rendered by the jury.

The evidence we have already detailed demonstrates that there was evidence from which it might be inferred that the end of the mail hook struck Haney in the back of the head, an inference that the Supreme Court admitted could be drawn. That inference is not rendered unreasonable by the fact that Haney apparently fell forward toward the main Frisco track so that his head was 5 1/2 feet north of the rail. He may well have been struck and then wandered in a daze to the point where he fell forward. The testimony as to blood marks some distance away from his head lends credence to that possibility, indicating that he did not fall immediately upon being hit. When that is added to the evidence most favorable to the petitioner

485

as to the height and swing-out of the hook, the height and location of the mound and the nature of Haney's duties, the inference that Haney was killed by the hook cannot be said to be unsupported by probative facts or to be so unreasonable as to warrant taking the case from the jury.

It is true that there is evidence tending to show that it was physically and mathematically impossible for the hook to strike Haney. And there are facts from which it might reasonably be inferred that Haney was murdered. But such evidence has become irrelevant upon appeal, there being a reasonable basis in the record for inferring that the hook struck Haney. The jury having made that inference, the respondents were not free to relitigate the factual dispute in a reviewing court. Under these circumstances it would be an undue invasion of the jury's historic function for an appellate court to weigh the conflicting evidence, judge the credibility of witnesses and arrive at a conclusion opposite from the one reached by the jury.

It is no answer to say that the jury's verdict involved speculation and conjecture. Whenever facts are in dispute or the evidence is such that fair-minded men may draw different inferences, a measure of speculation and conjecture is required on the part of those whose duty it is to settle the dispute by choosing what seems to them to be the most reasonable inference. Only when there is a complete absence of probative facts to support the conclusion reached does a reversible error appear. But where, as here, there is an evidentiary basis for the jury's verdict, the jury is free to discard or disbelieve whatever facts are inconsistent with its conclusion. And the appellate court's function is exhausted when that evidentiary basis becomes apparent, it being immaterial that the court might draw a contrary inference or feel that another conclusion is more reasonable.

We are unable, therefore, to sanction a reversal of the jury's verdict against Frisco's trustees. Nor can we approve any disturbance in the verdict as to Illinois Central. The evidence was uncontradicted that it was very dark at the place where Haney was working[,] and the surrounding ground was high and uneven. The evidence also showed that this area was entirely within the domination and control of Illinois Central despite the fact that the area was technically located in a public street of the City of Memphis. It was not unreasonable to conclude that these conditions constituted an unsafe and dangerous working place and that such conditions contributed in part to Haney's death, assuming that it resulted primarily from the mail hook striking his head.

In view of the foregoing disposition of the case, it is unnecessary to decide whether the allegedly hearsay testimony was admissible under the res gestae rule. Rulings on the admissibility of evidence must normally be left to the sound discretion of the trial judge in actions under the Federal Employers' Liability Act. But inasmuch as there is adequate support in the record for the jury's verdict apart from the hearsay testimony, we need not determine whether that discretion was abused in this instance. The judgment of the Supreme Court of Missouri is reversed[,] and the case is remanded for whatever further proceedings may be necessary not inconsistent with this opinion.

Reversed.

PENNSYLVANIA RAILROAD CO. v. CHAMBERLAIN
Supreme Court of the United States, 1933
288 U.S. 333

MR. JUSTICE SUTHERLAND delivered the opinion of the Court.

This is an action brought by respondent against petitioner to recover for the death of a brakeman, alleged to have been caused by petitioner's negligence. The complaint alleges that the deceased, at the time of the accident resulting in his death, was assisting in the yard work of breaking up and making up trains and in the classifying and assorting of cars operating in interstate commerce; that in pursuance of such work, while riding a cut of cars, other cars ridden by fellow employees were negligently caused to be brought into violent contact with those upon which deceased was riding, with the result that he was thrown therefrom to the railroad track and run over by a car or cars, inflicting injuries from which he died. At the conclusion of the evidence, the trial court directed the jury to find a verdict in favor of petitioner. Judgment upon a verdict so found was reversed by the court of appeals.

That part of the yard in which the accident occurred contained a lead track and a large number of switching tracks branching therefrom. The lead track crossed a "hump," and the work of car distribution consisted of pushing a train of cars by means of a locomotive to the top of the "hump," and then allowing the cars, in separate strings, to descend by gravity, under the control of hand brakes, to their respective destinations in the various branch tracks. Deceased had charge of a string of two gondola cars, which he was piloting to track 14. Immediately ahead of him was a string of seven cars, and behind him a string of nine cars, both also destined for track 14. Soon after the cars ridden by deceased had passed to track 14, his body was found on that track some distance beyond the switch. He had evidently fallen onto the track and been run over by a car or cars.

The case for respondent rests wholly upon the claim that the fall of deceased was caused by a violent collision of the string of nine cars with the string ridden by deceased. Three employees, riding the nine-car string, testified positively that no such collision occurred. They were corroborated by every other employee in a position to see, all testifying that there was no contact between the nine-car string and that of the deceased. The testimony of these witnesses, if believed, establishes beyond doubt that there was no collision between these two strings of cars, and that the nine-car string contributed in no way to the accident. The only witness who testified for the respondent was one Bainbridge; and it is upon his testimony alone that respondent's right to recover is sought to be upheld. His testimony is concisely stated, in its most favorable light for respondent, in the prevailing opinion below by Judge Learned Hand, as follows:

"The plaintiff's only witness to the event, one Bainbridge, then employed by the road, stood close to the yardmaster's office, near the 'hump.' He professed to have paid little attention to what went on, but he did see the deceased riding at the rear of his cars, whose speed when they passed him he took to be about eight or ten miles. Shortly thereafter a second string passed which was shunted into another track and this was followed by the nine, which, according to the plaintiff's theory, collided with the deceased's. After the nine cars had passed at a somewhat greater speed than the deceased's, Bainbridge paid no more attention to either string for a while, but looked again when the deceased, who was still standing in his place, had passed the switch and onto the assorting track where he was bound. At that time his speed had been checked to about three miles, but the speed of the following nine cars had increased. They were just passing the switch, about four or five cars behind the deceased. Bainbridge looked away again and soon heard what he described as a 'loud crash,' not however an unusual event in a switching yard. Apparently[,] this did not cause him at once to turn, but he did so shortly thereafter, and saw the two strings together, still moving, and the deceased no longer in sight. Later still his attention was attracted by shouts and he went to the spot and saw the deceased between the rails. Until he left to go to the accident, he had stood fifty feet to the north of the track where the accident happened, and about nine hundred feet from where the body was found."

The court, although regarding Bainbridge's testimony as not only "somewhat suspicious in itself, but it's contradiction . . . so manifold as to leave little doubt," held, nevertheless, that the question was one

487

of fact depending upon the credibility of the witnesses, and that it was for the jury to determine, as between the one witness and the many, where the truth lay. The dissenting opinion of Judge Swan proceeds upon the theory that Bainbridge did not testify that in fact a collision had taken place, but inferred it because he heard a crash, and because thereafter the two strings of cars appeared to him to be moving together. It is correctly pointed out in that opinion, however, that the crash might have come from elsewhere in the busy yard and that Bainbridge was in no position to see whether the two strings of cars were actually together; that Bainbridge repeatedly said he was paying no particular attention; and that his position was such, being 900 feet from the place where the body was found and less than 50 feet from the side of the track in question, that he necessarily saw the strings of cars at such an acute angle that it would be physically impossible even for an attentive observer to tell whether the forward end of the nine-car cut was actually in contact with the rear end of the two-car cut. The dissenting opinion further points out that all the witnesses who were in a position to see testified that there was no collision; that respondent's evidence was wholly circumstantial, and the inferences which might otherwise be drawn from it were shown to be utterly erroneous unless all of petitioner's witnesses were willful perjurers. "This is not a case," the opinion proceeds, "where direct testimony to an essential fact is contradicted by direct testimony of other witnesses, though even there it is conceded a directed verdict might be proper in some circumstances. Here, when all the testimony was in, the circumstantial evidence in support of negligence was thought by the trial judge to be so insubstantial and insufficient that it did not justify submission to the jury."

. . .

It, of course, is true, generally, that where there is a direct conflict of testimony upon a matter of fact, the question must be left to the jury to determine, without regard to the number of witnesses upon either side. But here there really is no conflict in the testimony as to the facts. The witnesses for petitioner flatly testified that there was no collision between the nine-car and the two-car strings. Bainbridge did not say there was such a collision. What he said was that he heard a "loud crash," which did not cause him at once to turn, but that shortly thereafter he did turn and saw the two strings of cars moving together with the deceased no longer in sight; that there was nothing unusual about the crash of cars--it happened every day; that there was nothing about this crash to attract his attention except that it was extra loud; that he paid no attention to it; that it was not sufficient to attract his attention. The record shows that there was a continuous movement of cars over and down the "hump," which were distributed among a large number of branch tracks within the yard, and that any two strings of these cars moving upon the same track might have come together and caused the crash which Bainbridge heard. There is no direct evidence that in fact the crash was occasioned by a collision of the two strings in question; and it is perfectly clear that no such fact was brought to Bainbridge's attention as a perception of the physical sense of sight or of hearing. At most there was an inference to that effect drawn from observed facts which gave equal support to the opposite inference that the crash was occasioned by the coming together of other strings of cars entirely away from the scene of the accident, or of the two-car string ridden by deceased and the seven-car string immediately ahead of it.

We, therefore, have a case belonging to that class of cases where proven facts give equal support to each of two inconsistent inferences; in which event, neither of them being established, judgment, as a matter of law, must go against the party upon whom rests the necessity of sustaining one of these inferences as against the other, before he is entitled to recover. . . .

The rule is . . . stated in *Smith v. First National Bank in Westfield*:[688]

---

[688] 99 Mass. 605, 611–12.

There being several inferences deducible from the facts which appear, and equally consistent with all those facts, the plaintiff has not maintained the proposition upon which alone he would be entitled to recover. There is strictly no evidence to warrant a jury in finding that the loss was occasioned by negligence and not by theft. When the evidence tends equally to sustain either of two inconsistent propositions, neither of them can be said to have been established by legitimate proof. A verdict in favor of the party bound to maintain one of those propositions against the other is necessarily wrong.

That Bainbridge concluded from what he himself observed that the crash was due to a collision between the two strings of cars in question is sufficiently indicated by his statements. But this, of course, proves nothing, since it is not allowable for a witness to resolve the doubt as to which of two equally justifiable inferences shall be adopted by drawing a conclusion, which, if accepted, will result in a purely gratuitous award in favor of the party who has failed to sustain the burden of proof cast upon him by the law. And the desired inference is precluded for the further reason that respondent's right of recovery depends upon the existence of a particular fact which must be inferred from proven facts, and this is not permissible in the face of the positive and otherwise uncontradicted testimony of unimpeached witnesses consistent with the facts actually proved, from which testimony it affirmatively appears that the fact sought to be inferred did not exist. This conclusion results from a consideration of many decisions . . . . A rebuttable inference of fact . . . must necessarily yield to credible evidence of the actual occurrence." And, as stated by the court in *George v. Missouri Pac. R. Co.*, "It is well settled that where plaintiff's case is based upon an inference or inferences, that the case must fail upon proof of undisputed facts inconsistent with such inferences." . . . In Southern Ry. Co. v. Walters, supra, the negligence charged was failure to stop a train and flag a crossing before proceeding over it. The court concluded that the only support for the charge was an inference sought to be drawn from certain facts proved. In rejecting the inference, this court said:

"It is argued that it may be inferred from the speed of the train when some of the witnesses observed it crossing other streets as well as Bond Avenue, and from a guess of the engineer as to the time required to get up such speed after a full stop, that none could have been made at Bond Avenue. But the argument amounts to mere speculation in view of the limited scope of the witnesses' observation, the down grade of the railway tracks at the point, and the time element involved. . . . Five witnesses for defendant [employees] testified that a full stop was made and the crossing flagged, and that no one was hit by the rear of the tender, which was the front of the train.

"An examination of the record requires the conclusion that the evidence on the issue whether the train was stopped before crossing Bond Avenue was so insubstantial and insufficient that it did not justify a submission of that issue to the jury."

Not only is Bainbridge's testimony considered as a whole suspicious, insubstantial and insufficient, but his statement that when he turned shortly after hearing the crash the two strings were moving together is simply incredible, if he meant thereby to be understood as saying that he saw the two in contact; and if he meant by the words "moving together" simply that they were moving at the same time in the same direction but not in contact, the statement becomes immaterial. As we have already seen he was paying slight and only occasional attention to what was going on. The cars were eight or nine hundred feet from where he stood and moving almost directly away from him, his angle of vision being only 3 degrees 33 minutes from a straight line. At that sharp angle and from that distance, near dusk of a misty evening (as the proof shows), the practical impossibility of the witness being able to see whether the front of the nine-car string was in contact with the back of the two-car string is apparent. And, certainly . . . no verdict based upon a statement so unbelievable reasonably could be sustained as against the positive testimony to the contrary of unimpeached witnesses, all in a position to see, as this witness was not, the precise relation of

489

the cars to one another. The fact that these witnesses were employees of the petitioner, under the circumstances here disclosed, does not impair this conclusion.

We think, therefore, that the trial court was right in withdrawing the case from the jury. It repeatedly has been held by this court that before evidence may be left to the jury, "there is a preliminary question for the judge, not whether there is literally no evidence, but whether there is any upon which a jury can properly proceed to find a verdict for the party producing it, upon whom the onus of proof is imposed." And where the evidence is "so overwhelmingly on one side as to leave no room to doubt what the fact is, the court should give a peremptory instruction to the jury." The rule is settled for the federal courts, and for many of the state courts, that whenever in the trial of a civil case the evidence is clearly such that if a verdict were rendered for one of the parties the other would be entitled to a new trial, it is the duty of the judge to direct the jury to find according to the views of the court. Such a practice, this court has said, not only saves time and expense, but "gives scientific certainty to the law in its application to the facts and promotes the ends of justice." The scintilla rule has been definitely and repeatedly rejected so far as the federal courts are concerned.

Leaving out of consideration, then, the inference relied upon, the case for respondent is left without any substantial support in the evidence, and a verdict in her favor would have rested upon mere speculation and conjecture. This, of course, is inadmissible.

The judgment of the Circuit Court of Appeals is reversed and that of the District Court is *affirmed*.

Follow-Up Questions and Comments

1. Can you reconcile the results in *Lavender* and *Chamberlain*? Why or why not?

2. To what is the "scintilla of the evidence" discussion in Chamberlain referring? If a scintilla of evidence was sufficient to get past the JMOL phase, what effect would that have on the system?

3. Is the court on a JMOL applying the same standard it applies in determining whether sufficient evidence should allow the case to go forward as we learned in pretrial summary judgment? Thus, referring to the diagram with the three points (p. 446)—one to the far left being 'summary Judgment Burden" which mays seem odd but demonstrates that sufficiency of the evidence is the same test on a summary judgment motion and a Rule 50 JMOL. The JMOL motions will occur at trial, and the court will have heard the witnesses and seen the other evidence. However, the court on a JMOL—whether during or after the trial—is supposed to disregard witnesses' credibility and decide whether reasonable jurors could disagree on the claim or claims. If so, even if the court personally does not find witnesses convincing, she is supposed to deny the JMOL motion.

4. Recall that an atypical summary judgment burden would be where the claimant moves for JMOL because the evidence is so overwhelming on her claim that reasonable jurors could not rule against her. Because it is hard for the party with the burden of proof to show that reasonable jurors could reach no conclusion but that the claimant proved the case and should win, such a motion is rarely granted. That is why the term "atypical" is used.

Practice Problem

Practice Problem 17-1

Pete worked at an asphalt plant on the night shift. A coal bin was at the top of a sloped ramp and a large wheel loader went up the ramp, loaded coal into the scoop of the machine, and took it down the ramp to unload at the location where the asphalt was made. Pete was found at the bottom of the ramp with his leg crushed. He cannot recall what happened, but everyone believes that the loader must have accidentally run over him in the dark. The loader has headlights and lights at the top of the cab. Pete's lawyers find an expert that opines that the lights on top of the cab do not shed light as much as they could if positioned in front of the loader, though they generally do allow the operator to see in front of the loader. Pete brings a product liability claim against the manufacturer of the loader. His theory is that the lighting pattern on the loader is negligently designed because it could have set a greater swath of light. Defendant contents that, even assuming for purposes of argument that the loader was defectively designed, plaintiff has failed to show sufficient evidence on which reasonable jurors could disagree that the lighting—even if altered as the expert suggested—would have made any difference. In other words, the defendant asserts that there is insufficient evidence of proximate cause. Should the court grant a JMOL?

C. Motion for a New Trial

An alternative to a renewed JMOL is to move for a new trial under Federal Rule of Civil Procedure 59. Indeed, most lawyers move for a renewed JMOL or, alternatively for a new trial. As we will see, the standard is more flexible for a court in granting a new trial. Thus, the court may well deny a renewed JMOL but grant a motion for a new trial under Rule 59.

MOLSKI v. M.J. CABLE, INC.
United States Court of Appeals for the Ninth Circuit, 2007
481 F. 3d 724

FERGUSON, Circuit Judge.

Jarek Molski ("Molski") appeals the District Court's denial of his motion for a new trial following a jury verdict in favor of M.J. Cable Inc., owner of Cable's Restaurant ("Cable's"). Molski, who is paraplegic, sued Cable's for violations of the Americans with Disabilities Act ("ADA") and California's Unruh Civil Rights Act ("Unruh Act"), alleging that Cable's failed to accommodate the disabled. Although Molski provided uncontradicted evidence that Cable's did not identify and remove architectural barriers, the jury returned a verdict for the restaurant. The District Court denied Molski's motion for a new trial, speculating that the jury could have reasonably concluded that because of Molski's record of litigiousness, he was a "business" and not an "individual" entitled to the ADA's protections. We reverse.

FACTUAL AND PROCEDURAL BACKGROUND

Molski is a paraplegic who has been confined to a wheelchair since a motorcycle accident paralyzed him at the age of 18. Considered by some to be a controversial figure, Molski has brought hundreds of lawsuits against inaccessible public accommodations throughout California. Molski considers himself a civil rights activist who uses litigation to force compliance with the ADA; California businesses and a federal district court consider him a vexatious litigant who exploits the ADA and its state law counterpart for pecuniary gain.

On January 26, 2003, Molski took his grandmother to church, then to lunch at Cable's Restaurant in Woodland Hills, California, where he spent thirty-five dollars on their meal. After eating lunch, Molski excused himself to use the restaurant's public restroom.

Upon entering the restroom, Molski noticed numerous architectural barriers to his accessing the facilities. The door pressure on the bathroom door was too heavy, and the door lacked a handicap accessible sign. Inside, the stall doors could not close with Molski's wheelchair in the stall. The stall lacked grab bars on both the rear wall and side wall, which prevented Molski from maneuvering from his wheelchair to the toilet. The toilet seat cover dispenser was unreachable. The pipes underneath the sink were not insulated, and therefore, according to Molski, posed a special risk to those without feeling in their legs, as hot pipes could burn them without their realization. The sink also lacked levered hardware, a type of fixture that is easily moveable without strong grip strength. Molski was unable to reach at least one of the paper towel dispensers. Molski testified that the hygienic violations were especially important in his case because, due to his chest-down paralysis, he uses a catheter and a urine bag that must be emptied frequently. He explained that failure to empty the urine bag can cause autonomic dysreflexia, a condition that can result in whole body spasms and even cardiac arrest. Handling the bag with unwashed hands can also lead to bladder infections.

On March 7, 2003, Rick Sarantschin ("Sarantschin"), the principal of Access Investigation Monitoring, conducted an inspection of Cable's and confirmed Molski's observations using the ADA Accessibility Guidelines for Buildings and Facilities ("ADAAG"). Four months later, Molski brought a lawsuit against Cable's in the Central District of California, alleging violations of the ADA and state laws. The District Court held a three-day trial.

At trial, Molski, Sarantschin, and construction expert Michael Beall ("Beall") testified on behalf of Molski, and Cable's vice president Anthony Dalkas ("Dalkas") testified as an adverse witness. Molski testified primarily about his experience at Cable's, his prior lawsuits, and his views on disability access discrimination. Sarantschin testified about his investigation of Cable's and the ADA violations he observed.

Beall testified about the construction costs of making Cable's compliant with the ADA. He estimated that the approximate total cost to remodel both the men's and women's bathrooms would be $8,600, or $6,000 for just the men's bathroom. Beall noted that incremental steps were even cheaper: lowering the toilet seat cover dispenser would cost $20 and take about 15 minutes; insulating the pipes would cost under $20 and take "about a minute and a half to do." Other repairs were as inexpensive as $30.

In his testimony, Dalkas acknowledged that the company had not attempted to identify barriers to the disabled. He admitted that Cable's had not made the renovations because "[w]e weren't compelled to do it." Dalkas testified that Cable's could afford each of the repairs but stated, "once you start down that path[,] you're opening a can of worms that will cost a lot of money." Dalkas described issues with Cable's landlord, as well as the economic costs of remodeling, such as the need to close the restaurant during renovations. Dalkas said he had received estimates of $40,000 to "bring the two bathrooms up to the current [c]ode," although Cable's had not disclosed any such remodeling bids during discovery.

The defendant did not call any witnesses[] but relied primarily on its cross-examination of Molski and Dalkas. The defendant's strategy was to discredit Molski by exposing an ulterior motive for bringing suit: Molski and his lawyer Thomas Frankovich ("Frankovich") were purportedly in the business of tracking down public accommodations with ADA violations and extorting settlements out of them. On cross examination, Molski acknowledged that: he did not complain to any of Cable's employees about his access problems; he had filed 374 similar ADA lawsuits as of October 8, 2004; Frankovich had filed 232 of the 374 lawsuits; even more lawsuits had been filed since that date; Molski and Frankovich averaged $4,000 for each case that settled; Molski did not pay any fees to Frankovich; Molski maintained no employment besides prosecuting ADA cases, despite his possession of a law degree; Molski's projected annual income from settlements was $800,000; Molski executed blank verification forms for Frankovich to submit with responses to interrogatories; they had also filed lawsuits against two other restaurants owned by Cable's; they had filed a lawsuit against a nearby restaurant; and Sarantschin obtained up to 95% of his income from Frankovich's firm for performing investigations for ADA lawsuits.

During closing arguments, Molski focused primarily on the ADA violations, and Cable's focused primarily on Molski. The Court instructed the jury on, inter alia, the elements of an ADA claim, and gave it a Special Verdict Form. The jury returned a verdict for Cable's, responding "No" to the threshold question: "Do you find that the defendant failed to identify and remove architectural barriers at Cable's restaurant?"

Pursuant to Rule 59(a) of the Federal Rules of Civil Procedure, Molski moved for a new trial on the grounds that the verdict was against the weight of the evidence. The District Court denied the motion. Molski timely appealed.

DISCUSSION

Standard of Review

We review a district court's denial of a motion for a new trial under Federal Rule of Civil Procedure 59(a) for an abuse of discretion.[689]

"The district court's denial of the motion for a new trial is reversible only if the record contains no evidence in support of the verdict."[690] We may reverse the denial of the motion where the District Court has "made a mistake of law."[691]

Rule 59 (a)

Rule 59(a) states, "A new trial may be granted . . .in an action in which there has been a trial by jury, for any of the reasons for which new trials have heretofore been granted in actions at law in the courts of the United States."[692] As this circuit has noted, "Rule 59 does not specify the grounds on which a motion for a new trial may be granted." Rather, the court is "bound by those grounds that have been historically recognized." Historically recognized grounds include, but are not limited to, claims "that the verdict is against the weight of the evidence, that the damages are excessive, or that, for other reasons, the trial was not fair to the party moving." We have held that "[t]he trial court may grant a new trial only if the verdict is contrary to the clear weight of the evidence, is based upon false or perjurious evidence, or to prevent a miscarriage of justice."

Upon the Rule 59 motion of the party against whom a verdict has been returned, the district court has "the duty . . .to weigh the evidence as [the court] saw it, and to set aside the verdict of the jury, even

---

[689] Dorn v. Burlington N. Santa Fe R.R. Co., 397 F.3d 1183, 1189 (9th Cir.2005); *see also* Gilbrook v. City of Westminster, 177 F.3d 839, 856 (9th Cir.1999) (applying abuse of discretion standard where the motion for a new trial was "grounded on the assertion that the jury's verdict was against the clear weight of evidence").

[690] Farley Transp. Co. v. Santa Fe Trail Transp. Co., 786 F.2d 1342, 1347 (9th Cir.1985).

[691] 12 JAMES WM. MOORE ET AL., MOORE'S FEDERAL PRACTICE § 59.54 (3d ed. 2006).

[692] FED. R. CIV. P. 59(a) (1).

though supported by substantial evidence, where, in [the court's] conscientious opinion, the verdict is contrary to the clear weight of the evidence."

Because determining "the clear weight of the evidence" is a fact-specific endeavor, appeals courts are reluctant to second-guess district court's conclusions. An appellate court generally will not reverse the denial of a new trial motion if there was some "reasonable basis" for the jury's verdict. If there is no reasonable basis, however, "the absolute absence of evidence to support the jury's verdict makes [refusal to grant a new trial] an error in law."

Americans with Disabilities Act

Congress passed the ADA,[693] in 1990 "to provide clear, strong, consistent, enforceable standards addressing discrimination against individuals with disabilities." Title III of the ADA prohibits discrimination by public accommodations. Title III provides, "No individual shall be discriminated against on the basis of disability in the full and equal enjoyment of the goods, services, facilities, privileges, advantages, or accommodations of any place of public accommodation by any person who owns, leases (or leases to), or operates a place of public accommodation." Discrimination includes "a failure to remove architectural barriers . . .in existing facilities . . .where such removal is readily achievable." Readily achievable means "easily accomplishable and able to be carried out without much difficulty or expense."

Federal regulations clarify which barrier removals are likely to be readily achievable and provide examples in 28 C.F.R. § 36.304. They include installing grab bars in toilet stalls, rearranging toilet partitions to increase maneuvering space, insulating lavatory pipes under sinks to prevent burns, installing raised toilet seats, installing full-length bathroom mirrors, and repositioning paper towel dispensers. The Department of Justice has referred to these examples as "the types of modest measures that may be taken to remove barriers and that are likely to be readily achievable."

To prevail on a Title III discrimination claim, the plaintiff must show that (1) she is disabled within the meaning of the ADA; (2) the defendant is a private entity that owns, leases, or operates a place of public accommodation; and (3) the plaintiff was denied public accommodations by the defendant because of her disability.

Aggrieved individuals or the Attorney General may enforce the ADA. Private parties may utilize the remedies and procedures made available by the Civil Rights Act of 1964. They may obtain injunctive relief against public accommodations with architectural barriers, including "an order to alter facilities to make such facilities readily accessible to and usable by individuals with disabilities." In suits brought by the Attorney General, courts may grant both equitable relief and monetary damages. Monetary damages are not available in private suits under Title III of the ADA, . . . but the ADA gives courts the discretion to award attorney's fees to prevailing parties.

California's Unruh Civil Rights Act

In the disability context, California's Unruh Civil Rights Act operates virtually identically to the ADA. It states,

> All persons within the jurisdiction of this state are free and equal, and no matter what their sex, race, color, religion, ancestry, national origin, disability, medical condition, marital status, or sexual orientation are entitled to the full and equal accommodations, advantages, facilities, privileges, or services in all business

---

[693] 42 U.S.C. § 12101 et seq.

establishments of every kind whatsoever.[694]

The Unruh Act, however, does allow for monetary damages. Victims of discrimination may obtain actual damages, as well as "any amount that may be determined by a jury . . .up to a maximum of three times the amount of actual damage but in no case less than four thousand dollars." The litigant need not prove she suffered actual damages to recover the independent statutory damages of $4,000. The Unruh Act also allows for attorney's fees.

Because the Unruh Act is coextensive with the ADA and allows for monetary damages, litigants in federal court in California often pair state Unruh Act claims with federal ADA claims.[695]

Analysis

The issue in this case is whether the District Court abused its discretion when it denied Molski's motion for a new trial. The first question is whether there was an absence of evidence to support the jury's conclusion that "defendant[s did not] fail[ ] to identify and remove architectural barriers at Cable's Restaurant." The second question is whether the District Court's explanation of the verdict, that Molski was a business and not an individual, somehow justifies the jury's conclusion.

. . .

The District Court structured the Special Verdict Form to track the elements of a Title III claim. First, as a threshold question, it asked, "Do you find that the defendant failed to identify and remove architectural barriers at Cable's Restaurant?" The form then instructed the jury, if it answered "yes," to answer three questions for each of the purported violations: "(1) Did this barrier exist at the Cable's Restaurant on January 26, 2003? (2) If 'yes,' did defendant M.J. Cable fail to identify and remove the barrier? (3) If 'yes,' was it readily achievable to remove?" After these questions, the form asked, "Should plaintiff be awarded statutory damages in the sum of $4,000?" The jury answered "no" to the first question and therefore did not go on to answer any of the subsequent questions.

Reviewing the trial transcript, "the record contains no evidence in support of the verdict." The testimony of Molski and Sarantschin established a laundry list of architectural barriers, including: the absence of accessibility signage, excessive door pressure, stalls that were neither wide enough nor long enough, the absence of side and rear grab bars, the absence of looped handles for opening or closing the stall door, no sliding lock, no automatic door opener, a toilet seat cover dispenser that was too high, a paper towel dispenser that was too high, a height-compliant paper towel dispenser that was blocked by a sink, sinks without levered hardware, no insulation on the pipes, urinals that were too close and too high, stall doors that were too narrow, and toilets that were too short.

Dalkas, the vice president of Cable's, acknowledged the continued existence of these violations and flatly admitted that neither he nor anyone else at Cable's had attempted to identify or remove architectural barriers.

The only issue about which there was any disagreement was whether the removal of the barriers was "readily achievable." This issue is separate from whether Cable's identified and removed the barriers.

---

[694] CAL. CIV. CODE § 51(B). Any violation of the ADA necessarily constitutes a violation of the Unruh Act. § 51(f).
[695] *Molski*, 347 F.Supp.2d at 862–63.

495

The Special Verdict Form specifically distinguished those questions, allowing the jury to find initially that Cable's had failed to identify or remove the barriers, but then that removal was not readily achievable. It did not do so.

The jury's determination, in response to the threshold question, that Cable's had not failed to identify and remove barriers was against the clear weight of the evidence, given the undisputed testimony from both Molski and Dalkas. Accordingly, the District Court abused its discretion in denying Molski's motion for a new trial.

. . .

In denying Molski's motion, the District Court accepted the defendant's "reasonable explanation for the jury's verdict: the jury determined that Molski was not an 'individual' under the ADA, and therefore could not recover against Defendants." This conclusion is unreasonable and legally flawed.

First, the District Court's explanation is inconsistent with the plain language, structure, and spirit of the ADA. Neither the District Court nor the defendant provide any support for concluding that a person may be considered a business and not an individual because of a history of litigiousness.

Title III of the ADA protects "individuals" who are disabled. It is clear that Molski, who is paraplegic, falls within that term. "Statutory interpretation begins with the plain meaning of the statute's language. Where the statutory language is clear and consistent with the statutory scheme at issue, the plain language of the statute is conclusive and the judicial inquiry is at an end."

The defendant, . . . contends that the ADA defines individuals as referring only "to the clients and customers of the covered public accommodation." This argument is unavailing for two reasons: first, it misinterprets the relevant provision of the ADA; second, even if its interpretation of the statute were correct, as a factual matter, it does not exclude Molski.

First, § 12182(b) (1) (A) (iv), which defines "individuals" as "clients or customers," applies only "[f]or purposes of clauses (i) through (iii) of . . .subparagraph [(b) (1) (A)]." Sections (i) through (iii) of subparagraph (b) (1) (A) generally prohibit public accommodations from denying participation to the disabled, providing disabled participants an unequal benefit, or providing disabled participants a separate benefit. However, it is subsection (a), not subsection (b), that provides the general prohibition against discrimination on the basis of disability. As the Supreme Court has pointed out, "clause (iv) [of subparagraph (b) (1) (A)] is not literally applicable to Title III's general rule [in subsection (a)] prohibiting discrimination against disabled individuals. Title III's broad general rule contains no express 'clients or customers' limitation ...." Aside from being inapplicable to subsection (a)'s general prohibition, the limited definition of "individual" in § 12182(b) (1) (A) (iv) is also inapplicable to § 12182(b) (2) (A) (iv), which defines discrimination to include the failure to remove architectural barriers.

This interpretation is in accord with at least one other circuit. In *Menkowitz v. Pottstown Memorial Medical Center,*[696] the Third Circuit held that Title III applied to a medical doctor working as an independent contractor at a hospital, despite the fact that he was neither a client nor a customer, nor even a member of the general public. The court concluded that "both the language of Title III and its legislative history clearly demonstrate [that] the phrase 'clients or customers,' which only appears in 42 U.S.C. §

_____

[696] 154 F.3d 113, 122 (3d Cir.1998).

12182(b)(1) (A) (iv), is not a general circumscription of Title III and cannot serve to limit the broad rule announced in 42 U.S.C. § 12182(a)." Rather, the court noted, "[t]he operative rule announced in Title III speaks not in terms of 'guests,' 'patrons,' 'clients,' 'customers,' or 'members of the public' but instead broadly uses the word 'individuals.'"

Accordingly, Molski did not need to have been a client or customer of Cable's to be an "individual" entitled to the protections of Title III. One need not be a client or customer of a public accommodation to feel the sting of its discrimination.

But even if the defendant's reading of the ADA were proper, it would not exclude Molski. Molski was plainly a "customer" of Cable's Restaurant. He brought a guest to the restaurant, ordered food, ate it, paid thirty-five dollars for it, tried to use the restroom, and left. He even returned the day before the trial for some ice cream. In Martin, the Supreme Court held that a one-time payment is sufficient to make a disabled person a client or customer of a public accommodation.

Even assuming it would have been a viable legal theory for Molski to have been a business and not an individual, the jury instructions provide no basis for making such a finding. Cable's did not put forth any evidence that Molski was incorporated, paid salaries, advertised, held himself out as a business, or conducted any activities that could make him a business as a matter of law. In fact, the Joint Pre–Trial Conference Order identifies the plaintiff as "JAREK MOLSKI, an individual" and states as an "admitted fact" that "Plaintiff Jarek Molski is a person with disabilities as defined by the ADA." The jury could not have then come to the opposite conclusion.

The jury instructions do not give any support to the District Court's explanation of the verdict, either. The jury was never instructed on the Molski-as-business theory. Although the District Court gave the jury definitions for "disability," "major life activities," "public accommodation," "denial of access," "architectural barrier," and "readily achievable," it never discussed the possibility that Molski was not an "individual" under the ADA, nor did it provide any definition of that term.

Finally, the test provided in the jury instructions stated only the following requirements for finding an ADA violation: (1) that Molski be disabled, (2) that Cable's be a public accommodation, and (3) that "Plaintiff was denied access to elements of the Defendants' public accommodation due to Defendants' failure to remove architectural barriers." The parties stipulated to the first two elements, and Molski unequivocally proved the third. The jury instructions therefore provide no support for the District Court's speculation that the jury concluded that Molski was not an individual.

CONCLUSION

We conclude that the record provides no evidence whatsoever for the jury's verdict. The District Court abused its discretion in denying Molski's motion for a new trial. Accordingly, we reverse the District Court's denial of the motion, vacate the judgment against Molski, including that for incurred costs, and remand for a new trial. Costs on appeal are awarded to appellant.

Reversed; Vacated and Remanded.

Follow-Up Questions and Comments

1. What test did the court state as the criteria for determining whether the trial court should have granted a new trial?

2. How does the court's analysis under that test differ from the analysis of a court examining the sufficiency of the evidence? Why is the standard for a new trial that allows the trial court to evaluate the weight of evidence and other matters unavailable on a JMOL not an affront to the jury system, whereas allowing such an aggressive approach on JMOL motions would be?

3. If the only thing that is contrary to the weight of the evidence is the amount of damages awarded, the court can grant a new trial limited to damages. The typical language a court relies on when it believes the damages are out of kilter with the evidence is that it "shocks the conscience of the court."[697] Alternatively, instead of granting new trial, the court can order remittitur so as to provide a reduced amount that the court deems reasonable under the evidence.[698] Remittitur is the term used when the court orders the amount awarded to be reduce to an amount the court believes the evidence supported. Plaintiff has the option of accepting the remitted amount or of seeking a new trial.

III. Jury Selection Procedures

After completing the pretrial process, usually on the first day of trial, counsel select a jury from the pool of potential jurors called to the court. Selecting a jury is a two-step process: assembling the list (venire) of prospective jurors and questioning the potential jurors (voir dire).

A. Venire

Generally, a "master roll" of the venire reflects a representative sample of the population and serves as the starting point from which to choose the jurors who will be summoned for trial.[699] Courts rely on a variety of means to select a cross-section of the community for jury service, including voter registration lists, lists of licensed drivers, lists of taxpayers, etc.

B. Voir Dire

The purpose of the voir dire is to gather information from the venire members (the prospective jurors) that would reveal potential biases, knowledge, opinions, or interests in the case that would disqualify them for cause. For instance, a judge may strike a juror for cause if she has a close connection with any party or witness to the case, or if a juror's too-firmly entrenched and immutable opinions would render an impartial judgment impossible.[700] Usually, the parties may exercise an unlimited number of these challenges, known as "for-cause" challenges.[701]

---

[697] Nye v. Fenton, 496 F. Supp. 136, 139 (D. Kan. 1980).

[698] *See* Hetzel v. Prince William County, 523 U.S. 208 (1998) (per curiam) (upholding constitutionality of remittitur as not violating the Seventh Amendment so long as claimant is given the option of a new trial).

[699] *See* Taylor v. Louisiana, 419 U.S. 522, 528–32 (1975) (holding that jury lists may not exclude certain groups, such as women or minorities, but instead must reflect a fair cross-section of the population).

[700] Patton v. Yount, 467 U.S. 1025, 1035 (1984).

[701] *See* J. GOBERT & W. JORDAN, JURY SELECTION § 7.01 (2010).

C. Peremptory Challenges

Unlike for-cause challenges, which are not limited, peremptory challenges—challenges which typically allow the lawyer to strike (or remove) a juror without the need to state a reason—are limited in number.[702] Traditionally, lawyers could exercise these challenges without offering any reason or explanation. The following case explores the Supreme Court's prior ruling that peremptory challenges based on a juror's race violated the equal protection clause and addresses whether strikes based on gender also represented an equal protection violation.

J.E.B. v. ALABAMA
Supreme Court of the United States, 1994
511 U.S. 127

JUSTICE BLACKMUN delivered the opinion of the Court.

In *Batson v. Kentucky*,[703] this Court held that the Equal Protection Clause of the Fourteenth Amendment governs the exercise of peremptory challenges by a prosecutor in a criminal trial. The Court explained that although a defendant has "no right to a 'petit jury composed in whole or in part of persons of his own race,'"[704] the "defendant does have the right to be tried by a jury whose members are selected pursuant to nondiscriminatory criteria,"[705] Since Batson, we have reaffirmed repeatedly our commitment to jury selection procedures that are fair and nondiscriminatory. We have recognized that whether the trial is criminal or civil, potential jurors, as well as litigants, have an equal protection right to jury selection procedures that are free from state-sponsored group stereotypes rooted in, and reflective of, historical prejudice.

Although premised on equal protection principles that apply equally to gender discrimination, all our recent cases defining the scope of Batson involved alleged racial discrimination in the exercise of peremptory challenges. Today we are faced with the question whether the Equal Protection Clause forbids intentional discrimination on the basis of gender, just as it prohibits discrimination on the basis of race. We hold that gender, like race, is an unconstitutional proxy for juror competence and impartiality.

I

On behalf of relator T. B., the mother of a minor child, respondent State of Alabama filed a complaint for paternity and child support against petitioner J. E. B. in the District Court of Jackson County, Alabama. On October 21, 1991, the matter was called for trial and jury selection began. The trial court assembled a panel of 36 potential jurors, 12 males and 24 females. After the court excused three jurors for cause, only 10 of the remaining 33 jurors were male. The State then used 9 of its 10 peremptory strikes to remove male jurors; petitioner used all but one of his strikes to remove female jurors. As a result, all the selected jurors were female.

Before the jury was empaneled, petitioner objected to the State's peremptory challenges on the ground that they were exercised against male jurors solely on the basis of gender, in violation of the Equal

---

[702] *See* 28 U.S.C. § 1870; GOBERT & W. JORDAN, JURY SELECTION § 8.02 (2010) (noting that the federal number in civil cases is three peremptory challenges and that there is no constitutionally mandated minimum number).
[703] 476 U.S. 79 (1986).
[704] *Id.* at 85, quoting Strauder v. West Virginia, 100 U.S. 303, 305 (1880).
[705] 476 U.S. at 85–86.

Protection Clause of the Fourteenth Amendment. Petitioner argued that the logic and reasoning of *Batson v. Kentucky*, which prohibits peremptory strikes solely on the basis of race, similarly forbids intentional discrimination on the basis of gender. The court rejected petitioner's claim and empaneled the all-female jury. The jury found petitioner to be the father of the child, and the court entered an order directing him to pay child support. On post-judgment motion, the court reaffirmed its ruling that Batson does not extend to gender-based peremptory challenges.

We granted certiorari . . . to resolve a question that has created a conflict of authority--whether the Equal Protection Clause forbids peremptory challenges on the basis of gender as well as on the basis of race. Today we reaffirm what, by now, should be axiomatic: Intentional discrimination on the basis of gender by state actors violates the Equal Protection Clause, particularly where, as here, the discrimination serves to ratify and perpetuate invidious, archaic, and overbroad stereotypes about the relative abilities of men and women.

II

Discrimination on the basis of gender in the exercise of peremptory challenges is a relatively recent phenomenon. Gender-based peremptory strikes were hardly practicable during most of our country's existence, since, until the 20th century, women were completely excluded from jury service. So well entrenched was this exclusion of women that in 1880 this Court, while finding that the exclusion of African-American men from juries violated the Fourteenth Amendment, expressed no doubt that a State "may confine the selection [of jurors] to males."[706]

Many States continued to exclude women from jury service well into the present century, despite the fact that women attained suffrage upon ratification of the Nineteenth Amendment in 1920. States that did permit women to serve on juries often erected other barriers, such as registration requirements and automatic exemptions, designed to deter women from exercising their right to jury service. . . .

The prohibition of women on juries was derived from the English common law which, according to Blackstone, rightfully excluded women from juries under "the doctrine of propter *defectum sexus*, literally, the 'defect of sex.'" In this country, supporters of the exclusion of women from juries tended to couch their objections in terms of the ostensible need to protect women from the ugliness and depravity of trials. Women were thought to be too fragile and virginal to withstand the polluted courtroom atmosphere.[707]

. . .

This Court in *Ballard v. United States*,[708] first questioned the fundamental fairness of denying women the right to serve on juries. Relying on its supervisory powers over the federal courts, it held that women may not be excluded from the venire in federal trials in States where women were eligible for jury service under local law. In response to the argument that women have no superior or unique perspective, such that defendants are denied a fair trial by virtue of their exclusion from jury panels, the Court explained:

---

[706] *Strauder*, 100 U.S. at 310.

[707] *See* Bailey v. State, 215 Ark. 53, 61, 219 S.W.2d 424, 428 (1949) ("Criminal court trials often involve testimony of the foulest kind, and they sometimes require consideration of indecent conduct, the use of filthy and loathsome words, references to intimate sex relationships, and other elements that would prove humiliating, embarrassing and degrading to a lady"); In re Goodell, 39 Wis. 232, 245–46 (1875) (endorsing statutory ineligibility of women for admission to the bar because "reverence for all womanhood would suffer in the public spectacle of women . . . so engaged").

[708] 329 U.S. 187 (1946).

"It is said . . . that an all-male panel drawn from the various groups within a community will be as truly representative as if women were included. The thought is that the factors which tend to influence the action of women are the same as those which influence the action of men--personality, background, economic status--and not sex. Yet it is not enough to say that women when sitting as jurors neither act nor tend to act as a class. Men likewise do not act like a class. . . . The truth is that the two sexes are not fungible; a community made up exclusively of one is different from a community composed of both; the subtle interplay of influence one on the other is among the imponderables. To insulate the courtroom from either may not in a given case make an iota of difference. Yet a flavor, a distinct quality is lost if either sex is excluded."

Fifteen years later, however, the Court still was unwilling to translate its appreciation for the value of women's contribution to civic life into an enforceable right to equal treatment under state laws governing jury service. In *Hoyt v. Florida*,[709], the Court found it reasonable, "despite the enlightened emancipation of women," to exempt women from mandatory jury service by statute, allowing women to serve on juries only if they volunteered to serve. The Court justified the differential exemption policy on the ground that women, unlike men, occupied a unique position "as the center of home and family life."

In 1975, the Court finally repudiated the reasoning of *Hoyt* and struck down, under the Sixth Amendment, an affirmative registration statute nearly identical to the one at issue in *Hoyt*.[710] We explained: "Restricting jury service to only special groups or excluding identifiable segments playing major roles in the community cannot be squared with the constitutional concept of jury trial." The diverse and representative character of the jury must be maintained "'partly as assurance of a diffused impartiality and partly because sharing in the administration of justice is a phase of civic responsibility.'"

III

Taylor relied on Sixth Amendment principles, but the opinion's approach is consistent with the heightened equal protection scrutiny afforded gender-based classifications. Since *Reed v. Reed*,[711] this Court consistently has subjected gender-based classifications to heightened scrutiny in recognition of the real danger that government policies that professedly are based on reasonable considerations in fact may be reflective of "archaic and overbroad" generalizations about gender,[712] or based on "outdated misconceptions concerning the role of females in the home rather than in the 'marketplace and world of ideas.'"[713]

Despite the heightened scrutiny afforded distinctions based on gender, respondent argues that gender discrimination in the selection of the petit jury should be permitted, though discrimination on the basis of race is not. Respondent suggests that "gender discrimination in this country . . . has never reached the level of discrimination" against African-Americans, and therefore gender discrimination, unlike racial discrimination, is tolerable in the courtroom.

While the prejudicial attitudes toward women in this country have not been identical to those held toward racial minorities, the similarities between the experiences of racial minorities and women, in some

---

[709] 368 U.S. at 61.
[710] *See* Taylor v. Louisiana, 419 U.S. 522 (1975).
[711] 404 U.S. 71 (1971).
[712] *See* Schlesinger v. Ballard, 419 U.S. 498, 506–07 (1975).
[713] Craig v. Boren, 429 U.S. 190, 198–99 (1976).

contexts, "overpower those differences." As a plurality of this Court observed in *Frontiero v. Richardson*,[714] Throughout much of the 19th century the position of women in our society was, in many respects, comparable to that of blacks under the pre-Civil War slave codes. Neither slaves nor women could hold office, serve on juries, or bring suit in their own names, and married women traditionally were denied the legal capacity to hold or convey property or to serve as legal guardians of their own children. . . . And although blacks were guaranteed the right to vote in 1870, women were denied even that right--which is itself 'preservative of other basic civil and political rights'--until adoption of the Nineteenth Amendment half a century later.

Certainly, with respect to jury service, African-Americans and women share a history of total exclusion, a history which came to an end for women many years after the embarrassing chapter in our history came to an end for African-Americans.

We need not determine, however, whether women or racial minorities have suffered more at the hands of discriminatory state actors during the decades of our Nation's history. It is necessary only to acknowledge that "our Nation has had a long and unfortunate history of sex discrimination," a history which warrants the heightened scrutiny we afford all gender-based classifications today. Under our equal protection jurisprudence, gender-based classifications require "an exceedingly persuasive justification" in order to survive constitutional scrutiny. Thus, the only question is whether discrimination on the basis of gender in jury selection substantially furthers the State's legitimate interest in achieving a fair and impartial trial. In making this assessment, we do not weigh the value of peremptory challenges as an institution against our asserted commitment to eradicate invidious discrimination from the courtroom. Instead, we consider whether peremptory challenges based on gender stereotypes provide substantial aid to a litigant's effort to secure a fair and impartial jury.

Far from proffering an exceptionally persuasive justification for its gender-based peremptory challenges, respondent maintains that its decision to strike virtually all the males from the jury in this case "may reasonably have been based upon the perception, supported by history, that men otherwise totally qualified to serve upon a jury in any case might be more sympathetic and receptive to the arguments of a man alleged in a paternity action to be the father of an out-of-wedlock child, while women equally qualified to serve upon a jury might be more sympathetic and receptive to the arguments of the complaining witness who bore the child."

We shall not accept as a defense to gender-based peremptory challenges "the very stereotype the law condemns." Respondent's rationale, not unlike those regularly expressed for gender-based strikes, is reminiscent of the arguments advanced to justify the total exclusion of women from juries. Respondent offers virtually no support for the conclusion that gender alone is an accurate predictor of juror's attitudes; yet it urges this Court to condone the same stereotypes that justified the wholesale exclusion of women from juries and the ballot box. Respondent seems to assume that gross generalizations that would be deemed impermissible if made on the basis of race are somehow permissible when made on the basis of gender.

Discrimination in jury selection, whether based on race or on gender, causes harm to the litigants, the community, and the individual jurors who are wrongfully excluded from participation in the judicial process. The litigants are harmed by the risk that the prejudice that motivated the discriminatory selection of the jury will infect the entire proceedings.[715] The community is harmed by the State's participation in the

---

[714] 411 U.S. at 685.

[715] *See Edmonson*, 500 U.S. at 628 (discrimination in the courtroom "raises serious questions as to the fairness of the

perpetuation of invidious group stereotypes and the inevitable loss of confidence in our judicial system that state-sanctioned discrimination in the courtroom engenders.

When state actors exercise peremptory challenges in reliance on gender stereotypes, they ratify and reinforce prejudicial views of the relative abilities of men and women. Because these stereotypes have wreaked injustice in so many other spheres of our country's public life, active discrimination by litigants on the basis of gender during jury selection "invites cynicism respecting the jury's neutrality and its obligation to adhere to the law."[716] The potential for cynicism is particularly acute in cases where gender-related issues are prominent, such as cases involving rape, sexual harassment, or paternity. Discriminatory use of peremptory challenges may create the impression that the judicial system has acquiesced in suppressing full participation by one gender or that the "deck has been stacked" in favor of one side.[717]

In recent cases we have emphasized that individual jurors themselves have a right to nondiscriminatory jury selection procedures. Contrary to respondent's suggestion, this right extends to both men and women. All persons, when granted the opportunity to serve on a jury, have the right not to be excluded summarily because of discriminatory and stereotypical presumptions that reflect and reinforce patterns of historical discrimination. Striking individual jurors on the assumption that they hold particular views simply because of their gender is "practically a brand upon them, affixed by the law, an assertion of their inferiority."[718] It denigrates the dignity of the excluded juror, and, for a woman, reinvokes a history of exclusion from political participation. The message it sends to all those in the courtroom, and all those who may later learn of the discriminatory act, is that certain individuals, for no reason other than gender, are presumed unqualified by state actors to decide important questions upon which reasonable persons could disagree.

IV

Our conclusion that litigants may not strike potential jurors solely on the basis of gender does not imply the elimination of all peremptory challenges. Neither does it conflict with a State's legitimate interest in using such challenges in its effort to secure a fair and impartial jury. Parties still may remove jurors who they feel might be less acceptable than others on the panel; gender simply may not serve as a proxy for bias. Parties may also exercise their peremptory challenges to remove from the venire any group or class of individuals normally subject to "rational basis" review. Even strikes based on characteristics that are disproportionately associated with one gender could be appropriate, absent a showing of pretext.

If conducted properly, voir dire can inform litigants about potential jurors, making reliance upon stereotypical and pejorative notions about a particular gender or race both unnecessary and unwise. Voir dire provides a means of discovering actual or implied bias and a firmer basis upon which the parties may exercise their peremptory challenges intelligently.[719]

The experience in the many jurisdictions that have barred gender-based challenges belies the claim that litigants and trial courts are incapable of complying with a rule barring strikes based on gender. As

---

proceedings conducted there").

[716] *Powers*, 499 U.S. at 412.

[717] *See id.*, at 413 ("The verdict will not be accepted or understood [as fair] if the jury is chosen by unlawful means at the outset").

[718] *Strauder*, 100 U.S. at 308.

[719] *See, e. g.*, Nebraska Press Assn. v. Stuart, 427 U.S. 539, 602 (1976) (Brennan, J., concurring) (voir dire "facilitate[s] intelligent exercise of peremptory challenges and [helps] uncover factors that would dictate disqualification for cause").

with race-based Batson claims, a party alleging gender discrimination must make a prima facie showing of intentional discrimination before the party exercising the challenge is required to explain the basis for the strike.[720] When an explanation is required, it need not rise to the level of a "for cause" challenge; rather, it merely must be based on a juror characteristic other than gender, and the proffered explanation may not be pretextual.

Failing to provide jurors the same protection against gender discrimination as race discrimination could frustrate the purpose of Batson itself. Because gender and race are overlapping categories, gender can be used as a pretext for racial discrimination. Allowing parties to remove racial minorities from the jury not because of their race, but because of their gender, contravenes well-established equal protection principles and could insulate effectively racial discrimination from judicial scrutiny.

V

Equal opportunity to participate in the fair administration of justice is fundamental to our democratic system. It not only furthers the goals of the jury system. It reaffirms the promise of equality under the law that all citizens, regardless of race, ethnicity, or gender, have the chance to take part directly in our democracy.[721] When persons are excluded from participation in our democratic processes solely because of race or gender, this promise of equality dims, and the integrity of our judicial system is jeopardized.

In view of these concerns, the Equal Protection Clause prohibits discrimination in jury selection on the basis of gender, or on the assumption that an individual will be biased in a particular case for no reason other than the fact that the person happens to be a woman or happens to be a man. As with race, the "core guarantee of equal protection, ensuring citizens that their State will not discriminate . . . would be meaningless were we to approve the exclusion of jurors on the basis of such assumptions, which arise solely from the jurors'[gender]."[722]

The judgment of the Court of Civil Appeals of Alabama is reversed, and the case is remanded to that court for further proceedings not inconsistent with this opinion.

It is so ordered.

Follow-Up Questions and Comments

1. What is the purpose of thorough but random selection of the pool of potential jurors? Which do you believe produces the most impartial and unbiased jury: (a) voir dire by counsel alone; (b) voir dire by the judge with questions proposed and selected by the judge to ask along with others from counsel if the judge deems them appropriate; or (c) voir dire solely by the judge? Why?

2. Peremptory challenges are an important part of the jury selection process. Counsel would be wise to remove a potential juror she believes has an "unacknowledged or unconscious basis" that could affect the juror's ability to render a fair judgment.[723] If a party objects to use of a peremptory strike

---

[720] *Batson*, 476 U.S. at 97.
[721] Powers v. Ohio, 499 U.S. at 407 ("Indeed, with the exception of voting, for most citizens the honor and privilege of jury duty is their most significant opportunity to participate in the democratic process").
[722] *Batson*, 476 U.S. at 97–98.
[723] *See* 9-47 PRENTICE H. MARSHALL, MOORE'S FEDERAL PRACTICE § 47.30 (Matthew Bender 3d ed. 2018); *cf.* 1

as based on race or gender, the court must make a determination of whether there is a prima facie showing of selection based on race or gender. The burden then shifts to the party exercising the strike to offer a race-neutral or gender-neutral reason for the strike. The lawyer can actually be put under oath and required to testify on such a matter. The court then decides whether the reason offered is legitimate, in which case the strike would be allowed, or pretextual, in which case the juror would be re-seated.[724] Although *Batson* was a criminal case, the Court extended its application to civil trials in *Edmondson v. Leesville Concrete Company*.[725] While *J.E.B* was a paternity case, it is applied in both criminal and civil trials.[726] Before a jury is discharged, jurors can be individually "polled" by the court at the request of counsel.[727] Under Rule 48(c), "if the poll reveals lack of unanimity or lack of assent" by the number of requisite jurors needed to reach the verdict, the court may order a new trial.[728]

Practice Problem

Practice Problem 17-2

Mike is an African-American who sued Don for negligence in a car accident. In choosing the jury, Don's lawyers struck an African American juror based on a peremptory strike. Mike's lawyer objects and challenges the strike under Batson. How will the issue be resolved?

KEVIN F. O'MALLEY ET. AL, FED. JURY PRAC. & INSTR.§ 4.9 (6th ed. 2018) (reiterating the purpose of peremptory challenges "is to reject not select, jurors.").

[724] *See* 2 CHARLES ALAN WRIGHT & ARTHUR R. MILLER, FEDERAL PRACTICE AND PROCEDURE CRIM. § 384 (2018).

[725] 500 U.S. 614 (1991).

[726] *See, e.g.*, United States v. Martinez, 621 F.3d 101 (2d Cir. 2010); *see also* Batson v. Kentucky, 476 U.S. 79, 89 (1986) (recognizing while peremptory challenges are typically allowed for any reason, challenge for race is not allowed under the Equal Protection Clause).

[727] FED. R. CIV. P. 48(c).

[728] *Id.*

CHAPTER 18:
CLAIM AND ISSUE PRECLUSION

I. Where We Are in the Study of Civil Procedure and the Progress of a Civil Case

The topic addressed in this last chapter presumes that one suit has gone to a final judgment ("First Suit") and that one or more of the same parties in a subsequent lawsuit ("Second Suit") were litigants in the First Suit. In general, the American system of civil litigation gives parties a fair chance to have their opportunity for a day in court. We have seen how the notice pleading threshold, though at this point somewhat in flux, is typically not too great a challenge to overcome in the straight-forward case. We have also seen how parties can develop evidence in discovery that, if challenged on summary judgment, will allow the party to go to trial so long as reasonable jurors could disagree about her claim. We will assume here that the First Suit has become final—either through settlement and a consent dismissal order with prejudice, a final judgment not appealed, or a final judgment whose appeals have all run.

Once we arrive at this stage, the civil justice system become more rigid. The concept known traditionally as "res judicata" will bar a Second Suit if the same parties were in litigation over the same transaction or occurrence in the First Suit. The more modern and precise term we will use for this type of res judicata is "claim preclusion." The effect of claim preclusion, if applicable, is that the Second Suit is stopped in its tracks. It will be dismissed with prejudice on the grounds that the litigation sought to be brought should have been litigated in the First Suit. The policies supporting claim preclusion include judicial economy. There is yet a deeper reason for insisting that parties not be permitted to bring multiple suits for claims that could have been litigated in the First Suit. The parties to the suits become attached to their claims. Indeed, some litigants are so attached to their claims that they hardly can think of anything else while the litigation is pending. Claim preclusion provides finality to disputes. If a party could bring some claims arising from a transaction or occurrence in the First Suit, and then later bring other claims arising from the same occurrences, the litigants—not to mention the courts and lawyers—could be tied up for years. Regardless of whether the result of litigation is what each party wanted, the one benefit it has for all is resolution of the dispute. With that, parties can move on with their lives. They can be productive again, not hampered by preoccupation with litigation.

The second type of preclusion involves a scenario in which one or more of the elements of Claim Preclusion did not apply but the potential for an issue litigated in the First Suit being precluded from relitigation does apply. In such a case, the findings in that First Suit can preclude relitigation of the issue or issues in the Second Suit. Known in the past as "collateral estoppel," the modern term for this—one which nicely complements claim preclusion—is "issue preclusion." The doctrine of issue preclusion will, even if claim preclusion does not apply, limit the issues in a Second Suit already litigated in the First Suit. Again, judicial economy is one of the policies. A streamlined Second Suit, in which only issues not previously litigated are at issue, is preferable to relitigating those already resolved. One might say that whereas claim preclusion operates like a sledgehammer to knock out all claims. Throughout this chapter, the phrase "First Suit" will be used to refer to the initial litigation on which either Claim Preclusion or Issue Preclusion is being sought. Throughout this chapter, the phrase "Second Suit" will be used to refer to the later litigation, after an initial suit, in which someone is seeking to bind another to Claim Preclusion or to Issue Preclusion. As compared to the sledgehammer of claim preclusion, issue preclusion is more like a pin hammer that knocks out specific issues from the First Suit already litigated.

II. Claim Preclusion ("Res Judicata")

Claim preclusion has a three-step series of questions, each of which must be answered "yes" for the doctrine to apply. If claim preclusion does apply, the Second Suit will be dismissed with prejudice and thus not allowed to proceed.

The three questions to ask when analyzing claim preclusion are:

(1) Do both suits involve the same claim?

(2) Are both suits asserted by the same claimant or one in privity with the claimant?

(3) Was the first claim resolved in a valid final judgment on the merits?

A. First Requirement: Same Claim

Determining whether the same claim is being asserted in the Second Suit as was in the First Suit may initially seem like a straightforward step. However, the meaning of "claim" changes depending on the test applied. Below is a Virginia case (that is still law in Virginia courts) in which the court's definition of "claim" ends up allowing a party to the First Suit to sue another party to the First Suit in later litigation. The result hinged entirely on how the court defined "claim." Pay attention to the different tests the court applies and consider why the one it chooses to apply allows the Second Suit to proceed.

CARTER v. HINKLE
Supreme Court of Virginia, 1949
52 S.E.2d 135

GREGORY, J., delivered the opinion of the court.

A taxicab owned and driven by Hinkle was involved in a head-on collision with an automobile owned by the defendant, Smith, and operated by his agent, the defendant, Carter. The collision occurred in Alleghany County, on U.S. Route 60, near the town of Covington, on December 20, 1946, and it is conceded that it was the proximate result of the negligence of the defendant, Carter. The taxi was damaged and an action was instituted by the plaintiff, Hinkle, against the defendant, Smith, for $1,000, $750 of which represented damage to the taxi and $250 damages for the loss of the use of it. Judgment was recovered, the full amount paid thereon and it was marked satisfied.

Later, Hinkle instituted another action against the two named defendants seeking to recover for personal injuries received by him by reason of the collision. The defendants pleaded that the judgment and its satisfaction in the first action was a bar to Hinkle's right to bring the second action for the personal injuries. The court overruled that contention and permitted the case to go to the jury. A verdict was returned in favor of the plaintiff for the sum of $1,000, and judgment was entered, from which this writ of error was obtained.

The question involved is one of law: May one who has suffered both damage to his property and injury to his person as the result of a single wrongful act maintain two separate actions therefor, or is a

507

judgment obtained in the first action a bar to the second? We have no Virginia decision upon the point. The question has been presented to the courts many times and there is a direct conflict of American authority on the subject. The majority of the American courts of last resort are of the view that but one single cause of action exists and that but one action may be brought therefor. Typical of this view is the case of *King v. Chicago, etc., Railway Company.*[729]

On the other hand[,] a respectable and increasing minority of the courts are of the view that a single tort, resulting in damage to both person and property, gives rise to two distinct causes of action, and that, therefore, recovery in one is no bar to an action subsequently commenced for the other. The minority view is based upon the English case of *Brunsden v. Humphrey.*

. . .

Typical of the minority rule are the cases of *Vasu v. Kohlers, Inc.*[730] and *Reilly v. Sicilian Asphalt Paving Co.*[731] In the latter case, which is a leading one, the court had this to say: "The question now before us has been the subject of conflicting decisions in different jurisdictions. In England it has been held by the court of appeals (Lord Coleridge, C.J., dissenting) that damages to the person and to property, though occasioned by the same wrongful act, give rise to different causes of action[732] while in Massachusetts, Minnesota, and Missouri the contrary doctrine has been declared. The argument of those courts which maintain that an injury to person and property creates but a single cause of action is that, as the defendant's wrongful act was single, the cause of action must be single, and that the different injuries occasioned by it are merely items of damage proceeding from the same wrong, while that of the English court is that the negligent act of the defendant in itself constitutes no cause of action, and becomes an actionable wrong only out of the damage which it causes 'One wrong was done as soon as the plaintiff's enjoyment of his property was substantially interfered with. A further wrong arose as soon as the driving also caused injury to the plaintiff's person.' *Brunsden v. Humphrey.*"

The court, in that case (Reilly v. Sicilian Asphalt Paving Co.), concluded that injury to person and injury to property were essentially different and gave rise to two causes of action; that to hold that only one cause of action exists would be impractical or at least very inconvenient in the administration of justice, and that they should not be blended. The court noted that different periods of limitation applied; that the plaintiff cannot assign his right of action for the injury to his person, while he could assign that for injury to his property; that action for injury to his person would abate or be lost by his death before a recovery; and that injury to property would be an action that would survive and might be seized by creditors or pass to an assignee in bankruptcy.

The court, in conclusion, referred to the common law in this language: "the history of the common law shows that the distinction between torts to the person and torts to property has always obtained. Lord Justice Bowen, in the *Brunsden* Case, has pointed out that there is no authority in the books for the proposition that a recovery for trespass to the person is a bar to an action for trespass to goods, or vice versa. It is true that at common law the necessity of bringing two suits could, at the election of the plaintiff, be obviated in some cases, . . . Therefore, for reason of the great difference between the rules of law applicable to injuries of the person and those relating to injuries to property, we conclude that an injury to person and one to property, though resulting from the same tortious act, constitute different causes of action."

---

[729] 82 N.W. 1113 (1900).
[730] 61 N.E.2d 707 (1945).
[731] 62 N.E. 772 (1902).
[732] *Brunsden v. Humphrey,* 14 Q.B. Div. 141 (1884).

In *Vasu v. Kohlers, Inc.*, the Ohio court, in an opinion distinguished for its thoroughness and notable for its logic and apt reasoning rendering it a leading case, adopted the minority view, and in speaking of the common law incorporated the statement from *Reilly v. Sicilian Asphalt Paving Co.*, to the effect that the history of the common law has always recognized and distinguished between torts to the person and torts to property. The court expressed the thought in this language: "A critical and analytical study of the two-causes-of-action rule will demonstrate that it is in harmony and keeping with the historical and logical development of the common law on that subject . . . The distinctions involved are most important because they involve not only the determination of what constitutes causes of action but the necessary relation of such causes of action to the doctrine of res judicata."

The right of personal security and the right of property which are invaded by a single wrong give rise to two remedial rights, said the court, and further, in giving the reason for the rule, it said that consideration must be given to the fact that where a property right is invaded the title to the property must be shown to be in the plaintiff, whereas there is no such requirement as to personal injuries. The court then referred to the same elements of inconvenience and the same differences as those stated in *Reilly v. Sicilian Asphalt Paving Company*.

The court further called attention to the fact that nearly all of the cases which support the single-cause-of action rule involve situations where the plaintiff brought the action in his own right to recover both his property and personal injury damages, and that the rule against splitting demands which would limit the plaintiff to a single action is based on the idea of unreasonable vexation of the defendant rather than upon a discrimination conception of a cause of action. However, when a tortfeasor has committed a tort resulting in damage to both person and property there is nothing vexatious or unreasonable in prosecuting separate actions against him.

. . .

It will be observed that an argument to support the majority view is that the single-cause-of-action rule will prevent the crowding of courts with unnecessary litigation, prevent vexatious litigation, eliminate added court costs and delay, and expeditiously end litigation.

That argument is answered in *Vasu v. Kohlers, Inc.*, where the court said: "Short cuts and improvisations may be appealing, but if certainty and predictability, qualities so necessary in the law, are to be maintained, the logical and symmetrical distinctions of the substantive common law, carefully developed through the necessities of experience, should be preserved and not destroyed. In the complexity of life[,] the combinations of fact which give rise to legal liability are infinite, and as a consequence a heavy burden is necessarily imposed upon procedural processes. Nevertheless, rights are too important and liability is too oppressive to be determined and administered in wholesale fashion."

The minority view follows a less practical but a more logical path. Each jurisdiction concerned has chosen a measuring stick regarded by it as the most important. When it is remembered that the plaintiff usually institutes an action in order to obtain compensation for damages done to his rights rather than to punish the defendant for the wrong, it would seem that the question of the number of rights invaded would be the more important one. This is the Ohio view and places Ohio on the side of a growing minority of States.

In the English case of *Brunsden v. Humphrey*, the plaintiff brought an action to recover for damages

509

done to his cab in a collision caused by the negligence of the defendant's servant, and after having recovered the amount claimed he brought another action against the defendant claiming damages for personal injury sustained through the same negligent act. After he obtained a verdict the court ruled in favor of the defendant on the ground that the action was not for a new wrong but for a consequence of the same wrongful act which was the subject of the former suit. On appeal the judgment was reversed and the judgment on the verdict for the plaintiff was restored. The Master of the Rolls said that the causes of action were distinct and therefore the court was not called upon to apply the doctrine of res judicata. It was suggested that different evidence would be required to support the respective claims for injury to property and to the person of the plaintiff, and on this point Lord Justice Bowen said, "In the one case the identity of the man injured and the character of his injuries would be in issue, and justifications might conceivably be pleaded as to the assault, which would have nothing to do with the damage done to the goods and chattels."

In speaking of the gist of the action, Lord Justice Bowen said, "Without remounting to the Roman law, or discussing the refinements of scholastic jurisprudence and the various uses that have been made, either by judges or juridical writers, of the terms 'injuria' and 'damnum', it is sufficient to say that the gist of an action for negligence seems to me to be the harm to person or property negligently perpetrated. . . . Two separate kinds of injury were in fact inflicted, and two wrongs done. The mere negligent driving in itself, if accompanied by no injury to the plaintiff, was not actionable at all, for it was not a wrongful act at all till a wrong arose out of the damage which it caused. One wrong was done as soon as the plaintiff's enjoyment of his property was substantially interfered with. A further wrong arose as soon as the driving also caused injury to the plaintiff's person. Both causes of action, in one sense, may be said to be founded upon one act of the defendant's servant, but they are not on that account identical causes of action. The wrong consists in the damage done without lawful excuse, not the act of driving, which (if no damage had ensued) would have been legally unimportant."

Lord Chief Justice Coleridge dissented, taking the other view. He said: "It appears to me that whether the negligence of the servant or the impact of the vehicle which the servant drove, be the technical cause of action, equally the cause of action is one and the same; that the injury done to the plaintiff is injury done to him at one and the same moment by one and the same act in respect to different rights, i.e., his person and his goods, I do not in the least deny; but it seems to me a subtlety not warranted by law to hold that a man cannot bring two actions, if he is injured in his arm and in his leg, but can bring two, if besides his arm and leg being injured, his trousers which contain his leg, and his coat sleeve which contains his arm, have been torn."

This case does not hold that it would have been improper join the two causes of action in one, subject to certain exceptions not important here. The English rule permits a plaintiff to unite in the same action several causes of action, but he is not compelled to do so.

The weight of American authority, as we have previously stated, disagrees with the decision in *Brunsden v. Humphrey*, but we believe that the principles announced in that case, upon which the minority rule is founded, are more logical and better suited to our practice in Virginia.

510

Follow-Up Questions and Comments

1. The Virginia Supreme Court in Carter chose the "primary rights" approach to defining the "claim" in the initial suit. The court states that this approach is "more logical" than the "single-cause-of-action rule" (more commonly known as the "single wrongful act" approach). What does the court contend makes the primary rights approach more logical than the other approach?

2. How does the single wrongful act definition of claims produce a broader definition of "claim" in the initial suit and, thus, a result that will more likely bar a later claim in a subsequent suit?

3. In discussing the *Brunsden* case, the court refers to yet another approach courts have used in analyzing the scope of the claim in the First Suit and whether it is the same in the Second Suit—i.e., the sameness of the evidence to support the claim. If the court in *Carter* applied the sameness-of-the-evidence test, would Hinkle's claim in the First Suit bar his claim in the Second Suit?

1. Restatement (Second) of Judgments Approach

The approaches explored in *Carter* are not the dominant approaches. Instead, most jurisdictions follow the Restatement (Second) of Judgments approach to defining the scope of a claim in the initial suit. Following is § 24 of this Restatement:

When a valid and final judgment rendered in an action extinguishes the plaintiff's claim pursuant to the rules of merger or bar, the claim extinguished includes all rights of the plaintiff to remedies against the defendant with respect to all or any part of the transaction, or series of connected transactions, out of which the action arose.

What factual grouping constitutes a "transaction", and what groupings constitute a "series", are to be determined pragmatically, giving weight to such considerations as whether the facts are related in time, space, origin, or motivation, whether they form a convenient trial unit, and whether their treatment as a unit conforms to the parties' expectations or business understanding or usage.[733]

Follow-Up Questions and Comments

1. The Restatement (Second) drafters commented that a transaction is "a natural grouping or common nucleus of operative facts."[734] This approach obviously echoes the Federal Rules' use of "transaction or occurrence" as a litigation unit by which courts can decide whether, for instance, to allow joinder, require a counterclaim, or allow relation back of an amended complaint.

2. Despite the breadth of the Restatement (Second) approach, one needs to remember not to forget that, even if two or more persons are involved in the same event (e.g., an accident), their claims are each personal. Thus, if Larry and Curly are both injured when Moe puts oil on the porch to Larry and Curly's house and they slip, fall, and are injured at the same time, Larry's claim is distinct from

---

[733] RESTATEMENT (SECOND) OF JUDGMENTS § 24 (1982).
[734] *Id.* cmt. b (1982).

Curly's. Thus, if Larry pre-vailed against Moe, Curly would still have to bring his own claim against Moe.

Practice Problems

Practice Problem 18-1

The State Department of Game and Inland Fisheries had a trout hatchery where it bred trout and, as they grew, transferred them to different pools until they were large enough to be taken in tank trucks to stock rivers, ponds, and streams. The State decided it could save money by hiring an independent contractor to supervise the breeding, care, and feeding of the trout. Fish Care, Inc. was the company hired to handle the State's hatchery. Unfortunately, an employee of Fish Care, instead of pouring in fish food, mistakenly poured in the chemical pellets Fish Care used to "clean out" bacteria from the pools prior to placing fish inside them. When the wrong pellets were poured into all the ponds at the hatchery, the fish were all killed and some of the equipment in the ponds used to monitor water temperature was damaged. Finally, the water, having been contaminated, was going to have to be replaced by the State so that new fish—brought in from another location—could be put in. Under the primary rights approach used in Carter, how many claims arose from the incident? Under the single wrongful act approach, how many claims arose from the incident? Under the sameness of the evidence approach, how many claims arose from the incident? Under the Restatement (Second) approach, how many claims arose from the incident?

Practice Problem 18-2

Recall the *Rex v. Hurry* case. Assume that Rex, while driving his motorcycle and having Ena slam into him, was wearing a pocket watch that had been handed down for generations and was an antique. In addition, Rex was wearing a $10,000 Armani suit. He was not only injured personally (broken ribs), but also his antique watch was smashed, and Armani suit was in shreds. Under the primary rights approach used in Carter, how many claims arose from the incident? Under the single wrongful act approach, how many claims arose from the incident? Under the sameness of the evidence approach, how many claims arose from the incident? Under the Restatement (Second) approach, how many claims arose from the incident?

Finally, what if Max was a passenger riding on the rear seat of the motorcycle Rex was driving. Max was injured when Hurry negligently ran the red light and hit the motorcycle. Assume Rex's suit has already gone to a final judgment. Max then brings a timely suit against Hurry. Hurry raises claim preclusion in an effort to bar Max's suit. Will Hurry be successful? Why or why not?

---

2. Special Rules for Defining "Contract" For Purposes of Claim Preclusion

Contract scenarios present special circumstances.

a. Separate Contracts

The *Restatement (Second) of Judgments* is clear that, even if the same parties have separate contracts, suit on one contract will not represent a claim that encompasses the other contract.[735]

3. Installment Contracts

The rule regarding installment contracts is that the party asserting a claim under an installment contract must assert all installments due at the time of the suit, but that installments not yet due are not part of the claim.[736]

Practice Problems

Practice Problem 18-3

Alan has a contract with Bill to handle the landscaping on his property. Alan also agrees in a separate contract to open, maintain, and close Bill's pool. Bill sues Alan over the landscaping contract because he has not been paid and the payment date is past due. Bill recovers against Alan. Later, after Alan has closed Bill's pool, Alan sues for nonpayment on the pool contract. Bill asserts that claim preclusion prevents Alan from bringing separate actions against Bill and that Alan received a final judgment in the first contract dispute and cannot thus sue again. Will the pool contract be deemed part of the claim in the First Suit that went to a final judgment?

Practice Problem 18-4

Tom Tenant entered a lease agreement with Larry Landlord under which Tom would pay $1,000 monthly installments to live in the plush condo Larry owned. Tom missed his second month's installment but paid $1,000 after the third month. Tom then missed the fourth installment at the end of the fourth month. Larry sued him for $1,000 for failure to pay in the fourth installment and recovers $1,000. Later Larry realized he'd left out the second installment amount. Will he be able to bring a suit for the second installment?

What if Tom paid the first month installment but missed the second month upon which Tom immediately sued and won a $1,000 judgment. Later, Tom missed the eighth month installment and Larry sues over that. Tom claims that Larry is barred because of the prior suit. Is Tom correct? Why or why not?

Second Requirement: Claimant in First Suit (or Someone in Privity with Claimant) Asserting a Claim in the Second Suit. One can never have claim preclusion raised against her if she was not a claimant (or someone in privity asserted a claim on her behalf) in the First Suit. Thus, we will first consider the requirement that a party be a claimant before claim preclusion can apply to that party. We will then consider examples of someone in the First Suit who, through the doctrine of privity, will be deemed to be the "same" party in a Second Suit.

The following Practice Problems illustrate the crucial requirement that, unless a party in the First Suit asserted a claim—the party was a claimant in the First Suit—then claim preclusion will never bar that party from bringing a claim in a Second Suit. Following are variations on the *Rex v. Hurry* intersection

---

[735] *See* RESTATEMENT (SECOND) OF JUDGMENTS § 26 cmt. d (1982); *see also* 18-131 LAWRENCE B. SOLUM, MOORE'S FEDERAL PRACTICE § 131.23 (2018).
[736] LAWRENCE B. SOLUM, MOORE'S FEDERAL PRACTICE § 131.23 (2018).

accident used at various points above. Assume that, in the jurisdiction in which suit is brought, the compulsory counterclaim rule does not apply.

Practice Problem 18-5

Brad sues Ena for negligence. Ena files only an answer. The jury rules for Ena at trial and judgment is entered for her. Six months later, Ena sues Brad for negligence in the accident. Brad raises claim preclusion as a defense. Will Ena be barred by claim preclusion? If not, could Brad raise another defense that will bar Ena's claim?

Practice Problem 18-6

Now assume Rex sues only Hurry even though the facts show that both Hurry and Kagasaki, Inc. are liable. Hurry is liable for negligence causing the collision and Kagasaki is liable for the defective design of its motorcycle airbag which resulted in Brad having greater injuries than he would have had if the airbag worked properly. Further assume that Hurry had her car in the shop before the accident to have her brakes worked on and believes they were not fixed properly—something that contributed to her inability to stop at the intersection. Rex sues Hurry. Hurry brings a third-party claim against Kagasaki, Inc. for contribution. The suit goes to a judgment in which Rex recovers against Hurry and Hurry recovers on her third-party claim against Kagasaki for contribution. Six months later, Hurry sues Gary's Garage, Inc.—the garage that failed to repair her brakes. Gary's Garage raises claim preclusion and argues that, under the Restatement (Second) of Judgments, Hurry, as a claimant in the First Suit, needed to bring all claims related to the same transaction or occurrence or series of transactions or occurrences. Is Gary's Garage correct? Hurry was not obliged to bring the third-party claim and, thus, become a "claimant." Does that matter?

Practice Problem 18-7

Now assume Rex's girlfriend, Rhonda, was on his bike when Hurry slammed into them. Rex sues Hurry for personal injuries, property damage, and defamation. That case settles and consent final judgment is entered. Rhonda then sues Hurry within the statute of limitations for personal injury claims. Is her claim barred by the final judgment in Rex's suit?

B. Parties Represented by Legal Representative (Privity)

A more complicated question arises when parties with interests aligned with those of the claimant assert the claims in the First Suit. The law refers to such parties as being in privity. The Restatement (Second) of Judgments has this to say on the subject:

A person who is not a party to an action but who is represented by a party is bound by and entitled to the benefits of a judgment as though he were a party. A person is represented by a party who is: The trustee of an estate or interest of which the person is a beneficiary; or Invested by the person with authority to represent him in an action; or The executor, administrator, guardian, conservator, or similar fiduciary manager of an interest of which the person is a beneficiary; or An official or agency invested by law with authority to represent the person's interests; or the representative of a class of persons similarly situated, designated as such with the approval of the court, of which the person is a member. A person represented by a party to an action is bound by the judgment even though the person himself does not have notice of the action, is not served with process, or is not subject to service of process.[737]

---

[737] RESTATEMENT (SECOND) OF JUDGEMENTS § 41 (1982).

Practice Problem

Practice Problem 18-8

Elaine Executrix was named in the will of Dan Deceased to be the representative to represent his estate and distribute his assets to heirs. Ned Nopay owed a $100,000 debt to Dan. Elaine sued Ned for the $100,000. When she realized that litigating the case and going to trial would cost at least $10,000, she agreed to a settlement in which Ned paid $90,000 and judgment was marked paid in full. Bev Beneficiary, one of the heirs in Dan's will, sued Ned for $100,000 believing that Ned should have to pay his full debt. Ned raised claim preclusion to bar Bev's claim. Would it apply here?

---

1. Successive Landowner Bound by Prior Rulings

Another classic privity scenario is when a landowner has a judgment entered affecting the property and then a successive landowner comes to own the property. Restatement (Second) of Judgments has the following to say about such a scenario:

> A judgment in an action that determines interests in real or personal property:
> With respect to the property involved in the action: Conclusively determines the claims of the parties to the action regarding their interests; and has preclusive effects upon a person who succeeds to the interest of a party to the same extent as upon the party himself. With respect to other property held by a party to the action, does not preclude a person who is a successor in interest thereof from subsequently litigating issues determined in the action.[738]

Practice Problem

Practice Problem 18-9

Bill owns Greenacre. Hank owns Yellowacre, which abuts Greencare. Bill claims that the fence between Greenacre and Yellowacre is his property because it is on Greenacre. Hand disputes Bill's claim and argues the fence is on Yellowacre. Bill brings on a boundary dispute action and a surveyor determines that the fence is on Greenacre, not Yellowacre. Hank sells Yellowacre to Halley. Halley then sues Bill in a boundary dispute action claiming the fence is on Yellowacre, not Greenacre. Bill asserts claim preclusion against Halley. Is she precluded by the prior judgment?

C. Third Requirement: Valid, Final Judgment on the Merits

Let's say you have a claim being asserted in the Second Suit that is part of the same transaction or occurrence as the initial suit. In addition, the party asserting the claim in the Second Suit was a claimant in the First Suit. Thus, two of the three required elements of claim preclusion have been met. The final question is whether the first trial resulted in a valid, final judgment on the merits.

---

[738] *Id.*

1. Valid Judgment

Valid judgment does not mean a correct judgment. "[T]he res judicata consequences of a final, unappealed judgment on the merits [are] not altered by the fact that the judgment may have been wrong or rested on legal principles overruled in another case."[739] Instead, the questions here are simple. First did the court have personal jurisdiction over the party against whom judgment is entered?[740] If a party makes a voluntary appearance or otherwise waives the personal jurisdiction the court will be deemed to have personal jurisdiction.[741]

The other question is whether the court that entered a judgment had subject matter jurisdiction.[742] If the court lacked such jurisdiction, the judgment could be deemed invalid, though in some circumstances (e.g., the question was litigated) courts have enforced judgments that arguably lack such jurisdiction.[743] For our purposes, and for the sake of simplicity, we will assume that any judgment where the court lacked personal jurisdiction that was not waived, or lacked subject matter jurisdiction, is not a valid judgment.

2. Final Judgment "On the Merits"

The more litigated question is whether a final judgment is "on the merits" for the purposes of claim preclusion. The phrase is less than ideal because it suggests a judgment must have gone to trial—where one usually expects the merits to be heard—when that is not in fact a requirement. The better way to think of this aspect of the validity requirement is to ask whether the party against whom judgment has been entered had an "opportunity to get to the merits."

Thus, summary judgments are considered to be on the merits.[744] The Restatement (Second) of Judgments considers a judgment to be on the merits unless the dismissal is "for lack of jurisdiction, for improper venue, or misjoinder of the parties."[745] Thus, a great many dismissals can fall within the "on the merits" category. Rule 41 allows the court to specify that a dismissal is "with prejudice" or "without prejudice."[746] Absent language making clear whether a judgment is with or without prejudice, the criteria suggested above will guide one in determining whether the judgment is on the merits. First, did the party have an opportunity to get to the merits? Second, and this is the more specific criteria, is the judgment for something other than lack of jurisdiction, improper venue, or misjoinder or nonjoinder of parties? If so, then the dismissal ought to be deemed on the merits.

---

[739] Federated Dep't Stores, Inc. v. Moitie, 452 U.S. 394, 398 (1981).

[740] *See* 18A CHARLES ALAN WRIGHT & ARTHUR R. MILLER, FEDERAL PRACTICE AND PROCEDURE § 4430 (2d ed. 2018).

[741] *See id.*

[742] *See id.* § 4428.

[743] *See id.*

[744] 18A CHARLES ALAN WRIGHT & ARTHUR R. MILLER, FEDERAL PRACTICE AND PROCEDURE § 4444 (2d ed. 2018).

[745] RESTATEMENT (SECOND) OF JUDGMENTS § 20(1) (a) (1982).

[746] *See* FED R. CIV. P. 41.

Practice Problem

Practice Problem 18-10

The plaintiff in a lawsuit consistently failed to abide by the Rules of Court concerning discovery. Moreover, the plaintiff disobeyed the court's orders on discovery. Ultimately, as permitted by Rule 37, the court entered judgment dismissing the plaintiff's case. By the criteria outlined above, reason through whether the dismissal meets the criteria for being "on the merits."

III. Issue Preclusion ("Collateral Estoppel")

If claim preclusion applies, it will preclude the entire case from being heard. However, the second case may not involve the same transaction or occurrence as the first—thus failing the first requirement of claim preclusion. Or, the party asserting the Second Suit may either not have been a claimant in the First Suit or not a party at all (or represented by someone in privity)—thus failing the second requirement of claim preclusion. Finally, the First Suit may not have been a valid final judgment on the merits—thus failing the third condition of claim preclusion. As already stated, every one of the requirements must be met for claim preclusion to apply. If one or more are not, then claim preclusion will not apply—but issue preclusion may.

Thus, the analytical framework above analyzed claim preclusion first for a good reason. If it applies, issue preclusion is irrelevant because the suit will be barred. However, if having worked through the claim preclusion analysis, one of the requirements is not met, or even arguably is not met, one should proceed with the issue preclusion analysis. The goal of the issue preclusion analysis will be to determine, even if the suit can proceed, whether one or more issues were previously litigated and ought to be binding in the current case.

The five questions analyzing issue preclusion are:

(1) Was the identical issue litigated and determined in the First Suit?

(2) Was the issue essential to the judgment?

(3) Was the holding embodied in a valid final judgment on the merits?

(4) Is preclusion being asserted against a party to the First Suit or one in privity with a party to the First Suit?

(5) Is preclusion being asserted by a party authorized to assert it?

For issue preclusion to apply, the answer to each of these questions must be "yes." The first four questions apply in every jurisdiction. The last question deals with a question that has only in recent years become pertinent. We will see, however, that the federal system (and many other jurisdictions) have adopted this part of the analysis.

A. First Requirement: Was the Identical Issue Actually Litigated and Determined in the First Suit?

The following case illustrates the requirement that an issue in the Second Suit must be identical to an issue actually litigated and determined in the First Suit for issue preclusion to apply.

LATIN AMERICAN MUSIC CO. INC. v. MEDIA POWER GROUP, INC.
United States Court of Appeals for the First Circuit, 2013
705 F.3d 34

HOWARD, Circuit Judge.

Appellants Latin American Music Company ("LAMCO") and Associación de Compositores y Editores de Música Latino Americana ("ACEMLA")1 sued Media Power Group, Inc. ("MPG") and its president Eduardo Rivero Albino for infringement of copyright with respect to twenty-one songs. The United States District Court for the District of Puerto Rico granted the defendants' motion for summary judgment as to twelve songs. Claims as to the remaining nine songs went to trial, resulting in a jury verdict for the defendants. LAMCO challenges both the summary judgment and the unfavorable jury verdict. Finding no error, we affirm.

I.

MPG owns four radio stations, branded "Radio Isla," in Puerto Rico and has a number of affiliated stations that rebroadcast its programming. In 2005, LAMCO notified MPG that LAMCO owned copyrights to many songs played on Radio Isla and that MPG was infringing the copyrights by using the songs on-air without a license. After unsuccessful licensing negotiations, LAMCO filed suit against MPG and its president, seeking money damages for violations of the Copyright Act as to twenty-one songs. Segments of the songs were allegedly broadcast during various news and talk-show programs on Radio Isla. LAMCO alleged that the composers or their heirs had assigned copyrights in the songs to LAMCO. MPG did not hold licenses from LAMCO or from the composers.

The parties' cross-motions for summary judgment were referred to a magistrate judge for a report and recommendation. Adopting most of the magistrate judge's findings and recommendations, the district court denied LAMCO's motion and granted the defendants' motion as to twelve songs, concluding that LAMCO: (1) was collaterally estopped from litigating ownership of valid copyrights in four songs; (2) failed to show compliance with the registration requirement of 17 U.S.C. § 411(a) with respect to four other songs; (3) failed to establish an infringing use as to three songs; and (4) lacked ownership in one song. Infringement claims as to the remaining nine songs were tried before a jury. The jury found that LAMCO failed to prove that it owned the songs, resulting in a verdict for the defendants.

II.

LAMCO . . . maintains that the district court erred when it ruled that LAMCO was collaterally estopped from litigating its claims as to four songs.

. . .

In *Brown v. Latin Am. Music Company*,[747] we affirmed the district court's dismissal of LAMCO's claims of infringement of copyright in eleven songs by Juan Antonio Corretjer on the basis that LAMCO failed to establish a prima facie case of ownership of valid copyrights in the songs. In the instant litigation, LAMCO alleged infringement of four of those songs. The district court dismissed the claims on collateral estoppel grounds, noting that LAMCO had presented the same evidence of copyright ownership that the Brown court deemed insufficient. LAMCO argues that the dismissal was in error, because in this case LAMCO provided additional evidence of ownership that the district court in Brown refused to consider due to tardy submission. We review de novo a district court's dismissal of a claim on collateral estoppel grounds. Because the judgment in Brown was entered by a federal court exercising federal question jurisdiction, the applicability of collateral estoppel is a matter of federal law.

Collateral estoppel, or issue preclusion, applies when: "(1) the issue sought to be precluded in the later action is the same as that involved in the earlier action; (2) the issue was actually litigated; (3) the issue was determined by a valid and binding final judgment; and (4) the determination of the issue was essential to the judgment." The dismissal of LAMCO's infringement claims in Brown for failure to establish ownership of valid copyrights in the Corretjer works, including the four songs subject to the instant litigation, plainly satisfies all four elements, and LAMCO does not argue otherwise.

Instead, LAMCO maintains that the Brown court dismissed the claims without the benefit of additional evidence that LAMCO submitted too late in that case, namely a certificate of recordation that included the assignment of copyrights from Corretjer's heirs to LAMCO. The argument is misguided party cannot circumvent the doctrine's preclusive effect merely by presenting additional evidence that was available to it at the time of the first action. As we noted in Brown, the assignment contract was not newly-discovered evidence and it did not signal a change in facts essential to the judgment. Despite having the contract in its possession at all relevant times, LAMCO failed to timely submit it to the Brown district court at the summary judgment stage.[748] That it timely produced the contract in the instant litigation is inapposite. The district court correctly concluded that LAMCO was collaterally estopped from litigating the claims as to the four Corretjer songs.

. . .

For the foregoing reasons, we affirm the judgments of the district court.

Follow-Up Questions and Comments

1. What was the issue previously litigated in the Brown case? Did the parties asserting copyrights in the songs fail in their proof in the First Suit, though the issue was part of the litigation? What does this case tell you, then, about what it takes to trigger the "actually litigated" requirement?

2. Some jurisdictions have, as the case below will show, a rule that if the plaintiff suing for negligence is himself contributorily negligent, he will be barred from recovery. In such a suit, the plaintiff must win on both the finding that he or she was not contributorily negligent and that the defendant was negligent. Thus, there will be an adverse finding and an adverse judgment against the defendant. If

---

[747] 498 F.3d 18 (1st Cir. 2007).
[748] Brown v. Latin Am. Music Co., No. 05–CV–1242 (JAF), 2006 WL 2059606, at *2 (D.P.R. July 21, 2006).

counsel has requested a special verdict form, the jury's findings as to every issue in the case would be recorded in the verdict. Therefore, there would be no ambiguity regarding what was "essential" to the jury's verdict. However, if the jury delivers a general verdict that verdict will reflect only a finding for the Defendant. The defense verdict could have been based on the jury finding the plaintiff's being contributorily negligent or, independently, on a finding that the defendant was negligent. However, the general verdict does not reflect subsidiary findings, only the finding for defendant. As you can see, and we will discuss further, this type of suit is thus a useful one to illustrate not only the actually litigated requirement—and when it can and cannot be determined—as well as the essentiality-of-the-issue requirement. To see when we can determine whether an issue was actually litigated and determined, we will explore here a number of variations in such a negligence suit.

Practice Problems

The following Practice Problems illustrate variations on the *Rex v. Hurry* case. Brad T. Rex's suit against Ena Hurry over the car accident in the intersection is a negligence action. If he sues in a jurisdiction, such as Virginia, in which contributory negligence is a bar to the plaintiff's recovery, then any negligence by plaintiff Brad—even he is only one percent contributorily negligent—would bar his suit. Please assume that after the First Suit in each Practice Problem a valid, final judgment is entered consistent with the verdicts. Assume that plaintiff's negligence is an absolute bar to recovery even if defendant is also found negligent. Also, assume no compulsory counterclaim rule applies in this jurisdiction. With that in mind, let's examine several scenarios:

Practice Problem 18-11

Brad sues Ena for negligence. Ena raises the defense of contributory negligence. The jury returns a general verdict in favor of Brad. A general verdict on which the court enters a judgment for Brad would look like this:

IN THE UNITED STATES DISTRICT COURT
FOR THE EASTERN DISTRICT OF ILLYRIA

BRAD T. REX
Plaintiff(s)

v.

Case No. 2016cv10

ENA HURRY & KAGASAKI, INC.
Defendant(s)

JURY VERDICT

We, the jury, hereby find:

_____for Brad Rex, the plaintiff, and award the plaintiff $100,000 in compensatory damages.

_____
[Name of jury foreperson]
[Date]

Now Ena sues Brad for negligence. Brad raises the defense of contributory negligence. Can Brad assert issue preclusion against Ena as to (1) Ena's negligence or (2) his freedom from negligence? Before you look at the general verdict and dismiss these questions too quickly, ask whether you can deduce from the general verdict in the first case the issues that must have been determined. For the jury to return a verdict for Brad, it had to make two findings, right? Do you see what findings had to be made in favor of Brad?

Practice Problem 18-12

Brad sues Ena for negligence. Ena raises the defense of contributory negligence. The jury returns a general verdict for which the court enters judgment in favor of Ena. A general jury verdict on which the court enters a judgment for Ena would look like this:

IN THE UNITED STATES DISTRICT COURT
FOR THE EASTERN DISTRICT OF ILLYRIA

BRAD T. REX	)
Plaintiff(s)	)
v.	)
	Case No. 2016cv10
ENA HURRY & KAGASAKI, INC.	
Defendant(s)	

JURY VERDICT

We, the jury, hereby find:

For [ ] Brad T. Rex, the plaintiff. For [X] Ena Hurry, the defendant.

_____
[Name of jury foreperson]
[Date]

Then Ena sues Brad for negligence to recover her damages from the same accident. Can Brad assert issue preclusion against Ena based on his freedom from negligence? If not, why not? If so, why? Can Brad assert issue preclusion against Ena precluding relitigation of her negligence? If so, why? If not, why not?

Practice Problem 18-13

Brad sues Ena for negligence. Ena raises the defense of contributory negligence. The jury returns a special verdict finding that Brad was negligent. A special verdict indicates in the verdict form the findings of the jury on each of the elements of the plaintiff's case, and each of the findings on defendants' defense, as well as for whom the judgment is entered. Here is what that special verdict would look like in a jurisdiction in which the plaintiff's contributory negligence barred recovery by the plaintiff, regardless of whether the defendant was negligent.

521

)
)
)
BRAD T. REX)
Plaintiff(s))
      v.)   **Case No.** 2016cv10
)
ENA HURRY & KAGASAKI, INC.
Defendant(s)

JURY VERDICT

We, the jury, hereby find:

Plaintiff was negligent	[X] YES	[ ] NO
Plaintiff's negligence proximately caused plaintiff's injuries	[X] YES	[ ] NO
Defendant was negligent	[ ] YES	[ ] NO
Defendant's negligence proximately caused plaintiff's injuries	[ ] YES	[ ] NO

The jury thus finds for   [ ] Plaintiff
The jury thus finds for   [X] Defendant.

_____
[Name of jury foreperson],
[Date]

    In other words, the jury may choose not to fill in anything in response to the last two questions in returning a special verdict in this type of case. (The jury fills in the first two questions and is smart enough to figure out, based on the instructions it heard, that contributory negligence barred plaintiff from winning and that a finding of contributory negligence thus meant the defendant had to prevail.) The plaintiff, Ena, then sues Brad based on negligence for her damages from the same accident. What finding from Suit 1 can be precluded, in favor of which party and against which party? What issue(s) must still be litigated in the Second Suit.

B. Second Requirement: Was the Issue That Was Actually Litigated Essential to the Judgment in the First Suit?

RIOS v. DAVIS
Court of Civil Appeals of Texas, 1963
373 S.W.2d 386

COLLINGS, Justice.

    Juan C. Rios brought this suit against Jessie Hubert Davis in the District Court to recover damages in the sum of $17,500.00, alleged to have been sustained as a result of personal injuries received on December 24, 1960, in an automobile collision. Plaintiff alleged that his injuries were proximately caused by negligence on the part of the defendant. The defendant answered alleging that Rios was guilty of contributory negligence. Also, among other defenses, the defendant urged a plea of res judicata and collateral estoppel based upon the findings and the judgment entered on December 17, 1962, in a suit between the same parties in the County Court at Law of El Paso County. The plea of res judicata was sustained and judgment was entered in favor of the defendant Jessie Hubert Davis. Juan C. Rios has appealed.

It is shown by the record that on April 11, 1961, Popular Dry Goods Company brought suit against appellee Davis in the El Paso County Court at Law, seeking to recover for damages to its truck in the sum of $443.97, alleged to have been sustained in the same collision here involved. Davis answered alleging contributory negligence on the part of Popular and joined appellant Juan C. Rios as a third-party defendant and sought to recover from Rios $248.50, the alleged amount of damages to his automobile. The jury in the County Court at Law found that Popular Dry Goods Company and Rios were guilty of negligence proximately causing the collision. However, the jury also found that Davis was guilty of negligence proximately causing the collision, and judgment was entered in the County Court at Law denying Popular Dry Goods any recovery against Davis and denying Davis any recovery against Rios.

Appellant Rios in his third point contends that the District Court erred in sustaining appellee's plea of res judicata based upon the judgment of the County Court at Law because the findings on the issues regarding appellant's negligence and liability in the County Court at Law case were immaterial because the judgment entered in that case was in favor of appellant. We sustain this point. We are unable to agree with appellee's contention that the findings in the County Court at Law case that Rios was guilty of negligence in failing to keep a proper lookout and in driving on the left side of the roadway, and that such negligent acts were proximate causes of the accident were essential to the judgment entered therein. The sole basis for the judgment in the County Court at Law as between Rios and Davis was the findings concerning the negligence of Davis. The finding that Rios was negligent was not essential or material to the judgment and the judgment was not based thereon. On the contrary, the finding in the County Court at Law case that Rios was negligent proximately causing the accident would, if it had been controlling, led to a different result. Since the judgment was in favor of Rios he had no right or opportunity to complain of or to appeal from the finding that he was guilty of such negligence even if such finding had been without any support whatever in the evidence. The right of appeal is from a judgment and not from a finding. The principles controlling the fact situation here involved are, in our opinion, stated in the following quoted authorities and cases. The annotation in 133 A.L.R. 840, page 850 states:

> According to the weight of authority, a finding of a particular fact is not res judicata in a subsequent action, where the finding not only was not essential to support the judgment but was found in favor of the party against whom the judgment was rendered, and, if allowed to control, would have led to a result different from that actually reached.

In the case of *Word v. Colley*,[749] at page 634 of its opinion (Error Ref.), the court stated as follows:

> It is the judgment, and not the verdict or the conclusions of fact, filed by a trial court which constitutes the estoppel, and a finding of fact by a jury or a court which

---

[749] Tex. Civ. App., 173 S.W. 629.

does not become the basis or one of the grounds of the judgment rendered is not conclusive against either party to the suit.

. . .

For the reasons stated the court erred in entering judgment for Jessie Hubert Davis based upon his plea of res judicata and collateral estoppel. The judgment is, therefore, *reversed and the cause is remanded.*

Follow-Up Questions and Comments

1. In jurisdictions such as Texas at the time of the Rios decision, contributory negligence of a plaintiff in a suit by that plaintiff for negligence absolutely barred the plaintiff from recovering. In such suits, the initial and essential finding is whether the plaintiff was contributorily negligent. If the plaintiff was contributorily negligent, then the jury can also make a finding on whether the defendant was negligent, but it is considered a superfluous finding.

2. As we learned in *Rios*, an adverse finding entered against a party who "wins" the First Suit cannot be appealed and is thus not essential. If the verdict was that Brad was negligent and that Ena was too, for whom must the judgment be entered? What test does the court in Rios suggest as a way of determining whether a finding in such a verdict as above was essential? If you apply that test to the findings in Rios, you should be able to zero in on the essential finding. Why is that finding essential? Why are the other findings superfluous—essentially like dicta?

3. If the party against whom an issue was decided won the First Suit, the rule stated in Note 2 above will resolve the lack of essentiality of the finding and preclude issue preclusion in a later suit seeking to bind the party who won the judgment but had no chance to appeal the prior judgment. If, however, the judgment in the First Suit was in favor of a party, a finding in that First Suit—even if actually litigated and decided— may still be unnecessary to the judgment in the first case and thus not entitled to issue preclusion. For instance, in *In re Randa Coal Company*,[750] the debtor brought adversary proceeding asserting 12 claims for relief. Prior to the bankruptcy, however, the debtor had filed suit in federal court against the same defendant as in the adversary proceedings (essentially a suit within bankruptcy proceedings in which claims are resolved). In addition to finding claim preclusion, the bankruptcy court held that the debtor was collaterally estopped from litigating claims in the adversary proceeding. The U.S. District Court for the Western District of Virginia held that several findings against the debtor would not be entitled to issue preclusion in later proceedings because they were not essential to the judgment in the action that had been dismissed (i.e., the First Suit). In other words, though the debtor obviously lost the First Suit by having it dismissed, the issues it was now raising in the adversary proceeding were not essential to the basis on which the First Suit was dismissed.

The special verdict in *Rios* would look like this:

---

[750] 128 B.R. 421 (Bankr. W.D. Va. 1991).

IN THE COURT OF APPEALS ELEVENTH DISTRICT
OF TEXAS AT EASTLAND, TEXAS

POPULAR DRY GOODS, INC,)
Plaintiff,)
)
v.)
)
JESSIE H. DAVIS,)   **Case No. 1963-CV-83528**
Defendant/)
Third-Party Plaintiff,)
)
and)
)
JUAN C. RIOS,)
Third-Party Defendant.)

JURY VERDICT

We, the jury, hereby find:

Defendant was negligent	[X] YES	[ ] NO
Defendant's negligence proximately caused plaintiff's injuries	[X] YES	[ ] NO
Plaintiff was negligent	[X] YES	[ ] NO
Plaintiff's negligence proximately caused plaintiff's injuries	[X] YES	[ ] NO
Third-Party Defendant was negligent	[X]YES	[ ] NO
Third-Party Plaintiff was negligent	[X] YES	[ ] NO

Accordingly, the judgment is for the Defendant on Plaintiff's claim and for the Third-Party Defendant on Defendant/Third-Party Plaintiff's Claim.

_____
[Name of jury foreperson],
[Date]

Practice Problem

Practice Problem 18-14

Brad sues Ena for negligence. Ena raises the defense of contributory negligence. The jury returns a special verdict finding that both Brad was contributorily negligent and Ena was negligent. The special verdict in this scenario would look like this:

525

IN THE UNITED STATES DISTRICT COURT
FOR THE EASTERN DISTRICT OF ILLYRIA

)) BRAD T. REX) **Plaintiff(s)**) **v.**)) ENA HURRY & KAGASAKI, INC.) **Defendant(s)**	**Case No.** 2016cv10

JURY VERDICT

We, the jury, hereby find:

Plaintiff was negligent	[X] YES	[ ] NO
Plaintiff's negligence proximately		
caused plaintiff's injuries	[X] YES	[ ] NO
Defendant was negligent	[X] YES	[ ] NO
Defendant's negligence proximately caused plaintiff's injuries	[X] YES	[ ] NO

According, the jury finds for the Defendant.

_____
[Name of jury foreperson]
[Date]

Now in a Second Suit Ena sues Brad for negligence resulting in her injuries from the same accident. Can Ena assert issue preclusion against Brad as to his negligence? If so, why? If not, why not? Can Brad assert issue preclusion against Ena as to her negligence? If so, why? If not, why not?

C. Third Requirement: Was the Finding on the Issue Embodied in a Valid, Final Judgment on the Merits?

The analysis at this point in the issue preclusion analysis is identical to the analysis of whether a claim was included in a valid, final judgment on the merits. Thus, one can refer to the discussion above under claim preclusion for the criteria to determine (a) validity, and (b) whether a decision is "on the merits."

D. Fourth Requirement: Is the One Against Whom Issue Preclusion Is Being Asserted a Party to the First Suit or One in Privity With the Party to the First Suit?

Just as a party cannot have claim preclusion asserted against her unless either she was part of the First Suit or had someone with whom she was in privity, she cannot have issue preclusion asserted against

526

her unless she as a party or in privity with a party to the First Suit. The principle here is plain old due process. It would not be fair to bind someone to a finding in litigation in which she did not have a full and fair opportunity to litigate, either as a party or by one in privity. One of the best cases to illustrate this principle follows. It involves one of the many cases that arose out of litigation over the effects of asbestos. "Asbestos is a naturally occurring mineral that once was lauded for its versatility, recognized for its heat resistance, tensile strength and insulating properties, and used for everything from fire-proof vests to home and commercial construction. It was woven into fabric, and mixed with cement."[751] Tragically, inhalation of asbestos fibers was found to cause asbestosis, mesothelioma, and other deadly lung diseases. The discovery of the deleterious effects of exposure to asbestos lead to four decades of litigation related to products containing the material, the longest mass tort litigation to date.[752]

HARDY v. JOHNS-MANVILLE SALES CORP.
United States Court of Appeals for the Fifth Circuit, 1982
681 F.2d 334

GEE, Circuit Judge:

This appeal arises out of a diversity action brought by various plaintiffs-insulators, pipefitters, carpenters, and other factory workers-against various manufacturers, sellers, and distributors of asbestos-containing products. The plaintiffs, alleging exposure to the products and consequent disease, assert various causes of action, including negligence, breach of implied warranty, and strict liability. The pleadings in each of the cases are substantially the same. No plaintiff names a particular defendant on a case-by-case basis but, instead, includes several-often as many as twenty asbestos manufacturers-in his individual complaint. . . . [Plaintiff] relies on the prior decision in the case, *Borel v. Fibreboard Paper Products Corporation.* [753] *Borel* was a diversity lawsuit in which manufacturers of insulation products containing asbestos were held strictly liable to an insulation worker who developed asbestosis and mesothelioma and ultimately died. The trial court construed *Borel* as establishing as a matter of law and/or of fact that: (1) insulation products containing asbestos as a generic ingredient are "unavoidably unsafe products," (2) asbestos is a competent producing cause of mesothelioma and asbestosis, (3) no warnings were issued by any asbestos insulation manufacturers prior to 1964, and (4) the "warning standard" was not met by the *Borel* defendants in the period from 1964 through 1969. [Six of the manufacturers named as defendants in the *Borel* case. However, the present case by Hardy added thirteen other manufacturers of asbestos and sought to have the court hold them precluded from relitigating issues decide in *Borel*.]

. . .

This is the first and, in our view, insurmountable problem with the trial court's application of collateral estoppel in the case *sub judice*. The omnibus order under review here does not distinguish between defendants who were parties to *Borel* and those who were not; it purports to estop all defendants because all purportedly share an "identity of interests" sufficient to constitute privity. The trial court's action stretches "privity" beyond meaningful limits. While we acknowledge the manipulability of the notion of "privity," . . . this has not prevented courts from establishing guidelines on the permissibility of binding nonparties through res judicata or collateral estoppel. Without such guidelines, the due process guarantee

---

[751] Mesothelioma Center, Asbestos, ASBESTOS.COM, http://www.asbestos.com/asbestos/ (last visited July 6, 2017).
[752] *See* 3 LAWRENCE G. CERTRULO, TOXIC TORT LITIGATION GUIDE § 33:4 (2016).
[753] 493 F.2d 1076 (5th Cir. 1973), *cert. denied*, 419 U.S. 869, 95 (1974).

of a full and fair opportunity to litigate disappears. Thus, we noted in *Southwest Airlines Co. v. Texas International Airlines*:[754]

Federal courts have deemed several types of relationships "sufficiently close" to justify preclusion. First, a nonparty who has succeeded to a party's interest in property is bound by any prior judgments against that party. . . . Second, a nonparty who controlled the original suit will be bound by the resulting judgment. . . . Third, federal courts will bind a nonparty whose interests were represented adequately by a party in the original suit.

The rationale for these exceptions-all derived from Restatement (Second) of Judgments § 30, 31, 34, 39-41 (1982)-is obviously that in these instances the nonparty has in effect had his day in court. In this case, the exceptions elaborated in Southwest Airlines and in the Restatement are inapplicable. First, the *Borel* litigation did not involve any property interests. Second, none of the non-*Borel* defendants have succeeded to any property interest held by the *Borel* defendants. Finally, the plaintiffs did not show that any non-*Borel* defendant had any control whatever over the *Borel* litigation. "To have control of litigation requires that a person have effective choice as to the legal theories and proofs to be advanced in behalf of the party to the action. He must also have control over the opportunity to obtain review." In, for example, *Sea-Land Services v. Gaudet*,[755] the Supreme Court held that a nonparty may be collaterally estopped from relitigating issues necessarily decided in a suit by a party who acted as a fiduciary responsible for the beneficial interests of the nonparties. Even in this context, however, the Court placed the exception within strict confines: "In such cases, 'the beneficiaries are bound by the judgment with respect to the interest which was the subject of the fiduciary relationship." Many of our circuit's cases evince a similar concern with keeping the nonparties' exceptions to res judicata and collateral estoppel within strict confines.

The fact that all the non-*Borel* defendants, like the *Borel* defendants, are engaged in the manufacture of asbestos-containing products does not evince privity among the parties. The plaintiffs did not demonstrate that any of the non-*Borel* defendants participated in any capacity in the *Borel* litigation-whether directly or even through a trade representative-or were even part of a trustee-beneficiary relationship with any *Borel* defendant. On the contrary, several of the defendants indicate on appeal that they were not even aware of the *Borel* litigation until those proceedings were over and that they were not even members of industry or trade associations composed of asbestos product manufacturers.

Plaintiffs can draw little support from the doctrine of "virtual representation" of cases such as *Aerojet-General Corp. v. Askew*, in which we stated that "(u)nder the federal law of res judicata, a person may be bound by a judgment even though not a party if one of the parties to the suit is so closely aligned with his interests as to be his virtual representative" and that "the question whether a party's interests in a case are virtually representative of the interests of a nonparty is one of fact for the trial court." In that case we approved a district court's determination that the interests of two government entities were so closely aligned that a prior judgment against one entity bound the other. The proposition that governments may represent private interests in litigation, thereby precluding relitigation, while uncertain at the margin, appears to be an unexceptional special instance of the examples noted in Restatement (Second) of Judgments s 41(1) (1982). The facts here permit no inference of virtual representation of interest. As we explained in *Pollard v. Cockrell*.[756]

---

[754] 546 F.2d 84, 95 (5th Cir. 1977).
[755] 414 U.S. 573 (1974).
[756] 578 F.2d 1002, 1008–09 (5th Cir. 1978).

Virtual representation demands the existence of an express or implied legal relationship in which parties to the first suit are accountable to nonparties who file a subsequent suit raising identical issues. . . . In the instant case . . .the (first) plaintiffs were in no sense legally accountable to the (second) plaintiffs; they shared only an abstract interest in enjoining enforcement of the ordinance. The (first) plaintiffs sued in their individual capacities and not as representatives of a judicially certified class. Representation by the same attorneys cannot furnish the requisite alignment of interest. . . .

Thus, in Pollard we rejected the contention that one group of massage parlor owners were bound by a judgment in a prior lawsuit brought by another group. Virtual representation was rejected despite nearly identical pleadings filed by the groups and representation by common attorneys. The court's omnibus order here amounts to collateral estoppel based on similar legal positions-a proposition that has been properly rejected by at least one other district court that considered the identical issue. We agree with the Texas Supreme Court that "privity is not established by the mere fact that persons may happen to be interested in the same question or in proving the same state of facts," . . . and hold that the trial court's actions here transgress the bounds of due process.

Our conclusion likewise pertains to those defendants who, while originally parties to the Borel litigation, settled before trial. The plaintiffs here did not show that any of these defendants settled out of the Borel litigation after the entire trial had run its course and only the judicial act of signing a final known adverse judgment remained. Such action would suggest settlement precisely to avoid offensive collateral estoppel and, in an appropriate case, might preclude relitigation. All the indications here are, however, that the defendants in question settled out of the case early because of, for example, lack of product identification. Like the non-*Borel* defendants, these defendants have likewise been deprived of their day in court by the trial court's omnibus order.

. . .

Reversed.

Follow-Up Questions and Comments

1. What is the due process violation that troubled the court in Hardy?

2. In rejecting the notion that the thirteen manufacturers not a party to the *Borel* case could have been "in effect" represented, the court referred to the Restatement (Second) of Judgments definition of privity discussed above under Claim Preclusion quoting RESTATEMENT SECOND OF JUDGMENTS § 41(1)), which identifies parties such as trustees and executors as parties with whom those who have a legal relationship can be bound due to privity. Clearly, the court did not see the manufacturer's representation to be analogous to that of trustees and executors in *Borel*.

3. The court refers to the concept of virtual representation that for some years the U.S. Court of Appeals for the Fifth Circuit had recognized in some contexts. In *Taylor v. Sturgill*,[757] the United States Supreme Court put a stake in the heart of the virtual representation concept. The concept too easily could avoid the due process concerns at the heart of the requirement of a party having a full

---

[757] 553 U.S. 880 (2008).

and fair opportunity to litigate an issue in the First Suit before being bound to it in the second.[758]

Practice Problem

Practice Problem 18-15

Fire retardant treated plywood ("FRTP") is a product developed for use in multi-dwelling buildings as opposed to more expensive fire walls. The product is supposed to, when exposed to flame, char immediately and prevent the spread of fire. Some FRTP in multi-family homes in hot, humid climates had charred even without a fire, leaving the building less structurally sound. Multi-Homes, Inc. had sued over its multi-family dwelling in Montgomery County, Maryland. The plaintiff sued Oswood, Inc, the manufacturer of FRTP that had been found in most of the dwelling. Part of the evidence in the trial, however, showed that WestWood, Inc.'s FRTP had been used in some homes. The jury found the FRTP defective and ruled for Multi-Homes, Inc. Later, in another multi-family dwelling that had experienced unexpected FRTP charring, Multi-Homes sued Westwood because most of the FRTP in that dwelling was from that FRTP manufacturer. Multi-Homes argued that the issue of defectiveness of West-Wood's FRTP had been resolved in the prior case and should be precluded from relitigation. Is that position correct or not? Why or why not?

E. Fifth Requirement: Is Issue Preclusion Being Asserted by Someone Who Can Properly Assert It?

1. The Traditional Rule of Mutuality and Its Exceptions

Traditionally, someone could assert issue preclusion only if that party would have been bound by the judgment on which he or she was relying. As one leading treatise observes:

For many years, most courts followed the general rule that the favorable preclusion effects of a judgment were available only to a person who would have been bound by any unfavorable preclusion effects. This rule, known as the rule of mutuality, established a pleasing symmetry—a judgment was binding only on parties and persons in privity with them, and a judgment could be invoked only by parties and their privies.[759]

The mutuality rule always has had some exceptions. The most common arose from indemnification scenarios, particularly in vicarious liability fact patterns. For instance, if an employer could be held liable for the actions of its employee, then even if the employer was not in the First Suit (the employee was), the employer could benefit from a favorable finding.[760] Later, courts extended this exception to vicarious liability scenarios in which the employer was the first sued. Even though the employee could not seek indemnification from the employer, the courts considered it anomalous that an employer could be sued based on an employee's acts or omissions, that the employer could win, but that when the third party sued the employee in a second action the employee could not raise issue preclusion because the employee was

---

[758] *See id.* at 903–04.
[759] 18A EDWARD H. COOPER, WRIGHT AND MILLER'S FEDERAL PRACTICE AND PROCEDURE § 4463 (2d ed. 2017).
[760] *See* 18A CHARLES ALAN WRIGHT & ARTHUR R. MILLER, FEDERAL PRACTICE AND PROCEDURE § 4463 (2d ed. 2018).

not a party to the First Suit. Hence, even without the right of indemnification as a basis for an exception, the courts began to recognize the broader exception to mutuality. One might say that this line of cases eroded the mutuality doctrine, and it will do no harm to think of them in that way. The mutuality doctrine has been eroded in many jurisdictions as well as in the federal system. We will see the extent of such erosion in the sections that follow.

2. Acceptance of Non-Mutual Defensive Use of Issue Preclusion

The mutuality rule is not one based on due process, but rather a judge-made rule. As noted, the rule had already eroded to some extent. In one of the most influential cases in civil procedure, well-respected jurist Roger Traynor had an ideal opportunity to illustrate why mutuality should not be required in certain instances where (a) a party defending a claim (b) is raising issue preclusion to preclude a party who has already lost from relitigating an issue.

In *Bernhard v. Bank of America*,[761] an elderly woman in failing health moved in with a couple, Mr. and Mrs. Cook. The woman gave Mr. Cook permission to write checks on her behalf against one of her accounts. At one point, Mr. Cook withdrew a large amount from the woman's account and deposited it in his own account. The woman had directed him to do so as a gift in light of Mr. and Mrs. Cook's having taking care of her. Mr. Cook became the executor of the woman's estate when she died. The woman's relatives sued him over the amount deposited into his account and sought return of the money. However, the court found that the woman had authorized Mr. Cook to withdraw the money and deposit it in his account as a gift to him and his wife. Judgment was thus entered for the executor, Mr. Cook.

Mr. Cook then withdrew as executor and one of the decedent's daughters became the executrix of the estate. The executrix sued the bank that had dealt with the accounts in question. She contended that her mother would not have authorized the withdrawal of funds. The bank asserted issue preclusion, arguing that the finding in the prior suit against Mr. Cook had established that the withdrawal was authorized.

If the court stuck to the mutuality doctrine, the bank would not have been able to assert issue preclusion. Because the bank was not a party to the First Suit and could not be bound to findings in it, mutuality would prevent the bank from relying on favorable findings in the First Suit. Nor were any of the classic exceptions to the mutuality doctrine available. Thus, the court in Bernhard had the opportunity to address whether issue preclusion should be applied simply because it made sense to do so even if there was a lack of mutuality. Justice Traynor explained the reason for abandoning the mutuality doctrine as follows:

Many courts have stated the facile formula that the plea of res judicata is available only when there is privity and mutuality of estoppel. Under the requirement of privity, only parties to the former judgment or their privies may take advantage of or be bound by it. A party in this connection is one who is 'directly interested in the subject matter, and had a right to make defense, or to control the proceeding, and to appeal from the judgment.' A privy is one who, after rendition of the judgment, has acquired an interest in the subject matter affected by the judgment through or under one of the parties, as by inheritance, succession, or purchase. The estoppel is mutual if the one taking advantage of the earlier adjudication would have been bound by it, had it gone against him.

The criteria for determining who may assert a plea of res judicata differ fundamentally from the criteria for determining against whom a plea of res judicata may be asserted. The requirements of due

---

[761] 122 P.2d 892 (Cal. 1942).

process of law forbid the assertion of a plea of res judicata against a party unless he was bound by the earlier litigation in which the matter was decided. He is bound by that litigation only if he has been a party thereto or in privity with a party thereto. There is no compelling reason, however, for requiring that the party asserting the plea of res judicata must have been a party, or in privity with a party, to the earlier litigation.

No satisfactory rationalization has been advanced for the requirement of mutuality. Just why a party who was not bound by a previous action should be precluded from asserting it as res judicata against a party who was bound by it is difficult to comprehend. Many courts have abandoned the requirement of mutuality and confined the requirement of privity to the party against whom the plea of res judicata is asserted . . . The courts of most jurisdictions have in effect accomplished the same result by recognizing a broad exception to the requirements of mutuality and privity, namely, that they are not necessary where the liability of the defendant asserting the plea of res judicata is dependent upon or derived from the liability of one who was exonerated in an earlier suit brought by the same plaintiff upon the same facts. Typical examples of such derivative liability are master and servant, principal and agent, and indemnitor and indemnitee.

In determining the validity of a plea of res judicata three questions are pertinent: Was the issue decided in the prior adjudication identical with the one presented in the action in question? Was there a final judgment on the merits? Was the party against whom the plea is asserted a party or in privity with a party to the prior adjudication?

In the present case, therefore, the defendant is not precluded by lack of privity or of mutuality of estoppel from asserting the plea of res judicata against the plaintiff. Since the issue as to the ownership of the money is identical with the issue raised in the probate proceeding, and since the order of the probate court settling the executor's account was a final adjudication of this issue on the merits . . . it remains only to determine whether the plaintiff in the present action was a party or in privity with a party to the earlier proceeding. The plaintiff has brought the present action in the capacity of administratrix of the estate. In this capacity she represents the very same persons and interests that were represented in the earlier hearing on the executor's account. In that proceeding plaintiff and the other legatees who objected to the executor's account represented the estate of the decedent. They were seeking not a personal recovery but, like the plaintiff in the present action, as administratrix, a recovery for the benefit of the legatees and creditors of the estate, all of whom were bound by the order settling the account. The plea of res judicata is therefore available against plaintiff as a party to the former proceeding despite her formal change of capacity. "Where a party though appearing in two suits in different capacities is in fact litigating the same right, the judgment in one estops him in the other."[762]

The impact of Bernhard has been profound, at least in terms of situations in which non-parties to an initial suit seek to use issue preclusion defensively to prevent a party who lost an issue in the First Suit from relitigating it. The influence has extended to the U.S. Supreme Court. In the following opinion, the Court recognized the logic of Bernhard as supporting non-mutual defensive issue preclusion.

---

[762] Bernhard v. Bank of America, 122 P.2d 892, 894–96 (Cal. 1942) (internal citations omitted).

BLONDER-TONGUE LABORATORIES, INC. v. UNIVERSITY OF ILLINOIS FOUNDATION
Supreme Court of the United States, 1971
402 U.S. 313

MR. JUSTICE WHITE delivered the opinion of the Court.

Respondent University of Illinois Foundation (hereafter Foundation) is the owner by assignment of U.S. Patent No. 3,210,767, issued to Dwight E. Isbell on October 5, 1965. The patent is for "Frequency Independent Unidirectional Antennas," and Isbell first filed his application May 3, 1960. The antennas covered are designed for transmission and reception of electromagnetic radio frequency signals used in many types of communications, including the broadcasting of radio and television signals.

The patent has been much litigated since it was granted, primarily because it claims a high-quality television antenna for color reception. One of the first infringement suits brought by the Foundation was filed in the Southern District of Iowa against the Winegard Co., an antenna manufacturer. Trial was to the court, and after pursuing the inquiry mandated by *Graham v. John Deere Company*,[763] Chief Judge Stephenson held the patent invalid since "it would have been obvious to one ordinarily skilled in the art and wishing to design a frequency independent unidirectional antenna to combine these three old elements, all suggested by the prior art references previously discussed." Accordingly, he entered judgment for the alleged infringer and against the patentee. On appeal, the Court of Appeals for the Eighth Circuit unanimously affirmed Judge Stephenson. We denied the patentee's petition for certiorari.

In March 1966, well before Judge Stephenson had ruled in the *Winegard* case, the Foundation also filed suit in the Northern District of Illinois charging a Chicago customer of petitioner, Blonder-Tongue Laboratories, Inc. (hereafter B-T), with infringing two patents it owned by assignment: the Isbell patent and U.S. Patent No. Re. 25,740, reissued March 9, 1965, to P. E. Mayes et al. The Mayes patent was entitled "Log Periodic Backward Wave Antenna Array," and was, as indicated, a reissue of No. 3,108,280, applied for on September 30, 1960. B-T chose to subject itself to the jurisdiction of the court to defend its customer, and it filed an answer and counterclaim against the Foundation and its licensee, respondent JFD Electronics Corp., charging: (1) that both the Isbell and Mayes patents were invalid; (2) that if those patents were valid, the B-T antennas did not infringe either of them; (3) that the Foundation and JFD were guilty of unfair competition; (4) that the Foundation and JFD had violated the "anti-trust laws of the United States, including the Sherman and Clayton Acts, as amended"; and (5) that certain JFD antenna models infringed B-T's patent No. 3,259,904, "Antenna Having Combined Support and Lead-In," issued July 5, 1966.

Trial was again to the court, and on June 27, 1968, Judge Hoffman held that the Foundation's patents were valid and infringed, dismissed the unfair competition and antitrust charges, and found claim 5 of the B-T patent obvious and invalid. Before discussing the Isbell patent in detail, Judge Hoffman noted that it had been held invalid as obvious by Judge Stephenson in the *Winegard* litigation. He stated:

> This court is, of course, free to decide the case at bar on the basis of the evidence before it. Although a patent has been adjudged invalid in another patent infringement action against other defendants, patent owners cannot be deprived 'of the right to show, if they can, that, as against defendants who have not previously been in court, the patent is valid and infringed.' On the basis of the evidence before it, this court disagrees with the conclusion reached in the *Winegard* case and finds

---

[763] 383 U.S. 1, 17–18 (1966).

both the Isbell patent and the Mayes et al. patent valid and enforceable patents.

B-T appealed, and the Court of Appeals for the Seventh Circuit affirmed: (1) the findings that the Isbell patent was both valid and infringed by B-T's products; (2) the dismissal of B-T's unfair competition and antitrust counterclaims; and (3) the finding that claim 5 of the B-T patent was obvious. However, the Court of Appeals reversed the judgment insofar as Judge Hoffman had found the Mayes patent valid and enforceable, enjoined infringement thereof, and provided damages for such infringement.

B-T sought certiorari, assigning the conflict between the Courts of Appeals for the Seventh and Eighth Circuits as to the validity of the Isbell patent as a primary reason for granting the writ. We granted certiorari and subsequently requested the parties to discuss the following additional issues not raised in the petition for review:

> 1. Should the holding of *Triplett v. Lowell*,[764] that a determination of patent invalidity is not res judicata as against the patentee in subsequent litigation against a different defendant, be adhered to?"

> 2. If not, does the determination of invalidity in the *Winegard* litigation bind the respondents in this case?

[T]he California Supreme Court, in *Bernhard v. Bank of America Nat. Trust & Savings Assn.*, unanimously rejected the doctrine of mutuality, stating that there was "no compelling reason . . . for requiring that the party asserting the plea of res judicata must have been a party, or in privity with a party, to the earlier litigation." Justice Traynor's opinion, handed down the same year the Restatement was published, listed criteria since employed by many courts in many contexts:

> "In determining the validity of a plea of res judicata three questions are pertinent: Was the issue decided in the prior adjudication identical with the one presented in the action in question? Was there a final judgment on the merits? Was the party against whom the plea is asserted a party or in privity with a party to the prior adjudication?"

Although the force of the mutuality rule had been diminished by exceptions and Bernhard itself might easily have been brought within one of the established exceptions, "Justice Traynor chose instead to extirpate the mutuality requirement and put it to the torch."

Bernhard had significant impact. Many state and federal courts rejected the mutuality requirement, especially where the prior judgment was invoked defensively in a second action against a plaintiff bringing suit on an issue he litigated and lost as plaintiff in a prior action. The trend has been apparent in federal-question cases. The federal courts found Bernhard persuasive.

. . .

The cases and authorities discussed above connect erosion of the mutuality requirement to the goal of limiting relitigation of issues where that can be achieved without compromising fairness in particular cases. The courts have often discarded the rule while commenting on crowded dockets and long delays preceding trial. Authorities differ on whether the public interest in efficient judicial administration is a

---

[764] 297 U.S. 638 (1936).

sufficient ground in and of itself for abandoning mutuality, but it is clear that more than crowded dockets is involved. The broader question is whether it is any longer tenable to afford a litigant more than one full and fair opportunity for judicial resolution of the same issue. The question in these terms includes as part of the calculus the effect on judicial administration, but it also encompasses the concern exemplified by Bentham's reference to the gaming table in his attack on the principle of mutuality of estoppel. In any lawsuit where a defendant, because of the mutuality principle, is forced to present a complete defense on the merits to a claim which the plaintiff has fully litigated and lost in a prior action, there is an arguable misallocation of resources. To the extent the defendant in the second suit may not win by asserting, without contradiction, that the plaintiff had fully and fairly, but unsuccessfully, litigated the same claim in the prior suit, the defendant's time and money are diverted from alternative uses--productive or otherwise--to relitigation of a decided issue. And, still assuming that the issue was resolved correctly in the first suit, there is reason to be concerned about the plaintiff's allocation of resources. Permitting repeated litigation of the same issue as long as the supply of unrelated defendants holds out reflects either the aura of the gaming table or "a lack of discipline and of disinterestedness on the part of the lower courts, hardly a worthy or wise basis for fashioning rules of procedure." Although neither judges, the parties, nor the adversary system performs perfectly in all cases, the requirement of determining whether the party against whom an estoppel is asserted had a full and fair opportunity to litigate is a most significant safeguard.

Some litigants--those who never appeared in a prior action--may not be collaterally estopped without litigating the issue. They have never had a chance to present their evidence and arguments on the claim. Due process prohibits estopping them despite one or more existing adjudications of the identical issue which stand squarely against their position. Also, the authorities have been more willing to permit a defendant in a second suit to invoke an estoppel against a plaintiff who lost on the same claim in an earlier suit than they have been to allow a plaintiff in the second suit to use offensively a judgment obtained by a different plaintiff in a prior suit against the same defendant. But the case before us involves neither due process nor "offensive use" questions. Rather, it depends on the considerations weighing for and against permitting a patent holder to sue on his patent after it has once been held invalid following opportunity for full and fair trial.

It is clear that judicial decisions have tended to depart from the rigid requirements of mutuality. In accordance with this trend, there has been a corresponding development of the lower courts' ability and facility in dealing with questions of when it is appropriate and fair to impose an estoppel against a party who has already litigated an issue once and lost. As one commentator has stated:

"Under the tests of time and subsequent developments, the Bernhard decision has proved its merit and the mettle of its author. The abrasive action of new factual configurations and of actual human controversies, disposed of in the common-law tradition by competent courts, far more than the commentaries of academicians, leaves the decision revealed for what it is, as it was written: a shining landmark of progress in justice and law administration."[765]

When these judicial developments are considered in the light of our consistent view--last presented in *Lear, Inc. v. Adkins*--that the holder of a patent should not be insulated from the assertion of defenses and thus allowed to exact royalties for the use of an idea that is not in fact patentable or that is beyond the scope of the patent monopoly granted, it is apparent that the uncritical acceptance of the principle of mutuality of estoppel expressed in *Triplett v. Lowell* is today out of place. Thus, we conclude that *Triplett* should be overruled to the extent it forecloses a plea of estoppel by one facing a charge of infringement of

---

[765] Currie, 53 Calif. L. Rev., at 37.

a patent that has once been declared invalid.

Res judicata and collateral estoppel are affirmative defenses that must be pleaded.[766] The purpose of such pleading is to give the opposing party notice of the plea of estoppel and a chance to argue, if he can, why the imposition of an estoppel would be inappropriate. Because of *Triplett v. Lowell*, petitioner did not plead estoppel and respondents never had an opportunity to challenge the appropriateness of such a plea on the grounds set forth in Part III-A of this opinion. Therefore, given the partial overruling of *Triplett*, we remand the case. Petitioner should be allowed to amend its pleadings in the District Court to assert a plea of estoppel. Respondents must then be permitted to amend their pleadings, and to supplement the record with any evidence showing why an estoppel should not be imposed in this case. If necessary, petitioner may also supplement the record. In taking this action, we intimate no views on the other issues presented in this case. The judgment of the Court of Appeals is vacated[,] and the cause is remanded to the District Court for further proceedings consistent with this opinion.

Follow-Up Questions and Comments

1. Why is there is no due process issue here when the question is whether a non-party to the initial suit is raising issue preclusion to bind a party to the First Suit to a ruling there?

2. Are you persuaded that non-mutual defensive issue preclusion ought to apply at least as broadly as the *Bernhard* and *Parklane Hosiery* decisions suggest? Is the application of non-mutual defensive issue preclusion consistent with the policies of claim and issue preclusion?

Practice Problem

Practice Problem 18-16
Plaintiff, Hut Dogs, Inc. sued Pork Dogs, Inc. for unfair competition on the basis that Pork Dogs sold the same food (burgers, hot dogs, and fries) in the public area surrounding a baseball stadium. The court ruled against Plaintiff, holding that sale of such food was not protected by unfair competition and could be sold by anyone. Hut Dogs then sued Frankie's Dogs, Inc., yet another vendor in the area of the baseball stadium, for unfair competition on the grounds that it sold the identical food as Plaintiff—again, burgers, hot dogs, and fries. Frankie's Dogs, Inc. raised issue preclusion as a defense to this action, arguing that issue preclusion bound Hut Dogs to the finding in its First Suit that sale of hot dogs, burgers, and fries in the stadium vicinity was not something Hut Dugs could claim to be unfair competition. How should the court rule?

---

3. Modest Recognition of Non-Mutual Offensive Use of Issue Preclusion

With greater acceptance of non-mutual defensive issue preclusion, the question was bound to be examined: Why not expand offensive non-mutual issue preclusion? The difference between defensive use of non-mutual issue preclusion and offensive use of the doctrine is not insignificant. We can see the logic that a party who has litigated and lost on an issue in prior litigation ought not to be able to litigate over and

---

[766] FED. R. CIV. P. 8(c).

over until that party prevails. However, with offensive non-mutual issue preclusion, a new plaintiff (not a party to the First Suit) seeks to assert offensively preclusion of a finding to prevent a party to the First Suit from relitigating the issue.

Due process again is not an issue because the party against whom issue preclusion is being asserted in offensive non-mutual issue preclusion was a party to the initial suit. However, other concerns have led courts to be more cautious when non-parties are seeking to assert nonmutual offensive issue preclusion because the arguments are not as compelling as with defensive use.

The following decision of the Supreme Court reflects its concerns and the conditions it imposes before non-mutual offensive issue preclusion can be applied.

PARKLANE HOSIERY CO. v. SHORE
Supreme Court of the United States, 1979
439 U.S. 322

MR. JUSTICE STEWART delivered the opinion of the Court.

This case presents the question whether a party who has had issues of fact adjudicated adversely to it in an equitable action may be collaterally estopped from relitigating the same issues before a jury in a subsequent legal action brought against it by a new party. The respondent brought this stockholder's class action against the petitioners in a Federal District Court. The complaint alleged that the petitioners, Parklane Hosiery Co., Inc. (Parklane), and 13 of its officers, directors, and stockholders, had issued a materially false and misleading proxy statement in connection with a merger. The proxy statement, according to the complaint, had violated §§ 14 (a), 10 (b), and 20 (a) of the Securities Exchange Act of 1934, 48 Stat. 895, 891, 899, as amended, 15 U. S. C. §§ 78n (a), 78j (b), and 78t (a), as well as various rules and regulations promulgated by the Securities and Exchange Commission (SEC). The complaint sought damages, rescission of the merger, and recovery of costs.

Before this action came to trial, the SEC filed suit against the same defendants in the Federal District Court, alleging that the proxy statement that had been issued by Parklane was materially false and misleading in essentially the same respects as those that had been alleged in the respondent's complaint. Injunctive relief was requested. After a 4-day trial, the District Court found that the proxy statement was materially false and misleading in the respects alleged and entered a declaratory judgment to that effect. The Court of Appeals for the Second Circuit affirmed this judgment.

The respondent in the present case then moved for partial summary judgment against the petitioners, asserting that the petitioners were collaterally estopped from relitigating the issues that had been resolved against them in the action brought by the SEC. The District Court denied the motion on the ground that such an application of collateral estoppel would deny the petitioners their Seventh Amendment right to a jury trial. The Court of Appeals for the Second Circuit reversed, holding that a party who has had issues of fact determined against him after a full and fair opportunity to litigate in a nonjury trial is collaterally estopped from obtaining a subsequent jury trial of these same issues of fact. The appellate court concluded that "the Seventh Amendment preserves the right to jury trial only with respect to issues of fact, [and] once those issues have been fully and fairly adjudicated in a prior proceeding, nothing remains for trial, either with or without a jury." Because of an inter-circuit conflict, we granted certiorari.

I

537

The threshold question to be considered is whether, quite apart from the right to a jury trial under the Seventh Amendment, the petitioners can be precluded from relitigating facts resolved adversely to them in a prior equitable proceeding with another party under the general law of collateral estoppel. Specifically, we must determine whether a litigant who was not a party to a prior judgment may nevertheless use that judgment "offensively" to prevent a defendant from relitigating issues resolved in the earlier proceeding.

A

Collateral estoppel, like the related doctrine of res judicata, has the dual purpose of protecting litigants from the burden of relitigating an identical issue with the same party or his privy and of promoting judicial economy by preventing needless litigation.[767] Until relatively recently, however, the scope of collateral estoppel was limited by the doctrine of mutuality of parties. Under this mutuality doctrine, neither party could use a prior judgment as an estoppel against the other unless both parties were bound by the judgment. Based on the premise that it is somehow unfair to allow a party to use a prior judgment when he himself would not be so bound, the mutuality requirement provided a party who had litigated and lost in a previous action an opportunity to relitigate identical issues with new parties.

By failing to recognize the obvious difference in position between a party who has never litigated an issue and one who has fully litigated and lost, the mutuality requirement was criticized almost from its inception. Recognizing the validity of this criticism, the Court in Blonder-Tongue Laboratories, Inc. University of Illinois Foundation abandoned the mutuality requirement, at least in cases where a patentee seeks to relitigate the validity of a patent after a federal court in a previous lawsuit has already declared it invalid. The "broader question" before the Court, however, was "whether it is any longer tenable to afford a litigant more than one full and fair opportunity for judicial resolution of the same issue." The Court strongly suggested a negative answer to that question.

B

The Blonder-Tongue case involved defensive use of collateral estoppel--a plaintiff was estopped from asserting a claim that the plaintiff had previously litigated and lost against another defendant. The present case, by contrast, involves offensive use of collateral estoppel--a plaintiff is seeking to estop a defendant from relitigating the issues which the defendant previously litigated and lost against another plaintiff. In both the offensive and defensive use situations, the party against whom estoppel is asserted has litigated and lost in an earlier action. Nevertheless, several reasons have been advanced why the two situations should be treated differently.

First, offensive use of collateral estoppel does not promote judicial economy in the same manner as defensive use does. Defensive use of collateral estoppel precludes a plaintiff from relitigating identical issues by merely "switching adversaries." Thus[,] defensive collateral estoppel gives a plaintiff a strong incentive to join all potential defendants in the first action if possible. Offensive use of collateral estoppel, on the other hand, creates precisely the opposite incentive. Since a plaintiff will be able to rely on a previous judgment against a defendant but will not be bound by that judgment if the defendant wins, the plaintiff has every incentive to adopt a "wait and see" attitude, in the hope that the first action by another plaintiff will result in a favorable judgment. Thus[,] offensive use of collateral estoppel will likely increase rather than decrease the total amount of litigation, since potential plaintiffs will have everything to gain and nothing to lose by not intervening in the first action.

---

[767] Blonder-Tongue Laboratories, Inc. v. University of Illinois Foundation, 402 U.S. 313, 328–29 (1971).

A second argument against offensive use of collateral estoppel is that it may be unfair to a defendant. If a defendant in the first action is sued for small or nominal damages, he may have little incentive to defend vigorously, particularly if future suits are not foreseeable. Allowing offensive collateral estoppel may also be unfair to a defendant if the judgment relied upon as a basis for the estoppel is itself inconsistent with one or more previous judgments in favor of the defendant. Still another situation where it might be unfair to apply offensive estoppel is where the second action affords the defendant procedural opportunities unavailable in the first action that could readily cause a different result.

C

We have concluded that the preferable approach for dealing with these problems in the federal courts is not to preclude the use of offensive collateral estoppel, but to grant trial courts broad discretion to determine when it should be applied. The general rule should be that in cases where a plaintiff could easily have joined in the earlier action or where, either for the reasons discussed above or for other reasons, the application of offensive estoppel would be unfair to a defendant, a trial judge should not allow the use of offensive collateral estoppel.

In the present case, however, none of the circumstances that might justify reluctance to allow the offensive use of collateral estoppel is present. The application of offensive collateral estoppel will not here reward a private plaintiff who could have joined in the previous action, since the respondent probably could not have joined in the injunctive action brought by the SEC even had he so desired. Similarly, there is no unfairness to the petitioners in applying offensive collateral estoppel in this case. First, in light of the serious allegations made in the SEC's complaint against the petitioners, as well as the foreseeability of subsequent private suits that typically follow a successful Government judgment, the petitioners had every incentive to litigate the SEC lawsuit fully and vigorously.

Second, the judgment in the SEC action was not inconsistent with any previous decision. Finally, there will in the respondent's action be no procedural opportunities available to the petitioners that were unavailable in the first action of a kind that might be likely to cause a different result.

We conclude, therefore, that none of the considerations that would justify a refusal to allow the use of offensive collateral estoppel is present in this case. Since the petitioners received a "full and fair" opportunity to litigate their claims in the SEC action, the contemporary law of collateral estoppel leads inescapably to the conclusion that the petitioners are collaterally estopped from relitigating the question of whether the proxy statement was materially false and misleading.

Follow-Up Questions and Comments

1. The Court was willing to accept the potential for application of non-mutual offensive issue preclusion, but only by giving courts broad discretion and several guidelines to determine whether nonmutual offensive issue preclusion should apply. Each of these guidelines is important when analyzing whether to allow offensive non-mutual issue preclusion. They are:

- **Ease of Joinder in the First Case.** By joinder here, the court is referring to joinder by the stranger's intervention. Joinder would thus be through the non-party (stranger) moving to intervene in (i.e., join) the first case. The rationale for this factor is that the non-party ought not to be able to sit back and watch litigation in which that non-party could have joined, wait for the results, and then use findings preclusively if they end up favoring the non-party. In other words, if a party could join easily, then that will cut against the court's allowing offensive use of non-mutual issue preclusion. Why did the Court in *Parklane* conclude that the private plaintiff likely could not have joined in the suit brought by the government agency, the Security and Exchange Commission?

- **Foreseeability of Litigation / Incentive to Litigate.** If the party in the first case would have had a strong incentive to litigate the issues, then that favors application of offensive non-mutual issue preclusion. Conversely, what does the Court in *Parklane* suggest would be unfair in cases where the stakes may not lead the party to the First Suit to litigate vigorously? If the incentive is not strong, does that cut against application of offensive use of non-mutual issue preclusion?

- **Inconsistency of Judgments.** The Court in *Parklane* stated that, if there are judgments in favor of the defendant—inconsistent decisions reached prior to the case in which the finding the non-party wishes to rely—that could argue against offensive non-mutual issue preclusion. Here, the Court is recognizing that, for instance, there could be a mass tort scenario. What if the first ten plaintiffs sue the defendant and the findings and result are favorable to the defendant but then, in the eleventh case, the defendant is found liable for the same accident? Allowing a non-party to the prior cases to offensively used the findings in the eleventh case, despite inconsistent rulings prior to that case, would not be fair. (Such a scenario is postulated in a well-known article.[768] In such a scenario, that would cut against application of offensive non-mutual issue preclusion.

- **Procedural Opportunities Available in the Second Suit but Not in the First Suit Likely to Cause a Different Result.** If the original suit was brought in a small claims court, or some other court that lacked all the procedural capabilities usually available, the Court suggests that this difference would cut against applying offensive non-mutual issue preclusion.

2. The challenge to this form of nonmutual offensive issue preclusion is that the criterial for application are not clearly defined. Those learning it for the first time are often frustrated by its lack of clarity. Moreover, the four criteria that the Court in *Parklane* set forth are not conjunctive. In other words, all of them do not need to apply for nonmutual offensive issue preclusion to apply. A court applying the analysis will take each criterion, examine the facts, and determine whether each criterion support—or counsels against—applying nonmutual offensive issue preclusion. Some contend that *Parklane* was the "perfect" case for applying nonmutual offensive issue preclusion because so many of the criteria supported application of the doctrine. The doctrine is less applied than defensive nonmutual issue preclusion.

3. Realize that in state practice you will need to evaluate whether mutuality still is the rule. You cannot assume that the Supreme Court's approach applies in every state. If the federal court is applying a

---

[768] *See* Brainerd Currie, *Mutuality of Estoppel: Limits of the Bernhard Doctrine*, 9 STAN. L. REV. 281 (1957).

federal statutory claim, the federal court will apply the Supreme Court precedent. However, in diversity of citizenship cases, the state approach will govern

---

Practice Problem

Practice Problem 18-17

Curtis and Katie rode a two-person bike everywhere. They even rode great distances, from Norfolk, Virginia to Elizabeth City, North Carolina, on some days. One time when they did so, they hit a hole in Elizabeth City's sidewalk and had a great fall. The fall damaged the bike. Curtis, the owner of the bike, sued in small claims court for damage to the bike. The judge found the City at fault and awarded Curtis the damages for his bike. Katie developed serious, chronic headaches from the fall even though she was wearing a helmet and had no other injuries. She sued the City in U. S. District Court for $500,000 and sought to establish the City's negligence by relying on the finding against the City in Curtis' bike case. Consider the *Parklane* analysis and whether offensive non-mutual issue preclusion should be applied.

Made in the USA
Monee, IL
09 November 2019

16554161R10308